Lecture Notes in Computer Science   **9364**

Commenced Publication in 1973
Founding and Former Series Editors:
Gerhard Goos, Juris Hartmanis, and Jan van Leeuwen

More information about this series at http://www.springer.com/series/7408

Bernd Finkbeiner · Geguang Pu
Lijun Zhang (Eds.)

Automated Technology for Verification and Analysis

13th International Symposium, ATVA 2015
Shanghai, China, October 12–15, 2015
Proceedings

 Springer

Editors

Bernd Finkbeiner
Universität des Saarlandes
Saarbrücken
Germany

Lijun Zhang
Chinese Academy of Sciences
Beijing
China

Geguang Pu
East China Normal University
Shanghai
China

ISSN 0302-9743   ISSN 1611-3349   (electronic)
Lecture Notes in Computer Science
ISBN 978-3-319-24952-0   ISBN 978-3-319-24953-7   (eBook)
DOI 10.1007/978-3-319-24953-7

Library of Congress Control Number: 2015950888

LNCS Sublibrary: SL2 – Programming and Software Engineering

Springer Cham Heidelberg New York Dordrecht London
© Springer International Publishing Switzerland 2015

Printed on acid-free paper

Springer International Publishing AG Switzerland is part of Springer Science+Business Media
(www.springer.com)

Preface

This volume contains the papers presented at ATVA 2015, the 13th International Symposium on Automated Technology for Verification and Analysis, held during October 12–15, 2015, in Shanghai. The purpose of ATVA is to promote research on theoretical and practical aspects of automated analysis, verification, and synthesis by providing an international forum for interaction among researchers in academia and industry.

This year, 82 regular and 13 tool papers were submitted to the conference. The Program Committee (PC) decided to accept 33 papers (six of them are tool papers). The program also included three invited talks and three invited tutorials given by Prof. Dino Distefano (Facebook and Queen Mary University of London), Prof. Martin Fränzle (Carl von Ossietzky University), Prof. Joost-Pieter Katoen (RWTH Aachen University), and Prof. J Strother Moore (University of Texas at Austin).

Many worked hard and offered their valuable time generously to make ATVA 2015 successful. First of all, the conference organizers thank the researchers who worked hard to complete and submit papers to the conference. We would like to thank the PC members: more than 300 reviews (four for each submission on average) were written by PC members and additional reviewers in order to select the papers to be presented at the conference. Without them, a competitive and peer-reviewed international symposium simply could not take place. We also thank the Steering Committee members for providing guidance on various aspects of planning of the symposium.

The Institute of Software, Chinese Academy of Sciences, and East China Normal University provided support and facilities for organizing the symposium and its tutorials. We are grateful for their support. Also, we give special thanks to Jian Guo and Jifeng He, local chair and general chair of the symposium, for providing helpful guidance whenever it was needed.

Finally, we thank EasyChair for providing us with the infrastructure to manage the submissions, the reviewing process, the PC discussion, and the preparation of the proceedings.

August 2015

Bernd Finkbeiner
Geguang Pu
Lijun Zhang

Organization

Program Committee

Alessandro Abate	University of Oxford, UK
Erika Ábrahám	RWTH Aachen University, Germany
Michael Backes	Saarland University and Max Planck Institute for Software Systems, Germany
Christel Baier	Technical University of Dresden, Germany
Ahmed Bouajjani	LIAFA, University of Paris Diderot, France
Tevfik Bultan	University of California at Santa Barbara, USA
Franck Cassez	NICTA, Australia
Rance Cleaveland	University of Maryland, USA
Hung Dang Van	Vietnam National University, Vietnam
Bernd Finkbeiner	Saarland University, Germany
Mark Greenstreet	University of British Columbia, Canada
Holger Hermanns	Saarland University, Germany
Pao-Ann Hsiung	National Chung Cheng University, Taiwan
Alan J. Hu	University of British Columbia, Canada
Michael Huth	Imperial College London, UK
Jie-Hong Roland Jiang	National Taiwan University, Taiwan
Orna Kupferman	Hebrew University, Israel
Kim Guldstrand Larsen	Aalborg University, Denmark
Xuandong Li	Nanjing University, China
Annabelle McIver	Macquarie University, Australia
Kenneth McMillan	Microsoft, USA
Madhavan Mukund	Chennai Mathematical Institute, India
Flemming Nielson	Technical University of Denmark, Denmark
Mizuhito Ogawa	Japan Advanced Institute of Science and Technology, Japan
Catuscia Palamidessi	Inria, France
Doron Peled	Bar Ilan University, Israel
Geguang Pu	East China Normal University, China
Jean-François Raskin	Université Libre de Bruxelles, Belgium
Kristin Yvonne Rozier	NASA Ames Research Center, USA
Sven Schewe	University of Liverpool, UK
Scott Smolka	Stony Brook Universtiy, USA
Bow-Yaw Wang	Academia Sinica, Taiwan
Farn Wang	National Taiwan University
Wang Yi	Uppsala University, Sweden

Naijun Zhan   Institute of Software, Chinese Academy of Sciences,
                          China
Lijun Zhang   Institute of Software, Chinese Academy of Sciences,
                          China

Additional Reviewers

Abdullah, Syed
Md. Jakaria
Almagor, Shaull
Artho, Cyrille Valentin
Avni, Guy
Bacci, Giorgio
Backeman, Peter
Barbot, Benoit
Beyer, Dirk
Bingham, Brad
Blazy, Sandrine
Brenguier, Romain
Bu, Lei
Buchholz, Peter
Cai, Xiaojuan
Calin, Georgel
Ceska, Milan
Chen, Mingshuai
Chen, Yu-Fang
Chiang, Hui-Ju Katherine
Cong, Tian
Corzilius, Florian
Defrancisco, Richard
Delzanno, Giorgio
Dräger, Klaus
Duggirala, Parasara
Sridhar
Ekberg, Pontus
Emmi, Michael
Enea, Constantin
Fehnker, Ansgar
Ferrer Fioriti, Luis María
Foshammer, Louise
Gao, Yang
Geeraerts, Gilles
Geulen, Sascha
Given-Wilson, Thomas
Godefroid, Patrice

González De Aledo, Pablo
Gorlin, Andrey
Haddad, Axel
Haesaert, Sofie
Hahn, Ernst Moritz
Hamza, Jad
Hartmanns, Arnd
Hashemi, Vahid
Hong, Chih-Duo
Howar, Falk
Hsu, Tzu-Chen
Hunter, Paul
Islam, Md. Ariful
Jansen, David N.
Jegourel, Cyrille
Jensen, Peter Gjøl
Jin, Xiaoqing
Julius, Agung
Kiniry, Joseph
Kong, Soonho
Kraehmann, Daniel
Krčál, Jan
Kremer, Gereon
Lal, Akash
Lampka, Kai
Le Roux, Stéphane
Lengal, Ondrej
Lesser, Kendra
Li, Guangyuan
Li, Guoqiang
Li, Jianwen
Lin, Shang-Wei
Liu, Jiang
Lynch, Christopher
Markey, Nicolas
Midtgaard, Jan
Mitsch, Stefan
Müller, David

Nayak, Abhaya
Nellen, Johanna
Nickovic, Dejan
Norman, Gethin
Ogata, Kazuhiro
Olesen, Mads Chr.
Olsen, Petur
Ozaki, Ana
Pan, Minxue
Partush, Nimrod
Poulsen, Danny Bøgsted
Rabehaja, Tahiry
Randour, Mickael
Roberts, Matt
Rozier, Eric
Ruemmer, Philipp
Sakai, Masahiko
Sangnier, Arnaud
Sankur, Ocan
Schupp, Stefan
Serwe, Wendelin
Soudjani, Sadegh
Steffen, Martin
Strzeboński, Adam
Su, Ting
Suresh, S.P.
Svoreňová, Mária
Taankvist, Jakob Haahr
Tang, Enyi
Tatsuta, Makoto
Truong, Hoang
Tsukada, Takeshi
Tupakula, Udaya
Turrini, Andrea
Valencia, Frank
van Glabbeek, Rob
Van Tang, Nguyen
Wang, Linzhang

Wang, Shuling
Wiltsche, Clemens
Wimmer, Ralf
Wunderlich, Sascha
Xia, Bican

Xue, Bingtian
Yang, Junxing
Yuen, Shoji
Zeljić, Aleksandar
Zhao, Hengjun

Zhao, Jianhua
Zhao, Yongxin
Zhu, Jiaqi
Zou, Liang
Zuliani, Paolo

Contents

Probabilistic Programming:
A True Verification Challenge

Joost-Pieter Katoen[1,2]([envelope])

[1] Software Modelling and Verification, RWTH Aachen University, Aachen, Germany
[2] Formal Methods and Tools, University of Twente, Enschede, The Netherlands
`katoen@cs.rwth-aachen.de`

Probabilistic Programming. Probabilistic programs [6] are sequential programs, written in languages like `C`, `Java`, `Scala`, or `ML`, with two added constructs: (1) the ability to draw values at random from probability distributions, and (2) the ability to condition values of variables in a program through observations. For a comprehensive treatment, see [3]. They have a wide range of applications. Probabilistic programming is at the heart of machine learning for describing distribution functions; Bayesian inference is pivotal in their analysis. Probabilistic programs are central in security for describing cryptographic constructions (such as randomised encryption) and security experiments. In addition, probabilistic programs are an active research topic in quantitative information flow. Quantum programs are inherently probabilistic due to the random outcomes of quantum measurements. Finally, probabilistic programs can be used for approximate computing, e.g., by specifying reliability requirements for programs that allocate data in unreliable memory and use unreliable operations in hardware (so as to save energy dissipation) [1]. Other applications include [4] scientific modeling, information retrieval, bio–informatics, epidemiology, vision, seismic analysis, semantic web, business intelligence, human cognition, and more. Microsoft has started an initiative to improve the usability of probabilistic programming which has resulted in languages such as `R2` [13] and `Tabular` [5] emerged.

What is special about probabilistic programs? They are typically small (up to a few hundred lines), but hard to understand and analyse, let alone algorithmically. For instance, the elementary question of almost-sure termination—for a given input, does a probabilistic program terminate with probability one?—is as hard as the universal halting problem—does an ordinary program halt on all possible inputs? [11]. Loop invariants of probabilistic programs typically involve quantitative statements and synthesizing them requires more involved techniques than for ordinary programs [12]. As a final indication of their complexity, we mention that probabilistic programs allow to draw values from parametric probability distributions. Obtaining quantitative statements such as "what is the expected value of program variable x on termination?" require non-trivial reasoning about such parametric distributions.

Analysing Probabilistic Programs. Bugs easily occur. We develop program analysis techniques, based on static program analysis, deductive verification, and

© Springer International Publishing Switzerland 2015
B. Finkbeiner et al. (Eds.): ATVA 2015, LNCS 9364, pp. 1–3, 2015.
DOI: 10.1007/978-3-319-24953-7_1

model checking, to make probabilistic programming more reliable, i.e., less buggy. Starting from a profound understanding from the intricate semantics of probabilistic programs (including features such as observations, possibly diverging loops, continuous variables, non-determinism, as well as unbounded recursion), we study fundamental problems such as checking program equivalence, loop-invariant synthesis, almost-sure termination, and pre- and postcondition reasoning. The aim is to study the computational hardness of these problems as well as to develop (semi-) algorithms and accompanying tool-support. The ultimate goal is to provide lightweight automated means to the probabilistic programmer so as check elementary program properties.

Formal Semantics and Verification. In this invited talk, I will survey recent progress on the formal semantics and verification of (parametric) probabilistic programs. This involves relating weakest pre-conditions and operational semantics [7,9], loop-invariant synthesis techniques by constraint solving [8,12], hardness results on almost-sure termination [11], and verifying parametric probabilistic models and their applications [2,10,14].

Acknowledgement. This work is funded by the EU FP7-projects SENSATION and MEALS, and the Excellence Initiative of the German federal and state government.

References

1. Carbin, M., Misailovic, S., Rinard, M.C.: Verifying quantitative reliability for programs that execute on unreliable hardware. In: Proceedings of OOPSLA, pp. 33–52. ACM Press (2013)
2. Dehnert, C., Junges, S., Jansen, N., Corzilius, F., Volk, M., Bruintjes, H., Katoen, J.-P., Ábrahám, E.: PROPhESY: a probabilistic parameter synthesis tool. In: Kroening, D., Păsăreanu, C.S. (eds.) CAV 2015. LNCS, vol. 9206, pp. 214–231. Springer, Heidelberg (2015)
3. Goodman, N.D., Stuhlmüller, A.: The Design and Implementation of Probabilistic Programming Languages (electronic) (2014). http://dippl.org
4. Gordon, A.D.: An agenda for probabilistic programming: Usable, portable, and ubiquitous (2013)
5. Gordon, A.D., Graepel, T., Rolland, N., Russo, C.V., Borgström, J., Guiver, J.: Tabular: a schema-driven probabilistic programming language. In: Proceedings of POPL, pp. 321–334. ACM Press (2014)
6. Gordon, A.D., Henzinger, T.A., Nori, A.V., Rajamani, S K.: Probabilistic programming. In: Proceedings of FOSE, pp. 167–181. ACM Press (2014)
7. Gretz, F., Jansen, N., Kaminski, B.L., Katoen, J.-P., McIver, A., Olmedo, F.: Conditioning in probabilistic programming. In: Proceedings of MFPS, ENTCS
8. Gretz, F., Katoen, J.-P., McIver, A.: PRINSYS—on a quest for probabilistic loop invariants. In: Joshi, K., Siegle, M., Stoelinga, M., D'Argenio, P.R. (eds.) QEST 2013. LNCS, vol. 8054, pp. 193–208. Springer, Heidelberg (2013)
9. Gretz, F., Katoen, J.-P., McIver, A.: Operational versus weakest pre-expectation semantics for the probabilistic guarded command language. Perform. Eval. **73**, 110–132 (2014)

10. Jansen, N., Corzilius, F., Volk, M., Wimmer, R., Ábrahám, E., Katoen, J.-P., Becker, B.: Accelerating parametric probabilistic verification. In: Norman, G., Sanders, W. (eds.) QEST 2014. LNCS, vol. 8657, pp. 404–420. Springer, Heidelberg (2014)
11. Kaminski, B.L., Katoen, J.-P.: On the hardness of almost–sure termination. In: Italiano, G.F., Pighizzini, G., Sannella, D.T. (eds.) MFCS 2015. LNCS, vol. 9234, pp. 307–318. Springer, Heidelberg (2015)
12. Katoen, J.-P., McIver, A.K., Meinicke, L.A., Morgan, C.C.: Linear-invariant generation for probabilistic programs. In: Cousot, R., Martel, M. (eds.) SAS 2010. LNCS, vol. 6337, pp. 390–406. Springer, Heidelberg (2010)
13. Nori, A.V., Hur, C.-K., Rajamani, S.K., Samuel, S.: R2: An efficient MCMC sampler for probabilistic programs. In: Proceedings of AAAI, AAAI Press (2014)
14. Pathak, S., Ábrahám, E., Jansen, N., Tacchella, A., Katoen, J.-P.: A greedy approach for the efficient repair of stochastic models. In: Havelund, K., Holzmann, G., Joshi, R. (eds.) NFM 2015. LNCS, vol. 9058, pp. 295–309. Springer, Heidelberg (2015)

Machines Reasoning About Machines: 2015

J Strother Moore[✉]

Department of Computer Science, University of Texas, Austin, USA
moore@cs.utexas.edu

Abstract. Computer hardware and software can be modeled precisely in mathematical logic. If expressed appropriately, these models can be executable, i.e., run on concrete data. This allows them to be used as simulation engines or rapid prototypes. But because they are formal they can be manipulated by symbolic means: theorems can be proved about them, directly, with mechanical theorem provers. But how practical is this vision of machines reasoning about machines? In this highly personal talk, I will describe the 45 year history of the "Boyer-Moore theorem prover," starting with its use in Edinburgh, Scotland, to prove simple list processing theorems by mathematical induction (e.g., the reverse of the reverse of x is x) to its routine commercial use in the microprocessor industry (e.g., the floating point operations of the Via Nano 64-bit X86 microprocessor are compliant with the IEEE standard). Along the way we will see applications in program verification, models of instruction set architectures including the JVM, and security and information flow. I then list some reasons this project has been successful. The paper also serves as an annotated bibliography of the key stepping stones in the applications of the prover.

1 Introduction

If we had some exact language ... or at least a kind of truly philosophic writing, in which the ideas were reduced to a kind of alphabet of human thought, then all that follows rationally from what is given could be found by a kind of calculus, just as arithmetical or geometrical problems are solved.
— *Leibniz (1646–1716)*

Instead of debugging a program, one should prove that it meets its specifications, and this proof should be checked by a computer program.
— *John McCarthy, "A Basis for a Mathematical Theory of Computation," 1961*

This paper is a highly personal recounting of 45 years spent in pursuit of the dream of building machines that can reason about machines. In my case, the machine doing the reasoning is the "Boyer-Moore theorem prover" and the machines about which it reasons are various algorithms, hardware designs, and software.

© Springer International Publishing Switzerland 2015
B. Finkbeiner et al. (Eds.): ATVA 2015, LNCS 9364, pp. 4–13, 2015.
DOI: 10.1007/978-3-319-24953-7_2

The first theorems proved by the "Boyer-Moore theorem prover," in Edinburgh, Scotland, in 1972, were simple list processing theorems such as

```
(equal (append (append a b) c)
       (append a (append b c)))
```

and

```
(implies (true-listp x)
         (equal (rev (rev x)) x))
```

where `append` and `rev` were defined recursively. The theorem prover automatically chose often-appropriate induction schemes and used axioms as rewrite rules. It could also generalize the conjecture being proved in order to set up successful inductions. By 2015, the "Boyer-Moore theorem prover" was being used nightly at a microprocessor company to verify functional correctness and other properties of various modules checked in the day before.

So how practical is the dream of machines reasoning about machines? Today, it is a reality.[1] But what were the stepping stones from the associativity of append to microprocessors?

2   A Quick History and Acknowledgments

There is no such thing as the "Boyer-Moore theorem prover." There have been a series of provers starting with the "Edinburgh Pure Lisp Theorem Prover" developed by Bob Boyer and me starting in 1971 in Edinburgh, Scotland. That prover was inspired by the ideas of John McCarthy (Lisp as a specification language and computational logic), Woody Bledsoe (how to build a heuristic theorem prover), Rod Burstall (induction as a routine proof step), A.P. Morse, and J.R. Shoenfield (logical foundations). It supported a home-grown untyped, first order, "pure Lisp" as the logic and was fully automatic; there was no way the user could change its behavior.

It evolved through QTHM (an unreleased version that supported quantification) to Nqthm ("New Quantified Theorem Prover") and then ACL2 ("A Computational Logic for Applicative Common Lisp"). All are known as the "Boyer-Moore theorem prover." But since about 1992, ACL2 has been developed and maintained by Matt Kaufmann and me, a fact recognized by the 2005 ACM Software System Award to Boyer, Kaufmann, and Moore for "the Boyer-Moore theorem prover."

ACL2 is available in open source form, without cost, under the terms of a 3-clause BSD license. See the ACL2 home page [31]. Many megabytes of documentation are available online and I refer to it sometimes in this paper by writing "see:DOC x," which means: go to the ACL2 home page, click on The User's Manual link, then click on the ACL2+Books Manual link and type x into the **Jump to** box.

While only three people, Bob Boyer, Matt Kaufmann, and me, are responsible for the code of those provers, many people have contributed to their success.

---

[1] For a discussion of why I consider this "reasoning" see [41].

Most often these contributors are users of the tools who pushed them beyond their intended limits, suggested ideas for overcoming those limits, tested proto-types, re-worked large proof scripts, etc., and demonstrated the flexibility and capacity of the provers. A quick scan of the bibliography will reveal some of their names.

Warren Hunt deserves special mention here. He formalized various hardware description languages in Nqthm and then ACL2 [23–25,43], demonstrated the potential of our tools to model and verify commercial microprocessor designs [25,28], trained many students in those techniques, helped start and build the verification teams at AMD, Centaur, and Oracle, and procured funding to main-tain and develop ACL2.

Given this brief history it should be clear that neither "the Boyer-Moore the-orem prover" nor most of the applications cited in this paper are my work alone. Indeed, I have had little or nothing to do with most of the recent applications other than co-authoring ACL2 with Bob Boyer and Matt Kaufmann. But I am in a unique position to report 45 years of formal methods history.

This paper will sketch the maturation of formal methods as seen from the perspective of the Boyer-Moore community by citing major verification projects carried out in our community with the Edinburgh Pure Lisp Theorem Prover, Nqthm, and ACL2.[2]

3   1970s – Simple List Processing

The most impressive theorem proved by the Edinburgh Pure Lisp Theorem prover [3,37] was probably the correctness of an insertion sort algorithm: the result is ordered and the number of times any object is listed in the output is equal to the number of times it is listed in the input. This was proved fully automatically from the recursive definitions of insertion and sort and involved interesting generalizations. But two things made the Edinburgh Pure Lisp Theo-rem prover stand out at a time when most other theorem provers were resolution based: it routinely proved theorems by induction and it proved a wide variety of theorems automatically. For a complete list of the theorems proved automatically by 1973 see [3].

By 1979, we had added the use of previously proved theorems as rewrite (and other kinds of) rules, allowing the user to steer the prover by suggesting lemmas [4]. For a description of the prover as it stood in 1979 and a summary of the important theorems proved see [5]. The important theorems included the existence and uniqueness of prime factorizations [5], the correctness of a ripple carry adder [38], the termination of the Takeuchi function [39], the correctness of a McCarthy-Painter-like expression compiler with respect to an assembly lan-guage formalized with an operational semantics [5], the correctness of the Boyer-Moore fast string searching algorithm in FORTRAN 77 [5], the correctness of

---

[2] For a wonderful narrative of one person's journey through formal methods appli-cations, mainly with Nqthm and ACL2, see Russinoff's page http://www.russinoff.com/papers/.

a linear-time majority vote algorithm in FORTRAN 77 [11], the soundness and completeness of a propositional tautology checker [5], and the correctness of a simple 1-dimensional real-time control algorithm ("cruise control") [13]. It was truly possible to reason mechanically about a wide variety of simple computing "machines."

The most important change to the prover in the 1970s, after the addition of lemmas, was the adoption of quote notation to represent constants in the logic. No longer was 3 represented by (ADD1 (ADD1 (ADD1 (ZERO)))); it was represented by (QUOTE 3). This change of term representation (and underlying logical changes) was described in [6] (the publication date of which belies when the work was actually done). The opened the door to much bigger models; for example, the opcodes for machine code instructions formalized with operational semantics were no longer huge terms.

4   1980s – Academic Math and Computer Science

In the 1980s Boyer and I moved to the University of Texas at Austin and started teaching and working with students. The use of QUOTE for constants allowed the efficient use of verified metafunctions [6]. We also integrated a linear arithmetic decision procedure (a process that took 4 years and, in our minds, did not warrant journal publication because it was "just engineering" since we had not invented a new decision procedure) [10].

Matt Kaufmann started calling this prover "Nqthm" which was originally just the name of the directory on which it was stored; the name stood for "New Quantified Theorem Prover." The name "Nqthm" stuck.

Boyer and I proved the invertibility of the RSA encryption algorithm [9], the unsolvability of the halting problem [8], and the Turing completeness of Pure Lisp [7].

By the mid-1980s, using Nqthm, Russinoff had proved Wilson's theorem [45], Shankar had proved Gödel's incompleteness theorem [47, 48], and Hunt had proved the correctness of a microprocessor described at the gate level [23, 24].

In 1987, Computational Logic, Inc. (CLI or more fondly "Clinc"), was founded and we left UT to continue our work there.

Hunt's microprocessor work positioned us to do "system verification," i.e., the verification of a hardware/software stack. The transition from hardware to software was facilitated by the implementation of a stack based assembly language, called Piton, which could be translated into Hunt's machine code for a register-based machine with a linear memory, but which was a convenient target for higher-level language compilers [2, 40]. I designed, implemented, and verified the correctness of the assembly/link/load process. Bevier verified an operating system [1], Flatau and Young verified compilers [18, 53], and Wilding verified some applications [52]. Furthermore, all the pieces were proved to "fit together:" the assumptions made at one level were verified at the next level so that one theorem ensured that if the preconditions of an application were satisfied then compiling, assembling, linking, and loading it on the gate machine and running it produced the results predicted by the high-level language. The entire "verified stack" was first published in a special issue of the **Journal of Automated Reasoning** in 1989 [2].

In the early 1990 s the stack was ported to a machine design by Hunt and Brock that was fabricated by LSI Logic from an NDL netlist verified with Nqthm [25,40]. Also in that time frame, Yu and Boyer proved the functional correctness of 21 of the 22 routines in the Berkeley Unix C String Library – performed by compiling the library with `gcc -o` to obtain binary machine code for the Motorola 68020 and then verifying that with respect to a formal operational semantics capturing 80 % of the user-level 68020 instructions [14], and, by the same technique, they proved a variety of other C programs, including the C code for binary search and Hoare's *in situ* Quick Sort from [34].

Boyer's website http://www.cs.utexas.edu/users/boyer/ftp/nqthm/ contains the sources for the 1992 version of Nqthm and all the proof scripts mentioned above and many others. See also [12].

However, the size of the models being formalized with Nqthm, the acceptance of the Common Lisp standard [50], and the inefficiency of our homegrown pure Lisp motivated us to adopt an applicative subset of Common Lisp as our logic. Boyer and I started the development of ACL2 in August, 1989.

5   1990s – Commercial Breakthrough

Two key projects with ACL2 convinced us and others that it was suitable for proving properties of commercially interesting models. One was the modeling and proofs about a Motorola digital signal processor and the other was the verification of the pseudocode for floating point division on the AMD K5 micro-processor before it was fabricated. Both projects are described in the 1996 paper [17]. The first project lasted 31 months starting in late 1993, the second project lasted about 2 months starting in June, 1995. For technical details see [16,42].

All of the elementary floating point arithmetic for the AMD Athlon was verified to be IEEE compliant by Russinoff using ACL2 [44]; this proof was done before the Athlon was fabricated and was based on a mechanical translation of the RTL (a variant of Verilog) description of the design. At the same time at Rockwell Collins, an ACL2 microarchitectural simulator for the first silicon-implemented JVM (the design became the JEM1 of aJile Systems, Inc.) was produced [22].

6   2000s – Gradual Acceptance

By this time ACL2 was in fairly routine if *ad hoc* use at a variety of companies manufacturing microprocessors and low level software. Scholarly papers were not always written because the work was not regarded as research so much as "just" verification that designs were correct. For example, at AMD properties of the Opteron and other desktop microprocessors were verified, and a verified ACL2

BDD package was built [51] that achieved about 60 % of the speed of the CUDD package (however, it did not support dynamic variable reordering).

At IBM, the algorithms used for floating point division and square root on the IBM Power 4 were verified [46]. At Rockwell Collins, the instruction equivalence of different implementations of a commercial microprocessor [20] was proved; in addition they proved that the microcode for the Rockwell Collins AAMP7 implements a given security policy having to do with process separation [21] allowing the AAMP7 to be certified for Multiple Independent Levels of Security (MILS).

At UT Austin, the Sun Java Virtual Machine was formalized and certain properties of Sun bytecode verifier as described in JSR-139 for J2ME JVMs [35] and the class loader [36] were verified.

Largely in response to the needs of users, ACL2 continued to evolve with the addition of such proof techniques as equivalence relations (see :DOC equivalence), congruence-based rewriting (see :DOC congruence), support for nonlinear arithmetic [27], extended metafunctions and clause processors (allowing the use of external proof tools like SAT solvers) [26,33], proof debugging tools [30], and many system programming facilities to support faster execution, faster loading of files, and the use of ACL2 both as a prototyping language and a language in which efficient, verified verification tools can be produced [19,29,32]. In addition, Bob Boyer, Warren Hunt, Jared Davis, Sol Swords and Matt Kaufmann prototyped the use of hash cons (unique representation of Lisp conses) and memoization which Matt Kaufmann and I eventually added to the standard release of ACL2 [15].

7   2010 – Integrated with the Design Process

ACL2 continues to be used on an *ad hoc* basis at many companies (including now Intel) to help gain confidence in designs. But there is one company where ACL2 is deeply integrated into the microprocessor design workflow: Centaur Technology.

Centaur produces x86 microprocessors (and is the third largest such manufacturer after Intel and AMD). In 2009, Hunt and Swords used ACL2 to verify the media unit of the Centaur (VIA) Nano 64-bit x86 CPU [28], which is part of Centaur's QuadCore processor. More significantly, the ACL2 team at Centaur has built an infrastructure that re-verifies designs nightly, running on hundreds of machines. In addition, ACL2-verified tools check wire-level engineering changes and clock trees. Errors introduced one day are addressed the next. This infrastructure is described in [49].

The cost of their ACL2 staff is less than the license fees previously paid for regression testing.

8   Lessons

Why has ACL2 succeeded to the extent that it has? Among the reasons are

- Everything is done in a single logic and that logic is an efficient, executable, ANSI standard programming language; models have dual use as emulators and formal semantics, and properties can be composed.
- We put a "human in the loop" doing things humans do well – inventing concepts and lemmas – allowing new proofs of modified modules to be found (often) automatically.
- We have spent decades engineering the system to be rugged and to handle large models.
- We encourage modelers to focus on problems that are appropriate for modeling with a programming language and to be bit- and cycle-accurate; conventional mathematical techniques are used to hide or expose the resulting complexity and to glue results together.
- We have an extremely talented and dedicated user community.
- Industry has no other option: modern machines are too complicated to be designed accurately without mechanized reasoning.

9 Conclusion

Formal methods saves times and costs less than informal ones – once sufficient investment is made in formalizing past designs and the terminology of the design group.

Complexity is not an argument against formal methods; it is an argument for formal methods.

References

1. Bevier, W.R.: A verified operating system kernel. Ph.D. dissertation, University of Texas at Austin (1987)
2. Bevier, W., Hunt Jr., W.A., Moore, J.S., Young, W.: Special issue on system verification. J. Autom. Reasoning **5**(4), 409–530 (1989)
3. Boyer, R.S., Moore, J.S.: Proving theorems about pure lisp functions. JACM **22**(1), 129–144 (1975)
4. Boyer, R.S., Moore, J.S.: A lemma driven automatic theorem prover for recursive function theory. In: 5th International Joint Conference on Artificial Intelligence, pp. 511–519 (1977)
5. Boyer, R.S., Moore, J.S.: A Computational Logic. Academic Press, New York (1979)
6. Boyer, R.S., Moore, J.S.: Metafunctions: Proving them correct and using them efficiently as new proof procedures. In: Boyer, R.S., Moore, J.S. (eds.) The Correctness Problem in Computer Science. Academic Press, London (1981)
7. Boyer, R.S., Moore, J.S.: A mechanical proof of the turing completeness of pure lisp. In: Bledsoe, W.W., Loveland, D.W. (eds.) Contemporary Mathematics: Automated Theorem Proving: After 25 Years, vol. 29, pp. 133–168. American Mathematical Society, Providence (1984)
8. Boyer, R.S., Moore, J.S.: A mechanical proof of the unsolvability of the halting problem. J. Assoc. Comput. Mach. **31**(3), 441–458 (1984)

9. Boyer, R.S., Moore, J.S.: Proof checking the rsa public key encryption algorithm. Am. Math. Monthly **91**(3), 181–189 (1984)
10. Boyer, R.S., Moore, J.S.: Integrating decision procedures into heuristic theorem provers: a case study of linear arithmetic. In: Hayes, J.E., Richards, J., Michie, D. (eds.) Machine Intelligence 11, pp. 83–124. Oxford University Press, Oxford (1988)
11. Boyer, R.S., Moore, J.S.: Mjrty - a fast majority vote algorithm. In: Boyer, R.S. (ed.) Automated Reasoning: Essays in Honor of Woody Bledsoe. Automated Reasoning Series, pp. 105–117. Kluwer Academic Publishers, Dordrecht (1991)
12. Boyer, R.S., Moore, J.S.: A Computational Logic Handbook, 2nd edn. Academic Press, New York (1997)
13. Boyer, R.S., Moore, J.S., Green, M.W.: The use of a formal simulator to verify a simple real time control program. In: Beauty is Our Business: A Birthday Salute to Edsger W. Dijkstra. pp. 54–66. Springer-Verlag Texts and Monographs in Computer Science (1990)
14. Boyer, R.S., Yu, Y.: Automated proofs of object code for a widely used microprocessor. J. ACM **43**(1), 166–192 (1996)
15. Boyer, R.S., Warren A., Hunt, J.: Function memoization and unique object representation for acl2 functions. In: ACL2 2006: Proceedings of the Sixth International Workshop on the ACL2 Theorem Prover and Its Applications, pp. 81–89. ACM, New York (2006)
16. Brock, B., Hunt Jr., W.A.: Formal analysis of the motorola CAP DSP. In: Hinchey, M.G., Bowen, J.P. (eds.) Industrial-Strength Formal Methods, pp. 81–115. Springer-Verlag, London (1999)
17. Brock, B., Kaufmann, M., Moore, J.S.: ACL2 theorems about commercial microprocessors. In: Srivas, M., Camilleri, A. (eds.) FMCAD 1996. LNCS, vol. 1166, pp. 275–293. Springer, Heidelberg (1996). http://www.cs.utexas.edu/users/moore/publications/bkm96.ps.Z
18. Flatau, A.D.: A verified implementation of an applicative language with dynamic storage allocation. Ph.D. thesis, University of Texas at Austin (1992)
19. Goel, S., Hunt, W., Kaufmann, M.: Simulation and formal verification of x86 machine-code programs that make system calls. In: Claessen, K., Kuncak, V. (eds.) FMCAD 2014: Proceedings of the 14th Conference on Formal Methods in Computer-Aided Design, pp. 91-98. EPFL, Switzerland (2014). http://www.cs.utexas.edu/users/hunt/FMCAD/FMCAD14/proceedings/final.pdf
20. Greve, D., Wilding, M.: Evaluatable, high-assurance microprocessors. In: NSA High-Confidence Systems and Software Conference (HCSS), Linthicum, MD, March 2002. http://hokiepokie.org/docs/hcss02/proceedings.pdf
21. Greve, D., Wilding, M.: A separation kernel formal security policy (2003)
22. Greve, D.A.: Symbolic simulation of the JEM1 microprocessor. In: Gopalakrishnan, G.C., Windley, P. (eds.) FMCAD 1998. LNCS, vol. 1522, pp. 321–333. Springer, Heidelberg (1998)
23. Hunt, Jr., W.A.: FM8501: a verified microprocessor. Ph.D. thesis, University of Texas at Austin (1985). (Published as a book by the same title, Cambridge University Press 1994)
24. Hunt Jr., W.A. (ed.): FM8501: A Verified Microprocessor. LNCS, vol. 795. Springer, Heidelberg (1994)
25. Hunt, Jr., W.A., Brock, B.: A formal HDL and its use in the FM9001 verification. In: Proceedings of the Royal Society, April 1992
26. Hunt Jr., W.A., Kaufmann, M., Krug, R.B., Moore, J.S., Smith, E.W.: Meta reasoning in ACL2. In: Hurd, J., Melham, T. (eds.) TPHOLs 2005. LNCS, vol. 3603, pp. 163–178. Springer, Heidelberg (2005)

27. Hunt Jr., W.A., Krug, R.B., Moore, J.: Linear and nonlinear arithmetic in ACL2. In: Geist, D., Tronci, E. (eds.) CHARME 2003. LNCS, vol. 2860, pp. 319–333. Springer, Heidelberg (2003)

28. Hunt Jr., W.A., Swords, S.: Centaur technology media unit verification. In: Bouajjani, A., Maler, O. (eds.) CAV 2009. LNCS, vol. 5643, pp. 353–367. Springer, Heidelberg (2009)

29. Kaufmann, M.: – Invited Talk – ACL2 support for verification projects. In: Kirchner, C., Kirchner, H. (eds.) CADE 1998. LNCS (LNAI), vol. 1421, pp. 220–238. Springer, Heidelberg (1998)

30. Kaufmann, M., Moore, J.S.: Proof search debugging tools in ACL2. In: A Festschrift in Honour of Prof. Michael J. C. Gordon FRS. Royal Society, London, March 2008

31. Kaufmann, M., Moore, J.S.: The ACL2 home page. In: Dept. of Computer Sciences, University of Texas at Austin (2014). http://www.cs.utexas.edu/users/moore/acl2/

32. Kaufmann, M.: Abbreviated output for input in ACL2: an implementation case study. In: Proceedings of ACL2 Workshop 2009, May 2009. http://www.cs.utexas.edu/users/sandip/acl2-09

33. Kaufmann, M., Moore, J.S., Ray, S., Reeber, E.: Integrating external deduction tools with ACL2. J. Appl. Logic **7**(1), 3–25 (2009)

34. Kernighan, B.W., Ritchie, D.M.: The C Programming Language, 2nd edn. Prentice Hall, Englewood Cliff (1988)

35. Liu, H., Moore, J.S.: Executable JVM model for analytical reasoning: a study. In: Workshop on Interpreters, Virtual Machines and Emulators 2003 (IVME 2003). ACM SIGPLAN, San Diego, June 2003

36. Liu, H.: Formal Specification and Verification of a JVM and its Bytecode Verifier. Ph.D. thesis, University of Texas at Austin (2006)

37. Moore, J.S.: Computational logic: Structure sharing and proof of program properties. Ph.D. dissertation, University of Edinburgh (1973). http://www.era.lib.ed.ac.uk/handle/1842/2245

38. Moore, J.S.: Automatic proof of the correctness of a binary addition algorithm. ACM SIGARG Newslett. **52**, 13–14 (1975)

39. Moore, J.S.: A mechanical proof of the termination of takeuchi's function. Inf. Process. Lett. **9**(4), 176–181 (1979)

40. Moore, J.S.: Piton: A Mechanically Verified Assembly-Level Language. Automated Reasoning Series. Kluwer Academic Publishers, Dordrecht (1996)

41. Moore, J.S.: A mechanized program verifier. In: Meyer, B., Woodcock, J. (eds.) VSTTE 2005. LNCS, vol. 4171, pp. 268–276. Springer, Heidelberg (2008)

42. Moore, J.S., Lynch, T., Kaufmann, M.: A mechanically checked proof of the correctness of the kernel of the AMD5K86 floating point division algorithm. IEEE Trans. Comput. **47**(9), 913–926 (1998)

43. Hunt Jr., W.A., Reeber, E.: Formalization of the DE2 language. In: Borrione, D., Paul, W. (eds.) CHARME 2005. LNCS, vol. 3725, pp. 20–34. Springer, Heidelberg (2005)

44. Russinoff, D.: A mechanically checked proof of IEEE compliance of a register-transfer-level specification of the AMD-K7 floating-point multiplication, division, and square root instructions. London Math. Soc. J. Comput. Math. **1**, 148–200 (1998). http://www.onr.com/user/russ/david/k7-div-sqrt.html

45. Russinoff, D.M.: An experiment with the boyer-moore theorem prover: a proof of wilson's theorem. J. Autom. Reasoning **1**(2), 121–139 (1985)

46. Sawada, J.: Formal verification of divide and square root algorithms using series calculation. In: Proceedings of the ACL2 Workshop, 2002, Grenoble, April 2002. http://www.cs.utexas.edu/users/moore/acl2/workshop-2002

47. Shankar, N.: Proof-checking metamathematics. Ph.D. thesis, University of Texas at Austin (1986). (Published as the book Metamathematics, Machines, and Gödel's Proof, Cambridge University Press, 1994)

48. Shankar, N.: Metamathematics, Machines, and Godel's Proof. Cambridge University Press, Cambridge (1994)

49. Slobodova, A., Davis, J., Swords, S., Warren Hunt, J.: A flexible formal verification framework for industrial scale validation. In: Singh, S. (ed.) 9th IEEE/ACM International Conference on Formal Methods and Models for Codesign (MEMOCODE), pp. 89–97. IEEE (2011)

50. Steele Jr., G.L.: Common Lisp The Language, 2nd edn. Digital Press, Burlington (1990)

51. Sumners, R.: Correctness proof of a BDD manager in the context of satisfiability checking. In: Proceedings of ACL2 Workshop 2000, Department of Computer Sciences, Technical report TR-00-29, November 2000. http://www.cs.utexas.edu/users/moore/acl2/workshop-2000/final/sumners2/paper.ps

52. Wilding, M.: A mechanically verified application for a mechanically verified environment. In: Courcoubetis, C. (ed.) CAV 1993. LNCS, vol. 697, pp. 268–279. Springer, Heidelberg (1993)

53. Young, W.D.: A verified code generator for a subset of Gypsy. Technical report 33, Computational Logic. Inc., Austin, Texas (1988)

Using SMT for Solving Fragments
of Parameterised Boolean Equation Systems

Ruud P.J. Koolen, Tim A.C. Willemse$^{(\boxtimes)}$, and Hans Zantema

Eindhoven University of Technology, Eindhoven, The Netherlands
{R.P.J.Koolen,T.A.C.Willemse,H.Zantema}@tue.nl

Abstract. Fixpoint logics such as parameterised Boolean equation systems (PBESs) provide a unifying framework in which a number of practical decision problems can be encoded. Efficient evaluation methods (*solving* methods in the terminology of PBESs) are needed to solve the encoded decision problems. We present a sound pseudo-decision procedure that uses SMT solvers for solving *conjunctive* and *disjunctive* PBESs. These are important fragments, allowing to encode typical verification problems and planning problems. Our experiments, conducted with a prototype implementation, show that the new solving procedure is complementary to existing techniques for solving PBESs.

1 Introduction

Fixpoint extensions of first-order logic, such as *Least Fixpoint Logic (LFP)* and *parameterised Boolean equation systems (PBESs)* have applications in database theory, computer aided verification and planning. For instance, PBESs have been used to solve Datalog queries in [1]; modern toolsets for computer aided verification, such as CADP [8] and mCRL2 [5], automatically generate and subsequently solve PBESs when solving their model checking and behavioural equivalence checking problems. The range of applications of PBESs calls for techniques for efficiently (partially or fully) solving PBESs as solving them answers the encoded decision problems.

A variety of techniques for partially or fully solving PBESs exist, see [10]. A commonly used technique to partially solve a PBES is by first instantiating it to a *Boolean equation system (BES)* [15], and subsequently solving the latter. Instantiation bears close similarities to generating a behavioural state space from a high-level specification; in particular, it is often hampered by a similar combinatorial explosion. While static analysis techniques for PBESs such as those in [13], as implemented by tools in mCRL2 can help to combat the explosion, cases remain for which all known techniques fail, and the only practical solution seems to be to resort to symbolic reasoning.

SMT solvers are one kind of general tool for symbolic reasoning, but so far, they have not been used for solving PBESs. The *satisfiability modulo theories* or *SMT* problem is the problem of computing for a particular first-order logical theory whether that theory has a model. That is, for a given set of function symbols and a given set of first-order axioms over those function symbols,

© Springer International Publishing Switzerland 2015
B. Finkbeiner et al. (Eds.): ATVA 2015, LNCS 9364, pp. 14–30, 2015.
DOI: 10.1007/978-3-319-24953-7_3

the problem consists of determining whether an interpretation of those function symbols exists such that the axioms hold. The SMT problem is, like the PBES solving problem, undecidable in general. However, algorithms exist that can efficiently solve particular fragments of it, and modern SMT solvers are often quite effective at solving practical SMT problems.

Our contribution is an efficient decision procedure for partially solving an important fragment of PBESs. The decision procedure is built on SMT technology, borrowing ideas from bounded model checking. This procedure is:

- *sound* in the sense that upon termination, the answer it provides is correct.
- *complete*, up to the completeness of the SMT solver that is used, for PBESs with a *dependency space* admitting only bounded acyclic paths. This completeness criterion is determined dynamically, in a way that is similar to the technique of [14] for finite state systems.

Our SMT-based solver is able to partially solve PBESs that are out of reach for existing solving methods. Indeed, in Sect. 3, we describe a typical planning problem that cannot reasonably be solved using existing PBES solving techniques, and in Sect. 6, we further compare our prototype implementation of the decision procedure with existing solving techniques for a larger set of cases, illustrating that the technique is complementary to these.

The fragment of PBESs covered by our solver, which we refer to as the *disjunctive* and *conjunctive* fragment of PBESs, captures typical decision problems such as LTL model checking, but also real-time and first-order extensions of such model checking problems.

Related Work. There have been two previous attempts to solving PBESs symbolically, both using technology inspired by BDDs and variations thereof; see [9] and, more recently [11]. These approaches have proved to substantially scale and speed up solving PBESs, but practical cases remain where those tools do not help or even perform worse than standard instantiation-based tools.

Within the domain of computer aided verification, *bounded model checking (BMC)*, pioneered by Clarke, Biere, Raimi and Zhu [4] has been steadily gaining popularity. This technique is strongly related to the approaches used in this paper. Bounded model checking is commonly based on SAT solvers as the tool of choice; a consequence of this is that these techniques can only work with model checking problems for which all domains are finite. Model checkers such as nuXmv [3], and dedicated software model checkers that sport SMT solvers can potentially deal with domains that are infinite. For select properties, using dedicated techniques such as k-induction, BMC sometimes extends from refuting to proving properties. Such techniques are not guaranteed to lead to success; *e.g.*, unlike our procedure, nuXmv currently seems unable to prove the absence of a planning for our example in Sect. 3.

Structure of the Paper. In Sect. 2, we give a brief overview of parameterised Boolean equation systems, and in Sect. 3 we give an example of a small PBES that is typically hard to solve using existing techniques for solving PBESs.

Section 4 introduces a fragment of PBESs and develops the theory underlying our SMT-based decision procedure for solving PBESs, presented in Sect. 5. In Sect. 6 we provide an experimental evaluation of our contribution and in Sect. 7 we reflect on our results and discuss possibilities for future research.

2   Preliminaries

Throughout this paper, we work in a setting of *abstract data types* with non-empty data sorts $D, E, \ldots$, operations on these, and a set $\mathcal{D}$ of data variables.

With every sort D, we associate a semantic set $\mathbb{D}$, such that each term of sort D, and all operations on D are mapped to the elements and operations of $\mathbb{D}$ they represent. Terms not containing data variables are referred to as *ground terms*. For terms that contain data variables, we use an environment δ that maps each variable from $\mathcal{D}$ to a value of the associated type. We assume an interpretation function $\llbracket \_ \rrbracket$ that maps every term t of sort D to the data element $\llbracket t \rrbracket \delta$ it represents, where the extensions of δ to open terms is standard. Environment updates are denoted $\delta[v/d]$, where $\delta[v/d](d') = v$ if $d' = d$, and $\delta(d')$ otherwise.

We specifically assume the existence of a sort B with elements *true* and *false* representing the Booleans $\mathbb{B}$, a sort $N = \{0, 1, 2, \ldots\}$ representing the natural numbers $\mathbb{N}$ and a sort $Z = \{\ldots, -2, -1, 0, 1, 2, \ldots\}$ representing the integers $\mathbb{Z}$. For these sorts, we assume that the usual operators are available and, for readability, these are written the same as their semantic counterparts.

Parameterised Boolean equation systems [10] are sequences of fixed-point equations ranging over *predicate formulae*. The latter are first-order formulae extended with sorted predicate variables, in which the non-logical symbols are taken from the data language. Without loss of generality, we assume that all predicate variables range over the same sort D; in concrete examples, we sometimes deviate from this convention for the sake of readability.

Definition 1. *Predicate formulae are defined through the following grammar:*

$$\varphi ::= b \mid X(e) \mid \varphi \wedge \varphi \mid \varphi \vee \varphi \mid \forall d \colon E.\varphi \mid \exists d \colon E.\varphi$$

in which b is a data term of sort B, possibly containing negation, X is a predicate variable of sort $D \to B$ taken from some sufficiently large set $\mathcal{P}$ of predicate variables, e is a data term of sort D, and d is a data variable of sort E. The interpretation of a predicate formula φ in the context of a predicate environment $\eta \colon \mathcal{P} \to 2^{\mathbb{D}}$ and a data environment δ is denoted as $\llbracket \varphi \rrbracket \eta \delta$, where:

$$\llbracket b \rrbracket \eta \delta = \begin{cases} true \ if \ \llbracket b \rrbracket \delta \\ false \ otherwise \end{cases} \qquad \llbracket X(e) \rrbracket \eta \delta = \begin{cases} true \ if \ \llbracket e \rrbracket \delta \in \eta(X) \\ false \ otherwise \end{cases}$$

$$\llbracket \varphi \wedge \psi \rrbracket \eta \delta = \llbracket \varphi \rrbracket \eta \delta \ and \ \llbracket \psi \rrbracket \eta \delta \ hold \qquad \llbracket \varphi \vee \psi \rrbracket \eta \delta = \llbracket \varphi \rrbracket \eta \delta \ or \ \llbracket \psi \rrbracket \eta \delta \ hold$$

$$\llbracket \forall d \colon E. \ \varphi \rrbracket \eta \delta = for \ all \ v \in E, \ \llbracket \varphi \rrbracket \eta \delta[v/d] \ holds$$

$$\llbracket \exists d \colon E. \ \varphi \rrbracket \eta \delta = for \ some \ v \in E, \ \llbracket \varphi \rrbracket \eta \delta[v/d] \ holds$$

We assume the usual precedence rules for the logical operators.

Definition 2. *PBESs are defined by the following grammar:*

$$\mathcal{E} ::= \emptyset \mid (\nu X(d\colon D) = \varphi)\mathcal{E} \mid (\mu X(d\colon D) = \varphi)\mathcal{E}$$

in which $\emptyset$ denotes the empty PBES; μ and ν are the least and greatest fixed point signs, respectively; X is a sorted predicate variable of sort $D \to B$, d is a formal parameter, and φ is a predicate formula.

The set of *bound predicate variables* of some PBES $\mathcal{E}$, denoted $\mathsf{bnd}(\mathcal{E})$, is the set of predicate variables occurring at the left-hand sides of the equations in $\mathcal{E}$. Throughout this paper, we deal with PBESs that are both *well-formed, i.e.* for every $X \in \mathsf{bnd}(\mathcal{E})$ there is exactly one equation in $\mathcal{E}$.

Notation. *By convention φ_X denotes the right-hand side of the equation for X in a PBES $\mathcal{E}$. By subscripting a formal parameter with the predicate variable to which it belongs, we distinguish between formal parameters for different predicate variables, i.e., we write d_X for the formal parameter of X. The fixpoint sign μ or ν, associated with the equation for X is denoted σ_X. We omit a trailing $\emptyset$.*

We say that PBES $\mathcal{E}$ is *closed* iff for every $X \in \mathsf{bnd}(\mathcal{E})$, only predicate variables taken from $\mathsf{bnd}(\mathcal{E})$ occur in φ_X; throughout this paper, we restrict ourselves to closed PBESs. Moreover, we assume that no free variables other than d_X occur in φ_X, and that d_X does not occur as a variable bound by a quantifier in φ_X.

We next define a PBES's semantics. From hereon, let $\mathcal{E}$ be an arbitrary closed PBES. For the sake of completeness, we first give the standard, inductively defined fixpoint semantics. In the remainder of this paper we will use a graph-based characterisation of this semantics, which we introduce on the next page. For a given pair of environments δ, η, a predicate formula φ_X gives rise to a predicate transformer T_X on the complete lattice $(2^{\mathbb{D}}, \subseteq)$ as follows: $T_X(R) = \{v \in \mathbb{D} \mid [\![\varphi_X]\!]\eta[R/X]\delta[v/d]\}$, where $R \subseteq \mathbb{D}$. Since the predicate transformers defined this way are monotone, their extremal fixed points exist. We denote the least fixed point of a given predicate transformer T_X by μT_X, and the greatest fixed point of T_X is denoted νT_X. The semantics of a single equation then extends to sequences of equations.

Definition 3. *The* solution *of a PBES, in the context of a predicate environment η and data environment δ, is a predicate environment defined inductively:*

$$[\![\emptyset]\!]\eta\delta = \eta$$
$$[\![(\mu X(d\colon D) = \varphi_X)\mathcal{E}]\!]\eta\delta = [\![\mathcal{E}]\!]\eta[\mu T_X/X]\delta$$
$$[\![(\nu X(d\colon D) = \varphi_X)\mathcal{E}]\!]\eta\delta = [\![\mathcal{E}]\!]\eta[\nu T_X/X]\delta$$

with $T_X(R) = \lambda v \in \mathbb{D}.[\![\varphi_X]\!]([\![\mathcal{E}]\!]\eta[R/X]\delta)\delta[v/d]$

We refer to the problem of computing whether $v \in [\![\mathcal{E}]\!]\eta\delta(X)$ as (partially) solving a PBES. For a closed PBES, the solution to its bound predicate variables is independent of the environments used to compute the solution; we therefore write $[\![\mathcal{E}]\!](X)$ instead of $[\![\mathcal{E}]\!]\eta\delta(X)$.

Example 1. Consider $(\nu X(n\colon N) = Y(n+1))(\mu Y(n\colon N) = X(n) \vee Y(n+1))$. The solution for X is the set of all natural numbers. This can be seen by unfolding the semantics and using a transfinite approximation for computing the least and greatest fixpoints of the transformers associated to the right-hand side formulae.

Within the context of this paper we will use a characterisation of the semantics of PBESs in terms of *proof graphs*: particular types of graphs that capture the dependencies among the predicate variables of the equation systems. This characterisation will be more convenient to use in the context of this paper. While proof graphs were introduced in [6] for the purpose of certification of PBES solutions, we will be using SMT solving for *finding*, instead of *checking*, these certificates in the next sections.

We will be needing a few additional notions before we can define the notion of a proof graph. The *signature* of $\mathcal{E}$, denoted $\mathsf{sig}(\mathcal{E})$, is the set $\{(X,v) \mid X \in \mathsf{bnd}(\mathcal{E}), v \in \mathbb{D}\}$. For given set $S \subseteq \mathsf{sig}(\mathcal{E})$, we write $S_{\mathsf{true}}(X)$ for the predicate environment induced by S as follows: $S_{\mathsf{true}}(X) = \{v \in \mathbb{D} \mid (X,v) \in S\}$. We furthermore assume a mapping $\mathsf{rank}_{\mathcal{E}}(\_)$ which assigns to every bound predicate variable of $\mathcal{E}$ a unique natural number that satisfies:

- $\mathsf{rank}_{\mathcal{E}}(X) \leq \mathsf{rank}_{\mathcal{E}}(Y)$ iff the equation for X precedes Y's equation in $\mathcal{E}$;
- $\mathsf{rank}_{\mathcal{E}}(X)$ is even iff $\sigma_X = \nu$.

Definition 4. *Let $G = (V, E)$ be a directed graph on $V \subseteq \mathsf{sig}(\mathcal{E})$. For $v \in V$, $v^{\bullet}$ denotes the set $\{w \in V \mid (v,w) \in E\}$. Then G is a* dependency graph *just whenever for all $(X,v) \in V$: for all δ, $[\![\varphi_X]\!]\eta\delta[v/d_X]$ holds, where $\eta = (X,v)^{\bullet}_{\mathsf{true}}$.*

For an infinite path $\pi = (X_0, v_0)(X_1, v_1) \ldots$ in a dependency graph, let $V^{\infty}(\pi)$ denote the set of predicate variables X_i occurring infinitely often along the path π. Note that since the set $\mathsf{bnd}(\mathcal{E})$ is finite, $V^{\infty}(\pi)$ is not empty.

Definition 5. *Let $G = (V, E)$ be a dependency graph for $\mathcal{E}$. Then G is a* proof graph *for $\mathcal{E}$ iff for all infinite paths π in G, $\min\{\mathsf{rank}_{\mathcal{E}}(X) \mid X \in V^{\infty}(\pi)\}$ is even.*

The existence of a proof graph for $\mathcal{E}$ is related to the solution of $\mathcal{E}$ in the following way.

Theorem 1 ([6]). *Let $X \in \mathsf{bnd}(\mathcal{E})$. Then $v \in [\![\mathcal{E}]\!](X)$ iff there is a proof graph (V, E) such that $(X, v) \in V$.*

Example 2. Reconsider the PBES of the previous example. To see that the solution to X (and that of Y) is indeed the set of all natural numbers, a (fragment of a) proof graph testifying this is as follows:

$$(Y,0) \rightarrow (X,0) \rightarrow (Y,1) \rightarrow (X,1) \rightarrow (Y,2) \rightarrow (X,2) \longrightarrow \cdots$$
$$\quad 1 \qquad\quad 0 \qquad\quad 1 \qquad\quad 0 \qquad\quad 1 \qquad\quad 0$$

Here, for the purpose of illustration we used a rank function assigning 0 to X and 1 to Y. Observe that this is indeed a correct rank function, and it is such that the least rank of all the predicate variables occurring infinitely often on the above path is even.

3   A Motivating Example

A common technique for solving a PBES is through *instantiation* [15], which, if it terminates, generates a *Boolean equation system (BES)*. The latter is a fragment of PBESs with equations ranging over propositions only and for which solving is decidable. A drawback of instantiation is that it suffers from a combinatorial explosion that is similar to the state space explosion.

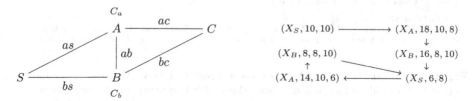

Fig. 1. Left: Configuration of a planning problem. Right: proof graph for the PBES using a small instance of the planning problem with maximal capacities $C_a = C_b = 10$, time to travel between villages $as = bs = ab = 2$, $ac = bc = 8$ and maximal truckload capacity $M = 20$.

We illustrate the combinatorial explosion through a simple *planning problem*. Given are four villages S, A, B, C, of which S is self-sufficient, A and B need to be periodically supplied with food produced by supply center S, and C needs to be periodically supplied with medicine also produced by S. Supplies are distributed by a single truck that drives around between the different villages, loading and unloading goods at each location. The truck has a bounded food cargo capacity M, but an unbounded cargo capacity for medicine, whose size is assumed to be negligible. Similarly, the amount of food that A and B can store is bounded by C_a and C_b, respectively, whereas the medicine store in C is unbounded. It takes time for the truck to travel between two places, during which each village consumes a unit of food from its stockpile per time unit; see Fig. 1 (left) for an abstract depiction of the problem.

The PBES in Fig. 2 encodes a decision problem based on this scenario. The equation for X_v, where v is one of the villages S, A, B or C, encodes the problem of whether there is a driving and unloading schedule for the truck (when currently in village v) to follow such that A and B never run out of food, without considering the fate of C. Such a PBES is obtained automatically by encoding a modal μ-calculus formula of the form $\nu X.(A \geq 0 \wedge B \geq 0 \wedge \Box X).$[1] Using a small instance of the planning problem for which there is a positive answer, the proof graph, depicted in Fig. 1 (right), shows that there is indeed a planning that meets the requirements. Intuitively, the proof graph represents the driving schedule $(S\ A\ B)^\omega$; the unwinding in the proof graph is due to the fact that we can never return to the starting state in which both villages have a supply of 10.

Our planning problem becomes more difficult if we consider larger instances of our planning problem, and, in addition, we also require the truck to visit

---

[1] In LTL one would write $G(A \geq 0 \wedge B \geq 0)$.

$\nu X_S(A, B: Z) =$
$\quad \exists m : N.(as \leq A \wedge as \leq B \wedge A - as + m \leq C_A \wedge m \leq M \wedge X_A(M - m, A - as + m, B - as))$
$\vee \ \exists m : N.(bs \leq A \wedge bs \leq B \wedge B - bs + m \leq C_B \wedge m \leq M \wedge X_B(M - m, A - bs, B - bs + m))$

$\nu X_A(T, A, B: Z) =$
$\quad \exists m : N.(ab \leq A \wedge ab \leq B \wedge B - ab + m \leq C_B \wedge m \leq T \wedge X_B(T - m, A - ab, B - ab + m))$
$\vee \ (ac \leq A \wedge ac \leq B \wedge X_C(T, A - ac, B - ac))$
$\vee \ (as \leq A \wedge as \leq B \wedge X_S(A - as, B - as))$

$\nu X_B(T, A, B: Z) =$
$\quad \exists m : N.(ab \leq A \wedge ab \leq B \wedge A - ab + m \leq C_A \wedge m \leq T \wedge X_A(T - m, A - ab + m, B - ab))$
$\vee \ (bc \leq A \wedge bc \leq B \wedge X_C(T, A - bc, B - bc))$
$\vee \ (bs \leq A \wedge bs \leq B \wedge X_S(A - bs, B - bs))$

$\nu X_C(T, A, B: Z) =$
$\quad \exists m : N.(bc \leq A \wedge bc \leq B \wedge B - bc + m \leq C_B \wedge m \leq T \wedge X_B(T - m, A - bc, B - bc + m))$
$\vee \ \exists m : N.(ac \leq A \wedge ac \leq B \wedge A - ac + m \leq C_A \wedge m \leq T \wedge X_A(T - m, A - ac + m, B - ac))$

Fig. 2. A PBES that encodes whether there is a planning for visiting villages A and B so that neither village runs out of stock. The PBES is generated automatically using the mCRL2 toolset [5]; it encodes the (first-order) modal μ-calculus model checking problem expressing that there is an infinite path along which, at any point in time, food supply is non-negative: $\nu X.(A \geq 0 \wedge B \geq 0 \wedge \Box X)$.

village C infinitely often. The existence of a driving schedule that meets these requirements can be expressed by a PBES with both μ and ν-equations, encoding a modal μ-calculus model checking problem for an alternating formula such as $\nu X.\mu Y.(A \geq 0 \wedge B \geq 0 \wedge (\Diamond (X \wedge loc = C) \vee \Diamond Y)).$[2]

To illustrate the complexity of the resulting problem: using an instance with two villages that can store up to 1071 (C_a) and 1071 (C_b) units of food and a truck that can carry up to 2200 (M) units of food at any time, and $as = 290, ab = 400, ac = 230, bs = 380$ and $bc = 190$, a naive upper bound on the size of the reachable state space is about $1071 \times 1071 \times 2200 \approx 2.5 \times 10^9$ states with a rather dense transition relation.

As a result the PBES encoding the planning problem faces the same complexities. Proving that there is no schedule that meets the constraints of visiting C infinitely often using conventional tooling turns out to be impossible. State-of-the-art tools for solving the resulting PBES using instantiation, such as those described in [15], work by brute-force enumeration and require an exceedingly long time to solve the food distribution problem; our experiment running a PBES instantiation tool was aborted after running for several days. The same is true for BDD-based PBES solving tools such as those described in [11], but also the SMT-based solver of nuXmv [3] appears to be incapable of showing the non-existence of a schedule that meets all constraints. In contrast, the solution we describe in the next sections successfully quickly shows that there is no schedule that meets the requirements, see also Sect. 6.

4   Disjunctive and Conjunctive PBESs

Disjunctive and conjunctive PBESs are important fragments of PBESs, capturing decision problems such as model checking LTL and various extensions

---

[2] In LTL one would write $G(A \geq 0 \wedge B \geq 0 \wedge F(loc = C))$.

thereof. In essence, the right-hand side predicate formulae occurring in a disjunctive PBES are restricted so as to only allow predicate variables to occur within the scope of disjunctions and existential quantifications.

Definition 6. *A formula φ is* disjunctive *if it follows the following grammar:*

$$\varphi ::= X(e) \mid \varphi \wedge \psi \mid \varphi \vee \varphi \mid \exists d\colon E.\varphi$$
$$\psi ::= b \mid \psi \wedge \psi \mid \psi \vee \psi \mid \forall d\colon E.\psi \mid \exists d\colon E.\psi$$

Formulae defined by the grammar ψ are called simple. *A PBES is* disjunctive *if all its right-hand side formulae are disjunctive predicate formulae.*

Let $\mathcal{E}$ be an arbitrary disjunctive PBES. We next show that it suffices to look for the existence (or absence) of *minimal* proof graphs for $\mathcal{E}$ of a particular shape. Arbitrary proof graphs may contain redundancy. For instance, a proof graph witnessing that $0 \in [\![\mathcal{E}]\!](X)$ for $\mathcal{E} \equiv (\nu X(n\colon \mathbb{N}) = X(n+1))(\nu Z(n\colon \mathbb{N}) = X(n))$ may have vertices (Z, i) and edges from vertex (X, i) to vertices (Z, j). A proof graph that contains no such irrelevant information is said to be minimal.

Definition 7. *Let $G = (V, E)$ be a proof graph for $\mathcal{E}$. Let $v \in V$. Then G is a* minimal *proof graph containing v iff there is no strict subgraph $G' = (V', E')$ with $v \in V'$, that is also a proof graph for $\mathcal{E}$.*

Proposition 1. *We have $v \in [\![\mathcal{E}]\!](X)$ iff there is a minimal proof graph $G = (V, E)$ with $(X, v) \in V$, satisfying $|(Y, w)^{\bullet}| \leq 1$ for all $(Y, w) \in V$.*

Proof. Since $v \in [\![\mathcal{E}]\!](X)$, there must be a proof graph containing (X, v). This proof graph can be minimised by showing that for an arbitrary vertex $(Y, w) \in V$ it suffices to pick at most one of the successors of (Y, w). The latter follows from the fact that φ_Y is disjunctive. The reverse implication follows from Theorem 1.

Following the above proposition, it thus suffices to search for proof graphs with particular characteristics. We next characterise the search space—we call this search space the *dependency space*—that contains all proof graphs of that characteristic, and we proceed to claim that any minimal proof graph is contained in this search space. This means that any disjunctive PBES can be solved by searching for a minimal proof graph within the confined space: finding a minimal proof graph containing some vertex (X, v) means we can establish that the PBES $\mathcal{E}$ defining X satisfies $v \in [\![\mathcal{E}]\!](X)$; the absence of a minimal proof graph containing (X, v) within the search space implies the absence of any proof graph containing (X, v), and as a result, $v \notin [\![\mathcal{E}]\!](X)$.

Definition 8. *The* dependency space *of $\mathcal{E}$ is a graph $G = (V, E)$, where:*

- *$V = \mathsf{sig}(\mathcal{E})$;*
- *$E \subseteq V \times V$ is defined by $(X, v)\ E\ (Y, w)$ iff for $\eta = \{(Y, w)\}_{true}$ we have $[\![\varphi_X]\!]\eta\delta[v/d_X]$ and for $\eta = \emptyset_{true}$, $[\![\varphi_X]\!]\eta\delta[v/d_X]$ does not hold.*

Intuitively, the dependency space contains all vertices and edges a minimal proof graph for a disjunctive PBES needs to have. Indeed, the proposition below formalises this.

Proposition 2. *Let $G = (V, E)$ be the dependency space for $\mathcal{E}$ and $(X, v) \in V$.*

1. G is a dependency graph;
2. All minimal proof graphs containing vertex (X, v) are subgraphs of G.

Following the above proposition, we can thus restrict our attention to the paths in a dependency space. Before we proceed, we introduce a normal form for disjunctive PBESs which we will use for ease of reasoning, and which allows us to further restrict the shape of the dependency space. PBESs in general can be automatically rewritten to a variation of the prefix-normal form of [13]. For disjunctive PBESs, a simplification of this normal form is adequate.

Definition 9. *A disjunctive predicate formula is in* disjunctive normal form *(DNF) iff it is a disjunction of existential clauses, i.e. it is of the following form:*

$$\bigvee_{i \in I} \exists e_i \colon E_i.\ f_i(d, e_i) \wedge X_i(g_i(d, e_i))$$

where I is a non-empty index set and f_i is a simple formula, possibly containing variables e_i and d, and g_i is an expression, possibly containing variables e_i and d. $\mathcal{E}$ is in DNF iff all its right-hand side predicate formulae are in DNF.

Example 3. The PBES $\nu X(n\colon N) = (n < 1 \wedge X(n)) \vee (n \geq 1 \wedge X(n-1))$ is in DNF; on the other hand, the PBES $\nu X(n\colon N) = (n < 1 \vee X(n-1))$ is not.

Lemma 1. *For every disjunctive PBES $\mathcal{E}$, there is an $\mathcal{E}'$ in DNF such that $[\![\mathcal{E}]\!](X) = [\![\mathcal{E}']\!](X)$ for all $X \in \mathsf{bnd}(\mathcal{E})$.*

Proof. Observe that equations of the form $\mu X(d\colon D) = \varphi_X$ can be rewritten to $\mu X(d\colon D) = \varphi_X \vee X(d)$, and equations of the form $\nu(Xd\colon D) = \varphi_X$ can be rewritten to $\nu X(d\colon D) = \varphi_X \vee X_{\mathsf{false}}(d)$ where $\mu X_{\mathsf{false}}(d\colon D) = X_{\mathsf{false}}(d)$, representing 'false' and with solution $\emptyset$ is a new equation following X's. Assuming a PBES is rewritten such as above, the desired result then follows by a straightforward induction on the structure of the predicate formulae.

It follows immediately that the dependency space for $\mathcal{E}$ in DNF only consists of infinite paths. By Proposition 1 this implies that we can determine the solution of a PBES in DNF by zooming in on infinite paths only.

Assume from hereon that $\mathcal{E}$ is in DNF. In case a proof graph consisting of an infinite path is finite, it must be of the form of a lasso. Note that minimal proof graphs need not be finite; in fact no finite proof graphs need exist, as illustrated by the example below.

Example 4. Let $\mathcal{E} \equiv (\nu X(n\colon \mathbb{N}) = X(n+1))$. A proof graph must at least contain the infinite path $(X, 0)\ (X, 1)\ (X, 2) \ldots$ to show that $0 \in [\![\mathcal{E}]\!](X)$.

Even in case we can find a lasso-shaped dependency graph, such a graph need not be a proof graph: this is only the case if the cycle is ν-*dominated*.

Definition 10. *Let $G = (V, E)$ be a dependency space for $\mathcal{E}$ and let π be the finite sequence of vertices $(X_0, v_0)\,(X_1, v_1) \ldots (X_n, v_n)$ in G. Then:*

- *π is called a* lasso *if there is an $i < n$ such that $(X_n, v_n) = (X_i, v_i)$;*
- *A lasso π is ν-dominated iff* $\min\{rank_{\mathcal{E}}(X_j) \mid i \leq j < n\}$ *is even.*

The proposition below follows instantly from Propositions 1 and 2.

Proposition 3. *If the dependency space of $\mathcal{E}$ contains a ν-dominated lasso starting in a vertex (X, v), then $v \in [\![\mathcal{E}]\!](X)$.*

As a result of the above proposition, we find that a witness to a ν-dominated lasso in the dependency space suffices to prove that a particular value belongs to the solution of a predicate variable in $\mathcal{E}$. The converse of the above lemma does not hold in general as Example 4 illustrates: if $v \in [\![\mathcal{E}]\!](X)$ for $\mathcal{E}$, no ν-dominated lassoes containing (X, v) need exist. The proposition below phrases a sufficient condition guaranteeing that the converse *does* hold.

Proposition 4. *Assume that in the dependency space $G = (V, E)$, all paths of length exceeding n, and starting in vertex (X, v), are lassoes. If $v \in [\![\mathcal{E}]\!](X)$, then there is a proof graph, containing vertex (X, v), that is a ν-dominated lasso.*

Proof. Suppose that all paths in G, starting in (X, v) and of length larger than n, are lassoes. Assume $v \in [\![\mathcal{E}]\!](X)$. By Theorem 1, there is a proof graph $G' = (V', E')$ for which $(X, v) \in V'$. But then there is also a proof graph $G'' \subseteq G'$ that is minimal. By Proposition 2, G'' must be contained in G. Since all paths in G of length exceeding n are lasso-shaped, G'' is necessarily lasso-shaped. Since G'' is a proof graph, the lasso must be ν-dominated.

We remark that conjunctive PBESs can be defined dually to disjunctive PBESs. All results for disjunctive PBESs in this and the next section have straightforward dual counterparts for conjunctive PBESs.

5   Solving Disjunctive and Conjunctive PBESs Using SMT

For disjunctive PBESs, Proposition 3 suggests PBESs can be solved using SMT solvers: find a ν-dominated lasso in the dependency space. Finding an arbitrary lasso is problematic in general; the best one can achieve is encoding that there is a ν-dominated lasso of a maximal size. Through a stepwise increase in size, a 'witness' may then be found. Showing that a witness does *not* exist is a different matter which cannot be demonstrated using this technique; after all, a witness of a length larger than any length tested so far could always exist. Therefore, an independent method, based on Proposition 4, for finding out when to stop searching for ever-larger witnesses is necessary to (partially) complete the above technique. In this section, we develop a pseudo-decision procedure for solving PBESs in DNF using the approach described above.

5.1   Finding Lasso-Shaped Proof Graphs

We first express the existence of a transition between two vertices in a dependency space as an SMT proposition. Building on these SMT propositions, we can then express the existence of a ν-dominated lasso within the dependency space.

Definition 11. *Let* $(\sigma_1 X_1(d_1 : D) = \varphi_1(d_1)) \ldots (\sigma_m X_m(d_m : D) = \varphi_m(d_m))$ *be in DNF, i.e. for all* $1 \leq k \leq m$:

$$\varphi_k(d_k) = \bigvee_{l \in I_k} \exists e_l \colon E_l.\ f_l(d_k, e_l) \wedge X_l(g_l(d_k, e_l))$$

For variables X^i, X^j *ranging over the set* $\{X_k \mid 1 \leq k \leq m\}$ *and variables* d^i, d^j *ranging over sort* D, *we define the SMT proposition* $occurs(X^i, d^i, X^j, d^j)$ *as follows:*

$$occurs(X^i, d^i, X^j, d^j)$$
$$\equiv$$
$$\bigvee_{1 \leq k \leq m} \bigvee_{l \in I_k} \left((X^i = X_k) \wedge (X^j = X_l) \wedge \exists e_l \colon E_l \Big[f_l(d^i, e_l) \wedge (d^j = g_l(d^i, e_l)) \Big] \right)$$

The lemma below relates the existence of edges in the dependency space to the evaluation of the above-defined SMT proposition. Let $\mathcal{E}$ be in DNF.

Lemma 2. *For* $\mathcal{E}$ *and its dependency space* $G = (V, E)$, *we have* $(X, v)\ E\ (Y, w)$ *iff* $occurs(X^0, d^0, X^1, d^1)$ *is true for the assignment* $X^0 = X$, $X^1 = Y$, $d^0 = v$ *and* $d^1 = w$.

SMT proposition occurs extends naturally to one for a symbolic n-step path $(X^0, d^0) \ldots (X^n, d^n)$, where each X^i is a variable representing a predicate variable and d^i represents X^i's formal parameter value. We refer to these symbolic n-step paths as n-unrollings.

Definition 12. *For* $\mathcal{E}$ *and a sequence* $(X^0, d^0) \ldots (X^n, d^n)$, *we define the SMT proposition* $unrolling_n((X^0, d^0) \ldots (X_n, d^n))$ *as:*

$$unrolling_n((X^0, d^0) \ldots (X^n, d^n))$$
$$\equiv$$
$$\bigwedge_{i < n} occurs(X^i, d^i, X^{i+1}, d^{i+1})$$

Intuitively, an n-unrolling is a lasso if the last element of the symbolic sequence $(X^0, d^0) \ldots (X^n, d^n)$, viz. (X^n, d^n), is equivalent to an element that occurred earlier in that sequence. We will use a variable k to indicate the starting point of the loop on the lasso. If such a lasso is ν-dominated, we have, according to Proposition 3, a proof graph. Encoding that the lasso is ν-dominated can be achieved by requiring that if $(X^n, d^n) = (X^i, d^i)$ for some $i < m$, then there is some (X^j, d^j), for $i \leq j < n$ with an even rank and it is the lowest rank among the ranks on the loop. We will use a variable m to record the rank of the dominating predicate variable.

Definition 13. *Let G be the dependency space of $\mathcal{E}$. The existence of a ν-dominated lasso of size at most n in G is encoded by the SMT proposition $\text{witness}_n((X^0, d^0)\ldots(X^n, d^n), k, m)$, defined as follows:*

$$\text{witness}_n((X^0, d^0)\cdots(X^n, d^n), k, m)$$

$$\equiv$$

$$\text{unrolling}_n((X^0, d^0)\cdots(X^n, d^n))$$

$$\wedge$$

$$\bigvee_{i<n} ((k = i) \wedge (X^i = X^n) \wedge (d^i = d^n))$$

$$\wedge$$

$$\bigvee_{i<n} ((k \leq i < n) \wedge (\sigma(X^i) = \nu) \wedge m = \text{rank}_\mathcal{E}(X^i))$$

$$\wedge$$

$$\bigwedge_{i<n} (k \leq i < n \Rightarrow m \leq \text{rank}_\mathcal{E}(X^i))$$

Theorem 2. *Let $G = (V, E)$ be $\mathcal{E}$'s dependency space. The SMT proposition $\text{witness}_n((X^0, d^0)\cdots(X^n, d^n), k, m)$ is satisfiable for some assignment that satisfies $(X^0, d^0) = (X, v)$ iff G contains a ν-dominated lasso starting in (X, v) and of size at most n.*

Computing whether the proposition $\text{witness}_n(\_)$ is satisfiable forms one out of two components of an algorithm for solving a given PBES.

5.2 Proving the Absence of Proof Graphs

Proving that $v \notin [\![\mathcal{E}]\!](X)$ requires that no proof graph containing a vertex (X, v) exists. While in general this problem cannot be solved using SMT, Proposition 4 provides a sufficient condition that allows us to restrict the search for lasso-shaped proof graphs of a particular size, thus providing the missing part for an algorithm for deciding whether $v \in [\![\mathcal{E}]\!](X)$. More specifically, the SMT proposition below encodes the decision problem that in the dependency space of $\mathcal{E}$ there is an acyclic path of a certain length.

Definition 14. *The existence of an acyclic path in the dependency space of $\mathcal{E}$ is encoded by the SMT proposition $\text{acyclic-unrolling}_n((X^0, d^0)\ldots(X^n, d^n))$, defined as follows:*

$$\text{acyclic-unrolling}_n((X^0, d^0)\ldots(X^n, d^n))$$

$$\equiv$$

$$\text{unrolling}_n((X^0, d^0)\ldots(X^n, d^n))$$

$$\wedge$$

$$\bigwedge_{i<j\leq n} (T_i, d_i) \neq (T_j, d_j)$$

We have the following lemma.

Lemma 3. *The dependency space of $\mathcal{E}$ contains an acyclic path of length $n + 1$, starting in some $(X, v) \in \text{sig}(\mathcal{E})$ iff $\text{acyclic-unrolling}_n((X^0, d^0)\ldots(X^n, d^n))$ holds for some assignment that satisfies $(X^0, d^0) = (X, v)$.*

5.3 A Pseudo-Decision Procedure

The SMT encodings described in the previous sections suggest a pseudo-decision procedure for deciding whether $v \in [\![\mathcal{E}]\!](X)$ for some v, X and $\mathcal{E}$ in DNF: we either attempt to prove that there is a proof graph of size n by checking for the satisfiability of $\mathsf{witness}_n$, or we attempt to prove that no witnesses of size larger than n exist by proving that $\mathsf{acyclic\text{-}unrolling}_n$ is not satisfiable. In the former case, an affirmative answer to the decision problem is given and in the latter, a negative answer is given.

Given that both witnesses and acyclic unrollings can be searched for arbitrarily increasing lengths, an obvious algorithm using this scheme is the following, where $\alpha > 1$ is a configurable multiplication factor:

> **Algorithm** $smt\text{-}unrolling_\alpha(\mathcal{E}, X, v)$
>
> 1 $n := 1$
> 2   **while** true:
> 3   **if** $\mathsf{witness}_n((X, v)(X^1, d^1) \ldots (X^n, d^n), k, m)$ is satisfiable:
> 4   **return** true
> 5   **elif** $\mathsf{acyclic\text{-}unrolling}_n((X, v)(X^1, d^1) \ldots (X^n, d^n))$ is not satisfiable:
> 6   **return** false
> 7   **else**
> 8 $n := n \times \alpha$

For this pseudo-decision procedure, the following properties hold; these essentially follow immediately from the theorems in the preceding sections.

Theorem 3. *For $\mathcal{E}$ in DNF, some $(X, v) \in \mathsf{sig}(\mathcal{E})$ and multiplication factor $\alpha > 1$, if* $smt\text{-}unrolling_\alpha(\mathcal{E}, X, v)$ *returns* true, *then $v \in [\![\mathcal{E}]\!](X)$ and if it returns* false *then $v \notin [\![\mathcal{E}]\!](X)$. In other words,* $smt\text{-}unrolling_\alpha$ *is sound.*

While the pseudo-decision procedure will not terminate in general, it is guaranteed to terminate under specific conditions.

Theorem 4. *For $\mathcal{E}$ in DNF, some $(X, v) \in \mathsf{sig}(\mathcal{E})$ and multiplication factor $\alpha > 1$, if the length of acyclic paths starting in (X, v) in the dependency space of $\mathcal{E}$ is bounded, then* $smt\text{-}unrolling_\alpha(\mathcal{E}, X^d)$ *terminates, provided that the individual SMT computations terminate.*

Together, these two properties show that *smt-unrolling* is a correct pseudo-decision procedure for determining whether $v \in [\![\mathcal{E}]\!](X)$; if furthermore (X, v) in the dependency space of $\mathcal{E}$ admits only bounded acyclic unrollings – which in particular is the case for any PBESs for which the reachable state space is finite – the decision procedure is complete, up to incompleteness of the SMT algorithm used.

We remark that showing that (X, v) admits only bounded acyclic unrollings is potentially as hard as solving the PBES itself, and undecidable in general. Fortunately, this is not required, as the *smt-unrolling* algorithm can be applied when one does not know whether (X, v) admits bounded acyclic unrollings. When applying the *smt-unrolling* procedure to some (X, v) that admits unbounded acyclic unrollings, the procedure may run indefinitely, without ever terminating; if it does terminate, the solution produced is correct. This characteristic is shared with many other model checking algorithms; for instance, any algorithm that relies on generating the explicit state space represented by an algebraic system description will fail to terminate for infinite state spaces.

6   Experiments

To give a feeling for the practical effectiveness of the procedure described in Sect. 5 we have implemented a prototype on top of the CVC4 [2] SMT solver and a prototype based on the Yices [7] SMT solver. Both prototypes were then used to solve, or attempt to solve:

- the (concurrent) alternating bit protocol and one bit sliding window protocol:
  - verify *payload-fairness*: each payload that can be sent infinitely often *is* sent infinitely often;
  - verify *infinite-loss*: a message can be lost infinitely often;
  - verify *infinite-sending*: a message can be sent infinitely often;
  - verify *fair-send-receive*: any payload is received eventually, as long as some messages eventually arrive correctly.
- two standard mutual exclusion protocols:
  - verify *starvation* for Lamport's Bakery protocol; *i.e.* does each requesting process eventually enter the critical section;
  - verify *fairness* of the access control for trains, implemented by Peterson's algorithm; *i.e.* do trains that want access to the critical section eventually get access.
- real-time model checking problems:
  - verify *infinitely-bright* for the timed light switch of Uppaal's tutorial; *i.e.* is it possible to infinitely often switch on the bright light;
  - verify *enter-cs* for Fischer's mutual exclusion protocol; *i.e.* is it possible to enter the critical section;
- the planning problem from Sect. 3, using the instance at the section end:
  - verify *no-starvation*: is there a driving and unloading scheme so that villages A and B do not deplete their supply;
  - verify *no-starvation-visit-c*: is there a driving and unloading scheme so that villages A and B do not deplete their supply while at the same time visiting C infinitely often.

The model checking problems are taken from the mCRL2 example distribution [5].[3] A larger set of experiments can be found in [12]. Our implementation was compared against the instantiation-based PBES solving tool *pbes2bool* of the mCRL2 distribution. For each investigated problem, we measured the running time of both implementations of the *smt-unrolling*$_2$ procedure. We also counted

---

[3] These can be found online via http://mcrl2.org.

the number of vertices in the dependency space in each problem, indicated as "$|V|$", as well as the size of the shortest witness or the longest acyclic unrolling characterising the solution of each problem ("|unrolling|"). For computations that are known not to terminate we denote a running time of ∞. A running time of "timeout" denotes a case where computation was aborted after 30 minutes, but the computation is expected to terminate eventually.

Table 1. Comparison between SMT-based PBES solving and traditional enumeration-based solving.

Problem	Proof graph	$|V|$	|unrolling|	Running time		
				pbes2bool	CVC4	Yices
ABP/payload-fairness	yes	594	22	0.04 s	8.82 s	timeout
ABP/infinite-loss	yes	119	10	0.03 s	1.20 s	2.16 s
ABP/infinite-sending	yes	78	19	0.03 s	1.73 s	12.1 s
ABP/fair-send-receive	no	131	unknown	0.07 s	timeout	timeout
CABP/payload-fairness	yes	3714	7	1:49 m	2.37 s	6.20, s
CABP/infinite-loss	no	753	unknown	0.08 s	timeout	timeout
CABP/infinite-sending	yes	514	23	5.95 s	8:01 m	3:37 m
CABP/fair-send-receive	yes	753	5	0.08 s	1.30 s	1.67 s
ONEBIT/payload-fairness	yes	655352	7	timeout	3.09 s	3.49 s
ONEBIT/infinite-loss	yes	199937	6	timeout	1.58 s	1.12 s
ONEBIT/infinite-sending	yes	88834	21	timeout	19:44 m	2:46 m
ONEBIT/fair-send-receive	yes	199937	4	23.3 s	0.43 s	0.21 s
BAKERY/starvation	yes	∞	6	∞	0.64 s	0.37 s
TRAINS/fairness	no	258	unknown	0.03 s	timeout	timeout
LIGHT/infinitely-bright	yes	∞	6	∞	0.22 s	0.13 s
FISCHER/enter-cs	yes	∞	5	∞	7.63 s	10.2 s
food/no-starvation	yes	$\approx 10^9$	7	timeout	0.44 s	0.28 s
food/no-starvation-visit-c	no	$\approx 10^9$	28	timeout	2:13 m	timeout

The test results for the above problems are summarised in Table 1. Our test results clearly illustrate that SMT solving for solving PBESs is largely complementary to the existing instantiation-based approach, allowing us to solve PBESs that would be out of reach otherwise. Another conclusion suggested by these results is that the running time of the *smt-unrolling*$_2$ algorithm seems to depend critically on the length of the shortest unrolling required to prove the solution to the model checking problem; *e.g.* problems with shortest proving unrollings larger than 30 steps are typically not solved in any reasonable amount of time. This is, in general, in line with other bounded model checking experiments.

7   Closing Remarks

We presented a novel procedure for solving fragments of PBESs, inspired by ideas from bounded model checking and by employing SMT solvers. Our procedure uses a completeness criterion that is checked dynamically, allowing the procedure to decide if it can terminate. This completeness criterion even works for PBESs with alternating fixpoints, which typically originate from liveness and fairness properties. Experiments show that our new solver is complementary to existing solvers and enables solving PBESs that could not reasonably be solved before.

Acknowledgement. We thank Jan Friso Groote (TU/e) for helpful discussions and feedback on our ideas, and the referees for their constructive feedback.

References

1. Alpuente, M., Feliú, M.A., Joubert, C., Villanueva, A.: Datalog-based program analysis with BES and RWL. In: de Moor, O., Gottlob, G., Furche, T., Sellers, A. (eds.) Datalog 2010. LNCS, vol. 6702, pp. 1–20. Springer, Heidelberg (2011)
2. Barrett, C., Conway, C.L., Deters, M., Hadarean, L., Jovanović, D., King, T., Reynolds, A., Tinelli, C.: CVC4. In: Gopalakrishnan, G., Qadeer, S. (eds.) CAV 2011. LNCS, vol. 6806, pp. 171–177. Springer, Heidelberg (2011)
3. Cavada, R., et al.: The NUXMV Symbolic Model Checker. In: Biere, A., Bloem, R. (eds.) CAV 2014. LNCS, vol. 8559, pp. 334–342. Springer, Heidelberg (2014)
4. Clarke, E., Biere, A., Raimi, R., Zhu, Y.: Bounded model checking using satisfiability solving. Form. Methods Syst. Des. **19**(1), 7–34 (2001)
5. Cranen, S., Groote, J.F., Keiren, J.J.A., Stappers, F.P.M., de Vink, E.P., Wesselink, W., Willemse, T.A.C.: An overview of the mCRL2 toolset and its recent advances. In: Piterman, N., Smolka, S.A. (eds.) TACAS 2013 (ETAPS 2013). LNCS, vol. 7795, pp. 199–213. Springer, Heidelberg (2013)
6. Cranen, S., Luttik, B., Willemse, T.A.C.: Proof graphs for parameterised boolean equation systems. In: D'Argenio, P.R., Melgratti, H. (eds.) CONCUR 2013 – Concurrency Theory. LNCS, vol. 8052, pp. 470–484. Springer, Heidelberg (2013)
7. Dutertre, B., De Moura, L.: The yices SMT solver. Technical report (2006)
8. Garavel, H., Lang, F., Mateescu, R., Serwe, W.: CADP 2010: a toolbox for the construction and analysis of distributed processes. In: Abdulla, P.A., Leino, K.R.M. (eds.) TACAS 2011. LNCS, vol. 6605, pp. 372–387. Springer, Heidelberg (2011)
9. Groote, J.F., Willemse, T.A.C.: Model-checking processes with data. Sci. Comput. Program **56**(3), 251–273 (2005)
10. Groote, J.F., Willemse, T.A.C.: Parameterised boolean equation systems. Theor. Comput. Sci. **343**(3), 332–369 (2005)
11. Kant, G., van de Pol, J.C.: Generating and solving symbolic parity games. In: GRAPHITE. EPTCS, vol. 159 , pp. 2–14 (2014)
12. Koolen, R.P.J.: Solving conjunctive and disjunctive parameterised Boolean equation systems using SMT solvers. Master's thesis, Eindhoven University of Technology (2014)
13. Orzan, S., Wesselink, W., Willemse, T.A.C.: Static analysis techniques for parameterised boolean equation systems. In: Kowalewski, S., Philippou, A. (eds.) TACAS 2009. LNCS, vol. 5505, pp. 230–245. Springer, Heidelberg (2009)

14. Oshman, R., Grumberg, O.: A new approach to bounded model checking for branching time logics. In: Namjoshi, K.S., Yoneda, T., Higashino, T., Okamura, Y. (eds.) ATVA 2007. LNCS, vol. 4762, pp. 410–424. Springer, Heidelberg (2007)
15. Ploeger, B., Wesselink, W., Willemse, T.A.C.: Verification of reactive systems via instantiation of parameterised Boolean equation systems. Inf. Comput. **209**(4), 637–663 (2011)

Unfolding-Based Process Discovery

Hernán Ponce-de-León[1]([✉]), César Rodríguez[2], Josep Carmona[3],
Keijo Heljanko[1], and Stefan Haar[4]

[1] Helsinki Institute for Information Technology HIIT and Department
of Computer Science, School of Science, Aalto University, Espoo, Finland
`hernan.poncedeleon@aalto.fi`
[2] Sorbonne Paris Cité, LIPN, CNRS, Université Paris 13, Villetaneuse, France
[3] Universitat Politècnica de Catalunya, Barcelona, Spain
[4] INRIA and LSV, École Normale Supérieure de Cachan and CNRS, Cachan, France

Abstract. This paper presents a novel technique for process discovery. In contrast to the current trend, which only considers an event log for discovering a process model, we assume two additional inputs: an independence relation on the set of logged activities, and a collection of negative traces. After deriving an intermediate net unfolding from them, we perform a controlled folding giving rise to a Petri net which contains both the input log and all independence-equivalent traces arising from it. Remarkably, the derived Petri net cannot execute any trace from the negative collection. The entire chain of transformations is fully automated. A tool has been developed and experimental results are provided that witness the significance of the contribution of this paper.

1 Introduction

The derivation of process models from partial observations has received significant attention in the last years, as it enables eliciting evidence-based formal representations of the real processes running in a system [1]. This discipline, known as *process discovery*, has similar premises as in *regression analysis*, i.e., only when moderate assumptions are made on the input data one can derive faithful models that represent the underlying system.

Formally, a technique for process discovery receives as input an *event log*, containing the footprints of a process' executions, and produces a model (e.g., a Petri net) describing the real process. Many process discovery algorithms in the literature make strong implicit assumptions. A widely used one is *log completeness*, requiring every possible trace of the underlying system to be contained in the event log. This is hard to satisfy by systems with cyclic or infinite behavior, but also for systems that evolve continuously over time. Another implicit assumption is the lack of *noise* in the log, i.e., traces denoting exceptional behavior that should not be contained in the derived process model. Finally, every discovery technique has a *representational bias*. For instance, the α-algorithm [2] can only discover Petri nets of a specific class (*structured workflow nets*).

© Springer International Publishing Switzerland 2015
B. Finkbeiner et al. (Eds.): ATVA 2015, LNCS 9364, pp. 31–47, 2015.
DOI: 10.1007/978-3-319-24953-7_4

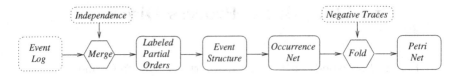

Fig. 1. Unfolding-based process discovery.

Few attempts have been made to remove the aforementioned assumptions. One promising direction is to relieve the discovery problem by assuming that more knowledge about the underlying system is available as input. On this line, the works in [3–5] are among the few that use domain knowledge in terms of *negative information*, expressed by traces which do not represent process behavior. In this paper we follow this direction, but additionally incorporate a crucial information to be used for the task of process discovery: when a pair of activities are *independent* of each other. One example could be the different tests that a patient should undergo in order to have a diagnosis: blood test, allergy test, and radiology test, which are independent each other. We believe that obtaining this coarse-grain independence information from a domain expert is an easy and natural step; however, if they are not available, one can estimate them from analysing the log with some of the techniques in the literature, e.g., the relations computed by the α-algorithm [1].

The approach of this paper is summarized in Fig. 1. Starting from an event log and an independence relation on its set of activities, we conceptually construct a collection of *labeled partial orders* whose linearizations include both the sequences in the log as well those in the same Mazurkiewicz trace [6], i.e., those obtained via successive permutations of independent activities. We then merge (the common prefixes of) this collection into an *event structure* which we next transform into an occurrence net representing the same behavior. Finally, we perform a controlled generalization by selectively folding the occurrence net into a Petri net. This step yields a net that (a) can execute all traces contained in the event log, and (b) generalizes the behavior of the log in a controlled manner, introducing no execution given in the collection of negative traces. The folding process is driven by a *folding equivalence relation*, which we synthesize using SMT. Different folding equivalences guarantee different properties about the final net. The paper proposes three different classes of equivalences and studies their properties. In particular we define a class of *independence-preserving* folding equivalences, guaranteeing that the natural independence relation in the final net will equal the one given by the expert.

In summary, the main contributions of the paper are:

- A general and efficient translation from prime event structures to occurrence nets (Sect. 3).
- Three classes of folding equivalences of interest not only in process discovery but also in formal verification of concurrent systems (Sect. 4).
- A method to synthesize folding equivalences using SMT (Sect. 5).

– An implementation of our approach and experimental results witnessing its capacity to even rediscover the original model (Sect. 6).

Remarkably, the discovery technique of this paper solves for the first time one of the foreseen operations in [7], which advocates for the unified use of event structures to support process mining operations.

Proofs for all formal results stated in the paper can be found in [8].

2   Preliminaries

Events: Given an alphabet of actions A, several occurrences of a given action can happen on a run or execution. In this paper we consider a set E of events representing the occurrence of actions in executions. Each event $e \in E$ has the form $e := \langle a, H \rangle$, where $a \in A$ and $H \subseteq E$ is a subset of events causing e (its history). The label of an event is given by a function $\lambda \colon E \to A$ defined as $\lambda(\langle a, H \rangle) := a$.

Labeled Partial Orders (lpos): We represent a labelled partial order by a pair $(E, \leq)$, where $\leq \subseteq E \times E$ is a reflexive, antisymmetric and transitive relation on the set E of events. Two distinct events $e, e' \in E$ can be either ordered ($e \leq e'$ or $e' \leq e$) or concurrent ($e \nleq e'$ and $e' \nleq e$). Observe that all events are implicitly labelled by λ.

Petri Nets: A net consists of two disjoint sets P and T representing respectively places and transitions together with a set F of flow arcs. The notion of state of the system in a net is captured by its markings. A marking is a multiset M of places, i.e., a map $M \colon P \to \mathbb{N}$. We focus on the so-called safe nets, where markings are sets, i.e., $M(p) \in \{0, 1\}$ for all $p \in P$. A Petri net (PN) is a net together with an initial marking and a total function that labels its transitions over an alphabet A of observable actions. Formally a PN is a tuple $\mathcal{N} := (P, T, F, \lambda, M_0)$ where *(i)* $P \neq \varnothing$ is a set of places; *(ii)* $T \neq \varnothing$ is a set of transitions such that $P \cap T = \varnothing$; *(iii)* $F \subseteq (P \times T) \cup (T \times P)$ is a set of flow arcs; *(iv)* $\lambda \colon T \to A$ is a labeling mapping; and *(v)* $M_0 \subseteq P$ is an initial marking. Elements of $P \cup T$ are called the nodes of $\mathcal{N}$. For a transition $t \in T$, we call $^\bullet t := \{p \mid (p, t) \in F\}$ the preset of t, and $t^\bullet := \{p \mid (t, p) \in F\}$ the postset of t. In figures, we represent as usual places by empty circles, transitions by squares, F by arrows, and the marking of a place p by black tokens in p. A transition t is enabled in marking M, written $M \xrightarrow{t}$, iff $^\bullet t \subseteq M$. This enabled transition can fire, resulting in a new marking $M' := (M \backslash ^\bullet t) \cup t^\bullet$. This firing relation is denoted by $M \xrightarrow{t} M'$. A marking M is reachable from M_0 if there exists a firing sequence, i.e. transitions, $t_1, \ldots, t_n$ such that $M_0 \xrightarrow{t_1} \ldots \xrightarrow{t_n} M$. The set of reachable markings from M_0 is denoted by $reach(\mathcal{N})$. The set of co-enabled transitions is $coe(\mathcal{N}) := \{(t, t') \mid \exists M \in reach(\mathcal{N}) \colon ^\bullet t \subseteq M \wedge ^\bullet t' \subseteq M\}$. The set of observations of a net is the image over λ of its fireable sequences, i.e., $\sigma \in obs(\mathcal{N})$ iff $M_0 \xrightarrow{t_1} \ldots \xrightarrow{t_n} M$ and $\lambda(t_1) \ldots \lambda(t_n) = \sigma$.

Occurrence Nets: Occurrence nets can be seen as infinite Petri nets with a special acyclic structure that highlights conflict between transitions that compete for resources. Places and transitions of an occurrence net are usually called conditions and events. Formally, let $N := (P, T, F)$ be a net, $<$ the transitive closure of F, and $\leq$ the reflexive closure of $<$. We say that transitions t_1 and t_2 are in structural conflict, written $t_1 \#_s t_2$, if and only if $t_1 \neq t_2$ and ${}^\bullet t_1 \cap {}^\bullet t_2 \neq \varnothing$. Conflict is inherited along $<$, that is, the conflict relation $\#$ is given by $a \# b \Leftrightarrow \exists t_a, t_b \in T : t_a \#_s t_b \wedge t_a \leq a \wedge t_b \leq b$. Finally, the concurrency relation **co** holds between nodes $a, b \in P \cup T$ that are neither ordered nor in conflict, i.e. a **co** $b \Leftrightarrow \neg(a \leq b) \wedge \neg(a \# b) \wedge \neg(b \leq a)$.

A net $\beta := (B, E, F)$ is an occurrence net iff *(i)* $\leq$ is a partial order; *(ii)* for all $b \in B$, $|{}^\bullet b| \in \{0, 1\}$; *(iii)* for all $x \in B \cup E$, the set $[x] := \{y \in E \mid y \leq x\}$ is finite; *(iv)* there is no self-conflict, i.e. there is no $x \in B \cup E$ such that $x \# x$. The initial marking M_0 of an occurrence net is the set of conditions with an empty preset, i.e. $\forall b \in B : b \in M_0 \Leftrightarrow {}^\bullet b = \varnothing$. Every $\leq$-closed and conflict-free set of events C is called a configuration and generates a reachable marking defined as $Mark(C) := (M_0 \cup C^\bullet) \setminus {}^\bullet C$. We also assume a labeling function $\lambda : E \to A$ from events in β to alphabet A. Conditions are of the form $\langle e, X \rangle$ where $e \in E$ is the event generating the condition and $X \subseteq E$ are the events consuming it. Occurrence nets are the mathematical form of the partial order unfolding semantics of a Petri net [9]; we use indifferently the terms occurrence net and unfolding.

Conditions in an occurrence net can be removed by keeping the causal dependencies and introducing a conflict relation; the obtained object is an event structure [10].

Event Structures: An event structure is a tuple $\mathcal{E} := (E, \leq, \#)$ where E is a set of events; $\leq \subseteq E \times E$ is a partial order (called causality) satisfying the property of finite causes, i.e. $\forall e \in E : |[e]| < \infty$ where $[e] := \{e' \in E \mid e' \leq e\}$; $\# \subseteq E \times E$ is an irreflexive symmetric relation (called conflict) satisfying the property of conflict heredity, i.e. $\forall e, e', e'' \in E : e \# e' \wedge e' \leq e'' \Rightarrow e \# e''$. Note that in most cases one only needs to consider reduced versions of relations $\leq$ and $\#$, which we will denote $\lessdot$ and $\#_d$, respectively. Formally, $\lessdot$ (which we call direct causality) is the transitive reduction of $\leq$, and $\#_d$ (direct conflict) is the smallest relation inducing $\#$ through the property of conflict heredity. A configuration is a computation state represented by a set of events that have occurred; if an event is present in a configuration, then so must all the events on which it causally depends. Moreover, a configuration does not contain conflicting events. Formally, a configuration of $(E, \leq, \#)$ is a set $C \subseteq E$ such that $e \in C \Rightarrow (\forall e' \leq e : e' \in C)$, and $(e \in C \wedge e \# e') \Rightarrow e' \notin C$. The set of configurations of $\mathcal{E}$ is denoted by $\Omega(\mathcal{E})$.

Mazurkiewicz Traces: Let A be a finite alphabet of letters and $\Diamond \subseteq A \times A$ a symmetric and irreflexive relation called independence. The relation $\Diamond$ induces an equivalence relation $\equiv_\Diamond$ over A^*. Two words σ and σ' are equivalent $(\sigma \equiv_\Diamond \sigma')$ if there exists a sequence $\sigma_1 \ldots \sigma_k$ of words such that $\sigma = \sigma_1, \sigma' = \sigma_k$ and for all

$1 \le i \le k$ there exists words σ_i', σ_i'' and letters a_i, b_i satisfying

$$\sigma_i = \sigma_i' a_i b_i \sigma_i'', \qquad \sigma_{i+1} = \sigma_i' b_i a_i \sigma_i'', \quad \text{and } (a_i, b_i) \in \Diamond$$

Thus, two words are equivalent by $\equiv_\Diamond$ if one can be obtained from the other by successive commutation of neighboring independent letters. For a word $\sigma \in A^*$ the equivalence class of σ under $\equiv_\Diamond$ is called a Mazurkiewicz trace [6].

We now describe the problem tackled in this paper, one of the main challenges in the *process mining* field [1].

Process Discovery: A log $\mathcal{L}$ is a finite set of traces over an alphabet A representing the footprints of the real process executions of a system $\mathcal{S}$ that is only (partially) visible through these runs. Process discovery techniques aim at extracting from a log $\mathcal{L}$ a process model $\mathcal{M}$ (e.g., a Petri net) with the goal to elicit the process underlying in $\mathcal{S}$. By relating the behaviors of $\mathcal{L}$, $obs(\mathcal{M})$ and $\mathcal{S}$, particular concepts can be defined [11]. A log is *incomplete* if $\mathcal{S} \backslash \mathcal{L} \ne \varnothing$. A model $\mathcal{M}$ *fits* log $\mathcal{L}$ if $\mathcal{L} \subseteq obs(\mathcal{M})$. A model is *precise* in describing a log $\mathcal{L}$ if $obs(\mathcal{M}) \backslash \mathcal{L}$ is small. A model $\mathcal{M}$ represents a *generalization* of log $\mathcal{L}$ with respect to system $\mathcal{S}$ if some behavior in $\mathcal{S} \backslash \mathcal{L}$ exists in $obs(\mathcal{M})$. Finally, a model $\mathcal{M}$ is *simple* when it has the minimal complexity in representing $obs(\mathcal{M})$, i.e., the well-known *Occam's razor principle*. It is widely acknowledged that the size of a process model is the most important simplicity indicator. Let $\mathcal{U}^\mathcal{N}$ be the universe of nets, we define a function $\hat{c} : \mathcal{U}^\mathcal{N} \to \mathbb{N}$ to measure the simplicity of a net by counting the number of some of its elements, e.g., its transitions and/or places.

3   Independence-Preserving Discovery

Let $\mathcal{S}$ be a system whose set of actions is A. Given two actions $a, b \in A$ and one state s of $\mathcal{S}$, we say that a and b *commute* at s when

- if a can fire at s and its execution reaches state s', then b is possible at s iff it is possible at s'; and
- if both a and b can fire at s, then firing ab and ba reaches the same state.

Commutativity of actions at states identifies an equivalence relation in the set of executions of the system $\mathcal{S}$; it is a *ternary* relation, relating two transitions with one state.

Since asking the expert to provide the commutativity relation of $\mathcal{S}$ would be difficult, we restrict ourselves to unconditional independence, i.e., a conservative overapproximation of the commutativity relation that is a sole property of transitions, as opposed to transitions and states. An *unconditional independence* relation of $\mathcal{S}$ is any *binary*, symmetric, and irreflexive relation $\Diamond \subseteq A \times A$ satisfying that if $a \Diamond b$ then a and b commute at *every reachable state* of $\mathcal{S}$. If a, b are not independent according to $\Diamond$, then they are dependent, denoted by $a \otimes b$.

In this section, given a log $\mathcal{L} \subseteq A^*$, representing some behaviors of $\mathcal{S}$, and an arbitrary unconditional independence $\Diamond$ of $\mathcal{S}$, provided by the expert, we construct an occurrence net whose executions contain $\mathcal{L}$ together with all sequences in A^* which are $\equiv_\Diamond$-equivalent to some sequence in $\mathcal{L}$.

If commuting actions are not declared independent by the expert (i.e., $\diamond$ is smaller than it could be), then $\mathcal{M}$ will be more sequential than $\mathcal{S}$; if some actions that did not commute are marked as independent, then $\mathcal{M}$ will not be a truthful representation of $\mathcal{S}$. The use of expert knowledge in terms of an independence relation is a novel feature not considered before in the context of process discovery. We believe this is a powerful way to fight with the problem of log incompleteness in a practical way since it is only needed to observe in the log one trace representative of a class in $\equiv_\diamond$ to include the whole set of traces of the class in the process model's executions.

Our final goal is to generate a Petri net that represents the behavior of the underlying system. We start by translating $\mathcal{L}$ into a collection of partial orders whose shape depends on the specific definition of $\diamond$.

Definition 1. *Given a sequence $\sigma \in A^*$ and an independence relation $\diamond \subseteq A \times A$, we associate to σ a labeled partial order $lpo_\diamond(\sigma)$ inductively defined by:*

1. *If $\sigma = \varepsilon$, then let $\bot := \langle \tau, \varnothing \rangle$ and set $lpo_\diamond(\sigma) := (\{\bot\}, \varnothing)$.*
2. *If $\sigma = \sigma'a$, then let $lpo_\diamond(\sigma') := (E', \leq')$ and let $e := \langle a, H \rangle$ be the single event such that H is the unique $\subseteq$-minimal, causally-closed set of events in E' satisfying that for any event $e' \in E'$, if $\lambda(e') \otimes a$, then $e' \in H$. Then set $lpo_\diamond(\sigma) := (E, \leq)$ with $E := E' \cup \{e\}$ and $\leq := \leq' \cup (H \times \{e\})$.*

Since a system rarely generates a single observation, we need a compact way to model all the possible observations of the system. We represent all the partially ordered executions of a system with an event structure.

Definition 2. *Given a set of partial orders $S := \{(E_i, \leq_i) \mid 1 \leq i \leq n\}$, we define $ES(S) := (E, \leq, \#)$ where:*

1. $E := \bigcup_{1 \leq i \leq n} E_i$,
2. $\leq := (\bigcup_{1 \leq i \leq n} \leq_i)^*$, *and*
3. *for $e := \langle a, H \rangle$ and $e' := \langle b, H' \rangle$, we have that $e \mathrel{\#_d} e'$ (read: e and e' are in direct conflict) iff $e' \notin H, e \notin H'$ and $a \otimes b$. The conflict relation $\#$ is the smallest relation that includes $\#_d$ and is inherited w.r.t. $\leq$, i.e., for $e \mathrel{\#} e'$ and $e \leq f$, $e' \leq f'$, one has $f \mathrel{\#} f'$.*

Given a set of finite partial orders S, we now show that S is included in the configurations of the event structure obtained by Definition 2. This means that our event structure is a fitting representation of $\mathcal{L}$.

Proposition 1. *If S is finite, then $S \subseteq \Omega(ES(S))$.*

Since we want to produce a Petri net, we now need to "attach conditions" to the result of Definition 2. Event structures and occurrence nets are conceptually very similar objects so this might seem very easy for the acquainted reader. However, this definition is crucial for the success of the subsequent folding step (Sect. 4), as we will be constrained to merge conditions in the preset and postset of an event when we merge the event. As a result, the conditions that we produce now should constraint as little as possible the future folding step.

Definition 3. *Given an event structure $\mathcal{E} := (E, \leq, \#)$ we construct the occurrence net $\beta := (B, E\backslash\{\bot\}, F)$ in two steps*

1. *Let $G := (V, A)$ be a graph where $V := E$ and $(e_1, e_2) \in A$ iff $e_1 \#_d e_2$. For each clique (maximal complete subgraph) $K := \{e_1, \ldots, e_n\}$ of G, let $C_K := [e_1] \cap \cdots \cap [e_n]$ and $e_K \in \max(C_K)$. We add a condition b to B and set $b \in e_K{}^\bullet$ and $b \in {}^\bullet e_i$ for $i = 1 \ldots n$.*
2. *For each $e \in E$, let $G_e := (V_e, A_e)$ be a graph where $V_e := \{e' \in E \mid e \lessdot e'\}$ and $(e_1, e_2) \in A_e$ iff $\lambda(e_1) \circledast \lambda(e_2)$. For each clique $K_e := \{e_1, \ldots, e_n\}$ of G_e, we add a condition b to B and set $b \in e^\bullet$ and $b \in {}^\bullet e_i$ for $i = 1 \ldots n$.*

Definition 3.1. adds a condition for every set of pairwise direct conflicting events; the condition is generated by some event e_K which is in the past of every conflicting event and consumed by all of them; by the latter the conflict of the event structure is preserved in the occurrence net. For each event and its immediate successors, Definition 3.2. adds conditions between them to preserve causality. To minimize the number of conditions, for the successor events having dependent labels only one condition is generated. This step does not introduce new conflicts in the occurrence net since the events have dependent labels and none is in the past of the other, then by Definition 2 they are also in conflict in the event structure.

We note that Winskel already explained, in categorical terms, how to relate an event structure with an occurrence net [12]. However, his definition is of interest only in that context, while ours focus on a practical and efficient translation.

Given a log $\mathcal{L}$ and an independence relation $\Diamond$, the net obtained applying Definitions 1, 2 and 3, in this order, is denoted by $\beta_{\mathcal{L},\Diamond}$. Since every trace in $\mathcal{L}$ is a linearization of some of the partial orders in the set S obtained by Definition 1 and these partial orders are included by Proposition 1 in the configurations of $ES(S)$ (which are the same as the configurations in $\beta_{\mathcal{L},\Diamond}$), the obtained net is fitting.

Proposition 2. *Let $\mathcal{L}$ be a log and $\Diamond$ an independence relation, for every $\sigma \in \mathcal{L}$ we have $\sigma \in obs(\beta_{\mathcal{L},\Diamond})$.*

It is worth noticing that the obtained net generalizes the behavior of the model, but in a controlled manner imposed by the independence relation. For instance, if $\mathcal{L} := \{ab\}$ and $a \Diamond b$, then $ba \in obs(\beta_{\mathcal{L},\Diamond})$, even if this behavior was not present in the log. If the expert rightly declared a and b independent (i.e., if they commute at all states of $\mathcal{S}$), then necessarily ba is a possible observation of $\mathcal{S}$, even if it is not in $\mathcal{L}$. The extra information provided by the expert allows us to generalize the discovered model in a provably sound manner, thus coping with the log incompleteness problem.

The independence relation between labels gives rise to an arbitrary relation between transitions of a net (not necessarily an independence relation):

Definition 4. *Let $\Diamond \subseteq A \times A$ be an independence relation, $\mathcal{N} := (P, T, F, \lambda, M_0)$ a net, and $\lambda: T \to A$. We define relation $\Diamond_N \subseteq T \times T$ between transitions of N as*

$$t \Diamond_N t' \Leftrightarrow \lambda(t) \Diamond \lambda(t').$$

In the next section we will define an approach to fold $\beta_{\mathcal{L},\diamond}$ into a Petri net whose natural independence relation equals $\diamond$. To formalize our approach we first need to define such natural independence.

Definition 5. *Let $N := (P, T, F)$ be a net. We define the* natural independence *relation $\bowtie_N \subseteq T \times T$ on N as*

$$t \bowtie_N t' \Leftrightarrow {}^\bullet t \cap {}^\bullet t' = \varnothing \wedge t^\bullet \cap {}^\bullet t' = \varnothing \wedge {}^\bullet t \cap t'^\bullet = \varnothing.$$

In fact, one can prove that when N is safe, then $\bowtie_N$ is the notion of independence underlying the unfolding semantics of N. In other words, the equivalence classes of $\equiv_{\bowtie_N}$ are in bijective correspondence with the configurations in the unfolding of N. The following result shows that the natural independence on the discovered occurrence net corresponds to the relation provided by the expert, when both we restrict to the set of co-enabled transitions.

Theorem 1. *Let $\beta_{\mathcal{L},\diamond}$ be the occurrence net from the log $\mathcal{L}$ with $\diamond$ as the independence relation, then*

$$\diamond_{\beta_{\mathcal{L},\diamond}} \cap coe(\beta_{\mathcal{L},\diamond}) = \bowtie_{\beta_{\mathcal{L},\diamond}} \cap coe(\beta_{\mathcal{L},\diamond})$$

4   Introducing Generalization

The construction described in the previous section guarantees that the unfolding obtained is fitting (see Proposition 1). However, the difference between $\mathcal{S}$ and $\mathcal{L}$ may be significant (e.g., $\mathcal{S}$ can contain cyclic behavior that can be instantiated an arbitrary number of times whereas only finite traces exist in $\mathcal{L}$) and the unfolding may be poor in generalization. The goal of this section is to generalize $\beta_{\mathcal{L},\diamond}$ in a way that the right patterns from $\mathcal{S}$, partially observed in $\mathcal{L}$ (e.g., loops), are incorporated in the generalized model. To generalize, we fold the discovered occurrence net. This folding is driven by an equivalence relation $\sim$ on $E \cup B$ that dictates which events merge into the same transition, and analogously for conditions; events cannot be merged with conditions. We write $[x]_\sim := \{x' \mid x \sim x'\}$ for the equivalence class of node x. For a set X, $[X]_\sim := \{[x]_\sim \mid x \in X\}$ is a set of equivalence classes.

Definition 6 (Folded net [13]). *Let $\beta := (B, E, F)$ be an occurrence net and $\sim$ a equivalence relation on the nodes of β. The folded Petri net (w.r.t. $\sim$) is defined as $\beta^\sim := (P_\sim, T_\sim, F_\sim, M_{0_\sim})$ where*

$$P_\sim := \{[b]_\sim \mid b \in B\}, \qquad F_\sim := \{([x]_\sim, [y]_\sim) \mid (x, y) \in F\},$$
$$T_\sim := \{[e]_\sim \mid e \in E\}, \qquad M_{0_\sim}([b]_\sim) := |\{b' \in [b]_\sim \mid {}^\bullet b' = \varnothing\}|.$$

Notice that the initial marking of the folded net is not necessarily safe. Safeness of the net depends on the chosen equivalence relation (see Proposition 3).

4.1   Language-Preserving Generalization

Different folding equivalences guarantee different properties on the folded net. From now on we focus our attention on three interesting classes of folding equivalences. The first preserves sequential executions of $\beta_{\mathcal{L},\diamond}$.

Definition 7 (Sequence-preserving folding equivalence). *Let β be an occurrence net; an equivalence relation $\sim$ is called a sequence preserving (SP) folding equivalence iff $e_1 \sim e_2$ implies $\lambda(e_1) = \lambda(e_2)$ and $[{}^\bullet e_1]_\sim = [{}^\bullet e_2]_\sim$ for all events $e_1, e_2 \in E$.*

From the definition above it follows that $e_1 \sim e_2$ implies $\forall b \in {}^\bullet e_1 : \exists b' \in {}^\bullet e_2$ with $b \sim b'$. Since for every folded net obtained from a SP folding equivalence only equally labeled events are merged; we define then $\lambda([e]_\sim) := \lambda(e)$.

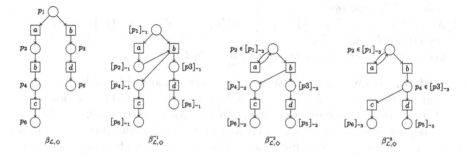

Fig. 2. Folding equivalences and folded nets.

Example 1. Consider the log $\mathcal{L} = \{abc, bd\}$ and the independence relation $\diamond = \varnothing$. Figure 2 shows the obtained unfolding $\beta_{\mathcal{L},\diamond}$ (left) and three of its folded nets. The equivalence relation $\sim_1$ merges events labeled by b, but it does not merge their presets, i.e. is not a SP folding equivalence. It can be observed that bd is not fireable in $\beta_{\mathcal{L},\diamond}^{\sim_1}$. Whenever two events are merged, their preconditions need to be merged to preserved sequential executions. The equivalence relation $\sim_2$ does not only merge events labeled by b, but it also sets $p_1 \sim_2 p_2$ and is a SP folding equivalence. The folded net $\beta_{\mathcal{L},\diamond}^{\sim_2}$ can replay every trace in the log $\mathcal{L}$, but it also adds new traces of the form $a^*, a^*b, a^*bc, a^*bd, a^*bcd$ and a^*bdc.

Given an unfolding, every SP folding equivalence generates a net that preserves its sequential executions.

Theorem 2. *Let β be an occurrence net and $\sim$ a SP folding equivalence, then every fireable sequence $M_0 \xrightarrow{e_1} \ldots \xrightarrow{e_n} M_n$ from β generates a fireable sequence $[M_0]_\sim \xrightarrow{[e_1]_\sim} \ldots \xrightarrow{[e_n]_\sim} [M_n]_\sim$ from $\beta^\sim$.*

As a corollary of the result above and Proposition 2, the folded net obtained from $\beta_{\mathcal{L},\diamond}$ with a SP folding equivalence is fitting.

Corollary 1. *Let $\mathcal{L}$ be a log, $\Diamond$ an independence relation and $\sim$ a SP folding equivalence, then for every $\sigma \in \mathcal{L}$ we have $\sigma \in obs(\beta^{\sim}_{\mathcal{L},\Diamond})$.*

Example 2. We saw in Example 1 that every trace from $\mathcal{L}$ can be replayed in $\beta^{\sim_2}_{\mathcal{L},\Diamond}$, but (as expected) the net accepts more traces. However this net also adds some independence between actions of the system: after firing b the net puts tokens at $[p_3]_{\sim_2}$ and $[p_4]_{\sim_2}$ and the reached marking enables concurrently actions c and d which contradicts $c \otimes d$ (the independence relation $\Diamond = \varnothing$ implies $c \otimes d$). In order to avoid this extra independence, we now consider the following class of equivalences.

Definition 8 (Independence-preserving folding equivalence). *Let β be an occurrence net and $\Diamond$ an independence relation; an equivalence relation $\sim$ is called an independence preserving (IP) folding equivalence iff*

1. *$\sim$ is a SP folding equivalence,*
2. *$\lambda(e_1) \Diamond \lambda(e_2) \Leftrightarrow [{}^\bullet e_1]_\sim \cap [{}^\bullet e_2]_\sim = \varnothing \wedge [{}^\bullet e_1]_\sim \cap [e_2{}^\bullet]_\sim = \varnothing \wedge [e_1{}^\bullet]_\sim \cap [{}^\bullet e_2]_\sim = \varnothing$ for all events $e_1, e_2 \in E$.*
3. *$b_1 \mathbf{co} b_2$ implies $b_1 \not\sim b_2$ for all conditions $b_1, b_2 \in B$.*

IP folding equivalences not only preserve the sequential behavior of β, but also ensure that $\beta^{\sim}$ and β exhibit the same natural independence relation.

The definition above differs from the folding equivalence definition given in [13]; they consider occurrence nets coming from an unfolding procedure which takes as an input a net. This procedure generates a mapping between conditions and events of the generated occurrence net and places and transitions in the original net. Such mapping is necessary to define their folding equivalence. In our setting, the occurrence net does not come from a given net and therefore the mapping is not available.

Example 3. The equivalence $\sim_2$ from Fig. 2 is not an IP folding equivalence since the intersection of the equivalent classes of the preset of c and d is empty ($[{}^\bullet c]_{\sim_2} = \{[p_4]_{\sim_2}\}, [{}^\bullet d]_{\sim_2} = \{[p_3]_{\sim_2}\}$ and $\{[p_4]_{\sim_2}\} \cap \{[p_3]_{\sim_2}\} = \varnothing$), but c and d are not independent. Consider the equivalence relation $\sim_3$ which merges events labeled by b and it sets $p_1 \sim_3 p_2$ and $p_3 \sim_3 p_4$; this relation is an IP folding equivalence. It can be observed in the net $\beta^{\sim_3}_{\mathcal{L},\Diamond}$ of Fig. 2 that all the traces from the log can be replayed, but new independence relations are not introduced.

The occurrence net $\beta_{\mathcal{L},\Diamond}$ is clearly safe. We show that $\beta^{\sim}_{\mathcal{L},\Diamond}$ is also safe when $\sim$ is an IP folding equivalence. In this work, we constraint IP equivalences to generate safe nets because their natural independence relation is well understood (Definition 5), thus allowing us to assign a solid meaning to the class IP. It is unclear what is the natural unconditional independence of an unsafe net, and extending our definitions to such nets is subject of future work.

Proposition 3. *Let $\beta_{\mathcal{L},\Diamond}$ be the unfolding obtained from the log $\mathcal{L}$ with $\Diamond$ as the independence relation and $\sim$ an IP folding equivalence. Then $\beta^{\sim}_{\mathcal{L},\Diamond}$ is safe.*

Theorem 1 shows that the structural relation between events of the unfolding and the relation generated by the independence given by the expert coincide (when we restrict to co-enabled events); the result also holds for the folded net when an IP folding equivalence is used.

Theorem 3. *Let $\beta_{\mathcal{L},\diamond}$ be the unfolding obtained from the log $\mathcal{L}$ with $\diamond$ as the independence relation and $\sim$ an IP folding equivalence, then $\diamond_{\beta_{\mathcal{L},\diamond}^{\sim}} = \bowtie_{\beta_{\mathcal{L},\diamond}^{\sim}}$.*

4.2   Controlling Generalization via Negative Information

We have shown that IP folding equivalences preserve independence. However, they could still introduce new unintended behaviour not present in $\mathcal{S}$. In this section we limit this phenomena by considering *negative information*, denoted by traces that should not be allowed by the model. Concretely, we consider negative information which is also given in the form of sequences $\sigma \in \mathcal{L}^- \subseteq A^*$. Negative information is often provided by an expert, but it can also be obtained automatically by recent methods [14]. Very few techniques in the literature use negative information in process discovery [5]. In this work, we assume a minimality criterion on the negative traces used:

Assumption 1. *Let $\mathcal{L} := \mathcal{L}^+ \uplus \mathcal{L}^-$ be a pair of positive and negative logs and $\diamond$ the independence relation given by the expert. Any negative trace $\sigma \in \mathcal{L}^-$ corresponds to the local configuration of some event e_σ in $\beta_{\mathcal{L},\diamond}$.*

This assumption implies that each negative trace is of the form $\sigma'a$ where σ' only contains the actions that are necessarily to fire a. If a can happen without them, they should not be consider part of σ. By removing all events e_σ from $\beta_{\mathcal{L},\diamond}$ (one for each negative trace $\sigma \in \mathcal{L}^-$), we obtain a new occurrence net denoted by $\beta_{\mathcal{L},\diamond,*}$. The goal of this section is to fold this occurrence net without re-introducing the negative traces in the generalization step. If the expert is unable to provide negative traces satisfying this assumption, the discovery tool can always let him/her choose e_σ from a visual representation of the unfolding.

Definition 9 (Removal-aware folding equivalence). *Let $\beta := (B, E, F)$ be an occurrence net and $\mathcal{L}^-$ a negative log; an equivalence relation $\sim$ is called removal aware (RA) folding equivalence iff*

1. $\sim$ is a SP folding equivalence, and
2. for every $\sigma \in \mathcal{L}^-$ and $e' \in E$ we have $\lambda(e') = \lambda(e_\sigma)$ implies $[^\bullet e']_\sim \notin [^\bullet e_\sigma]$.

The folded net obtained from $\beta_{\mathcal{L},\diamond,*}$ with a RA folding equivalence does not contain any of the negative traces.

Theorem 4. *Let $\beta_{\mathcal{L},\diamond,*}$ be the unfolding obtained from the log $\mathcal{L} := \mathcal{L}^+ \uplus \mathcal{L}^-$ with $\diamond$ as the independence relation after removing the corresponding event of each negative trace and $\sim$ a RA folding equivalence,[1] then*

$$obs(\beta_{\mathcal{L},\diamond,*}^{\sim}) \cap \mathcal{L}^- = \varnothing$$

---

[1] Since Definition 9 refers to the events that generates the local configurations of the negative traces, the folding equivalence must be defined over the nodes of $\beta_{\mathcal{L},\diamond}$ and not those of $\beta_{\mathcal{L},\diamond,*}$.

5 Computing Folding Equivalences

Section 3 presents a discovery algorithm that generates fitting occurrence nets and Sect. 4 defines three classes of folding criteria, SP, IP, and RA, that ensure various properties. This section proposes an approach to synthesize SP, IP and RA folding equivalences using SMT.

5.1 SMT Encoding

We use an SMT encoding to find folding equivalences generating a net $\beta^{\sim}$ satisfying specific metric properties. Specifically, given a measure $\hat{c}$ (cf., Sect. 2), decidable in polynomial time, and a number $k \in \mathbb{N}$, we generate an SMT formula which is satisfiable iff there exists a folding equivalence $\sim$ such that $\hat{c}(\beta^{\sim}) = k$. We consider the number of transitions in the folded net as the measure $\hat{c}$, however, theoretically, any other measure that can be computed in polynomial time could be used. As explained in Sect. 2 simple functions like counting the number of nodes/arcs provide in practice reasonable results.

Given an occurrence net $\beta := (B, E, F)$, for every event $e \in E$ and condition $b \in B$ we have integer variables v_e and v_b. The key intuition is that two events (conditions) whose variables have equal number are equivalent and will be merged into the same transition (place). The following formulas state, respectively, that every element of a set X is related with at least one element of a set Y, and that every element of X is not related with any element of Y:

$$\phi_{X,Y}^{sub} := \bigwedge_{x \in X} \bigvee_{y \in Y} (v_x = v_y) \qquad \phi_{X,Y}^{disj} := \bigwedge_{x \in X, y \in Y} (v_x \neq v_y)$$

We force any satisfying assignment to represent an SP folding equivalence (Definition 7) with the following two constraints:

$$\phi_{\beta}^{SP} := \phi_{\beta}^{lab} \wedge \phi_{\beta}^{pre}.$$

Formulas ϕ_{β}^{lab} and ϕ_{β}^{pre} impose that only equally labeled events should be equivalent and that if two events are equivalent, then their presets should generate the same equivalence class:

$$\phi_{\beta}^{lab} := \bigwedge_{\substack{e,e' \in E \\ \lambda(e) \neq \lambda(e')}} (v_e \neq v_{e'}) \qquad \phi_{\beta}^{pre} := \bigwedge_{e,e' \in E} (v_e = v_{e'} \Rightarrow (\phi_{{}^{\bullet}e,{}^{\bullet}e'}^{sub} \wedge \phi_{{}^{\bullet}e',{}^{\bullet}e}^{sub}))$$

In addition to the properties encoded above, an IP folding equivalence (Definition 8) should satisfy some other restrictions:

$$\phi_{\beta}^{IP} := \phi_{\beta}^{SP} \wedge \phi_{\beta}^{ind} \wedge \phi_{\beta}^{co}$$

where ϕ_{β}^{ind} imposes that the presets and postsets of events with independent labels should generate equivalence classes that do not intersect and ϕ_{β}^{co} forbids concurrent conditions to be merged:

$$\phi_{\beta}^{ind} := \bigwedge_{e,e' \in E} (\lambda(e) \diamond \lambda(e') \Leftrightarrow (\phi_{{}^{\bullet}e,{}^{\bullet}e'}^{disj} \wedge \phi_{{}^{\bullet}e,e'{}^{\bullet}}^{disj} \wedge \phi_{e{}^{\bullet},e'{}^{\bullet}}^{disj})) \qquad \phi_{\beta}^{co} := \bigwedge_{\substack{b,b' \in B \\ b\,co\,b'}} (v_b \neq v_{b'})$$

Given a negative log $\mathcal{L}^-$, to encode a RA folding equivalence (Definition 9) we define:

$$\phi_{\beta,\mathcal{L}^-}^{RA} := \phi_\beta^{SP} \wedge (\bigwedge_{\substack{\sigma \in \mathcal{L}^-, e' \in E \\ \lambda(e') = \lambda(e_\sigma)}} \neg \phi_{\bullet e', \bullet e_\sigma}^{sub})$$

where the right part of the conjunction imposes that for every e_σ generated by a negative trace and any other event with the same label, their presets cannot generate the same equivalence class.

We now encode the optimality (w.r.t. the number of transitions) of the mined net. Given an occurrence net $\beta := (B, E, F)$, each event $e \in E$ generates a transition v_e in the folded net $\beta^\sim$. To impose that the number of transitions in $\beta^\sim$ should be at most $k \in \mathbb{N}$, we define:

$$\phi_{\beta,k}^{MET} := \bigwedge_{e \in E} (1 \le v_e \le k)$$

To find an IP and RA folding equivalence that generates a net with at most k transitions we propose the following encoding:

$$\phi_{\beta,\mathcal{L}^-,k}^{OPT} := \phi_\beta^{IP} \wedge \phi_{\beta,\mathcal{L}^-}^{RA} \wedge \phi_{\beta,k}^{MET}$$

Theorem 5. *Let $\mathcal{L} := \mathcal{L}^+ \uplus \mathcal{L}^-$ be a set of positive and negative logs, $\diamond \subseteq A \times A$ and independence relation and $k \in \mathbb{N}$. The formula $\phi_{\beta,\mathcal{L}^-,k}^{OPT}$ is satisfiable iff there exists an IP and RA folding equivalence $\sim$ such that $\beta_{\mathcal{L},\diamond,*}^\sim$ contains at most k transitions.*

5.2   Finding an Optimal Folding Equivalence

Section 5.1 explains how to compute a folding equivalence that generates a folded net with a bounded number of transitions; this section explain how to obtain the optimal folded net, i.e. the one with minimal number of transitions satisfying the properties of Theorems 3 and 4.

Iterative calls to the SMT solver can be done for a binary search with k between min_k and max_k; since only equally labeled events can be merged by the folding equivalence, the minimal number of transitions in the folded net is $min_k := |A|$; in the worst case, when events cannot be merged, $max_k := |E|$.

As a side remark, we have noted that the optimal folding equivalence can be encoded as a MaxSMT problem [15] where some clauses which are called hard must be true in a solution (in our case ϕ_β^{IP} and $\phi_{\beta,\mathcal{L}^-}^{RA}$) and some soft clauses may not ($\phi_{\beta,k}^{MET}$ for $|A| \le k \le |E|$); a MaxSMT solver maximizes the number of soft clauses that are satisfiable and thus it obtains the minimal k generating thus the optimal folded net.

6   Experiments

As a proof of concept, we implemented our approach into a new tool called POD (Partial Order Discovery).[2] It supports synthesis of SP and IP folding

---

[2] Tool and benchmarks: http://lipn.univ-paris13.fr/~rodriguez/exp/atva15/.

Table 1. Experimental results.

Original Benchmark	$|T|$	$|P|$	POD (max. places)				POD (60% places)			
			$r_{\mathcal{S}\subseteq\mathcal{M}}$	$r_{\mathcal{M}\subseteq\mathcal{S}}$	%Prec	$|P|$	$r_{\mathcal{S}\subseteq\mathcal{M}}$	$r_{\mathcal{M}\subseteq\mathcal{S}}$	%Prec	$|P|$
A(22)	22	20	0.99	1.00	0.77	19	0.57	1.00	0.22	11
A(32)	32	32	1.00	1.00	0.80	32	0.46	1.00	0.19	19
A(42)	42	47	0.98	1.00	0.54	40	0.79	1.00	0.21	28
T(32)	33	31	1.00	1.00	0.88	31	0.54	1.00	0.19	18
ANGIO(1)	64	39	0.39	0.94	0.18	21	0.10	0.92	0.06	13
COMPLEX	19	13	0.98	1.00	0.62	12	0.62	1.00	0.39	7
CONFDIMB	11	10	1.00	1.00	1.00	10	0.62	1.00	0.39	6
CYCLES(5)	20	16	1.00	1.00	1.00	16	0.60	1.00	0.40	6
DBMUT(2)	32	38	0.98	0.98	0.94	32	0.76	0.98	0.21	19
DC	32	35	0.99	0.99	0.77	27	0.84	0.99	0.38	21
PETERS(2)	126	102	0.45	1.00	0.07	51	0.30	1.00	0.05	30

equivalences using a restricted form of our SMT encoding. In particular POD merges all events with equal label, in contrast to the encoding in Sect. 5 which may in general yield more than one transition per log action. While this ensures a minimum (optimal as per Sect. 5.2) number of folded transitions, the tool could sometimes not find a suitable equivalence (unsatisfiable SMT encoding). Since the number of transitions in the folded net is fixed, it turns out that the quality of the mined model increases as we increase the number of folded places, as we show below. Using POD we evaluate the ability of our approach to rediscover the original process model, given its independence relation and a set of logs. For this we have used standard benchmarks from the verification and process mining literature [16,17].

In our experiments, Table 1, we consider a set of original processes faithfully modelled as safe Petri nets. For every model $\mathcal{S}$ we consider a log $\mathcal{L}$, i.e. a subset of its traces. We extract from $\mathcal{S}$ the (best) independence relation $\sqcup_{\mathcal{S}}$ that an expert could provide. We then provide $\mathcal{L}$ and $\sqcup_{\mathcal{S}}$ to POD and find an SP folding equivalence with the largest number of places (cols. "max. places") and with 60% of the places of $\mathcal{S}$ (last group of cols.), giving rise to two different mined models. All three models, original plus mined ones, have perfect fitness but varying levels of precision, i.e. traces of the model not present in the log. For the mined models, we report (cols. "%Prec.") on the ratio between their precision and the precision of the original model $\mathcal{S}$. All precisions were estimated using the technique from [18]. All POD running times were below 10 s.

Additionally, we measure how much independence of the original model is preserved in the mined ones. For that, we define the ratios $r_{\mathcal{S}\subseteq\mathcal{M}} := |\sqcup_{\mathcal{S}}\cap\sqcup_{\mathcal{M}}|/|\sqcup_{\mathcal{S}}|$ and $r_{\mathcal{M}\subseteq\mathcal{S}} := |\sqcup_{\mathcal{S}}\cap\sqcup_{\mathcal{M}}|/|\sqcup_{\mathcal{M}}|$. The closer $r_{\mathcal{S}\subseteq\mathcal{M}}$ is to 1, the larger is the number of pairs in $\sqcup_{\mathcal{S}}$ also contained in $\sqcup_{\mathcal{M}}$ (i.e., the more independence was preserved), and conversely for $r_{\mathcal{M}\subseteq\mathcal{S}}$ (the less independence was *"invented"*). Remark that $\sqcup_{\mathcal{S}} = \sqcup_{\mathcal{M}}$ iff $r_{\mathcal{S}\subseteq\mathcal{M}} = r_{\mathcal{M}\subseteq\mathcal{S}} = 1$.

In 7 out of the 11 benchmarks in Table 1 our proof-of-concept tool rediscovers the original model or finds one with only minor differences. This is even more encouraging when considering that we only asked POD to find SP equivalences which, unlike IP, do not guarantee preservation of independence. In 9 out of 11 cases both ratios $r_{S\subseteq M}$ and $r_{M\subseteq S}$ are above 98 %, witnessing that independence is almost entirely preserved. Concerning the precision, we observe that it is mostly preserved for these 9 models. We observe a clear correlation between the number of discovered places and the precision of the resulting model. The running times of POD on all benchmarks in Table 1 were under few seconds.

In PETERS(2) and ANGIO(1) our tool could not increase the number of places in the folded net, resulting in a significant loss of independence and precision. We tracked the reason down to (a) the additional restrictions on the SMT encoding imposed by our implementation and (b) the algorithm for transforming event structures into unfoldings (i.e., introducing conditions). We plan to address this in future work. This also prevented us from of employing IP equivalences instead of SP for these experiments: POD could find IP equivalences for only 5 out of 11 cases. Nonetheless, as we said before, in 9 out of 11 the found SP equivalences preserved at least 98 % of the independence.

Finally, we instructed POD to synthesize SP equivalences folding into an arbitrarily chosen low number of places (60 % of the original). Here we observe a large reduction of precision and significant loss of independence (surprisingly only $r_{S\subseteq M}$ drops, but not $r_{M\subseteq S}$). This witnesses a strong dependence between the number of discovered places and the ability of our technique to preserve independence.

7   Related Work

To the best of our knowledge, there is no technique in the literature that solves the particular problem we are considering in this paper: given a set of positive and negative traces and an independence relation on events, derive a Petri net that both preserves the independence relation and satisfies the quality dimensions enumerated in Sect. 2. However, there is related work that intersects partially with the techniques of this paper. We now report on it.

Perhaps the closest work is [13], where the simplification of an initial process model is done by first unfolding the model (to derive an overfitting model) and then folding it back in a controlled manner, thus generalizing part of the behavior. The approach can only be applied for fitting models, which hampers its applicability unless alignment techniques [19] are used. The folding equivalences presented in this paper do not consider a model and therefore are less restrictive than the ones presented in [13].

Synthesis is a problem different from discovery: in synthesis, the underlying system is given and therefore one can assume $S = \mathcal{L}$. Considering a synthesis scenario, Bergenthum *et al.* have investigated the synthesis of a p/t net from partial orders [20]. The class of nets considered in this paper (safe Petri nets) is less expressive than p/t nets, which in practice poses no problems in the context of business processes. The algorithms in [20] are grounded in the *theory of regions* and split the problem into two steps *(i)* the p/t net $\mathcal{M}$ is generated which, by construction, satisfies $\mathcal{L} \subseteq obs(\mathcal{M})$, and *(ii)* it is checked whereas $\mathcal{L} = obs(\mathcal{M})$. Actually, by avoiding *(ii)*, a discovery scenario is obtained where the generalization feature is not controlled, in contrast to the technique of this paper. With the same goal but relying on ad-hoc operators tailored to compose lpos (choice, sequentialization, parallel compositions and repetition), a discovery technique is presented in [21]. Since the operators may in practice introduce wrong generalizations, a domain expert is consulted for the legality of every extra run.

8   Conclusions

A fresh look at process discovery is presented in this paper, which establishes theoretical basis for coping with some of the challenges in the field. By automating the folding of the unfolding that covers traces in the log but also combinations thereof derived from the input independence relation, problems like log incompleteness and noise may be alleviated. The approach has been implemented and the initial results show the potential of the technique in rediscovering a model, even for the simplest of the folding equivalences described in this paper.

Next steps will focus on implementing the remaining folding equivalences, and in general improving the SMT constraints for computing folding equivalences. Also, incorporating the notion of trace frequency in the approach will be considered, to guide the technique to focus on principal behavior. This will allow to also test the tool in presence of incomplete or noisy logs.

References

1. van der Aalst, W.M.P.: Process Mining - Discovery, Conformance and Enhancement of Business Processes. Springer, New York (2011)
2. van der Aalst, W.M.P.: On the representational bias in process mining. In: 20th IEEE International Workshops on Enabling Technologies: Infrastructures for Collaborative Enterprises, WETICE 2011, France, pp. 2–7 (2011)
3. Ferreira, H., Ferreira, D.: An integrated life cycle for workflow management based on learning and planning. Int. J. Coop. Inf. Syst. **15**(4), 485–505 (2006)
4. Lamma, E., Mello, P., Riguzzi, F., Storari, S.: Applying inductive logic programming to process mining. In: Blockeel, H., Ramon, J., Shavlik, J., Tadepalli, P. (eds.) ILP 2007. LNCS (LNAI), vol. 4894, pp. 132–146. Springer, Heidelberg (2008)
5. Goedertier, S., Martens, D., Vanthienen, J., Baesens, B.: Robust process discovery with artificial negative events. J. Mach. Learn. Res. **10**, 1305–1340 (2009)
6. Mazurkiewicz, A.W.: Trace theory. In: Petri Nets: Central Models and Their Properties, Advances in Petri Nets 1986, Part II, Proceedings of an Advanced Course, Bad Honnef, pp. 279–324 (1986)
7. Dumas, M., García-Bañuelos, L.: Process mining reloaded: event structures as a unified representation of process models and event logs. In: Devillers, R., Valmari, A. (eds.) PETRI NETS 2015. LNCS, vol. 9115, pp. 33–48. Springer, Heidelberg (2015)

8. Ponce-de-León, H., Rodríguez, C., Carmona, J., Heljanko, K., Haar, S.: Unfolding-based process discovery. CoRR abs/1507.02744 (2015)
9. Esparza, J., Römer, S., Vogler, W.: An improvement of McMillan's unfolding algorithm. Formal Methods Syst. Des. **20**(3), 285–310 (2002)
10. Nielsen, M., Plotkin, G.D., Winskel, G.: Petri nets, event structures and domains, part I. Theor. Comput. Sci. **13**, 85–108 (1981)
11. Buijs, J.C.A.M., van Dongen, B.F., van der Aalst, W.M.P.: Quality dimensions in process discovery: The importance of fitness, precision, generalization and simplicity. Int. J. Coop. Inf. Syst. **23**(1), 1–39 (2014)
12. Winskel, G.: Categories of models for concurrency. In: Brookes, S.D., Roscoe, A.W., Winskel, G. (eds.) Seminar on Concurrency. LNCS. Springer, Heidelberg (1984)
13. Fahland, D., van der Aalst, W.M.P.: Simplifying discovered process models in a controlled manner. Inf. Syst. **38**(4), 585–605 (2013)
14. van den Broucke, S.K.L.M., Weerdt, J.D., Vanthienen, J., Baesens, B.: Determining process model precision and generalization with weighted artificial negative events. IEEE Trans. Knowl. Data Eng. **26**(8), 1877–1889 (2014)
15. Nieuwenhuis, R., Oliveras, A.: On SAT modulo theories and optimization problems. In: Biere, A., Gomes, C.P. (eds.) SAT 2006. LNCS, vol. 4121, pp. 156–169. Springer, Heidelberg (2006)
16. The Model Checking Contest: Website. http://mcc.lip6.fr/
17. van der Werf, J.M.E.M., van Dongen, B.F., Hurkens, C.A.J., Serebrenik, A.: Process discovery using integer linear programming. In: van Hee, K.M., Valk, R. (eds.) PETRI NETS 2008. LNCS, vol. 5062, pp. 368–387. Springer, Heidelberg (2008)
18. Adriansyah, A., Munoz-Gama, J., Carmona, J., van Dongen, B.F., van der Aalst, W.M.P.: Measuring precision of modeled behavior. Inf. Syst. E-Bus. Manag. **13**(1), 37–67 (2015)
19. Adriansyah, A.: Aligning observed and modeled behavior. Ph.D. thesis, Technische Universiteit Eindhoven (2014)
20. Bergenthum, R., Desel, J., Lorenz, R., Mauser, S.: Synthesis of petri nets from finite partial languages. Fundam. Inform. **88**(4), 437–468 (2008)
21. Bergenthum, R., Desel, J., Mauser, S., Lorenz, R.: Construction of process models from example runs. In: Jensen, K., van der Aalst, W.M.P. (eds.) Transactions on Petri Nets and Other Models of Concurrency II. LNCS, vol. 5460, pp. 243–259. Springer, Heidelberg (2009)

Improving Interpolants for Linear Arithmetic

Ernst Althaus[1,2], Björn Beber[1]([✉]), Joschka Kupilas[1],
and Christoph Scholl[3]

[1] Max Planck Institute for Informatics, Campus E 14, 66123 Saarbrücken, Germany
bbeber@mpi-inf.mpg.de
[2] Johannes Gutenberg University, Staudinger Weg 9, 55128 Mainz, Germany
[3] Albert-Ludwigs-Universität, Georges Köhler Allee, Gebäude 51,
79110 Freiburg im Breisgau, Germany

Abstract. Craig interpolation for satisfiability modulo theory formulas have come more into focus for applications of formal verification. In this paper we, introduce a method to reduce the size of linear constraints used in the description of already computed interpolant in the theory of linear arithmetic with respect to the number of linear constraints. We successfully improve interpolants by combining satisfiability modulo theory and linear programming in a local search heuristic. Our experimental results suggest a lower running time and a larger reduction compared to other methods from the literature.

Keywords: Craig-interpolation · Linear arithmetic · Satisfiability modulo theory · Linear programming

1 Introduction

First efficients methods were introduced for computing such interpolants for Boolean systems out of the resolution proofs from DPLL-based SAT solvers [1,2]. McMillan [2] introduced interpolants to formal verification as over-approximations of state sets.

Due to the fact that such interpolants are in general not unique, many researchers try to find *good* interpolants. The measurement for interpolants differs depending on the context. In Boolean formulas it is often the size of the representation of the interpolant, i.e. the size the And-Inverter-Graph representing the interpolant. In the theory of linear arithmetic with rational coefficients $\mathcal{LA}(\mathbb{Q})$ the measurement of the number of linear constraints in the representation is often used, e.g. in [3] the authors showed that this measurement is beneficial for an improved generation of program invariants in software verification. This measurement is motivated by the verification of hybrid systems where operations are applied on state sets whose complexity strongly depends on the number of linear constraints, e.g. quantifier elimination in the worst-case leads to a quadratic blow-up of linear constraints after the elimination. Damm et al. showed [4] that such a measurement is the key for avoiding an explosion in the complexity of the state set representation.

© Springer International Publishing Switzerland 2015
B. Finkbeiner et al. (Eds.): ATVA 2015, LNCS 9364, pp. 48–63, 2015.
DOI: 10.1007/978-3-319-24953-7_5

In this paper we will only consider interpolants for the theory $\mathcal{LA}(\mathbb{Q})$. Therefore our measurement for *good* interpolants is the number of linear constraints. The problem of finding the best interpolant in this sense is NP-hard, which can be shown by a reduction from *k-Polyhedral Separability* [5], i.e. given two sets of points P and Q and an integer k, recognize whether there exist k hyperplanes that separate the sets P and Q through a Boolean formula. Therefore, we will here present a heuristic approach that simplifies a given interpolant. Additionally, there is no known algorithm that can compute reasonable lower bounds for this problem to measure the quality of an interpolant, so benchmarks exist where the initial interpolant is optimal, without a chance of verifying this situation.

Most approaches in this case were done by constructing an interpolant out of the resolution proof and then simplifying the proof by removing or combining theory lemmas [4,6], but maintaining the resolution proof correctly. Our approach differs in the way that we do not try to maintain the resolution proof. In fact, we only derive the set of linear constraints used in the interpolant by such proofs and then try to reduce this set in a local search heuristic. The invariant we preserve is based on an extension of Proposition 3 in [5], i.e. our set of interpolant constraints L fulfill that for every pair of points $a \in A$ and $b \in B$, there exists a linear constraint $l \in L$ such that l separates the points a and b. The proposition states that then there exists a Boolean formula, i.e. the interpolant, that separates A and B.

The paper is structured as follows: In Sect. 2 we will briefly describe previous methods to construct interpolants and the data-structure used in our benchmarks. Then we present our approach in Sect. 3, and some optimizations in Sect. 4. After that we present the evaluation of our method compared to three different other approaches in Sect. 5.

2 Preliminaries

2.1 Notations

For a point $p \in \mathbb{B}^n \times \mathbb{R}^m$, we denote the first n components, i.e. the Boolean components, by $p_\mathbb{B}$ and the last m, i.e. the real components, by $p_\mathbb{R}$. We describe a single linear constraint l by a formula $d^T x \le d_0$ with rational coefficients $d_0, d_1, \ldots, d_m \in \mathbb{Q}^{m+1}$ over rational variables $x_1, \ldots, x_m$. For a point $p \in \mathbb{B}^n \times \mathbb{R}^m$ and a linear constraint l, we associate with $l(p)$ the Boolean variable that is true, if $d^T p_\mathbb{R} \le d_0$ and false if $d^T p_\mathbb{R} > d_0$. We write $Dx \le d_0$ for a conjunction of u linear constraints over rational variables $(x_1, \ldots, x_m)^T = x$ with $D \in \mathbb{Q}^{u \times m}$ and $d_0 \in \mathbb{Q}^u$.

2.2 Computing Interpolants by Resolution Proofs

A (quantifier-free) formula F in the theory of linear arithmetic with rational coefficients $(\mathcal{LA}(\mathbb{Q}))$ is a Boolean combination of *atoms*. Each atom is potentially a linear constraint with rational coefficients d over a fixed set of rational variables

$x_1, \ldots, x_m$, denoted by $d^T x \leq d_0$, or a Boolean variable of a fixed set $y_1, \ldots, y_n$. A *literal* κ is either an atom or the negation of an atom. A *clause* is a disjunction of literals $\kappa_1 \vee \cdots \vee \kappa_s$. For a set of literals C and a formula F, we denote by $C \setminus F$ the set containing the literals in C by removing all atoms occurring in F, and by $C \downarrow F$ the set of literals created from C by removing all atoms *not* occurring in F.

Definition 1 (Craig Interpolant [7]). *Let A and B be two formulas, such that $A \wedge B \models \bot$. A Craig interpolant I is a formula such that $A \models I$, $I \wedge B \models \bot$ and the uninterpreted symbols in I occur both in A and B, the free variabels in I can occur freely both in A and B.*

Typically an SMT-Solver solves such formulas stepwise, first handling the non Boolean atoms like Boolean variables and solving this formula with a SAT approach. After finding a satisfiable assignment for the Boolean variables, e.g. $\kappa_1 \wedge \cdots \wedge \kappa_s$, the solver starts a decision procedure for the rational variables, i.e. computes if there exists one assignment of x such that all inequalities in the assignment simultaneously imply their given Boolean assignment. If this is not possible, we call $\eta = \{\kappa_1, \ldots, \kappa_s\}$ a $\mathcal{LA}(\mathbb{Q})$-*conflict*, the SMT-solver then adds a subset of $\kappa_1, \wedge \cdots \wedge \kappa_s$ described as a clause called $\mathcal{LA}(\mathbb{Q})$-*lemma*, to its set of clauses and starts backtracking, this will provide the procedure from selecting the invalid assignment again. These subsets are often called *minimal infeasible subsets* and are optimized in the way that the number of literals is minimized but still maintaining the $\mathcal{LA}(\mathbb{Q})$-unsatisfiability.

Definition 2 (Resolution Proof). *Let $S = \{c_1, \ldots, c_t\}$ be a set of clauses. $P = (V_P, E_P)$ is a directed acyclic graph partitioned in inner nodes and leaves. P is a resolution proof of the unsatisfiability of $c_1 \wedge \cdots \wedge c_t$ in $\mathcal{LA}(\mathbb{Q})$, if*

1. *each leaf in P is either a clause in S or a $\mathcal{LA}(\mathbb{Q})$-lemma (corresponding to some $\mathcal{LA}(\mathbb{Q})$-conflict η);*
2. *each inner node v in P has exactly two parents v^R and v^L, such that v^R and v^L share a common variable p (pivot variable) in the way that $p \in v^L$ and $\neg p \in v^R$. We derive v by computing the conjunction of $v^R \wedge v^L$;*
3. *the unique root node r in P is the empty clause.*

Let $S = \{c_1, \ldots, c_t\}$ be a $\mathcal{LA}(\mathbb{Q})$-unsatisfiable set of clauses, (A, B) a disjoint partition of S, and P a proof for the unsatisfiability of S in $\mathcal{LA}(\mathbb{Q})$. Then an interpolant I for (A, B) can be constructed by the following procedure [8]:

Initiate I as a copy of P, we then change the association of the nodes accordingly.

1. For every leaf $v_P \in P$ associated with a clause in S,
   set $v_I = v_P \downarrow B$, if $v_P \in A$, and set $v_I = \top$, if $v_P \in B$.
2. For every leaf $v_P \in P$ associated with a $\mathcal{LA}(\mathbb{Q})$-conflict η,
   set $v_I = \texttt{Interpolant}(\eta \setminus B, \eta \downarrow B)$.
3. For every inner node $v_P \in P$,
   set $v_I = v_I^L \vee v_I^R$ if $v_P \notin B$, and set $v_I = v_I^L \wedge v_I^R$ if $v_P \in B$.

The unique root node r_I then represents the formula of an interpolant of A and B. Several methods are known to construct $\mathcal{LA}(\mathbb{Q})$-interpolants, e.g. [9], all have in common that they construct a single linear constraint based on the convex regions given to the function. One basic idea is to use Farkas Lemma to construct a linear constraint separating these convex regions computed by linear programming. If those calls are handled separately, this will add for each $\mathcal{LA}(\mathbb{Q})$-conflict in the proof a linear constraint with a fixed normal [6] to the interpolant, and therefore will lead to a substantial blow up in the complexity. To find *simpler* interpolants the authors in [6] try to combine those calls by enlarging their degrees of freedom, i.e. extending the $\mathcal{LA}(\mathbb{Q})$-lemmas and relaxing specific constraints in the linear program to find shared interpolants for different theory lemmas in one proof.

2.3 Computing Interpolants by DC-Removability Checks

In the description of a formula F we could ask whether it is possible to remove redundant constraints. This is not as straightforward as in the situation of convex polyhedra. A linear constraint l is redundant for a formula F if there exists a formula G that depends on the same linear constraints except of l and F and G represents the same predicates. To achieve this we introduce a "don't care set" DC for F, which consists of all Boolean configurations which are not $\mathcal{LA}(\mathbb{Q})$-sufficient, and then efficiently construct G, which holds $F = G$ for every configuration not in DC. This method was introduced by [10] and expanded in [11] to compute an interpolant of A and B. Assume we have two disjoint formulas A, B, i.e. $A \wedge B$ is unsatisfiable. We then set $F = A$ and extend the set DC from above by the set $\neg A \wedge \neg B$. By the usage of the same construction now the new formula G can differ in all regions that are not specified by either A or B. This turns the method of redundancy removal in a method of interpolation.

For both the basic approach of constructing an interpolant from a resolution proof and the reduncancy removal, the fundamental problem is that there is no freedom in the choice of linear constraints. The approach introduced in [6] is more flexible, but lacks the fact that it does not notice if a linear constraint is redundant.

2.4 Description of a State Set

A formula A can be interpreted as a specific subset of $\mathbb{B}^n \times \mathbb{R}^m$, e.g. a representation of a state set. There are several possibilities to describe state sets, e.g. the LinAIG data structure [11] where such formulas are saved as an extension of a classical And-Inverter-Graph. An And-Inverter-Graphs is a directed, acyclic graph partitioned in inner nodes and leaves. Each inner node has exactly two predecessors, representing a logical conjunction. Each leaf represents a Boolean variable $y \in \mathbb{B}^n$ or in LinAIGs a lesser-or-equal constraint over the rational variables $x \in \mathbb{Q}^m$. Additionally, the edges can contain markers indicating a logical negation. The formula A is then the association of the unique root.

This representation is also often used as a data structure for resolution proofs.

Our method does not depend on the way the state sets are described, but we assume that we can negate and intersect state sets and that we can compute whether a state set is non-empty and if so, obtain a point within the state set. All these operations are executable by common SMT solvers. Furthermore, we can easily create a set of all linear constraints used in the description of the state set.

Note that the state sets are not in disjunctive normal form, where convex regions would be easily accessible, and a transformation would not be practicable due to a potentially exponential blow-up in the description.

3   The General Algorithm

The problem we are solving can be briefly described as follows. Let two state sets A, B and an interpolant of these be given. Try to minimize the number of linear constraints used in the interpolant.

Example 1. Figure 1(a) shows two state sets A, B, with no Boolean complexity, i.e. $n = 0$. One representation of those sets is $A = (l_1 \wedge l_2) \vee l_3 \vee l_4$ and $B = (l_5 \wedge l_6) \vee (l_7 \wedge l_8)$. In this case, A itself is an interpolant of A and B.

Our algorithm is based on the following extension of Proposition 3 in [5].

Proposition 1. *The set of (linear) constraints $L = \{L_1, \ldots, L_h\}$ separates the state sets A and B through some Boolean formula if and only if for every pair of points $p \in A$ and $q \in B$ with $p_\mathbb{B} = q_\mathbb{B}$ there exists an i ($1 \leq i \leq h$) such that $L_i(p) \neq L_i(q)$.*

The proof of the extension is basically the same as the one given in [5] despite two differences. Firstly, we have a finite set of (convex) regions instead of points. But since we also used L to construct these regions they behave like points, i.e. the points in such a (convex) region are constant under the associated Boolean variables. Secondly, in the extension this only holds for pairs of points in the same Boolean space, since we can distinguish the Boolean spaces by m other Boolean variables easily in a formula easily. We use this proposition in our algorithm as follows.

The algorithm iteratively improves the set L by replacing two linear constraints by one, while preserving the invariant that L satisfy Proposition 1. The linear constraints in L are called *interpolant constraints*. Every new constraint added to L can be described separately by a linear combination of constraints in A and B. This lead to the fact that if the initial L only contains constraints described over local variables of A and B, the output of our algorithm only contains such constraints, for details we refer to the linear constraints of the LP (4) and (5) in Sect. 3.4. Hence, our algorithm is a local search heuristic. In this section, we describe the test whether two linear constraints can be replaced by one and in Sect. 4, we describe some techniques to improve the performance. In particular, we describe our approach to reduce the number of pairs of linear constraints that are tested. Most approaches are of a heuristic nature.

The interpolant itself is constructed by using the method described in Sect. 2.3. We therefore deliver a sufficient set of constraints to construct the interpolant, so in the constraint minimization the part of finding redundant constraints can be skipped. This together with the fact that all interpolant constraints are defined over local variables of A and B lead to the fact that the resulting interpolant is in fact an Craig-Interpolant.

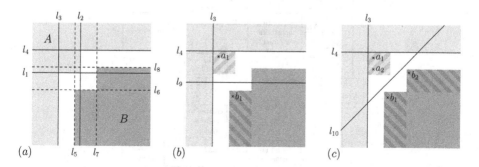

Fig. 1. Running example for our algorithm

3.1 Test Whether One Additional Linear Constraint Is Sufficient

This is the core part of the heuristic, where we determine if we can reduce the size of the interpolant. It will test if it is possible to substitute two given interpolant constraints by one new linear constraint l^*. Notice, that when removing two interpolant constraints, there will be pairs $a \in A, b \in B$ of points with $a_{\mathbb{B}} = b_{\mathbb{B}}$ that can not be distinguished by the remaining interpolant constraints L, i.e. $l(a) = l(b)$ for all $l \in L$. We will test whether all those pairs of points can be distinguished by a single new linear constraint.

Basically, we iteratively collect such pairs of points and construct a linear constraint l^* separating all pairs of points already found, until either all pairs of points can be distinguished with the additional help of l^* or no such linear constraint can be found. Figure 2 gives a sketch of the algorithm.

In order to guarantee termination, it does not satisfy to collect pairs of points, as there can be an infinite number. Therefore, we construct convex regions C_a and C_b around the points a and b described only by constraints known to the system, i.e. for C_a we only use linear constraints used in the description of A and additionally all remaining interpolant constraints. The convex sets are contained in the respective sets, i.e. $C_a \subseteq A$ and $C_b \subseteq B$. Since there are only a finite number of linear constraints in the description of the state sets and interpolant constraints, there are only a finite number of possible convex sets describable by these constraints. This lead to a termination of this part of the algorithm in a finite number of steps.

Hence, we need three sub-algorithms. One for finding pairs of points that can not be distinguished, one for constructing the convex regions around them, and one for constructing a linear constraint separating a given set of pairs of convex regions. An algorithm for the first problem which is based on SMT is given in Sect. 3.2. A simple solution for the second problem is given in Sect. 3.3. Finally, we give a solution for the third problem based on linear programming (LP) in Sect. 3.4.

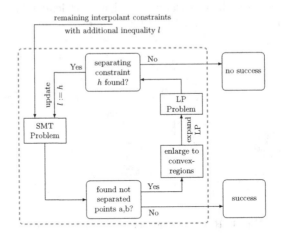

Fig. 2. Sketch of the core part of the heuristic

Example 2. As mentioned in the previous part the set of linear constraints $L = \{l_1, \ldots, l_4\}$ of A is a valid set of interpolant constraints, i.e. satisfy Proposition 1. Figure 1(b) and (c) show the solutions of the three sub-algorithms from the test, whether l_1 and l_2 can be substituted by a single new constraint. In the first iteration, shown in (b) we find a pair of points a_1, b_1 that are indistinguishable, once $L = \{l_3, l_4\}$, after that we compute convex regions around those points, shown as highlighted areas, and finally compute a linear constraint l_9 that separates this pair of convex regions. $L \cup \{l_9\}$ do not satisfy Proposition 1, therefore the algorithm starts a second iteration, shown in (c), and finally computes a linear constraint l_{10}, that simultaneously separates both pairs of convex regions found in the first and the current iteration. Finally $L \cup \{l_{10}\}$ satisfy Proposition 1 and therefore one constraint less is needed in the interpolant.

3.2   Finding Pairs of Indistinguishable Points with SMT

Notice, that we are in the situation that we have to test whether our tentative new linear constraints l^* together with the remaining linear constraints L of the interpolant satisfies to construct an interpolant between state sets A and B. The linear constraints are not sufficient if and only if we can find points $a \in A, b \in B$ with $a_{\mathbb{B}} = b_{\mathbb{B}}$ that are not distinguishable, i.e. for all $l \in L \cup \{l^*\} l(a) = l(b)$ holds.

To solve this by an SMT solver we use the following formula:

$$(a \in A) \wedge (b \in B) \wedge (a_{\mathbb{B}} = b_{\mathbb{B}}) \wedge \left(\bigwedge_{l \in L \cup \{l^*\}} l(a) = l(b) \right) \qquad (1)$$

Either we found a valid solution and therefore two points a, b that are not separable by any linear constraint in $L \cup \{l^*\}$ or we found that $L \cup \{l^*\}$ is a valid set of interpolant constraints. The problem has only minor changes in every iteration, because we only substitute the old condition $l^*(p) = l^*(q)$ with an updated linear constraint l^*. This gives us the opportunity to use the advantage of incremental SMT.

3.3 Enlarge Pairs of Indistinguishable Points to Convex Regions

If we have found a pair of points a, b as described in the previous section, we want to find a set of points $C_a \subseteq A$ around a that is preferably large, such that no point in C_a can be distinguished from b and vice versa.

We achieve this by computing convex regions around a, such that all points within C_a are equal with respect to all linear constraints in $L \setminus \{l^*\}$ and all linear constraints used in the description of A.

For computing C_a test for every linear constraint l that is used in the description of A, if a satisfies this linear constraint, i.e. we compute $l(a)$. We therefore collect linear constraints in a set C. We add l to C when $l(a)$ is *true*, or $\neg l$ if $l(a)$ is *false*. After evaluating that for every linear constraint in A, we compute the same for every interpolant constraint. We do not use the current l^* in the description of the convex region, since we change this constraint in the next step, where we search for a new candidate. C_a is then computed as a conjunction of . all constraints in C.

3.4 Finding a Linear Constraint Separating Pairs of Convex Regions with LP

We try to find a solution to this problem by constructing a linear program whose solution represents a separating linear constraint. The LP does not solve the problem in general, as it will fix all convex regions of A on one side and the convex regions of B on the other side, which is not necessarily required. Furthermore, it assumes that all inequalities in A and B are non-strict, i.e. convex regions are enlarged by their boundary. Both deficiencies are handled heuristically later. We use an LP-solver that handles rational arithmetic as errors in the coefficients prevent the algorithm from termination since we could be forced to separate the same pair of convex region multiple times.

The construction of the LP is similar to the one that computes the linear constraints in resolution proofs, hence based on Farkas' Lemma. We expanded the approach to separate multiple pairs of convex regions.

Therefore, we define the variables $d \in \mathbb{Q}^m$ and $d_0 \in \mathbb{Q}$ that describe the new linear constraint l^* in the form $d^T x \leq d_0$. Pairs of convex sets (A^i, B^i) for $i \in \{1, \ldots, k\}$, which are present in the k-th iteration of the LP-problem for finding a new constraint for one test described in Sect. 3.1, all constructed by the enlargement of points to convex regions described in Sect. 3.3. The constraint $d^T x \leq d_0$ is implied by A^i, if there is a non-negative linear combination of the inequalities of A^i leading to $d^T x \leq d_0$. Similarly, the constraint $a^T x > b$ is implied by B^i, if there is a positive ε such that there is a non-positive linear combination of the inequalities of B^i leading to $d^T x \geq d_0 + \varepsilon$. All constraints can easily be formulated as linear constraints.

A detailed description of the LP is given in the appendix. If the LP is solvable and $\varepsilon > 0$ the computed linear constraint l^* separates each pair of convex regions.

Extension to Non-Closed Polyhedra. Obviously, the former statement is also true in the case that some of the inequalities are strict. When the LP is solvable but $\varepsilon = 0$, at least one of the convex regions of each set touches the inequality if all inequalities are non-strict. Hence, the LP solution does not give a linear constraint in this case, as the negation of the non-strict inequality is not implied by one convex set of B and its strict version is not implied by one convex set of A. If there are strict inequalities in the description of the convex regions, we test whether the computed linear constraint still separates the convex regions either in the non-strict or in the strict version. This is done by computing if the non-strict or the strict version is a valid choice for each pair. Only if a solution is valid for every pair it is a solution for the problem. Details are given in Section B in the appendix. Alternatively, a linear program that is forced to use a strict inequality of the right-hand side of the linear combination evaluates if d_0 can be used.

Greedy Approach. The LP is trying to separate all regions by always forcing A^i on one side of l^* and all B^i on the other side of l^*. This is more than we actually need in order to satisfy Proposition 1. So we expand our LP problem by a greedy approach as follows. Assume we find a linear constraint separating the pairs (A^i, B^i) for the first $k - 1$ convex pairs, but the LP does not find a solution when trying to set A^k on the one side and B^k on the other. Then we try to switch the sides of A^k and B^k, i.e. we modify the variable bounds and the constraints concerning the last added pair of regions, such that the convex regions will change the sides on l^*.

This is a greedy approach, as we only change the positions of the convex regions of the last iteration.

The LP and Proposition 2 given in Section B in the appendix can be adopted easily for this greedy approach.

4   Optimizations

Our main goal with the optimizations is to reduce the number of tested pairs of linear constraints to a reasonable amount. For this goal, we first introduce the concept of Non-Redundancy-Certificate-points (NRC-points) for interpolant constraints, which are then used to choose interesting candidates of pairs of linear constraints. The idea behind this heuristic is, that it is more likely to combine constraints when they are needed to separate the same regions. There will be situations where we will not choose the correct pair. To check the potency of the heuristic choice of specific pairs and the overall heuristical algorithm we computed all benchmarks in Sect. 5 with the heuristical choice and by testing every pair of interpolant constraints. Furthermore, we give some other optimizations to the general approach.

NRC-Points. An NRC-Point (a, b) is a pair of points, where $a \in A$ and $b \in B$ are only distinguishable by one interpolant constraint h and are indistinguishable for every other interpolant constraint, we call (a, b) a NRC-point of h. Formally, an NRC-point (a, b) of h is a solution of the formula

$$(a \in A) \wedge (b \in B) \wedge (a_\mathbb{B} = b_\mathbb{B}) \wedge \left(\bigwedge_{l \in L \setminus h} l(a) = l(b) \right). \tag{2}$$

Since there can be more than one NRC-point of h, we first solve (2), then we compute convex regions C_a, C_b around a and b, with the method described in Sect. 3.3. After this, we solve (2) with the additional conjunction, that $(a \notin C_a) \wedge (b \notin C_b)$. This can be done multiple times, and with the advantage of an incremental SMT since we only add clauses to the formula.

It is worth mentioning that the search for the NRC-points detects if an interpolant constraint is redundant, i.e. it is not needed to fulfill Proposition 1. This is the case, when (2) is not satisfiable in the first iteration. When this occurs, we delete the inequality from the interpolant constraints. To keep the computational effort low, we only compute a maximum of three NRC-points for each interpolant constraint, this is motivated by experimental results.

Example 3. Consider Example 2, we want to compute all NRC-points for l_3. Therefore we search for points (a_3, b_3), that are a solution to the problem $(a_3 \in A) \wedge (b_3 \in B) \wedge (\bigwedge_{i \in \{1,2,4\}} l_i(a_3) = l_i(b_3))$. The pair (a_3, b_3) is shown in Fig. 3(a). The highlighted areas are again the convex regions built around the points a_3, b_3. There is no other solution that is not in the convex regions, therefore (a_3, b_3) is the only NRC-point for l_3. Additionally it is easy to see in Fig. 1, that the pair (a_1, b_1) is an NRC-point of l_1, and (a_2, b_2) an NRC-point of l_2.

The Choice of Interesting Pairs of Inequalities. After we calculated the NRC-points for every interpolant constraint, we compare the constructed convex regions around these points. A pair of inequalities (s, t) is chosen by our heuristic, if there exist two NRC-points (a_s, b_s) and (a_t, b_t) for interpolant constraints s and t, such that either a_s and a_t or b_s and b_t are equal in respect to all $l \in L \setminus \{s, t\}$.

In this case, our heuristic chooses the pair (s, t) as a pair that is promising, and therefore will be tested by the method described in Sect. 3.1.

If it was possible to improve the interpolant by testing the pair (s, t), all other constraints that where chosen to be tested with either s or t are then tested with the newly found interpolant constraint.

Example 4. Consider Example 3, we already computed NRC-points for l_1, l_2 and l_3. The heuristic for interesting pairs now compares these points, i.e. the

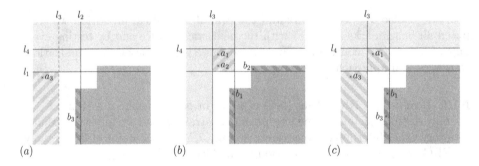

Fig. 3. Example of NRC-points and the heuristic choice of pairs.

convex regions around these points only build by interpolant constraints. In Fig. 3(b), we see that the convex regions around a_1 and a_2 are the same, the heuristic therefore chooses the pair l_1, l_2 as a promising candidate. The heuristic does not choose the pair l_1, l_3 since none of the convex regions are equal as we can see in Fig. 3(c).

Using NRC-Points to Save SMT-Calls. Assume we want to replace the interpolant constraints l_1 and l_2 by a new linear constraint l^*. The algorithm in Sect. 3.1 would first compute a pair of points, that is now not separable. With the precomputation of NRC-points, we can skip this since we already have at least two pairs of convex regions at hand that need to be distinguished by l^*.

5   Experimental Results

We implemented our algorithm in the C++ language, using Yices [12] to solve the SMT problems and QSopt-Exact [13] to solve the rational LP problems. All computations were done on a single core of an Intel I7 with 3.20 GHz, and a memory limit of 2 GB. The maximal time used for a computation of a single interpolant for a method was 15minutes, the average overall was around 2 s. The benchmarks are intermediate state sets of over 150 different model checker runs, mainly two different categories of models. We tested 62 models of the category *Flap/Slat System (FS)*, during take-off (and landing) flaps and slats of the aircraft are extended to generate more lift at low velocity and have to be retracted in time as they are not robust enough for high velocities. The models have different numbers of flaps/slats, explained in more detail in [15]. Another 90 models of the category of *ACC*, where a controllers objective is to set the acceleration of the controlled car to make it reach the goal velocity in a distance equal to or greater than the goal distance. Additionally, we tested 15 other models of other categories. Damm et al. [4] provided the model checker and models, which created the intermediate state sets. Independent of the model which is tested the intermediate state sets are divided in two different classes. In the first class, formula A describes a state set and formula B describes the negation of a bloated version of A. This is used in the model checker, if the descriptions of the state sets become too difficult. Hence, we look for a state set with a simpler description that is slightly larger than the given state set. Due to the bloating factor this will lead to different degrees of freedom. In all our benchmarks the bloating factor for each linear constraint was set to 10 %, so every linear constraint of the bloated state set is pushed by 10 % of the total variable range of all variables used in the constraint, which is applicable, since all benchmarks are bounded in every variable. The second class comes from the so-called abstraction refinement, where specific points are excluded in a previous computed interpolant computation. In this set of benchmarks the two state sets A and B "touch" each other, i.e. they use the same linear constraint in different orientations.

All benchmarks are compared with *Constraint Minimization* [4], which basically removes redundant constraints out of the description, a version of *Simple Interpolants* [6], which creates shared constraints in the proof, and the standard interpolation method of *MathSat* [14]. To compare the quality of the solutions of *Simple interpolants* and *MathSat* we additionally executed a Constraint Minimization at the end of their computation. We were not able to compare our approach with the method described in [3], as their description of the state sets differs from ours.

We implemented four types of our approach. Approaches g_all and n_all test all pairs of linear constraints, while g_h and n_h only test pairs of interpolant constraints selected by our heuristic described in Sect. 3.4. Further g_all and g_h use the greedy approach described in Sect. 3.4, while n_all and n_h do not use it. A computed interpolant obtained by *Constraint Minimization* was used to compute the initial set of interpolant constraints L.

Table 1 shows a comparison of $g_{all}, n_{all}, g_h, n_h$s, *Simple Interpolants* (SI), *MathSat* (MS), and *Constraint Minimization* (CM).

The benchmarks are all sorted by categories (FS, ACC, other models) and classes (bloated, refinement). The key specifics of each benchmarks are given with the number instances, the number of Boolean variables n, and the number of real variables m in the table. To compare the approaches, we state the average number of linear constraints ($\# LC$) and its variance (var. $\# LC$). Then the relative size of the interpolant (rel. $\# LC$) is compared to the approach of Constraint Minimization, since this method only removes redundant constraints. Additionally, we state the number of instances where the method improved the interpolant ($\#$ better), again compared to the Constraint Minimization. In the cell of the Constraint Minimization "$\#$ better" states the number of instances where no method constructed an interpolant better than the one computed by the Constraint Minimization. At last, the average runtime (time) of each method is stated.

From the table we can see that most of the benchmarks in the refinement context independent of the model could usually not be improved by any method. The distinct test where this can be seen is *ACC - refinement*. In this set of benchmarks for every of the 180 instances all methods computed an equal interpolant. We assume that this is the result of the fact that the state sets "touch" each

Table 1. Experimental results

	g_{all}	n_{all}	g_h	n_h	SI	MS	CM
FS - bloated (2255 instances, $n \in \{0,\ldots,34\}$, $m \in \{1,\ldots,3\}$)							
#LC	6.18	6.30	6.76	6.79	7.33	7.39	7.43
var. #LC	7.72	8.51	10.434	10.66	9.78	9.70	9.97
rel. #LC	0.83	0.85	0.90	0.90	0.99	1.00	1
#better	1533	1453	969	938	336	196	717
time	3.14 s	2.35 s	0.92 s	0.82 s	1.78 s	0.83 s	0.37 s
FS - refinement (915 instances, $n \in \{0,\ldots,36\}$, $m \in \{2,\ldots,3\}$)							
#LC	8.00	8.01	8.12	8.12	8.22	8.23	8.22
var. #LC	11.28	11.32	11.19	11.21	11.22	11.23	11.13
rel. #LC	0.97	0.97	0.98	0.99	1.00	1.00	1
#better	138	134	81	79	15	10	776
time	2.59 s	2.10 s	0.69 s	0.64 s	0.95 s	0.62 s	0.30 s
ACC - bloated (1575 instances, $n \in \{0,\ldots,7\}$, $m \in \{3,\ldots,5\}$)							
#LC	2.28	2.28	2.51	2.51	4.41	5.71	5.54
var. #LC	0.38	0.38	0.25	0.25	2.19	11.84	6.06
rel. #LC	0.51	0.51	0.55	0.55	0.87	1.01	1
#better	1305	1305	1305	1305	724	258	270
time	2.60 s	2.09 s	1.33 s	1.12 s	0.35 s	0.24 s	0.24 s
ACC - refinement (180 instances, $n \in \{4,\ldots,7\}$, $m \in \{7\}$)							
#LC	3	3	3	3	3	3	3
var. #LC	0	0	0	0	0	0	0
rel. #LC	1	1	1	1	1	1	1
#better	0	0	0	0	0	0	180
time	0.36 s	0.29 s	0.34 s	0.26 s	0.06 s	0.04 s	0.06 s
other models - bloated (740 instances, $n \in \{0,\ldots,31\}$, $m \in \{1,\ldots,5\}$)							
#LC	7.32	7.43	8.13	8.16	8.28	8.47	8.50
var. #LC	13.84	14.83	18.32	18.72	19.78	20.54	20.16
rel. #LC	0.87	0.88	0.95	0.95	1.00	1.00	1
#better	464	435	209	196	64	64	276
time	7.77 s	6.30 s	3.48 s	3.40 s	11.33 s	8.36 s	1.83 s
other models - refinement (96 instances, $n \in \{4,\ldots,24\}$, $m \in \{2,\ldots,3\}$)							
#LC	12.09	12.11	12.11	12.13	12.31	12.34	12.19
var. #LC	21.62	21.79	21.87	21.84	22.32	22.61	21.73
rel. #LC	0.99	0.99	0.99	0.99	1.01	1.01	1
#better	9	7	7	6	2	2	86
time	8.30 s	6.65 s	2.37 s	2.30 s	11.78 s	8.73 s	1.23 s

other and therefore reduce the degree of freedom. On the other hand, all of our algorithms were able to improve most of the bloated benchmarks. Again the obvious test where this can be seen is in the ACC models. There, all of our methods could improve 1305 of 1575 instances, with an overall relative improvement of 49 % for the algorithms that tested every pair of interpolant constraints, and 45 % for the two algorithms that tested only *interesting* pairs computed by our heuristic.

The experiments also indicate that our greedy approach for the LP problem is not often helpful in improving interpolants, i.e. there were only 162 of total 5761 instances where the greedy algorithm (g_{all}, g_{tps}) was better than the appropriate normal algorithm (n_{all}, n_{tps}). Overall, our algorithm n_{tps} achieves the best ratio in improving interpolants compared to the time effort, with a overall factor of ~ 4.71 in exceeded running time and an improvement of around 20 %.

6   Conclusion and Further Research

In this paper, we showed how the number of linear constraints in interpolants for linear arithmetic can be reduced by a fair amount. The experiments showed that in the context of intermediate state sets in hybrid model checking the success of our algorithm closely related to the model in which this problem occurs. Further, we plan to improve our running times by replacing the rational LP solver by a state of the art LP solver and use rational arithmetic only to verify the feasibility of the solutions. Additionally, we want to improve our heuristic for the choice of "interesting" pairs of interpolant constraints. Furthermore, we will try to compute lower bounds for the amount of interpolant constraints needed in this context.

Acknowledgment. The results presented in this paper were developed in the context of the Transregional Collaborative Research Center 'Automatic Verification and Analysis of Complex Systems' (SFB/TR 14 AVACS) supported by the German Research Council (DFG). We worked in close coorperation with our colleagues from the 'First Order Model Checking Team' within the subproject H3 and we would like to thank W. Damm, B. Wirtz, W. Hagemann, and A. Rakow from the University of Oldenburg, U. Waldmann from the Max Planck Institute for Informatics at Saarbrücken and S. Disch from the University of Freiburg for numerous ideas and discussions

A Detailed Description of the Linear Program

Recall the variables given in Sect. 3.4. Let A^i, B^i be the convex sets of the i-th iteration, constructed by s_{A^i}, respectively s_{B^i}, conjunctions of linear constraints. Then A^i is formally defined by $A^i = \{x \in \mathbb{R}^m | \mathcal{A}^i x \leq \alpha^i\}$, with $\mathcal{A}^i \in \mathbb{Q}^{m \times s_{A^i}}$ and $B^i = \{x \in \mathbb{R}^m | \mathcal{B}^i x \leq \beta^i\}$, with $\mathcal{B}^i \in \mathbb{Q}^{m \times s_{B^i}}$. We additionally introduce s_{A^i} variables λ^i and s_{B^i} variables μ^i for every iteration $i \in \{1, \ldots, k\}$.

We look for an inequality that maximizes a simple measure of the distance of the constructed inequality to the convex regions. We do this by subtracting the ε to the positive convex combination of the inequalities from A^i for l, i.e. the convex combination leads to $d^T x \leq d_0 - \varepsilon$. As we can scale any LP-solution by an arbitrary positive scalar so far, we have to normalize the solution. Therefore, we restrict the linear combination of one region to be a convex combination.

Hence, we obtain the following LP, where all linear constraints except (6) and (11) are introduced for all $i \in \{1, \ldots, k\}$:

$$\max \quad \varepsilon \tag{3}$$
$$\text{s.t.} \quad (A^i)^T \lambda^i = d \tag{4}$$
$$(B^i)^T \mu^i = d \tag{5}$$
$$\sum \lambda^1 = 1 \tag{6}$$
$$(\alpha^i)^T \lambda^i \leq d_0 - \varepsilon \tag{7}$$
$$(\beta^i)^T \mu^i \geq d_0 + \varepsilon \tag{8}$$
$$\lambda^i \geq 0 \tag{9}$$
$$\mu^i \leq 0 \tag{10}$$
$$\varepsilon \geq 0 \tag{11}$$

Constraints (4) and (5) force that the direction of the new constraint, described by d, is representable by the linear constraint of the convex regions. Conditions (7–11) verify that convex regions are on the right side of l^*. Condition (6) normalizes the solutions.

B Detailed Distinction for Non-Closed Polyhedra

The following proposition states when we have found a separating constraint in case of $\varepsilon = 0$.

Proposition 2. *Assume the LP (4–11) has optimal value 0 and let $(\bar{d}, \bar{d}_0)$ be the solution of the LP for the variables d and d_0.*

1. *If for all $i \in \{1, \ldots, k\}$ either $(\beta^i)^T \mu^i - d_0 > 0$ or there exists a strict inequality $s \neq \mathbf{0}$ in B^i with variable $(\mu^i)_s$ such that $(\mu^i)_s < 0$, then $\bar{a}^T x \leq \bar{d}_0$ separates the regions.*
2. *If for all $i \in \{1, \ldots, k\}$ either $(\alpha^i)^T \lambda^i - d_0 < 0$ or there exists a strict inequality $s \neq \mathbf{0}$ in A^i with variable $(\lambda^i)_s$ such that $(\lambda^i)_s > 0$, then $\bar{a}^T x < \bar{d}_0$ separates the regions.*

The proof for this proposition is straight forward and will not be given in the paper.

References

1. Pudlák, P.: Lower bounds for resolution and cutting plane proofs and monotone computations. J. Symbolic Logic **62**(3), 981–998 (1997)
2. McMillan, K.L.: Interpolation and sat-based model checking. In: Hunt Jr., W.A., Somenzi, F. (eds.) CAV 2003. LNCS, vol. 2725, pp. 1–13. Springer, Heidelberg (2003)
3. Albarghouthi, A., McMillan, K.L.: Beautiful interpolants. In: Sharygina, N., Veith, H. (eds.) CAV 2013. LNCS, vol. 8044, pp. 313–329. Springer, Heidelberg (2013)
4. Damm, W., Dierks, H., Disch, S., Hagemann, W., Pigorsch, F., Scholl, C., Waldmann, U., Wirtz, B.: Exact and fully symbolic verification of linear hybrid automata with large discrete state spaces. Sci. Comput. Program. **77**(10–11), 1122–1150 (2012)
5. Megiddo, N.: On the complexity of polyhedral separability. Discrete Comput. Geom. **3**(1), 325–337 (1988)
6. Scholl, C., Pigorsch, F., Disch, S., Althaus, E.: Simple interpolants for linear arithmetic. In: Design, Automation and Test in Europe Conference and Exhibition (DATE), 2014, pp. 1–6. IEEE (2014)
7. William, C.: Three uses of the Herbrand-Gentzen theorem in relating model theory and proof theory. J. Symbolic Logic **22**(03), 269–285 (1957)
8. McMillan, K.L.: An interpolating theorem prover. Theoret. Comput. Sci. **345**(1), 101–121 (2005)
9. Rybalchenko, A., Sofronie-Stokkermans, V.: Constraint solving for interpolation. In: Cook, B., Podelski, A. (eds.) VMCAI 2007. LNCS, vol. 4349, pp. 346–362. Springer, Heidelberg (2007)
10. Scholl, C., Disch, S., Pigorsch, F., Kupferschmid, S.: Using an SMT solver and craig interpolation to detect and remove redundant linear constraints in representations of non-convex polyhedra. In: Proceedings of the Joint Workshops of the 6th International Workshop on Satisfiability Modulo Theories and 1st International Workshop on Bit-Precise Reasoning, pp. 18–26. ACM (2008)
11. Damm, W., Disch, S., Hungar, H., Jacobs, S., Pang, J., Pigorsch, F., Scholl, C., Waldmann, U., Wirtz, B.: Exact state set representations in the verification of linear hybrid systems with large discrete state space. In: Namjoshi, K.S., Yoneda, T., Higashino, T., Okamura, Y. (eds.) ATVA 2007. LNCS, vol. 4762, pp. 425–440. Springer, Heidelberg (2007)
12. Dutertre, B., De Moura, L.: The yices SMT solver (2006). http://yices.csl.sri.com/tool-paper.pdf
13. Applegate, D.L., Cook, W., Dash, S., Espinoza, D.G.: Exact solutions to linear programming problems. Oper. Res. Lett. **35**(6), 693–699 (2007)
14. Griggio, A.: A practical approach to satisfiability modulo linear integer arithmetic. JSAT **8**, 1–27 (2012)
15. Rakow, A.: Flap/Slat System. http://www.avacs.org/fileadmin/Benchmarks/Open/FlapSlatSystem.pdf

A Mechanically Checked Generation
of Correlating Programs Directed
by Structured Syntactic Differences

Thibaut Girka[1,2], David Mentré[1], and Yann Régis-Gianas[2(✉)]

[1] Mitsubishi Electric R&D Centre Europe, 35708 Rennes, France
[2] University of Paris Diderot, Sorbonne Paris Cité, PPS, UMR 7126 CNRS,
PiR2, INRIA Paris-Rocquencourt, 75205 Paris, France
yrg@pps.univ-paris-diderot.fr

Abstract. We present a new algorithm for the construction of a correlating program from the syntactic difference between the original and modified versions of a program. This correlating program exhibits the semantics of the two input programs and can then be used to compute their semantic differences, following an approach of Partush and Yahav [12]. We show that Partush and Yahav's correlating program is unsound on loops that include an early exit. Our algorithm is defined on an imperative language with **while**-loops, **break**, and **continue**. To guarantee its correctness, it is formalized and mechanically checked within the Coq proof assistant. On a series of examples, we experimentally find that the static analyzer dizy is at least as precise on our correlating program as on Partush and Yahav's.

1 Introduction

Most of current software engineering practices are using textual differences – as provided by the Unix diff tool – to examine changes made on a program. However, many development tasks [9] would take benefit from *semantic differences*, i.e. a representation of the *meaning* of each change made on a program. Such a piece of information would be very helpful to check that refactoring does not change current program behavior [15], to minimize replay of tests after a change [1], to check that a change indeed modified the expected parts of the program [7,8], to generate synthetic patches for code reviews, to determine security impact of a change [2], etc.

Moreover, the tool computing and presenting such semantic differences to a final user should be *sound*, i.e. no change should be missed, so that the user can safely elaborate further software engineering tasks on top of the reported differences. Building such a sound tool implies that the underlying theory is itself sound and that it is correctly used to specify and implement the tool. This is an error-prone task which can be nonetheless guided by modern proof assistants. This approach leads to Correct-by-Construction tools like the CompCert C compiler [10].

© Springer International Publishing Switzerland 2015
B. Finkbeiner et al. (Eds.): ATVA 2015, LNCS 9364, pp. 64–79, 2015.
DOI: 10.1007/978-3-319-24953-7_6

We follow Partush's and Yahav [12]'s approach to compute semantic differences between two variants P and P' of the same program: (i) we generate a *correlating program* C that tightly interleaves the instructions to simulate the parallel executions of P and P'; (ii) we apply a dedicated Abstract Interpretation [3] technique on C to approximate the correlation between the variables of P and P'.

Even though we reuse an existing approach, we propose a new algorithm to build the correlating program and we formally verified this algorithm within the Coq proof assistant [11]. Incidentally, this allowed us to find that Partush and Yahav's approach produces incorrect results for loop constructions with early exit. In our opinion, Parush and Yahav's approach is flawed by design because their generation algorithm is directed by a *textual* difference between the two versions of the program. This textual representation is not structured enough to correctly perform a static scheduling of the two programs instructions. On the contrary, our generation algorithm is directed by a *structured* difference between abstract syntax trees which is a better input for a static scheduling because it gives a structured relationship between the control flow graphs of the two programs. Besides, our tool is extracted from our Coq formalization and is thus Correct-by-Construction. To sum up, the contributions of our paper are as follow: (i) we identify errors in previous work of Partush and Yahav [12]; (ii) we propose a new sound algorithm for the production of a correlating program from a syntactic structural difference; (iii) both the underlying theory and our algorithm are formalized and mechanically checked within the Coq proof assistant; (iv) we experimentally compare the quality of our approach against Partush and Yahav's work.

Plan. In Sect. 2, we give an overview of our analysis chain structure along with an example. In Sect. 3, we present our input language and its guarded form as well as their semantics. In Sect. 4, we show how we represent syntactic differences between the original and modified programs. In Sect. 5, we present the core of our approach to generate a sound correlating program. In Sect. 6, we discuss our implementation and some experiments. In Sect. 7, we present related work and finally present our conclusion and future work in Sect. 8.

2   Overview

The original analysis described by Nimrod Partush and Eran Yahav [12] can be decomposed in two main components: a set of program transformations (implemented in a tool called ccc) yielding a *correlating program*, and a static analysis on this correlating program (implemented in a tool called dizy). Our work mainly consists in a restricted (but proven correct) replacement for the first part (ccc) while producing an output that remains compatible with the second part (dizy). This new algorithm called correlating_program uses structured syntactic differences to correctly interleave the instructions of the two programs while factoring their control flow as much as possible. In this section, we compare Partush's and Yahav's algorithm and our algorithm on the following examples where the line "a = a + 10;" is moved.

```
——————— Original version ———————
void f(int a, int b) {
  if (a < b) {
    a = a + 10; // moved line
    b = b - 10;
  } else {
    b = b + 1;
  };
}
```

```
——————— Modified version ———————
void f(int a, int b) {
  if (a < b) {
    b = b - 10;
  } else {
    a = a + 10; // moved line
    b = b + 1;
  };
}
```

Textual Diff-directed Tool ccc. First, ccc turns the two programs into a semantically equivalent guarded form where every assignment is guarded by a condition. Thus, conditional statements are useless and the only remaining control structures are loops. On the example, this step produces the following two programs where the if(a < b) statement has been translated as a guard for each statement:

```
—— Guarded original program (ccc) ——
void f(int a, int b) {

  Guard G0 = (a < b);
  if (G0) a = a + 10;
  if (G0) b = b - 10;
  if (!G0) b = b + 1;
}
```

```
—— Guarded modified program (ccc) ——
void f(int a, int b) {
  int T_a = a; int T_b = b;
  Guard T_G0 = (T_a < T_b);
  if (T_G0) T_b = T_b - 10;
  if (!T_G0) T_a = T_a + 10;
  if (!T_G0) T_b = T_b + 1;
}
```

Second, ccc interleaves the instructions of these two guarded programs according to their *textual difference* into the following correlating program.

```
———————————— Correlating program (ccc) ————————————
void f(int a, int b) {
  int T_a = a; int T_b = b;
  Guard G0 = (a < b);              // if condition (original version)
  Guard T_G0 = (T_a < T_b);        // if condition (modified version)
  if (G0) a = a + 10;              // then branch (original version)
  if (G0) b = b - 10;              // then branch (original version)
  if (T_G0) T_b = T_b - 10;        // then branch (modified version)
  if (!T_G0) T_a = T_a + 10;       // else branch (modified version)
  if (!G0) b = b + 1;              // else branch (original version)
  if (!T_G0) T_b = T_b + 1;        // else branch (modified version)
}
```

Syntactic Difference-directed Tool correlating_program. Instead of a textual difference, our algorithm takes a *syntactic difference between the abstract syntax trees* of two programs as defined in Sect. 4. First, it *tags* variables in this syntax difference to avoid naming conflicts. Tagging consists in prefixing names of the original program with O_ and names of the modified program with T_O_:

```
——————— Structured difference ———————
  void f(int a, int b) {
    if (a < b) {
-     a = (a + 10);
      b = (b - 10);
    } else {
+     a = (a + 10);
      b = (b + 1);
    };
  }
```

```
——————— Tagged structured difference ———————
  void test(int O_a, int O_b) {
    if ([O_a < O_b] → [T_O_a < T_O_b]) {
-     O_a = (O_a + 10);
      O_b = O_b - 10 → T_O_b = T_O_b - 10;
    } else {
+     T_O_a = (T_O_a + 10);
      O_b = O_b + 1 → T_O_b = T_O_b + 1;
    };
  }
```

The correlating program is then obtained by recursively translating to guarded form the original and modified programs represented by the structured difference, and interlacing them following the difference structure, as defined in Sect. 5, leading in this case to the same correlating program as produced by ccc.

Motivating Example. The correctness proof of the above program transformations ensures that the execution of the correlating program correctly simulates the input programs parallel execution. Such transformations are error-prone, and it is easy to overlook corner cases, which is what happens in ccc regarding early exits of loops. Indeed, consider the following example, in which the user simply adds a **break** statement so that the loop is iterated at most once in the modified version of the program:

```
————— Original version —————          ————— Modified version —————
void fail(int x) {                     void fail(int x) {
  i = 0;                                 i = 0;
  while (i <= 1) {                       while (i <= 1) {
    i = i + 1;                             i = i + 1;
    x = x + 1;                             x = x + 1;
                                           break; // added break statement
  }                                      }
}                                      }
```

In this case, we observe that the following correlating program produced by ccc will return as soon as the code corresponding to the modified version reaches the **break** statement (translated to a **goto** statement on line 15), thus incorrectly simulating the original version of the program. Meanwhile, our tool correlating_program produces a sound correlating program by translating the **break** statement into a guard affectation (T_G0 = 0 on line 15) inhibiting further execution of the code corresponding to the modified version of the loop without impacting the execution of the code corresponding to the original version of the loop:

```
          ———— ccc ————                           ———— correlating_program ————
1    void fail(int x) {                    void fail(int 0_x) {
2      int T_x = x;                           int T_0_x = 0_x;
3      int i = 0; int T_i = 0;                int 0_i = 0; int T_0_i = 0;
4
5                                             Guard G1 = 1; Guard T_G1 = 1;
6    L1: T_L1:;                               Guard G0 = (0_i <= 1);
7      Guard G0 = (i <= 1);                   Guard T_G0 = (T_0_i <= 1);
8      Guard T_G0 = (T_i <= 1);            L1:
9                                             if (G0) G1 = 1; // unused here (used to
10                                            if (T_G0) T_G1 = 1; // encode continue)
11     if (G0) i = i + 1;                     if (G0) if (G1) 0_i = 0_i + 1;
12     if (T_G0) T_i = T_i + 1;               if (T_G0) if (T_G1) T_0_i = T_0_i + 1;
13     if (G0) x = x + 1;                     if (G0) if (G1) 0_x = 0_x + 1;
14     if (T_G0) T_x = T_x + 1;               if (T_G0) if (T_G1) T_0_x = T_0_x + 1;
15     if (T_G0) goto T_L3;                   if (T_G0) if (T_G1) T_G0 = 0;
16                                            if (G0) G0 = (0_i <= 1);
17                                            if (T_G0) T_G0 = (T_0_i <= 1);
18     if (G0) goto L1;                       if (G0) goto L1;
19     if (T_G0) goto T_L1;                   if (T_G0) goto L1;
20   L3: T_L3:                              }
21   }
```

3   Source Language and Its Guarded Form

In this section, we define the syntax and semantics of our input language as well as its guarded form, that will later be used in our translation functions.

3.1   Input Language

Syntax. We write x for a variable identifier taken in an enumerable set of identifiers $\mathcal{I}$, $\mathbf{n}$ for an integer value taken in $\mathbb{Z}$ and $\mathbf{b}$ for a Boolean value in $\{\textbf{true}, \textbf{false}\}$. As shown in Fig. 1, the input language is a standard imperative programming language with **while**-loops and **if**-statements which also includes the non-local control-flow operators **break** and **continue**.

Semantics. The input language enjoys a standard big-step semantics: a program transforms the store by means of commands and commands make use of pure expressions to perform arithmetic and boolean computations. A store $S : \mathcal{I} \to \mathbb{Z}$ is a partial map from variable identifiers to integer values. The empty store is written $\emptyset$, $\forall x \in \mathrm{dom}(S)$ quantifies over the finite domain of S, and $S[x \mapsto v]$ is the store defined on $\mathrm{dom}(S) \cup \{x\}$ such that $S[x \mapsto v](y) = v$ if $x = y$ and $S(y)$ otherwise. The judgment "$S \vdash e \Downarrow \mathbf{n}$" is read "In the store S, the arithmetic expression e evaluates into the integer $\mathbf{n}$." and the judgment "$S \vdash b \Downarrow \mathbf{b}$" is read "In the store S, the boolean expression b evaluates into the boolean $\mathbf{b}$." The interpretation of a command yields a return *mode* m which is either *normal* (written $\square$), *interrupted* (written $\star$, used to handle **break** statements) or *continuing* (written $\circ$, used to handle **continue** statements). The judgment "$S_0 \vdash c \Downarrow_m S_1$" is read "The command c transforms S_0 into S_1 in mode m" (Fig. 1).

3.2   Guarded Language

We derive a guarded language from the input language of the previous section. Every condition is now stored into a boolean variable called a *guard variable* and every atomic instruction is guarded by a conjunction of guard variables (called a *guard* in the sequel). This specific form effectively abstracts execution paths into guard variables, as the values of the guard variables precisely determine a single block in the control flow graph of the input program. Thus, assigning specific values to these guard variables activates specific instructions of the input program. In Sect. 5, this mechanism will be at the heart of the static interleaving of programs instructions.

Syntax. To simplify the proof of some technical lemmas, the identifiers of guard variables are taken in the set $\mathcal{I}_\mathcal{G}$ of words over the alphabet $\{0, 1\}$. We will use the fact that a word in this alphabet can encode a path in an abstract syntax tree. We write g for such guard identifiers.

Definition 1 (Guard identifier independance). *A guard g is independant for a path π, written $g \# \pi$, if it does not end with π.*

Syntax

$$c ::= a \mid c;\, c \mid \textbf{while}\ (b)\ c \mid \textbf{if}\ (b)\ c\ \textbf{else}\ c \qquad\qquad \text{(COMMANDS)}$$
$$a ::= \textbf{skip} \mid x = e \mid \textbf{break} \mid \textbf{continue} \qquad\qquad \text{(ATOMIC COMMANDS)}$$
$$b ::= \textbf{true} \mid \textbf{false} \mid b\ \&\&\ b \mid !b \mid e \leq e \qquad\qquad \text{(BOOLEAN EXPRESSIONS)}$$
$$e ::= x \mid \mathbf{n} \mid e + e \qquad\qquad\qquad\qquad \text{(ARITHMETIC EXPRESSIONS)}$$

Big-step semantics for arithmetic expressions

CST
$$\overline{S \vdash \mathbf{n} \Downarrow \mathbf{n}}$$

VAR
$$\overline{S \vdash x \Downarrow S(x)}$$

SUM
$$\dfrac{S \vdash e_1 \Downarrow \mathbf{n_1} \qquad S \vdash e_2 \Downarrow \mathbf{n_2}}{S \vdash e_1 + e_2 \Downarrow \mathbf{n_1} +_{z} \mathbf{n_2}}$$

Big-step semantics for boolean expressions

CST
$$\overline{S \vdash \mathbf{b} \Downarrow \mathbf{b}}$$

NOT
$$\dfrac{S \vdash b \Downarrow \mathbf{b}}{S \vdash !b \Downarrow \neg \mathbf{b}}$$

AND
$$\dfrac{S \vdash b_1 \Downarrow \mathbf{b_1} \qquad S \vdash b_2 \Downarrow \mathbf{b_2}}{S \vdash b_1\ \&\&\ b_2 \Downarrow \mathbf{b_1} \wedge \mathbf{b_2}}$$

LESSEQUAL
$$\dfrac{S \vdash e_1 \Downarrow \mathbf{n_1} \qquad S \vdash e_2 \Downarrow \mathbf{n_2}}{S \vdash e_1 \leq e_2 \Downarrow \mathbf{n_1} \leq_{z} \mathbf{n_2}}$$

Big-step semantics for commands

SKIP
$$\overline{S \vdash \textbf{skip} \Downarrow_{\square} S}$$

ASSIGN
$$\dfrac{S \vdash e \Downarrow \mathbf{n}}{S \vdash x = e \Downarrow_{\square} S[x \mapsto \mathbf{n}]}$$

SEQ
$$\dfrac{S \vdash c_1 \Downarrow_{\square} S' \qquad S' \vdash c_2 \Downarrow_m S''}{S \vdash c_1;\, c_2 \Downarrow_m S''}$$

SEQ INTERRUPTED
$$\dfrac{S \vdash c_1 \Downarrow_m S'}{S \vdash c_1;\, c_2 \Downarrow_m S'} \quad m \neq \square$$

THEN
$$\dfrac{S \vdash c_1 \Downarrow_m S' \qquad S \vdash b \Downarrow \textbf{true}}{S \vdash \textbf{if}\ (b)\ c_1\ \textbf{else}\ c_2 \Downarrow_m S'}$$

ELSE
$$\dfrac{S \vdash c_2 \Downarrow_m S' \qquad S \vdash b \Downarrow \textbf{false}}{S \vdash \textbf{if}\ (b)\ c_1\ \textbf{else}\ c_2 \Downarrow_m S'}$$

WHILE FALSE
$$\dfrac{S \vdash b \Downarrow \textbf{false}}{S \vdash \textbf{while}\ (b)\ c \Downarrow_{\square} S}$$

WHILE TRUE
$$\dfrac{S \vdash b \Downarrow \textbf{true} \qquad S \vdash c \Downarrow_m S' \qquad S' \vdash \textbf{while}\ (b)\ c \Downarrow_{\square} S''}{S \vdash \textbf{while}\ (b)\ c \Downarrow_{\square} S''} \quad m \neq \star$$

WHILE BREAK
$$\dfrac{S \vdash b \Downarrow \textbf{true} \qquad S \vdash c \Downarrow_{\star} S'}{S \vdash \textbf{while}\ (b)\ c \Downarrow_{\square} S'}$$

BREAK
$$\overline{S \vdash \textbf{break} \Downarrow_{\star} S}$$

CONTINUE
$$\overline{S \vdash \textbf{continue} \Downarrow_{\circ} S}$$

Fig. 1. Syntax and semantics of the input language.

The syntax of the guarded language includes an assignment statement ac_G guarded by a conjunction of (positive or negative) guard variables and a **while**-loop statement guarded by a disjunction of guard conjunctions. Notice that **break** and **continue** are not present in the guarded language.

Semantics. Besides the store S of integer variables, a program in the guarded language also transforms a store G of guarded variables, which is a partial map from guard identifiers to boolean values. The operations over standard memories are naturally transported to guard memories. The judgment "$S_0, G_0 \vdash c_G \Downarrow S_1, G_1$" is read "The guarded command c_G transforms the store S_0 and the guard store G_0 into a new store S_1 and a new guard store G_1". The rules for the evaluation of guards and disjunctions of guards are straightforward and thus omitted.

$\boxed{\text{Syntax}}$

$$
\begin{aligned}
c_G &::= c_G;\ c_G \mid \textbf{skip} \mid \textbf{while}\,(g_\vee)\,c_G \mid \textbf{if}\,(g_\wedge)\,ac_G & (\text{Commands}) \\
ac_G &::= x = e \mid g = b & (\text{Atomic commands}) \\
g_\wedge &::= g_\ell \mid g_\ell \wedge g_\wedge & (\text{Guard conjunctions}) \\
g_\vee &::= g_\wedge \mid g_\wedge \vee g_\vee & (\text{Guard disjunctions}) \\
g_\ell &::= g \mid \neg g & (\text{Guard literals})
\end{aligned}
$$

$\boxed{\text{Big-step operational semantics for commands}}$

$$
\textsc{Seq} \quad \frac{S, G \vdash c_1 \Downarrow S', G' \quad S', G' \vdash c_2 \Downarrow S'', G''}{S, G \vdash c_1;\ c_2 \Downarrow S'', G''}
$$

$$
\textsc{Skip} \quad \frac{}{S, G \vdash \textbf{skip} \Downarrow S, G}
$$

$$
\textsc{Ignore} \quad \frac{G \vdash g_\wedge \Downarrow \textbf{false}}{S, G \vdash \textbf{if}\,(g_\wedge)\,ac_G \Downarrow S, G}
$$

$$
\textsc{Activate} \quad \frac{G \vdash g_\wedge \Downarrow \textbf{true} \quad S, G \vdash ac_G \Downarrow S', G'}{S, G \vdash \textbf{if}\,(g_\wedge)\,ac_G \Downarrow S', G'}
$$

$$
\textsc{GAssignment} \quad \frac{S \vdash b \Downarrow \textbf{b}}{S, G \vdash g = b \Downarrow S, G[g \mapsto \textbf{b}]}
$$

$$
\textsc{Assignment} \quad \frac{S \vdash e \Downarrow \textbf{n}}{S, G \vdash x = e \Downarrow S[x \mapsto \textbf{n}], G}
$$

$$
\textsc{While False} \quad \frac{G \vdash g_\vee \Downarrow \textbf{false}}{S, G \vdash \textbf{while}\,(g_\vee)\,c \Downarrow S, G}
$$

$$
\textsc{While True} \quad \frac{G \vdash g_\vee \Downarrow \textbf{true} \quad S, G \vdash c \Downarrow S', G' \quad S', G' \vdash \textbf{while}\,(g_\vee)\,c \Downarrow S'', G''}{S, G \vdash \textbf{while}\,(g_\vee)\,c \Downarrow S'', G''}
$$

Fig. 2. Syntax and semantics of the guarded language.

3.3 Translation to Guarded Form

We transform input programs into guarded form using a recursive translation function CI defined as follows:

c	o	$CI(gl, \pi, c, o)$
skip	o	**skip**
$x = e$	o	**if** (gl) $x = e$
$c_1; c_2$	o	$CI(gl, 0 \cdot \pi, c_1, o);\ CI(gl, 1 \cdot \pi, c_1, o)$
if (b) c_1 **else** c_2	o	**if** (gl) $\pi = b$; $CI(gl \wedge \pi, 1 \cdot \pi, c_1, o)$; $CI(gl \wedge \neg\pi, 0 \cdot \pi, c_2, o)$

while (b) c	o	**if** (gl) $\pi = b$;
		while $(gl \wedge \pi)$ {
		    if $(gl \wedge \pi)$ $1 \cdot \pi = $ **true**;
		        $CI(gl \wedge \pi \wedge (1 \cdot \pi), 1 \cdot 1 \cdot \pi, c, $ **Some** $\pi)$;
		    if $(gl \wedge \pi)$ $\pi = b$ }

break	**Some** π'	**if** (gl) $\pi' = $ **false**
continue	**Some** π'	**if** (gl) $1 \cdot \pi' = $ **false**

$CI(gl, \pi, c, o)$ is a guarded program simulating the input program c ; π is the path of the sub-program c in the whole program and is used as a fresh name for new guard variables ; gl is the guard conjunction guarding c in the program ; o equals "**Some** π'" if the innermost loop under which c is executed is at path π' or "**None**" if there is no such loop. o is used in the translation of **break** and **continue** statements by keeping track of the guard variables π' and $1 \cdot \pi'$ controlling the execution of the innermost loop.

Let us consider the case where c is "**if** (b) c_1 **else** c_2". We first create a new guard of name π to which we conditionally assign the value b under the guard conjunction gl: "**if** (gl) $\pi = b$". This guard represents the condition used to select the branch of the **if** statement. Then we recursively call CI on c_1 (the **then** part), guarded by the conjunction of the previous guards and the newly created guard ("$gl \wedge \pi$"). We create a new unique path "$1 \cdot \pi$" for the program translated under this path. We do the same for c_2 (the **else** part), negating the guard π ("$gl \wedge \neg\pi$") and creating another unique path "$0 \cdot \pi$".

The soundness of CI is expressed by the following technical Lemma. Roughly speaking, this lemma states that $CI(gl, \pi, c, o)$ simulates c correctly assuming that the guard gl is active (i). The assumptions (ii) and (iii) are extra invariants that makes the transformation work: o must provide the guard for the innermost loop (ii) and the guard identifiers in gl must be independent with respect to the path π. The extra conclusions (a),(b) and (c) ensure that the invariants are maintained by each evaluation step of the guarded program.

Lemma 1 (CI is sound on active guards). *Coq:* `CP.CI_sound`
If $S \vdash c \Downarrow_m S'$ *holds; (i)* $G \vdash gl \Downarrow$ **true** *holds; (ii)* $m \neq \square \implies \exists \pi_l, o = $ **Some** π_l; *(iii)* $\forall \pi_l, o = $ **Some** $\pi_l \implies G(\pi_l) = G(1 \cdot \pi_l) = $ **true** *; and (iv)* $\forall g \in gl, g \# \pi$; *then there exists a guard store* G' *such that* $S, G \vdash CI(gl, \pi, c, o) \Downarrow S', G'$ *holds and (a)* $\forall g \in dom(G), g \# \pi \implies G'(g) = G(g)$; *(b)* $m = \star \implies G'(\pi_l) = $ **false** *; and (c)* $m = \circ \implies G'(1 \cdot \pi_l) = $ **false**.

4 Structured Differences Between Programs

The syntactic differences between the abstract syntax trees of two syntactically correct programs is denoted by a special representation of a whole program together with a patch. This representation will be processed in a purely recursive way by the algorithm that generates the correlating program.

Syntax. The structured difference language is derived from the input language, in such a way that each internal node of the abstract syntax tree is associated with a local mutation Δ (where $\pm :: = - \mid +$):

$$\Delta :: = \pm[c]; \Delta \mid \pm\Delta; [c] \mid \Delta; \Delta \mid a \to a'$$
$$\mid \text{if } (b \to b') \; \Delta \text{ else } \Delta \mid \text{while } (b \to b') \; \Delta$$
$$\mid \pm[\text{if } (b) \; c \text{ else}] \; \Delta \mid \pm[\text{if } (b)] \; \Delta \text{ [else } c] \mid \pm[\text{while } (b)] \; \Delta$$

The notation "$\pm[c]; \Delta$" means that the command c is removed from the original program ("$-[c]; \Delta$") or inserted into the modified program ("$+[c]; \Delta$") while the right side is kept with a local mutation Δ. The notation "$a \to a'$" means that the leaf command a of the original program is replaced by "a'". "$+[\text{if } (b) \; c \text{ else}] \; \Delta$" means that an **if** statement is inserted in the modified program with the command c as its **then** branch and using the existing code (with a local mutation) Δ as its **else** branch.

Semantics. A structured difference represents the full original program along with the differences leading to the modified program. The projection function Π_0 (resp. Π_1) returns the original (resp. modified) embedded program:

Δ	$\Pi_0(\Delta)$	$\Pi_1(\Delta)$
$-[c]; c'$	$c; \Pi_0(c')$	$\Pi_1(c')$
$-c; [c']$	$\Pi_0(c); c'$	$\Pi_1(c)$
$+[c]; c'$	$\Pi_0(c')$	$c; \Pi_1(c')$
$+c; [c']$	$\Pi_0(c)$	$\Pi_1(c); c'$
$c; c'$	$\Pi_0(c); \Pi_0(c')$	$\Pi_1(c); \Pi_1(c')$
if $(b \to b') \; c$ else c'	if $(b) \; \Pi_0(c)$ else $\Pi_0(c')$	if $(b') \; \Pi_1(c)$ else $\Pi_1(c')$
while $(b \to b') \; c$	while $(b) \; \Pi_0(c)$	while $(b') \; \Pi_1(c)$
$+[\text{if } (b) \; c \text{ else}] \; c'$	$\Pi_0(c')$	if $(b) \; c$ else $\Pi_1(c')$
$+[\text{if } (b)] \; c \text{ [else } c']$	$\Pi_0(c)$	if $(b) \; \Pi_1(c)$ else c'
$-[\text{if } (b) \; c \text{ else}] \; c'$	if $(b) \; c$ else $\Pi_0(c')$	$\Pi_1(c')$
$-[\text{if } (b)] \; c \text{ [else } c']$	if $(b) \; \Pi_0(c)$ else c'	$\Pi_1(c)$
$+[\text{while } (b)] \; c$	$\Pi_0(c)$	while $(b) \; \Pi_1(c)$
$-[\text{while } (b)] \; c$	while $(b) \; \Pi_0(c)$	$\Pi_1(c)$
$a \to a'$	a	a'

A difference between two programs can always be found. Section 6 explains how we tackled this problem.

Theorem 1 (Completeness of the diff. language). *Coq: CP.diff_complete ness*

For all pair of programs (p, p'), there exists a difference Δ such that $\Pi_0(\Delta) = p$ and $\Pi_1(\Delta) = p'$.

5   Generation Algorithm Directed by Structured Differences

We define in Figs. 3 and 4 a correlating program generation algorithm directed by structured differences as a recursive function CP. The program $CP(\Delta, \pi_0, \pi_1, gl_0, gl_1, o_0, o_1)$ is a correlating program of $\Pi_0(\Delta)$ and $\Pi_1(\Delta)$, corresponding to an interleaving of the guarded forms $CI(gl_0, \pi_0, \Pi_0(\Delta), o_0)$ and $CI(gl_1, \pi_1, \Pi_1(\Delta), o_1)$. π_0 and π_1 are the paths of the subprograms $\Pi_0(\Delta)$ and $\Pi_1(\Delta)$ in the whole correlating program. They are used as fresh names for new guard variables, which also eases Coq proofs by encoding path information in the name of the guards. gl_0 and gl_1 are the guard conjunctions guarding $\Pi_0(\Delta)$ and $\Pi_1(\Delta)$ in the whole correlating program, while o_0 and o_1 represent the optional innermost loop under which $\Pi_0(\Delta)$ and $\Pi_1(\Delta)$ are executed, and are used to translate **break** and **continue** statements.

For example, consider the definition of "$-[\mathbf{if}\ (b)\ c\ \mathbf{else}]\ \Delta$" in Fig. 3, corresponding to the removal of an **if** statement and its **then** part while keeping its **else** part. We first create a new guard π_0 to which we conditionally assign the value b under the conjunction gl_0 of the original program ("**if** $(gl_0)\ \pi_0 = b$") because the **if** statement is only executed in the first program. We then call CI to output the guarded form of the statement c under the removed **then** part: "$CI(gl_0 \wedge \pi_0, 1 \cdot \pi_0, c, o_0)$". It will be conditionally executed under the conjunction of gl_0 and the new guard π_0, under a new unique path "$1 \cdot \pi_0$". We then continue the translation of the remaining structured difference Δ by recursively calling CP on it: "$CP(\Delta, 0 \cdot \pi_0, \pi_1, gl_0 \wedge \neg\pi_0, gl_1, o_0, o_1)$". For the original program, we create a new unique path "$0 \cdot \pi_0$". This part is guarded by "$gl_0 \wedge \neg\pi_0$" as it is executed under the **else** part of the original program. For the modified program, we keep the guard gl_1 and the path π_1 which is still unique. o_0 and o_1 are reused unmodified as we are not translating a **while** statement.

Definition 2 (Store splitting). *Two stores S_0 and S_1 are said to split a store S if $\forall n \in \{0,1\}$, $\forall x \in dom(S_n)$, $S(x) = S_n(x)$; and S_0 contains only variables starting with "$0\_$", and S_1 with "$T\_0\_$".*

Definition 3 (Guarded store splitting). *Two guarded stores G_0 and G_1 are said to split a guarded store G if $\forall n \in \{0,1\}$, $\forall x \in dom(G_n)$, $G(x) = G_n(x)$; and G_0 contains only variables ending with 0, and G_1 with 1.*

Lemma 2 (CP is sound under context). *Coq: CP.cp_sound*
For all S_0, S_0', S_1, S_1', S, S', G_0, G_0', G_1, G_1', G, G', π_0, π_1, gl_0, gl_1, o_0, o_1, if (i) $\forall n \in \{0,1\}$, $S_n, G_n \vdash CI(gl_n, \pi_n, \Pi_n(\Delta), o_n) \Downarrow S_n', G_n'$ holds ; (ii) S_0 and S_1 split S ; (iii) G_0 and G_1 split G ; (iv) Variables appearing in $\Pi_0(\Delta)$ start with "$0\_$", those of $\Pi_1(\Delta)$ with "$T\_0\_$" ; (v) gl_0 contains only variables ending with 0, and gl_1 with 1 ; then there exist a store S' and a guard store G' such that (a) $S, G \vdash CP(\Delta, \pi_0, \pi_1, gl_0, gl_1, o_0, o_1) \Downarrow S', G'$ holds ; (b) S_0' and S_1' split S' ; (c) G_0' and G_1' split G'.

Δ	$CP(\Delta, \pi_0, \pi_1, gl_0, gl_1, o_0, o_1)$
$-[c]; \Delta$	$CI(gl_0, 0 \cdot \pi_0, c, o_0);$ $CP(\Delta, 1 \cdot \pi_0, \pi_1, gl_0, gl_1, o_0, o_1)$
$-\Delta; [c]$	$CP(\Delta, 0 \cdot \pi_0, \pi_1, gl_0, gl_1, o_0, o_1);$ $CI(gl_0, 1 \cdot \pi_0, c, o_0)$
$+[c]; \Delta$	$CI(gl_1, 0 \cdot \pi_1, c, o_1);$ $CP(\Delta, \pi_0, 1 \cdot \pi_1, gl_0, gl_1, o_0, o_1)$
$+\Delta; [c]$	$CP(\Delta, \pi_0, 0 \cdot \pi_1, gl_0, gl_1, o_0, o_1);$ $CI(gl_1, 1 \cdot \pi_1, c, o_1)$
$\Delta_0; \Delta_1$	$CP(\Delta_0, 0 \cdot \pi_0, 0 \cdot \pi_1, gl_0, gl_1, o_0, o_1)$ $CP(\Delta_1, 1 \cdot \pi_0, 1 \cdot \pi_1, gl_0, gl_1, o_0, o_1)$
if $(b_0 \rightarrow b_1) \, \Delta_0$ **else** Δ_1	**if** $(gl_0) \; \pi_0 = b_0;$ **if** $(gl_1) \; \pi_1 = b_1;$ $CP(\Delta_0, 1 \cdot \pi_0, 1 \cdot \pi_1, gl_0 \wedge \pi_0, gl_1 \wedge \pi_1, o_0, o_1);$ $CP(\Delta_1, 0 \cdot \pi_0, 0 \cdot \pi_1, gl_0 \wedge \neg\pi_0, gl_1 \wedge \neg\pi_1, o_0, o_1)$

while $(b_0 \rightarrow b_1) \, \Delta$	**if** $(gl_0) \; \pi_0 = b_0;$
	 if $(gl_1) \; \pi_1 = b_1;$
	 while $((gl_0 \wedge \pi_0) \vee (gl_1 \wedge \pi_1)) \, \{$
	    if $(gl_0 \wedge \pi_0) \; 1 \cdot \pi_0 = $ **true**;
	    if $(gl_1 \wedge \pi_1) \; 1 \cdot \pi_1 = $ **true**;
	    $CP(\Delta, 1 \cdot 1 \cdot \pi_0, 1 \cdot 1 \cdot \pi_1, gl_0 \wedge \pi_0 \wedge (1 \cdot \pi_0),$
	          $gl_1 \wedge \pi_1 \wedge (1 \cdot \pi_1), $ **Some** $\pi_0,$ **Some** $\pi_1);$
	    if $(gl_0 \wedge \pi_0) \; \pi_0 = b_0;$
	    if $(gl_1 \wedge \pi_1) \; \pi_1 = b_1;$
	 $\}$

$a_0 \rightarrow a_1$	$CI(gl_0, \pi_0, a_0, o_0);$ $CI(gl_1, \pi_1, a_1, o_1)$
$-[$**if** $(b) \; c$ **else**$] \, \Delta$	**if** $(gl_0) \; \pi_0 = b;$ $CI(gl_0 \wedge \pi_0, 1 \cdot \pi_0, c, o_0);$ $CP(\Delta, 0 \cdot \pi_0, \pi_1, gl_0 \wedge \neg\pi_0, gl_1, o_0, o_1)$
$+[$**if** $(b) \; c$ **else**$] \, \Delta$	**if** $(gl_1) \; \pi_1 = b;$ $CI(gl_1 \wedge \pi_1, 1 \cdot \pi_1, c, o_1);$ $CP(\Delta, \pi_0, 0 \cdot \pi_1, gl_0, gl_1 \wedge \neg\pi_1, o_0, o_1)$
$-[$**if** $(b)] \, \Delta \, [$**else** $c]$	**if** $(gl_0) \; \pi_0 = b;$ $CP(\Delta, 1 \cdot \pi_0, \pi_1, gl_0 \wedge \pi_0, gl_1, o_0, o_1);$ $CI(gl_0 \wedge \neg\pi_0, 0 \cdot \pi_0, c, o_0)$
$+[$**if** $(b)] \, \Delta \, [$**else** $c]$	**if** $(gl_1) \; \pi_1 = b;$ $CP(\Delta, \pi_0, 1 \cdot \pi_1, gl_0, gl_1 \wedge \pi_1, o_0, o_1);$ $CI(gl_1 \wedge \neg\pi_1, 0 \cdot \pi_1, c, o_1)$

Fig. 3. Difference directed correlating program generation function CP.

While the above key lemma mentions the invariants ((ii), (iii), (iv), (v), (b) and (c)) used in the induction, CP is typically used with fixed initial values for most of its arguments, hence the following theorem.

Theorem 2 (`correlating_program` is sound). *Coq:* `correlating_program_sound`

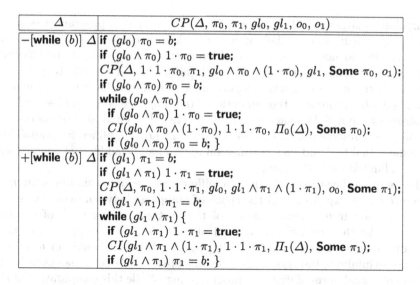

Δ	$CP(\Delta, \pi_0, \pi_1, gl_0, gl_1, o_0, o_1)$

$-[\textbf{while } (b)] \ \Delta$	**if** $(gl_0) \ \pi_0 = b;$
	 if $(gl_0 \wedge \pi_0) \ 1 \cdot \pi_0 = \textbf{true};$
	 $CP(\Delta, 1 \cdot 1 \cdot \pi_0, \pi_1, gl_0 \wedge \pi_0 \wedge (1 \cdot \pi_0), gl_1, \textbf{Some } \pi_0, o_1);$
	 if $(gl_0 \wedge \pi_0) \ \pi_0 = b;$
	 while $(gl_0 \wedge \pi_0) \{$
	    if $(gl_0 \wedge \pi_0) \ 1 \cdot \pi_0 = \textbf{true};$
	    $CI(gl_0 \wedge \pi_0 \wedge (1 \cdot \pi_0), 1 \cdot 1 \cdot \pi_0, \Pi_0(\Delta), \textbf{Some } \pi_0);$
	    if $(gl_0 \wedge \pi_0) \ \pi_0 = b; \}$

$+[\textbf{while } (b)] \ \Delta$	**if** $(gl_1) \ \pi_1 = b;$
	 if $(gl_1 \wedge \pi_1) \ 1 \cdot \pi_1 = \textbf{true};$
	 $CP(\Delta, \pi_0, 1 \cdot 1 \cdot \pi_1, gl_0, gl_1 \wedge \pi_1 \wedge (1 \cdot \pi_1), o_0, \textbf{Some } \pi_1);$
	 if $(gl_1 \wedge \pi_1) \ \pi_1 = b;$
	 while $(gl_1 \wedge \pi_1) \{$
	    if $(gl_1 \wedge \pi_1) \ 1 \cdot \pi_1 = \textbf{true};$
	    $CI(gl_1 \wedge \pi_1 \wedge (1 \cdot \pi_1), 1 \cdot 1 \cdot \pi_1, \Pi_1(\Delta), \textbf{Some } \pi_1);$
	    if $(gl_1 \wedge \pi_1) \ \pi_1 = b; \}$

Fig. 4. Difference directed correlating program generation function CP (cont.).

For all S, S_0, S_0', S_1, S_1', a diff Δ and a guard store G such that the judgments $S_0 \vdash \Pi_0(\Delta) \Downarrow_\square S_0'$ and $S_1 \vdash \Pi_1(\Delta) \Downarrow_\square S_1'$ hold ; S_0 and S_1 split S ; G_0 and G_1 split G, then there exists a store S' and a guard store G' such that $S, G \vdash CP(\Delta^{T,T'}, 0, 1, \textbf{true}, \textbf{true}, \textbf{None}, \textbf{None}) \Downarrow S', G'$ hold ; S_0' and S_1' split S ; and G_0 and G_1 split G'.

Roughly speaking, this theorem states that the correlating program simulates the original and the modified programs correctly. As we are using big-step semantics, this theorem only characterizes terminating evaluations. In our opinion, a similar result can be proved in a small-step semantics to encompass non terminating evaluations. This is left as future work.

6   Implementation and Experiments

Implementation. As said previously, we proved our algorithm within the Coq proof assistant. Our development is about 3,800 lines of Coq, 10 % of which are definitions of the input and guarded languages, as well as the definition of what a correct correlating program is. The remaining lines are used for the algorithm and its soundness proof. The Coq development is available online at www.pps.univ-paris-diderot.fr/~thib/atval15/coq/.

This code is then extracted from Coq to OCaml. In addition to the extracted code, we wrote 1,000 lines of OCaml to parse the input language, to construct the syntactic difference and to print the correlating program in C syntax. One should notice that the generated C program semantics does not exactly match the semantics of our formalized development. For example, our input language manipulates mathematical integers while the generated C program uses fixed-length machine integers. Albeit it was not done because outside the core of our work, we do not consider it would be conceptually difficult to integrate into our input language the semantics of the generated C code (e.g. 32 bits integers) because the generation algorithm manipulates the syntax of expressions abstractly. Moreover, the semantics of our language is compatible with the semantics of input C language expected by dizy. It should also be noted that the language presented in this paper has been slightly simplified for readability, while the actual tool and its formalization in Coq handle additional operators as well as a limited form of arrays.

To compute the structural syntactic differences, we aim at finding a minimal difference by an exploration of the space of mappings between abstract syntax trees. We start from the root nodes of the abstract syntax trees of the two programs. We then recursively descend along those trees, comparing at each level all possible differences and keeping the minimal one (using an heuristics that tries to minimize insertion or deletion of loops). We use some memoization to implement a weak form of dynamic programming. While this computation of the syntactic difference is not proven correct neither optimal in Coq, a mechanically verified checker dynamically ensures that the projections of the chosen structural difference are indeed the two input programs.

Regarding correlating points, which are an important aspect of Partush and Yavah's work and are essential for scalability, we have implemented a basic heuristics similar to theirs: we insert a correlating point in the generated program after two equivalent instructions of the input programs. However finding the best place to put them is orthogonal to the soundness of the correlating program generation itself which is our primary concern. Furthermore, we observed that in some instances, placing correlating points actually increases computation time due to increased complexity in the analyzer's sub-states. Therefore, we disabled them in our experiments.

Gap with Real Language Like C. Our language roughly corresponds to a small subset of the C language equipped with idealized integers and arrays. It would not be very difficult to handle C's "struct" and other kinds of type definition as our algorithm is only concerned about the control-flow of programs. "switch" and "for" constructs could also be easily integrated. Regarding pointers and "union" structure, we would have to ensure proper correspondence between pointed variables at abstract interpretation initialization as well as proper memory partitioning. dizy currently does not handle such issues. Regarding "goto" and "setjmp"/"longjmp", we are currently unable to handle them because that would require to encode any arbitrary displacement in the control-flow graph using guard variables. Even if such an encoding is possible in theory, there is little hope that an abstract interpretation could effectively infer interesting correlations out of the resulting correlating program.

Experiments. To compare the *quality* of our correlating programs with the ones produced by ccc, a series of 23 examples (most between 10 and 20 lines long, with the exception of one around 140 lines long) were analyzed by `dizy`. While doing so, we found no instance where the correlating program produced by `ccc` enabled a more precise analysis than that permitted by the correlating program generated by `correlating_program`. On the contrary, we found several examples where `correlating_program` outperformed `ccc` (examples 6, 7 and 23). We also implemented a binary search algorithm in a sorted array, with the modified version introducing early loop exits. We can generate the correlating program and analyze it with `dizy` (by slightly modifying it to correctly handle read access to arrays). We also attempted to test more complex examples but were limited by `dizy`'s capabilities (e.g., no handling of C's bit-wise logical operations). All those tests are available online at www.pps.univ-paris-diderot.fr/~thib/atva15/examples/. and can be reproduced. In practice, the computation of structural differences and the generation of the correlating program was almost instantaneous on our examples. Most of the computation time is spent in `dizy`.

7   Related Work

Formal treatment of equivalence between algorithms dates back to the 60s' (references [1–3] in [5]). However, the specific topic of semantic differences between program variants was only considered in 1990 by Susan Horwitz [6]. Like us, she focuses on intra-procedural differences and she compares a structured intermediate representation of the programs, a so-called Program Representation Graph, which is a graph mixing control and data flow information.

Strichman and Godlin pioneered the use of uninterpreted functions for doing inter-procedural analysis [15]. They use the CBMC bounded model checker to establish the equivalence between two variants of a C program, thus limiting analysis to bounded loops. In case the two programs semantically differs, a counter-example is proposed. The user needs to provide a list of program points when the two variants should be equivalent. Like us, they do not handle neither complex data structure nor pointers.

Lahiri et al. proposed the SymDiff tool to check equivalence between program and display semantic differences [8]. As they rely on the intermediate logical language Boogie, their approach can handle multiple imperative languages like C, C# or even x86 assembly through appropriate front-end. Their approach is interprocedural, using uninterpreted functions or inlining to handle function calls. For C language, they handle pointers and arrays but assume there is no aliasing. The underlying technology is based on generation of verification conditions and use the Z3 SMT solver to solve them. In case differences are found, a counterexample is generated. The approach does not scale when the number of different intra-procedural paths is too important (beyond 1,000 paths).

Symbolic execution has also been used to characterize semantic differences. Person et al. [14] propose an inter-procedural analysis with two notions of equivalences: *functional equivalence* with same black-box behavior and *partition-effect equivalence* where the program variants have the same sets of paths in their implementations. They are using uninterpreted functions to handle function calls. They need to store the analysis of the variants of analyzed programs. Yang et al. [16] also use symbolic execution but simultaneously analyze two variants of a program. Their approach considers unaffected program parts to increase the scalability and precision of the analysis. In both papers, the Java language is handled however proposed approaches are limited to bounded loops.

Gao et al. addressed the finding of semantic differences over binary files [4]. There are using a combination of Control Flow Graph, Symbolic Execution and Theorem proving to find similarities between basic blocks. However their approach is unsound due to approximations when they abstract x86 instructions.

An obvious reference for our work is the one of Partush and Yahav [12] as we built directly on top of it. They proposed an intra-procedural approach capable of handling unbounded loops over simple C programs without complex data structures or pointers. They propose both a way to interleave two variants of a program and an abstract interpretation technique focusing on establishing program equivalence or characterizing precise differences. In this paper, we show their approach is unsound and described a sound, mechanically checked, variant of their work. Partush and Yahav initial work has recently been improved with a technique to dynamically establish the best interleaving of the two programs during their analysis [13]. They use uninterpreted functions to analyze arrays or function calls. They are no longer using guards assertion to build interleaving programs, process that we have shown to be erroneous.

8   Conclusion

In this paper, we tackle the issue of characterizing the semantic differences between two versions of a program. We follow an approach similar to Partush and Yahav [12], building a correlating program representing the semantics of the two programs and then analyzing it using an Abstract Interpretation technique. This approach can handle unbounded loops. However, we show through counter-examples that the Partush and Yahav construction of correlating program is unsound for certain forms of loop and goto constructions.

We thus present an original and sound algorithm to build a correlating program from the structured syntactic difference of two programs. While we do not handle free form goto, we handle **break** and **continue** statements. We formalize and prove our algorithm within the Coq proof assistant, from which we extract our tool to ensure it is Correct by Construction. We compare our tool with the one of Partush and Yahav, observing that it is at least as precise as theirs.

This work only consider intra-procedural analysis of a simple language, without complex data structures, arrays or pointers. In the future, we would like to define intra-procedure semantic differences on other kinds of programs like functional, object-oriented or modular ones. We also want to have a wider and more structural view on a program, characterizing inter-procedural semantic differences through programmer level constructions like "adding a method to a class" or "adding a parameter to a function". Our long-term objective is to propose a tool capable of describing semantic differences of a real-world development like the Linux kernel or the Firefox web browser.

References

1. Binkley, D.: Using semantic differencing to reduce the cost of regression testing. In: Proceedings of Conference on Software Maintenance, pp. 41–50, November 1992
2. Brumley, D., Poosankam, P., Song, D., Zheng, J.: Automatic patch-based exploit generation is possible: Techniques and implications. In: 2008 IEEE Symposium on Security and Privacy (SP 2008), pp. 143–157. IEEE Computer Society (2008)
3. Cousot, P., Cousot, R.: Abstract interpretation: a unified lattice model for static analysis of programs by construction or approximation of fixpoints. In: Fourth Annual ACM SIGPLAN-SIGACT Symposium on Principles of Programming Languages, pp. 238–252. ACM Press (1977)
4. Gao, D., Reiter, M.K., Song, D.: BinHunt: automatically finding semantic differences in binary programs. In: Chen, L., Ryan, M.D., Wang, G. (eds.) ICICS 2008. LNCS, vol. 5308, pp. 238–255. Springer, Heidelberg (2008)
5. Hoare, C.A.R.: An axiomatic basis for computer programming. Commun. ACM 12(10), 576–580 (1969)
6. Horwitz, S.: Identifying the semantic and textual differences between two versions of a program. SIGPLAN Not. 25(6), 234–245 (1990)
7. Jackson, D., Ladd, D.A.: Semantic diff: A tool for summarizing the effects of modifications. In: Proceedings of the International Conference on Software Maintenance (ICSM 1994), pp. 243–252, Washington, DC. IEEE Computer Society (1994)
8. Lahiri, S.K., Hawblitzel, C., Kawaguchi, M., Rebêlo, H.: SYMDIFF: a language-agnostic semantic diff tool for imperative programs. In: Madhusudan, P., Seshia, S.A. (eds.) CAV 2012. LNCS, vol. 7358, pp. 712–717. Springer, Heidelberg (2012)
9. Lahiri, S.K., Vaswani, K., Hoare, C.A.R.: Differential static analysis: opportunities, applications, and challenges. In: Proceedings of the FSE/SDP Workshop on Future of Software Engineering Research (FoSER 2010), pp. 201–204, ACM. New York (2010)
10. Leroy, X.: Formal verification of a realistic compiler. Commun. ACM 52(7), 107–115 (2009)
11. The Coq development team: The Coq proof assistant reference manual. LogiCal Project. Version 8.0 (2004)
12. Partush, N., Yahav, E.: Abstract semantic differencing for numerical programs. In: Logozzo, F., Fähndrich, M. (eds.) Static Analysis. LNCS, vol. 7935, pp. 238–258. Springer, Heidelberg (2013)
13. Partush, N., Yahav, E.: Abstract semantic differencing via speculative correlation. In: ACM International Conference on Object Oriented Programming Systems Languages and Applications(OOPSLA 2014), pp. 811–828, ACM. New York (2014)
14. Person, S., Dwyer, M.B., Elbaum, S., Păsăreanu, C.S.: Differential symbolic execution. In: 16th ACM SIGSOFT International Symposium on Foundations of Software Engineering(SIGSOFT 2008/FSE-16), pp. 226–237, ACM (2008)
15. Strichman, O., Godlin, B.: Regression verification - a practical way to verify programs. In: Meyer, B., Woodcock, J. (eds.) VSTTE 2005. LNCS, vol. 4171, pp. 496–501. Springer, Heidelberg (2008)
16. Yang, G., Person, S., Rungta, N., Khurshid, S.: Directed incremental symbolic execution. ACM Trans. Softw. Eng. Methodol. 24(1), 3:1–3:42 (2014)

On Automated Lemma Generation
for Separation Logic with Inductive Definitions

Constantin Enea[1], Mihaela Sighireanu[1(✉)], and Zhilin Wu[1,2]

[1] LIAFA, Université Paris Diderot and CNRS, Paris, France
mihaela.sighireanu@liafa.univ-paris-diderot.fr
[2] State Key Laboratory of Computer Science, Institute of Software,
Chinese Academy of Sciences, Beijing, China

Abstract. Separation Logic with inductive definitions is a well-known approach for deductive verification of programs that manipulate dynamic data structures. Deciding verification conditions in this context is usually based on user-provided lemmas relating the inductive definitions. We propose a novel approach for generating these lemmas automatically which is based on simple syntactic criteria and deterministic strategies for applying them. Our approach focuses on iterative programs, although it can be applied to recursive programs as well, and specifications that describe not only the shape of the data structures, but also their content or their size. Empirically, we find that our approach is powerful enough to deal with sophisticated benchmarks, e.g., iterative procedures for searching, inserting, or deleting elements in sorted lists, binary search tress, red-black trees, and AVL trees, in a very efficient way.

1 Introduction

Program verification requires reasoning about complex, unbounded size data structures that may carry data ranging over infinite domains. Examples of such structures are multi-linked lists, nested lists, trees, etc. Programs manipulating such structures perform operations that may modify their shape (due to dynamic creation and destructive updates) as well as the data attached to their elements. An important issue is the design of logic-based frameworks that express assertions about program configurations (at given control points), and then to check automatically the validity of these assertions, for all computations. This leads to the challenging problem of finding relevant compromises between expressiveness, automation, and scalability.

An established approach for scalability is the use of *Separation logic* (SL) [18,24]. Indeed, its support for local reasoning based on the "frame rule" leads to compact proofs, that can be dealt with in an efficient way. However, finding expressive fragments of SL for writing program assertions, that enable

Zhilin Wu is supported by the NSFC projects (No. 61100062, 61272135, and 61472474), and the visiting researcher program of China Scholarship Council. This work was supported by the ANR project Vecolib (ANR-14-CE28-0018).

© Springer International Publishing Switzerland 2015
B. Finkbeiner et al. (Eds.): ATVA 2015, LNCS 9364, pp. 80–96, 2015.
DOI: 10.1007/978-3-319-24953-7_7

efficient automated validation of the verification conditions, remains a major issue. Typically, SL is used in combination with *inductive definitions*, which provide a natural description of the data structures manipulated by a program. Moreover, since program proofs themselves are based on induction, using inductive definitions instead of universal quantifiers (like in approaches based on first-order logic) enables scalable automation, especially for recursive programs which traverse the data structure according to their inductive definition, e.g., [22]. Nevertheless, automating the validation of the verification conditions generated for **iterative programs**, that traverse the data structures using while loops, remains a challenge. The loop invariants use inductive definitions for *fragments of data structures*, traversed during a partial execution of the loop, and proving the inductiveness of these invariants requires non-trivial *lemmas* relating (compositions of) such inductive definitions. Most of the existing works require that these lemmas be provided by the user of the verification system, e.g., [8,17,22] or they use translations of SL to first-order logic to avoid this problem. However, the latter approaches work only for rather limited fragments [20,21]. In general, it is difficult to have lemmas relating complex user-defined inductive predicates that describe not only the shape of the data structures but also their content.

To illustrate this difficulty, consider the simple example of a sorted singly linked list. The following inductive definition describes a sorted list segment from the location E to F, storing a multiset of values M:

$$lseg(E, M, F) ::= E = F \wedge M = \emptyset \wedge \mathtt{emp} \tag{1}$$

$$lseg(E, M, F) ::= \exists X, v, M_1.\ E \mapsto \{(\mathtt{next}, X), (\mathtt{data}, v)\} * lseg(X, M_1, F)$$
$$\wedge\ v \le M_1 \wedge M = M_1 \cup \{v\} \tag{2}$$

where $\mathtt{emp}$ denotes the empty heap, $E \mapsto \{(\mathtt{next}, X), (\mathtt{data}, v)\}$ states that the pointer field $\mathtt{next}$ of E points to X while its field $\mathtt{data}$ stores the value v, and $*$ is the separating conjunction. Proving inductive invariants of typical sorting procedures requires such an inductive definition and the following lemma:

$$\exists E_2.\ lseg(E_1, M_1, E_2) * lseg(E_2, M_2, E_3) \wedge M_1 \le M_2 \Rightarrow \exists M.\ lseg(E_1, M, E_3).$$

The data constraints in these lemmas, e.g., $M_1 \le M_2$ (stating that every element of M_1 is less or equal than all the elements of M_2), which become more complex when reasoning for instance about binary search trees, are an important obstacle for trying to synthesize them automatically.

Our work is based on a new class of inductive definitions for describing fragments of data structures that (i) supports lemmas **without additional** data constraints like $M_1 \le M_2$ and (ii) allows to **automatically synthesize** these lemmas using efficiently checkable, almost syntactic, criteria. For instance, we use a different inductive definition for *lseg*, which introduces an additional parameter M' that provides a "data port" for appending another sorted list segment, just like F does for the shape of the list segment:

$$lseg(E, M, F, M') ::= E = F \wedge M = M' \wedge \mathtt{emp} \tag{3}$$

$$lseg(E, M, F, M') ::= \exists X, v, M_1.\ E \mapsto \{(\mathtt{next}, X), (\mathtt{data}, v)\} * lseg(X, M_1, F, M')$$
$$\wedge\ v \le M_1 \wedge M = M_1 \cup \{v\} \tag{4}$$

The new definition satisfies the following simpler lemma, which avoids the introduction of data constraints:

$$\exists E_2, M_2.\, lseg(E_1, M_1, E_2, M_2) * lseg(E_2, M_2, E_3, M_3) \Rightarrow lseg(E_1, M_1, E_3, M_3). \quad (5)$$

Besides such "composition" lemmas (formally defined in Sect. 4), we define (in Sect. 5) other classes of lemmas needed in program proofs and we provide efficient criteria for generating them automatically. Moreover, we propose (in Sect. 6) a proof strategy using such lemmas, based on simple syntactic matchings of spatial atoms (points-to atoms or predicate atoms like $lseg$) and reductions to SMT solvers for dealing with the data constraints. We show experimentally (in Sect. 7) that this proof strategy is powerful enough to deal with sophisticated benchmarks, e.g., the verification conditions generated from the iterative procedures for searching, inserting, or deleting elements in binary search trees, red-black trees, and AVL trees, in a very efficient way. The proofs of theorems and additional classes of lemmas are provided in [12].

2 Motivating Example

Figure 1 lists an iterative implementation of a search procedure for binary search trees (BSTs). The property that E points to the root of a BST storing a multiset of values M is expressed by the following inductively-defined predicate:

$$bst(E, M) ::= E = \mathsf{nil} \land M = \emptyset \land \mathsf{emp} \quad (6)$$

$$bst(E, M) ::= \exists X, Y, M_1, M_2, v.\, E \mapsto \{(\mathtt{left}, X), (\mathtt{right}, Y), (\mathtt{data}, v)\} \quad (7)$$
$$* \ bst(X, M_1) * bst(Y, M_2)$$
$$\land \ M = \{v\} \cup M_1 \cup M_2 \land M_1 < v < M_2$$

```
int search(struct Tree* root,
            int key) {
  struct Tree *t = root;
  while (t != NULL) {
    if (t->data == key)
      return 1;
    else if (t->data > key)
      t = t->left;
    else
      t = t->right;
  }
  return 0;
}
```

Fig. 1. Searching a key in BST

The predicate $bst(E, M)$ is defined by two rules describing empty (Eq. (6)) and nonempty trees (Eq. (7)). The body (right-hand side) of each rule is a conjunction of a pure formula, formed of (dis)equalities between location variables (e.g. $E = \mathsf{nil}$) and data constraints (e.g. $M = \emptyset$), and a spatial formula describing the structure of the heap. The data constraints in Eq. (7) define M to be the multiset of values stored in the tree, and state the sortedness property of BSTs.

The precondition of search is $bst(\mathtt{root}, M_0)$, where M_0 is a ghost variable denoting the multiset of values stored in the tree, while its postcondition is $bst(\mathtt{root}, M_0) \land (\mathtt{key} \in M_0 \to ret = 1) \land (\mathtt{key} \notin M_0 \to ret = 0)$, where ret denotes the return value.

The while loop traverses the BST in a top-down manner using the pointer variable t. This variable decomposes the heap into two domain-disjoint subheaps: the tree rooted at t, and the truncated tree rooted at root which contains a "hole" at t. To specify the invariant of this loop, we define another predicate $bsthole(E, M_1, F, M_2)$ describing "truncated" BSTs with one hole F as follows:

$$bsthole(E, M_1, F, M_2) ::= E = F \land M_1 = M_2 \land \texttt{emp} \tag{8}$$

$$bsthole(E, M_1, F, M_2) ::= \exists X, Y, M_3, M_4, v.\ E \mapsto \{(\texttt{left}, X), (\texttt{right}, Y), (\texttt{data}, v)\}$$
$$* \ bst(X, M_3) * bsthole(Y, M_4, F, M_2) \tag{9}$$
$$\land \ M_1 = \{v\} \cup M_3 \cup M_4 \land M_3 < v < M_4$$

$$bsthole(E, M_1, F, M_2) ::= \exists X, Y, M_3, M_4, v.\ E \mapsto \{(\texttt{left}, X), (\texttt{right}, Y), (\texttt{data}, v)\}$$
$$* \ bsthole(X, M_3, F, M_2) * bst(Y, M_4) \tag{10}$$
$$\land \ M_1 = \{v\} \cup M_3 \cup M_4 \land M_3 < v < M_4$$

Intuitively, the parameter M_2, interpreted as a multiset of values, is used to specify that the structure described by $bsthole(E, M_1, F, M_2)$ could be extended with a BST rooted at F and storing the values in M_2, to obtain a BST rooted at E and storing the values in M_1. Thus, the parameter M_1 of $bsthole$ is the union of M_2 with the multiset of values stored in the truncated BST represented by $bsthole(E, M_1, F, M_2)$.

Using $bsthole$, we obtain a succinct specification of the loop invariant:

$$Inv ::= \exists M_1.\ bsthole(\texttt{root}, M_0, \texttt{t}, M_1) * bst(\texttt{t}, M_1) \land (\texttt{key} \in M_0 \Leftrightarrow \texttt{key} \in M_1). \tag{11}$$

We illustrate that such inductive definitions are appropriate for automated reasoning, by taking the following branch of the loop: `assume(t != NULL);` `assume(t->data > key); t' = t->left` (as usual, if statements are transformed into `assume` statements and primed variables are introduced in assignments). The postcondition of Inv w.r.t. this branch, denoted $post(Inv)$, is computed as usual by unfolding the bst predicate:

$$\exists M_1, Y, v, M_2, M_3.\ bsthole(\texttt{root}, M_0, \texttt{t}, M_1) * \texttt{t} \mapsto \{(\texttt{left}, \texttt{t}'), (\texttt{right}, Y), (\texttt{data}, v)\}$$
$$* \ bst(\texttt{t}', M_2) * bst(Y, M_3) \land M_1 = \{v\} \cup M_2 \cup M_3 \land M_2 < v < M_3$$
$$\land \ (\texttt{key} \in M_0 \Leftrightarrow \texttt{key} \in M_1) \land v > \texttt{key}. \tag{12}$$

The preservation of Inv by this branch is expressed by the entailment $post(Inv) \Rightarrow Inv'$, where Inv' is obtained from Inv by replacing t with t'.

Based on the lemmas, this paper also proposes a deterministic proof strategy for proving the validity of entailments of the form $\varphi_1 \Rightarrow \exists \vec{X}.\varphi_2$, where φ_1, φ_2 are quantifier-free and $\vec{X}$ contains only data variables[1]. The strategy comprises two steps: (i) enumerating spatial atoms A from φ_2, and for each of them, carving out a sub-formula φ_A of φ_1 that entails A, where it is required that these subformulas do not share spatial atoms (due to the semantics of separation conjunction), and (ii) proving that the data constraints from φ_A imply those from φ_2 (using SMT solvers). The step (i) may generate constraints on the variables in φ_A and φ_2 that are used in step (ii). If the step (ii) succeeds, then the entailment holds.

For instance, by applying this strategy to the entailment $post(Inv) \Rightarrow Inv'$ above, we obtain two goals for step (i) which consist in computing two sub-formulas of $post(Inv)$ that entail $\exists M_1'.\ bsthole(\texttt{root}, M_0, \texttt{t}', M_1')$ and respectively,

---

[1] The existential quantifiers in φ_1 are removed using skolemization.

$\exists M_1''.\ bst(\mathbf{t}', M_1'')$. This renaming of existential variables requires adding the equality $M_1 = M_1' = M_1''$ to Inv'. The second goal, for $\exists M_1''.\ bst(\mathbf{t}', M_1'')$, is solved easily since this atom almost matches the sub-formula $bst(\mathbf{t}', M_2)$. This matching generates the constraint $M_1'' = M_2$, which provides an instantiation of the existential variable M_1'' useful in proving the entailment between the data constraints in step (ii).

Computing a sub-formula that entails $\exists M_1'.\ bsthole(\mathtt{root}, M_0, \mathbf{t}', M_1')$ requires a non-trivial lemma. Thus, according to the syntactic criteria defined in Sect. 4, the predicate $bsthole$ enjoys the following *composition lemma*:

$$\big(\exists F, M.\ bsthole(\mathtt{root}, M_0, F, M) * bsthole(F, M, \mathbf{t}', M_1')\big) \qquad (13)$$
$$\Rightarrow bsthole(\mathtt{root}, M_0, \mathbf{t}', M_1').$$

Intuitively, this lemma states that composing two heap structures described by $bsthole$ results in a structure that satisfies the same predicate. The particular relation between the arguments of the predicate atoms in the left-hand side is motivated by the fact that the parameters F and M are supposed to represent "ports" for composing $bsthole(\mathtt{root}, M_0, F, M)$ with some other similar heap structures. This property of F and M is characterized syntactically by the fact that, roughly, F (resp. M) occurs only once in the body of each inductive rule of $bsthole$, and F (resp. M) occurs only in an equality with $\mathtt{root}$ (resp. M_0) in the base rule (we are referring to the rules (8)–(10) with the parameters of $bsthole$ substituted by $(\mathtt{root}, M_0, F, M)$).

Therefore, the first goal reduces to finding a sub-formula of $post(Inv)$ that implies the premise of (13) where M_1' remains existentially-quantified. Recursively, we apply the same strategy of enumerating spatial atoms and finding sub-formulas that entail them. However, we are relying on the fact that all the existential variables denoting the root locations of spatial atoms in the premise of the lemma, e.g., F in lemma (13), occur as arguments in the only spatial atom of the conclusion whose root location is the same as that of the consequent, i.e., $bsthole(\mathtt{root}, M_0, F, M)$ in lemma (13). Therefore, the first sub-goal, $\exists F, M.\ bsthole(\mathtt{root}, M_0, F, M)$ matches the atom $bsthole(\mathtt{root}, M_0, \mathbf{t}, M_1)$, under the constraint $F = \mathbf{t} \wedge M = M_1$. This constraint is used in solving the second sub-goal, which now becomes $\exists M_1'.\ bsthole(\mathbf{t}, M_1, \mathbf{t}', M_1')$.

The second sub-goal is proved by unfolding $bsthole$ twice, using first the rule (10) and then the rule (8), and by matching the resulting spatial atoms with those in $post(Inv)$ one by one. Assuming that the existential variable M_1 from Inv' is instantiated with M_2 from $post(Inv)$ (fact automatically deduced in the first step), the data constraints in $post(Inv)$ entail those in Inv'. This completes the proof of $post(Inv) \Rightarrow Inv'$.

3   Separation Logic with Inductive Definitions

Let LVar be a set of *location variables*, interpreted as heap locations, and DVar a set of *data variables*, interpreted as data values stored in the heap, (multi)sets of values, etc. In addition, let Var = LVar ∪ DVar. The domain of heap locations is denoted by $\mathbb{L}$ while the domain of data values stored in the heap is generically denoted by $\mathbb{D}$. Let $\mathcal{F}$ be a set of pointer fields, interpreted as functions $\mathbb{L} \rightharpoonup \mathbb{L}$, and $\mathcal{D}$ a set of data fields, interpreted as functions $\mathbb{L} \rightharpoonup \mathbb{D}$. The syntax of the Separation Logic fragment considered in this paper is defined in Table 1.

Formulas are interpreted over pairs (s, h) formed of a *stack* s and a *heap* h. The stack s is a function giving values to a finite set of variables (location or data variables) while the heap h is a function mapping a finite set of pairs (ℓ, pf), where ℓ is a location and pf is a pointer field, to locations, and a finite set of pairs (ℓ, df), where df is a data field, to values in $\mathbb{D}$. In addition, h satisfies the condition that for each $\ell \in \mathbb{L}$, if $(\ell, df) \in \mathsf{dom}(h)$ for some $df \in \mathcal{D}$, then $(\ell, pf) \in \mathsf{dom}(h)$ for some $pf \in \mathcal{F}$. Let $\mathsf{dom}(h)$ denote the domain of h, and $\mathsf{ldom}(h)$ denote the set of $\ell \in \mathbb{L}$ such that $(\ell, pf) \in \mathsf{dom}(h)$ for some $pf \in \mathcal{F}$.

Table 1. The syntax of the Separation Logic fragment

$X, Y, E \in \mathsf{LVar}$ location variables	$\rho \subseteq (\mathcal{F} \times \mathsf{LVar}) \cup (\mathcal{D} \times \mathsf{DVar})$
$\vec{F} \in \mathsf{Var}^*$ vector of variables	$P \in \mathcal{P}$ predicates
$x \in \mathsf{Var}$ variable	Δ formula over data variables

$$\Pi ::= X = Y \mid X \neq Y \mid \Delta \mid \Pi \wedge \Pi \qquad \text{pure formulas}$$
$$\Sigma ::= \mathsf{emp} \mid E \mapsto \rho \mid P(E, \vec{F}) \mid \Sigma * \Sigma \qquad \text{spatial formulas}$$
$$\varphi ::= \Pi \wedge \Sigma \mid \varphi \vee \varphi \mid \exists x.\, \varphi \qquad \text{formulas}$$

Formulas are conjunctions between a pure formula Π and a spatial formula Σ. Pure formulas characterize the stack s using (dis)equalities between location variables, e.g., a stack models $x = y$ iff $s(x) = s(y)$, and constraints Δ over data variables. We let Δ unspecified, though we assume that they belong to decidable theories, e.g., linear arithmetic or quantifier-free first order theories over multisets of values. The atom emp of spatial formulas holds iff the domain of the heap is empty. The *points-to atom* $E \mapsto \{(f_i, x_i)\}_{i \in \mathcal{I}}$ specifies that the heap contains exactly one location E, and for all $i \in \mathcal{I}$, the field f_i of E equals x_i, i.e., $h(s(E), f_i) = s(x_i)$. The *predicate atom* $P(E, \vec{F})$ specifies a heap segment rooted at E and shaped by the predicate P; the fragment is parameterized by a set $\mathcal{P}$ of *inductively defined predicates*, formally defined hereafter.

Let $P \in \mathcal{P}$. An *inductive definition* of P is a finite set of rules of the form $P(E, \vec{F}) ::= \exists \vec{Z}.\Pi \wedge \Sigma$, where $\vec{Z} \in \mathsf{Var}^*$ is a tuple of variables. A rule R is called a *base rule* if Σ contains no predicate atoms. Otherwise, it is called an *inductive rule*. A base rule R is called *spatial-empty* if $\Sigma = \mathsf{emp}$. Otherwise, it is called a *spatial-nonempty* base rule. For instance, the predicate bst in Sect. 2 is defined by one spatial-empty base rule and one inductive rule.

We consider a class of restricted inductive definitions that are expressive enough to deal with intricate data structures (see Sect. 7) while also enabling efficient proof strategies for establishing the validity of the verification conditions (see Sect. 6). For each rule $R : P(E, \vec{F}) ::= \exists \vec{Z}.\Pi \wedge \Sigma$ in the definition of a predicate $P(E, \vec{F}) \in \mathcal{P}$, we assume that:

- If R is inductive, then $\Sigma = \Sigma_1 * \Sigma_2$ and the following conditions hold:
  - *the root atoms*: Σ_1 contains only points-to atoms and a *unique* points-to atom starting from E, denoted as $E \mapsto \rho$. Also, all the *location* variables from $\vec{Z}$ occur in Σ_1. Σ_1 is called the *root* of R and denoted by $root(R)$.
  - *connectedness*: the Gaifman graph of Σ_1, denoted by G_{Σ_1}, is a connected DAG (directed acyclic graph) with the root E, that is, every vertex is reachable from E,
  - *predicate atoms*: Σ_2 contains only atoms of the form $Q(Z, \vec{Z}')$, and for each such atom, Z is a vertex in G_{Σ_1} without outgoing arcs.
- If R is a spatial-nonempty base rule, then Σ contains exactly one points-to atom $E \mapsto \rho$, for some ρ.

The classic acyclic list segment definition [24] satisfies these constraints as well as the first rule below; the second rule below falsifies the "root atoms" constraint:

$$lsegeven(E, F) ::= \exists X, Y.\ E \mapsto (\mathtt{next}, X) * X \mapsto (\mathtt{next}, Y) * lsegeven(Y, F)$$
$$lsegb(E, F) ::= \exists X.\ lsegb(E, X) * X \mapsto (\mathtt{next}, F).$$

Since we disallow the use of negations on top of the spatial atoms, the semantics of the predicates in $\mathcal{P}$ is defined as usual as a least fixed-point. The class of inductive definitions defined above is in general undecidable, since with data fields, inductive definitions can be used to simulate two-counter machines.

A *variable substitution* η is a mapping from a finite subset of Var to the set of terms over the respective domains. For instance, if $X \in$ LVar and $v, v_1 \in$ DVar be integer variables then the mapping $\eta = \{X \to \mathtt{nil}, v \to v_1 + 5\}$ is a variable substitution. We denote by $\mathtt{free}(\psi)$ the set of free variables of a formula ψ.

4   Composition Lemmas

As we have seen in the motivating example, the predicate $bsthole(E, M_1, F, M_2)$ satisfies the property that composing two heap structures described by this predicate results in a heap structure satisfying the same predicate. We call this property a *composition lemma*. We define simple and uniform syntactic criteria which, if they are satisfied by a predicate, then the composition lemma holds.

The main idea is to divide the parameters of inductively defined predicates into three categories: The *source* parameters $\vec{\alpha} = (E, C)$, the *hole* parameters $\vec{\beta} = (F, H)$, and the *static* parameters $\vec{\xi} \in$ Var*, where $E, F \in$ LVar are called the source and resp., the hole location parameter, and $C, H \in$ DVar are called the cumulative and resp., the hole data parameter[2].

Let $\mathcal{P}$ be a set of inductively defined predicates and $P \in \mathcal{P}$ with the parameters $(\vec{\alpha}, \vec{\beta}, \vec{\xi})$. Then P is said to be *syntactically compositional* if the inductive definition of P contains *exactly one base rule*, and *at least one inductive rule*, and the rules of P are of one of the following forms:

---

[2] For simplicity, we assume that $\vec{\alpha}$ and $\vec{\beta}$ consist of exactly one location parameter and one data parameter.

- Base rule: $P(\vec{\alpha}, \vec{\beta}, \vec{\xi}) ::= \alpha_1 = \beta_1 \wedge \alpha_2 = \beta_2 \wedge \mathsf{emp}$. Note that here the points-to atoms are disallowed.
- Inductive rule: $P(\vec{\alpha}, \vec{\beta}, \vec{\xi}) :: = \exists \vec{Z}.\ \Pi \wedge \Sigma$, with (a) $\Sigma \triangleq \Sigma_1 * \Sigma_2 * P(\vec{\gamma}, \vec{\beta}, \vec{\xi})$, (b) Σ_1 contains only and at least one points-to atoms, (c) Σ_2 contains only and possibly none predicate atoms, (d) $\vec{\gamma} \subseteq \vec{Z}$, and (d) the variables in $\vec{\beta}$ *do not occur elsewhere* in $\Pi \wedge \Sigma$, i.e., not in Π, or Σ_1, or Σ_2, or $\vec{\gamma}$. Note that the inductive rule also satisfies the constraints "root atom" and "connectedness" introduced in Sect. 3. In addition, Σ_2 may contain P atoms.

One may easily check that both the predicate $lseg(E, M, F, M')$ in Eqs. (3)–(4) and the predicate $bsthole(E, M_1, F, M_2)$ in Eqs. (8)–(10) are syntactically compositional, while the predicate $lseg(E, M, F)$ in Eqs. (1)–(2) is not.

A predicate $P \in \mathcal{P}$ with the parameters $(\vec{\alpha}, \vec{\beta}, \vec{\xi})$ is said to be *semantically compositional* if the entailment $\exists \vec{\beta}.\ P(\vec{\alpha}, \vec{\beta}, \vec{\xi}) * P(\vec{\beta}, \vec{\gamma}, \vec{\xi}) \Rightarrow P(\vec{\alpha}, \vec{\gamma}, \vec{\xi})$ holds.

Theorem 1. *Let $\mathcal{P}$ be a set of inductively defined predicates. If $P \in \mathcal{P}$ is syntactically compositional, then P is semantically compositional.*

The Proof of Theorem 1 is done by induction on the size of the domain of the heap structures. Suppose $(s, h) \models P(\vec{\alpha}, \vec{\beta}, \vec{\xi}) * P(\vec{\beta}, \vec{\gamma}, \vec{\xi})$, then either $s(\vec{\alpha}) = s(\vec{\beta})$ or $s(\vec{\alpha}) \neq s(\vec{\beta})$. If the former situation occurs, then $(s, h) \models P(\vec{\alpha}, \vec{\gamma}, \vec{\xi})$ follows immediately. Otherwise, the predicate $P(\vec{\alpha}, \vec{\beta}, \vec{\xi})$ is unfolded by using some inductive rule of P, and the induction hypothesis can be applied to a sub-heap of smaller size. Then $(s, h) \models P(\vec{\alpha}, \vec{\gamma}, \vec{\xi})$ can be deduced by utilizing the property that the hole parameters occur only once in each inductive rule of P.

Remark 1. The syntactically compositional predicates are rather general in the sense that they allow nestings of predicates, branchings (e.g. trees), as well as data and size constraints. Therefore, composition lemmas can be obtained for complex data structures like nested lists, AVL trees, red-black trees, and so on. In addition, although lemmas have been widely used in the literature, we are not aware of any work that uses the composition lemmas as simple and elegant as those introduced above, when data and size constraints are included.

5   Derived Lemmas

Theorem 1 provides a mean to obtain lemmas for one single syntactically compositional predicate. In the following, based on the syntactic compositionality, we demonstrate how to derive additional lemmas describing relationships between different predicates. We present here two categories of derived lemmas: "completion" lemmas and "stronger" lemmas; more categories are provided in [12]. Based on our experiences in the experiments (cf. Sect. 7) and the examples from the literature, we believe that the composition lemmas as well as the derived ones are natural, essential, and general enough for the verification of programs manipulating dynamic data structures. For instance, the "composition" lemmas and "completion" lemmas are widely used in our experiments, the "stronger" lemmas are used to check the verification conditions for rebalancing AVL trees and red-black trees.

5.1   The "Completion" Lemmas

We first consider the "completion" lemmas which describe relationships between incomplete data structures (e.g., binary search trees with one hole) and complete data structures (e.g., binary search trees). For example, the following lemma is valid for the predicates *bsthole* and *bst*:

$$\exists F, M_2. \; bsthole(E, M_1, F, M_2) * bst(F, M_2) \Rightarrow bst(E, M_1).$$

Notice that the rules defining $bst(E, M)$ can be obtained from those of $bsthole(E_1, M_1, F, M_2)$ by applying the variable substitution $\eta = \{F \to nil, M_2 \to \emptyset\}$ (modulo the variable renaming M_1 by M). This observation is essential to establish the "completion lemma" and it is generalized to arbitrary syntactically compositional predicates as follows.

Let $P \in \mathcal{P}$ be a syntactically compositional predicate with the parameters $(\vec{\alpha}, \vec{\beta}, \vec{\xi})$, and $P' \in \mathcal{P}$ a predicate with the parameters $(\vec{\alpha}, \vec{\xi})$. Then P' is a *completion* of P with respect to a pair of constants $\vec{c} = c_1 c_2$, if the rules of P' are obtained from the rules of P by applying the variable substitution $\eta = \{\beta_1 \to c_1, \beta_2 \to c_2\}$. More precisely,

- let $\alpha_1 = \beta_1 \wedge \alpha_2 = \beta_2 \wedge \texttt{emp}$ be the base rule of P, then P' contains only one base rule, that is, $\alpha_1 = c_1 \wedge \alpha_2 = c_2 \wedge \texttt{emp}$,
- the set of inductive rules of P' is obtained from those of P as follows: Let $P(\vec{\alpha}, \vec{\beta}, \vec{\xi}) ::= \exists \vec{Z}. \; \Pi \wedge \Sigma_1 * \Sigma_2 * P(\vec{\gamma}, \vec{\beta}, \vec{\xi})$ be an inductive rule of P, then $P'(\vec{\alpha}, \vec{\xi}) ::= \exists \vec{Z}. \; \Pi \wedge \Sigma_1 * \Sigma_2 * P'(\vec{\gamma}, \vec{\xi})$ is an inductive rule of P' (Recall that $\vec{\beta}$ does not occur in $\Pi, \Sigma_1, \Sigma_2, \vec{\gamma}$).

Theorem 2. *Let $P(\vec{\alpha}, \vec{\beta}, \vec{\xi}) \in \mathcal{P}$ be a syntactically compositional predicate, and $P'(\vec{\alpha}, \vec{\xi}) \in \mathcal{P}$. If P' is a completion of P with respect to $\vec{c}$, then $P'(\vec{\alpha}, \vec{\xi}) \Leftrightarrow P(\vec{\alpha}, \vec{c}, \vec{\xi})$ and $\exists \vec{\beta}. \; P(\vec{\alpha}, \vec{\beta}, \vec{\xi}) * P'(\vec{\beta}, \vec{\xi}) \Rightarrow P'(\vec{\alpha}, \vec{\xi})$ hold.*

5.2   The "Stronger" Lemmas

We illustrate this class of lemmas on the example of binary search trees. Let $natbsth(E, M_1, F, M_2)$ be the predicate defined by the same rules as $bsthole(E, M_1, F, M_2)$ (i.e., Eqs. (8)–(10)), except that $M_3 \geq 0$ (M_3 is an existential variable) is added to the body of each inductive rule (i.e., Eqs. (9) and (10)). Then we say that $natbsth$ is *stronger* than $bsthole$, since for each rule R' of $natbsth$, there is a rule R of $bsthole$, such that the body of R' entails the body of R. This "stronger" relation guarantees that the following lemmas hold:

$$natbsth(E, M_1, F, M_2) \Rightarrow bsthole(E, M_1, F, M_2)$$
$$\exists E_2, M_2. \; natbsth(E_1, M_1, E_2, M_2) * bsthole(E_2, M_2, E_3, M_3) \Rightarrow bsthole(E_1, M_1, E_3, M_3).$$

In general, for two syntactically compositional predicates $P, P' \in \mathcal{P}$ with the same set of parameters $(\vec{\alpha}, \vec{\beta}, \vec{\xi})$, P' is said to be *stronger* than P if for each inductive rule $P'(\vec{\alpha}, \vec{\beta}, \vec{\xi}) ::= \exists \vec{Z}. \; \Pi' \wedge \Sigma_1 * \Sigma_2 * P'(\vec{\gamma}, \vec{\beta}, \vec{\xi})$, there is an inductive rule $P(\vec{\alpha}, \vec{\beta}, \vec{\xi}) ::= \exists \vec{Z}. \; \Pi \wedge \Sigma_1 * \Sigma_2 * P(\vec{\gamma}, \vec{\beta}, \vec{\xi})$ such that $\Pi' \Rightarrow \Pi$ holds. The following result is a consequence of Theorem 1.

Theorem 3. *Let* $P(\vec{\alpha}, \vec{\beta}, \vec{\xi}), P'(\vec{\alpha}, \vec{\beta}, \vec{\xi}) \in \mathcal{P}$ *be two syntactically composi-tional predicates. If* P' *is stronger than* P, *then the entailments* $P'(\vec{\alpha}, \vec{\beta}, \vec{\xi}) \Rightarrow P(\vec{\alpha}, \vec{\beta}, \vec{\xi})$ *and* $\exists\vec{\beta}. P'(\vec{\alpha}, \vec{\beta}, \vec{\xi}) * P(\vec{\beta}, \vec{\gamma}, \vec{\xi}) \Rightarrow P(\vec{\alpha}, \vec{\gamma}, \vec{\xi})$ *hold.*

The "stronger" relation defined above requires that the spatial formulas in the inductive rules of P and P' are the same. This constraint can be relaxed by only requiring that the body of each inductive rule of P' is stronger than a formula obtained by unfolding an inductive rule of P for a *bounded number of times*. This relaxed constraint allows generating additional lemmas, e.g., the lemmas relating the predicates for list segments of even length and list segments.

6 A Proof Strategy Based on Lemmas

We introduce a proof strategy based on lemmas for proving entailments $\varphi_1 \Rightarrow \exists\vec{X}.\varphi_2$, where φ_1, φ_2 are quantifier-free, and $\vec{X} \in \mathsf{DVar}^*$. The proof strategy treats uniformly the inductive rules defining predicates and the lemmas defined in Sects. 4 and 5. Therefore, we call lemma also an inductive rule. W.l.o.g. we assume that φ_1 is quantifier-free (the existential variables can be skolemized). In addition, we assume that *only data variables are quantified in the right-hand side*[3].

W.l.o.g., we assume that every variable in $\vec{X}$ occurs in at most one spatial atom of φ_2 (multiple occurrences of the same variable can be removed by intro-ducing fresh variables and new equalities in the pure part). Also, we assume that φ_1 and φ_2 are of the form $\Pi \wedge \Sigma$. In the general case, our proof strategy checks that for every disjunct φ_1' of φ_1, there is a disjunct φ_2' of φ_2 s.t. $\varphi_1' \Rightarrow \exists\vec{X}.\varphi_2'$.

We present the proof strategy as a set of rules in Fig. 2. For a variable sub-stitution η and a set $\mathcal{X} \subseteq \mathsf{Var}$, we denote by $\eta|_{\mathcal{X}}$ the restriction of η to $\mathcal{X}$. In addition, $\mathsf{EQ}(\eta)$ is the conjunction of the equalities $X = t$ for every X and t such that $\eta(X) = t$. Given two formulas φ_1 and φ_2, a substitution η with $\mathsf{dom}(\eta) = \vec{X}$, the judgement $\varphi_1 \models_\eta \exists\vec{X}.\varphi_2$ denotes that the entailment $\varphi_1 \Rightarrow \eta(\varphi_2)$ is valid. Therefore, η provides an instantiation for the quantified variables $\vec{X}$ which wit-nesses the validity.

The rules MATCH1 and MATCH2 consider a particular case of $\models_\eta$, denoted using the superscript SUB, where the spatial atoms of φ_2 are syntactically matched[4] to the spatial atoms of φ_1 modulo a variable substitution θ. The substitution of the existential variables is recorded in η, while the substitu-tion of the free variables generates a set of equalities that must be implied by $\Pi_1 \wedge \mathsf{EQ}(\eta)$. For example, let $\Pi_1 \wedge \Sigma_1 ::= w = w' \wedge E \mapsto \{(f, Y), (d_1, v), (d_2, w)\}$, and $\exists\vec{X}. \Sigma_2 ::= \exists X, v'. E \mapsto \{(f, X), (d_1, v'), (d_2, w')\}$, where d_1 and d_2 are data fields. If $\theta = \{X \rightarrow Y, v' \rightarrow v, w' \rightarrow w\}$, then $\Sigma_1 = \theta(\Sigma_2)$. The substitution of the free variable w' from the right-hand side is sound since the equality $w = w'$ occurs in the left-hand side. Therefore, $\Pi_1 \wedge \Sigma_1 \models_{\theta|_{\{X,v'\}}}^{SUB} \exists X, v'. \Sigma_2$ holds.

---

[3] We believe that this restriction is reasonable for the verification conditions appearing in practice and all the benchmarks in our experiments are of this form.
[4] In this case, the right-hand side contains no pure constraints.

$$(\text{MATCH1}) \quad \frac{\Sigma_1 = \theta(\Sigma_2) \qquad \eta = \theta|_{\vec{X}} \qquad \Pi_1 \wedge \text{EQ}(\eta) \models \text{EQ}(\theta|_{\text{free}(\exists \vec{X}.\Sigma_2)})}{\Pi_1 \wedge \Sigma_1 \models_{\eta}^{SUB} \exists \vec{X}.\ \Sigma_2}$$

$$(\text{MATCH2}) \quad \frac{\Pi_1 \wedge \Sigma_1 \models_{\eta}^{SUB} \exists \vec{X}.\ \Sigma_2}{\Pi_1 \wedge \Sigma_1 \models_{\eta} \exists \vec{X}.\ \Sigma_2}$$

$$(\text{LEMMA}) \quad \frac{\Pi_1 \wedge \Sigma_1 \models_{\eta_1}^{SUB} \exists \vec{Z}'.\ root(L) \qquad \Pi_1 \wedge \Sigma_1' \models_{\eta_2} \exists \vec{Z}''.\ \eta_1(\Pi \wedge \Sigma)}{\Pi_1 \wedge \Sigma_1 * \Sigma_1' \models_{\eta|_{\vec{X}}} \exists \vec{X}.\ A}$$

- $L ::= \exists \vec{Z}.\ \Pi \wedge root(L) * \Sigma \Rightarrow A$ is a lemma,
- $\vec{Z}' = (\vec{X} \cup \vec{Z}) \cap \text{free}(root(L))$, $\vec{Z}'' = (\vec{X} \cup \vec{Z}) \cap \text{free}(\eta_1(\Pi \wedge \Sigma))$,
- $\eta = ext_{\Pi}(\eta_1 \cup \eta_2)$ is the extension of $\eta_1 \cup \eta_2$ with Π s.t. $\text{dom}(\eta) = \vec{X} \cup \vec{Z}$.

$$(\text{SLICE}) \quad \frac{\Pi_1 \wedge \Sigma_1 \models_{\eta_1} \exists \vec{Z}'.A \qquad \Pi_1 \wedge \Sigma_2 \models_{\eta_2} \exists \vec{Z}''.\Sigma \qquad \Pi_1 \wedge \text{EQ}(\eta) \models \Pi_2}{\Pi_1 \wedge \Sigma_1 * \Sigma_2 \models_{\eta} \exists \vec{X}.\ \Pi_2 \wedge A * \Sigma}$$

- $\vec{Z}' = \vec{X} \cap \text{free}(A)$, $\vec{Z}'' = \vec{X} \cap \text{free}(\Sigma)$,
- $\eta = ext_{\Pi_2}(\eta_1 \cup \eta_2)$ is the extension of $\eta_1 \cup \eta_2$ with Π_2 s.t. $\text{dom}(\eta) = \vec{X}$.

Fig. 2. The proof rules for checking the entailment $\varphi_1 \Rightarrow \exists \vec{X}.\ \varphi_2$

The rule LEMMA applies a lemma $L ::= \exists \vec{Z}.\ \Pi \wedge root(L) * \Sigma \Rightarrow A$. It consists in proving that φ_1 implies the LHS of the lemma where the variables in $\vec{X}$ are existentially quantified, i.e., $\exists \vec{X} \exists \vec{Z}.\ \Pi \wedge root(L) * \Sigma$. Notice that $\vec{Z}$ may contain existential location variables. Finding suitable instantiations for these variables relies on the assumption that $root(L)$ in the LHS of L is either a *unique predicate atom* or a *separating conjunction of points-to atoms* rooted at E (the first parameter of A) and $root(L)$ includes all the location variables in $\vec{Z}$. This assumption holds for all the inductive rules defining predicates in our fragment (a consequence of the root and connectedness constraints) and for all the lemmas defined in Sects. 4 and 5. The proof that φ_1 implies $\exists \vec{X} \exists \vec{Z}.\ \Pi \wedge root(L) * \Sigma$ is split into two sub-goals (i) proving that a sub-formula of φ_1 implies $\exists \vec{X} \exists \vec{Z}.\ root(L)$ and (ii) proving that a sub-formula of φ_1 implies $\exists \vec{X} \exists \vec{Z}.\ \Pi \wedge \Sigma$. The sub-goal (i) relies on syntactic matching using the rule MATCH1, which results in a quantifier instantiation η_1. The substitution η_1 is used to instantiate existential variables in $\exists \vec{X} \exists \vec{Z}.\ \Pi \wedge \Sigma$. Notice that according to the aforementioned assumption, the location variables in $\vec{Z}$ are not free in $\eta_1(\Pi \wedge \Sigma)$. Let η_2 be the quantifier instantiation obtained from the second sub-goal. The quantifier instantiation η is defined as the extension of $\eta_1 \cup \eta_2$ to the domain $\vec{X} \cup \vec{Z}$ by utilizing the pure constraints Π from the lemma[5]. This extension is necessary since some existentially quantified variables may only occur in Π, but not in $root(L)$ nor

---

[5] The extension depends on the pure constraints Π and could be quite complex in general. In the experiments of Sect. 7, we use the extension obtained by the propagation of equalities in Π.

in Σ, so they are not covered by $\eta_1 \cup \eta_2$. For instance, if Π contains a conjunct $M = M_1 \cup M_2$ such that $M_1 \in \text{dom}(\eta_1)$, $M_2 \in \text{dom}(\eta_2)$, and $M \notin \text{dom}(\eta_1 \cup \eta_2)$, then $\eta_1 \cup \eta_2$ is extended to η where $\eta(M) = \eta_1(M_1) \cup \eta_2(M_2)$.

The rule SLICE chooses a spatial atom A in the RHS and generates two sub-goals: (i) one that matches A (using the rules MATCH2 and LEMMA) with a spatial sub-formula of the LHS (Σ_1) and (ii) another that checks that the remaining spatial part of the RHS is implied by the remaining part of the LHS. The quantifier instantiations η_1 and η_2 obtained from the two sub-goals are used to check that the pure constraints in the RHS are implied by the ones in LHS. Note that in the rule SLICE, it is possible that $\Sigma_2 = \Sigma = \text{emp}$.

The rules in Fig. 2 are applied in the order given in the figure. Note that they focus on disjoint cases w.r.t. the syntax of the RHS. The choice of the atom A in SLICE is done arbitrary, since it does not affect the efficiency of proving validity. We apply the above proof strategy to the entailment $\varphi_1 \Rightarrow \exists M.\ \varphi_2$ where:

$$\varphi_1 ::= x_1 \neq \text{nil} \land x_2 \neq \text{nil} \land v_1 < v_2 \land x_1 \mapsto \{(\text{next}, x_2), (\text{data}, v_1)\}$$
$$* \ x_2 \mapsto \{(\text{next}, \text{nil}), (\text{data}, v_2)\}$$
$$\varphi_2 ::= lseg(x_1, M, \text{nil}, \emptyset) \land v_2 \in M,$$

and $lseg$ has been defined in Sect. 1 (Eqs. (3) and (4)). The entailment is valid because it states that two cells linked by next and storing ordered data values form a sorted list segment. The RHS φ_2 contains a single spatial atom and a pure part so the rule SLICE is applied and it generates the sub-goal $\varphi_1 \models_\eta \exists M.\ lseg(x_1, M, \text{nil}, \emptyset)$ for which the syntactic matching (rule MATCH1) can not be applied. Instead, we apply the rule LEMMA using as lemma the inductive rule of $lseg$, i.e., Eq. (4) (page II). We obtain the RHS $\exists M, X, M_1, v.\ x_1 \mapsto \{(\text{next}, X), (\text{data}, v)\} * lseg(X, M_1, \text{nil}, \emptyset) \land M = \{v\} \cup M_1 \land v \leq M_1$, where $x_1 \mapsto \{(\text{next}, X), (\text{data}, v)\}$ is the root. The rule MATCH1 is applied with $\Pi_1 \land \Sigma_1 ::= x_1 \neq \text{nil} \land x_2 \neq \text{nil} \land v_1 < v_2 \land x_1 \mapsto \{(\text{next}, x_2), (\text{data}, v_1)\}$ and it returns the substitution $\eta_1 = \{X \to x_2, v \to v_1\}$. The second sub-goal is $\Pi_1 \land \Sigma_2 \models_{\eta_2} \exists M, M_1.\psi'$ where $\Pi_1 \land \Sigma_2 ::= x_1 \neq \text{nil} \land x_2 \neq \text{nil} \land v_1 < v_2 \land x_2 \mapsto \{(\text{next}, \text{nil}), (\text{data}, v_2)\}$ and $\psi' ::= M = \{v_1\} \cup M_1 \land v_1 \leq M_1 \land lseg(x_2, M_1, \text{nil}, \emptyset)$. For this sub-goal, we apply the rule SLICE, which generates a sub-goal where the rule LEMMA is applied first, using the same lemma, then the rule SLICE is applied again, and finally the rule LEMMA is applied with a lemma corresponding to the base rule of $lseg$, i.e., Eq. (3) (page II). This generates a quantifier instantiation $\eta_2 = \{M \to \{v_1, v_2\}, M_1 \to \{v_2\}\}$. Then, $\eta_1 \cup \eta_2$ is extended with the constraints from the pure part of the lemma, i.e., $M = \{v\} \cup M_1 \land v_1 \leq M_1$. Since $M \in \text{dom}(\eta_1 \cup \eta_2)$, this extension has no effect. Finally, the rule SLICE checks that $\Pi_1 \land \text{EQ}(\eta|_{\{M\}}) \models \Pi_2$ holds, where $\text{EQ}(\eta|_{\{M\}}) ::= M = \{v_1, v_2\}$ and $\Pi_2 ::= v_2 \in M$. The last entailment holds, so the proof of validity is done.

The following theorem states the correctness of the proof rules. Moreover, since we assume a finite set of lemmas, and every application of a lemma L removes at least one spatial atom from φ_1 (the atoms matched to $root(L)$), the termination of the applications of the rule LEMMA is guaranteed.

Table 2. Experimental results on benchmark RDBI

Data structure	Procedure	#VC	Lemma (#b, #r, #p, #c, #d)	$\Rightarrow_\mathbb{D}$	Time (s) SPEN	SMT
sorted lists	search	4	(1, 3, 3, 1, 3)	5	1.108	0.10
	insert	8	(4, 6, 3, 1, 2)	7	2.902	0.15
	delete	4	(2, 2, 4, 1, 1)	6	1.108	0.10
BST	search	4	(2, 3, 6, 2, 2)	6	1.191	0.15
	insert	14	(15, 18, 27, 4, 6)	19	3.911	0.55
	delete	25	(13, 19, 82, 8, 5)	23	8.412	0.58
AVL	search	4	(2, 3, 6, 2, 2)	6	1.573	0.15
	insert	22	(18, 28, 74, 6, 8)	66	6.393	1.33
RBT	search	4	(2, 3, 6, 2, 2)	6	1.171	0.15
	insert	21	(27, 45, 101, 7, 10)	80	6.962	2.53

Theorem 4. *Let φ_1 and $\exists \vec{X}.\varphi_2$ be two formulas such that $\vec{X}$ contains only data variables. If $\varphi_1 \models_\eta \exists \vec{X}.\varphi_2$ for some η, then $\varphi_1 \Rightarrow \exists \vec{X}.\varphi_2$.*

7 Experimental Results

We have extended the tool SPEN [25] with the proof strategy proposed in this paper. The entailments are written in an extension of the SMTLIB format used in the competition SL-COMP'14 for separation logic solvers. It provides as output SAT, UNSAT or UNKNOWN, and a diagnosis for all these cases.

The solver starts with a normalization step, based on the boolean abstractions described in [11], which saturates the input formulas with (dis)equalities between location variables implied by the semantics of separating conjunction. The entailments of data constraints are translated into satisfiability problems in the theory of integers with uninterpreted functions, discharged using an SMT solver dealing with this theory.

We have experimented the proposed approach on two sets of benchmarks[6]:

RDBI: verification conditions for proving the correctness of iterative procedures (delete, insert, search) over recursive data structures storing integer data: sorted lists, binary search trees (BST), AVL trees, and red black trees (RBT).

SL-COMP'14: problems in the SL-COMP'14 benchmark, without data constraints, where the inductive definitions are syntactically compositional.

Table 2 provides the experiment results[7] for **RDBI**. The column #VC gives the number of verification conditions considered for each procedure. The column Lemma provides statistics about the lemma applications as follows: #b and #r are the number of the applications of the lemmas corresponding to base resp.

---

[6] http://www.liafa.univ-paris-diderot.fr/spen/benchmarks.html.

[7] The evaluations used a 2.53 GHz Intel processor with 2 GB, running Linux on VBox.

Table 3. Experimental results on benchmark SL-COMP'14

Data structure	#VC	Lemma(#b, #r, #p, #c, #d)	Time-SPEN(s)	
			SPEN	SPEN-TA
Nested linked lists	16	(17,47,14,8,0)	4.428	4.382
Skip lists 2 levels	4	(11,16,1,1,0)	1.629	1.636
Skip lists 3 levels	10	(16,32,29,17,0)	3.858	3.485

inductive rules, #c and #d are the number of the applications of the composition resp. derived lemmas, and #p is the number of predicates matched syntactically, without applying lemmas. Column $\Rightarrow_{\mathbb{D}}$ gives the number of entailments between data constraints generated by SPEN. Column Time-SPEN gives the "system" time spent by SPEN on all verification conditions of a function[8] excepting the time taken to solve the data constraints by the SMT solver, which is given in the column Time-SMT.

Table 3 provides a comparison of our approach (column SPEN) with the decision procedure in [11] (column SPEN-TA) on the same set of benchmarks from SL-COMP'14. The times of the two decision procedures are almost the same, which demonstrates that our approach, as an extension of that in [11], is robust.

8 Related Work

There have been many works on the verification of programs manipulating mutable data structures in general and the use of separation logic, e.g., [1–5,7–11,13–17,21,23,26]. In the following, we discuss those which are closer to our approach.

The prover SLEEK [7,17] provides proof strategies for proving entailments of SL formulas. These strategies are also based on lemmas, relating inductive definitions, but differently from our approach, these lemmas are supposed to be given by the user (SLEEK can prove the correctness of the lemmas once they are provided). Our approach is able to discover and synthesize the lemmas systematically, efficiently, and automatically.

The natural proof approach DRYAD [19,22] can prove automatically the correctness of programs against the specifications given by separation logic formulas with inductive definitions. Nevertheless, the lemmas are still supposed to be provided by the users in DRYAD, while our approach can generate the lemmas automatically. Moreover, DRYAD does not provide an independent solver to decide the entailment of separation logic formulas, which makes difficult to compare the performance of our tool with that of DRYAD. In addition, the inductive definitions used in our paper enable succinct lemmas, far less complex than those used in DRYAD, which include complex constraints on data variables and the magic wand.

---

[8] SPEN does not implement a batch mode, each entailment is dealt separately, including the generation of lemma. The SMT solver is called on the files generated by SPEN.

The method of cyclic proofs introduced by [5] and extended recently in [9] proves the entailment of two SL formulas by using induction on the paths of proof trees. They are not generating the lemma, but the method is able to (soundly) check intricate lemma given by the user, even ones which are out of the scope of our method, e.g., lemmas concerning the predicate *RList* which is defined by unfolding the list segments from the end, instead of the beginning. The cyclic proofs method can be seen like a dynamic lemma generation using complex reasoning on proof trees, while our method generates lemma statically by simple checks on the inductive definitions. We think that our lemma generator could be used in the cyclic proof method to cut proof trees.

The tool SLIDE [14,15] provides decision procedures for fragments of SL based on reductions to the language inclusion problem of tree automata. Their fragments contain no data or size constraints. In addition, the EXPTIME lower bound complexity is an important obstacle for scalability. Our previous work [11] introduces a decision procedure based on reductions to the membership problem of tree automata which however is not capable of dealing with data constraints.

The tool GRASShopper [21] is based on translations of SL fragments to first-order logic with reachability predicates, and the use of SMT solvers to deal with the latter. The advantage is the integration with other SMT theories to reason about data. However, this approach considers a limited class of inductive definitions (for linked lists and trees) and is incapable of dealing with the size or multiset constraints, thus unable to reason about AVL or red-black trees.

The truncation point approach [13] provides a method to specify and verify programs based on separation logic with inductive definitions that may specify truncated data structures with multiple holes, but it cannot deal with data constraints. Our approach can also be extended to cover such inductive definitions.

9   Conclusion

We proposed a novel approach for automating program proofs based on Separation Logic with inductive definitions. This approach consists of (1) efficiently checkable syntactic criteria for recognizing inductive definitions that satisfy crucial lemmas in such proofs and (2) a novel proof strategy for applying these lemmas. The proof strategy relies on syntactic matching of spatial atoms and on SMT solvers for checking data constraints. We have implemented this approach in our solver SPEN and applied it successfully to a representative set of examples, coming from iterative procedures for binary search trees or lists.

In the future, we plan to investigate extensions to more general inductive definitions by investigating ideas from [9,22] to extend our proof strategy. From a practical point of view, apart from improving the implementation of our proof strategy, we plan to integrate it into the program analysis framework Celia [6].

References

1. Abdulla, P.A., Holík, L., Jonsson, B., Lengál, O., Trinh, C.Q., Vojnar, T.: Verification of heap manipulating programs with ordered data by extended forest automata. In: Van Hung, D., Ogawa, M. (eds.) ATVA 2013. LNCS, vol. 8172, pp. 224–239. Springer, Heidelberg (2013)
2. Antonopoulos, T., Gorogiannis, N., Haase, C., Kanovich, M., Ouaknine, J.: Foundations for decision problems in separation logic with general inductive predicates. In: Muscholl, A. (ed.) FOSSACS 2014 (ETAPS). LNCS, vol. 8412, pp. 411–425. Springer, Heidelberg (2014)
3. Balaban, I., Pnueli, A., Zuck, L.D.: Shape analysis by predicate abstraction. In: Cousot, R. (ed.) VMCAI 2005. LNCS, vol. 3385, pp. 164–180. Springer, Heidelberg (2005)
4. Berdine, J., Calcagno, C., O'Hearn, P.W.: Symbolic execution with separation logic. In: Yi, K. (ed.) APLAS 2005. LNCS, vol. 3780, pp. 52–68. Springer, Heidelberg (2005)
5. Brotherston, J., Distefano, D., Petersen, R.L.: Automated cyclic entailment proofs in separation logic. In: Bjørner, N., Sofronie-Stokkermans, V. (eds.) CADE 2011. LNCS, vol. 6803, pp. 131–146. Springer, Heidelberg (2011)
6. CELIA. http://www.liafa.univ-paris-diderot.fr/celia
7. Chin, W.-N., David, C., Nguyen, H.H., Qin, S.: Automated verification of shape, size and bag properties via user-defined predicates in separation logic. Sci. Comput. Program. **77**(9), 1006–1036 (2012)
8. Chlipala, A.: Mostly-automated verification of low-level programs in computational separation logic. In: PLDI, vol. 46, pp. 234–245. ACM (2011)
9. Chu, D., Jaffar, J., Trinh, M.: Automating proofs of data-structure properties in imperative programs. CoRR, abs/1407.6124 (2014)
10. Cook, B., Haase, C., Ouaknine, J., Parkinson, M., Worrell, J.: Tractable reasoning in a fragment of separation logic. In: Katoen, J.-P., König, B. (eds.) CONCUR 2011. LNCS, vol. 6901, pp. 235–249. Springer, Heidelberg (2011)
11. Enea, C., Lengál, O., Sighireanu, M., Vojnar, T.: Compositional entailment checking for a fragment of separation logic. In: Garrigue, J. (ed.) APLAS 2014. LNCS, vol. 8858, pp. 314–333. Springer, Heidelberg (2014)
12. Enea, C., Sighireanu, M., Wu, Z.: On automated lemma generation for separation logic with inductive definitions. Technical report hal-01175732, HAL (2015)
13. Guo, B., Vachharajani, N., August, D.I.: Shape analysis with inductive recursion synthesis. In: PLDI, pp. 256–265. ACM (2007)
14. Iosif, R., Rogalewicz, A., Simacek, J.: The tree width of separation logic with recursive definitions. In: Bonacina, M.P. (ed.) CADE 2013. LNCS, vol. 7898, pp. 21–38. Springer, Heidelberg (2013)
15. Iosif, R., Rogalewicz, A., Vojnar, T.: Deciding entailments in inductive separation logic with tree automata. In: Cassez, F., Raskin, J.-F. (eds.) ATVA 2014. LNCS, vol. 8837, pp. 201–218. Springer, Heidelberg (2014)
16. Itzhaky, S., Banerjee, A., Immerman, N., Lahav, O., Nanevski, A., Sagiv, M.: Modular reasoning about heap paths via effectively propositional formulas. In: POPL, pp. 385–396. ACM (2014)
17. Nguyen, H.H., Chin, W.-N.: Enhancing program verification with lemmas. In: Gupta, A., Malik, S. (eds.) CAV 2008. LNCS, vol. 5123, pp. 355–369. Springer, Heidelberg (2008)

18. O'Hearn, P.W., Reynolds, J.C., Yang, H.: Local reasoning about programs that alter data structures. In: Fribourg, L. (ed.) CSL 2001 and EACSL 2001. LNCS, vol. 2142, pp. 1–19. Springer, Heidelberg (2001)
19. Pek, E., Qiu, X., Madhusudan, P.: Natural proofs for data structure manipulation in C using separation logic. In: PLDI, pp. 440–451. ACM (2014)
20. Piskac, R., Wies, T., Zufferey, D.: Automating separation logic using SMT. In: Sharygina, N., Veith, H. (eds.) CAV 2013. LNCS, vol. 8044, pp. 773–789. Springer, Heidelberg (2013)
21. Piskac, R., Wies, T., Zufferey, D.: Automating separation logic with trees and data. In: Biere, A., Bloem, R. (eds.) CAV 2014. LNCS, vol. 8559, pp. 711–728. Springer, Heidelberg (2014)
22. Qiu, X., Garg, P., Stefănescu, A., Madhusudan, P.: Natural proofs for structure, data, and separation. In: PLDI, pp. 231–242. ACM (2013)
23. Rakamarić, Z., Bingham, J.D., Hu, A.J.: An inference-rule-based decision procedure for verification of heap-manipulating programs with mutable data and cyclic data structures. In: Cook, B., Podelski, A. (eds.) VMCAI 2007. LNCS, vol. 4349, pp. 106–121. Springer, Heidelberg (2007)
24. Reynolds, J.C.: Separation logic: a logic for shared mutable data structures. In: LICS, pp. 55–74. ACM (2002)
25. SPEN. http://www.liafa.univ-paris-diderot.fr/spen
26. Zee, K., Kuncak, V., Rinard, M.: Full functional verification of linked data structures. In: PLDI, pp. 349–361. ACM (2008)

Severity Levels of Inconsistent Code

Martin Schäf[✉] and Ashish Tiwari[✉]

SRI International, Menlo Park, CA 94025, USA
martin.schaef@sri.com, tiwari@csl.sri.com

Abstract. Inconsistent code detection is a variant of static analysis that detects statements that never occur on feasible executions. This includes code whose execution ultimately must lead to an error, faulty error handling code, and unreachable code. Inconsistent code can be detected locally, fully automatically, and with a very low false positive rate. However, not all instances of inconsistent code are worth reporting. For example, debug code might be rendered unreachable on purpose and reporting it will be perceived as false positive.

To distinguish relevant from potentially irrelevant inconsistencies, we present an algorithm to categorize inconsistent code into (a) code that must lead to an error and may be reachable, (b) code that is unreachable because it must be preceded by an error, and (c) code that is unreachable for other reasons. We apply our algorithm to several open-source project to demonstrate that inconsistencies of the first category are highly relevant and often lead to bug fixes, while inconsistencies in the last category can largely be ignored.

1 Introduction

In this paper, we present a severity ranking for *inconsistent code*. Inconsistent code refers to a statement that is never executed on a normal terminating execution. That is, this statement is either unreachable, or any execution containing this statement leads to an error[1]. The concept of inconsistent code is appealing because it lends itself to be detected using static analysis – one simply has to prove that none of the paths containing the statement of interest is feasible. Hence, by using a sound over-approximation of the feasible paths of a program, one can build a tool to detect inconsistent code that never raises false alarms (at least in theory). Over the past years, several static analysis tools have been developed that detect, among other things, inconsistent code (e.g., [2,12,18,20]). We have seen interesting bugs rooted in inconsistent code being detected, e.g., in the Linux kernel [7], in Eclipse [11], or in Tomcat [16]. However, not all inconsistent code is worth reporting. For example, unreachable code, which is a special case of inconsistent code, is often used deliberately or is unavoidable. Reporting harmless instances of unreachable code would be perceived as false positives.

---

[1] E.g., the violation of an assertion or a (user-provided) safety property. The concrete definition of error depends on the tool.

B. Finkbeiner et al. (Eds.): ATVA 2015, LNCS 9364, pp. 97–113, 2015.
DOI: 10.1007/978-3-319-24953-7_8

Hence, it is vital to distinguish different reasons why code is inconsistent and prioritize warnings based on this.

In this paper, we introduce three tiers of inconsistent code – doomed, demood (doomed spelt backward), and unr code. Inconsistent code is categorized as doomed if it is possibly reachable (i.e., we cannot prove that it is unreachable), but any execution passing through it must lead to an error (violation of a safety property). Inconsistent code is categorized as demood if it is unreachable because any execution that would reach it must necessarily trigger an error earlier. Inconsistent code is categorized as unr if it is unreachable and not demood. We present an inconsistent code detection algorithm that can categorize inconsistent code as doomed, demood, or unr.

We show on a set of open-source benchmarks that this categorization can be made with very small computational overhead, and that the proposed severity levels help to identify critical inconsistencies easily. In most cases, code categorized as doomed indicates a patchable bug in the program while code categorized as unr tends to be less interesting and in the vast majority of cases not worth patching. Our experiments further indicate that inconsistent code of category doomed and demood is rare compared to unreachable code of category unr. Another observation is that false alarms, caused by imprecise handling of advanced language features, such as multi-threading and reflection, are always categorized as unr. Hence, by only reporting warnings of type doomed and demood, we obtain a highly usable inconsistent code detection tool.

2   Overview

We motivate our severity levels for inconsistent code using the illustrative examples in Fig. 1. Each of the four procedures, f1 to f4, has inconsistent code in the then-block of the conditional choice. The reason why this code is inconsistent, however, is different for each procedure.

In procedure f1, line 3 is inconsistent because on any execution passing through line 3, o is guaranteed to be null which violates the (implicit) run-time assertion in line 5 that o must be properly allocated before it can be de-referenced. We categorize this type of inconsistent code doomed because it may be (forward) reachable and inevitably leads to an error. This category comprises what we want to report with the highest severity. For this category of inconsistent code, the developer has to be notified because the only way to prevent an error is to make this code unreachable. Later in this section we will show some real-world examples of this case.

Procedure f2 contains inconsistent code in line 4. To reach this line, o has to be null. This, however, would violate the implicit run-time assertion that o must not be null in line 2. We categorize this case, where code is rendered unreachable by an (implicit) safety property, as demood. Code in this category often indicates that error handling is in the wrong place (e.g., a null-check of a pointer that has already been de-referenced). While this is not necessarily a bug, it certainly indicates confusion about the necessary error handling, which often

```
1  void f1(Object o) {
2    if (o == null) {
3      // inconsistent
4    }
5    o.toString();
6  }
```

```
1  void f2(Object o) {
2    o.toString();
3    if (o == null) {
4      // inconsistent
5    }
6  }
```

```
1  void f3() {
2    Object o =
3      new Integer(123);
4    if (o == null) {
5      // inconsistent
6    }
7  }
```

```
1  void f4(Object o) {
2    int i=0;
3    if (o == null) {
4      i++ // inconsistent
5    }
6    assert (i==0);
7  }
```

Fig. 1. Four examples of inconsistent code. In each procedure, the **then**-block is inconsistent. The procedures **f1**, **f2**, and **f3** represent the shortest possible examples for inconsistent code of category **doomed**, **demood**, and **unr** respectively. We added the procedure **f4** to clarify that inconsistent code is more than just forward or backward reachability.

is an indicator for bit rot or unclear specifications. Code categorized as **demood** will be reported with the second highest severity. While technically being plain unreachable code, it still indicates there may be a potential risk of an assertion violation.

In procedure **f3**, we have an example of unreachable code. Line 5 is unreachable because, in Java, **new** cannot return **null**. In this case, no run-time assertion is involved in making line 5 unreachable and we categorize it as **unr**. We report unreachable code of this category with the lowest severity (or even hide it completely). There are many reasons why code in this category should not be reported: in languages without pre-processor, such as Java, code is often rendered unreachable on purpose (e.g., debug code). Furthermore, translating high-level languages into simpler three-address code formats often introduces unreachable code, e.g., through translation of conjunctions into nested conditional choices, or inlining of **finally**-blocks in exception handling (see [1]). Also, unsound abstractions, such as ignoring possible interleaving in multi-threaded code, may introduce false positives which manifest as unreachable code.

Procedure **f4** has inconsistent code in line 4. This procedure illustrates the difference between unreachability and inconsistency. Unlike the previous examples, where the inconsistent code was either forward- or backward-unreachable, the inconsistent code in this example is both forward- and backward-reachable. Since line 4 is inconsistent and forward reachable, our algorithm will categorize it as **doomed** and report it with a high priority.

Motivating Examples. Figure 2 shows two occurrences of inconsistent code categorized as **doomed** by our approach. Both cases have been reported to the

```
1  //@org.apache.jasper.el.JasperELResolver
2  public synchronized void add(ELResolver elResolver) {
3    super.add(elResolver);
4    if (resolvers.length < size) {
5      resolvers[size] = elResolver;
6    //...
```

```
1  //@org.apache.maven.repository.MetadataResolutionResult
2  public MetadataResolutionResult addError(Exception e) {
3    if (exceptions==null)
4      initList( exceptions );
5    exceptions.add( e );
6    return this;
7  }
```

Fig. 2. Two examples of inconsistent code in the wild. The first example was found and fixed in Tomcat. Line 4 guarantees that line 5 access the array out of bounds and line 4 is forward reachable. The second example was found and fixed in Maven. Line 4 uses the list initializing incorrectly, thus, line 5 must throw an exception. In both cases, our algorithm categorizes the inconsistent code as doomed because it is reachable and must lead to an exception.

developers and our fixes have been accepted. In the first example taken from the application server Tomcat, the operator in line 4 is flipped resulting in an inevitable out-of-bounds exception being thrown in line 5. By inspecting the code, it was easy to see that this was just a typo and the operands merely had to be flipped. The second example is taken from Maven. Here, the procedure initList is used in the wrong way. The author of this code assumed that initList has a side effect on the field exceptions which is not the case. Even though our analysis is not really inter-procedural, it detects that exceptions cannot be modified by this call and hence detects that executing line 4 must lead to a NullPointerException in line 5.

These are just two examples of the type of problems that are categorized and reported as doomed by our algorithm. These are bugs that seem trivial but do occur in practice. In fact, they even occur on the main branches of well tested long standing open-source projects. In our evaluation, we will discuss in more detail which projects we analyzed, and how the severity levels helped us to stay focused on genuine bugs and ignore false positives.

3   Inconsistent Code

In this section, we formally define the notion of inconsistent code and present our static analysis approach for detecting inconsistent code. In subsequent sections, we will define the three categories of inconsistent code and then we will present an inconsistent code detection procedure that also outputs the category with each instance of inconsistent code.

We present our approach using the simple unstructured language shown in Fig. 3. The language is a simplified version of Boogie [4] and is sufficient for demonstration purposes. Even though it is simple, it is expressive enough to encode a large class of programs in high-level languages such as Java [1].

$$
\begin{aligned}
Program \;\; &::= \;\; Block^* \\
Block \;\; &::= \;\; label: \; Stmt;^* \; \textbf{goto } label^*; \\
Stmt \;\; &::= \;\; VarId := Expr; \;\; | \;\; \textbf{assert } Expr; \;\; | \;\; \textbf{assume } Expr;
\end{aligned}
$$

Fig. 3. The syntax of our simple (unstructured) Language

A program in this language is a set of *Blocks*, with one unique entry block, b_e, where execution of the program starts, and a unique sink block, b_x, where execution terminates. Each block is connected to possibly multiple other blocks using (non-deterministic) gotos. A block is a piece of sequential code containing assignments, assertions, and assumptions. Assertions have no effect if the asserted condition evaluates to true and abort the execution with an error, otherwise. Assume statements behave similar to assertions except that execution *blocks* if the assumed condition evaluates to false. Assume statements are used to reduce non-determinism introduced by gotos and model common control-flow constructs such as conditional choices or loops. Assignments update the value of program variables. We do not explicitly present the syntax for expressions. We do allow the assignment of non-deterministic values to variables (e.g., for abstraction).

A (complete) path in a program is a sequence of blocks $b_e b_1 \ldots b_x$ such that each block in the sequence is connected (via *goto*) to the next block in the sequence. Throughout this paper, the term *path* always refers to a complete path, starting in b_e and ending in b_x. For our purposes here, the semantics of a path in a program is just a Boolean value indicating if the path is *feasible*; that is, if the sequence of assignment statements on this path can be executed without violating any assumption or assertion. Formally, we define the semantics of a path, feasibility of a path, and inconsistent code as follows.

Definition 1. *The function* $[\cdot]$ *mapping a sequence of statements* $s_1; \cdots ; s_m$ *to a first-order formula is defined recursively as follows:*

$$[s_1; s_2] = [s_1] \wedge [s_2] \qquad [v := e] = v = e \qquad [\textbf{assume } e] = e \qquad [\textbf{assert } e] = e$$

The <u>*semantics*</u> $[b_e b_1 \ldots b_x]$ *of a path* $b_e b_1 \ldots b_x$ *is the formula* $[s_{b_e}; s_{b_1}; \ldots; s_{b_x}]$, *where* $s_{b_e}; s_{b_1}; \ldots; s_{b_x}$ *is a static single assignment form for the straight-line program* $Stmt_{b_e}; Stmt_{b_1}; \ldots; Stmt_{b_x}$ *obtained using the statements* $Stmt_{b_i}$ *in the definition of block* b_i.

A path π is feasible if the formula $[\pi]$ is satisfiable.

A block (and each statement in that block) is inconsistent in a program, if there is no feasible path inside the program containing this block.

Feasibility of a path π can be checked using SMT solvers to check satisfiability of $[\pi]$; see also [13].

Finding Inconsistent Code

Since the number of paths in the program can be unbounded (due to loops), most existing algorithms for detecting inconsistent code perform *program abstraction* to remove loops from the program, and then use a satisfiability checker on the abstract program; see for example [10,12,18]. We discuss these steps next.

Program Abstraction. The goal of the program abstraction step is to eliminate loops and procedure calls from the program. This is usually done by replacing the corresponding code by non-deterministic assignments to (an over-approximation of) all variables modified in the original code surrounded by a (possibly trivial) pair of pre- and postcondition. The property guaranteed by the abstraction step is that it only adds executions to the program but never removes one (see [10, 18]). We use $\mathsf{abs}(P)$ to denote an abstraction of program P.

Static Single Assignment. In the second step, we apply static single assignment transformation [5] to $\mathsf{abs}(P)$ to get a program $\mathsf{ssa}(\mathsf{abs}(P))$. The program $\mathsf{ssa}(\mathsf{abs}(P))$ is a loop-free program in which each variable is only written once. We refer to such a program as *passive program*.

Inconsistent Code Detection. Finally, the passive program $\mathsf{ssa}(\mathsf{abs}(P))$ is encoded into a first-order logic formula $[\mathsf{ssa}(\mathsf{abs}(P))]$ such that each model of this formula maps to some feasible paths in the passive program. Formally, given a passive program in our language from Fig. 3, its encoding into first-order logic is done as follows:

Statement	First-order representation
$[Program:: = Block_0\,Block_1 \ldots Block_n]$	$\bigwedge_{0 \le i \le n}([Block_i])$
$[Block:: = \ label: \ Stmt_i^* \ \textbf{goto}\ label_1 \ldots label_n;]$	$label = ([Stmt_i^*] \wedge \bigvee_{0 \le i \le n} label_i)$
$[Stmt_0; \ldots Stmt_n;]$	$\bigwedge_{0 \le i \le n}([Stmt_i])$
[**assume** e], [**assert** e], [$v := e$]	As in Definition 1

The most important step is the translation of *Block*. Each block comes with a *label* which becomes a Boolean variable in the first-order representation. This variable is true (in any model) if and only if there exists a feasible suffix from that block to a terminal block of the program. Since the program is already in single assignment form, each program variable can be translated into a variable in the first-order formula of appropriate (SMT) type. Going from program types to SMT types may require inserting additional assertions (or be a source of unsoundness); for example, when fixed size integers are encoded as natural numbers. We do not discuss this last point in this paper.

Given program P, the procedure for detecting inconsistent code in P first computes the formula $\phi := [\mathsf{ssa}(\mathsf{abs}(P))]$, and then it checks satisfiability of $\phi \wedge label_e$, where $label_e$ is the label for the initial block $block_e$. If the formula is satisfiable and M is a model, then we can extract *at least one* complete path with labels, say $label_e, label_1, \ldots, label_n, label_x$, where each label in the path is mapped to *True* in the model M. Each block in this path is marked "consistent". We iterate this process after adding an additional constraint to ϕ that eliminates M from the set of models of the new formula. The new constraint could either be a blocking clause that excludes this path (i.e., $\neg \bigwedge label_i$), or it could just set the label of one of the unmarked blocks to *True*. Iterating this process excludes at least one feasible path in each iteration. Since the number of feasible paths in a passive program is finite (because we removed loops and procedure calls), eventually the new formula becomes unsatisfiable and the process terminates. At termination, all unmarked blocks are output as "inconsistent code". Since the abstraction of loops and procedure calls only adds executions, we have the guarantee that all inconsistent code found by the above procedure on $\mathsf{abs}(P)$ is also inconsistent in the original program P.

The above procedure describes the basic steps necessary to build a tool that detects inconsistent code as described in [2,16,18]. In the following, we show how this basic inconsistent code detection can be extended to distinguish different categories of inconsistency.

Note that, for inconsistent code detection, assumptions and assertions are treated in the same way because, for the proof of inconsistency, it is not relevant why paths through a block are not feasible.

4   Severity Levels of Inconsistency

The key contribution of this paper is the introduction of the concept of severity levels for inconsistent code. This categorization is intended to reflect the confidence of the static analysis tool in its claim about the presence of a bug in the software and its severity.

We categorize inconsistent code in two dimensions. First, we distinguish between inconsistent code that is possibly reachable versus inconsistent code that is provably unreachable. Second, we also distinguish inconsistent code based on whether executions along paths containing that code results in assertion violation. Figure 4 shows the categories resulting from the distinction along these two dimensions: doomed, for inconsistent code that is possibly reachable and leads to an assertion violation error; demood, for inconsistent code that is provably unreachable because it must be preceded by an exception; and unr, for code that is provably unreachable, but executions along paths containing it do not cause assertion violations (that is, they all block due to assume violations).

		Statement s is possibly reachable.	
Executions containing s lead to an error.		Yes	No
	Yes	s is doomed	s is demood
	No	-	s is unr

Fig. 4. Categories of inconsistent code.

Definition 2 (Severity Levels). *Given a program P, let P' denote the program obtained from P by removing all* **assert** *statements.*

An inconsistent block in a program is unr *if for every complete path π in P' containing this block, the formula $[\pi]$ is unsatisfiable.*

An inconsistent block in a program is doomed *if for some complete path π in P' containing this block, the formula $[\pi]$ is satisfiable and for some path π in P from an initial block to this block, the formula $[\pi]$ is satisfiable.*

An inconsistent block in a program is demood *if for some complete path π in P' containing this block, the formula $[\pi]$ is satisfiable and for every path π in P from an initial block to this block, the formula $[\pi]$ is unsatisfiable.*

Intuitively, if all paths through some block cause an assertion violation, then that block is either doomed or demood. It is doomed if that block is reachable, and it is demood if it that block is not reachable. All other instances of inconsistent code are categorized as unr.

We remark here that **assert** statements in our program can arise either from explicit assert statements in the source, or from implicit assert statements that arise, for example, when dereferencing a pointer or dividing by a number.

Since our inconsistent code detection and categorization procedure will necessarily run on an *abstraction* of some concrete program, we relate a categorization on an abstraction to a categorization on the concrete in Lemma 3. For our purposes, abstractions can just add behaviors: formally, program Q is an abstraction of P, if Q and P share the same blocks, and for every path π in P, there is a corresponding path σ in Q (containing the same blocks) such that $[\pi] \Rightarrow [\sigma]$ is valid in both cases – when we retain the **assert** blocks in P and Q and also in the case when we remove the **assert** blocks from P and Q.

Lemma 3. *Let Q be an abstraction of P. Then, if a block is* unr *in Q, then it is* unr *in P. If a block is* demood *in Q, then it is either* demood *or* unr *in P. If a block is* doomed *in Q, then it is either* doomed *or* demood *or* unr *in P.*

Proof. Suppose a block b is unr in Q. Consider any complete path π through that block in P. We know there is a corresponding path σ in Q such that $[\pi] \Rightarrow [\sigma]$. Since block b is unr in Q, the formula $[\sigma]$ (with all asserts removed) is unsatisfiable; and hence $[\pi]$ (with all asserts removed) is also unsatisfiable.

Next, suppose block b is demood in Q. Consider any partial path π in P from an initial block to block b. Since b is demood in Q, for the corresponding partial path σ in Q, $[\sigma]$ is unsatisfiable. Since $[\pi] \Rightarrow [\sigma]$, this implies that $[\pi]$ is unsatisfiable. This shows that b can not be doomed. Hence, b is either demood or unr. □

Since abstractions add behaviors and inconsistent code is about the absence of feasible behaviors, it is clear (also from Lemma 3) that if we use sound abstractions to compute inconsistent code, we will never get a "false positive" instance of inconsistent code. In reality, however, a static analyzer in general and our tool in particular, has to use all kinds of abstractions – both over (sound) and under (unsound) – to enable scalable analysis [15]. Under-approximations can cause false positives. An even more interesting feature of inconsistent code is that false positives for inconsistent code can also arise from perfect semantic-preserving transformations (i.e. no abstractions) because introducing inconsistent code does not change semantics of programs. Preprocessors and transformers used in compilers and analysis tools can often introduce inconsistent code, which is irrelevant for the developer. Our categorization is significant also because all such false-positive inconsistencies get categorized as unr in our approach. Pragmatically, irrespective of whether an inconsistency is a true one or a false positive, it will be counted as a false positive in practise if it is not fixed by a developer, and this aspect will guide our evaluation in Sect. 6.

In the following, we discuss how the inconsistent code detection algorithm outlined in Sect. 3 can be extended to distinguish the three severity levels.

5   Algorithm for Categorizing Inconsistent Code

We refine the inconsistent code detection algorithm from Sect. 3 to also report the categories doomed, demood, and unr, of inconsistent code.

Recall that to appropriately categorize inconsistent code, we need to be able to (1) detect if a statement is inconsistent because the executions containing it lead to an error, and (2) check if a statement is forward reachable.

Statement	First-order representation
[assume e]	e
[assert e]	$e \vee \text{ignore}$
[$v := e$]	$v = e$

Fig. 5. To detect which code is inconsistent because

The first check can be easily integrated in the existing algorithm. After the algorithm has covered all feasible paths, we simply remove all assertions from the program and check if there are statements that can be covered now but couldn't be covered before. These are the statements that are inconsistent because of assertion errors (i.e., doomed or demood). Everything that still cannot be covered after removing the assertions falls into the category unr. To implement this step efficiently, we modify the way we encode programs into first-order logic as shown in Fig. 5. The only change is that we translate assertions of the form **assert**(e) into $e \vee$ *ignore* instead of just e. Here, *ignore* is an uninitialized Boolean variable that we introduce. That is, if *ignore* is true, the whole expression becomes true and thus the assertion e is ignored.

Our refined algorithm works as follows: first, we compute the first-order formula ϕ_{new} using the new encoding with the alternative treatment of assertions. Then, in Phase 1, we run the algorithm from Sect. 3, but in place of the old ϕ, we use ϕ_{new} and, before we start searching for models, we push the axiom *ignore* $= false$ on the theorem prover stack (for our implementation we use Princess [17], but other SMT solvers can be used equally well). That is, in Phase 1, we do inconsistent code detection exactly as before. Once we have marked all feasible blocks, we pop *ignore* $= false$ from the prover stack (thus allowing the solver to pick *ignore* $= true$ which removes all asserts), and continue our search for (more) feasible paths in Phase 2. Every block that is marked in this second phase (and was left unmarked in the first phase) is inconsistent solely due to assert violations; that is, it either falls into doomed, or demood. Everything that is unmarked even after the second phase is categorized as unr.

With this small extension, we are already able to distinguish unr from the other two categories. What is left is to distinguish doomed from demood. To that end, we need to check if the inconsistent code is reachable. This step can be implemented by a single theorem prover query (e.g., [12]) by encoding the subprogram containing all traces from the program's source to this statement using the simple encoding from Sect. 3, and checking the satisfiability of the resulting formula. If the formula is SAT, then the statement is reachable, and the inconsistent code is categorized as doomed. If it is unsatisfiable, the statement is unreachable and it is categorized as demood.

Theorem 4. *The procedure outlined above correctly categorizes code as* doomed, demood, *or* unr.

We recall that, in practice, the categorization is performed on some abstraction, and even though Lemma 3 informs us that our categorization as doomed and demood (computed on the abstract) may not hold for the concrete, we still report the severity level computed on the abstract as the severity level for the concrete. Now, we have to show experimentally that these categories are useful and that our intuition is correct that doomed is the most important, followed by demood, and that unr can mostly be ignored.

6   Evaluation

We show experimentally that the three severity levels introduced above can be effectively used to differentiate inconsistencies that are deemed relevant by developers from the ones that are considered irrelevant. Specifically, we answer the following research questions:

1. Does our categorization improve usability of inconsistent code detection? Are reports in the doomed category rare and highly relevant to developers? Are reports in demood rare and interesting (but less relevant than the previous category)? Does the bulk of reports fall into the unr category, and are the reports non-critical so that we can hide them from the user unless she deliberately asks to see them?
2. Can we categorize inconsistent code at a reasonable cost?

Experimental Setup. We implemented the proposed extensions from Sect. 5 on top of our Bixie tool [16]. Bixie is based on Soot [19] and performs intra-procedural inconsistent code detection on Java bytecode. The tool and all scripts necessary to repeat the presented results are available on the tool website.

Table 1. Results of applying our approach on several open-source programs. The table shows per benchmark the number of detected inconsistencies, the categories they fall into, the time for analyzing the benchmark, and the overhead introduced by our approach. For Flume and Tomcat, which use custom run-time assertions libraries, we needed to specify their assertion procedure to avoid false alarms.

Benchmark	Inconsistencies	doomed	demood	unr	Total time	Overhead
Apache Cassandra	127	0	0	127	415.142s	5.636s
Apache Flume	12	5(1)	0	7	1475.955s	31.412s
Apache Hive	534	11	7	516	12623.264s	179.478s
Apache jMeter	9	0	0	9	1389.117s	29.394s
Apache Maven	15	1	0	14	777.079s	10.78s
Apache Tomcat	62	7(2)	0	56	5141.671s	170.065
Bouncy Castle	23	2	0	21	2067.994s	22.358s
WildFly (JBoss)	31	7	0	24	3130.415s	41.268s

We evaluate our extensions to Bixie on a set of popular open-source Java projects with a total of over a million lines of code. We picked the projects without having a particular pattern in mind. Mostly, we picked projects because we could build them easily. The projects include popular projects from the Apache foundation, such as Cassandra, Flume, Hive, jMeter, Maven, and Tomcat. We also applied our analysis to the crypto library Bouncy Castle and the application-server WildFly (formally known as jBoss).

The upside of picking real open-source projects is that we will find real bugs that we can report and we avoid the confirmation bias that would arise from handcrafted examples. The downside is that popular open-source projects tend to be of good quality and rather well-tested meaning that inconsistent code will be rare. However, as we will see, it still exists.

For each project, Bixie scans one procedure at a time for inconsistent code with a timeout of 40 s. If Bixie is not conclusive within the given time limit, it reports nothing for that procedure. We analyze all projects on a standard desktop PC. Table 1 summarizes our results, showing the number of inconsistent code snippets detected in total, and by category, as well as the total computation time per benchmark and the extra time spent by our extensions to put inconsistent code into the different categories.

Table 2. Number of inconsistencies from Table 1 for which we proposed a patch per category and in total, and number of inconsistencies that have been fixed by the time of writing this paper.

Benchmark	doomed	demood	unr	Total	fixed
Apache Cassandra	0	0	1	1	1
Apache Flume	1	0	0	1	1
Apache Hive	3	1	0	4	11
Apache jMeter	0	0	2	2	2
Apache Maven	1	0	0	1	1
Apache Tomcat	1	0	0	1	1
Bouncy Castle	1	0	4	5	5
WildFly (JBoss)	6	0	0	6	6

Discussion. With our experimental results, we try to answer our first research question, whether the proposed categories make sense and help to identify relevant inconsistent code quickly. Looking at the distribution of inconsistent code over the different categories in Table 1, we can see that, as expected, a large part of the detected code falls into the unr category. A welcomed side effect is that all false positive that arise from our unsound abstraction of multi-threading or reflection fall into this category. That is, none of the doomed inconsistencies qualify as false positive. To our surprise, demood inconsistencies are very rare. We assume that this can be largely attributed to the fact that the most common Java IDEs, Eclipse and IntelliJ, use constant propagation to warn the user about a subset of demood inconsistent code (but Eclipse, for example, often does not warn about doomed inconsistent code).

Table 2 shows for how many inconsistencies of each category we have proposed a patch, and how many of those got accepted by developers. Further down, we will discuss these findings for each benchmark individually. Out of the total 24 doomed inconsistencies (after removing the inconsistencies related to Guava calls as described in the caption of the table), we provided patches for 13, and by the time of writing this paper, 22 have been fixed (in the 9 cases where we did not provide patches, the developers fixed the bugs by themselves). That is, 91 % of doomed inconsistent code has been fixed. We only reported 1 out of 7 demood inconsistencies (all of which have been found in Hive). We did not report the remaining 6 because the developers did not respond to our earlier pull requests for this project and we did not want to spam their Git. Three of the remaining six demood inconsistencies were unnecessary null-checks. The other three occurred in three instances of the same cloned code and resulted from a bug in Bixie which we were not able to fix by the time of submission. In total, we found 774 unr inconsistencies out of which we reported 7 that we found worth patching. The remaining inconsistencies were either deliberately unreachable code, unreachable code that occurred in bytecode but not in source code (see [1]), or false positives from unsound translation of multi-threading, reflection, or other programming bugs. Out of the 7 reported unr inconsistency, only one had an effect on the program behavior which we discuss below (in the findings for Cassandra), the others were mostly cosmetic.

In the following we discuss, benchmark by benchmark, what we found, what we patched and the developer feedback that we got.

For Cassandra, we reported one inconsistent statement from unr. The code computed a random Boolean by computing rnd%1==0. Since modulo 1 is constant, the Boolean expression is constant, which caused unreachable code. None of the other 127 statements in unr was worth reporting.

For Flume, we reported one of five inconsistent statements from doomed where a variable of reference type was checked for nullness and later, one of it's fields was accessed. The four remaining inconsistent statements from doomed were found because Flume uses the Guava library for run-time assertions. Without inter-procedural analysis, our analysis does not see that Guava throws an exception if an assertion fails. Thus the analysis assumes that, if the assertion fails, the code behind it is still reachable (and, in these cases, inconsistent). For code that uses custom assertion libraries, our analysis will produce these 'false alarms', unless we provide contracts (which can be done manually), or perform inter-procedural analysis.

For Hive, we reported several bugs but since there was no feedback from the developers so we decided not to submit patches for the remaining bugs. However, by the time of writing this paper, all doomed inconsistent code had been removed by the developers (without acknowledging our pull requests). We assume that the developers only mirror their git to GitHub and hence could not integrated our pull requests. The large number of unr inconsistent code in Hive is rooted in generated code that contains a lot of deliberately unreachable code.

For jMeter, we reported two occurrences of unr. Both were duplicated cases in case splits. While these cases were not changing the behavior of the code they were obvious mistakes that had a straight forward patch, so we decided to report them anyway.

For Maven, we reported the one bug found by our tool which is shown in the second listing of Fig. 2. Our patch got accepted.

For Bouncy Castle, we report 5 occurrences of inconsistent code and all fixes got accepted. We only report one of the two doomed inconsistencies. We did not report second inconsistency which was a pointer de-reference that inevitably failed if the loop, which iterated over a list, was not entered. However, we (and our algorithm) could not immediately decide if this list may be empty. While adding an additional check may help to harden the code we decided not to write a patch. For the other doomed inconsistency, which was a possible array out-of-bounds read after loop, we submitted a patch. We further submitted patches for four unr inconsistencies which were obviously unreachable because of duplication. None of these were actual bugs but since they were easy to fix, we decided to patch them anyway.

For Tomcat, we reported one out of seven instances of doomed inconsistent code. Similar to Flume, five of the seven entries in doomed are inconsistent because Tomcat uses its own run-time assertion library. Once we provide a specification for these procedures, these five reports disappear. One reported doomed inconsistent code was rooted in an implicit else-case that would lead to an inevitable run-time exception. However, since we believe this case cannot occur, we decided not to propose a patch.

For WildFly, we submitted patches for 6 out of 7 occurrences of doomed. All got accepted (but have not been merged at the time of writing the paper). We did not report one occurrence, which was an implicit else-block in a switch whose execution must cause an exception. However, it looked like the developers decided to use an else if-block instead of the else to make the code more readable so we decided not to propose a patch.

To summarize, we can answer our first research question with yes. Our categories significantly improve the usability of our inconsistent code detection tool: distinguishing doomed inconsistencies from which over 90 % are relevant and worth fixing, from unr inconsistencies where less than 1 % was fixed and which may contain false positives, dramatically improves the user experience of the tool. To our surprise, demood inconsistencies did not play a role at all. As discussed above, we believe that modern IDE support is sufficient to detect and eliminate demood inconsistencies before they find their way into the repository. To answer our second research question, we look at the computational overhead in last column of Table 1 to see if our extensions are prohibitively expensive. This is not the case. For our benchmarks the time overhead for putting inconsistent code into categories is in the single digit percentage. Even for projects like Cassandra and Hive where many inconsistencies are found the overhead is small. This is because a large percentage of the detected inconsistent code falls into the unr category for the (potentially expensive) reachability check in our algorithm does not need to be performed. Hence, we can give a positive answer to our second research question: categorizing inconsistent code can be done at a reasonable computational overhead. In particular, given the number of non-interesting reports it can suppress, the overhead time clearly pays off for the user.

Threats to Validity. We identify the following three threats to validity in our experimental setup. First, we only picked the master-branches of each project. Most of these projects use some form of continuous integration (CI), so the master-branch is usually well tested. This may distort how inconsistencies are distributed across the categories during development. The CI system may have commit hooks that reject contributions according to various rules. WildFly, for example, enforces coding conventions for each commit, which potentially affects the number of demood inconsistencies. However, in general, we assume that, without CI, we would just find more relevant inconsistencies and our finding that the proposed categorization improves usability still holds.

Second, the selection of benchmark projects may be biased because we selected only projects which we could compile (and hence analyze) easily. However, since all projects are major open-source projects, we believe that it is still possible to generalize from the results.

Finally, the selection of tools, theorem prover, etc. can be seen as a threat to validity. However, since there is no competing tool to detect inconsistent code we can only assume that our implementation is not biased towards or against the finding in this paper. For transparency, we make the code and experimental setup available online [16].

7   Related Work

Algorithm that detect, among other things, inconsistent code have been published in several previous papers (e.g., [2,6,18]). The term inconsistent code is used by [2,10,18], in other papers, the same phenomenon is called doomed program points [10], or deviant behavior [7].

A similar technique to detect unreachable code in the programs with annotations has been presented in [12]. Like our approach, their technique is based on deductive verification, but only detects a subset of demood and unr, but would not detect doomed inconsistent code.

Our approach of using Boolean flags to disable assertions is inspired by the work of [14] which uses a similar encoding to obtain error traces and the assertions that cause them to fail from SMT solver counterexamples.

Other papers have discussed the value of post-processing reports from static analysis tools. In [8], warnings produced by Coverity Static Analysis and FindBugs are clustered by similarity. The authors show that the grouping significantly reduces the reports that have to be considered. In [9], a set of benchmarks is proposed to evaluate categorization of static analysis reports. Unfortunately, these benchmarks target light-weight analysis and are not comparable to our approach. FindBugs uses a set of detectors that detect a particular category of potential bugs. In a case study in [3] the authors discuss the value of categorizing warnings and its impact in an industrial cases study. While all these papers share our motivation that categorizing static analysis warnings increases usability of tools, their work is based on light-weight analysis tools that notoriously produce many false alarms. We operate on inconsistent code (which is not detected as such by their tools).

8   Conclusion

We have presented an efficient way to categorize inconsistencies in source code. With a small extension to existing inconsistent code detection algorithms, we are able to distinguish three categories doomed, demood, and unr of inconsistent code. Our experiments show that the doomed category contains only few, but highly relevant warnings, while the unr category contains hardly any critical warning but collects all false alarms. Hence, the proposed approach dramatically increases the usability of inconsistent code detection.

Our experiments indicate that demood inconsistent code is rare which would suggest that making a distinction between demood and doomed inconsistent code is not necessary as this step is relatively costly. However, this observation may be biased by using only master-branches and further experiments on code in active development will be necessary.

For our future work, we have identified that custom assertion libraries like Guava can still introduce false alarms which can easily be avoided by adding very simple contracts. These contracts could be generated automatically, or we could extend our tool to inline procedures up to a certain size.

If nothing else, we have fixed several bugs in open-source projects that run on many web servers that we talk to every day, and thus, we can claim that we have made the world a bit safer.

Acknowledgement. This work was supported in part by the National Science Foundation under grant contracts CCF 1423296 and CNS 1423298, and DARPA under agreement number FA8750-12-C-0225.

References

1. Arlt, S., Rümmer, P., Schäf, M.: Joogie: From java through jimple to boogie. In: SOAP (2013)
2. Arlt, S., Schäf, M.: Joogie: infeasible code detection for java. In: Madhusudan, P., Seshia, S.A. (eds.) CAV 2012. LNCS, vol. 7358, pp. 767–773. Springer, Heidelberg (2012)
3. Ayewah, N., Pugh, W., Morgenthaler, J.D., Penix, J., Zhou, Y.: Evaluating static analysis defect warnings on production software. In: PASTE (2007)
4. Barnett, M., Chang, B.-Y.E., DeLine, R., Jacobs, B., M. Leino, K.R.: Boogie: a modular reusable verifier for object-oriented programs. In: de Boer, F.S., Bonsangue, M.M., Graf, S., de Roever, W.-P. (eds.) FMCO 2005. LNCS, vol. 4111, pp. 364–387. Springer, Heidelberg (2006)
5. Cytron, R., Ferrante, J., Rosen, B.K., Wegman, M.N., Zadeck, F.K.: Efficiently computing static single assignment form and the control dependence graph. In: TOPLAS (1991)
6. Dillig, I., Dillig, T., Aiken, A.: Static error detection using semantic inconsistency inference. In: PLDI (2007)
7. Engler, D., Chen, D.Y., Hallem, S., Chou, A., Chelf, B.: Bugs as deviant behavior: A general approach to inferring errors in systems code. In: SOSP (2001)
8. Fry, Z.P., Weimer, W.: Clustering static analysis defect reports to reduce maintenance costs. In: WCRE (2013)
9. Heckman, S., Williams, L.: On establishing a benchmark for evaluating static analysis alert prioritization and classification techniques. In: ESEM (2008)

10. Hoenicke, J., Leino, K.R., Podelski, A., Schäf, M., Wies, T.: Doomed program points. In: FMSD (2010)
11. Hovemeyer, D., Pugh, W.: Finding more null pointer bugs, but not too many. In: PASTE (2007)
12. Janota, M., Grigore, R., Moskal, M.: Reachability analysis for annotated code. In: SAVCBS (2007)
13. Leino, K.R.M.: Efficient weakest preconditions. Inf. Process. Lett. **93**(6) (2005)
14. Leino, K.R.M., Millstein, T., Saxe, J.B.: Generating error traces from verification-condition counterexamples. Sci. Comput. Program. **55**(1–3), 209–226 (2005)
15. Livshits, B., Sridharan, M., Smaragdakis, Y., Lhoták, O., Amaral, J.N., Chang, B.-Y.E., Guyer, S.Z., Khedker, U.P., Møller, A., Vardoulakis, D.: In defense of soundiness: A manifesto. In: CACM, vol. 56(1), February 2015
16. McCarthy, T., Rümmer, P., Schäf, M.: Bixie: Finding and understanding inconsistent code (2015). http://www.csl.sri.com/bixie-ws/
17. Rümmer, P.: A constraint sequent calculus for first-order logic with linear integer arithmetic. In: Cervesato, I., Veith, H., Voronkov, A. (eds.) LPAR 2008. LNCS (LNAI), vol. 5330, pp. 274–289. Springer, Heidelberg (2008)
18. Tomb, A., Flanagan, C.: Detecting inconsistencies via universal reachability analysis. In: ISSTA (2012)
19. Vallée-Rai, R., Hendren, L., Sundaresan, V., Lam, P., Gagnon, E., Co., P.: Soot - a Java Optimization Framework. In: CASCON (1999)
20. Wang, X., Zeldovich, N., Kaashoek, M.F., Solar-Lezama, A.: Towards optimization-safe systems: analyzing the impact of undefined behavior. In: SOSP (2013)

Learning the Language of Error

Martin Chapman[1], Hana Chockler[1]([✉]), Pascal Kesseli[2], Daniel Kroening[2], Ofer Strichman[3], and Michael Tautschnig[4]

[1] Department of Informatics, King's College London, London, UK
{martin.chapman,hana.chockler}@kcl.ac.uk
[2] Department of Computer Science, University of Oxford, Oxford, UK
{pascal.kesseli,kroening}@cs.ox.ac.uk
[3] Information Systems Engineering, Technion, Haifa, Israel
ofers@ie.technion.ac.il
[4] EECS, Queen Mary University of London, London, UK
mt@eecs.qmul.ac.uk

Abstract. We propose to harness Angluin's L^* algorithm for learning a deterministic finite automaton that describes the possible scenarios under which a given program error occurs. The alphabet of this automaton is given by the user (for instance, a subset of the function call sites or branches), and hence the automaton describes a user-defined abstraction of those scenarios. More generally, the same technique can be used for visualising the behavior of a program or parts thereof. This can be used, for example, for visually comparing different versions of a program, by presenting an automaton for the behavior in the symmetric difference between them, or for assisting in merging several development branches. We present initial experiments that demonstrate the power of an abstract visual representation of errors and of program segments.

1 Introduction

Many automated verification tools produce a counterexample trace when an error is found. These traces are often unintelligible because they are too long (an error triggered after a single second can correspond to a path with millions of states), too low-level, or both. Moreover, a trace focuses on just one specific scenario. Thus, error traces are frequently not general enough to help focus the attention of the programmer on the root cause of the problem.

A variety of methods have been proposed for the *explanation of counterexamples*, such as finding similar paths that satisfy the property [16] and analysing causality [8], but these focus on a single counterexample. The analysis of *multiple* counterexamples has been suggested in the hardware domain by Copty et al. [13], who propose to compute all counterexamples and present those states that occur in all of them to the user. Multiple counterexample analysis has also been suggested in the context of a push-down automaton (PDA) (representing software) and a deterministic finite automaton (DFA) (representing a

---

This work was supported in part by the Google Faculty Research Award 2014.

B. Finkbeiner et al. (Eds.): ATVA 2015, LNCS 9364, pp. 114–130, 2015.
DOI: 10.1007/978-3-319-24953-7_9

negated property) by Basu et al. [7], who describe the generation of all loop-free counterexamples of a certain class, and the presentation of them to the user in a tree-like structure. In software, another notable example is the model checker MS-SLAM, which reports multiple counterexamples if they are believed to relate to different causes [6], and each example is 'localized' by comparing it to a trace that does not violate the property.

We believe that developers can benefit from seeing the multiple ways in which a given assertion can fail, and that raw counterexamples quickly become unhelpful. In this article we suggest that a user should be presented with a DFA that summarizes all the ways (up to a given bound, as will be explained) in which an assertion can fail. Furthermore, the alphabet of this automaton is user-defined, e.g., the user can give some subset of the function calls in a program. We argue that this combination of user-defined abstraction with a compact representation of multiple counterexamples addresses all three problems mentioned above. Moreover, the same idea can be applied to *describing* a program or, more realistically, parts of a program by adding an 'assert(false)' at the end of the subprogram to be explained. Fig. 1, for instance, gives an automaton that describes the operation of a merge-sort program in terms of its possible function calls.[1] We obtained it by inserting such a statement at the end of the main function.

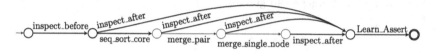

Fig. 1. An abstract description of a merge-sort program, where the letters are the function calls.

Our method is based on Angluin's L^*-learning algorithm [3]. L^* is a framework for learning a minimal DFA that captures the (regular) language of a model $\mathcal{U}$ over a given alphabet Σ, the behavior of which is communicated to L^* via an interface called the 'teacher'. L^* asks the teacher *membership* queries over Σ, namely whether $w \in \mathcal{U}$, where w is a word and $\mathcal{U}$ is the language (the model), and *conjecture* queries, namely whether for a given DFA $\mathcal{A}$, $L(\mathcal{A}) = \mathcal{U}$. The number of queries that the algorithm performs is polynomial in the size of the alphabet, in the number of states of the resulting minimal DFA, and in the length of the longest counterexample (feedback) to a conjecture query returned by the oracle (see Sect. 2 for a more in-detail description).

The use of L^* in the verification community, to the best of our knowledge, has been restricted so far to the verification process itself: to model components in an assume-guarantee framework, e.g., [15], or to model the input-output relation in specific types of programs, in which that relation is sufficient for verifying certain properties [11].

---

[1] Source code for all the programs mentioned in this article is available online from [1].

Trivially, the language that describes a part of a program, or the behaviors that fail an assertion, is neither finite nor regular in the general case. We therefore bound the length of the traces we consider by a constant, and thereby obtain a finite set of finite words. The automaton that we learn may accept unbounded words, but our guarantee to the user is limited: any word in $L(\mathcal{A})$, up to the given bound, corresponds to a real trace in the program. We will formalize this concept in Sect. 3. The fact that $\mathcal{A}$ may have loops has both advantages and disadvantages. Consider, for example, the program in Fig. 2 (left). Suppose that Σ is the set of functions that are called. With a small bound on the word length we may get the automaton in Fig. 2 (right), which among others, accepts the word $g^{120} \cdot f$. The bound is not long enough to exclude this word. On the other hand, if g had no effect on the reachability of f, then the automaton would capture the language of error precisely, despite the fact that we are only examining bounded traces.

```
void g(int x) { if (x > 100) exit (0); }

void f() { assert(0); }

int main(int argc, char* argv[]) {
    for (int i=0; i < argc; i++) g(argc);
    f ();
}
```

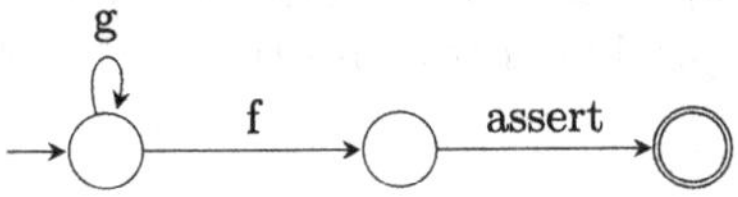

Fig. 2. A program and an automaton that we learn from it when using a low bound (< 100) on the word length.

We note that the automaton we generate is conceptually different from a control-flow graph (CFG) of a program mapped on a set of interesting events. This is because a CFG is based on the structure of a program, whereas the automaton generated by L^* is based on the actual executions, and in general, cannot be deduced from the CFG.

In the next sections, we briefly describe the L^* algorithm and define the language we learn precisely. We follow with a detailed description of our method, which is based on the L^* algorithm, using it mostly as a black box. We describe various aspects of our system and our empirical evaluation of it in Sect. 6, and conclude with some ideas for future research in Sect. 7. More examples can be found on the project's website [1].

2   Preliminaries – the L^* Algorithm

We start by revisiting the well-known definition of deterministic finite automata (cf. [18]).

Definition 1 (Determinisic Finite Automaton). *A deterministic finite automaton (DFA) $\mathcal{A}$ is a 5 tuple $\langle S, init, \Sigma, \delta, F \rangle$, where S is a finite set of states, $init \in S$ is the initial state, Σ is the alphabet, $\delta : S \times \Sigma \rightarrow S$ is the transition function, and $F \subseteq S$ is the set of accepting states. We denote by $L(\mathcal{A})$ the language accepted by the automaton $\mathcal{A}$.*

The *complement* operation on DFA $\mathcal{A}$ is naturally defined as $\bar{\mathcal{A}} = \langle S, init, \Sigma, \delta, S \setminus F \rangle$, that is, an automaton in which the accepting and non-accepting states are switched. A complement automaton accepts a complement language: $L(\bar{\mathcal{A}}) = \Sigma^* \setminus L(\mathcal{A})$.

The *intersection* operation $\mathcal{A}_1 \cap \mathcal{A}_2$, where $\mathcal{A}_1 = \langle S_1, init_1, \Sigma, \delta_1, F_1 \rangle$ and $\mathcal{A}_2 = \langle S_2, init_2, \Sigma, \delta_2, F_2 \rangle$, assuming the same alphabet, results in the automaton $\mathcal{A} = \langle S, init, \Sigma, \delta, F \rangle$, with the set of states S being a cross-product $S_1 \times S_2$ of the sets of states of $\mathcal{A}_1$ and $\mathcal{A}_2$, and the transition relation following the same letter on both parts of the state-pair. The initial state $init$ is defined as $init_1 \times init_2$, and the set of accepting states F is $F_1 \times F_2$ (that is, both $\mathcal{A}_1$ and $\mathcal{A}_2$ need to accept in order for $\mathcal{A}$ to accept). The language $L(\mathcal{A})$ is the intersection of languages $L(\mathcal{A}_1) \cap L(\mathcal{A}_2)$.

The *difference* operation between two languages of DFA, $L(\mathcal{A}_1) \setminus L(\mathcal{A}_2)$, is computed as the language of $\mathcal{A}_1 \cap \bar{\mathcal{A}}_2$, that is, an intersection of $\mathcal{A}_1$ with the complement of $\mathcal{A}_2$. The *symmetric difference* between $\mathcal{A}_1$ and $\mathcal{A}_2$ is computed as the union of $L(\mathcal{A}_1) \setminus L(\mathcal{A}_2)$ and $L(\mathcal{A}_2) \setminus L(\mathcal{A}_1)$. In understanding the behavior of programs, we find that it is easier to analyze both sides of the difference separately, hence we do not produce the automaton for the union of differences (though it can easily be done).

The L^* algorithm, developed by Angluin [3], introduces a framework for iterative learning of DFA. Essentially, L^* learns an unknown regular language $\mathcal{U}$ by iteratively constructing a minimal DFA $\mathcal{A}$ such that $L(\mathcal{A}) = \mathcal{U}$. The algorithm includes two types of queries: *membership queries* and conjecture queries. Angluin's original description of the entities that answer the two queries uses the terms 'teacher' and 'oracle'; for simplicity we unify them here under the name 'teacher'. Figure 3 describes the interaction of L^* with the teacher. L^* learns $\mathcal{U}$, by querying the teacher with two types of questions:

- *membership queries* (top arrow), namely whether for a given word $w \in \Sigma^*$, $w \in \mathcal{U}$, and
- *conjecture queries* (third arrow from top), namely whether a given conjectured automaton $\mathcal{A}$ has the property $L(\mathcal{A}) = \mathcal{U}$. If the answer is yes, L^* terminates with $\mathcal{A}$ as the answer. Otherwise it expects the teacher to provide a counterexample string σ such that $\sigma \in \mathcal{U} \setminus L(\mathcal{A})$ or $\sigma \in L(\mathcal{A}) \setminus \mathcal{U}$. In the first case, we call σ *positive* feedback, because it should be added to $L(\mathcal{A})$. In the second case, we call σ *negative* feedback since it should be removed from $L(\mathcal{A})$. Based on the counterexample, L^* initiates a new series of queries, until it converges on a DFA $\mathcal{A}$ such that $L(\mathcal{A}) = \mathcal{U}$.

L^* maintains a table (called an 'observation table') that records transitions and states, and is used to construct the resulting automaton $\mathcal{A} = \langle S, init, \Sigma, \delta, F \rangle$.

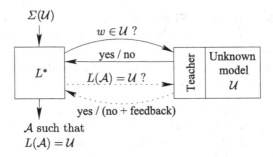

Fig. 3. The input and output of L^*, and its interaction with the teacher.

The states are defined by the prefixes they accept, and for each state s and each letter σ, the table defines whether $\delta(s, \sigma) \in F$. Let S' be a set of states currently in this table. A table is said to be *closed* if $\forall s \in S'. \forall \sigma \in \Sigma. \delta(s, \sigma) \in S'$. In other words, the table is closed when it represents a complete transition function. To close its table, L^* asks the teacher multiple membership queries. By construction, once the table is closed it represents a DFA. L^* presents this DFA as a conjecture query to the teacher. If the answer to the query is 'no', it analyzes the counterexample σ and adds states and transitions to accommodate it, which makes the table 'open' again. This leads to additional membership queries, and the process continues.

The underlying principle ensuring the convergence of the L^* algorithm is the Myhill-Nerode theorem [18], which provides a sufficient and necessary condition for a language to be regular. Since we assume that $\mathcal{U}$ is regular, L^* uses the Myhill-Nerode theorem to compute the equivalence classes of $\mathcal{U}$, which are mapped to the states of the final DFA. The number of queries is bounded by $O(km^2n^3)$, where k is the size of the alphabet, n is the number of states of the resulting (minimal) DFA, and m is the length of the longest feedback (counterexample).[2]

3   The Language We Learn

Our learning scheme is based on user-defined *events*, which are whatever a user chooses as their atoms for describing the behaviors that lead to an assertion violation. At source level, events are identified by instrumenting the code with a `Learn(id)` instruction at the desired position, where `id` is an identifier of the event. Typical locations for such instrumentation are at the entry to functions and branches, both of which can be done automatically by our tool. Each location obtains its own unique id.

The set of event identifiers constitutes the alphabet Σ of the automaton $\mathcal{A}$ that we construct. A sequence of events is a Σ-*word* that may or may not be in $L(\mathcal{A})$, the language of $\mathcal{A}$. For an instrumented program P, a trace π of P

---

[2] This is a simplified upper bound of the complexity of the L^* algorithm.

(further denoted as $\pi \in P$) induces a Σ-word, which we denote by $\alpha(\pi)$. The language of such a program, denoted $L(P)$, is defined naturally by

$$L(P) \doteq \{\alpha(\pi) \mid \pi \in P\}. \tag{1}$$

Recall that our goal is to obtain a representation over Σ of P's traces that violate a given assertion. Let φ be that assertion, and denote by $\pi \not\models \varphi$ the fact that a given trace violates φ. We now define

$$Fail(P) \doteq \{\alpha(\pi) \mid \pi \in P \land \pi \not\models \varphi\}. \tag{2}$$

In general, this set is irregular and incomputable and, even in cases in which it is computable, it is likely to contain too much information to be useful. However, if we bound the loops and recursion in P, this set becomes finite, and hence regular and computable. Let b be such a bound, and let

$$Fail(P, b) \doteq \{\alpha(\pi) \mid \pi \in P \land |\pi| \le b \land \pi \not\models \varphi\}, \tag{3}$$

where $|\pi|$ denotes the maximal number of loop iterations or recursive calls made along π. Restricting the set of paths this way implicitly restricts the length of the abstract traces that we consider, i.e., $|\alpha(\pi)| \le b'$, where b' can be computed from P and b. We also allow users to bound the word length $|\alpha(\pi)|$ directly with another value b^{wl}. In Sect. 6 we will describe strategies for obtaining such bounds automatically. Based on these bounds we define

$$Fail(P, b, b^{wl}) \doteq \{\alpha(\pi) \mid \pi \in P \land |\pi| \le b \land |\alpha(\pi)| \le b^{wl} \land \pi \not\models \varphi\}. \tag{4}$$

The DFA, $\mathcal{A}$, that we learn and present to the user has the following property for all $\pi \in P$:

$$|\pi| \le b \land |\alpha(\pi)| \le b^{wl} \land \alpha(\pi) \in L(\mathcal{A}) \iff \alpha(\pi) \in Fail(P, b, b^{wl}). \tag{5}$$

4 L^* and the Queries

Consider the automaton in Fig. 2, which is learned by our system from the program on the left of the same figure, when $b = b^{wl} = 4$. This automaton is the second conjecture of L^*. Let us briefly review the steps L^* follows that lead to this conjecture. Initially it has a single state with no transitions. Then it asks the teacher three single-letter membership queries: whether f, g and assert are in $\mathcal{U}$. The answer is 'no' to all three since, e.g., we cannot reach an assertion failure on a path hitting f alone (in fact the first two are trivially false because they do not end with assert).

After answering these queries, L^* has a closed table corresponding to the automaton on the right: an automaton with one non-accepting state. It poses this automaton as a conjecture to the teacher, which answers 'no' and returns $\sigma = $ f $\cdot$ assert as positive feedback, i.e., this word should be added to $L(\mathcal{A})$. Now L^* poses 12 more membership queries and conjectures the automaton in Fig. 2. The teacher answers 'yes', which terminates the algorithm.   □

We continue by describing the teacher in our case, namely how we answer those queries. The source code of P is instrumented with two functions: LEARN(ID) at a location of each Σ-event (recall that ID is the identifier of the event), and LEARN_ASSERT at the location of the assertion that is being investigated. The implementation of these functions depends on whether we are checking a membership or a conjecture query, as we will now show.

4.1 Membership Queries

A membership query is as follows: "given a word w, is there a $\pi \in P$ such that $\alpha(\pi) = w$ and $\pi \not\models \varphi$?" Fig. 4 gives sample code that we generate for a membership query — in this case for the word $(3 \cdot 3 \cdot 6 \cdot 2 \cdot 0)$. The letter '0' always symbolizes an assertion failure event, and indeed queries that do not end with '0' are trivially rejected. This code, which is an implementation of the instrumented functions mentioned above, is added to P, and the combined code is then checked with the Bounded Model Checker for software CBMC [12]. CBMC supports 'assume($pred$)' statements, which block any path that does not satisfy the predicate $pred$. In lines 4–5 we use this feature to block paths that are not compatible with w.

LEARN_ASSERT is called when the path arrives at the checked assertion, and declares the membership to be true (i.e., $w \in L(\mathcal{A})$) if the assertion fails exactly at the end of the word.

```
 1: int word[|w|] = {3, 3, 6, 2, 0};                    ▷ The checked word w
 2: int idx = 0;
 3: function VOID LEARN(int x)                           ▷ Event
 4:    if idx ≥ |w| ∨ word[idx] ≠ x then
 5:       assume(FALSE);                  ▷ Block paths incompatible with query
 6:    idx = idx + 1;
 7: function LEARN_ASSERT(bool assertCondition)
 8:    if ¬assertCondition then                          ▷ Assertion fail
 9:       if idx = |w| − 1 then assert(FALSE);   ▷ w ∈ L(A). Answer 'true' to query
10:       assume(FALSE);                  ▷ Arrived here at the wrong time: block path.
```

Fig. 4. Sample (pseudo) code generated for a particular membership query.

Optimisations. We bypass a CBMC call and answer 'no' to a membership query if one of the following holds:

- The query does not end with a call to assert,
- The query contains more than one call to assert,
- w is incompatible with the control-flow graph.

4.2   Conjecture Queries

A conjecture query is: "given a DFA $\mathcal{A}$, is there a $\pi \in P$ such that

- $\alpha(\pi) \in L(\mathcal{A}) \wedge \pi \models \varphi$, or
- $\alpha(\pi) \notin L(\mathcal{A}) \wedge \pi \not\models \varphi$?"

The two cases correspond to negative and positive feedback to L^*, respectively.

Figure 5 presents the code that we add to P when checking a conjecture query. The candidate $\mathcal{A}$ is given in a two-dimensional array, A, and the accepting states of $\mathcal{A}$ are given in an array *accepting* (both are not shown here). *path* is an array that captures the abstract path, as can be seen in the implementation of LEARN. LEARN_ASSERT simulates the path accumulated so far (lines 6–7) on $\mathcal{A}$ in order to find the current state. It then aborts if one of the two conditions above holds. In both cases the path *path* serves as the feedback to L^*.

```
1:  function LEARN(int x)                                         ▷ Event
2:     path[++idx] = x;
3:  function LEARN_ASSERT(bool assertCondition)
4:     if ¬assertCondition then LEARN(0);              ▷ 0 = the 'assert' letter
5:     char state = 0;
6:     for (int i = 0; i < idx; ++i) do
7:        state = A[state][path[i]];                           ▷ Finding current state.
8:     if assertCondition ∧ accepting[state] then assert(FALSE);   ▷ neg. feedback
9:     if ¬assertCondition ∧ ¬accepting[state] then assert(FALSE);  ▷ pos. feedback
```

Fig. 5. Code added to P for checking conjecture queries.

Eliminating Spurious Words. The conjecture-query mechanism described above only applies to paths ending with LEARN_ASSERT. Other paths should be rejected, and for this we add a 'trap' at the exit points of the program. The implementation of this function appears in Fig. 6. It ends with negative feedback if the current path is a prefix of a path that a) reaches an accepting state in $\mathcal{A}$ (line 6), and b) was not marked earlier as belonging to $L(\mathcal{A})$ (line 7). The reason for this filtering is that the same abstract path (word) can belong to both a real abstract path $p \in P$ and to a path $p' \notin P$ that we chose nondeterministically in this function (see line 9). For example, a path $p = 1 \cdot 1 \cdot 2 \cdot 0$ can exist in P (recall that the '0' at the end of this path means that it violates the assertion), but there is another path p' that does not go via any of these locations and reaches LEARN_TRAP, which nondeterministically chooses this path.

We now show that the above implementation indeed guarantees the properties described in Eq. (5):

Theorem 1. *The implementations of Figs. 5 and 6 ensure that for all $\pi \in P$:*

$$|\pi| \leq b \wedge |\alpha(\pi)| \leq b^{wl} \wedge \alpha(\pi) \in L(\mathcal{A}) \iff \alpha(\pi) \in Fail(P, b, b^{wl}) \,.$$

```
1: function LEARN_TRAP
2:    char state = 0;
3:    for (; idx < b^{wl}; ++idx) do
4:       for (int i = 0; i ≤ idx; ++i) do              ▷ Compute current state in A
5:          state = A[state][path[i]];
6:       if accepting[state] then                      ▷ state is an accepting state
7:          if path ∈ L(A) is known then assume(FALSE);   ▷ Block path
8:       assert(FALSE);                                 ▷ Negative feedback
9:       path[idx] = non-deterministic element from Σ;
```

Fig. 6. LEARN_TRAP is called at P's exit points. It gives negative feedback to conjecture queries in which $\exists w \in L(\mathcal{A})$ such that w does not correspond to any path in P.

Proof. $\Rightarrow$ We need to show that for all $\pi \in P$

$$|\pi| \le b \wedge |\alpha(\pi)| \le b^{wl} \wedge \alpha(\pi) \in L(\mathcal{A}) \quad \Rightarrow \quad |\pi| \le b \wedge |\alpha(\pi)| \le b^{wl} \wedge \pi \not\models \varphi$$

The first two conjuncts are trivially true. We prove the third by contradiction. Thus assume that $\pi \models \varphi$. We separate the discussion to two cases:

- $\alpha(\pi)$ ends with a LEARN_ASSERT statement. In the (last) conjecture query π calls that function, which appears in Fig. 5. Since $\pi \models \varphi$ the guard in line 4 is false. In line 7 $state$, in the last iteration of the for loop, is accepting, because we know from the premise that $\alpha(\pi) \in L(\mathcal{A})$. This fails the assertion in line 8, and the conjecture is rejected. Contradiction.

- Otherwise, in the (last) conjecture query, π calls the trap function of Fig. 6. In line 5 $state$, in the end of the for loop, is accepting, again because we know from the premise that $\alpha(\pi) \in L(\mathcal{A})$. The condition in line 7 is false, and the assert(0) in the following line is reached. The conjecture is rejected. Contradiction.

$\Leftarrow$ We need to show that for all $\pi \in P$

$$|\pi| \le b \wedge |\alpha(\pi)| \le b^{wl} \wedge \alpha(\pi) \in L(\mathcal{A}) \quad \Leftarrow \quad |\pi| \le b \wedge |\alpha(\pi)| \le b^{wl} \wedge \pi \not\models \varphi$$

Again, the first two conjuncts are trivially true, and we prove the third by contradiction: assume that $\alpha(\pi) \notin L(\mathcal{A})$. Since $\pi \not\models \varphi$, π must end with a call to LEARN_ASSERT. Hence in the (last) conjecture query π calls that function, which appears in Fig. 5. By our premise, the state is not accepting. Hence the condition in line 9 is met, and $\alpha(\pi)$ is returned as a positive feedback to L^*, which adds it to $\mathcal{A}$. Contradiction. □

The trap function has an additional benefit: it brings us close to the following desired property for every word $w \in \Sigma^*$:

$$w \in L(\mathcal{A}) \wedge |w| \le b^{wl} \implies \exists \pi \in P. \, \alpha(\pi) = w \,. \tag{6}$$

That is, ideally we should exclude from $L(\mathcal{A})$ any word w, $|w| \le b^{wl}$ that does *not* correspond to a path in P. The reason that this trap function does not guarantee (6) is that it only catches a word $w \in L(\mathcal{A})$ if there is a path $\pi \in P$ to an exit point, such that $\alpha(\pi)$ is a prefix of w. In other cases, the user can check the legality of $w \in L(\mathcal{A})$ either manually or with a membership query.

Optimisation. We can bypass a CBMC call in the following case: consider an automaton $\mathcal{A}_{cfg}$ in which the states and transitions are identical to those of the control-flow graph (CFG) of P, and every state is accepting. Since the elements of Σ correspond to locations in the program we can associate them with nodes in the CFG. Hence, we can define $L_\Sigma(\mathcal{A}_{cfg})$, the language of $\mathcal{A}_{cfg}$ projected to Σ. Then if $L(\mathcal{A}) \not\subseteq L_\Sigma(\mathcal{A}_{cfg})$, return 'no', with an element of $L(\mathcal{A}) \setminus L_\Sigma(\mathcal{A}_{cfg})$ as the negative feedback.

5   Usage Scenarios for the Learning Framework

The framework presented in the paper is constructed in order to understand the language of software errors. That is, given a program with errors reported from the verification process, applying the learning algorithm results in a DFA that presents an abstraction of the bounded language of error traces of the program to important events, as defined in Theorem 1. The automaton represents the set of error traces in a concise and compact way and is amenable to standard analyses on DFAs, such as the computation of *dominators* and *doomed states and transitions*. These analyses aid in understanding the *root cause* of errors.

Beyond the language of software errors, our framework can be applied, without changes, to the task of *program explanation*. As illustrated by the Docking software example in Sect. 6.2, modern-day programs are often very difficult to understand. This is either because of the sheer complexity of the implementation, because of a change in ownership of the code, or because the program was, at least in part, generated automatically. By adding a failing assertion to the exit point of the program, our framework produces a DFA that represents a bounded regular abstraction of the program behavior with respect to important events (as defined by the user or defined automatically).

Finally, we extend our framework to assist in merging several software development branches. In this common scenario, several developers make changes to different branches of the same (version controlled) source code. Often, when the developers attempt to merge their changes back into the parent branch, *automatic merging* is performed by the version control system. This can introduce unexpected behavior. For example, consider the source code in Fig. 7, representing an original program, its two branches developed independently, and the result of a widely used automatic merge (this example is taken from [20]). Note that the merge operation creates an unexpected behavior, where `functionZ()` calls `functionC()`, despite this not being either developer's intent.

Using our framework, both versions and the merged program are represented as DFAs, and the difference between the merged program and each branch is computed as a difference between automata (see Sect. 2). Figures 8 and 9 draw attention to the new behavior introduced by the automatic merge.

```
main {              main {              main {              main {
  ...                 ...                 ...                 ...
  functionA();        functionA();        functionA();        functionA();
  functionB();        ...                 functionB();        ...
  ...}                functionZ();}       functionC();        functionZ();
                                          ... }               }
                    functionZ() {
                      functionB();}                         functionZ() {
                                                              functionB();
                                                              functionC();
                                                              ...}

   (a) Source        (b) Branch A         (c) Branch B         (d) Merged
```

Fig. 7. The effects of automatic merge in a version control system.

Fig. 8. Behavior not in Branch A   **Fig. 9.** Behavior not in Branch B

The changes are easy to see in small examples; in arbitrarily large programs, however, the issues introduced by an automatic merge could be hard to identify. Moreover, this behavior in larger programs might be difficult to understand due to a lack of single ownership over the code. This mechanism can also be applied to merge *conflicts* (i.e., when different versions of code cannot be merged automatically), in order to visually display differences between branches, rather than annotating the repository code directly with conflict markers.

6   System Description and Empirical Evaluation

In this section, we discuss the possible optimisations of the algorithm and present experimental results of executing our framework on standard benchmarks.

6.1   Optimisations

Determining the Bounds. The automatic estimation of suitable values for both the loop bound b and the word length b^{wl} contributes significantly to the usability of our framework. Our strategy for this is illustrated in Fig. 10. We let b range between 1 and b_{max}, where b_{max} is relatively small (4 in our default configuration). This reflects the fact that higher values of b may have a negative impact on performance, and that in practice, with CBMC low values of b are sufficient for triggering the error. As an initial value for b^{wl} (b_{min}^{wl}), we take a

```
1: function LEARNUPTOBOUND(Program P)
2:    for b ∈ [1 ... b_max] do
3:       for b^{wl} ∈ [b^{wl}_{min} ... b^{wl}_{max}] do
4:          A = learn P with b and b^{wl};
5:          if A = A_{prev} and A does not have back edges then return A;
6:       A_{prev} = A;
```

Fig. 10. The autonomous discovery of the appropriate bounds.

conservative estimation of the shortest word possible, according to a light-weight analysis of the control-flow graph of P. We increase the value of b^{wl} up to a maximum of b^{wl}_{max}, which is user-defined. The value of b^{wl}_{max} reflects an estimation of how long these words can be before the explanation becomes unintelligible.

Recall that the value of b implies a bound on the word length (we denoted it b' in Sect. 3), and hence for a given b, increasing the explicit bound on the word length b^{wl} beyond a certain value is meaningless. In other words, for a given b, the process of increasing b^{wl} converges. Until convergence, the number of states of A can both increase and decrease as a result of increasing b^{wl} (it can decrease because paths not belonging to the language are caught in the conjecture query, which may lead to a smaller automaton).

Figure 11 demonstrates this fact for one of the benchmarks (bubble sort with $b = 2$). We are not aware of a way to detect convergence in PTIME, so in practice we terminate when two conditions hold (see line 5): a) A has not changed from the previous iteration, and b) A does not contain edges leaving an accepting state ('back edges'). Recall that a failing assertion aborts execution, and hence no path can continue beyond it. Therefore, the existence of such edges in A indicates that increasing b, b^{wl} or both should eventually remove them.

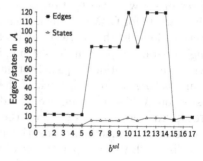

Fig. 11. Size of A (bubble sort example).

Incrementality. The incremental nature of LEARNUPTOBOUND is exploited by our system for improving performance. We maintain a cache of words that have already been proven to be in U, and consult it as the first step of answering membership queries. Negative results from membership queries can only be cached and reused if this result does not depend on the bound. For example, the optimisation mentioned in Sect. 4, by which we reject words that are not compatible with the control-flow graph, does not depend on the bound and hence can be cached and reused. In our experiments caching reduces the number of membership queries sent to CBMC by an average of 32 %.

Post-processing. Our system performs the following post-processing on $\mathcal{A}$ in order to assist the user:

- Marking *dominating edges*: edges that represent events that must occur in order to reach the accepting state. In order to detect these edges, we remove each event in turn (recall that the same event can label more than one edge), and check whether the accepting state is still reachable from the root.
- Marking *doomed states*: states such that the accepting state is inevitable [17].
- Removing the (non-accepting) sink state and its incoming edges: Such a state always exists, because the outgoing edges of the accepting state must transition to it (because, recall, an assertion failure corresponds to aborting the execution). Missing transitions, then, are interpreted as rejection.

6.2   Implementation and Evaluation

Our implementation of the learning framework is based on the automata library libalf [10] as the L^* component and the bounded software model-checker for C CBMC [12] as the 'teacher' component and includes the optimisations described in Sect. 6.1. The modular implementation allows to replace both the L^* and the teacher component with other alternatives, which we discuss in Sect. 7.

We applied our framework to learn the language of error associated with a set of software verification benchmarks (that are relatively easy as verification targets for CBMC) drawn from three sources: the Competition on Software Verification [9], the Software-artifact Infrastructure Repository[3], and a 'docking' program: a program describing the behavior of a space shuttle as it docks with the International Space Station (an open-source version of the NASA system *Docking_Approach*). Each of these programs contain a single instrumented assertion. Whilst learning, we record our estimated $b_{\min}^{wl}$, and when LEARNUP-TOBOUND terminates we record the values of b^{wl}, the number of iterations, b, the total CPU time in seconds, the number of states and edges in $\mathcal{A}$, the number of calls to CBMC as a percentage of the total membership queries, and the total number of conjecture queries. All experiments were conducted on a computer with a 3.2 GHz quad-core processor and 6 GB of DDR3 RAM. The results are summarized in Table 1. We also tested a strategy by which we do not return at line 5 of Fig. 10 (recall that the condition there does not guarantee convergence), and rather only print $\mathcal{A}$. The multiple entries of b^{wl} and b for the same example in Table 1 reflect this.

Next, we present several examples of $\mathcal{A}$ from this benchmark set. Bold edges in our figures indicate dominating events, e.g., the function inspect in Fig. 12 is marked as dominating because a path to the error *must* call it. Doomed states are labelled with 'D'. (In this and later examples all states have paths to the non-accepting sink-state which we remove in post-processing, as explained above. Hence only the accepting state is marked doomed).

Figures 12 and 13 give $\mathcal{A}$ in the bubble sort example with bounds $(b, b^{wl}) = (2, 12)$ and $(b, b^{wl}) = (3, 15)$ respectively. The example constructs a linked list

---

[3] http://sir.unl.edu/.

Table 1. Experimental results. b_{min}^{wl} is our initial bound estimation. b^{wl}, *It.*, b and Time pertain to the process in LEARNUPTOBOUND, which produces $\mathcal{A}$. We give the number of states and edges of $\mathcal{A}$. We also list the percentage of membership queries made to CBMC, and the total number of conjecture queries.

Target	b_{min}^{wl}	b^{wl}	*It.*	b	Time [sec]	States	Edges	C BMC Queries memb.	conj.
tcas	3	17	14	1	7.76	25	28	0.51 %	34
bubble_sort	8	16	8	2	1.61	10	10	0.17 %	66
bubble_sort	8	19	19	3	4.24	19	21	0.13 %	96
merge_sort	4	8	4	1	0.13	4	3	0.92 %	12
merge_sort	4	12	12	2	0.74	7	9	2.90 %	40
sll_to_dll_rev	8	28	20	1	2.83	14	13	0.18 %	39
sll_to_dll_rev	8	28	40	2	7.28	17	19	0.15 %	78
defroster	25	29	4	1	32.92	14	18	0.01 %	26
docking	5	8	3	1	0.49	7	6	0.86 %	9
docking	5	8	6	2	0.72	7	6	0.86 %	18
docking	5	11	12	2	1.65	11	11	1.04 %	27

of non-deterministic size and contains a bug where the root node linkage is not initialized correctly. The bug can thus occur after an arbitrary amount of node insertions by the `gl_insert` operation. Using Fig. 12 we can conjecture that the bug either occurs after one or two insertions. In Fig. 13 L^* then correctly conjectures a loop and represents the whole nature of the bug with $b^{wl} = 15$. Whether L^* is able to conjecture a loop is dependent on multiple factors, but ultimately linked to the word length bound b^{wl}. Our membership query oracle will reject any word which is longer than b^{wl}. However, this limitation does not apply in the conjecture oracle. Since L^* at $b^{wl} = 15$ does not pose any membership queries exceeding this limit, the result in Fig. 13 ensues. The membership query list posed by L^* is dependent on the counter-examples provided by CBMC, which vary for different values of b and b^{wl}.

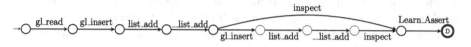

Fig. 12. Automaton produced for the 'bubble_sort' example. $b^{wl} = 12$. $b = 2$.

Figure 14 shows the 'docking' benchmark, with $b = 4, b^{wl} = 15$. This automaton is an example of a *program explanation* usage scenario. The C source code of the program was automatically generated from an existing MatLab module and is thus not optimized for readability. Furthermore, the original MatLab model may

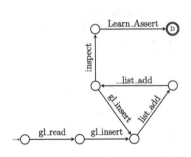

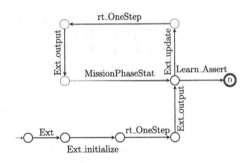

Fig. 13. Automaton produced for the 'bubble_sort' example. $b^{wl} = 15$. $b = 3$.

Fig. 14. Automaton produced for the 'docking' benchmark. $b^{wl} = 15$. $b = 4$.

not accurately describe how the respective program semantics was mapped to C. The automaton in Fig. 14 can explain the core behavior of the mapped program. It consists of a stepwise main simulation loop in which the logic of all mission-related phases is handled in the operation `MissionPhaseStat`. The source code and the learned automata of all our benchmarks are available online [1], where the reader may observe the effect of an interactive change of bounds.

7 Conclusions and Future Work

Our definition of $Fail(P)$ in (2) captures the 'language of error', but this language is, in the general case, not computable. We have presented a method for automatically learning a DFA, $\mathcal{A}$, that captures a well-defined subset of this language (see Theorem 1), for the purpose of assisting the user in understanding the cause of the error. More generally, the same technique can be used for visualising the behavior of a program or parts thereof, hence aiding in program understanding – a direction that becomes especially relevant when the software in question is prohibitively large to be examined manually, or when the code owner is not available (or, as in our docking software example, the software was generated automatically). We demonstrated that the same technique can also be used for visually comparing different versions of a program (by presenting an automaton that captures the behavior in the symmetric difference between them), or for assisting in merging several development branches.

A possible extension is to adapt the framework to learn ω-regular languages, represented by Büchi automata (see [4,14] for the extension of L^* to ω-regular languages). This extension would enable the learning of behaviors that violate the liveness properties of non-terminating programs.

Another future direction is learning non-regular languages, as it will enable the learning of richer abstract representations of the language of error for a given program. Context-free grammars are of particular interest because of the natural connection between context-free grammars and the syntax of programming languages; some subclasses of context-free grammars have been shown to be learnable, such as k-bounded context free grammars [2], (though in general, the class of context-free grammars is not believed to be learnable [5]), providing us with the possibility of harnessing these algorithms in our framework.

As mentioned in Sect. 6.2, the modularity of our implementation allows us to replace CBMC with another component, acting as a 'teacher' in our framework. In particular, we can use a software testing tool as a 'teacher', thus potentially improving the scalability of the framework. The learned language, however, will likely differ from the one in Theorem 1 if the answers to queries are based on the results of software testing.

One of the main goals of our framework is to present the language of error (or interesting behavior) in a compact, easy to analyze and understandable way. Hence, small automata are preferable, at least for manual analysis. Even for a given alphabet Σ, we believe it should be possible to reduce the size of the learned DFA $\mathcal{A}$, based on the observation that we *do not care* whether a word w such that $\forall \pi \in P.|\pi| \leq b \wedge |\alpha(\pi)| \leq b^{wl} \Rightarrow \alpha(\pi) \neq w$ is accepted or rejected by the automaton. Adding a 'don't care' value to the learning scheme requires a learning mechanism that can recognize three-valued answers (see [19] for a learning algorithm with inconclusive answers).

References

1. http://www.cprover.org/learning-errors/
2. Angluin, D.: Learning k-bounded context-free grammars. Technical report, Dept. of Computer Science, Yale University (1987)
3. Angluin, D.: Learning regular sets from queries and counterexamples. Inf. Comput. **75**(2), 87–106 (1987)
4. Angluin, D., Fisman, D.: Learning regular omega languages. In: Auer, P., Clark, A., Zeugmann, T., Zilles, S. (eds.) ALT 2014. LNCS, vol. 8776, pp. 125–139. Springer, Heidelberg (2014)
5. Angluin, D., Kharitonov, M.: When won't membership queries help? (extended abstract). In: Proceedings of 23rd STOC, pp. 444–454. ACM (1991)
6. Ball, T., Naik, M., Rajamani, S.K.: From symptom to cause: localizing errors in counterexample traces. In: Proceedings of 30th POPL, pp. 97–105 (2003)
7. Basu, S., Saha, D., Lin, Y.-J., Smolka, S.A.: Generation of all counter-examples. In: König, H., Heiner, M., Wolisz, A. (eds.) FORTE 2003. LNCS, vol. 2767, pp. 79–94. Springer, Heidelberg (2003)
8. Beer, I., Ben-David, S., Chockler, H., Orni, A., Trefler, R.J.: Explaining counterexamples using causality. Formal Methods Syst. Des. **40**(1), 20–40 (2012)
9. Beyer, D.: Software verification and verifiable witnesses. In: Baier, C., Tinelli, C. (eds.) TACAS 2015. LNCS, vol. 9035, pp. 401–416. Springer, Heidelberg (2015)
10. Bollig, B., Katoen, J.-P., Kern, C., Leucker, M., Neider, D., Piegdon, D.R.: libalf: the automata learning framework. In: Touili, T., Cook, B., Jackson, P. (eds.) CAV 2010. LNCS, vol. 6174, pp. 360–364. Springer, Heidelberg (2010)
11. Botinčan, M., Babić, D.: Sigma*: symbolic learning of input-output specifications. In: Proc. of 40th POPL, pp. 443–456. ACM (2013)
12. Clarke, E., Kroning, D., Lerda, F.: A tool for checking ANSI-C programs. In: Jensen, K., Podelski, A. (eds.) TACAS 2004. LNCS, vol. 2988, pp. 168–176. Springer, Heidelberg (2004)

13. Copty, F., Irron, A., Weissberg, O., Kropp, N.P., Kamhi, G.: Efficient debugging in a formal verification environment. STTT **4**(3), 335–348 (2003)
14. Farzan, A., Chen, Y.-F., Clarke, E.M., Tsay, Y.-K., Wang, B.-Y.: Extending automated compositional verification to the full class of omega-regular languages. In: Ramakrishnan, C.R., Rehof, J. (eds.) TACAS 2008. LNCS, vol. 4963, pp. 2–17. Springer, Heidelberg (2008)
15. Giannakopoulou, D., Rakamarić, Z., Raman, V.: Symbolic learning of component interfaces. In: Miné, A., Schmidt, D. (eds.) SAS 2012. LNCS, vol. 7460, pp. 248–264. Springer, Heidelberg (2012)
16. Groce, A., Chaki, S., Kroening, D., Strichman, O.: Error explanation with distance metrics. STTT **8**(3), 229–247 (2006)
17. Hoenicke, J., Leino, K., Podelski, A., Schäf, M., Wies, T.: Doomed program points. Formal Methods Syst. Des. **37**(2–3), 171–199 (2010)
18. Hopcroft, J., Motwani, R., Ullman, J.: Introduction to Automata Theory, Languages, and Computation, 2nd edn. Addison-Wesley, Reading (2000)
19. Leucker, M., Neider, D.: Learning minimal deterministic automata from inexperienced teachers. In: Margaria, T., Steffen, B. (eds.) ISoLA 2012, Part I. LNCS, vol. 7609, pp. 524–538. Springer, Heidelberg (2012)
20. The problem of automatic code merging (2012). http://www.personal.psu.edu/txl20/blogs/tks_tech_notes/2012/03/the-problem-of-automatic-code-merging.html

Explicit Model Checking of Very Large MDP Using Partitioning and Secondary Storage

Arnd Hartmanns[(✉)] and Holger Hermanns

Department of Computer Science, Saarland University, Saarbrücken, Germany
{arnd,hermanns}@cs.uni-saarland.de

Abstract. The applicability of model checking is hindered by the state space explosion problem in combination with limited amounts of main memory. To extend its reach, the large available capacities of secondary storage such as hard disks can be exploited. Due to the specific performance characteristics of secondary storage technologies, specialised algorithms are required. In this paper, we present a technique to use secondary storage for probabilistic model checking of Markov decision processes. It combines state space exploration based on partitioning with a block-iterative variant of value iteration over the same partitions for the analysis of probabilistic reachability and expected-reward properties. A sparse matrix-like representation is used to store partitions on secondary storage in a compact format. All file accesses are sequential, and compression can be used without affecting runtime. The technique has been implemented within the MODEST TOOLSET. We evaluate its performance on several benchmark models of up to 3.5 billion states. In the analysis of time-bounded properties on real-time models, our method neutralises the state space explosion induced by the time bound in its entirety.

1 Introduction

Model checking [9] is a formal verification technique to ensure that a given model of the states and behaviours of a safety- or performance-critical system satisfies a set of requirements. We are interested in models that consider *nondeterminism* as well as quantitative aspects of systems in terms of *time* and *probabilities*. Such models can be represented as Markov decision processes (MDP [32]) and verified with *probabilistic model checking*. However, the applicability of model checking is limited by the state space explosion problem: The number of states of a model grows exponentially in the number of variables and parallel components, yet they have to be represented in limited computer memory in some form. Probabilistic model checking is particularly affected due to its additional numerical complexity. Several techniques are available to stretch its limits: For example, symbolic

---

This work is supported by the EU 7th Framework Programme under grant agreements 295261 (MEALS) and 318490 (SENSATION), by the DFG as part of SFB/TR 14 AVACS, by the CAS/SAFEA International Partnership Program for Creative Research Teams, and by the CDZ project CAP (GZ 1023).

© Springer International Publishing Switzerland 2015
B. Finkbeiner et al. (Eds.): ATVA 2015, LNCS 9364, pp. 131–147, 2015.
DOI: 10.1007/978-3-319-24953-7_10

probabilistic model checking [2], implemented in the PRISM tool [25], uses variants of binary decision diagrams (BDD) to compactly represent the state spaces of well-structured models in memory at the cost of verification runtime. Partial order [4] and confluence reduction [35] deliver smaller-but-equivalent state spaces and work particularly well for highly symmetric models. When trading accuracy for tractability or efficiency is acceptable, abstraction and refinement techniques like CEGAR [23] can be applied. The common theme is that these approaches aim at reducing the state space or its representation such that it fits, in its entirety, into the main memory of the machine used for model checking. An alternative is to store this data on secondary storage such as hard disks or solid state drives and only load small parts of it into main memory when and as needed. This is attractive due to the vast difference in size between main memory and secondary storage: Typical workstations today possess in the order of 4–8 GB of main memory, but easily 1 TB or more of hard disk space. Moreover, with the advent of dynamically scalable cloud storage, virtually unlimited off-site secondary storage has become easily accessible. For conciseness, we from now on refer to main memory as *memory* and to any kind of secondary storage as *disk*.

In this paper, we present a method and tool implementation for disk-based probabilistic model checking of MDP. Any such approach must solve two tasks: State space *exploration*, the generation and storage on disk of a representation of the reachable part of the state space, and the disk-based *analysis* to verify the given properties of interest based on this representation. The core challenge is that the most common type of secondary storage, magnetic hard disks, exhibits extremely low random-access performance, yet standard memory-based methods for exploration and analysis access the state space in a practically random way.

Previous Work. Exploration is an implicit graph search problem, and a number of solutions that reduce the amount of random accesses during search have been proposed in the literature. These fall into three broad categories: (*i*) exploiting the layered structure of breadth-first search (BFS) by keeping only the current BFS layer in memory while delaying duplicate detection w.r.t. previous layers until the current one has been fully explored [12,33]; (*ii*) partitioning the state space according to some given or automatically computed partitioning function over the states and then loading only one partition into memory at a time in an iterative process [5,16]; (*iii*) treating memory purely as a cache for a disk-based search, but using clever hashing and hash partitioning techniques to reduce and sequentialise disk accesses [19]. Exploration can naturally be combined on-the-fly with checking for the reachability of error states, and methods to perform on-the-fly verification of liveness and LTL properties exist [6,13,15].

The analysis of other logics, such as CTL model checking with satisfaction sets, and of other models, such as probabilistic model checking of MDP with value iteration, inherently require the entire state space for a dedicated analysis step following exploration. Previous work on disk-based probabilistic model checking considers purely stochastic models and focusses on the analysis phase:

In absence of nondeterminism, classical block-iterative methods [34] can be used with disk-based (sparse) matrix representations of Markov models. They proceed by loading into memory and analysing one matrix block at a time (plus those that it depends on) iteratively until the method has converged for all blocks. Implementations can be divided into *matrix-out-of-core* and *complete out-of-core* approaches [30]. In the former, the vector of state values being iteratively computed is still kept in memory in its entirety [11]. It is similar to how PRISM [25] uses BDD in its "HYBRID" engine for the model only, while both model and values are represented symbolically in its "MTBDD" engine. The symbolic and disk-based approaches for Markov chains can be combined [24]. Further work on the disk-based analysis of purely stochastic models includes different implementations that are both disk-based and parallelised or distributed [7,20].

For the nondeterministic-probabilistic model of MDP that we are concerned with, the default scalable analysis algorithm used in model checking is value iteration, an iterative fixpoint method that updates the values of each state based on a function over the values of its immediate successors until all changes remain below a given error. We are aware of only one explicitly disk-based approach to value iteration, which associates the values to the transitions instead of the states and is based on sequentially traversing two files containing the transitions that have been externally sorted by source and target states in each iteration [14]. However, external sorting is a costly operation, leading to high runtime.

The correctness of value iteration depends neither on the order in which the updates are performed nor on how many updates a state receives in one iteration. This can be exploited to improve its performance by taking the graph structure of the underlying model into account to perform more updates for "relevant" states in a "good" order. One such technique is topological value iteration [10], based on a division of the MDP into strongly connected components. More generally, this means that value iteration can also be performed in a block-iterative manner.

Our Contribution. The technique for disk-based probabilistic model checking of MDP that we present in this paper is a complete out-of-core method. It combines the state space partitioning approach from disk-based search with a block-iterative variant of value iteration based on a very compact sparse matrix-like representation of the partitions on disk. In light of the disk space available, compactness seems at first sight to be a non-issue, but in fact is a crucial aspect due to the low throughput of hard disks compared to main memory. Based on a given partitioning function, our approach proceeds by first exploring the partitions of the state space using an explicit state representation while directly streaming the sparse matrix-like representation to disk. When exploration is completed, the stored partitions are analysed using a block-based variant of value iteration: It iterates in an outer loop over the partitions on disk, for each of which value iterations are performed in an inner loop until convergence. All read and write operations on the files we generate on disk are sequential. We can thus easily add compression, which in our experiments reduces the amount of disk space needed by a factor of up to 10 without affecting overall runtime.

Our method has been implemented by extending the mcsta tool [18] of the MODEST TOOLSET [22]. The implementation currently supports the computation of reachability probabilities and expected accumulated rewards. To the best of our knowledge, mcsta is at this point the only publicly available tool that provides disk-based verification of MDP. We have evaluated the approach and its implementation on five case studies. The largest model we consider has 3.5 billion states. It can be explored and analysed in less than 8 hours using no more than 2 GB of memory and 30 GB disk space. Our technique is particularly efficient for the analysis of time-bounded properties on real-time extensions of MDP. In these cases, the overhead of using the disk is small and the enormous state space explosion caused by the time bounds can be neutralised in its entirety.

2 Preliminaries

The central formal model that we use are Markov decision processes:

Definition 1. *A* probability distribution *over a countable set Ω is a function $\mu \in \Omega \to [0,1]$ such that $\sum_{\omega \in \Omega} \mu(\omega) = 1$. Its* support *is* $\mathrm{support}(\mu) = \{\, s \in S \mid \mu(s) > 0 \,\}$. *We denote by* $\mathrm{Dist}(\Omega)$ *the set of all probability distributions over Ω.*

Definition 2. *A* Markov decision process *(MDP) is a triple $\langle S, T, s_0 \rangle$ consisting of a countable set of* states *S, a* transition function *$T \in S \to 2^{\mathrm{Dist}(S \times R)}$ for a countable subset $R \subsetneq \mathbb{R}$ with $T(s)$ countable for all $s \in S$, and an* initial state *$s_0 \in S$. A* partitioning function *for an MDP is a function $f \in S \to \{\, 1, \ldots, k \,\}$ for some $k \in \mathbb{N}$ with $f(s_0) = 1$.*

For $s \in S$, we call $\mu \in T(s)$ a *transition* of s, and a pair $b = \langle s', r \rangle \in \mathrm{support}(\mu)$ a *branch* of μ, with s' being the *target state* of b and r being the associated *reward* value. MDP support both nondeterministic and probabilistic choices: A state can have multiple outgoing transitions, each of which leads into a probability distribution over pairs $\langle s, r \rangle$. A partitioning function $f \in S \to \{\, 1, \ldots, n \,\}, n \in \mathbb{N}$, divides the states of an MDP into partitions $P_i = \{\, s \in S \mid f(s) = i \,\}$. The *partition graph* is the directed graph $\langle P, U \rangle$ with nodes $P = \{\, P_i \mid 1 \leq i \leq k \,\}$ and edges $U = \{\, \langle P_i, P_j \rangle \mid i \neq j \wedge \exists\, s \in P_i, \mu \in T(s), \langle s', r \rangle \in \mathrm{support}(\mu) \colon s' \in P_j \,\}$. It is *forward-acyclic* if there is no $\langle P_i, P_j \rangle \in U$ with $j < i$.

We are interested in the probability of reaching certain states in an MDP and in the expected reward accumulated when doing so. Since an MDP may contain nondeterministic choices, these values are only well-defined under a *scheduler*, which provides a recipe to resolve the nondeterminism. The verification questions are thus: Given a set of states $F \subseteq S$, (*i*) what is the maximum/minimum probability of eventually reaching a state in F over all possible schedulers (*reachability probability*), and (*ii*) what is the maximum/minimum expected accumulated reward once a state in F is reached for the first time over all possible schedulers (*expected reward*)? These quantities can be formally defined using the usual cylinder set construction for the paths of the MDP [17].

The computation of these quantities is typically done using *value iteration*, as shown in Algorithm 1 for maximum reachability probabilities. For the minimum

```
1  values := { s ↦ 1 | s ∈ F } ∪ { s ↦ 0 | s ∈ S \ F }              // the value vector
2  repeat
3  |   error := 0
4  |   foreach s ∈ S \ F do
5  |   |   v_new := max { Σ_{⟨s',r⟩∈support(μ)} μ(s') · values(s') | μ ∈ T(s) }
6  |   |   if v_new > 0 then error := max{ error, |v_new − values(s)|/values(s) }
7  |   |   values(s) := v_new
8  until error < ε
9  return values(s_0)
```

Algorithm 1. Value iteration to compute max. reachability probabilities

case, we replace maximisation by minimisation in line 5. To compute expected rewards, a precomputation step is needed to determine those states from which F is reachable with probability one and zero, respectively. This can be done with straightforward fixpoint algorithms over the graph structure of the MDP [17].

Using MDP directly to build models of complex systems is cumbersome. Instead, higher-level formalisms such as PRISM's guarded command language are used. They add to MDP variables that take values from finite domains. In an *MDP with variables* (VMDP), each transition is associated with a *guard*, a Boolean expression that disables the transition when it is *false*. The probabilities and reward values of the branches are given as real-valued arithmetic expressions. Every branch has an *update* that assigns new values (given as expressions) to the variables of the process. The semantics of a VMDP M is the MDP $[\![M]\!]$ whose states are pairs $\langle s, v \rangle$ of a state s of M and a valuation v for the variables. Transitions out of s that are disabled according to v do not appear in $[\![M]\!]$, and the valuations of a branch's targets are computed by applying the update of the branch to the valuation of the transition's source state. A partitioning function f for a VMDP can be determined by an upper-bounded arithmetic expression e with values in $\mathbb{N}$: $f(\langle s, v \rangle) = e(v)$ where $e(v)$ is the evaluation of e in v. The reachability set F can likewise be characterised by a Boolean expression.

Real-Time Extensions of MDP. To model and analyse real-time systems, MDP can be extended with real-valued clock variables and state invariant expressions as in timed automata (TA [3]), leading to the model of probabilistic timed automata (PTA [27]). A number of techniques are available to model-check PTA [31], but only the digital clocks approach [26] allows the computation of both reachability probabilities and expected rewards: Clocks are replaced by bounded integer variables, and self-loop transitions are added to increment them synchronously as long as the state invariant is satisfied. This turns the (finite) PTA into a (finite) VMDP. The conversion preserves reachability probabilities and expected reward values whenever all clock constraints in the PTA are closed and diagonal-free. However, the size of the final MDP is exponential in the number of clock variables and the maximum constants that they are compared to.

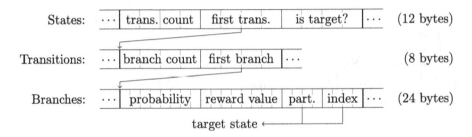

Fig. 1. In-memory representation of MDP for fast random access

For timed models, we are also interested in *time-bounded reachability*: Ranging over all possible schedulers, what is the maximum/minimum probability of eventually reaching a state in F within at most t time units? These probabilities can be computed by adding a new clock variable x to the PTA that is never reset and computing reachability probability for the set $F' = \{ \langle s, v \rangle \mid s \in F \wedge v(x) \leq t \}$ in the resulting digital clocks MDP [31].

A further extension of PTA are stochastic timed automata (STA [8]). They allow assignments of the form $x := \text{SAMPLE}(D)$ to sample from (continuous) probability distributions D, e.g. exponential or normal distributions, in updates. This allows for stochastic delays, such as the exponentially-distributed sojourn times of continuous-time Markov chains, in addition to the nondeterministic delays of (P)TA. A first model checking technique for STA has recently been described [18] and implemented within the mcsta tool of the MODEST TOOLSET [22]. It works by abstracting assignments that use continuous distributions into finite-support probabilistic choices plus continuous nondeterminism, turning the STA into a PTA that can be analysed with e.g. the digital clocks technique.

3   Disk-Based State Space Exploration with Partitioning

In this section, we describe the partitioned state space exploration approach that we use in our disk-based analysis technique for MDP. We assume that the MDP to be explored is given in some compact description that can be interpreted as a VMDP, and a partitioning function f is given as an expression over its variables. Disk-based exploration using partitioning has been the subject of previous work [5,16], so we focus on the novel aspect of generating a sparse matrix-like representation of the MDP on-the-fly during explicit-state exploration with low memory usage and in a compact format in a single file on disk.

3.1   Representation of MDP in Memory and on Disk

There are conceptually two ways to represent in memory an MDP that is the semantics of a VMDP: In an *explicit-state* manner, or in a *sparse matrix-style* representation. In the former, only the set of states of the MDP is kept, with

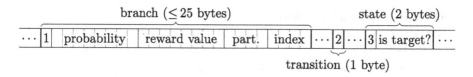

Fig. 2. Inverse-sequential format to compactly represent MDP on disk

each state stored as a vector $\langle s, v = \langle v_1, \dots, v_n \rangle \rangle$ where s identifies the state in the original VMDP and v_i the value of its i-th variable. Given a state and the compact description of the VMDP, we can recompute transitions and branches at any time on-demand. The other alternative is to identify each of the n states of the MDP with a value in $\{1, \dots, n\}$, its *index*, and explicitly store the set of transitions belonging to a state index and the transitions' branches. For each branch, its probability, its reward value, and the index of the target state need to be stored. This sparse matrix-style representation takes its name from the similar idea of storing a Markov chain as a sparse encoding of its probability matrix. All information about the inner structure of the states is discarded.

Figure 1 outlines the sparse matrix-style representation used by mcsta, which keeps three arrays to store the states, transitions and branches of a partition of the state space. For a state, "is target?" is *true* iff it is in the reachability set F that we consider. The target state of a branch is identified by its partition and its relative index within that partition. This format is more memory-efficient than an explicit-state representation when the model has many variables, and access to transitions and branches can be significantly faster because guards and other expressions in the model do not need to be evaluated on every access.

The format of Fig. 1 allows fast random access to all parts of the state space. However, when only sequential access is required, an MDP can be stored more compactly. Figure 2 shows the "inverse-sequential" format used by our technique to store state spaces on disk. States, transitions and branches are stored as a sequence of records, with the type of each record given by its first byte. Branches can be stored even more compactly by adding record types for common cases such as branches with probability 1. The key idea of the format is to first store all the branches of a transition before the transition record itself, and similarly store all the transitions (each preceded by its branches) of a state before the state record itself. In this way, we do not need to store the number of transitions and the index of the first transition for a state since its transitions are precisely those that appeared since the previous state record (and analogously for the branches of a transition). The random-access format of Fig. 1 can be reconstructed from a single sequential read of a file in the inverse-sequential format, and the file can be created sequentially with one simultaneous sequential pass through the arrays of the random-access format in memory.

3.2 Disk-Based Exploration Using Partitioning

Our disk-based exploration technique is given as Algorithm 2. It is based on the approach of [5,16]. Files on disk are indicated by subscript $_D$; when loaded into

```
1  int count := 1, queue_D^1.append(s_0)
2  repeat
3  │  changed := false
   │  // iterate over all partitions discovered so far
4  │  for i := 1 to count do
   │  │  // Phase 1: update preliminary target indices for cross transitions
5  │  │  foreach j ∈ successors^i do array updates_M^j := updates_D^j.load()
6  │  │  oldmatrix_D^i := matrix_D^i, matrix_D^i.clear()              // rename file
7  │  │  foreach r ∈ oldmatrix_D^i do                   // read records sequentially
8  │  │  │  if r = ⟨1, p, r, j, k⟩ ∧ k < 0 then
9  │  │  │  └  matrix_D^i.append(⟨1, p, r, j, updates_M^j[−k − 1]⟩))   // update index
10 │  │  │  else matrix_D^i.append(r)
11 │  │  unload updates_M^j for all j ∈ successors^i
   │  │  // Phase 2: explore more states in breadth-first manner
12 │  │  updates_D^i.clear()
13 │  │  queue queue_M^i := queue_D^i.load(), queue_D^i.clear(), qlen^i := 0
14 │  │  indexed-set states_M^i := states_D^i.load()
15 │  │  set done^i := states_M^i
16 │  │  while queue_M^i.length > 0 do
17 │  │  │  explicit-state s := queue_M^i.dequeue()
18 │  │  │  if s ∉ states_M^i then states_M^i.add(s), states_D^i.append(s)
19 │  │  │  updates_D^i.append(states_M^i.indexof(s))
20 │  │  │  if s ∈ done^i then continue else changed := true
21 │  │  │  foreach t ∈ s.transitions() do
22 │  │  │  │  if ¬ t.guard(s.v) then continue
23 │  │  │  │  foreach b ∈ t.branches() do
24 │  │  │  │  │  double p := b.probability(s.v), r := b.reward(s.v)
25 │  │  │  │  │  if p = 0 then continue
26 │  │  │  │  │  explicit-state s' := b.target(s.v)
27 │  │  │  │  │  if f(s') = i then                          // local transition
28 │  │  │  │  │  │  if s' ∉ states_M^i then states_M^i.add(s'), states_D^i.append(s')
29 │  │  │  │  │  │  queue_M^i.enqueue(s')
30 │  │  │  │  │  └  matrix_D^i.append(⟨1, p, r, i, states_M^i.indexof(s')⟩)
31 │  │  │  │  │  else                                       // cross transition
32 │  │  │  │  │  │  j := f(s'), successors^i.add(j), count := max { count, j }
33 │  │  │  │  │  │  queue_D^j.append(s'), qlen^j = qlen^j + 1
34 │  │  │  │  │  └  matrix_D^j.append(⟨1, p, r, j, −qlen^j⟩)   // prelim. index < 0
35 │  │  │  └  matrix_D^i.append(⟨2⟩)
36 │  │  │  matrix_D^i.append(⟨3, s ∈ F⟩)
37 │  │  └  done^i.add(s)
38 │  └  unload queue_M^i, states_M^i, done^i
39 while changed
```

Algorithm 2. Partitioned disk-based exploration with sparse matrix creation memory, the corresponding variable has subscript $_M$. For each partition, we use BFS to discover new states (lines 12 to 38) with the following data in memory:

- $states^i$: The set of states (explicit-state representation) of partition i is loaded into memory in its entirety when search begins for the partition (line 14). States are added in memory and appended on disk (lines 18 and 28).
- $queue^i$: The queue of states to explore in partition i. When a cross-transition is found during search in partition i, i.e. a branch leads to another partition $j \neq i$, then the target state is appended to $queue_D^j$ on disk (line 33). For local transitions, the target state is appended to $queue_M^i$ in memory (line 29).
- $done^i$: The in-memory set of fully explored states for the current iteration.

When an iteration of search in partition i ends, $states^i$ is backed on disk, $queue^i$ is empty, and $done^i$ is no longer needed, so we remove them from memory (line 38).

During search, we simultaneously create the sparse matrix-like representation of the partitions on disk in files $matrix_D^i$ using the inverse-sequential format. The files are not loaded into memory. The records for new branches, transitions and states are appended to the file in lines 30, 34, 35 and 36. The main complication is the correct treatment of cross transitions: A branch record stores the partition j of its target state s' and the index of s' within that partition. However, we cannot determine this index without loading all of $states_D^j$ into memory, and even then, s' may not have been explored yet. To solve this problem, we instead use the index of s' in $queue_D^j$, which is easily determined (line 33). To distinguish such a preliminary index, which needs to be corrected later, from a local or already corrected one, we store it as a negative value (line 34).

The correction of these preliminary indices inside $matrix_D^i$ happens at the beginning of an iteration for partition i (lines 5 to 11). The files $updates_D^j$ for all successor partitions j are loaded into memory. These files have been created by the previous iteration for partition j in lines 12 and 19 and contain the correct indices for all states that were previously in $queue_D^j$, at the same position. The preliminary queue-based indices in partition i can thus be corrected by a sequential pass through its sparse matrix-like representation in file $matrix_D^i$, replacing all negative indices $-k$ for partition j by the corrected value at $updates_M^j[k]$. This is a random-access operation on the files $updates_D^j$, which is why they were loaded into memory beforehand, but a sequential operation on the file $matrix_D^i$, of which we thus only need to load into memory one record at a time. Observe that this correction process relies on the availability of $updates^j$ for all successor partitions j. To assure this, we iterate over all partitions in a fixed order in line 4 instead of always moving to the partition with the longest queue as in [5,16].

To describe the memory usage and I/O complexity of this algorithm, let n_{max} denote the max. number of states, s_{max} the max. number of successor partitions (i.e. the max. outdegree of the partition graph), and c_{max} the max. number of *incoming* cross edges, over all partitions. Then the correction of preliminary indices in phase 1 needs memory in $O(s_{max} \cdot c_{max})$ for the $updates_M^i$ arrays and the exploration in phase 2 needs memory in $O(n_{max} + c_{max})$ for $states_M^i$ and $done^i$ plus $queue_M^i$. Additionally, we need memory for the sets of integers

```
 1  for i := 1 to count do                          // prepare value arrays on disk
 2      matrix_M^i := matrix_D^i.load()
 3      for k := 0 to matrix_M^i.states.length − 1 do
 4        ⌊ values_D^i.append(matrix_M^i.states[k].istarget ? 1 : 0)
 5      ⌊ unload matrix_M^i

 6  while changed do                                 // block-iterative value iteration
 7      changed := false                             // changed is initially true
 8      for i := count down to 1 do
 9          matrix_M^i := matrix_D^i.load(), values_M^i := values_D^i.load()
10          foreach j ∈ successors^i do values_M^j := values_D^j.load()
11          repeat
12              error := 0
13              for k := 0 to matrix_M^i.states.length − 1 do
14                  if matrix_M^i.states[k].istarget then continue
15                  v_new := max...    // as in Algoritm 1, but with values_M^i/values_M^j
16                  if v_new > 0 then error := ...// compute error as in Algorithm 1
17                  values_M^i[k] := v_new
18                ⌊ if error ≥ ε then changed := true
19          until error < ε
20        ⌊ unload matrix_M^i, values_M^i and the values_M^j for all j ∈ successors^i
21  return values_D^1[0]
```
```

**Algorithm 3.** Partitioned value iteration for max. reachability probabilities

$successors^i$, which we assume to be negligible compared to the other data items. A theoretical analysis of the I/O complexity [1] of a partitioning-based technique is problematic (and in fact absent from [5] and [16]) due to the way multiple files are used e.g. when cross transitions are encountered: For the (unusual) case of very small $n_{max}$ and very high $s_{max}$ and $c_{max}$, the disk accesses to append target states to different queues would be mostly random, but in practice (with low $s_{max}$ and I/O buffering) they are almost purely sequential. A theoretical worst-case analysis would thus be too pessimistic to be useful. We consequently abstain from such an analysis, too, and rely on the experimental evaluation of Sect. 5.

However, it is clear that the structure of the model w.r.t. the partitioning function will have a high impact on performance in general; in particular, a low number of cross edges is most desirable for the exploration algorithm presented here. Ideally, the partition graph is also forward-acyclic. In that case, two iterations of the outermost loop suffice: All states are explored in the first iteration, and the second only corrects the preliminary indices.

# 4  Disk-Based Partitioned Value Iteration

The result of the partitioned exploration presented in the previous section is a set of files in inverse-sequential format for the partitions of the state space.
```

As mentioned in Sect. 1, value iteration can update the states in any order, as long as the maximum error for termination is computed in a way that takes all states into account. We can thus apply value iteration in a block-iterative manner to the partitions of the state space as shown in Algorithm 3. The vector of values for each partition is stored in a separate file on disk. In lines 1 to 5, these files are created with the initial values based on whether a state is in the target set F. The actual value iterations are then performed in lines 6 to 20. For each partition, we need to load the sparse matrix-style representation of this part of the MDP into memory in the random-access format of Fig. 1, plus the values for the current partition (line 9), and those of its successors (lines 10). The values of the successor partitions are needed to calculate the current state's new value in line 15 in presence of cross transitions. Memory usage is thus in $O(m_{max} + s_{max} \cdot n_{max})$, where m_{max} is the maximum over all partitions of the sum of the number of states, transitions and branches. The I/O complexity is in $O(i \cdot p \cdot (\text{scan}(m_{max}) + (s_{max} + 1) \cdot \text{scan}(n_{max})))$ where i is the number of iterations of the outermost loop starting in line 6 and p is the total number of partitions.

In contrast to the exploration phase, the performance of this disk-based value iteration is not directly affected by the number of cross transitions. However, the number of successor partitions, i.e. s_{max}, is crucial. An additional consideration is the way that values propagate through the partitions. The ideal case is again a forward-acyclic partition graph, for which a single iteration of the outermost loop (line 6) suffices since we iterate over the partitions in reverse order (line 8).

For expected rewards, we additionally need to precompute the sets of states that reach the target set with probability one and zero as mentioned in Sect. 2. The standard graph-based fixpoint algorithms used for this purpose [17] can be changed to work in a block-iterative manner in the same way as value iteration.

5   Evaluation

In this section, we investigate the behaviour of our disk-based probabilistic model checking approach and its implementation in mcsta on five models from the literature. Experiments were performed on an Intel Core i7-4650U system with 8 GB of memory and a 2 TB USB 3.0 magnetic hard disk, running 64-bit Windows 8.1 for mcsta and Ubuntu Linux 14.10 for PRISM version 4.2.1. We used a timeout of 12 hours. Memory measurements refer to peak working/resident sets. Since mcsta (implemented in C#) and parts of PRISM are garbage-collected, however, the reported memory usages may fluctuate and be higher than what is actually necessary to solve the task at hand. Our experiments show what the disk-based approach makes possible on standard workstation configurations today; by using compute servers with more memory, we can naturally scale to even larger models.

Detailed performance results are shown in Table 1. State space sizes are listed in *millions* of states, so the largest model has about 3.5 *billion* states. Columns "exp" and "chk" show the runtime of the exploration and analysis phases, respectively, in *minutes*. Columns "GB" list the peak memory usage over both phases in *gigabytes*. We show the performance of mcsta without using the disk to judge the

overhead of partitioning and disk usage. Where possible, we also compare with
PRISM, which does not use the disk, but provides a semi-symbolic HYBRID engine
that uses BDD to compactly represent the states, transitions and branches while
keeping the entire value vector(s) in memory during value iteration (limiting its
scalability), and a fully symbolic MTBDD engine that also uses BDD for the value
vector. The HYBRID engine does not support expected rewards.

Compression. As all file accesses are sequential, we can use generic lossless compression to reduce disk accesses. Using the LZ4 algorithm [29], we achieved a
$7\times$ to $10\times$ reduction in disk usage on our examples. We observed almost no change
in runtime with compression enabled, so the extra CPU time is outweighed by
reduced disk I/O. Compression thus lowers disk usage at no runtime costs.

Partitioning Functions. The actual performance of our approach depends on the
structure of the model and its interplay with the partitioning function. Scalability hinges on the function's ability to distribute the states such that the largest
partition and the values of its successors fit into memory. The problem of automatically constructing a good partitioning function has largely been solved in
prior work, and many techniques, like the ones described and referenced in [16],
are available, but they are not yet implemented in mcsta. For our evaluation, we
thus use relatively simple manually specified partitioning functions.

CSMA/CD: The MDP model of the IEEE 802.3 CSMA/CD protocol from the
PRISM benchmark suite. It was manually constructed from a PTA model using
the digital clocks approach. It has parameters N, the number of communicating
nodes, and K, the maximum value of the backoff counter. The nodes count the
number of collisions they encounter when trying to send a message. We partition according to the sum of the collision counters of the nodes. The resulting
partition graph is forward-acyclic since these counters are only incremented, and
$s_{\max} = N$. However, due to using the sum of several values for partitioning, the
states are not evenly distributed over the partitions.

We first report on the performance of computing the minimum probability of
any node eventually delivering its message with fewer than K collisions (model
$\mathrm{CSMA/CD}_{1\times P}^{N,K}$ in Table 1, with $1 \times P$ indicating that one reachability probability
is computed), and then on computing the max. and min. expected times until all
nodes have delivered their message (model $\mathrm{CSMA/CD}_{2\times E}^{N,K}$, where $2 \times E$ indicates
that we compute two expected-reward values). All MDP are only medium-sized.
Our disk-based technique achieves performance comparable to the semi-symbolic
approach here, which however does not support expected rewards. The fully
symbolic approach has significantly higher runtimes for those properties.

Randomised Consensus: The PRISM benchmark of the randomised consensus
protocol of N actors doing random walks bounded by K to reach a common
decision. We partition according to the value of the shared counter variable. The
resulting partition graph is strongly connected with $s_{\max} = 2$. We use $\epsilon = 0.02$

Table 1. Evaluation results (millions of states, minutes, and gigabytes of memory)

model		in-memory (mcsta)			disk-based (mcsta -L)					semi-symbolic (Prism hybrid)			fully symbolic (Prism mtbdd)		
params	states	exp	chk	GB	p	n_{max}	exp	chk	GB	exp	chk	GB	exp	chk	GB
CSMA/CD$_{1\times P}^{N,K}$															
3,4	1.5	0.1	0.0	0.3	12	0.4	0.2	0.0	0.2	0.0	0.2	0.2	0.0	0.5	0.3
3,5	12.1	1.1	0.1	2.6	15	2.6	1.3	0.1	0.7	0.1	1.6	0.5	0.1	4.0	0.4
3,6	84.9	>8GB			18	15.3	9.3	1.3	5.0	0.3	13.1	2.3	0.3	22.9	3.0
4,3	8.2	1.0	0.1	1.7	12	2.7	1.1	0.1	0.8	0.1	0.8	0.4	0.1	2.2	0.4
4,4	133.3	>8GB			16	33.0	19.1	2.2	6.6	0.4	17.6	3.6	0.6	21.7	5.1
4,5	2596.0				>8GB					>8GB			>12h		
CSMA/CD$_{2\times E}^{N,K}$															
3,4	1.5	0.1	0.1	0.3	12	0.4	0.2	0.2	0.2	n/a			0.0	18.1	0.4
3,5	12.1	1.1	1.5	2.6	15	2.6	1.3	1.7	0.7				0.1	96.9	4.7
3,6	84.9	>8GB			18	15.3	9.3	19.4	5.0				0.3	707.0	5.1
4,3	8.2	1.0	0.9	1.7	12	2.7	1.1	0.9	0.8	n/a			0.1	92.4	0.5
4,4	133.3	>8GB			16	33.0	19.1	16.5	6.6				0.5	637.3	5.5
4,5	2596.0				>8GB								>12h		
Consensus$_{2\times P}^{N,K}$															
8,2	61.0				5	16.8	10.5	104.9	6.4	0.0	28.3	1.6	0.0	5.4	0.3
8,3	87.9				7	16.8	16.0	200.6	4.3	0.0	65.1	2.3	0.0	10.1	0.4
8,4	114.8	>8GB			8	16.8	21.8	347.5	7.3	0.0	121.4	2.9	0.0	17.5	0.4
8,5	141.6				10	16.8	27.2	484.9	6.8	0.0	193.4	3.6	0.0	25.1	0.4
8,6	168.5				12	16.8	33.9	660.3	6.9	0.0	260.6	4.2	0.0	38.9	0.4
8,7	195.4				>12h					0.0	361.6	4.9	0.0	49.9	0.4
WLAN$_{1\times P}^{K}$															
1	718.0				203	11.5	177.3	8.5	3.0				715.3	4.3	5.8
2	1197.9	>8GB			337	12.0	283.5	15.7	3.0	>8GB					
3	1685.0				471	13.1	392.2	23.4	3.0				>12h		
4	2186.7				605	15.1	502.6	30.7	3.5						
WLAN$_{1\times E}^{K}$															
1	718.0				203	11.5	177.3	52.4	3.0				>12h		
2	1197.9	>8GB			337	12.0	283.5	72.0	3.0	n/a					
3	1685.0				471	13.1	392.2	94.2	3.0						
4	2186.7				605	15.1	502.6	114.0	3.5						
BRP$_{6\times P}^{N,TD}$															
64,16	18.7	1.5	0.2	3.8	65	0.3	1.8	0.5	0.2	23.0	56.8	1.0	error		
128,16	37.4	3.1	0.5	7.3	129	0.3	3.7	0.9	0.2	34.7	150.4	1.4			
64,32	70.7	>8GB			65	1.2	7.4	1.8	0.5	89.4	345.2	2.4	error		
128,32	141.5				129	1.2	15.3	3.4	0.5	>12h					
BRP$_{2\times TP}^{N,D}$															
64,256	355.7	>8GB			577	1.5	40.7	3.3	0.6	>8GB			122.6	38.2	2.6
128,256	715.6				1153	1.5	93.0	60.6	0.6				>12h		
64,512	1773.7	>8GB			1089	4.8	203.1	18.8	1.6	>8GB			>8GB		
128,512	3573.3				2177	4.8	418.5	38.1	1.8						
File server$_{2\times TP}^{C,D}$															
5,100	18.0	1.4	0.5	5.4	102	0.2	2.0	0.4	0.2	n/a			n/a		
5,200	41.2				202	0.2	4.7	1.0	0.2						
5,400	87.8	>8GB			402	0.2	10.5	2.1	0.2						
5,800	180.9				802	0.2	22.4	4.3	0.2						
10,100	34.0				102	0.4	4.0	0.9	0.2	n/a			n/a		
10,200	77.1				202	0.4	9.6	1.9	0.2						
10,400	163.4	>8GB			402	0.4	20.4	4.1	0.3						
10,800	335.9				802	0.4	43.9	8.6	0.3						
params	states	exp	chk	GB	p	n_{max}	exp	chk	GB	exp	chk	GB	exp	chk	GB

during value iteration (instead of the default $\epsilon = 10^{-6}$ as in the other examples). The MDP appear medium-sized in terms of states, but have about 5× as many transitions and 7× as many branches as states, so should be considered large.

We check the two probabilistic reachability properties originally named "C_1" and "C_2". The fully symbolic technique completes exploration and analysis much faster than our disk-based approach. This is because this model is a benchmark for value iteration, with values propagating in very small increments back-and-forth through all the states and thus partitions. Still, we observe that n_{max} is invariant under K, so our technique will be able to check this model for $N = 8$ and any value of K without running out of memory—if given enough time.

Wireless LAN: The MODEST PTA model [21] of IEEE 802.11 WLAN, based on [28]. So far, this protocol has only been analysed with reduced timing parameters to contain state space explosion. We use the original values of the standard for a 2 Mbps transmission rate instead, including the max. transmission time of $15717\,\mu s$, with $1\,\mu s$ as one model time unit. Parameter K is the maximum value of the backoff counter. We partition according to the first station's backoff counter, its control location, and its clock. The resulting partition graph has some cycles with $s_{max} = 3$. Exploration needs 5 iterations of the outermost loop of Algorithm 2 in all cases. We compute the maximum probability that either station's backoff counter reaches K (model $\text{WLAN}_{1\times P}^{K}$ in Table 1) as well as the maximum expected time until one station delivers its packet ($\text{WLAN}_{1\times E}^{K}$).

BRP: The MODEST PTA model of the Bounded Retransmission Protocol (BRP) from [21]. Parameters are N, the number of data frames to be transmitted, MAX, the bound on the retries per frame, and TD, the maximum transmission delay. We fix $MAX = 12$. We partition by the number of the current data frame to analyse the model's six probabilistic reachability properties ($\text{BRP}_{6\times P}^{N,TD}$). This leads to the ideal case of a forward-acyclic partition graph with $s_{max} = 1$. We also analyse two time-bounded reachability properties ($\text{BRP}_{2\times TP}^{N,D}$) with deadline D and fixed $TD = 32$, partitioning additionally according to the values of the added global clock. This leads to $s_{max} = 2$. For the reachability probabilities, PRISM's MTBDD engine incorrectly reported probability zero in all cases. Our approach benefits hugely from having to perform far fewer total value iterations per state due to the favourable partitioning. In the reachability probabilities case, n_{max} is invariant under N, so we can scale N arbitrarily without running out of memory.

File Server: The STA file server model from [18]. C is the capacity of the request buffer. We compute the maximum and the minimum probability of a buffer overflow within time bound D. We cannot compare with PRISM because some features necessary to support STA cannot currently be translated into its input language from MODEST. Using our disk-based technique permits a finer abstraction for continuous probability distributions than before ($\rho = 0.01$ instead of 0.05). We partition according to the values of the global clock introduced to check the time bounds. This leads to the ideal case of an acyclic partition graph with $s_{max} = 1$. The state space and number of partitions grow linearly in the time bound while n_{max} remains invariant. We can thus check time-bounded properties for any large bound without exceeding the available memory, at a linear increase in runtime. This solves a major problem in STA model checking.

6 Conclusion

We have shown that the state space partitioning approach to using secondary storage for model checking combines well with analysis techniques built on graph fixpoint algorithms. We have used the example of MDP models and value iteration, but the same scheme is applicable to other techniques, too. In particular, the precomputation step for expected-reward properties is very close to what is needed for CTL model checking. Our technique is implemented in the mcsta tool of the MODEST TOOLSET, available at www.modestchecker.net. In our evaluation, we observed that it significantly extends the reach of probabilistic model checking. It appears complementary to the symbolic approach: On the model where our technique struggles, PRISM performs well, and where PRISM runs into memory or time limitations, our technique appears to work well. In particular, our approach appears to work better for expected-reward properties, and we have been able to defuse the crippling state space explosion caused by the deadlines of time-bounded reachability properties in PTA and STA models.

References

1. Aggarwal, A., Vitter, J.S.: The input/output complexity of sorting and related problems. Commun. ACM **31**(9), 1116–1127 (1988)
2. de Alfaro, L., Kwiatkowska, M., Norman, G., Parker, D., Segala, R.: Symbolic model checking of probabilistic processes using MTBDDs and the kronecker representation. In: Graf, S. (ed.) TACAS 2000. LNCS, vol. 1785, pp. 395–410. Springer, Heidelberg (2000)
3. Alur, R., Dill, D.L.: A theory of timed automata. Theor. Comput. Sci. **126**(2), 183–235 (1994)
4. Baier, C., D'Argenio, P.R., Größer, M.: Partial order reduction for probabilistic branching time. Electron. Notes Theor. Comput. Sci. **153**(2), 97–116 (2006)
5. Bao, T., Jones, M.: Time-efficient model checking with magnetic disk. In: Halbwachs, N., Zuck, L.D. (eds.) TACAS 2005. LNCS, vol. 3440, pp. 526–540. Springer, Heidelberg (2005)
6. Barnat, J., Brim, L., Šimeček, P.: I/O efficient accepting cycle detection. In: Damm, W., Hermanns, H. (eds.) CAV 2007. LNCS, vol. 4590, pp. 281–293. Springer, Heidelberg (2007)
7. Bell, A., Haverkort, B.R.: Distributed disk-based algorithms for model checking very large Markov chains. Formal Methods Syst. Des. **29**(2), 177–196 (2006)
8. Bohnenkamp, H.C., D'Argenio, P.R., Hermanns, H., Katoen, J.: MoDeST: a compositional modeling formalism for hard and softly timed systems. IEEE Trans. Softw. Eng. **32**(10), 812–830 (2006)
9. Clarke, E.M., Grumberg, O., Peled, D.A.: Model Checking. MIT Press, Cambridge (1999)
10. Dai, P., Goldsmith, J.: Topological value iteration algorithm for Markov decision processes. In: IJCAI, pp. 1860–1865 (2007)
11. Deavours, D.D., Sanders, W.H.: An efficient disk-based tool for solving very large Markov models. In: Marie, R., Plateau, B., Calzarossa, M., Rubino, G. (eds.) Computer Performance Evaluation Modelling Techniques and Tools. LNCS, vol. 1245, pp. 58–71. Springer, Heidelberg (1997)

12. Penna, G.D., Intrigila, B., Tronci, E., Zilli, M.V.: Exploiting transition locality in the disk based Murϕ verifier. In: Aagaard, M.D., O'Leary, J.W. (eds.) Formal Methods in Computer-Aided Design. LNCS, vol. 2517, pp. 202–219. Springer, Heidelberg (2002)

13. Edelkamp, S., Jabbar, S.: Large-scale directed model checking LTL. In: Valmari, A. (ed.) SPIN 2006. LNCS, vol. 3925, pp. 1–18. Springer, Heidelberg (2006)

14. Edelkamp, S., Jabbar, S., Bonet, B.: External memory value iteration. In: ICAPS, pp. 128–135. AAAI (2007)

15. Edelkamp, S., Sanders, P., Šimeček, P.: Semi-external LTL model checking. In: Gupta, A., Malik, S. (eds.) CAV 2008. LNCS, vol. 5123, pp. 530–542. Springer, Heidelberg (2008)

16. Evangelista, S., Kristensen, L.M.: Dynamic state space partitioning for external memory state space exploration. Sci. Comput. Program. **78**(7), 778–795 (2013)

17. Forejt, V., Kwiatkowska, M., Norman, G., Parker, D.: Automated verification techniques for probabilistic systems. In: Bernardo, M., Issarny, V. (eds.) SFM 2011. LNCS, vol. 6659, pp. 53–113. Springer, Heidelberg (2011)

18. Hahn, E.M., Hartmanns, A., Hermanns, H.: Reachability and reward checking for stochastic timed automata. ECEASST **70** (2014)

19. Hammer, M., Weber, M.: "To store or not to store" reloaded: reclaiming memory on demand. In: Brim, L., Haverkort, B.R., Leucker, M., van de Pol, J. (eds.) FMICS 2006 and PDMC 2006. LNCS, vol. 4346, pp. 51–66. Springer, Heidelberg (2007)

20. Harrison, P.G., Knottenbelt, W.J.: Distributed disk-based solution techniques for large Markov models. In: Numerical Solution of Markov Chains, pp. 58–75 (1999)

21. Hartmanns, A., Hermanns, H.: A Modest approach to checking probabilistic timed automata. In: QEST, pp. 187–196. IEEE Computer Society (2009)

22. Hartmanns, A., Hermanns, H.: The Modest Toolset: an integrated environment for quantitative modelling and verification. In: Ábrahám, E., Havelund, K. (eds.) TACAS 2014 (ETAPS). LNCS, vol. 8413, pp. 593–598. Springer, Heidelberg (2014)

23. Hermanns, H., Wachter, B., Zhang, L.: Probabilistic CEGAR. In: Gupta, A., Malik, S. (eds.) CAV 2008. LNCS, vol. 5123, pp. 162–175. Springer, Heidelberg (2008)

24. Kwiatkowska, M.Z., Mehmood, R., Norman, G., Parker, D.: A symbolic out-of-core solution method for Markov models. Electron. Notes Theor. Comput. Sci. **68**(4), 589–604 (2002)

25. Kwiatkowska, M., Norman, G., Parker, D.: PRISM 4.0: verification of probabilistic real-time systems. In: Gopalakrishnan, G., Qadeer, S. (eds.) CAV 2011. LNCS, vol. 6806, pp. 585–591. Springer, Heidelberg (2011)

26. Kwiatkowska, M.Z., Norman, G., Parker, D., Sproston, J.: Performance analysis of probabilistic timed automata using digital clocks. Formal Methods Syst. Des. **29**(1), 33–78 (2006)

27. Kwiatkowska, M.Z., Norman, G., Segala, R., Sproston, J.: Automatic verification of real-time systems with discrete probability distributions. Theoretical Comput. Sci. **282**(1), 101–150 (2002)

28. Kwiatkowska, M., Norman, G., Sproston, J.: Probabilistic model checking of the IEEE 802.11 wireless local area network protocol. In: Hermanns, H., Segala, R. (eds.) PROBMIV 2002, PAPM-PROBMIV 2002, and PAPM 2002. LNCS, vol. 2399, pp. 169–187. Springer, Heidelberg (2002)

29. LZ4. http://www.lz4.info/. Accessed 2 July 2015

30. Mehmood, R.: Serial disk-based analysis of large stochastic models. In: Baier, C., Haverkort, B.R., Hermanns, H., Katoen, J.-P., Siegle, M. (eds.) Validation of Stochastic Systems. LNCS, vol. 2925, pp. 230–255. Springer, Heidelberg (2004)

31. Norman, G., Parker, D., Sproston, J.: Model checking for probabilistic timed automata. Formal Methods Syst. Des. **43**(2), 164–190 (2013)
32. Puterman, M.L.: Markov Decision Processes: Discrete Stochastic Dynamic Programming. Wiley, New York (1994)
33. Stern, U., Dill, D.L.: Using magnetic disk instead of main memory in the Murφ verifier. In: Hu, A.J., Vardi, M.Y. (eds.) Computer Aided Verification. LNCS, vol. 1427, pp. 172–183. Springer, Heidelberg (1998)
34. Stewart, W.J.: Introduction to the Numerical Solution of Markov Chains. Princeton University Press, Princeton (1994)
35. Timmer, M., Stoelinga, M., van de Pol, J.: Confluence reduction for probabilistic systems. In: Abdulla, P.A., Leino, K.R.M. (eds.) TACAS 2011. LNCS, vol. 6605, pp. 311–325. Springer, Heidelberg (2011)

Model Checking Failure-Prone Open Systems Using Probabilistic Automata

Yue Ben[✉] and A. Prasad Sistla

University of Illinois, Chicago, USA
benyue06@gmail.com

Abstract. We consider finite-state Hierarchical Probabilistic Automata (HPA) to model failure-prone open systems. In an HPA, its states are stratified into a fixed number of levels. A k-HPA is an HPA with $k+1$ levels and it can be used to model open systems where up to k failures can occur. In this paper, we present a new forward algorithm that checks universality of a 1-HPA. This algorithm runs much faster than an earlier backward algorithm. We present the implementation and experimental results for verifying abstracted failure-prone web applications. We also prove a theoretical result showing that the problem of checking emptiness and universality for 2-HPA is undecidable answering an open question.

Keywords: Model checking · Verification tool · Failure-prone open systems · Emptiness and decision problems · Hierarchical Probabilistic Automata (HPA)

1 Introduction

Open concurrent systems, such as *web applications*, are usually deployed on multiple processors/servers. These systems take user inputs (thus called *open* systems), and service their requests. Failures may occur in such systems in the form of server/processor crashes. Once a processor fails, the other functioning processors take over the remaining tasks from the failed processor and continue their execution. In this paper, we model the failures probabilistically and assume that the probability of failure of a processor may depend on its current state as well as the input (inputs are usually submitted as a *form*) being processed. In such systems, it is critically important to verify that the system satisfies a correctness property with a minimum probability on all input sequences.

We employ *Open Probabilistic Transition Systems* (OPTSes) to model such failure-prone open concurrent systems. In general, an OPTS takes inputs from the environment and makes transitions to different states according to a probability distribution which may depend on the input as well as the current state. We consider systems abstracted as finite-state OPTSes. We consider the correctness property specified by a deterministic automaton on the computations of the system. The problem of checking that a system, specified by an OPTS $\mathbb{T}$, satisfies a specification given by an automaton $\mathcal{A}$ with a probability greater

© Springer International Publishing Switzerland 2015
B. Finkbeiner et al. (Eds.): ATVA 2015, LNCS 9364, pp. 148–165, 2015.
DOI: 10.1007/978-3-319-24953-7_11

than a given value x, reduces to the problem of checking if the Probabilistic Automaton (PA) $\mathbb{T} \times \mathcal{A}$, accepts all input sequences with probability greater than x. Therefore, checking correctness reduces to checking universality of the language accepted by a PA [1,8,9,11].

When we use the probabilistic behavior of the OPTS only for modeling processor failures, as described above, we get hierarchical OPTSes. A hierarchical OPTS is one in which its states are stratified into $k+1$ levels, say $0, 1, \ldots, k$, (for some $k \geq 0$) such that, from any state, on an input, at most one transition goes to a state at the same level and all other transitions go to higher levels, and the initial state is at level 0. Such an OPTS is called a k-OPTS. Intuitively, it captures the situation when up to k processors can fail probabilistically in some arbitrary sequence. The level of a state denotes the number of failures that occurred before reaching the state. Now checking correctness of a k-OPTS reduces to checking universality of the language accepted by an HPA (Hierarchical Probabilistic Automata). HPA introduced in [4] are a subclass of Probabilistic automata (PA). In that work it has been shown that the problem of checking the emptiness of $L_{>x}(\mathcal{A})$ ($L_{\geq x}(\mathcal{A})$) of an HPA $\mathcal{A}$ for a rational $x \in (0,1)$ is undecidable. (Here $L_{>x}(\mathcal{A})$ is the set of all strings accepted by $\mathcal{A}$ from the initial state with probability $> x$).

It has been shown in [6], that checking emptiness and universality problems for 1-HPA is decidable in exponential time by presenting an algorithm, called *backward* algorithm. In this paper, we give an alternative algorithm, called *forward* algorithm, for checking emptiness and universality of 1-HPA. This algorithm employs the given threshold value x critically in its logic. It is shown to have a better complexity (although it is also exponential time in the worst case), and runs much faster in practice as shown by our experimental results.

We also show that the emptiness problem for 2-HPA is undecidable. The undecidability result for HPA given in [4], proves the result for 6-HPA. Our result closes the gap between the levels of HPA for which decidability and undecidability results are proved. Our result employs a new elegant construction of a 2-HPA, to check equality of two counter values of a counter machine (more specifically, to recognize the context free language $\{a^n b^n \mid n \geq 0\}$), replacing the Freivalds' construction employed in [4].

We have implemented a tool that takes a PA, checks if it is an HPA. If it is an HPA it computes the minimum k such that it is a k-HPA and classifies its states into $k+1$ levels; this algorithm runs in time $O(k \cdot m)$ where m is the size of the PA. If $k = 1$, it also takes a threshold value x and checks for non-emptiness of $L_{>x}(\mathcal{A})$ using the forward and backward algorithm. We employed it to check the correctness of two abstracted web applications under a single failure. The experimental results confirm that the forward algorithm is orders of magnitude faster than the backward algorithm for these examples.

In summary, the main contributions of the paper are as follows.

- A new faster algorithm for checking non-emptiness of the language accepted by a 1-HPA with respect to a given rational threshold $x \in (0,1)$.

- Undecidability result for checking non-emptiness for 2-HPA, thus closing the gap in the known decidability results.
- A tool that takes a PA and checks if it is a 1-HPA and then checks for the non-emptiness of its language with respect to a given threshold value.
- A tool that takes the following as input: the specification of a single session of a web server as deterministic automaton, and a failure specification, and a correctness specification and checks for its correctness, under the assumption of at most one failure, of a system running two servers.

There has been much work done on verifying finite-state concurrent probabilistic programs [3,10]. All of them assume closed systems and model the system as a Markov Decision Process (MDP) and verify its correctness in an appropriate logic. To the best of our knowledge, ours is the first work that checks for correctness of a class of open probabilistic systems using probabilistic automata. The decidability problem for different classes of PA under different threshold conditions has been extensively studied [2,5,7]. Our algorithm for non-emptiness of 1-HPA is faster in practice than the one proposed in [6]. Our undecidability result for 2-HPA improves the result of [4] and closes the gap between known decidability/undecidability results for HPA.

The rest of the paper is organized as follows. Section 2 has basic definitions and notation used in the paper. In Sect. 3 we present our enhanced backward algorithm and the forward algorithm for deciding the non-emptiness of 1-HPA. In Sect. 4 we present the undecidability result for 2-HPA. Section 5 presents the model for OPTS. Section 6 presents implementation and application of the algorithms. Finally, Sect. 7 contains concluding remarks.

2   Preliminaries

We assume reader is familiar with finite-state automata, regular languages, and ω-regular languages. The closed unit interval is denoted by $[0, 1]$ and the open unit interval by $(0, 1)$. The power-set of a set X will be denoted by 2^X.

Sequences. Given a finite set S, $|S|$ denotes the cardinality of S. Given a finite sequence $\kappa = s_0 s_1 \ldots$ over S, $|\kappa|$ will denote the length of the sequence, $\kappa[i]$ will denote the element s_i of the sequence and $Pref(\kappa)$ denotes the set of prefixes of κ. As usual S^* will denote the set of all finite sequences/strings/words over S, S^+ will denote the set of all finite non-empty sequences/strings/words over S, and S^ω will denote the set of all infinite sequences/strings/words over S. A *language* over S is a subset of S^*.

Probabilistic Automata (PA). Informally, a PA is like a finite-state deterministic automaton except that the transition function from a state on a given input is described as a probability distribution which determines the probability of the next state.

Definition 1. A *finite-state probabilistic automaton* (PFA) over a finite alphabet Σ is a tuple $\mathcal{A} = (Q, q_0, \delta, \mathsf{Acc})$ where Q is a finite set of *states*, $q_0 \in Q$ is the *initial state*, $\delta : Q \times \Sigma \times Q \rightarrow [0,1]$ is the *transition relation* such that for all $q, q' \in Q$ and $a \in \Sigma$, $\delta(q, a, q')$ is a rational number and $\sum_{q' \in Q} \delta(q, a, q') = 1$, and $\mathsf{Acc} \subseteq Q$ is an *acceptance condition*, also called set of final/accepting states.

Notation: By default we mean PFA when we talk about PA in this paper. The transition function δ of PA $\mathcal{A}$ on input $a \in \Sigma$ can be seen as a square matrix δ_a of order $|Q|$ with the rows labeled by "current" state, columns labeled by "next state" and the entry $\delta_a(q, q')$ equal to $\delta(q, a, q')$. Given a word $u = a_0 a_1 \ldots a_n \in \Sigma^+$, δ_u is the matrix product $\delta_{a_0} \delta_{a_1} \ldots \delta_{a_n}$. For the empty word $\epsilon \in \Sigma^*$ we take δ_ϵ to be the identity matrix. Finally for any $Q_0 \subseteq Q$, we say that $\delta_u(q, Q_0) = \sum_{q' \in Q_0} \delta_u(q, q')$. Given a state $q \in Q$ and a word $u \in \Sigma^+$, $\mathsf{post}(q, u) = \{q' \mid \delta_u(q, q') > 0\}$ and $\mathsf{pre}(q, u) = \{q' \mid \delta_u(q', q) > 0\}$. For a set $C \subseteq Q$, $\mathsf{post}(C, u) = \cup_{q \in C} \mathsf{post}(q, u)$ and $\mathsf{pre}(C, u) = \cup_{q \in C} \mathsf{pre}(q, u)$.

Intuitively, a PA $\mathcal{A}$ starts in the initial state q_0, and if after reading $a_0, a_1, \ldots, a_i$ it results in state q, then it moves to state q' with probability $\delta_{a_{i+1}}(q, q')$ on symbol a_{i+1}. A *run* of $\mathcal{A}$ starting in a state $q \in Q$ on an input $\kappa \in \Sigma^*$ is a sequence $\rho \in Q^*$ such that $|\rho| = 1 + |\kappa|$, $\rho[0] = q_0$ and for each $i \geq 0$, $\delta_{\kappa[i]}(\rho[i], \rho[i+1]) > 0$. We say that ρ is an *accepting* run if $\rho[|\rho| - 1] \in \mathsf{Acc}$, i.e., the last state on ρ is an accepting state.

Given a word $\kappa \in \Sigma^*$, the PA $\mathcal{A}$ can be thought of as a Markov chain. The set of states of this Markov chain is the set $\{(q, v) \mid q \in Q, v \in \mathit{Pref}(\kappa)\}$, and the probability of transitioning from (q, v) to (q', u) is $\delta_a(q, q')$ if $u = va$ for some $a \in \Sigma$ and 0 otherwise.

PA Languages. Consider a PA $\mathcal{A} = (Q, q_0, \delta, \mathsf{Acc})$ over an alphabet Σ. Given a rational threshold $x \in [0, 1]$ and $\rhd \in \{\geq, >\}$, the language $\mathsf{L}_{\rhd x}(\mathcal{A}) = \{u \in \Sigma^* \mid \delta_u(q_0, \mathsf{Acc}) \rhd x\}$ is the set of finite words accepted by $\mathcal{A}$ from q_0 with probability $\rhd x$.

2.1   Hierarchical Probabilistic Automata

Intuitively, a hierarchical probabilistic automaton is a PA such that the set of its states can be stratified into (totally) ordered levels. From a state q, on each letter a, the machine can transit with non-zero probability to at most one state in the same level as q, and all other probabilistic successors belong to higher levels.

Definition 2. For an integer $k > 0$, a *k-hierarchical probabilistic automaton* (HPA) is a probabilistic automaton $\mathcal{A} = (Q, q_0, \delta, \mathsf{Acc})$ over alphabet Σ such that Q can be partitioned into $k+1$ sets $Q_0, Q_1, \ldots, Q_k$ satisfying the following properties:

- $q_0 \in Q_0$;
- for every i, $0 \leq i \leq k$ and every $q \in Q_i$ and $a \in \Sigma$, $|\mathsf{post}(q, a) \cap Q_i| \leq 1$; and,
- for every i, $0 < i \leq k$, $q \in Q_i$ and $a \in \Sigma$, $\mathsf{post}(q, a) \cap Q_j = \emptyset$ for every $j < i$.

For any k-HPA $\mathcal{A}$, as given above, for $0 \leq i \leq k$, we call elements of Q_i as level i states of $\mathcal{A}$. For the rest of the paper, by HPA we mean 1-HPA, unless otherwise stated.

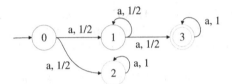

Fig. 1. 1-HPA example with initial state 0 and final state 3, and $Q_0 = \{0,1\}$, $Q_1 = \{2,3\}$.

Notation: Let $\mathcal{A} = (Q, q_0, \delta, Acc)$ be a 1-HPA over an input alphabet Σ, $\mathcal{A}$ has n states (i.e., $|Q| = n$) and m transitions where m is the cardinality of the set $\{(q, a, q') \mid \delta(q, a, q') > 0\}$. Let $s = |\Sigma|$. Q_0 and Q_1 are the level 0 and level 1 states respectively. It's easy to see that given any state $q \in Q_0$ and any word $\kappa \in \Sigma^*$, $\mathcal{A}$ has at most one run ρ on κ where all states in ρ belong to Q_0.

Witness Sets. A set $W \subseteq Q$ is said to be a *witness set* if W has at most one Q_0 state. Note that every subset of Q_1 is a witness set. For a witness set W such that $W \cap Q_0 \neq \emptyset$, we let q_W denote the unique state in $W \cap Q_0$. A word $\kappa \in \Sigma^*$ is *definitely accepted* from a witness set W iff for every $q \in W$ with $q \in Q_i$ (for $i \in \{0, 1\}$) there is an accepting run ρ on κ starting from q such that for every j, $\rho[j] \in Q_i$ and $\delta_{\kappa[j]}(\rho[j], \rho[j+1]) = 1$. In other words, κ is definitely accepted from a witness set W iff κ is accepted from every state q in W by a run where the HPA stays in the same level as q, and all transitions in the run are taken with probability 1. We say that a witness set W is *good* if there is at least one word that is definitely accepted from W.

Notation: Let $\mathcal{X}$ be the collection of all witness sets U such that $U \cap Q_1$ is a good witness set. Let $\mathcal{Y}$ be the collection of all good witness sets U such that $U \cap Q_0 = 1$.

3 Decision Algorithms and Robustness

For a 1-HPA $\mathcal{A}$, the problem of determining if $L_{>x}(\mathcal{A})$ is non-empty (i.e., non-emptiness problem) has been shown to be in **EXPTIME** in [6]. The above paper gave an algorithm, called *backward algorithm*, for the non-emptiness problem. In this section, we present a new algorithm called *forward algorithm* and an improved version of the backward algorithm. We show that the forward algorithm has better complexity than the backward algorithm. Both algorithms are based on the calculation of good witness sets for the HPA, which is covered in Sect. 6.1.

Let $x \in [0, 1]$ be a rational threshold of size at most r[1]. It has been shown in [6], that for an HPA $\mathcal{A}$, $L_{>x}(\mathcal{A}) \neq \emptyset$ iff there is a finite word u and a good non-empty witness set W, such that $|u| \leq 4rn8^n$ and $\delta_u(q_0, W) > x$. Now, let $L = 4rn8^n$.

---

[1] A rational number s has size r iff $s = \frac{m}{n}$ where m, n are integers, and the binary representation of m and n has at most r bits.

3.1   Forward Algorithm

The forward algorithm is based on a quantity $\mathsf{val}(C, x, u)$ defined for a set $C \subseteq Q_1$ of states in HPA $\mathcal{A}$, a threshold $x \in (0, 1)$, and a finite word u. The intuition of val is, starting from q_0, after the input string u, the probability that the automaton is in some state in C is $\delta_u(q_0, C)$; this means an additional probability of $(x - \delta_u(q_0, C))$ is needed to cross the threshold x; this additional probability can only come from the probability remaining at level 0, which is $\delta_u(q_0, Q_0)$. Thus, $\mathsf{val}(C, x, u)$, defined as the ratio of the above additional probability to that of $\delta_u(q_0, Q_0)$, is the fraction of $\delta_u(q_0, Q_0)$ that still needs to move to C so that the probability of reaching the accepting states at the end exceeds the threshold x. Formally, we have the following definition.

$$\mathsf{val}(C, x, u) = \begin{cases} \frac{x - \delta_u(q_0, C)}{\delta_u(q_0, Q_0)} & \text{if } \delta_u(q_0, Q_0) \neq 0 \\ +\infty & \text{if } \delta_u(q_0, C) < x, \delta_u(q_0, Q_0) = 0 \\ 0 & \text{if } \delta_u(q_0, C) = x, \delta_u(q_0, Q_0) = 0 \\ -\infty & \text{if } \delta_u(q_0, C) > x, \delta_u(q_0, Q_0) = 0 \end{cases} \tag{1}$$

From the definition of the function val, and using algebraic simplifications, the following properties are easily proved.

Lemma 1. *For $u, v \in \Sigma^+$, if $C, D \subseteq Q_1$, $q, q' \in Q_0$ be such that $C = \mathsf{pre}(D, v) \cap Q_1, \{q\} = \mathsf{post}(q_0, u), \{q'\} = \mathsf{post}(q, v), x' = \delta_v(q, D), z' = \delta_v(q, q'), y' = 1 - z'$ and $y', z' > 0$, then the following hold:*

1. $\mathsf{val}(D, x, uv) = \frac{\mathsf{val}(C, x, u) - x'}{z'}$, *and*
2. *If $C = D$ (i.e., $\mathsf{post}(C, v) = C$) and $q' = q$, then for any integer $p \geq 0$,* $\mathsf{val}(C, x, uv^p) = \frac{x'}{y'} + (\frac{1}{z'})^p (\mathsf{val}(C, x, u) - \frac{x'}{y'})$.

The val values play an important role in deciding whether a word κ is accepted by an HPA. It has been shown in [6] that κ is accepted with probability $> x$ iff κ can be divided into strings u, κ', i.e., $\kappa = u\kappa'$, and there is a witness W such that κ' is definitely accepted from W and one of the following conditions:

- $W \subseteq Q_1$, $\mathsf{val}(W, x, u) < 0$
- $W \cap Q_0 \neq \emptyset$ and $0 \leq \mathsf{val}(W \cap Q_1, x, u) < 1$.

Now, to check the existence of a string κ satisfying the above property, we define another quantity $\mathsf{minval}(W, i)$ for each $W \in \mathcal{X}$ and $i \geq 0$ as follows. Intuitively, this is the minimum of the values given by val over all strings of length at most i. Formally, we have the following definition where $\min\{\emptyset\} = +\infty$.

$$\mathsf{minval}(W, i) = \min\{\mathsf{val}(W \cap Q_1, x, u) \,|\, |u| \leq i\}.$$

The following lemma is easily proved using the observations above.

Lemma 2. $L_{>x}(\mathcal{A}) \neq \emptyset$ *iff for some $i \geq 0$, either $(\exists W \in \mathcal{X} : \mathsf{minval}(W, i) < 0)$ or $(\exists W \in \mathcal{Y} : 0 \leq \mathsf{minval}(W, i) < 1)$.*

For any $C \subset Q, u \in \Sigma^+$, recall that $\mathsf{pre}(C, u) = \cup_{q \in C} \mathsf{pre}(q, u)$ (see Sect. 2). Now, for any $W \in \mathcal{X}$, $a \in \Sigma$, and $q \in Q_0$, let $W_{a,q} = (\mathsf{pre}(W, a) \cap Q_1) \cup \{q\}$. It should be easy to see that $W_{a,q} \in \mathcal{X}$. To calculate the values $\mathsf{minval}(W, i)$ for $W \in \mathcal{X}$ and $i \geq 0$, we present the following incremental algorithm.

$$\mathsf{minval}(W, 0) = \begin{cases} x & if (q_0 \in W); \\ +\infty & else. \end{cases}$$

For $i > 0$, and $W \cap Q_0 \neq \emptyset$,

$$\mathsf{minval}(W, i) = \min\{\mathsf{minval}(W, i - 1), \qquad (2)$$
$$\min\{\frac{\mathsf{minval}(W_{a,q}, i - 1) - \delta_a(q, W \cap Q_1)}{\delta_a(q, q_W)} \mid$$
$$a \in \Sigma, q \in Q_0, \delta_a(q, q_W) > 0\}\}.$$

Further more, for $i > 0$ and $W \cap Q_0 = \emptyset$, $\mathsf{minval}(W, i)$ is updated as follows: if $\exists a \in \Sigma, q \in Q_0$ such that $\mathsf{minval}(W_{a,q}, i-1) < \delta_a(q, W \cap Q_1)$ then $\mathsf{minval}(W, i) = -\infty$; otherwise, $\mathsf{minval}(W, i) = \mathsf{minval}(W, i - 1)$. By induction on i, it can be shown the above algorithm computes $\mathsf{minval}(\cdot, \cdot)$ correctly, i.e., the computed values agree with the definition of $\mathsf{minval}(\cdot, \cdot)$ given earlier. Clearly, $\mathsf{minval}(W, i)$ is monotonically non-increasing with increasing values of i.

Let $w = |\mathcal{X}|$. It should be easy to see that $w \leq 2^n \leq L$. The algorithm computes the values of $\mathsf{minval}(W, i)$, for each witness set $W \in \mathcal{X}$, in increasing values of $i = 0, \ldots$ until one of the following conditions is satisfied: (a) $(\exists W \in \mathcal{X} : \mathsf{minval}(W, i) < 0)$ or $(\exists W \in \mathcal{Y} : 0 \leq \mathsf{minval}(W, i) < 1)$; (b) $i > 0$ and $\forall W \in \mathcal{X}$, $\mathsf{minval}(W, i) = \mathsf{minval}(W, i - 1)$; (c) $i = w$. Observe that once condition (b) holds, the values of $\mathsf{minval}(W, i)$ do not change from that point onwards, i.e., they reach a fixed point. The algorithm terminates for the smallest integer i such that either of the conditions (a) or (b) hold. If at termination, condition (a) holds then it answers "yes"; if (a) does not hold but (b) holds then it answers "no"; if both (a) and (b) do not hold, but (c) holds then it will answer "yes". Now we have the following theorem.

Theorem 1 (Correctness of Forward Algorithm). *Forward algorithm will definitely terminate after at most w iterations providing the correct answer, i.e., it outputs "yes" iff $\mathsf{L}_{>x}(\mathcal{A}) \neq \emptyset$.*

Proof. Clearly, the algorithm terminates within at most w iterations and outputs an "yes" or "no" answer. It is enough if we prove that it outputs the correct answer. Assume that the algorithm outputs an "yes" answer. Here there are two cases. The first one is condition (a) is satisfied. Clearly, from Lemma 2, we see that $\mathsf{L}_{>x}(\mathcal{A}) \neq \emptyset$. The second case, is that condition (c) is satisfied, i.e., $i = w$ at termination and neither of conditions (a), (b) is satisfied. Let $F_0 = \{W \in \mathcal{X} \mid q_0 \in W\}$. For $j > 0$, let $F_j = \{W \in \mathcal{X} \mid \mathsf{minval}(W, j) < \mathsf{minval}(W, j - 1)\}$. It is easily seen that for each $j > 0$, $F_j \neq \emptyset$, otherwise the fixed point condition (b) would have been satisfied before the wth iteration. Also for each $W \in F_j$, $W \cap Q_0 \neq \emptyset$ and there exists $V \in F_{j-1}$ and $a \in \Sigma$ such that $\text{minval}(W, j) = \frac{\text{minval}(V, j-1) - \delta_a(q_V, W \cap Q_1)}{\delta_a(q_V, W \cap Q_0)}$. Since $F_w \neq \emptyset$, the above property would imply that there exists $W_0 \in F_0$ and for each $0 < j \leq w$, there exists $W_j \in F_j$ and $a_j \in \Sigma$ such that $\text{minval}(W_j, j) = \frac{\text{minval}(W_{j-1}, j-1) - \delta_{a_j}(q, W_j \cap Q_1)}{\delta_{a_j}(q, W_j \cap Q_0)}$ where $q = q_{W_{j-1}}$. Let $\kappa_j = (a_1, \ldots, a_j)$ for $j > 0$. Then, by simple induction on j, it is seen that $\text{minval}(W_j, j) = \text{val}(W_j \cap Q_1, x, \kappa_j)$.

Now, using Pigeon Hole principle, we see there exist integers $0 \leq j < k \leq w$, such that $W_j = W_k$. Let $V = W_j$ and q be the state q_{W_j}. Clearly $\text{minval}(V, k) < \text{minval}(V, j)$. Now, let $u = \kappa_j$ as given above, and $v \in \Sigma^*$ be the string $(a_{j+1}, a_{j+2}, \ldots, a_k)$. Let $x' = \delta_v(q, V \cap Q_1), z' = \delta_v(q, q)$ and $y' = 1 - z'$. From the earlier observation, $\text{minval}(V, j) = \text{val}(V \cap Q_1, x, u)$ and $\text{minval}(V, k) = \text{val}(V \cap Q_1, x, uv)$. Using property (1) of Lemma 1, it is seen that $\text{minval}(V, j) - \text{minval}(V, k) = \frac{y'}{z'}(\frac{x'}{y'} - \text{minval}(V, j))$. Hence $\frac{x'}{y'} > \text{minval}(V, j)$. Observe that $|u| = j, |v| = k - j$. Now, for an integer $p > 0$, let $n_p = j + p(k - j)$. By considering the string uv^p, and using part (2) of Lemma 1, we see that $\text{minval}(V, n_p) = \rho + (\frac{1}{z'})^p(\text{minval}(V, j) - \rho)$ where $\rho = \frac{x'}{y'}$. Since $(\text{minval}(V, j) - \rho) < 0$ and $z' < 1$, we see that $\text{minval}(V, n_p) < 0$ for sufficiently large $p > 0$. Applying Lemma 2, we see that $L_{>x}(\mathcal{A}) \neq \emptyset$.

Now, assume the algorithm outputs a "no" answer on termination, which means condition (b) is satisfied but condition (a) is not. Assume the algorithm terminated after j iterations. Clearly, condition (a) is not satisfied for all $i \leq j$. Condition (b) implies for all $i \geq j$ and for all $W \in \mathcal{X}$, $\text{minval}(W, i) = \text{minval}(W, j)$. Hence for all $i \geq j$, condition (a) is not satisfied. By Lemma 2, we see that $L_{>x}(\mathcal{A}) = \emptyset$.

3.2 Backward Algorithm

The basic backward algorithm has been introduced in [6]. Here we present an enhanced algorithm supporting convergence and early termination before completing L iterations, not only for cases when $L_{>x}(\mathcal{A}) \neq \emptyset$, but also for some cases when $L_{>x}(\mathcal{A}) = \emptyset$.

Let $\mathcal{X}'$ be the set of all $W \in \mathcal{X}$ such that $W \cap Q_0 \neq \emptyset$. Let $\mathcal{Y}'$ be the set of all good witness sets. A function $Prob(\cdot, \cdot)$ which maps each pair (W, i), where $W \in \mathcal{X}'$ and $i \geq 0$, to a probability value, is defined as follows: Here we take $\max\{\emptyset\} = 0$;

$$Prob(W, i) = \max\{\delta_u(q_W, V) | u \in \Sigma^*, V \in \mathcal{Y}', \text{post}(W \cap Q_1, u) \subseteq V, |u| \leq i\}.$$

$Prob(W, i)$ denotes the maximum probability of reaching any set $V \in \mathcal{Y}'$ using an input of length at most i, from the state q_W. If $Prob(W, i) > x$, there is an input accepted from q_W with probability $> x$ (because from q_W using an input of length at most i, we can reach a good witness set V, with probability $> x$, and then we can use any sequence that is accepted from all states in V with probability 1; there exists at least one such sequence because $V \in \mathcal{X}'$). Clearly, $Prob(W, i)$ is monotonically non-decreasing with increasing values of i.

It has been shown in [6] that $L_{>x}(\mathcal{A}) \neq \emptyset$ iff $Prob(\{q_0\}, L) > x$. The following inductive algorithm is proposed to compute $Prob(\cdot, \cdot)$.

$$
\begin{aligned}
Prob(W, 1) &= \max\{\delta_a(q_W, V) | a \in \Sigma, V \in \mathcal{Y}', \mathsf{post}(W \cap Q_1, a) \subseteq V\}; \\
Prob(W, i+1) &= \max(\{Prob(W, i)\} \cup \qquad\qquad\qquad\qquad\qquad (3) \\
&\quad \{\delta_a(q_W, q_V) Prob(V, i) + \delta_a(q_W, V \cap Q_1) \\
&\quad |a \in \Sigma, V \in \mathcal{X}', \mathsf{post}(W \cap Q_1, a) \subseteq V\}).
\end{aligned}
$$

The backward algorithm works as follows. For increasing values of $i = 1, \ldots, L$, it computes $Prob(W, i)$ for each $W \in \mathcal{X}'$. The algorithm terminates at the smallest $i > 1$ such that one of the following conditions is satisfied: (a) $Prob(\{q_0\}, i) > x$, (b) for each $W \in \mathcal{X}'$, $Prob(W, i) = Prob(W, i-1)$, (c) $i = L$ and $Prob(\{q_0\}, i) \leq x$. It is not difficult to see that if the convergence condition (b) is satisfied for a particular value i, then for all $j \geq i$, $Prob(W, j) = Prob(W, i)$, i.e., the values given by $Prob(., .)$ do not change. On termination, if condition (a) is satisfied then the algorithm gives "yes" answer, otherwise it gives a "no" answer. We refer to condition (a) as positive termination, condition (b) and (c) as negative termination conditions.

The backward algorithm is in **EXPTIME** in the worst case. However, in case it converges and terminates early, it may take much less time than the theoretically worst time. The following theorem states the correctness of the algorithm and is proved by induction on i and using the result of [6].

Theorem 2 (Backward Termination). *The backward algorithm is correct, that is, it answers "yes", iff* $L_{>x}(\mathcal{A}) \neq \emptyset$.

Consider the HPA $\mathcal{A}$ in Figure 1, for $x = \frac{1}{2}$. It is easy to see that $L_{>\frac{1}{2}}(\mathcal{A})$ is empty. The backward algorithm will run all the L iterations and output a "no" answer.

3.3   Forward vs. Backward

Both forward and backward algorithms can be utilized to solve the decidability problem. Suppose the HPA $\mathcal{A}$ has n states, m transitions, $w = |\mathcal{X}|$ and the number of input symbols is s. After careful calculation, we see that in the worst case the forward algorithm runs in time $O((mn + L_f m^2)w)$, while backward algorithm runs in $O((L_b m + m + n)sw^2)$, where L_f and L_b denote the number of iterations before the respective algorithms terminate. Clearly $L_f \leq w$, while $L_b \leq L$. Since $w = O(2^n)$ and $L > w$ is also exponential in n, both these algorithms run in time exponential in n in the worst case. However, the above complexities show that the forward algorithm is quadratic in w, while that of the backward algorithm is cubic in w, considering the dependence of L_f, L_b on w. Thus, forward algorithm has better worst case complexity. Our experimental results, given in Sect. 6.3, show that the forward algorithm runs much faster than the backward algorithm. Also, the forward algorithm critically depends on x, i.e., the definition of $\mathsf{minval}(\cdot, \cdot)$ function depends on x, while the $Prob(\cdot, \cdot)$ used in the backward algorithm is independent of x. Also, forward algorithms often terminates much faster than the backward algorithm, especially when $L_{>x}(\mathcal{A}) = \emptyset$ and the latter terminates on condition (c), as is for the example in Fig. 1.

3.4 Robustness

So far we have given algorithms for the verification problem. When failure-prone systems are modeled as HPA, an equally important notion is *robustness*. As we will show later, we model the incorrectness of an open system under failures as a 1-HPA. In this case, we define the robustness of an HPA $\mathcal{A}$ as $(1-y)$ where y is the least upper bound of the set of values $\{x | L_{>x}(\mathcal{A}) \neq \emptyset\}$. This value is the greatest lower bound of $\{z | z$ is the probability of rejection of some input string by $\mathcal{A}\}$. The value of y, and hence the robustness, can be found within some accuracy by using binary search repeatedly employing the forward algorithm for various values of x. Although the backward algorithm is less efficient for the verification problem, it can be used to compute the exact value of the robustness in some cases. Suppose the backward algorithm reaches a fixed point after k iterations, then $y = Prob(\{q_0\}, k)$ where q_0 is the initial state of $\mathcal{A}$. In this case, robustness has the exact value $(1 - y)$.

4 Undecidability for 2-HPA

In this section, we consider 2-HPA and show that the problem of checking $L_{>x}(\mathcal{A}) \neq \emptyset$ is undecidable for the case when $\mathcal{A}$ is a 2-HPA. This result closes the gap between the decidability and undecidability results for HPA.

Theorem 3. *Given a 2-HPA $\mathcal{A}$, a rational threshold $x \in [0,1]$ the problem of determining if $L_{>x}(\mathcal{A}) \neq \emptyset$ is undecidable.*

Proof. We use the approach given in the [4], with major critical modifications. There the result was proved by reducing the halting problem of deterministic 2-counter machines to the non-emptiness problem of HPA with strict acceptance thresholds. The broad ideas behind that construction are as follows. Let T be deterministic 2-counter machine with control states Q and a special halting state q_h. It is assumed, without loss of generality, that each transition of T changes at most one counter and the initial counter values are 0. Recall that a configuration of such a machine is of the form (q, a^{i+1}, b^{j+1}), where $q \in Q$ is the current control state, and a^i (b^j) is the unary representation of the value stored in the first counter (second counter, respectively). The input alphabet Σ of the constructed HPA $\mathcal{A}_T$ will consist of the set Q as well as the 5 symbols- ",", "(", ")", a and b. The HPA $\mathcal{A}_T$ will have the following property: if $\rho = \sigma_1\sigma_2\cdots\sigma_n$ is a halting computation of T then $\mathcal{B}$ will accept the word ρ with probability $> \frac{1}{2}$; if $\rho = \sigma_1\sigma_2\cdots$ is a non-halting computation of T then $\mathcal{A}_T$ will accept every prefix of ρ with probability $< \frac{1}{2}$; and if ρ is an encoding of an invalid computation (i.e., if ρ is not of the right format or has incorrect transitions) and no prefix of ρ is a valid halting computation of T then $\mathcal{A}_T$ will accept ρ with probability

$< \frac{1}{2}$. Given this property we will be able to conclude that T halts iff $L_{>\frac{1}{2}}(\mathcal{A}_T)$ is non-empty, thus proving the theorem.

In order to construct an HPA $\mathcal{A}_T$ with the above properties, $\mathcal{A}_T$ must be able to check if there is a finite prefix α of input ρ that encodes a valid halting computation of T. This requires checking the following properties. (1) α is of the right format, i.e., it is a sequence of tuples of the form (q, a^i, b^j). (2) The first configuration is the initial configuration. (3) Successive configurations in the sequence follow because of a valid transition of T. (4) In the last configuration, T is in the halting state q_h.

Checking properties (1), (2) and (4) can be easily accomplished using only finite memory. On the other hand checking (3) requires checking that the counters are updated correctly which cannot be done deterministically using finite memory. Our major changes to the proof are for step (3). Our construction for step (3) is as follows. The main part of the 2-HPA $\mathcal{A}_T$, corresponding to step (3), is shown in Fig. 2. In this automaton, The level 0 states keep track of which part of each configuration the input sequence is in. The set of states of $\mathcal{A}_T$ is a super set of Q. After the input q of an input configuration (q, a^i, b^j), $\mathcal{A}_T$ will be in state q. On the following input symbol comma, $\mathcal{A}_T$ from state q, probabilistically decides to do: (a) check that the first set of counters (i.e., those denoted by a symbols) in the current and next configurations match; (b) check that the second set of counters (i.e., those denoted by b symbols) in the current and next configurations match; (c) continue and go to state q' at level 0. From state q', $\mathcal{A}_T$ has transitions as shown on inputs a, b, and at the end of the current configuration, on the input string of the form ")("u" (where $u \in Q$), it will go to state u with probability 1. From any state, if no transition on an input symbol is shown, it is assumed that the automaton stays in the same state on that input. In every state, whenever the input symbol is a state component of a configuration of T which is a halting state, $\mathcal{A}_T$ goes to the accepting state with probability 1. To check the second counter values in the current and next configurations, a similar mechanism with additional level 1 states s_1, s_2, s_3, etc., is employed.

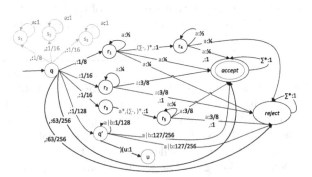

Fig. 2. Partial HPA used in the Undecidability Proof. Inputs and associated probabilities are shown on each transition separated by ":" symbol.

Now, we analyze probability of acceptance and rejection as follows. Suppose that the first counter values in the current and next configurations have values i, j respectively. Then, let p_{accept}, p_{reject} be the probabilities of $\mathcal{A}_T$ going to accept and reject states, respectively, after going to r_1, r_2 or r_3 at the beginning of the current configuration. Their values are shown below in Table 1.

Table 1. Probability analysis for Undecidability Proof.

	P_{accept}	P_{reject}	Sum
Through r_1	$\frac{1}{16}(1 + 2^{-(i+j)})$	$\frac{1}{16}(1 - 2^{-(i+j)})$	$\frac{1}{8}$
Through r_2	$\frac{1}{32}(1 - 2^{-2i})$	$\frac{1}{32}(1 + 2^{-2i})$	$\frac{1}{16}$
Through r_3	$\frac{1}{32}(1 - 2^{-2j})$	$\frac{1}{32}(1 + 2^{-2j})$	$\frac{1}{16}$

From this, we see that

$$p_{reject} - p_{accept} = \frac{1}{16}(2^{-2i} + 2^{-2j} - 2 \cdot 2^{-(i+j)}) = \frac{1}{16}(2^{-i} - 2^{-j})^2 \geq 0.$$

If $i = j$, then $p_{accept} - p_{reject} = 0$. Now consider the case when $i \neq j$. Assume with out loss of generality that $i > j$. In this case,

$$p_{reject} - p_{accept} \geq \frac{1}{16}(2^{-j} - 2^{-j-1})^2 \geq \frac{1}{16}2^{-2(j+1)} = \frac{1}{64} \cdot 2^{-2j}.$$

Now the probability that $\mathcal{A}_T$ is at a level 0 state (i.e., such as q) is $\frac{1}{128} \cdot (\frac{1}{128})^{(i+i')}$ where i, i' are the values of the first and second counters in the current configuration, which is $\leq (\frac{1}{64})^2 \cdot 2^{-(2 \cdot i + 7i')}$. This value is less than $\frac{1}{64} \cdot 2^{-2j}$ when $i > j$, and is less than $\frac{1}{64} \cdot 2^{-2i}$ when $j > i$. (The same reasoning is used to establish this property when we consider the second counter values using the values i', j'). This shows that $p_{reject} - p_{accept}$ is greater the probability that $\mathcal{A}_T$ is at a level 0 state plus the probabilities that $\mathcal{A}_T$ is in any of the intermediate level 1 states which go to the accepting state if the following configuration has a halt state in an illegal computation. From this, we see that even if we get an illegal computation that ends with a halting state, that computation will be accepted with probability $< \frac{1}{2}$. On the other hand a legal halting computation will be accepted with probability $> \frac{1}{2}$.

Here we are assuming the counter values in successive configurations are required to be equal. However, if a counter values in the next configurations need to be one less (or one more) than that in the current configuration, then the above mechanism is easily modified to achieve this.

5   Modeling Failure-Prone Open Systems

Many concurrent systems, such as web servers, run on multiple processors. They take inputs from the environment (e.g. users), and consume inputs by going through a sequence of states. However, they are subjected to processor failures. When such failures occur, exception handling is executed and usually the load on the failed processor, i.e., the processes running on it, are transferred to the remaining processors. Thus after occurrence of a failure, the computation of the system changes. We model the failures with probability distributions, and model the behavior as *Open Probabilistic Transition Systems* (OPTS).

An Open Probabilistic Transition System $\mathbb{T}$ is 6-tuple $(S, \Sigma, \eta, s_0, \mathcal{P}, \phi)$ where S is a set of states, Σ is an input alphabet, $\eta : S \times \Sigma \times S \rightarrow [0,1]$ is the *transition relation* so that for all $s, s' \in S$ and $a \in \Sigma$, $\eta(s, a, s')$ is a rational number and $\sum_{s' \in Q} \eta(s, a, s') = 1$, and $s_0 \in S$ is the initial state, $\mathcal{P}$ is a set of atomic propositions and $\phi : S \rightarrow 2^{\mathcal{P}}$ is a function assigning a set of atomic propositions to each state. We assume that $S, \mathcal{P}$ are finite sets. Observe that S, η, s_0 and Σ are similar to the corresponding components of a PA. However, $\mathbb{T}$ has additional information given by $\mathcal{P}$ and ϕ that label the states with atomic propositions. For a given OPTS $\mathbb{T}$ as given above, we can define a probability space $(S^{\omega}, \mathbb{E}, \psi)$ where S^{ω} is the set of infinite sequences of states, $\mathbb{E}$ is the set of measurable subsets of S^{ω} which is the σ-algebra generated by cylinders of the form $u S^{\omega}$ where $u \in S^*$, and ψ is a probability function defined on it. As pointed out earlier, we use OPTSes to model failure-prone open concurrent systems. An input to $\mathbb{T}$ is an infinite sequence $\beta \in \Sigma^{\omega}$. A computation σ of $\mathbb{T}$ on input β is an infinite sequence of states $(s_0, \ldots, s_i, \ldots)$ starting from the initial state s_0 such that $\eta(s_i, \beta[i], s_{i+1}) > 0$ for all $i \geq 0$. We let $\mathcal{C}(\mathbb{T}, \beta)$ denote the set of computations of $\mathbb{T}$ on β. For a computation σ as given above, we let $\phi(\sigma)$ to be the sequence $(\phi(s_0), \phi(s_1), \ldots)$.

We consider the problem of verifying OPTSes against correctness property specified by deterministic safety automata. The inputs to the safety automaton are elements of $2^{\mathcal{P}}$. Formally a safety specification $\mathcal{B}$ for a OPTS $\mathbb{T}$ as given above is a deterministic finite-state automaton $\mathcal{B} = (R, \delta_1, r_0, F_1)$ where R is a finite set of automaton states, $\delta_1 : R \times 2^{\mathcal{P}} \rightarrow R$ is the next state function such that $\delta_1(r_{error}, c) = r_{error}$ for all $c \in 2^{\mathcal{P}}$, $r_0 \in R$ is the initial state and $F_1 = R - \{r_{error}\}$ where r_{error} is unique state in R called the *error* state. As usual, we define a run ρ of $\mathcal{B}$ on an input $t = (t_0, \ldots) \in (2^{\mathcal{P}})^{\omega}$ to be an infinite sequence of states $(r_0, r_1, \ldots)$ starting from the initial state r_0 such that $r_{i+1} \in \delta_1(r_i, t_i)$. We say that the above run is an accepting run if $r_i \in F_1$ for all $i \geq 0$, i.e., r_{error} does not appear on the run.

Now, we define the probability of satisfaction of the property $\mathcal{B}$ by the OPTS $\mathbb{T}$ on an input sequence $\beta \in \Sigma^{\omega}$, denoted by $Pr(\mathbb{T}, \beta, \mathcal{B})$, to be the probability given by $\psi(D)$ where D is the set of all computations σ of $\mathbb{T}$ on the input β such that $\phi(\sigma)$ is accepted by $\mathcal{B}$. Note that $1 - Pr(\mathbb{T}, \beta, \mathcal{B})$ denotes the probability that $\mathbb{T}$ does not satisfy the property $\mathcal{B}$ on the input β. The *verification problem* for OPTSes is — given $\mathbb{T}, \mathcal{B}$ as above and a rational $x \in [0,1]$ – determine if $Pr(\mathbb{T}, \beta, \mathcal{B}) \geq x$ for all $\beta \in \Sigma^{\omega}$.

Now, we transform the above verification problem to checking emptiness problem for PAs. Given $\mathbb{T}, \mathcal{B}, x$ as specified above, we construct a PA, $\mathcal{A}(\mathbb{T}, \mathcal{B})$, over the set of input symbols Σ, which is a product of $\mathbb{T}, \mathcal{B}$, and is defined as follows: $\mathcal{A}(\mathbb{T}, \mathcal{B}) = (Q, q_0, \delta, F)$ where $Q = S \times R$, $q_0 = (s_0, r_0)$, $F = S \times \{r_{error}\}$ and δ is defined as follows: for any $s, s' \in S$ and $r, r' \in R$, $a \in \Sigma$, $\delta((s, r), a, (s', r')) = \eta(s, a, s')$ if $r' = \delta_1(r, \phi(s))$, and is 0 otherwise. The following theorem can be easily shown.

Theorem 4. *For any OPTS* $\mathbb{T} = (S, \Sigma, \eta, s_0, \mathcal{P}, \phi)$ *and safety automaton* $\mathcal{B} = (R, \delta_1, r_0, F)$ *over* $2^{\mathcal{P}}$ *and rational* $x \in [0, 1]$, *for all* $\beta \in \Sigma^\omega$, $\mathbb{T}$ *satisfies the specification* $\mathcal{B}$ *with probability* $\geq x$ *(i.e.,* $Pr(\mathbb{T}, \beta, \mathcal{B}) \geq x$*) iff for all* $u \in \Sigma^*$ *the PA* $\mathcal{A}(\mathbb{T}, \mathcal{B})$ *accepts* u *with probability* $\leq 1 - x$ *iff* $L_{>(1-x)}(\mathcal{A}(\mathbb{T}, \mathcal{B})) = \emptyset$.

We say that an OPTS $\mathbb{T}$ is a k-OPTS ($k > 0$) if its set of states S can be partitioned into $k + 1$ sets $S_0, S_1, \ldots, S_k$ satisfying the following conditions: (a) $s_0 \in S_0$; (b) for every integer $i \in [0, k]$, every $s \in S_i$, and every $a \in \Sigma$, there is at most one state $s' \in S_i$ such that $\eta(s, a, s') > 0$; (c) for every i, j such that $0 \leq j < i \leq k$, for every $s \in S_i, s' \in S_j$, $\eta(s, a, s') = 0$. k-OPTSes can be used to model web applications with at most k processor failures. Obviously, if $\mathbb{T}$ is a k-OPTS then $\mathcal{A}(\mathbb{T}, \mathcal{B})$ is a k-HPA. If $\mathbb{T}$ is a 1-OPTS, using the above theorem, we can verify that $Pr(\mathbb{T}, \beta, \mathcal{B}) \geq x$ for all $\beta \in \Sigma^\omega$ by checking $L_{>1-x}(\mathcal{A}(\mathbb{T}, \mathcal{B})) = \emptyset$. The latter property can be checked using the algorithms given in Sect. 3. We can define the *robustness* of $\mathbb{T}$ with respect to the correctness specification $\mathcal{B}$ to be the greatest lower bound of the set $\{Pr(\mathbb{T}, \beta, \mathcal{B}) \mid \beta \in \Sigma^\omega\}$. This value can be computed as the robustness of $\mathcal{A}(\mathbb{T}, \mathcal{B})$ which can be computed as presented in the previous section. Finally, the result of Sect. 4 also shows that the problem of checking if a given k-OPTS with $k \geq 2$ satisfies a safety specification with probability $> x$ on all inputs, for some rational threshold x, is undecidable.

6 Implementation and Experiment

In this section, we will present the implementation of various HPA related algorithms in our HPA tool[2]. We will also describe how we abstract 1-HPA models from web applications assuming at most one failure. We will present experimental results showing the effectiveness of our verification algorithms on the abstracted web applications.

6.1 Implementation of the Verification Algorithms

In our verification process, we first validate whether a given PA $\mathcal{A}$ is an HPA. If so, we compute the smallest integer k such that $\mathcal{A}$ is a k-HPA, and also classify the states of $\mathcal{A}$ into different levels. Then we obtain good witness sets for 1-HPA. Finally, we run the forward and backward verification algorithms on good witness sets for 1-HPA.

---

[2] HPA tool website: https://github.com/benyue/HPA.

Detect HPA and Assign Levels. In this section, we describe the algorithm for checking if a given PA is an HPA, and for classifying its states into different levels.

Given a PA $\mathcal{A} = (Q, q_0, \delta, \mathsf{Acc})$ over input alphabet Σ, we first construct a directed graph $G_{\mathcal{A}} = (Q, E)$ with Q as its set of nodes and $E = \{(q, q') \mid \exists a \in \Sigma, \delta(q, a, q') > 0\}$. Without loss of generality, we assume that all nodes in Q are reachable from the initial node q_0. A *strongly connected component* (SCC) of $G_{\mathcal{A}}$ is a maximal subset of Q such that there is a path in $G_{\mathcal{A}}$ between every pair of nodes in it; the *component graph* of $G_{\mathcal{A}}$ is the directed graph $F_{\mathcal{A}} = (\mathcal{C}, \mathbb{E})$ where $\mathcal{C}$ is the set of SCCs of $G_{\mathcal{A}}$, and $(C, D) \in \mathbb{E}$ iff $C \neq D$ and $\exists q \in C, q' \in D$ such that $(q, q') \in E$. It is known that $F_{\mathcal{A}}$ is acyclic. Let $n = |Q|$ and m be the number of triples (q, a, q') such that $\delta(q, a, q') > 0$. Using standard graph algorithms, $G_{\mathcal{A}}$ and $F_{\mathcal{A}}$ can be constructed in time $O(n + m)$. We refer to $C_0 \in \mathcal{C}$ where $q_0 \in C_0$ as the *initial* SCC. Under reachability assumption, every node in $F_{\mathcal{A}}$ is reachable from C_0.

A SCC node $C \in \mathcal{C}$ is said to be *conflicting* iff $\exists a \in \Sigma$ and $\exists q, q_1, q_2 \in C$ such that $q_1 \neq q_2$ and $\delta(q, a, q_1) > 0$ and $\delta(q, a, q_2) > 0$. All nodes in each $C \in \mathcal{C}$ are on the same level. It is not difficult to see that $\mathcal{A}$ is an HPA iff there are no conflicting nodes in $\mathcal{C}$, i.e., there are no conflicting SCCs in $G_{\mathcal{A}}$. This algorithm has time complexity $O(n + m)$.

For an HPA $\mathcal{A}$, let $Min\_level(\mathcal{A})$ be the minimum k such that $\mathcal{A}$ is k-HPA. Now, we present an algorithm to compute $Min\_level(\mathcal{A})$. For any $Q' \subseteq Q$ and any $q \in Q$, we say that q *is deterministic with respect to* Q', if for each $a \in \Sigma$, there is at most one state $q' \in Q'$ such that $\delta(q, a, q') > 0$. We say that an SCC $C \in \mathcal{C}$ is *deterministic* with respect to Q', if every state in C is deterministic with respect to Q'. For any sub-graph H of $F_{\mathcal{A}}$, let $States(H)$ be the union of all SCCs C such that C is a node in H and $TD(H)$ be the set of all nodes C in H such that all nodes in H, that are reachable from C (including C), are deterministic with respect to $States(H)$. Note that all terminal nodes of H are in $TD(H)$. Let $Level\_seq(\mathcal{A})$ be the unique maximum length sequence $(H_0, H_1, \ldots, H_\ell)$ of non-empty subgraphs of $F_{\mathcal{A}}$ such that $H_0 = F_{\mathcal{A}}$, for each $i, 0 \leq i < \ell$, H_{i+1} is the subgraph of H_i obtained by deleting all nodes in $TD(H_i)$. Since $Level\_seq(\mathcal{A})$ is the maximum length sequence, it is easy to see that every node in H_ℓ is a deterministic SCC with respect to $States(H_\ell)$. Now, we have the following theorem.

Theorem 5. *$\mathcal{A}$ is an ℓ–HPA iff $G_{\mathcal{A}}$ has no conflicting SCCs. Further more, if $G_{\mathcal{A}}$ has no conflicting SCCs and $Level\_seq(\mathcal{A}) = (H_0, \ldots, H_\ell)$ then Min_level $(\mathcal{A}) = \ell$ and $\mathcal{A}$ is a ℓ-HPA with $Q_i = States(H_{\ell-i})$ being the set of states at level i, for $0 \leq i \leq \ell$.*

It is easy to see that using standard graph algorithms, we can check whether $\mathcal{A}$ is an HPA in time $O(n + m)$; if it is an HPA, we compute $Level\_seq(\mathcal{A})$, $Min\_level(\mathcal{A})$ and partition the states of $\mathcal{A}$ into different levels in time $O(Min\_level(\mathcal{A}) \cdot (n + m))$.

Obtain Good Witness Sets. Now assume $\mathcal{A} = (Q, q_0, \delta, \mathsf{Acc})$ is a 1-HPA. In Sect. 2.1, we defined the set $\mathcal{Y}$ as the set of good witness sets U such that $U \cap Q_0 \neq \emptyset$, and set $\mathcal{X}$ as the set of all witness sets U such that $U \cap Q_1$ is a good witness set. To compute these sets, we start from the set Acc of final states of $\mathcal{A}$, and traverse backward using each input symbol and its predecessors, and compute $\mathcal{X}$ and $\mathcal{Y}$ incrementally. Equivalently, we construct a standard non-deterministic automaton $\mathcal{A}^{-1}$ which is a reversal of $\mathcal{A}$, i.e., $\mathcal{A}^{-1}$ has the same set of states as $\mathcal{A}$; there is a transition from q to q' on input a iff $\delta(q', a, q) > 0$; the set of its initial states is Acc. Our algorithm for computing $\mathcal{X}$ and $\mathcal{Y}$, is similar (with some critical modifications) to that of determinizing $\mathcal{A}^{-1}$ using standard subset-construction. The complexity of this algorithm is $O(wsmn)$ where $n = |Q|$, m is the number of transitions, $w = |\mathcal{X}|$ and $s = |\Sigma|$.

Run the Verification Algorithms on the Witness Sets. Now we can run the forward and backward algorithms (Sect. 3) on $\mathcal{A}$ and its witness sets. The algorithms use the threshold value x obtained from environment. In implementing the two algorithms, we precompute and store some of the values that are repeatedly used in the algorithm, such as the sets $W_{a,q}$ in the forward algorithm, for each $W \in \mathcal{X}$, $q \in Q$ and $a \in \Sigma$.

6.2   Abstracting Models of Web Applications

We consider web applications implemented on multiple servers. Only the server-side code of such web applications is abstracted. We assume a server accepts and processes a single session at a time. Concurrent sessions are executed by different servers. Each server is abstracted as a labeled deterministic finite-state automaton whose inputs are user-submitted *forms*; these include initiating a new session and ending the current session. These automata each have a special input symbol T that denotes elapse of one unit time (of course, we use discrete time and assume synchronized clocks). The states of these automata are labeled with atomic propositions denoting their properties.

We assume all servers are modeled by identical finite-state machines, since they run identical server code. We consider a system with only two servers. Our tool takes the automaton A describing the server logic as an input. It takes two such automata (distinguishing all input symbols of the two automata excepting T), and composes them by synchronizing on the T symbol and capturing their parallel execution until a failure occurs. This composition results in a 1-OPTS as described in Sect. 5. We assume that these two automata do not interfere with each other. The tool then takes a failure model as input. Only one server can fail, and its failure probabilities for each (state, input) pair are specified in the failure model. After a failure, the current session of the failed server is taken over by the good server until completed. During this period, the good server is executing its own session as well as that of the failed processor. The order in which these should be processed is also specified as part of the failure model. Once a good server completes the session of the failed server and its own current session, it will continue to accept one new session at a time and process it.

The correctness property to be verified is specified as a safety automaton whose input symbols are $2^{\mathcal{P}}$ where $\mathcal{P}$ are the atomic propositions labeling the nodes of the server automaton; actually $\mathcal{P}$ includes two sets of propositions corresponding to the two sessions and it also includes input symbols of the server automata. In the composed OPTS we abstract away the T transitions as these are not the actual user inputs. Using the approach given in Sect. 5, we obtain a 1-HPA and check its emptiness using both the forward and backward algorithms.

6.3 Experiment

In the experiment section, we abstracted several 1-HPA from server-end web applications using the methodology stated in Sect. 6.2, and our incorrectness property states that session one takes strictly more time when run normally without failures. We then ran verification algorithms on them. Experimental results are presented in Table 2. Each row represents a different 1-HPA obtained using a different combination of process, failure definition and threshold probability. For the rows where the answer is empty, the threshold probability x is 0.9, and for those with non-empty answer, it was 0.01 for the example "Larger HPA" and 0.1 for the others. Empty answer indicates there is no input sequence on which the probability of violating the correctness is greater x. The column "BKD/FWD" explicitly shows the ratio of the time taken by the backward algorithm to that of the improved forward algorithm. The table shows that the forward algorithm is any where from 8 to 4500 times faster than the backward algorithm. This supports our analysis in Sect. 3.3.

Table 2. Backward vs Forward on Time Efficiency. Recall notations in Sect. 3.3.

Web Application	n	m	s	w	Result	(CPU Time in ms)			L_f	L_b
						Forward	Backward	BKD/FWD		
eBay Auction	19	248	13	60	empty	16	140	**8.75**	4	2
					non-empty	0	125	**N/A**	2	2
On-line Shopping 1	86	1472	17	342	empty	78	4009	**51.40**	16	15
					non-empty	47	4165	**88.62**	13	14
On-line Shopping 2	87	1489	17	2051	empty	328	338273	**1031.32**	14	10
					non-empty	140	321362	**2295.44**	5	8
Medium HPA	191	4209	22	3402	empty	391	491719	**1257.59**	8	10
					non-empty	172	502984	**2924.33**	5	8
Larger HPA	399	797	12	3874	empty	47	210734	**4483.70**	1	5
					non-empty	156	221641	**1420.78**	2	7

7 Conclusions

In this paper, we have given a new faster algorithm (with better complexity) for checking non-emptiness of the language accepted by a 1-HPA on finite strings with probability greater than a given value. We can trivially extend this algorithm to the case of automata over infinite strings under Büchi as well as Muller acceptance conditions. We simply have to use a different algorithm for computing good witness sets. These extended algorithms can be used to verify correctness of 1-OPTSes when the correctness is specified by a Büchi or Muller automata. This allows us to verify general properties including liveness properties. Also, the faster algorithm can be extended to the case when the threshold is a non-strict threshold. We have also proved the undecidability result for 2-HPA and closed the gap between the known decidability/undecidability results. Possible future work include extending our tool to support the case when different web sessions can interfere, and also support verification of LTL formulas.

Acknowledgements. This research is supported by the NSF grants CCF-1319754, CNS-1314485 and CNS-1035914.

References

1. Baier, C., Größer, M.: Recognizing ω-regular languages with probabilistic automata. In: 20th IEEE Symposium on Logic in Computer Science, pp. 137–146 (2005)
2. Baier, C., Größer, M., Bertrand, N.: Probabilistic ω-automata. J. ACM **59**(1), 1–52 (2012)
3. Baier, C., Haverkort, B.R., Hermanns, H., Katoen, J.-P.: Efficient computation of time-bounded reachability probabilities in uniform continuous-time markov decision processes. In: Jensen, K., Podelski, A. (eds.) TACAS 2004. LNCS, vol. 2988, pp. 61–76. Springer, Heidelberg (2004)
4. Chadha, R., Sistla, A.P., Viswanathan, M.: Probabilistic Büchi automata with non-extremal acceptance thresholds. In: Jhala, R., Schmidt, D. (eds.) VMCAI 2011. LNCS, vol. 6538, pp. 103–117. Springer, Heidelberg (2011)
5. Chadha, R., Sistla, A.P., Viswanathan, M.: Power of randomization in automata on infinite strings. Log. Methods Comput. Sci. **7**(3), 1–22 (2011)
6. Chadha, R., Sistla, A.P., Viswanathan, M., Ben, Y.: Decidable and expressive classes of probabilistic automata. In: Pitts, A. (ed.) FOSSACS 2015. LNCS, vol. 9034, pp. 200–214. Springer, Heidelberg (2015)
7. Gimbert, H., Oualhadj, Y.: Probabilistic automata on finite words: decidable and undecidable problems. In: Abramsky, S., Gavoille, C., Kirchner, C., Meyer auf der Heide, F., Spirakis, P.G. (eds.) ICALP 2010. LNCS, vol. 6199, pp. 527–538. Springer, Heidelberg (2010)
8. Größer, M.: Reduction Methods for Probabilistic Model Checking. Ph.D. thesis, TU Dresden (2008)
9. Paz, A.: Introduction to Probabilistic Automata. Academic Press, Orlando (1971)
10. PRISM – Probabilistic Symbolic Model Checker. http://www.prismmodelchecker.org
11. Rabin, M.O.: Probabilistic automata. Inf. Control **6**(3), 230–245 (1963)

Optimal Continuous Time Markov Decisions

Yuliya Butkova[✉], Hassan Hatefi, Holger Hermanns, and Jan Krčál

Saarland University – Computer Science, Saarbrücken, Germany
{butkova,hhatefi,hermanns,krcal}@cs.uni-saarland.de

Abstract. In the context of Markov decision processes running in continuous time, one of the most intriguing challenges is the efficient approximation of finite horizon reachability objectives. A multitude of sophisticated model checking algorithms have been proposed for this. However, no proper benchmarking has been performed thus far.

This paper presents a novel and yet simple solution: an algorithm, originally developed for a restricted subclass of models and a subclass of schedulers, can be twisted so as to become competitive with the more sophisticated algorithms in full generality. As the second main contribution, we perform a comparative evaluation of the core algorithmic concepts on an extensive set of benchmarks varying over all key parameters: model size, amount of non-determinism, time horizon, and precision.

1 Introduction

Over the last two decades, a formal approach to quantitative performance and dependability evaluation of concurrent systems has gained maturity. At its root are continuous-time Markov chains (CTMC) for which efficient and quantifiably precise solution methods exist [2]. A CTMC can be viewed as a labelled transition system (LTS) whose transitions are delayed according to exponential distributions. CTMCs are stochastic processes and thus do not support non-determinism. Non-determinism, often present in classical concurrency and automata theory models, is useful for modelling uncertainty or for performing optimisation over multiple choices. The genuine extension of CTMCs with non-determinism are continuous time Markov decision processes (CTMDPs). The non-determinism is controlled by an object called *scheduler* (also policy or strategy).

Prominent applications of CTMDPs include power management and scheduling [28], networked, distributed systems [11,17], epidemic and population processes [21], economy [5] and others. Moreover, CTMDPs are the core semantic model [9] underlying formalisms such as generalised stochastic Petri nets [22], Markovian stochastic activity networks [23] and interactive Markov chains [18].

When model checking a CTMDP [6], one asks whether the behaviour of the model for *some* schedulers (if we control the non-determinism) or for *all* schedulers (if it is out of control) satisfies given performance or dependability criteria. A large variety of them can be expressed using logics such as CSL [1]. At the centre of model-checking problems for such criteria is time bounded reachability: *What is the maximal/minimal probability to reach a given set of states within a*

© Springer International Publishing Switzerland 2015
B. Finkbeiner et al. (Eds.): ATVA 2015, LNCS 9364, pp. 166–182, 2015.
DOI: 10.1007/978-3-319-24953-7_12

given time bound. Having an efficient approach for this optimisation (maximisation or minimisation) is crucial for successful large-scale applications.

In order to not discriminate against real situations, one usually assumes that the scheduler can base its decisions on *any* available information about the past. Restricting the information however tends to imply cheaper approximative algorithms [3,26]. For CTMDPs, we can distinguish (general) *timed* optimal scheduling and (restricted) *untimed* optimal scheduling [3,4]. In the latter case, the scheduler has no possibility, intuitively speaking, to look at a clock measuring time. Another distinction within timed optimality discussed in the literature is *early* optimal scheduling (where every decision is frozen in between state changes [16,27]) and *late* optimal scheduling (where every decision can change as time passes while residing in a state [7,10]).

A handful of sophisticated algorithms have been suggested for timed optimality (partly for early optimality, partly for late optimality) signifying both the importance and the difficulty of this problem [7,10,27]. This paper presents a substantially different algorithm addressing this very problem. The approach is readily applicable to both early and late optimality. It harvest a very efficient algorithm for untimed optimality [3] originally restricted to a subclass of models. By a simple twist, we make it applicable for the general timed optimality for arbitrary models. As a second contribution, we present an exhaustive empirical comparison of this novel algorithm with all other published algorithms for the (early or late) timed optimality problem. We do so on an extensive collection of scalable industrial and academic CTMDP benchmarks (that we also make available). Notably, all earlier evaluations did compare at most two algorithms on at most one or two principal cases. We instead cross-compare 5 algorithms on 7 application cases, yielding a total of about 2350 distinct configurations. The results demonstrate that our simple algorithm is highly efficient across the entire spectrum of models, except for some of the experiments where extreme precision is required. On the other hand, no algorithm is consistently dominating any other algorithm across the experiments performed.

Related Work. Timed optimal scheduling has been considered for many decades both theoretically [24,30] and practically by introducing approximative algorithms. Formal error bounds needed for verification have been studied only recently [7,10,16,27]. Fragmentary empirical evaluations of some of the published algorithms have been performed [6,10,16]. In a nutshell, the published knowledge boils down to [27] $<_{[16]}$ [16] and [27] $<_{[6]}$ [7] $<_{[10]}$ [10], where $a <_{[\cdot]} b$ denotes "*b* is shown empirically faster than *a* in [·]". A substantial cross-comparison of the newest three algorithms [7,10,16] is however lacking.

Contribution of the Paper. The paper (*i*) develops a novel and simple approximation method for time bounded CTMDP reachability, (*ii*) presents the first ever set of benchmarks for CTMDP model checking, and (*iii*) performs an empirical evaluation across benchmarks and algorithms. The evaluation suggests that the optimal timing of decisions for time bounded reachability can be solved effectively by a rather straightforward algorithm, unless extreme precision is needed.

2   Preliminaries

Definition 1. *A continuous-time Markov decision process (CTMDP) is a tuple* $\mathcal{C} = (S, Act, \mathbf{R})$ *where S is a finite set of states, Act is a finite set of actions, and* $\mathbf{R} : S \times Act \times S \rightarrow \mathbb{R}_{\geq 0}$ *is a rate function.*

We call an action a *enabled* in s, also denoted by $a \in Act(s)$, if $\mathbf{R}(s, a, s') > 0$ for some $s' \in S$. We require that all sets $Act(s)$ are non-empty. A continuous-time Markov chain (CTMC) is a CTMDP where all $Act(s)$ are singleton sets.

For a given state s and action $a \in Act(s)$, we denote by $E(s, a) = \sum_{s'} \mathbf{R}(s, a, s')$ the *exit* rate of a in s. Finally, we let $\mathbf{P}(s, a, s') := \mathbf{R}(s, a, s')/E(s, a)$.

The operational behaviour of a CTMDP is like in a CTMC. Namely, when performing a given action a_0 in a state s_0, the CTMDP waits for a transition, i.e. waits for a delay t_0 chosen randomly according to an exponential distribution with rate $E(s_0, a_0)$. The transition leads to a state s_1 again chosen randomly according to the probability distribution $\mathbf{P}(s_0, a_0, \cdot)$. When performing an action a_1 there, it similarly waits for time t_1 and makes a transition into a state s_2 and so on, forming an infinite *run* $s_0 t_0 s_1 t_1 \cdots$.

The difference to a CTMC lies in the need to choose actions to perform, done by a *scheduler*. There are two classes of schedulers, *early* and *late*. Whenever entering a state, an early scheduler needs to choose and commit to a next action, whereas late schedulers may change such choices at any time later while residing in the state. In this paper we restrict w.l.o.g. [25] to deterministic schedulers but we allow the decision to depend on the whole *history* $s_0 t_0 \cdots t_{n-1} s_n$ so far.

Definition 2. *A (timed late) randomised scheduler is a measurable[1] function σ that to any history $h = s_0 t_0 \cdots t_{n-1} s_n$ and time $t \geq 0$ spent in s_n so far assigns a distribution over enabled actions $Act(s_n)$. We call σ early if $\sigma(h, t) = \sigma(h, t')$ for all h, t, t'; and deterministic if $\sigma(h, t)$ assign 1 to some action a for all h, t.*

We denote the set of all (timed) late or early schedulers by $Time_\ell$ and $Time_e$, respectively. We use these subscripts $\nabla \in \{\ell, e\}$ throughout the paper to distinguish between the late and the early setting. Furthermore, a scheduler σ is called *untimed* if $\sigma(h, t) = \sigma(h', t')$ whenever h and h' contain the same sequence of states. By Unt we denote the set of all untimed schedulers. Note that $Unt \subseteq Time_e \subseteq Time_\ell$.

Fixing a scheduler σ and an initial state s in a CTMDP $\mathcal{C}$, we obtain the unique probability measure $\Pr_\sigma^{\mathcal{C},s}$ over the space of all runs by standard definitions [25], denoted also by $\Pr_\sigma^s$ when $\mathcal{C}$ is clear from context.

Problem 1 (Maximum Time-Bounded Reachability). *Let $\mathcal{C} = (S, Act, \mathbf{R})$, $G \subseteq S$ be a set of goal states, $T \in \mathbb{R}_{\geq 0}$ a time bound, and $\nabla \in \{\ell, e\}$. Approximate the values* $val_\mathcal{C}^\nabla \in [0,1]^S$, *where each* $val_\mathcal{C}^\nabla(s)$ *maximises the probability*

$$val_\mathcal{C}^\nabla(s) := \sup_{\sigma \in Time_\nabla} \Pr_\sigma^s [\lozenge^{\leq T} G]$$

of runs $\lozenge^{\leq T} G = \{s_0 t_0 \cdots \mid \exists i : s_i \in G \wedge \sum_{j=0}^{i-1} t_j \leq T\}$ *reaching G before T.*

---

[1] Measurable with respect to the standard σ-algebra on the set of finite histories [25].

Whenever $\mathcal{C}$ is clear from context, we write val^∇. We call $\sigma \in Tim_\nabla$ ϵ-*optimal* if $\mathrm{Pr}^s_\sigma[\lozenge^{\leq T} G] \geq \mathrm{val}^\nabla(s) - \varepsilon$ for all $s \in S$, and *optimal* if it is 0-optimal.

By minor changes, all results of the paper also address the dual problem of *minimum* time bounded reachability that we omit to simplify the presentation.

Remark 1. There exists a value preserving encoding of early scheduling into late scheduling in CTMDPs [29]. It has exponential space complexity (due to the number of induced transitions). This exponentiality does arise in practice, e.g. for the stochastic job scheduling problem considered later. Therefore we treat the two algorithmic settings separately. Early scheduling is natural for models derived from generalised stochastic Petri nets or interactive Markov chains.

3 Unif$^+$: Optimal Time-Bounded Reachability Revisited

In this section, we develop a novel and simple algorithm for Problem 1. We fix $\mathcal{C} = (S, Act, \mathbf{R})$, $G \subseteq S$, $T \in \mathbb{R}_{\geq 0}$, $\nabla \in \{\ell, e\}$ and an approximation error $\varepsilon > 0$. Furthermore, let $E_{max} := \max_{s,a} E(s, a)$ denote the maximal exit rate in $\mathcal{C}$.

In contrast to existing methods, our approach does not involve discretisation. The algorithm instead builds upon *uniformisation* [19] and *untimed* analysis [3,4,30]. It is outlined in Algorithm 1. Technically, it is based on an iterative computation of tighter and tighter lower and upper bounds on the values until the required precision is met. In the first iteration, a *uniformisation rate* λ is set to E_{max}, in every further iteration its value is doubled. In every iteration, we compute a lower bound $\underline{\mathrm{val}}$ and an upper bound $\overline{\mathrm{val}}$ by two types of untimed analyses on the CTMDP $\mathcal{C}^\nabla_\lambda$ obtained by uniformising $\mathcal{C}$ to the rate λ. In the remainder of this section, we explain the individual steps of Algorithm 1, and prove correctness and termination.

Informally, the lower bound is based on maximum time bounded reachability with respect to the untimed scheduler subclass [3]. The upper bound, similarly to the one in [7], is based on *prophetic* untimed schedulers that yield higher

---

Algorithm 1. UNIF$^+$

---

    input   : CTMDP $\mathcal{C} = (S, Act, \mathbf{R})$, goal states $G \subseteq S$, horizon $T \in \mathbb{R}_{>0}$,
               scheduler class $\nabla \in \{\ell, e\}$, and approximation error $\varepsilon > 0$
    params: truncation error ratio $\kappa \in (0, 1)$
    output : vector v such that $\|\mathrm{v} - \overline{\mathrm{val}}\|_\infty \leq \varepsilon$ and λ
1 $\lambda \leftarrow$ maximal exit rate E_{max} in $\mathcal{C}$
2 **repeat**
3      $\mathcal{C}^\nabla_\lambda \leftarrow \nabla$-uniformisation of $\mathcal{C}$ to the rate λ
4      $\underline{\mathrm{v}} \leftarrow$ approximation of the lower bound $\underline{\mathrm{val}}$ for $\mathcal{C}^\nabla_\lambda$ up to error $\varepsilon \cdot \kappa$
5      $\overline{\mathrm{v}} \leftarrow$ approximation of the upper bound $\overline{\mathrm{val}}$ for $\mathcal{C}^\nabla_\lambda$ up to error $\varepsilon \cdot \kappa$
6      $\lambda \leftarrow 2 \cdot \lambda$
7 **until** $\|\overline{\mathrm{v}} - \underline{\mathrm{v}}\|_\infty \leq \varepsilon \cdot (1 - \kappa)$
8 **return** $\underline{\mathrm{v}}, \lambda$

---

value than timed schedulers by knowing in advance how many steps will be taken within time T. The intuition is that an untimed scheduler can approximately observe the elapse of time by knowing the count of steps taken and the expected delay per every step. In uniformised models, these delay expectations are identical across all states (forming a Poisson process) and therefore allow easy access to the expected total elapsed time. By uniformising the model with higher and higher uniformisation rates, this implicit knowledge of untimed schedulers increases. On the other hand, the knowledge of prophetic untimed schedulers decreases; both approaching the power of timed schedulers.

3.1 Uniformisation to $\mathcal{C}_\lambda^\nabla$

CTMDP $\mathcal{C}$ may have transitions with very different rates across different states and actions. Here, we discuss how to perform *uniformisation* for such a model. This is a conceptually well-known idea [19]. Applying it to $\mathcal{C}$ intuitively makes transitions occur with a higher rate $\lambda \geq E_{max}$, uniformly across all states and actions.

To ensure that uniformisation does not change the schedulable behaviour, we need distinct uniformisation procedures for the early and the late setting. Late uniformisation is straightforward, it adds self-loops to states and actions where needed.

Definition 3 (Late uniformisation). *For $\lambda \geq E_{max}$ we define the* late *uniformisation of $\mathcal{C}$ to rate λ as a CTMDP $\mathcal{C}_\lambda^\ell = (S, Act, \mathbf{R}_\lambda^\ell)$ where*

$$\mathbf{R}_\lambda^\ell(s, a, s') := \begin{cases} \mathbf{R}(s, a, s') & \text{if } s \neq s', \\ \lambda - \sum_{s'' \neq s} \mathbf{R}(s, a, s'') & \text{if } s = s'. \end{cases}$$

Example 1. For the fragmentary CTMDP $\mathcal{C}$ depicted below on the left, its late uniformisation to rate 4.5 is depicted in the middle.

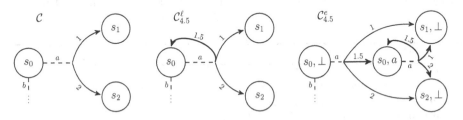

Using the same transformation for the early setting would give the scheduler the spurious possibility to "reconsider" the choice of the action in a state whenever a newly added self-loop is taken. To exclude that possibility, early uniformisation introduces a copy state (s, a) for each state s and action a so as to "freeze" the commitment of choosing action a until the next state change occurs. The construction is shown on the right. States of the form $(s, \perp)$ correspond to the original states, i.e. those where no action has been committed to yet.

Definition 4 (Early uniformisation). *For* $\lambda \geq E_{max}$, *the early uniformisation of* $\mathcal{C}$ *to rate* λ *is a CTMDP* $\mathcal{C}_\lambda^e = (S \times (\{\perp\} \cup Act), Act, \mathbf{R}_\lambda^e)$ *where for every state* $(s, \cdot)$, *action* $a \in Act$, *and every successor state* $(s', \circ)$ *we have*

$$\mathbf{R}_\lambda^e((s, \cdot), a, (s', \circ)) := \begin{cases} \mathbf{R}(s, a, s') & \text{if } \circ = \perp, \\ \lambda - E(s, a) & \text{if } \circ = a, s = s', \\ 0 & \text{elsewhere.} \end{cases}$$

Uniformisation preserves the value of time-bounded reachability for both early [25] and late schedulers [24].

Lemma 1. $\forall \lambda \geq E_{max}. \; \mathrm{val}_{\mathcal{C}}^\nabla = \mathrm{val}_{\mathcal{C}_\lambda^\nabla}^\nabla$, *i.e. uniformisation preserves the value.*

As a result, we can proceed by bounding the values of $\mathcal{C}_\lambda^\nabla$ for large enough λ instead of bounding the values of the original CTMDP $\mathcal{C}$.

3.2 Lower and Upper Bounds on the Value of $\mathcal{C}_\lambda^\nabla$

We now fix a λ and consider a uniform CTMDP $\mathcal{C}_\lambda^\nabla$. We denote by $\Diamond_{=i}^{\leq T} G$ the subset of runs $\Diamond^{\leq T} G$ reaching the target where exactly i steps are taken up to time T. With this, we define the bounds by ranging over Unt schedulers in $\mathcal{C}_\lambda^\nabla$:

$$\underline{\mathrm{val}}(s) := \sup_{\sigma \in Unt} \sum_{i=0}^{\infty} \{ \Pr[s]\sigma[\Diamond_{=i}^{\leq T} G], \qquad \overline{\mathrm{val}}(s) := \sum_{i=0}^{\infty} \sup_{\sigma \in Unt} \{ \Pr[s]\sigma[\Diamond_{=i}^{\leq T} G].$$

Since all $\Diamond_{=i}^{\leq T} G$ are disjoint and $\Diamond^{\leq T} G = \bigcup_{i \in \mathbb{N}_0} \Diamond_{=i}^{\leq T} G$, the value $\underline{\mathrm{val}}$ is the optimal reachability probability of standard untimed schedulers on the uniformised model. It will serve as a lower bound on the values val^∇. The value $\overline{\mathrm{val}}$, on the other hand, which has the supremum and summation swapped, does not correspond to the value of any realistic scheduler. Intuitively, it is the value of a *prophetic* untimed scheduler, which for each particular run knows how many steps will be taken (as for every i, a different standard scheduler σ may be used). This knowledge makes the scheduler more powerful than any other timed one:

Lemma 2. *It holds that* $\mathrm{val}^e \leq \mathrm{val}^\ell$, *and for any CTMDP* $\mathcal{C}_\lambda^\nabla$, $\underline{\mathrm{val}} \leq \mathrm{val}^\nabla \leq \overline{\mathrm{val}}$.

Approximating the Bounds. Since $\underline{\mathrm{val}}$ and $\overline{\mathrm{val}}$ are defined via infinite summations, we need to approximate these bounds. We do so by iterative algorithms truncating the sums. This is what is computed in line 4 and 5 of Algorithm 1. Each truncation induces an error of up to $\varepsilon \cdot \kappa$.

Let $\psi_\lambda(k)$ denote the Poisson distribution with parameter λT at point k, i.e. the probability that exactly k transitions are taken in the CTMDP $\mathcal{C}_\lambda^\nabla$ before time T. Furthermore, let $N = \lceil \lambda T e^2 - \ln(\varepsilon \cdot \kappa) \rceil$, where e is the Euler's number. We recursively define for every $0 \leq k \leq N$ and every state s, functions

$$\underline{v}_k(s) = \begin{cases} 0 & \text{if } k = N, \\ \sum_{i=k}^{N-1} \psi_\lambda(i) & \text{if } k < N \text{ and } s \in G, \\ \max_a \sum_{s'} \mathbf{P}_\lambda^\nabla(s, a, s') \cdot \underline{v}_{k+1}(s') & \text{if } k < N \text{ and } s \notin G, \end{cases}$$

$$\overline{w}_k(s) = \begin{cases} 0 & \text{if } k = N, \\ 1 & \text{if } k < N \text{ and } s \in G, \\ \max_a \sum_{s'} \mathbf{P}_\lambda^\nabla(s, a, s') \cdot \overline{w}_{k+1}(s') & \text{if } k < N \text{ and } s \notin G, \end{cases}$$

$$\overline{v}_k(s) = \sum_{i=k}^{N-1} \psi_\lambda(i) \cdot \overline{w}_{(N-1)-(i-k)}(s),$$

where $\mathbf{P}_\lambda^\nabla$ denotes the transition probability matrix of $\mathcal{C}_\lambda^\nabla$.

Lemma 3. *In any CTMDP $\mathcal{C}_\lambda^\nabla$, $\|\underline{v}0 - \underline{val}\|_\infty \leq \varepsilon \cdot \kappa$ and $\|\overline{v}0 - \overline{val}\|_\infty \leq \varepsilon \cdot \kappa$.*

We compute $\underline{v}[0]$ as in the untimed analysis of uniform models [3], which in turn agrees with the standard "uniformisation" algorithm for CTMCs when the maximisation is dropped. The computation of $\overline{w}_k$ is analogous to step-bounded reachability for *discrete-time* Markov decision processes, where the reachability probabilities for different step-bounds are weighted by the Poisson distribution in the end in $\overline{v}[0]$. Both vectors can be computed in time $O(N \cdot |S|^2 \cdot |Act|)$.

Numerical Aspects. In practice also $\underline{v}[0]$ and $\overline{v}[0]$ can only be approximated due to presence of $\psi_\lambda(k)$. For details how the overall error bound is met in an analogous setting, see [4]. For high values of λ and thus also N, the Poisson values $\psi_\lambda(k)$ are low for most $0 \leq k < N$ and also the values in $\mathbf{P}_\lambda^\nabla$ get close to 1 when on the diagonal and to 0 when off-diagonal. Where high precision is required and thus high λ may be needed, attention has to be paid to numerical stability.

3.3   Convergence of the Bounds for Increasing λ

An essential part for the correctness of Algorithm 1 is its convergence:

Lemma 4. *We have $\lim_{\lambda \to \infty} g_\lambda \to 0$ where g_λ denotes the gap $\|\underline{val} - \overline{val}\|_\infty$ in $\mathcal{C}_\lambda^\nabla$.*

Proof Idea. We here provide an intuition of the core of the proof, namely why uni-formisation with higher λ increases the power of untimed schedulers and decreases the power of prophetic ones: The count of transitions taken so far gives untimed schedulers approximate knowledge of how much time has elapsed. In situations with the *same expectation* of elapsed time, a higher uniformisation rate induces a *lower variance* of elapsed time. On the

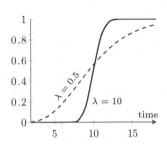

right, we illustrate comparable situations for different uniformisation rates, after 5 transitions with rate 0.5 and after 100 transitions with rate 10. Both depicted cumulative distribution functions of elapsed time have expectation 10 but the latter is way steeper, providing a more precise knowledge of time.

At the same time prophetic schedulers on the high-rate uniformised model are less powerful than on the original one. When taking decisions, the future evolution is influenced by two types of randomness: (a) continuous timing, i.e. how many further transitions will be taken before the time horizon and (b) discrete branching, i.e. which transitions will be taken. Even though the value stays the same for arbitrary λ, the "source of" randomness for high λ shifts from (a) to (b). Namely, the distribution of the number of future transitions also becomes steeper for higher λ, thus being "less random" by having smaller coefficient of variation. At the same time, the discrete branching for higher λ influences more the number of *actual* transitions taken (i.e. transitions that are not the added self-loops). As a result, the advantage of the prophetic scheduler is only little as (i) it boils down to observing the outcome of a less and less random choice and (ii) the observed quantity has little impact on how many actual transitions are taken.

As a result of Lemma 4, we obtain that Algorithm 1 terminates. Its correctness follows from Lemmas 1, 2 and 3, all summarized by the following theorem.

Theorem 1. *Algorithm 1 computes an approximation of* val^{∇} *up to error* ε.

Remark 2. Algorithm 1 determines a sufficiently large λ in an exponential search fashion. In practice, this approach is efficient w.r.t. the total number I of *iterations* needed, i.e. the total number of times $\underline{v}_k$ and $\overline{w}_k$ are computed from $\underline{v}_{k+1}$ and $\overline{w}_{k+1}$. Namely, in practice the error monotonously decreases when the rate increases (not in theory but we never encountered the opposite case on our extensive experiments.) As a result, λ found by Algorithm 1 satisfies $\lambda < 2 \cdot \lambda^*$ where λ^* is the minimal sufficiently large rate. As the number of iterations needed for one approximation is linear in the uniformisation rate used, we have $I = 2I_\lambda < 4 \cdot I_{\lambda^*}$, where each $I_{\lambda'}$ denotes the number of iterations needed for the computation for the fixed rate λ'.

3.4 Extracting the Scheduler

By computing the lower bound, Algorithm 1 also produces [3] an untimed scheduler σ_λ^∇ that is ε-optimal on the *uniformised* model $\mathcal{C}_\lambda^\nabla$. In the *original* CTMDP $\mathcal{C}$, we cannot use σ_λ^∇ directly as its choices are tailored to the high rate λ. We can however use a *stochastic update* scheduler attaining the same value. Informally, a (timed) *stochastic update scheduler* $\sigma = (\mathcal{M}, \sigma_u, \pi_0)$ operates over a countable set $\mathcal{M}$ of memory elements where the initial memory value is chosen randomly according to the distribution π_0 over $\mathcal{M}$. The stochastic update function σ_u, given the current memory element, state, and the time spent there, defines a distribution specifying the action to take and how to update the memory. Intuitively, the stochastic update is used for simulating the high-rate transitions that would be taken in $\mathcal{C}_\lambda^\nabla$; their total count so far is stored in the memory. For a formal definition of stochastic update and the construction, see [8].

Theorem 2. *The values* $(\underline{v}_k)_{0 \le k \le N}$ *computed by Algorithm 1 for given* $\mathcal{C}$, ∇, *and* $\varepsilon > 0$ *yield a stochastic update scheduler* $\tilde{\sigma}_{TD}^\nabla$ *that is* ε-*optimal in* $\mathcal{C}$.

4   Existing Algorithms

This section briefly reviews the various published algorithms solving Problem 1. In contrast to Algorithm 1 (called $\textsc{Unif}^+$ or $\textsc{u}^+$ for short), they all discretise time into a finite number of time points $t_0, t_1, \ldots, t_n$ where $t_0 = 0$ and $t_n = T$. They iteratively approximate the values $\text{val}^\nabla(s; t_i) := \sup_{\sigma \in Tim_\nabla} \Pr^s_\sigma[\Diamond^{\leq t_i} G]$ when t_i time units remain at state s. Three different iteration concepts have been proposed, each approximating $\text{val}^\nabla(s; t_{i+1})$ from approximations of $\text{val}^\nabla(s'; t_i)$.

Exponential Approximation – Early [16,27]. Assuming equidistant points t_i one can approximate the (early) value function by piece-wise exponential functions. A k-order approximation considers only runs where at most k steps are taken between any two time points. This can yield an a priori error bound. The higher k, the less time points are required for a given precision, but the more computation is needed per time point. We refer to these algorithms by $\textsc{ExpStep-}k$ or $\textsc{es-}k$ for short. Only $\textsc{es-}1$ [27] and $\textsc{es-}2$ [16] have been implemented so far.

Polynomial Approximation – Late [10]. Another way to approximate the (late) value function on equidistant time points uses polynomials. As before, the higher the degree of the polynomials, the higher is the computational effort, but the number of discretised time points required to assure an a priori error bound decreases. We call these algorithms $\textsc{PolyStep-}k$ or $\textsc{ps-}k$ in the sequel, only $\textsc{ps-}1$, $\textsc{ps-}2$, and $\textsc{ps-}3$ have been implemented. Among these, $\textsc{ps-}2$ has better worst-case behaviour, but $\textsc{ps-}3$ has been reported to often perform better in practice.

Adaptive Discretisation – Late [7]. This approach is not based on an a priori error bound but instead computes both under- and over-approximations of the values $\text{val}^\nabla(s; t_i)$. This allows one to lay out the time points *adaptively*. Depending on the shape of the value function, the time step can be prolonged until the error allowed for this step is reached. This greatly reduces the number of time points, relative to the worst case. We refer to this algorithm as $\textsc{AdaptStep}$ or $\textsc{as}$.

5   Empirical Evaluation and Comparison

In this section we present an exhaustive empirical comparison of the different algorithmic approaches discussed.

Benchmarks. The experiments are performed on a diverse collection of published benchmark models. This collection is the first of its kind for CTMDP, as far as we know and contains the following parametrised models:

PS-K-J The *Polling System* case [13,31] consists of two stations and one server. Incoming requests of J types are buffered in two queues of size K each, until they are processed by the server and delivered to their station. We consider the undesirable states with both queues being full to form the goal state set.

QS-K-J The *Queuing System* [15] stores requests of J different types into two queues of size K. Each queue is attached to a server. Two servers fetch requests from their corresponding queues and process them. One of them can non-deterministically decide to insert a request after processing into the other server's queue. Goal states are again those with both queues full.

DPMS-K-J The *Dynamic Power Management System* [28] is a CTMDP model of the internals of a Fujitsu disk drive. The model consists of four components: service requester (SR), service queue (SQ), service provider (SP), and power manager (PM). SR generates tasks of J types differing in energy demand that are buffered by the queue SQ of size K. Afterwards they are delivered to SP to be processed. SP can work in different modes ranging from sleep and stand-by to full processing mode, selected by PM. We define a state as goal if the queue of at least one task type is full.

GFS-N The *Google File System* [11,12] splits files into chunks of equal size, each chunk is maintained by one of N chunk servers. We fix the number of chunks a server may store to 5000 and the total number of chunks to 100000. While other benchmarks start in optimal conditions, the GFS starts in the broken state where no chunk is stored. A state is defined as goal if the system is back up and for each chunk at least one copy is available.

FTWC-N The *Fault Tolerant Workstation Cluster* [17], originally described by a GSPN, models two networks of N workstations each, interconnected by a switch. The two switches communicate via a backbone. Workstations, switches, and the backbone fail after exponentially distributed delays, and can be repaired only one at a time. We define a state as goal if in total less than N workstations are operational and connected to each other.

SJS-M-J The *stochastic job scheduling* [5] models a multiprocessor architecture running a sequence of independent jobs. It consists of M identical processors and J jobs, where each job's service time is governed by an exponential distribution. As goal we define the desirable states with all jobs completed.

ES-K-R The *Erlang Stages* is a synthetic model with known characteristics [32]. It has two different paths to reach the goal state: a fast but risky path or a slow but sure path. The slow path is an Erlang chain of length K and rate R.

Implementation Aspects. Unbiased performance evaluation of algorithms originally developed by different researchers is not easy even with all original implementations at hand. Namely, they may use different programming languages or rely on different platforms with incomparable performance and memory management. However, reimplementing a published algorithm may induce unfairness as the original implementation may use specific data structures or other optimisations that go beyond what is explained in the respective publication.

We adapted/implemented all algorithms in C/C++, trying to avoid the shortcomings. We used a common infrastructure from the IMCA/MAMA toolset [13]. Thus, we could directly use the original IMCA implementations of EXPSTEP-1 and of EXPSTEP-2 [16]. The original implementation [6] of ADAPT-STEP in MRMC [20] needed only minor adaptations, as MRMC uses a data

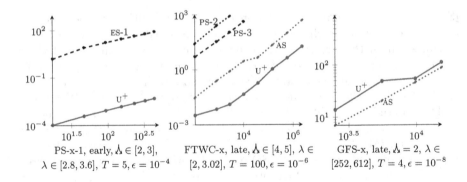

Fig. 1. Selected experiments: Increasing state space size.

structure identical to ours. Finally, for POLYSTEP, we closely followed the original Java code [10]. Our C version clearly outperforms the original Java version.

We implemented all algorithms with standard double precision arithmetic, observing no issues with numerical stability in our experiments. All values computed by different algorithms lie within the expected precision from each other.

We used parameter values $k^{\max} = 10$ and $\omega = 0.1$ for AS, as recommended. We always ran both adaptive and non-adaptive variant of AS and display the better results (mostly adaptive). Based on our tests, we fixed $\kappa := 0.1$ for U$^+$.

Empirical Results. In this section we present our empirical observations. We consider early and late scheduling problems separately (because the encoding mentioned in Remark 1 of Sect. 2, is exponential); only UNIF$^+$ can be directly run on both problems. All experiments were run on a single core of Intel Core i7-4790 with 16 GB of RAM, computing a total of about 2350 data points.

The memory requirements of all the considered algorithms do not deviate considerably and thus are not reported. This echoes that all space complexities are linear in the model size. We encountered no significant impact of additional dependencies of POLYSTEP on a hidden model parameter (number of "switching points", coarsely bounded in [10]).

In the following, we focus on the time requirements. We first show plots of a few selected experiments that represent well our general observations. Later, we give a short summary of all experiments. All plots presented below use logarithmic scale for the runtime (in seconds). Some data points are missing as we applied a time limit of 15 min for every computation and also because the original implementation of EXPSTEP-2 cannot handle models with more than two actions per state. We use symbol λ to denote the maximal number of action choices and λ for the maximal exit rate. We use the symbol "x" whenever the varying parameter is a part of the model name, e.g. PS-2-x.

State Space. In Fig. 1 we illustrate the effect of enlarging the state space. On the left there is a plot for early algorithms representing the general trend:

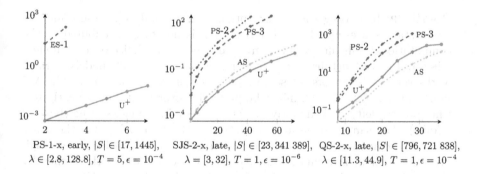

Fig. 2. Selected experiments: Increasing number of action choices.

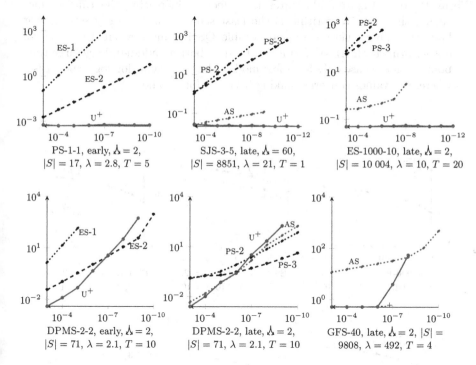

Fig. 3. Selected experiments: Increasing precision.

UNIF$^+$ outperforms EXPSTEP-1 (as well as EXPSTEP-2 where applicable). For late algorithms in the plots on the right, the situation is more diverse, with UNIF$^+$ and ADAPTSTEP outperforming the POLYSTEP algorithms. All algorithms exhibit similar dependency on the growth of the state space.

Action Choices. Figure 2 displays the effect of increasing the number of actions to choose from. For early schedulers (left) UNIF$^+$ generally dominates EXPSTEP-1. For late schedulers, again UNIF$^+$ and ADAPTSTEP dominate

POLYSTEP. Increasing the choice options in our models generally induces larger state spaces, so the observed growth is not to be attributed to the computational difficulty resulting from an increase in choice options alone.

Precision. Figure 3 details precision dependency. Across all models, UNIF$^+$ works very well, excepts for some high precision cases, such as the DPMS models, where EXPSTEP-2 might be preferable over UNIF$^+$ in the early setting (bottom left), and similarly for ADAPTSTEP in the late setting (bottom middle). The same is true for the GFS case (bottom right). On the other hand, for some models (examples in the first row) UNIF$^+$ delivers very high precision without any runtime increase. It is also interesting that generally the sensitivity of all algorithm to required precision is more than linear in the number of precision digits.

Time Bound. Figure 4 illustrates the effect of increasing the time bound. Again, the UNIF$^+$-algorithm is the least sensitive in the early setting. For late scheduling, there are some notable QS instances where POLYSTEP-3 outperforms both ADAPTSTEP and UNIF$^+$ (bottom middle). Very large time bounds make sense only for a few models (bottom right, log-log-scale). Elsewhere, the values converge making it trivial for AS and U$^+$.

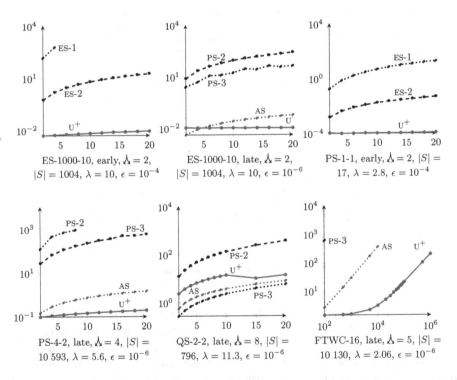

Fig. 4. Selected experiments: Increasing time bound.

Among the many instances we considered we found a few instances where the late UNIF⁺-algorithm shows surprising sensitivity to changes in time bound, particularly for high precision scenarios. This is exemplified on the right (GFS, late, $\lambda= 2$, $|S| = 9808$, $\lambda = 492$, $\epsilon = 10^{-8}$, increasing time bound, no log scale). In line with the apparent general tendency of the algorithms for increasing parameter 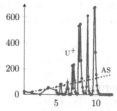 values, the work and thus time needed tends to increase monotonously. Instead, small variations in time bound may lead to great savings in runtime for UNIF⁺. This is rooted in the error calculated while running the algorithm coincidentally falling into the allowed margin. Less extreme examples of this behaviour are included in Fig. 3 top row and Fig. 4 bottom middle. We observed such time savings only for UNIF⁺, not for any other algorithm, though conceptually the runtime of ADAPTSTEP might profit from similar effects as well. The exact conditions of this behaviour are still to be found.

A complete list of model files, additional statistics, result tables as well as all prototype implementations are available at the following URL: http://depend. cs.uni-saarland.de/~hahate/atval5/.

Evaluation and Discussion. The results presented show that a general answer about the relative performance of the proposed algorithms is not easy to give, but appears very much dependent on model parameters outside the awareness of the modeller. Thus there is no clear winner across all models. Still, our benchmarking, summarised in Table 1, provides some general insights:

- All algorithms are naturally sensitive to increases in model parameters. Their runtime mostly behaves linear in the time bounds and the state space size, exponential in precision and superlinear (though still polynomial) in fanout.
- For early schedulers EXPSTEP-1 is not competitive. UNIF⁺ mostly outperforms EXPSTEP-2.
- For late schedulers POLYSTEP-1 is not competitive and POLYSTEP-3 is effectively faster than POLYSTEP-2. ADAPTSTEP and UNIF⁺ mostly outperform POLYSTEP-3. Still each of the late algorithms {ADAPTSTEP, UNIF⁺, POLYSTEP-3} is dominating the other two on at least one model instance. The particular algorithmic strengths have no obvious relation to model parameters available to the modeller.
- For low precision, UNIF⁺ appears to be the preferred choice. For high precision, ADAPTSTEP is a more stable choice than UNIF⁺. Yet its performance depends on non-obvious model particularities and algorithm parameters.

All in all, UNIF⁺ is easy to implement for both early and late, and competitive across a wide range of models. In settings where an a posteriori error bound is enough, a good approximation can be usually obtained by a variant of UNIF⁺ that computes only the first iteration and does not increase the uniformisation rate (see the accompanying web for the error bounds obtained in experiments).

Table 1. Overview of experiments summarising which algorithm performed best how many times; N/A indicates that no algorithm completed within 15 min.

	max. $|S|$	max. Λ	max. exit rate range	Best in early (# of cases)	Best in late (# of cases)
PS	743 969	7	5.6–129.6	U^+ (**32**)	U^+ (**47**)
QS	16 924	36	6.5–44.9	U^+ (**32**)	PS-3 (**18**), U^+ (17), AS (15)
DPMS	366 148	7	2.1–9.1	U^+ (**31**), ES-2(3), N/A(1)	AS (**24**), U^+ (14), PS-3 (6)
GFS	15 258	2	252–612	U^+ (**40**)	AS (**23**), U^+ (11)
FTWC	2 373 650	5	2–3.02	U^+ (**25**)	U^+ (**32**)
SJS	18 451	72	3–32	U^+ (**57**), ES-2(2)	U^+ (**70**), AS (29)
ES	30 004	2	10	U^+ (**23**), ES-2(4), N/A(1)	U^+ (**28**), PS-3(2)

6 Conclusion

This paper has introduced UNIF$^+$, a new and simple algorithm for time-bounded reachability objectives in CTMDPs. We studied this and all other published algorithms in an extensive comparative evaluation for both early and late scheduling. In general, UNIF$^+$ performs very well across the benchmarks, apart from late scheduling and high precision, where it appears hard to predict which of the algorithms UNIF$^+$, ADAPTSTEP, POLYSTEP-3 performs best. One might consider to follow an approach inspired by the distributed concurrent solver in GUROBI [14]. The idea is to launch all three implementations to run concurrently on distinct cores and report the result as soon as the first one terminates.

For researchers who want to extend an existing CTMC model checker to a CTMDP model checker, the obvious choice is the UNIF$^+$-algorithm: It works right away for early and for late optimisation, and it requires only a small change to the uniformisation subroutine used at the core of CTMC model checking.

Acknowledgements. We are grateful to Moritz Hahn (ISCAS Beijing), Dennis Guck (Universiteit Twente), and Markus Rabe (UC Berkeley) for discussions and technical contributions. This work is supported by the EU 7th Framework Programme projects 295261 (MEALS) and 318490 (SENSATION), by the Czech Science Foundation project P202/12/G061, the DFG Transregional Collaborative Research Centre SFB/TR 14 AVACS, and by the CDZ project 1023 (CAP).

References

1. Aziz, A., Sanwal, K., Singhal, V., Brayton, R.K.: Verifying continuous time Markov chains. In: Alur, R., Henzinger, T.A. (eds.) CAV 1996. LNCS, vol. 1102, pp. 269–276. Springer, Heidelberg (1996)
2. Baier, C., Haverkort, B.R., Hermanns, H., Katoen, J.: Model-checking algorithms for continuous-time Markov chains. IEEE Trans. Softw. Eng. **29**(6), 524–541 (2003)
3. Baier, C., Hermanns, H., Katoen, J., Haverkort, B.R.: Efficient computation of time-bounded reachability probabilities in uniform continuous-time Markov decision processes. Theor. Comput. Sci. **345**(1), 2–26 (2005)
4. Brázdil, T., Forejt, V., Krcál, J., Kretínský, J., Kucera, A.: Continuous-time stochastic games with time-bounded reachability. Inf. Comput. **224**, 46–70 (2013)

5. Bruno, J.L., Downey, P.J., Frederickson, G.N.: Sequencing tasks with exponential service times to minimize the expected flow time or makespan. J. ACM **28**(1), 100–113 (1981)
6. Buchholz, P., Hahn, E.M., Hermanns, H., Zhang, L.: Model checking algorithms for CTMDPs. In: Gopalakrishnan, G., Qadeer, S. (eds.) CAV 2011. LNCS, vol. 6806, pp. 225–242. Springer, Heidelberg (2011)
7. Buchholz, P., Schulz, I.: Numerical analysis of continuous time Markov decision processes over finite horizons. Comput. OR **38**(3), 651–659 (2011)
8. Butkova, Y., Hatefi, H., Hermanns, H., Krčál, J.: Optimal continuous time Markov decisions. CoRR abs/1507.02876 (2015). http://arxiv.org/abs/1507.02876
9. Eisentraut, Christian, Hermanns, Holger, Katoen, Joost-Pieter, Zhang, Lijun: A semantics for every GSPN. In: Colom, José-Manuel, Desel, Jörg (eds.) PETRI NETS 2013. LNCS, vol. 7927, pp. 90–109. Springer, Heidelberg (2013)
10. Fearnley, J., Rabe, M., Schewe, S., Zhang, L.: Efficient approximation of optimal control for continuous-time markov games. In: FSTTCS, pp. 399–410 (2011)
11. Ghemawat, S., Gobioff, H., Leung, S.T.: The Google file system. In: SOSP, pp. 29–43. ACM (2003)
12. Guck, D.: Quantitative Analysis of Markov Automata. Master's thesis, RWTH Aachen University, June 2012
13. Guck, D., Hatefi, H., Hermanns, H., Katoen, J.-P., Timmer, M.: Modelling, reduction and analysis of markov automata. In: Joshi, K., Siegle, M., Stoelinga, M., D'Argenio, P.R. (eds.) QEST 2013. LNCS, vol. 8054, pp. 55–71. Springer, Heidelberg (2013)
14. Gurobi Optimization Inc: Gurobi optimizer reference manual, version 6.0 (2015)
15. Hatefi, H., Hermanns, H.: Model checking algorithms for Markov automata. In: ECEASST, vol. 53 (2012)
16. Hatefi, H., Hermanns, H.: Improving time bounded reachability computations in interactive markov chains. In: Arbab, F., Sirjani, M. (eds.) FSEN 2013. LNCS, vol. 8161, pp. 250–266. Springer, Heidelberg (2013)
17. Haverkort, B.R., Hermanns, H., Katoen, J.: On the use of model checking techniques for dependability evaluation. In: SRDS 2000, pp. 228–237. IEEE CS (2000)
18. Hermanns, H., Katoen, J.-P.: The how and why of interactive markov chains. In: de Boer, F.S., Bonsangue, M.M., Hallerstede, S., Leuschel, M. (eds.) FMCO 2009. LNCS, vol. 6286, pp. 311–338. Springer, Heidelberg (2010)
19. Jensen, A.: Markoff chains as an aid in the study of Markoff processes. Scand. Actuarial J. **1953**, 87–91 (1953)
20. Katoen, J., Zapreev, I.S., Hahn, E.M., Hermanns, H., Jansen, D.N.: The ins and outs of the probabilistic model checker MRMC. Perform. Eval. **68**(2), 90–104 (2011)
21. Lefévre, C.: Optimal control of a birth and death epidemic process. Oper. Res. **29**(5), 971–982 (1981)
22. Marsan, M.A., Balbo, G., Conte, G., Donatelli, S., Franceschinis, G.: Modelling with Generalized Stochastic Petri Nets. Wiley, New York (1994)
23. Meyer, J.F., Movaghar, A., Sanders, W.H.: Stochastic activity networks: Structure, behavior, and application. In: PNPM, pp. 106–115 (1985)
24. Miller, B.L.: Finite state continuous time Markov decision processes with a finite planning horizon. SIAM J. Control **6**(2), 266–280 (1968)
25. Neuhäußer, M.R.: Model checking nondeterministic and randomly timed systems. Ph.D. thesis, RWTH Aachen University (2010)

26. Neuhäußer, M.R., Stoelinga, M., Katoen, J.-P.: Delayed nondeterminism in continuous-time markov decision processes. In: de Alfaro, L. (ed.) FOSSACS 2009. LNCS, vol. 5504, pp. 364–379. Springer, Heidelberg (2009)
27. Neuhäußer, M.R., Zhang, L.: Time-bounded reachability probabilities in continuous-time Markov decision processes. In: QEST, pp. 209–218 (2010)
28. Qiu, Q., Qu, Q., Pedram, M.: Stochastic modeling of a power-managed system-construction andoptimization. IEEE Trans. CAD Integr. Circ. Syst. 20(10), 1200–1217 (2001)
29. Rabe, M.N., Schewe, S.: Finite optimal control for time-bounded reachability in CTMDPs and continuous-time Markov games. Acta Inf. 48(5–6), 291–315 (2011)
30. Rabe, M.N., Schewe, S.: Optimal time-abstract schedulers for CTMDPs and continuous-time Markov games. Theor. Comput. Sci. 467, 53–67 (2013)
31. Timmer, M., van de Pol, J., Stoelinga, M.I.A.: Confluence reduction for markov automata. In: Braberman, V., Fribourg, L. (eds.) FORMATS 2013. LNCS, vol. 8053, pp. 243–257. Springer, Heidelberg (2013)
32. Zhang, L., Neuhäußer, M.R.: Model checking interactive markov chains. In: Esparza, J., Majumdar, R. (eds.) TACAS 2010. LNCS, vol. 6015, pp. 53–68. Springer, Heidelberg (2010)

Spanning the Spectrum from Safety to Liveness

Rachel Faran[✉] and Orna Kupferman

School of Computer Science and Engineering, The Hebrew University,
Jerusalem, Israel
`rachelmi@cs.huji.ac.il`

Abstract. Of special interest in formal verification are *safety* specifications, which assert that the system stays within some allowed region, in which nothing "bad" happens. Equivalently, a computation violates a safety specification if it has a "bad prefix" – a prefix all whose extensions violate the specification. The theoretical properties of safety specifications as well as their practical advantages with respect to general specifications have been widely studied. Safety is binary: a specification is either safety or not safety. We introduce a quantitative measure for safety. Intuitively, the *safety level* of a language L measures the fraction of words not in L that have a bad prefix. In particular, a safety language has safety level 1 and a liveness language has safety level 0. Thus, our study spans the spectrum between traditional safety and liveness. The formal definition of safety level is based on probability and measures the probability of a random word not in L to have a bad prefix. We study the problem of finding the safety level of languages given by means of deterministic and nondeterministic automata as well as LTL formulas, and the problem of deciding their membership in specific classes along the spectrum (safety, almost-safety, fraction-safety, etc.). We also study properties of the different classes and the structure of deterministic automata for them.

1 Introduction

Today's rapid development of complex and safety-critical systems requires reliable verification methods. In formal verification, we verify that a system meets a desired property by checking that a mathematical model of the system meets a formal specification that describes the property. Of special interest are specifications asserting that the observed behavior of the system always stays within some allowed region, in which nothing "bad" happens. For example, we may want to assert that every message sent is acknowledged in the next cycle. Such specifications of systems are called *safety specifications*. Intuitively, a specification ψ is a safety specification if every violation of ψ occurs after a finite execution

The research leading to these results has received funding from the European Research Council under the European Union's Seventh Framework Programme (FP7/2007-2013) / ERC grant agreement no 278410, and from The Israel Science Foundation (grant no 1229/10).

© Springer International Publishing Switzerland 2015
B. Finkbeiner et al. (Eds.): ATVA 2015, LNCS 9364, pp. 183–200, 2015.
DOI: 10.1007/978-3-319-24953-7_13

of the system. In our example, if in a computation of the system a message is sent without being acknowledged in the next cycle, this occurs after some finite execution of the system. Also, once this violation occurs, there is no way to "fix" the computation.

In order to define safety formally, we refer to computations of a non-terminating system as infinite words over an alphabet Σ. Consider a language L of infinite words over Σ. That is, $L \subseteq \Sigma^\omega$. A finite word $x \in \Sigma^*$ is a *bad prefix* for L iff for all infinite words $y \in \Sigma^\omega$, the concatenation $x \cdot y$ is not in L. Thus, a bad prefix for L is a finite word that cannot be extended to an infinite word in L. A language L is a *safety language* if every word not in L has a finite bad prefix[1].

The interest in safety started with the quest for natural classes of specifications. The theoretical aspects of safety have been extensively studied [2,18,19,25]. With the growing use of formal verification, safety has turned out to be interesting also from a practical point of view [8,10,14]. Indeed, the ability to reason about finite prefixes significantly simplifies both enumerative and symbolic algorithms. In the first, safety circumvents the need to reason about complex ω-regular acceptance conditions. For example, methods for synthesis, program repair, or parametric reasoning are much simpler for safety properties [9,23]. In the second, it circumvents the need to reason about cycles, which is significant in both BDD-based and SAT-based methods [3,4].

In addition to a rich literature on safety, researchers have studied additional classes, such as co-safety and liveness [2,18]. A language L is a *co-safety* language if the complement of L, namely the language of words not in L, is safety. Equivalently, every word in L has a *good prefix* – one all whose extensions result in a word in L. A language L is a *liveness* language if it does not have bad prefixes. Thus, every word in Σ^* can be extended to a word in L. For example, if $\Sigma = \{a, b\}$, then $L = \{a^\omega, b^\omega\}$ is a safety language, its complement is both co-safety and liveness, and $L = (a + b)^* \cdot b^\omega$ is a liveness language that is neither safety nor co-safety.

From a theoretical point of view, the importance of safety and liveness languages stems from their topological characteristics. Consider the natural topology on Σ^ω, where similarity between words corresponds to the length of the prefix they share. Formally, the distance between w and w' is 2^{-i}, where $i \geq 0$ is the position of the first letter in which w and w' differ. In this topology, safety languages are exactly the closed sets, co-safety languages are the open sets, and liveness languages are the dense sets (that is, they intersect every nonempty open set) [1]. This, for example, implies that every linear specification can be expressed as a conjunction of a safety and a liveness specification [1,2].

Safety is binary: a specification is either safety or not safety. In this work, we introduce a quantitative measure for safety. We define the *safety level* of a language L as the probability of a word not in L to have a bad prefix.

---

[1] The definition of safety we consider here is given in [1,2], it coincides with the definition of limit closure defined in [7], and is different from the definition in [16], which also refers to the property being closed under stuttering.

From a theoretical point of view, our study spans the spectrum between traditional safety and liveness. From a practical point of view, the higher the safety level of L is, the bigger is the chance that algorithms designed for safety languages would work appropriately for L.

Let us describe our framework and results in more detail. A random word over an alphabet Σ is a word in which for all indices i, the i-th letter is drawn uniformly at random. Thus, we assume a uniform probability distribution on Σ^ω, and the probability of a language $L \subseteq \Sigma^\omega$ is the probability of the event L. For example, the probability of $Pr(a \cdot (a + b)^\omega)$ is $\frac{1}{2}$. Now, for a language $L \subseteq \Sigma^\omega$, the safety level of L is the conditional probability of the event "words with a bad prefix for L" given the event "words not in L". That is, intuitively, the safety level measures the fraction of words not in L that have a bad prefix. When L is a safety language, all the words not in L have a bad prefix, thus the safety level of L is 1. When L is liveness, no word has a bad prefix, thus the safety level is 0. A language may have safety level 1 without being safety. For example, when $AP = \{a, b\}$, then the safety level of the non-safety specification $\psi = aUb$ (that is, a until b) is 1. Indeed, almost all computations (that is, all but $\{a\}^\omega$) that violate ψ have a bad prefix.[2] Also, languages may have a fractional safety level. For example, $\varphi = a \wedge FGb$ (that is, a and eventually always b) has safety level $\frac{1}{2}$, as only words that start with a letter satisfying $\neg a$ have a bad prefix for φ and almost all words that start with a letter satisfying a do not satisfy φ either.

We partition safety levels to four classes: safety, *almost-safety* (the safety level is 1 but the language is not safety), *frac-safety* (the safety level is in $(0, 1)$), and liveness. We define a dual classification for co-safety and examine possible combinations. For example, it is shown in [15] that the intersection of safety and co-safety languages is exactly the set of *bounded languages* – these that are recognizable by cycle-free automata, which correspond to *clopen* sets in topology. We study all intersections, some of which we prove to be empty. For example, there is no language that is both co-safety and frac-safety. We study the problem of calculating the safety level of a given language and prove that it can be solved in linear, exponential, and doubly-exponential time for languages given by deterministic parity automata, nondeterministic Büchi automata, and LTL formulas, respectively.

We then turn to study the classification problem, where the goal is to decide whether a given language belongs to a given class. The problem was studied for the classes of safety and liveness properties [13,25], and we study it for almost-safety and frac-safety. We show that the complexities for almost-safety coincide with these known for safety; that is, the problem is NLOGSPACE-complete for deterministic automata, and is PSPACE-complete for nondeterministic automata and LTL formulas. The complexities for frac-safety coincide with these known for livenesss, where the treatment of LTL formulas is exponentially

---

[2] Note that $\Sigma = 2^{AP}$ and our probability distribution is such that for each atomic proposition a and for each position in a computation, the probability that a holds in the position is $\frac{1}{2}$.

harder than that of nondeterministic automata and is EXPSPACE-complete. Our results are based on an analysis of the strongly connected components of deterministic automata for the language, and involve other results of interest on the expressive power of deterministic automata. In particular, we prove that frac-safety languages cannot be recognized by deterministic Büchi automata. This is in contrast with safety and almost-safety languages, which can always be recognized by deterministic Büchi automata, and liveness languages, some of which can be recognized by such automata. In Sect. 5 we discuss possible extensions of our approach as well as its practical applications.

Due to the lack of space, some of the proofs are missing and can be found in the full version, in the authors' URLs.

2   Preliminaries

Linear Temporal Logic. For a finite alphabet Σ, an infinite *word* $w = \sigma_1 \cdot \sigma_2 \cdots$ is an infinite sequence of letters from Σ. We use Σ^ω to denote the set of all infinite words over the alphabet Σ. A *language* $L \subseteq \Sigma^\omega$ is a set of words. When $\Sigma = 2^{AP}$, for a set AP of atomic propositions, each infinite word corresponds to a *computation* over AP. The logic *LTL* is a linear temporal logic [22]. Given a set AP of atomic propositions, LTL formulas are constructed from AP using the Boolean operators $\neg$ ("negation") and $\wedge$ ("and"), and the temporal operators X ("next time") and U ("until"). Writing LTL formulas, we also use the abbreviations $\vee$ ("or"), F ("eventually"), and G ("always"). The semantics of LTL is defined with respect to infinite computations $\pi = \sigma_1, \sigma_2, \sigma_3, \ldots \in (2^{AP})^\omega$. We use $\pi \models \psi$ to indicate that the computation π satisfies the LTL formula ψ. For the full syntax and semantics of LTL, see [22]. Each LTL formula ψ over AP defines a language $[\![\psi]\!] \subseteq (2^{AP})^\omega$ of the computations that satisfy ψ. Formally, $[\![\psi]\!] = \{\pi \in (2^{AP})^\omega : \pi \models \psi\}$.

Probability. Given a set S of elements, a *probability distribution* on S is a function $Pr : S \to [0,1]$ such that $\Sigma_{s \in S} Pr(s) = 1$. An *event* is a set $A \subseteq S$. The probability of A is then $\Sigma_{s \in A} Pr(s)$. Given two events A and B with $Pr(B) > 0$, the *conditional probability of A given B*, denoted $Pr(A \mid B)$, is defined as the ratio between the probability of the joint of events A and B, and the probability of B. That is, $Pr(A \mid B) = Pr(A \cap B)/Pr(B)$.

Consider an alphabet Σ. A *random word* over Σ is a word in which for all indices i, the i-th letter is drawn uniformly at random. In particular, when $\Sigma = 2^{AP}$, then a random computation π is such that for each atomic proposition q and for each position in π, the probability that q holds in the position is $\frac{1}{2}$. The probabilistic model above induces a probability distribution on Σ^ω, where the probability of a word is the product of the probabilities of its letters. The probability of a language $L \subseteq \Sigma^\omega$, denoted $Pr(L)$, is then the probability of the event L. It is known that regular languages have measurable probabilities [5]. For an LTL formula ψ, we use $Pr(\psi)$ to denote $Pr([\![\psi]\!])$. For example, the probabilities of Xp, Gp, and Fp are $\frac{1}{2}$, 0, and 1, respectively.

Automata. A *nondeterministic finite automaton* is a tuple $\mathcal{A} = \langle \Sigma, Q, Q_0, \delta, \alpha \rangle$, where Σ is a finite non-empty alphabet, Q is a finite non-empty set of *states*, $Q_0 \subseteq Q$ is a set of *initial states*, $\delta : Q \times \Sigma \rightarrow 2^Q$ is a *transition function*, and α is an *acceptance condition*. The automaton $\mathcal{A}$ is *deterministic* if $|Q_0| = 1$ and $|\delta(q, \sigma)| \leq 1$ for all states $q \in Q$ and letters $\sigma \in \Sigma$.

A *run* of $\mathcal{A}$ on an infinite input word $w = \sigma_1 \cdot \sigma_2 \cdots \in \Sigma^\omega$, is an infinite sequence of states $r = q_0, q_1, \ldots$ such that $q_0 \in Q_0$, and for all $i \geq 0$, we have $q_{i+1} \in \delta(q_i, \sigma_{i+1})$. The acceptance condition α determines which runs are accepting. For a run r, let $inf(r) = \{q : q_i = q \text{ for infinitely many } i\text{'s}\}$. That is, $inf(r)$ is the set of states that r visits infinitely often. Then, r is accepting iff $inf(r)$ satisfies α. We consider two acceptance conditions.

A set S of states satisfies a *Büchi* acceptance condition $\alpha \subseteq Q$ if $S \cap \alpha \neq \emptyset$. That is, a run r is accepting iff $inf(r) \cap \alpha \neq \emptyset$. A richer acceptance condition is *parity*, where $\alpha = \{\alpha_1, \alpha_2, \ldots, \alpha_k\}$, with $\alpha_1 \subseteq \alpha_2 \subseteq \cdots \subseteq \alpha_k = Q$, and a set S satisfies α if the minimal index i for which $S \cap \alpha_i \neq \emptyset$ is even. That is, a run r is accepting iff the minimal index i for which $inf(r) \cap \alpha_i \neq \emptyset$ is even.

A word w is accepted by an automaton $\mathcal{A}$ if there is an accepting run of $\mathcal{A}$ on w. The language of $\mathcal{A}$, denoted $L(\mathcal{A})$, is the set of words that $\mathcal{A}$ accepts. We use NBW, DBW, and DPW to abbreviate nondeterministic Büchi, deterministic Büchi, and deterministic parity word automata, respectively.

Theorem 1. [21, 24, 28]

- *Given an LTL formula ψ of lenght n, we can construct an NBW $\mathcal{A}_\psi$ such that $\mathcal{A}_\psi$ has $2^{O(n)}$ states and $L(\mathcal{A}_\psi) = [\![\psi]\!]$.*
- *Given an NBW with n states, we can construct an equivalent DPW with $2^{O(n \log n)}$ states.*

Consider a directed graph $G = \langle V, E \rangle$. A *strongly connected set* of G (SCS) is a set $C \subseteq V$ of vertices such that for every two vertices $v, v' \in C$, there is a path from v to v'. An SCS C is *maximal* if it cannot be extended to a larger SCS. Formally, for every nonempty set $C' \subseteq V \setminus C$, we have that $C \cup C'$ is not an SCS. The maximal strongly connected sets are also termed *strongly connected components* (SCC). An automaton $\mathcal{A} = \langle \Sigma, Q, Q_0, \delta, \alpha \rangle$ induces a directed graph $G_\mathcal{A} = \langle Q, E \rangle$ in which $\langle q, q' \rangle \in E$ iff there is a letter σ such that $q' \in \delta(q, \sigma)$. When we talk about the SCSs and SCCs of $\mathcal{A}$, we refer to these of $G_\mathcal{A}$.

An SCC C of a graph G is *ergodic* iff for all $\langle u, v \rangle \in E$, if $u \in C$ then $v \in C$. That is, an SCC is ergodic if no edge leaves it. We say that a path $\pi = \pi_0, \pi_1, \pi_2, \ldots$ in G *reaches* an ergodic SCC C, if there exists $i \geq 0$ such that for all $j \geq i$, we have that $\pi_j \in C$. Note that if $\pi_i \in C$ for some i, then π reaches the ergodic SCC C.

The following lemma states two fundamental properties of runs of automata (see, for example, [12]).

Lemma 1. *Consider an automaton $\mathcal{A}$.*

1. *A run of $\mathcal{A}$ on a random word reaches some ergodic SCC with probability 1.*
2. *An infinite run that reaches an ergodic SCC C of $\mathcal{A}$ visits all the states in C infinitely often with probability 1.*

We distinguish between several types of ergodic SCCs. Let $\mathcal{A}$ be an automaton. An ergodic SCC C of $\mathcal{A}$ is *accepting* if a random path that reaches C is accepting with probability 1. Similarly, C is *rejecting* if a random path that reaches C is rejecting with probability 1. Recall that for an acceptance condition α, a run r is accepting iff $inf(r)$ satisfies α. It follows from Lemma 1 that an ergodic SCC C is accepting iff it satisfies α. We say that an ergodic SCC C of $\mathcal{A}$ is *pure accepting* if every random path π that reaches C is accepting. Similarly, an ergodic SCC C of $\mathcal{A}$ is *pure rejecting* if every random path π that reaches C is rejecting. Note that pure accepting and pure rejecting ergodic SCCs are equivalent to accepting and rejecting sinks, respectively.

3   Classes of Safety

Consider a language $L \subseteq \Sigma^\omega$ of infinite words over an alphabet Σ. A finite word $x \in \Sigma^*$ is a *bad prefix* for L if for all infinite words $y \in \Sigma^\omega$, we have that $x \cdot y \notin L$. In other words, a bad prefix for L is a finite word that cannot be extended into an infinite word in L. Let $safe(L) = \{w : w \text{ has a bad prefix for } L\}$ and $comp(L) = \Sigma^\omega \setminus L$. Note that $safe(L) \subseteq comp(L)$. We define the *safety level* of a language L, denoted $slevel(L)$, as the probability of a word not in L to have a bad prefix. Formally, $slevel(L) = Pr(safe(L) \mid comp(L))$. When $slevel(L) = p$, we say that L is a *p-safety language*. By the definition of conditional probability, we have that

$$slevel(L) = Pr(safe(L) \mid comp(L)) = \frac{Pr(safe(L) \cap comp(L))}{Pr(comp(L))} = \frac{Pr(safe(L))}{Pr(comp(L))}.$$

Note that if $Pr(L) = 1$, then $Pr(comp(L)) = 0$ so $slevel(L)$ is undefined. In this case, we define the safety level of L to be 0, as justified in Proposition 1 below.[3]

Proposition 1. *For every language L, if $Pr(L) = 1$, then $safe(L) = \emptyset$.*

Proof. Consider a language L with $Pr(L) = 1$. Assume, by way of contradiction, that there is a bad prefix x of L. For every $y \in \Sigma^\omega$, we have that $x \cdot y \notin L$. It follows that $Pr(comp(L)) > 0$, contradicting the assumption that $Pr(L) = 1$. □

Remark 1. Note that the other direction of Proposition 1 does not hold. That is, there exists a language L such that L has no bad prefixes and still $Pr(L) \neq 1$. As an example, consider the language $L = \llbracket FGa \rrbracket$ with $AP = \{a\}$. Every finite prefix can be extended to a word in L by the suffix $\{a\}^\omega$, thus L has no bad prefixes. Nevertheless, it is easy to see that $Pr(L) = 0$.

We define four classes of languages, describing their safety level:

---

[3] An anomaly of this definition is the language $L = \Sigma^\omega$. While $Pr(L) = 1$, making its safety level 0, we also have that L is a safety language. Thus, L is the only language that is both safety and has safety level 0.

- *Safety* [2,25]. A language $L \subseteq \Sigma^\omega$ is a safety language if $safe(L) = comp(L)$. That is, every word not in L has a bad prefix. For example, $L = [\![Ga]\!]$ is a safety language, as every word not in L has a prefix in which a does not hold, and this prefix cannot be extended to a word in L.
- *Almost-safety.* A language $L \subseteq \Sigma^\omega$ is an almost-safety language if it is p-safety for $p = 1$ but is not safety. As an example, consider the language $L = [\![aUb]\!]$. The language L is not a safety language, as the word $a^\omega \notin L$ has no bad prefix. Indeed, we can concatenate b^ω to every prefix of a^ω and get a word in L. In addition, every word not in L except for a^ω has a bad prefix for L, and there are infinitely many such words. Accordingly, $\dfrac{Pr(safe(L))}{Pr(comp(L))} = 1$.
- *Frac-safety.* A language $L \subseteq \Sigma^\omega$ is a frac-safety language if it is p-safety for $0 < p < 1$. As an example, consider the language $L = [\![a \wedge FGa]\!]$. We show that L is $\frac{1}{2}$-safety. The words not in L are these that satisfy $\neg a \vee GF \neg a$. Since $Pr(GF \neg a) = 1$, we have that $Pr(comp(L)) = Pr(\neg a \vee GF \neg a) = 1$. Note that every prefix can be extended to a word that satisfies FGa, simply by concatenating the suffix a^ω. That is, words that do not satisfy FGa have no bad prefixes. On the other hand, every word that does not satisfy a has the bad prefix $\neg a$. It follows that a word has a bad prefix for L iff it does not satisfy a. Accordingly, $Pr(safe(L)) = Pr(\neg a) = \frac{1}{2}$. Hence, $\dfrac{Pr(safe(L))}{Pr(comp(L))} = \dfrac{\frac{1}{2}}{1} = \frac{1}{2}$, and L is $\frac{1}{2}$-safety.
- *Liveness.* A language $L \subseteq \Sigma^\omega$ is a liveness language if $safe(L) = \emptyset$. For example, the language $L = [\![Fa]\!]$ is liveness, as no word in $comp(L)$ has a bad prefix. Indeed, the only word in $comp(L)$ is $(\neg a)^\omega$, and it has no bad prefixes. Note that the definition is equivalent to the one in [1], according to which L is liveness if every word in Σ^* can be extended to a word in L.

We extend the classification to LTL formulas. We say that a formula φ is *p-safety* if $[\![\varphi]\!]$ is p-safety, and that φ is in one of the classes above if $[\![\varphi]\!]$ is in the class.

Recall that an almost-safety language is a language that is 1-safety but not safety. Dually, we can relate to 0-safety languages that are not liveness. While, however, 1-safety is distinct from safety, we have that 0-safety and liveness coincide:

Proposition 2. *A language is liveness iff it is 0-safety.*

Proof. Consider a language $L \subseteq \Sigma^\omega$. By the definition of liveness, if L is liveness, then $safe(L) = \emptyset$, so it is 0-safety. For the other direction, we prove that if L is not liveness then it is not 0-safety. Assume that L is not liveness, thus $safe(L) \neq \emptyset$. Let $w \in safe(L)$ and let u be a bad prefix for w. Every word that starts with u is both in $comp(L)$ and in $safe(L)$. Therefore, the measure of words in $safe(L)$ is at least the measure of words with prefix u, which is strictly greater than 0. Hence, if L is not liveness then it is not 0-safety. □

3.1   Co-safety

We turn to study the dual notion, of *co-safety languages*. A finite word $x \in \Sigma^*$ is a *good prefix* for a language $L \subseteq \Sigma^\omega$, if for all infinite words $y \in \Sigma^\omega$, we have that $x \cdot y \in L$. In other words, a *good prefix* is a finite word all whose extentions are in L. A language L is a *co-safety language* if every word in L has a good prefix. Equivalently, L is co-safety iff $comp(L)$ is safety. We define $co\text{-}safe(L) = \{w : w \text{ has a good prefix for } L\}$. The classes defined above for safety can be dualized to classes on co-safety. Thus, the *co-safety level* of a language L, denoted $co - slevel(L)$, is $Pr(co\text{-}safe(L) \mid L)$. Also, a language L is *co-liveness* if $co\text{-}safe(L) = \emptyset$. Propositions 1 and 2 can be dualized too. Formally, we have the following.

Lemma 2. *For every language L, we have $slevel(L) = co - slevel(comp(L))$.*

Proof. Consider a language L. By the definition of good and bad prefixes, every bad prefix for L is a good prefix for $comp(L)$, thus $Pr(safe(L)) = Pr(co\text{-}safe(comp(L)))$. Hence, $slevel(L) = Pr(safe(L) \mid comp(L)) = \dfrac{Pr(safe(L))}{Pr(comp(L))} = \dfrac{Pr(co\text{-}safe(comp(L)))}{Pr(comp(L))} = Pr(co\text{-}safe(comp(L)) \mid comp(L)) = co - slevel(comp(L))$, and we are done.   □

Table 1 describes LTL formulas of different safety and co-safety levels. The number within brackets next to a formula φ is $Pr(\varphi)$. For example, the LTL formula $aUb \vee Gc$ is almost-safety, almost-co-safety, and has probability $\frac{2}{3}$.

Note that, by Lemma 2, a language L is a member of the (i,j)-th cell in the table iff $comp(L)$ is a member of the (j,i)-th cell. In addition, it follows from the definition of a safety level that if $Pr(\varphi) = 1$, then φ is 0-safety, so, by Proposition 2, the formula φ is in the right column. Dually, if $Pr(\varphi) = 0$, then φ is 0-co-safety, so, by the dual of Proposition 2, it is in the bottom row. Propositions 3 and 6 below state some additional properties of the table, and they are based on some observations on automata.

Table 1. Examples to formulas of different safety and co-safety levels, with $\varphi_1 = a \wedge GFb$, $\varphi_2 = c \wedge FGd$, and $\varphi_3 = \neg a \wedge FGb$

	safety	almost-safety	frac-safety	liveness
co-safety	a $(\frac{1}{2})$	aUb $(\frac{2}{3})$	—	Fa (1)
		$a \wedge Fb$ $(\frac{1}{2})$	(see Lemma 6)	
almost-co-safety	$\neg(aUb)$ $(\frac{1}{3})$	$aUb \vee Gc$ $(\frac{2}{3})$	$\neg\varphi_1 \wedge c$ $(\frac{1}{4})$	$\neg\varphi_1$ $(\frac{1}{2})$
	$a \vee Gb$ $(\frac{1}{2})$		$a \vee \varphi_2$ $(\frac{1}{2})$	$Ga \vee Fb$ (1)
frac-co-safety	—	$\varphi_1 \vee c$ $(\frac{3}{4})$	$\varphi_1 \vee \varphi_2 \vee e$ $(\frac{3}{4})$	$\neg\varphi_2$ (1)
	(see Lemma 6)	$a \wedge \neg\varphi_2$ $(\frac{1}{2})$		$\neg\varphi_1 \wedge \neg\varphi_2$ $(\frac{1}{2})$
co-liveness	Ga (0)	φ_1 $(\frac{1}{2})$	φ_2 (0)	FGa (0)
		$Ga \wedge Fb$ (0)	$\varphi_1 \vee \varphi_2$ $(\frac{1}{2})$	GFa (1)
				$\varphi_1 \vee \varphi_3$ $(\frac{1}{2})$

3.2   Finding the Safety Level

We now study the problem of calculating the the safety level of a language given by a DPW, an NBW, or an LTL formula.

Theorem 2. *Calculating the safety level of a language L can be done in linear, exponential, and doubly-exponential time for L given by a DPW, an NBW, and an LTL formula, respectively.*

Proof. We describe a linear-time algorithm for DPWs. The complexity for the other classes then follows from Theorem 1. Consider a DPW $\mathcal{A}$. We calculate $slevel(L(\mathcal{A}))$ by calculating $Pr(safe(L(\mathcal{A})))$, $Pr(comp(L(\mathcal{A})))$, and the ratio between them. Let $\mathcal{C} = \{C_1, \ldots, C_m\}$ be the ergodic SCCs of $\mathcal{A}$. We can find $\mathcal{C}$ in linear time, and can also mark the ergodic SCCs that are rejecting and these that are pure rejecting [27]. Now, $Pr(safe(L(\mathcal{A})))$ is the probability that a random run reaches a pure rejecting SCC, and $Pr(comp(L))$ is the probability that a random run reaches a rejecting SCC. Both can be calculated by assigning to each SCC the probability that a random run reaches it. Finally, by Proposition 1, if $Pr(comp(L(\mathcal{A}))) = 0$, then the algorithm returns 0.   □

Remark 2. In this work, we assume a uniform probability distribution on Σ^ω. However, this assumption is not necessary. In general, we can assume that the probability of a computation π is defined by a Markov chain, such that for each atomic proposition q and for each position in π, the probability that q holds in the position is greater than 0 and less than 1. This assumption may affect the exact safety level of a language. However, it is easy to see that the class of safety level will be the same as for uniform distribution.

4   Finding the Safety Class

In this section we study the problem of classifying languages to the four classes of safety level, hoping to end up with algorithms that are simpler than the one described for finding the exact safety level. Deciding membership in the classes of safety and liveness have already been studied, and we focus on almost-safety and frac-safety. We first recall the known results for safety and liveness:[4]

Theorem 3. *[13,25] Consider a language $L \subseteq \Sigma^\omega$.*

- *Deciding whether L is safety is NLOGSPACE-complete for L given by a DPW and PSPACE-complete for L given by an NBW or an LTL formula.*
- *Deciding whether L is liveness is NLOGSPACE-complete for L given by a DPW, PSPACE-complete for L given by an NBW, and EXPSPACE-complete for L given by an LTL formula.*

---

[4] We did not find in the literature an NLOGSPACE-complete result for deciding liveness of a DPW. The proof, however, follows standard considerations, and we give it in the full version.

Theorem 3 hints that at least for one of the classes almost-safety and frac-safety, the classification for LTL formulas is going to be EXPSPACE-complete. We turn to study the problems in detail. We do this by analyzing the structure of deterministic automata for the language. As detailed in Sect. 4.2, the analysis leads to interesting results on the expressive power of deterministic automata beyond the classification to safety level. We first need some definitions and observations on automata.

4.1   Observations on Automata

Consider a deterministic automaton $\mathcal{A}$. Recall the partition of $\mathcal{A}$ to SCC as defined in Sect. 2. An ergodic SCC C of $\mathcal{A}$ is *mixed* if there exist both accepting and rejecting paths that reach C. Note that a mixed ergodic SCC of a DPW may be either accepting or rejecting, whereas a mixed ergodic SCC of a DBW is accepting. In terms of safety and co-safety, a run that reaches a pure accepting (rejecting) ergodic SCC is an accepting (rejecting) run and it is labeled by a word that has a good (bad, respectively) prefix. On the other hand, a run that reaches a mixed ergodic SCC is labeled by a word that has neither a good prefix nor a bad prefix. For an automaton $\mathcal{A}$ and an ergodic SCC C of $\mathcal{A}$, we define $reach(\mathcal{A}, C) = \{w : \text{the run of } \mathcal{A} \text{ on } w \text{ reaches } C\}$. For a language L, we define $mixed\text{-}in(L) = L \setminus co\text{-}safe(L)$. That is, $mixed\text{-}in(L)$ contains all words w such that $w \in L$ and w has no good prefix. Dually, we define $mixed\text{-}out(L) = comp(L) \setminus safe(L)$. That is, $mixed\text{-}out(L)$ contains all words w such that $w \notin L$ and w has no bad prefix.

Our goal is to characterize classes of safety level by the structure of deterministic automata that recognize them. Lemmas 3 and 4 below state relevant observations on the ergodic SCC of automata of languages in the different classes.

Lemma 3. *Consider a deterministic automaton $\mathcal{A}$, and let $L = L(\mathcal{A})$.*

1. *$safe(L) \neq \emptyset$ iff $\mathcal{A}$ has a pure rejecting ergodic SCC. Dually, $co\text{-}safe(L) \neq \emptyset$ iff $\mathcal{A}$ has a pure accepting ergodic SCC.*
2. *Consider a mixed ergodic SCC C of $\mathcal{A}$. Let $R_{in} = reach(\mathcal{A}, C) \cap mixed\text{-}in(L)$ and $R_{out} = reach(\mathcal{A}, C) \cap mixed\text{-}out(L)$. Then, R_{in} and R_{out} form a partition of $reach(\mathcal{A}, C)$ with $R_{in} \neq \emptyset$ and $R_{out} \neq \emptyset$. If C is rejecting, then $Pr(R_{in}) = 0$ and $Pr(R_{out}) > 0$. Dually, if C is accepting, then $Pr(R_{in}) > 0$ and $Pr(R_{out}) = 0$.*

Lemma 4. *Consider a deterministic automaton $\mathcal{A}$. If $Pr(mixed\text{-}out(L(\mathcal{A}))) = 0$ and $mixed\text{-}out(L(\mathcal{A})) \neq \emptyset$, then at least one of the following conditions holds:*

1. *$\mathcal{A}$ has a mixed accepting ergodic SCC.*
2. *There is a rejecting run of $\mathcal{A}$ that does not reach an ergodic SCC.*

We can now reduce questions about the class of a given language to questions about the structure of a deterministic automaton for it.

Theorem 4. *Consider a deterministic automaton $\mathcal{A}$, and let $L = L(\mathcal{A})$.*

1. The language L is *liveness* iff $\mathcal{A}$ does not have a pure rejecting ergodic SCC.
2. The language L is *frac-safety* iff $\mathcal{A}$ has a pure rejecting ergodic SCC and a mixed rejecting ergodic SCC.
3. The language L is *almost-safety* iff $\mathcal{A}$ has a pure rejecting ergodic SCC, does not have a mixed rejecting ergodic SCC, and has either a mixed accepting ergodic SCC or a rejecting path that does not reach a pure rejecting ergodic SCC.
4. The language L is *safety* iff $\mathcal{A}$ has a pure rejecting ergodic SCC and all its rejecting paths reach a pure rejecting ergodic SCC.

Proof. Consider a deterministic automaton $\mathcal{A}$ and let $L = L(\mathcal{A})$.

1. By Lemma 3(1), the automaton $\mathcal{A}$ has a pure rejecting ergodic SCC iff $safe(L) \neq \emptyset$. Recall that L is liveness iff it has no bad prefixes. It follows that L is liveness iff $\mathcal{A}$ does not have pure rejecting ergodic SCCs.
2. For the first direction, assume that L is frac-safety. By the definition of frac-safety languages, we have that $safe(L) \neq \emptyset$. According to Lemma 3(1), it follows that $\mathcal{A}$ has a pure rejecting ergodic SCC. In addition, for a frac-safety language L it holds that $Pr(mixed\text{-}out(L)) > 0$. Since an ergodic SCC may be either pure or mixed and either accepting or rejecting, it follows from Lemma 3(2) that a positive measure of words in $mixed\text{-}out(L)$ can be induced only by a mixed rejecting ergodic SCC. Therefore, $\mathcal{A}$ has a mixed rejecting ergodic SCC, so we are done. For the other direction, assume that $\mathcal{A}$ has both pure rejecting and mixed rejecting ergodic SCCs. By Lemma 3, it holds that $safe(L) \neq \emptyset$ and $Pr(mixed\text{-}out(L)) > 0$. Thus, we have that $0 < Pr(safe(L) \mid comp(L)) < 1$. In addition, since $safe(L) \neq \emptyset$, we have that $Pr(L) < 1$. Recall that for a language L with $Pr(L) \neq 1$, the level of safety is defined as $Pr(safe(L) \mid comp(L))$. Therefore, we have that the level of safety of L is greater than 0 and less than 1, so L is frac-safety, and we are done.
3. For the first direction, assume that L is almost-safety. Since L is almost-safety, we have that $Pr(mixed\text{-}out(L)) = 0$ and $mixed\text{-}out(L) \neq \emptyset$. By Lemma 4, the automaton $\mathcal{A}$ has either a mixed accepting ergodic SCC or a rejecting path that does not reach a pure rejecting ergodic SCC. By Lemma 3(2), $\mathcal{A}$ does not have mixed rejecting ergodic SCC. In addition, an almost-safety language has a bad prefix. Therefore, by Lemma 3(1), the automaton $\mathcal{A}$ has a pure rejecting ergodic SCC, and we are done. For the other direction, assume that $\mathcal{A}$ has a pure rejecting ergodic SCC, does not have a mixed rejecting ergodic SCC, and has either a mixed accepting ergodic SCC or a rejecting path that does not reach a pure rejecting ergodic SCC. From the first two conditions and Lemma 3 it follows that $Pr(safe(L) \mid comp(L)) = 1$. From the last condition, it follows that $mixed\text{-}out(L) \neq \emptyset$, and therefore L is not safety. Then, by the definition of almost-safety languages, the language L is almost-safety.
4. For the first direction, assume that L is safety. Since every word in $comp(L)$ has a bad prefix, the automaton $\mathcal{A}$ does not have mixed ergodic SCCs. Since $safe(L) \neq \emptyset$, by Lemma 3(1) $\mathcal{A}$ has a pure rejecting ergodic SCC. In other words, if L is safety then $\mathcal{A}$ has a pure rejecting ergodic SCC and all its rejecting paths reach a pure rejecting ergodic SCC. For the other direction,

assume that $\mathcal{A}$ has a pure rejecting ergodic SCC and all its rejecting paths reach a pure rejecting ergodic SCC. It follows that every word in $comp(L)$ has a bad prefix, thus L is safety.   □

4.2 Expressive Power

Before we study the decision procedure that follow from Theorem 4, let us point to some interesting conclusions regarding expressive power that follow from the theorem.

Consider a language L. By the dual of Remark 1, co-liveness of a language L is not a sufficient condition for $Pr(L) = 0$. It is easy to see that also safety is not a sufficient condition for $Pr(L) = 0$. For example, the language $\llbracket a \rrbracket$ is safety and $Pr(a) = \frac{1}{2}$. Proposition 3 below shows that the combination of co-liveness and safety is sufficient.

Proposition 3. *If a language L is safety and co-liveness, then $Pr(L) = 0$.*

Proof. Consider a deterministic automaton $\mathcal{A}$ for a safety and co-liveness language L. According to Theorem 4(4), since L is safety, the automaton $\mathcal{A}$ does not have mixed ergodic SCCs and has a pure rejecting ergodic SCC. According to the dual (for co-liveness) of Theorem 4(1), since L is co-liveness, the automaton $\mathcal{A}$ does not have pure accepting ergodic SCCs. Hence, $\mathcal{A}$ has only rejecting ergodic SCCs, so $Pr(L) = 0$.   □

It is known that safety languages can be recognized by looping automata (that is, Büchi automata in which all states are accepting). Propositions 4 and 5 below relate the other classes with recognizability by deterministic Büchi automata, which are known to be less expressive than deterministic parity automata [17].

Proposition 4. *The language of a DBW is safety, almost-safety, or liveness.*

Proof. Consider a DBW $\mathcal{A}$. By Lemma 1, if a path in $\mathcal{A}$ reaches an ergodic SCC C, it visits all states in C infinitely often with probability 1. Therefore, a mixed ergodic SCC of a DBW is accepting. On the other hand, by Theorem 4(2), a DBW of a frac-safety language has a mixed rejecting ergodic SCC.   □

Note that the other direction of Proposition 4 does not hold for liveness languages. That is, a liveness language may not have a DBW. For example, the language $\llbracket FGa \rrbracket$ is liveness, but it does not have a DBW [17]. Proposition 5 states that the other direction of Proposition 4 does hold for safety and almost-safety languages.

Proposition 5. *If a language is safety or almost-safety, then it can be recognized by a DBW.*

Proof. Consider a DPW $\mathcal{A}$ for a safety or almost-safety language. Let $\alpha = \{\alpha_1, \ldots, \alpha_k\}$. By Theorems 4(3) and (4), the DPW $\mathcal{A}$ does not have a mixed rejecting ergodic SCC. Recall that an ergodic SCC of a DBW is either pure accepting, pure rejecting, or mixed accepting. Let $\alpha' = \bigcup \alpha_i : i$ is even. Since $\mathcal{A}$ does not have a mixed rejecting ergodic SCC, the DBW obtained from $\mathcal{A}$ by defining the acceptance condition to be α' is equivalent to $\mathcal{A}$. Hence, L can be recognized by a DBW and we are done.   □

Recall that in Table 1, we left some intersections empty. We can now prove that the corresponding combinations are indeed impossible.

Proposition 6. *A language cannot be both safety and frac-co-safety or both frac-safety and co-safety.*

Proof. We prove that a language L cannot be both safety and frac-co-safety. The proof of the second claim is dual. Let L be a frac-co-safety language, and let $\mathcal{A}$ be a DPW for L. As follows from the dual of Theorem 4(2), the DPW $\mathcal{A}$ has a mixed accepting ergodic SCC. Since a mixed accepting ergodic SCC induces at least one word in $mixed\text{-}out(L)$, it follows that L is not safety, and we are done.   □

4.3   Decision Procedures

We now use Theorem 4 in order to find safety classes. Essentially, the characterization there reduces the problem to a search for "witness SCCs" or "witness paths". We elaborate on the algorithms for the specific cases.

Theorem 5. *Deciding whether a language $L \subseteq \Sigma^\omega$ is almost-safety is NLOGSPACE-complete for L given by a DPW and PSPACE-complete for L given by an NBW or an LTL formula.*

Proof. We start with the upper bounds and show that the problem is in NLOGSPACE for DPWs. The upper bound for NBWs then follow from Theorem 1. Consider a DPW $\mathcal{A}$. By Theorem 4(3), we have that $L(\mathcal{A})$ is almost-safety iff $\mathcal{A}$ has a pure rejecting ergodic SCC, does not have a mixed rejecting ergodic SCC, and has either a mixed accepting ergodic SCC or a rejecting path that does not reach a pure rejecting ergodic SCC. Since NLOGSPACE is closed under complementation, and since we can verify the classification of a given SCC in NLOGSPACE, checking whether $\mathcal{A}$ satisfies the condition above can be done in NLOGSPACE.

We turn to an upper bound for LTL. Note that a naive application of Theorems 4(3) and 1 only gives an EXPSPACE upper bound. Consider an LTL formula φ. First, we construct an NBW $\mathcal{A}_\varphi$ for φ and remove from it empty states (that is, states from which no word is accepted). We then construct an NBW $\mathcal{A}_\varphi^{loop}$ by making all of the states of $\mathcal{A}_\varphi$ accepting. As argued in [25], the language $[\![\varphi]\!]$ is safety iff $L(\mathcal{A}_\varphi^{loop}) = L(\mathcal{A}_\varphi)$. For almost-safety languages, this equality holds with probability 1. That is, $[\![\varphi]\!]$ is almost-safety iff it is not safety and $Pr(L(\mathcal{A}_\varphi^{loop}) \cap L(\mathcal{A}_{\neg\varphi})) = 0$. Indeed, every word without a bad prefix is accepted both by $\mathcal{A}_\varphi^{loop}$ and $\mathcal{A}_{\neg\varphi}$. Therefore, $[\![\varphi]\!]$ is almost-safety iff the set $L(\mathcal{A}_\varphi^{loop}) \cap L(\mathcal{A}_{\neg\varphi})$ is of measure 0. Accordingly, our algorithm constructs the

NBWs $\mathcal{A}_{\varphi}^{loop}$ and $\mathcal{A}_{\neg\varphi}$, and then check whether $Pr(L(\mathcal{A}_{\varphi}^{loop}) \cap L(\mathcal{A}_{\neg\varphi})) = 0$. The latter can be done in NLOGSPACE($|\mathcal{A}_{\varphi}|$), which is PSPACE($|\varphi|$), as required. Indeed, we only have to check that the product automaton does not have an accepting SCC.

We turn to the lower bounds, and start with DPWs. In fact, we show that the problem is NLOGSPACE-hard already for DBWs. We describe a reduction from the reachability problem, proven to be NLOGSPACE-hard in [11]. Given a graph G and two vertices u and v in V, we construct a DBW $\mathcal{A}$ such that $L(\mathcal{A})$ is almost-safety iff v is reachable from u. Intuitively (see details in the full version), the DBW $\mathcal{A}$ adds to G self loops in v and transitions to an accepting and a rejecting sink in such a way so that if v is not reachable from u, the language of $\mathcal{A}$ is safety. If, however, v is reachable from u, an infinite path that loops forever in v makes its language almost-safe.

For NBWs, we again show a reduction from the non-universality problem for safety NBWs, namely the problem of deciding, given an NBW $\mathcal{A}$ for a safety language, whether $L(\mathcal{A}) \neq \Sigma^{\omega}$. The latter is proven to be PSPACE-hard in [20]. Given an NBW $\mathcal{A}$ for a safety language, we define an NBW $\mathcal{B}$ such that $\mathcal{A}$ is not universal iff $L(\mathcal{B})$ is almost-safety. Let $\mathcal{A} = \langle \Sigma, Q, Q_0, \delta, \alpha \rangle$, and let $\mathcal{A}' = \langle \{a, b\}, Q', Q'_0, \delta', \alpha' \rangle$ be an NBW for the language $[\![aUb]\!]$. We define $\mathcal{B} = \langle \Sigma \times \{a, b\}, Q \times Q', Q_0 \times Q'_0, \delta'', \alpha'' \rangle$, where $\delta''(\langle q, q' \rangle, \langle \sigma, \sigma' \rangle) = \langle \delta(q, \sigma), \delta'(q', \sigma') \rangle$, and $\alpha'' = \{\langle Q, Q' \rangle : Q \in \alpha\} \cup \{\langle Q, Q' \rangle : Q' \in \alpha'\}$. For a word $w \in (\Sigma \times \{a, b\})^{\omega}$, let $w_1 \in \Sigma^{\omega}$ be the word obtained from w by projecting its letters on Σ, and similarly for w_2 and $\{a, b\}$. It is easy to see that $L(\mathcal{B}) = \{w : w_1 \in L(\mathcal{A}) \text{ or } w_2 \in [\![aUb]\!]\}$. In the full version, we prove that $\mathcal{A}$ is not universal iff $L(\mathcal{B})$ is almost-safety.

It is left to prove PSPACE-hardness the LTL setting. We do this by a reduction from the non-validity problem for safety LTL formulas, proven to be PSPACE-hard in [26]. Given a safety LTL formula φ over AP, let a and b be atomic propositions not in AP. In the full version, we prove that φ is not valid iff $\varphi \lor (aUb)$ is almost-safety.   □

Theorem 6. *Deciding whether a language $L \subseteq \Sigma^{\omega}$ is frac-safety is NLOGSPACE-complete for L given by a DPW, PSPACE-complete for L given by an NBW, and EXPSPACE-complete for L given by an LTL formula.*

Proof. We start with the upper bounds and show that the problem is in NLOGSPACE for DPWs. The upper bounds for NBWs and LTL formulas then follow from Theorem 1. Consider a DPW $\mathcal{A}$. By Theorem 4(2), we have that $L(\mathcal{A})$ is frac-safety iff $\mathcal{A}$ has a pure rejecting ergodic SCC and a mixed rejecting ergodic SCC. Since we can verify the classification of a given SCC in NLOGSPACE, checking whether $\mathcal{A}$ satisfies the condition above can be done in NLOGSPACE.

We proceed to the lower bounds. For DPWs, we describe a reduction from the reachability problem. Given a graph G and two vertices u and v in V, we construct a DPW $\mathcal{A}$ such that $L(\mathcal{A})$ is frac-safety iff v is reachable from u. Intuitively, the DPW is constructed in the following way. A new rejecting sink is added, with a transition from u. In addition, v is replaced by a mixed rejecting component. We get a DPW with a reachable pure rejecting ergodic SCC. In addition, it has mixed rejecting ergodic SCC which is reachable iff v is reachable from u. Recall that by Theorem 4(2), a language is frac-safety iff its automaton has a pure rejecting ergodic SCC and a mixed rejecting ergodic SCC. For details, see the full version.

We turn to prove that the problem is PSPACE-hard for NBWs, again by a reduction from the non-universality problem for safety NBWs. The reduction is similar to the one for NBWs in the proof of Theorem 5, except that now we take $\mathcal{A}'$ to be an NBW for the language $[\![a \wedge GFb]\!]$, which is a $\frac{1}{2}$-safety language. Consequently, $L(\mathcal{B}) = \{w : w_1 \in L(\mathcal{A})$ or $w_2 \in [\![a \wedge GFb]\!]\}$. In the full version we prove that $\mathcal{A}$ is not universal iff $L(\mathcal{B})$ is frac-safety.

It is left to prove that the problem is EXPSPACE-hard for LTL formulas. We show a reduction from the problem of deciding non-liveness of LTL formulas, which is EXPSPACE-hard [13]. Given an LTL formula ψ over AP of, we construct an LTL formula φ such that ψ is not liveness iff φ is frac-safety.

The construction of φ is as follows. Let a, b, and c be propositions not in AP. We define $\varphi = ((a \wedge b) \rightarrow \psi) \wedge ((\neg a \vee \neg b) \rightarrow FGc)$. We prove that ψ is not liveness iff φ is frac-safety. First, if ψ is liveness then φ is liveness, since nor ψ neither FGc have a bad prefix. Therefore, φ is not frac-safety. That is, if ψ is liveness then φ is not frac-safety. For the other direction, assume that ψ is not liveness. Then, $0 < Pr(safe([\![\psi]\!])) \leq 1$. Note that if a computation for φ starts with $\{a, b\}$, then the computation has a bad prefix with probability $Pr(safe([\![\psi]\!]))$. Otherwise, the computation has a bad prefix with probability $Pr(safe([\![FGp]\!]))$, which is 0. That is, $Pr(safe([\![\varphi]\!])) = \frac{Pr(safe([\![\psi]\!]))}{4}$, so $0 < Pr(safe([\![\varphi]\!])) \leq \frac{1}{4}$. In order to find the safety level of φ, it is left to find $Pr(comp([\![\varphi]\!]))$, which is equal to $Pr(\neg\varphi)$. If a computation for φ starts with $\{a, b\}$, then the computation satisfies φ with probability $Pr(\psi)$. Otherwise, the computation satisfies φ with probability $Pr(FGc)$, which is 0. That is, $Pr(\varphi) = \frac{Pr(\psi)}{4}$, so $0 \leq Pr(\varphi) \leq \frac{1}{4}$. Therefore, $\frac{3}{4} \leq Pr(\neg\varphi) \leq 1$. Since $0 < Pr(safe([\![\varphi]\!])) \leq \frac{1}{4}$, we have that $0 < \frac{Pr(safe([\![\varphi]\!]))}{Pr(\neg\varphi)} \leq \frac{1}{3}$. Note that the safety level of $L(\varphi)$ is equal to $\frac{Pr(safe([\![\varphi]\!]))}{Pr(\neg\varphi)}$, thus φ is frac-safety, and we are done. □

We note that the problem of deciding frac-safety for DBWs is in $O(1)$, as, by Proposition 4, the language of all DBWs is not frac-safety.

To conclude, the complexity of deciding almost-safety and safety coincide, and so does the complexity of deciding frac-safety and liveness. In the case of LTL formulas, the difference in the complexity of deciding safety and liveness is carried over to a difference in deciding almost-safety and frac-safety, and the latter is exponentially more expensive. Intuitively, it follows from the structural similarity between safety and almost-safety – both search a word with no bad prefix, which can be done in the nondeterministic automaton, and between frac-safety and liveness – both search for a word that cannot be extended to a word in the language, which should be done in the deterministic automaton for the language.

5   Discussion and Directions for Future Research

We defined and studied safety levels of ω-regular languages. One can define the *relative* safety level of a specification in a system. Then, rather than taking the probability distribution with respect to Σ^ω, we take it with respect to the set of computations generated by a system S. For example, if S does not generate the computation a^ω, then the specification aUb is safety with respect to S. Relative safety and liveness have been studied in [13]. It is interesting to extend the study and add relativity to the full spectrum between safety and liveness. In particular, relativity may both increase and decrease the safety level.

A different approach to span the spectrum between safety and liveness was taken in [6]. Recall that the probability of a specification is measured with respect to random computations in Σ^ω. Alternatively, one can also study the probability of formulas to hold in computations of random *finite-state* systems. Formally, for an integer $l \geq 1$, let $Pr_l(\varphi)$ denote the probability that φ holds in a random cycle of length l. Here too, the probability that each atomic proposition holds in a state is $\frac{1}{2}$, yet we have only l states to fix an assignment to. So, for example, while $Pr(Gp) = 0$, we have that $Pr_1(Gp) = \frac{1}{2}$, $Pr_2(Gp) = \frac{1}{4}$, and in general $Pr_j(Gp) = \frac{1}{2^j}$. Indeed, an l-cycle satisfies Gp iff all its states satisfy p. It is suggested in [6] to characterize safety properties by means of the asymptotic behavior of $Pr_l(\varphi)$. The idea is to define different levels of safety according to the rate the probability decreases or increases. For example, clearly $Pr_l(Gp)$ tends to 0 as l increases, whereas $Pr_l(Fp)$ tends to 1. As it turns out, however, the characterization is not clean. For example, FGp is a liveness formula, but $Pr_l(FGp)$ decreases as l increases. It is interesting to see whether a combination of the safety level studied here and the finite-state system approach of [6] can lead to a refined spectrum.

Given the importance of safety and liveness in the topological view to ω-regular languages, it is interesting to examine the meaning of safety level in this view. In particular, the notion of safety level suggests a continuous transition from closed sets to dense ones. Also, the same way the intersection of safety and co-safety languages correspond to clopen languages [15], it would be interesting to examine the different levels of "clopeness" of the different intersections in Table 1.

In practice, the safety level of a language L indicates how well algorithms that are designated for safety specifications can work for L. We propose two approximated model-checking algorithms for languages with a high safety level. In one, model checking proceeds using an automaton for the bad prefixes (c.f. [14]). Here, we may get a one-sided error in which model checking succeeds even though the system has a bad computation (evidently, one with no bad prefix). In the second, model checking ignores the acceptance condition of an automaton for the specification and views it as a looping automaton (that is, all infinite runs that do not reach an empty state are accepting). Here, we may get a one-sided error in which model checking fails even though the system has no computation that violates the specification (evidently, it has a computation all whose prefixes can be extended to computations that violates the specification).

When the specification is safety, no errors occur. Also, the higher its safety level is, the less probable the two types of errors are. Combining this with the relative approach described above can tighten our expectation of error further.

References

1. Alpern, B., Schneider, F.B.: Defining liveness. IPL **21**, 181–185 (1985)
2. Alpern, B., Schneider, F.B.: Recognizing safety and liveness. Distrib. Comput. **2**, 117–126 (1987)
3. Biere, A., Cimatti, A., Clarke, E., Zhu, Y.: Symbolic model checking without BDDs. In: Cleaveland, W.R. (ed.) TACAS 1999. LNCS, vol. 1579, p. 193. Springer, Heidelberg (1999)
4. Bloem, R., Gabow, H.N., Somenzi, F.: An algorithm for strongly connected component analysis in n log n symbolic steps. In: Johnson, S.D., Hunt Jr., W.A. (eds.) FMCAD 2000. LNCS, vol. 1954, pp. 37–54. Springer, Heidelberg (2000)
5. Courcoubetis, C., Yannakakis, M.: The complexity of probabilistic verification. J. ACM **42**, 857–907 (1995)
6. Ben-David, S., Kupferman, O.: A framework for ranking vacuity results. In: Van Hung, D., Ogawa, M. (eds.) ATVA 2013. LNCS, vol. 8172, pp. 148–162. Springer, Heidelberg (2013)
7. Emerson, E.A.: Alternative semantics for temporal logics. TCS **26**, 121–130 (1983)
8. Filiot, E., Jin, N., Raskin, J.-F.: An antichain algorithm for LTL realizability. In: Bouajjani, A., Maler, O. (eds.) CAV 2009. LNCS, vol. 5643, pp. 263–277. Springer, Heidelberg (2009)
9. Harel, D., Katz, G., Marron, A., Weiss, G.: Non-intrusive repair of reactive programs. In: ICECCS, pp. 3–12 (2012)
10. Havelund, K., Roşu, G.: Synthesizing monitors for safety properties. In: Katoen, J.-P., Stevens, P. (eds.) TACAS 2002. LNCS, vol. 2280, pp. 342–356. Springer, Heidelberg (2002)
11. Jones, N.D.: Space-bounded reducibility among combinatorial problems. J. Comput. Syst. Sci. **11**, 68–75 (1975)
12. Kemeny, J.G., Snell, J.L., Knapp, A.W.: Denumerable Markov Chains. Springer, New York (1976)
13. Kupferman, O., Vardi, G.: On relative and probabilistic finite counterabilty. In: Proceediongs of the 24th CSL. Springer (2015)
14. Kupferman, O., Vardi, M.Y.: Model checking of safety properties. Formal Methods Syst. Des. **19**(3), 291–314 (2001)
15. Kupferman, O., Vardi, M.Y.: On bounded specifications. In: Nieuwenhuis, R., Voronkov, A. (eds.) LPAR 2001. LNCS (LNAI), vol. 2250, pp. 24–38. Springer, Heidelberg (2001)
16. Lamport, L.: Logical foundation. In: Paul, M., Siegert, H.J. (eds.) Distributed Systems - Methods and Tools for Specification. LNCS, 190th edn. Springer, Heidelberg (1985)
17. Landweber, L.H.: Decision problems for ω-automata. Math. Syst. Theory **3**, 376–384 (1969)
18. Manna, Z., Pnueli, A.: The Temporal Logic of Reactive and Concurrent Systems: Specification. Springer, New York (1992)
19. Manna, Z., Pnueli, A.: The Temporal Logic of Reactive and Concurrent Systems: Safety. Springer, New York (1995)

20. Meyer, A.R., Stockmeyer, L.J.: The equivalence problem for regular expressions with squaring requires exponential time. In: Proceedings of the 13th SWAT, pp. 125–129 (1972)
21. Piterman, N.: From nondeterministic Büchi and Streett automata to deterministic parity automata. In: Proceedings of the 21st LICS, pp. 255–264 (2006)
22. Pnueli, A.: The temporal logic of programs. In: Proceedings of the 18th FOCS, pp. 46–57 (1977)
23. Pnueli, A., Shahar, E.: Liveness and acceleration in parameterized verification. In: Emerson, E.A., Sistla, A.P. (eds.) CAV 2000. LNCS, vol. 1855, pp. 328–343. Springer, Heidelberg (2000)
24. Safra, S.: On the complexity of ω-automata. In: Proceedings of the 29th FOCS, pp. 319–327 (1988)
25. Sistla, A.P.: Safety, liveness and fairness in temporal logic. FAC **6**, 495–511 (1994)
26. Sistla, A.P., Clarke, E.M.: The complexity of propositional linear temporal logic. J. ACM **32**, 733–749 (1985)
27. Tarjan, R.E.: Depth first search and linear graph algorithms. SIAM J. Comput. **1**(2), 146–160 (1972)
28. Vardi, M.Y., Wolper, P.: Reasoning about infinite computations. I& C **115**(1), 1–37 (1994)

Marimba: A Tool for Verifying Properties of Hidden Markov Models

Noé Hernández[1]([✉]), Kerstin Eder[3,4], Evgeni Magid[3,4], Jesús Savage[2],
and David A. Rosenblueth[1]

[1] Instituto de Investigaciones en Matemáticas Aplicadas y en Sistemas,
Universidad Nacional Autónoma de México,
México, D.F., México
no_hernan@ciencias.unam.mx, drosenbl@unam.mx

[2] Facultad de Ingeniería, Universidad Nacional Autónoma de México,
México, D.F., México
savage@servidor.unam.mx

[3] Department of Computer Science, University of Bristol, Bristol BS8 1UB, UK

[4] Bristol Robotics Laboratory, Bristol BS16 1QY, UK
{Kerstin.Eder,Evgeni.Magid}@bristol.ac.uk

Abstract. The formal verification of properties of Hidden Markov Models (HMMs) is highly desirable for gaining confidence in the correctness of the model and the corresponding system. A significant step towards HMM verification was the development by Zhang et al. of a family of logics for verifying HMMs, called POCTL*, and its model checking algorithm. As far as we know, the verification tool we present here is the first one based on Zhang et al.'s approach. As an example of its effective application, we verify properties of a handover task in the context of human-robot interaction. Our tool was implemented in HASKELL, and the experimental evaluation was performed using the humanoid robot BERT2.

1 Introduction

A Hidden Markov Model (HMM) is an extension of a Discrete Time Markov Chain (DTMC) where the states of the model are hidden but the observations are visible. Typically, an HMM is studied with respect to the three basic problems examined by Rabiner in [1]. However, to the best of our knowledge, no actual model checker exists for HMMs despite their broad range of applications, e.g., speech recognition, DNA sequence analysis, text recognition and robot control. We describe in this paper a tool for verifying HMM properties written in the Probabilistic Observation Computational Tree Logic* (POCTL* [2]), and use this tool for verifying properties of a robot-to-human handover interaction.

POCTL* is a specification language for HMM properties. It is a probabilistic version of CTL* where a set of observations is attached to the *next* operator. Zhang et al. [2] sketched two model checking algorithms for POCTL*, an "automaton based" approach, and a "direct" approach. We opted for the direct

B. Finkbeiner et al. (Eds.): ATVA 2015, LNCS 9364, pp. 201–206, 2015.
DOI: 10.1007/978-3-319-24953-7_14

approach both for its lower time complexity and for its clarity, facilitating its correctness proof and its implementation [3]. This approach produces a DTMC $\mathcal{D}$ and a Linear Temporal Logic (LTL) formula ϕ. So the PRISM [4] model checker could be used to verify ϕ on $\mathcal{D}$. Such a model checker follows an approach whose complexity is doubly exponential in $|\phi|$ and polynomial in $|\mathcal{D}|$, whereas the direct approach verifies ϕ on $\mathcal{D}$ with the method by Courcoubetis et al. [5] whose complexity is singly exponential in $|\phi|$ and polynomial in $|\mathcal{D}|$, which is also the final complexity of our tool. This latter method repeatedly constructs a DTMC and rewrites an LTL formula, such that one temporal operator is removed each time while preserving the probability of satisfaction.

We have named our model checker Marimba. A marimba is a xylophone-like musical instrument that is popular in south-east Mexico and Central America. Marimba was implemented in HASKELL and compiled with GHCi. Our tool is available for download from https://github.com/nohernan/Marimba.

2   Tool Architecture and Implementation

HASKELL was chosen to code this first version of Marimba since it allows us to work in a high-level abstract layer, by providing useful mechanisms like lazy evaluation and a pure functional paradigm. Furthermore, HASKELL excels at managing recursion; this is a valuable aspect because recursive calls are made continuously throughout the execution.

Marimba features a command-line interface. Moreover, instead of working with a command window, a more user friendly and preferable execution is accomplished through the *Emacs* text editor extended with the `Haskell-mode`.

2.1   Marimba's Input and Modules

The first input is a `.hmm` file with the six elements of an HMM $\mathcal{H}$, namely a finite set of states S, a state transition probability matrix A, a finite set of observations Θ, an observation probability matrix B, a function L that maps states to sets of atomic propositions from a set $AP_{\mathcal{H}}$, and an initial probability distribution π over S. The second input is a POCTL* state formula Φ typed in the command window according to the syntactic rules:

$$\Phi ::= \text{true} \mid \text{false} \mid a \mid (\neg\Phi) \mid (\Phi \vee \Phi) \mid (\Phi \wedge \Phi) \mid (\mathcal{P}_{\bowtie p}(\phi)),$$
$$\phi ::= \Phi \mid (\neg\phi) \mid (\phi \vee \phi) \mid (\phi \wedge \phi) \mid (\mathbf{X}_\mathsf{o}\phi) \mid (\phi\mathcal{U}^{\leq n}\phi) \mid (\phi\mathcal{U}\phi),$$

where $a \in AP_{\mathcal{H}}$, $\mathsf{o} \in \Theta$, $n \in \mathbb{N}$, $p \in [0,1]$, and $\bowtie \in \{\leq, <, \geq, >\}$. In addition, we define $\mathbf{X}_\Omega\phi$ as a shorthand for $\bigvee_{\mathsf{o}\in\Omega} \mathbf{X}_\mathsf{o}\phi$ provided $\Omega \subseteq \Theta$. We examine below the six HASKELL modules that constitute Marimba.

ModelChecker.hs performs the initial computations of the model checker for POCTL*. It recursively finds a most nested state subformula of Φ, not being a propositional variable, and the states of $\mathcal{H}$ that satisfy it. Finding the states that satisfy a state subformula is straightforward when such a subformula is propositional. If, however, the state subformula is probabilistic, the module *DirectApproach.hs* obtains the states satisfying this subformula. Next, we extend the labels of such states with a new atomic proposition a. In Φ, the state subformula being addressed is replaced by a. The base case occurs when we reach a propositional variable, so we return the states that have it in their label.

DirectApproach.hs transforms the HMM $\mathcal{H}$ into a DTMC $\mathcal{D}$, and removes from the specification the observation set attached to the *next* operator $\mathbf{X}$ by generating a conjunction of the observation-free $\mathbf{X}$ with a new propositional variable. Thus, we obtain an LTL formula that is passed, together with $\mathcal{D}$, to the module *Courcoubetis.hs*. The new propositional variables are drawn from the power set of observations. Remarkably, it is not necessary to compute such a power set since the label of a state in $\mathcal{D}$ is easily calculated.

Courcoubetis.hs implements a modified version of the method by Courcoubetis et al. to find the probability that an LTL formula is satisfied in a DTMC. In this module, when dealing with the $\mathcal{U}$ and $\mathcal{U}^{\leq n}$ operators, we apply ideas from [6] for computing a partition of states of $\mathcal{D}$. Moreover, to handle the $\mathcal{U}$ operator we have to solve a linear equation system. To that end, we use the *linearEqSolver* library [7], which in turn executes the *Z3* theorem prover [8].

Lexer.hs and *Parser.hs* are in charge of the syntactic analysis of the input. Finally, *Main.hs* is loaded to start Marimba. This module manages the interaction with the user, and starts the computation by passing control to *ModelChecker.hs*.

In a typical execution, Marimba prompts the user to enter a .hmm file path. Next, our tool asks whether or not the user wants to take into account the initial distribution in the computation of the probability of satisfaction. This choice corresponds to opposite ideas presented in [2,5], i.e., the method by Courcoubetis et al. uses the initial distribution to define their probability measure, contrary to that defined by Zhang et al. Afterwards, a POCTL* formula has to be entered. Marimba returns the list of states satisfying this formula, and asks the user whether there are more formulas to be verified on the same model.

The .hmm file is simply a text file where the elements of an HMM are defined, e.g., the set of states is defined by the reserved word States, and if the model consists of five states, we write States=5. Likewise, POCTL* formulas have a natural writing, for example, $\mathcal{P}_{<0.1}(\mathbf{X}_{\{o_1\}}a)$ is typed as P[< 0.1](X_{1}a).

Our implementation of Marimba in HASKELL makes extensive use of ordinary arrays, which are known for a lack of efficiency in this programming language [9]. Thus, Marimba presents limitations in practice when considering large models. To better deal with this situation, a future work would consist in coding Marimba in a language like JAVA and make it a symbolic model checker. Nevertheless, with a high degree of confidence, we can say that this current implementation correctly performs the steps dictated by our version of Zhang et al.'s algorithm, mostly because HASKELL provides an abstract and formal coding framework.

3   Verification of a Human-Robot Interaction

We applied Marimba to a real-world example, namely the verification of the robot-to-human handover task [10] using the robot BERT2 [11] at the Bristol

Robotics Laboratory (BRL). The robot's decision to release the object during the handover task is determined by an HMM [10]. Figure 1 presents the state diagram of the HMM corresponding to the basic handover interaction, where the label $L(s)$ is defined for each state s.

We initialise A, B and π of the HMM for later training as follows. Since the first state of the handover process is Robot not hold, the initial distribution π favours this state above the others. The initialisation of matrix A must encourage the transitions shown in Fig. 1. To initialise B, we consider as observations the ordered pairs whose first and second components are the index and middle finger metacarpophalangeal joint motor current values, respectively. By the Cartesian product of these values, we obtain 56,404 observations. Since these observations are merged with the states to generate the DTMC passed to *Courcoubetis.hs*, and the size of a formula could

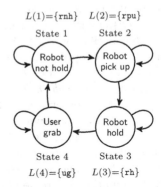

$L(1)=\{\text{rnh}\}$ $L(2)=\{\text{rpu}\}$

Fig. 1. The labelled states involved in the basic handover process.

grow considerably by associating the *next* operator with up to 56,404 observations, Marimba's execution is not practical under these circumstances. Vector quantisation [12] was used to reduce the number of observations to just 13. This method eliminates redundancy by grouping similar pairs in regions. So, we obtained 13 regions of the plane, which were regarded as the observations of the HMM and taken to initialise matrix B. Applying vector quantisation causes a loss in accuracy, as indicated by the computation of the root mean square error. However, we can effectively find observations that are likely to characterise each of the four states of this HMM (see first liveness property below, for example).

To make reliable estimates, we collected observations from 50 handover experiments on BERT2. These observations were used to train the initial HMM with the reestimation method found in the solution of Rabiner's Problem 3 [1].

Liveness Properties. A liveness property requires that a *good thing* happens during the execution of a system. For example, we would like to know whether *the model generates the sequence of observations* $\mathcal{O} = o_1, o_2, o_3, o_4$ *where* $o_1, o_2 \in \{3, 4, 6\}$ *and* $o_3, o_4 \in \{3, 4, 11\}$, *with probability greater than 0.88*, that is, $\mathcal{P}_{>0.88}(\mathbf{X}_{\{3,4,6\}}(\mathbf{X}_{\{3,4,6\}}(\mathbf{X}_{\{3,4,11\}}(\mathbf{X}_{\{3,4,11\}}\text{true}))))$. Interestingly, this property is a generalisation of Rabiner's Problem 1 [1]. Marimba's execution for this property is found in Fig. 2. The inputs are the trained HMM, defined in ModelBert2. hmm, and the previous formula. The output returned by Marimba is State 4. Hence, the model starting at state User grab is likely to generate $\mathcal{O}$.

A second liveness property states that *with probability at least 0.9, BERT2 releases the object when the user grabs it*. The POCTL* formula for this property is $\mathcal{P}_{\geq 0.9}(\text{rh} \wedge (\text{rh } \mathcal{U} (\text{ug} \wedge \text{ug } \mathcal{U} \text{rnh})))$. Marimba outputs State 3, i.e., the specification is satisfied when the starting state is Robot hold. So, we expect BERT2 to hold the object, and let it go when the user grabs it.

```
Main> main
Enter the file name where the HMM is located.
examples/ModelBert2.hmm
Would you like to consider each state as if it were the initial
state, i.e., as if it had initial distribution value equal to 1? y/n: y
Enter the POCTL* formula we are interested in.
P[>0.88]  (X_{3,4,6}(X_{3,4,6}(X_{3,4,11}(X_{3,4,11}T))))
The states that satisfy it are:
(Probability of satisfaction of each state:[4.998198505964186e-10,
          4.08659792160621e-6,7.508994137303159e-3,0.8915357419467848])
[4]
Do you want to continue checking more specifications? y/n: n
```

Fig. 2. Verifying a property with Marimba.

Safety Properties. A safety property establishes that a *bad thing* does not occur during the execution of a system. For instance, *with probability less than 0.05,* BERT2 *abandons its serving position with the user not grabbing the object,* that is, $\mathcal{P}_{<0.05}(\text{rh} \wedge \mathbf{X}_\Theta(\text{rnh} \vee \text{rpu}))$, where Θ is the set of observations. Our model checker returns $\{1, 2, 3, 4\}$ as the set of states satisfying this property. We conclude that it is unlikely that the model, being at state Robot hold, reaches a state other than User grab, that is, Robot not hold or Robot pick up.

The satisfaction of the previous three specifications provides us with confidence that BERT2 reliably performs the handover interaction specified above.

On an Intel® Core™ i3 1.70 GHz computer with 4 GB in memory, Marimba takes 28.55 s to compute the states satisfying the first liveness formula. The time required for checking the other two properties studied here is around 0.06 s.

Further examples are given in the *examples* folder and *user's manual* that come with Marimba's source code.

4   Conclusions

Since the automatic verification of properties of HMMs seems to be an unattended problem, we present here Marimba, a HASKELL implementation of the model checking algorithm for POCTL* [2]. This model checking algorithm was slightly modified to carry out its computations in a real program. Marimba's calculation is basically broken out in three stages that are coded in the modules *ModelChecker.hs*, *DirectApproach.hs* and *Courcoubetis.hs*, such that the involved components, steps and transformations are well arranged throughout the implementation. Finally, we have successfully applied Marimba to verify relevant properties of a handover interaction from the robot BERT2 to a human.

Acknowledgements. We gratefully acknowledge support from grants PAPIIT IN113013 and Conacyt 221341, and especially thank the BRL staff for their assistance operating the robot BERT2. E. Magid and K. Eder have been supported, in full and in part, respectively, by the UK EPSRC grant EP/K006320/1 ROBOSAFE: "Trustworthy Robotic Assistants".

References

1. Rabiner, L.R.: A tutorial on hidden Markov models and selected applications in speech recognition. Proc. IEEE **77**, 257–286 (1989)
2. Zhang, L., Hermanns, H., Jansen, D.N.: Logic and model checking for hidden Markov models. In: Wang, F. (ed.) FORTE 2005. LNCS, vol. 3731, pp. 98–112. Springer, Heidelberg (2005)
3. Hernández, N.: Model checking based on the hidden Markov model and its application to human-robot interaction. Master's thesis, Universidad Nacional Autónoma de México, México (2014). http://132.248.9.195/ptd2014/noviembre/303087692/Index.html
4. Kwiatkowska, M., Norman, G., Parker, D.: PRISM 4.0: Verification of probabilistic real-time systems. In: Gopalakrishnan, G., Qadeer, S. (eds.) CAV 2011. LNCS, vol. 6806, pp. 585–591. Springer, Heidelberg (2011)
5. Courcoubetis, C., Yannakakis, M.: The complexity of probabilistic verification. J. ACM **42**(4), 857–907 (1995)
6. Rutten, J.J.M.M., Kwiatkowska, M., Norman, G., Parker, D.: Mathematical techniques for analyzing concurrent and probabilistic systems. CRM monograph series. Am. Math. Soc. **23**, 101–116 (2004)
7. Erkok, L.: linearEqSolver: a library to solve systems of linear equations, using SMT solvers. https://github.com/LeventErkok/linearEqSolver
8. de Moura, L., Bjørner, N.S.: Z3: An efficient SMT solver. In: Ramakrishnan, C.R., Rehof, J. (eds.) TACAS 2008. LNCS, vol. 4963, pp. 337–340. Springer, Heidelberg (2008)
9. Chakravarty, M.M.T., Keller, G.: An approach to fast arrays in Haskell. In: Jeuring, J., Jones, S.L.P. (eds.) AFP 2002. LNCS, vol. 2638, pp. 27–58. Springer, Heidelberg (2003)
10. Grigore, E.C., Eder, K., Pipe, A.G., Melhuish, C., Leonards, U.: Joint action understanding improves robot-to-human object handover. In: IEEE/RSJ International Conference on Intelligent Robots and Systems, pp. 4622–4629. IEEE (2013)
11. Lenz, A., Skachek, S., Hamann, K., Steinwender, J., Pipe, A.G., Melhuish, C.: The BERT2 infrastructure: an integrated system for the study of human-robot interaction. In: 10th IEEE-RAS International Conference on Humanoid Robots, pp. 346–351. IEEE (2010)
12. Linde, Y., Buzo, A., Gray, R.M.: An algorithm for vector quantizer design. IEEE Trans. Commun. **28**, 84–95 (1980)

ParaVerifier: An Automatic Framework for Proving Parameterized Cache Coherence Protocols

Yongjian Li[1,3], Jun Pang[2]($\boxtimes$), Yi Lv[1], Dongrui Fan[4], Shen Cao[1], and Kaiqiang Duan[1]

[1] State Key Laboratory of Computer Science, Institute of Software, CAS, Beijing, China
[2] Computer Science and Communications, University of Luxembourg, Luxembourg, Luxembourg
jun.pang@uni.lu
[3] College of Information Engineering, Capital Normal University, Beijing, China
[4] State Key Laboratory of Computer Architecture, Institute of Computing Technology, CAS, Beijing, China

Abstract. Parameterized verification of cache coherence protocols is an important but challenging research problem. We present in this paper our automatic framework paraVerifier to handle this problem: (1) it first discovers auxiliary invariants and thecorresponding causal relations between invariants and protocol rules from a small reference instance of the verified protocol; (2) the discovered invariants and causal relations can then be generalized into their parameterized form to automatically construct a formal proof to establish the correctness of the protocol. paraVerifier has been successfully applied to a number of benchmarks.

1 Introduction

Verification of parameterized systems (e.g., see [1–11]) is interesting in the area of formal methods, mainly due to the practical importance of such systems. Parameterized systems exist in many application domains, including cache coherence protocols, security systems, and network communication protocols. In this work, we focus on cache coherence protocols, which play a key role in modern computer architecture. They require complex algorithms that deal with asynchrony, unpredictable message delays, and multiple communication paths between many nodes. Therefore, the highest possible assurance for the correctness of these systems should be guaranteed by formal reasoning techniques.

The challenge posed by parameterized verification of cache coherence protocols is that the desired safety properties, in terms of invariants, should hold for any instance of the studied protocol, not just for a single protocol instance. Model checking is automatic but is only able to verify an instance of the protocol. The correctness of the reference instance does not formally suffice to conclude the

© Springer International Publishing Switzerland 2015
B. Finkbeiner et al. (Eds.): ATVA 2015, LNCS 9364, pp. 207–213, 2015.
DOI: 10.1007/978-3-319-24953-7_15

correctness for all instances. Due to the extreme importance of cache coherence protocols, it is preferable to have a proof for any instance of such protocols.

Advanced verification techniques such as compositional [12] and abstraction model checking [6] have been proposed to handle this challenge. However, auxiliary invariants of a cache coherence protocol, which is usually provided by a human, based on his insights of the protocol, are needed to make these techniques work. How to find sufficient and necessary invariants is the main difficulty in the field of parameterized verification. Many works have focused on the construction of a set of auxiliary invariants, for example, see [4,6,8,10,11]. However, the theoretical foundation of these techniques and their soundness proofs are often only discussed in the respective papers. These theories themselves are not easy to understand, and are subjects to be mechanically checked, mainly due to the fact that their soundness needs to be guaranteed without any conditions.

The aim of our framework paraVerifier is to solve the parameterized verification of cache coherence protocols in a *unified*, *rigorous* and *automated* way. paraVerifier consists of two parts: an invariant finder invFinder and a proof generator proofGen. In order to verify that an invariant *inv* holds for any instance of a parameterized protocol, a reference model of the protocol with a fixed parameter is constructed first and successfully model checked, and invFinder tries to search for interesting auxiliary invariants and causal relations which are capable of proving *inv*. Next, proofGen explores the outputs of invFinder to construct a complete and parameterized formal proof in a theorem prover (e.g., Isabelle). Such a proof can eventually be checked automatically.

The originality of our work lies in the following aspects. First, paraVerifier is built on a simple but elegant theory. Three types of causal relations between protocol rules and invariants are identified, which are essentially the special cases of the general induction rule. The correctness of the three causal relations is captured by the so-called *consistency lemma*. It is heuristics-inspired by trying to construct the consistency relation that guides the tool invFinder to find auxiliary invariants. On the other hand, the consistency lemma provides a general guiding principle to prove invariants in the parameterized model of a cache coherence protocol. The lemma itself is verified as a formal theory in Isabelle [13].[1] Second, paraVerifier produces a list of invariants and a readable proof script for a given parameterized cache coherence protocol. The invariants are visible, in the sense that they can characterize the semantical features of the protocol and help users to precisely understand the design of the protocol. The formal proof script models the protocol rigorously and specifies its properties without any ambiguity, and more importantly it is mechanically checked. Third, paraVerifier is automatic, i.e., requiring little human intervention, and scalable. After the protocol is modeled in paraVerifier, auxiliary invariants are searched automatically via invFinder. The formal proof script in Isabelle is also automatically generated by proofGen, and

---

[1] We directly use parts of our Isabelles theories to introduce definitions and lemmas in the paper.

checked by Isabelle. paraVerifier is successfully applied to industrial case studies such as the Flash protocol [12,14].[2]

2 Consistency Lemma

In this section, we introduce the theoretical foundation underlining paraVerifier. Consider a set of state variables V, we use e, f and S to denote an expression, a formula, and a statement over the set of state variables V. Variables are divided into two classes: array variables or non-array (global) variables. A state s of a protocol is an instantaneous snapshot of its behavior given by a mapping from all variables in V to natural numbers. We write expEval e s (and formEval f s) to denote the evaluation of the expression e (and formula f) at the state s. With a parallel assignment $S = \{x_i := e_i | i > 0\}$, we define preCond S $f = f[x_i := e_i]$, which substitutes each occurrence of x_i by e_i.

Protocols. A cache coherence protocol is formalized as a pair $(ini, rules)$, where (1) ini is an initialization formula; and (2) $rules$ is a set of transition rules. Each rule $r \in rules$ is defined as $g \triangleright S$, where g is a predicate, and S is a parallel assignment to distinct variables v_i with expressions e_i. We write pre $r = g$, and act $r = S$ if $r = g \triangleright S$.

We identify three kinds of causal relations that are essentially the special cases of the general induction rule. Consider a transition rule r, a formula f, and a formula set F, the three causal relations are defined as follows:

Definition 1. We define the following relations

1. invHoldForRule$_1$ f $r \equiv$ pre $r \longrightarrow$ preCond f (act r);
2. invHoldForRule$_2$ f $r \equiv f =$ preCond f (act r);
3. invHoldForRule$_3$ f r $F \equiv \exists f' \in F$ s.t. $(f' \wedge (\text{pre } r)) \longrightarrow$ preCond f (act r);
4. invHoldForRule f r F represents a disjunction of invHoldForRule$_1$, invHoldForRule$_2$ and invHoldForRule$_3$.

The first relation (invHoldForRule$_1$ f r) means that after rule r is executed, f should hold. The second relation (invHoldForRule$_2$ f r) intuitively means that none of the state variables in f is changed and the execution of rule r does not affect the evaluation of f. The third relation (invHoldForRule$_3$ f r F) states that there exists another formula (invariant) $f' \in F$ such that the conjunction of the guard of r and f' implies that f holds after the election of rule r. Essentially, the causal relations capture whether and how the execution of a particular protocol rule changes the protocol state variables appearing in an invariant. More importantly, the relations can be considered as induction proof tactics designed for automatic proof generation (for example, used by proofGen).

---

[2] Flash is considered as a standard and difficult benchmark for any proposed method for parameterized verification, as Chou et al. [6] state "if the method works on Flash, then there is a good chance that it will also work on many real-world cache coherence protocols".

Intuitively, the disjunction of the above relations (invHoldForRule f r F) defines a causal relation, which can guarantee that if each formula f in F holds before the execution of the rule r, then f also holds after the execution of the rule. Secondly, it can be considered as a special inductive proof rule, which can be applied to prove that each formula in F holds for each protocol rule.

Definition 2. *A consistency relation, i.e.,* consistent *invs ini rules, that holds between a protocol (ini, rules) and a set of invariants invs = $\{inv_1, \ldots, inv_n\}$, is defined as:*

- *For any invariant inv $\in$ invs and state s, if ini is evaluated as true at state s (i.e.,* formEval *ini s = true), then inv is also evaluated as true at the state s.*
- *For any inv $\in$ invs and r $\in$ rules,* invHoldForRule *inv r invs.*

Now we proceed with formally stating the *consistency lemma* below. Namely, if the consistency relation consistent *invs ini rules* holds, then for any *inv $\in$ invs inv* holds for any reachable state s of a protocol (*ini, rules*).

Lemma 1. *For a protocol (ini, rules), we use* reachableSet *ini rules to denote the set of reachable states of the protocol. Given a set of invariants invs, we have*

[consistent *invs ini rules*; $s \in$ reachableSet *ini rules*] $\Longrightarrow \forall inv \in invs.$formEval *inv s*

We have built a general theory `cache.thy` in Isabelle to model cache coherence protocols [15], and the consistency lemma is also formally proved.

3   Overview of Our Approach

The steps of our framework paraVerifier to parameterized verification of cache coherence protocol is illustrated in Fig. 1. A small cache coherence protocol instance `protoocl.fl`, is fed into the tool invFinder, which will search for all necessary ground auxiliary invariants from the reference protocol instance. A table `protoocl.tbl` is used to store the set of ground invariants and causal relations, which will then be used by proofGen to create an Isabelle proof script which models and verifies the protocol in a parameterized form. In this step, ground invariants will be generalized into a parameterized form, and accordingly ground causal relations will be adopted to create parameterized proof commands which essentially prove the existence of the parameterized causal relations. At last, the Isabelle proof script `protoocl.thy` is given to Isabelle to check the protocol correctness automatically.

The consistency lemma plays a crucial role in paraVerifier. It behaves as a heuristics to construct a consistency relation that guides the tool invFinder to find auxiliary invariants. On the other hand, it gives a general guiding principle to prove invariants of a cache coherence protocol. The consistency lemma eliminates the need of directly using the induction proof method. It allows us to focus on the causal relationship between transition rules of the protocol and its invariants. It also enables us to divide the proof of the invariants to a series of subproofs to

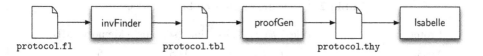

Fig. 1. The workflow of paraVerifier.

Table 1. An example fragment of `protocol.tbl` generated by invFinder.

protocol rule	ruleParas	invariant	causal relation	formula (f')
crit	[1]	inv1 1 2	invHoldForRule3	inv2 2
crit	[2]	inv1 1 2	invHoldForRule3	inv2 1
crit	[3]	inv1 1 2	invHoldForRule2	

verify whether one of the relations invHoldForRule$_{1---3}$ hold for a rule and an invariant. The strategy of 'divide and conquer' is the key step to make the series of sub-proofs to be automated because the proof patterns for the subproofs are similar and modular. The tool proofGen will then automatically generate a proof that applies the consistency lemma to prove correctness.

Starting from a given set of initial invariants, invFinder repeatedly tries to find new invariants, in the form of ground formulas, by constructing the causal relation between the invariants and the protocol rules. It uses an oracle[3] that checks whether a ground formula is an invariant in the small reference model of the protocol. invFinder stops until no new invariants can be found. The output of invFinder is stored in file `protocol.tbl`. Each line of the table records the index of an invariant, the name of a parameterized rule, the rule parameters to instantiate the rule, a causal relation between the invariant and a causal relation The table also records the proper formulas f' which is used to construct the third causal relation invHoldForRule$_3$. An example of such table is shown in Table 1.

The formal Isabelle proof script `protoocl.thy` generated by proofGen includes the definitions of control signals, rules, invariants, initializing formula, lemmas and their proofs. Here, we briefly explain the generalization principle involved in proofGen. For a ground invariant inv with parameters, proofGen analyzes the number of ground parameters in it and defines a parameterized invariant $pInv$ by replacing the ground parameters with their corresponding symbolic parameters accordingly. Then proofGen explores symmetry relations and uses the following three relations ex1P or ex2p or ex3P to define all the actually parameterized invariants, where ex1P N $P \equiv \exists i.(i \leq N \wedge P\ i)$, ex2P N $P \equiv \exists i\ j.(i \leq N \wedge j \leq N \wedge i \neq j \wedge P\ i\ j)$, and ex3P N $P \equiv \exists i\ j\ k.(i \leq N \wedge j \leq N \wedge k \leq N \wedge i \neq j \wedge i \neq k \wedge j \neq k \wedge P\ i\ j\ k)$. For instance, for the formula $\neg(n[1] = C \wedge n[2] = C)$, two ground parameters 1 and 2 are extracted, and a formal invariant formula $inv_1\ i1\ i2 = \neg(n[i1] = C \wedge n[i2] = C)$ is defined by replacing 1 and 2 with symbolic parameters $i1$ and $i2$, and $\{f.\text{ex2P } N\ \lambda i1 i2.f = inv_1\ i1\ i2\}$ defines the set of all the formulas, each of

---

[3] Implemented with SMV and the SMT solver Z3.

Table 2. Verification results on benchmarks.

Protocols	#rules	#invariants	time (seconds)	Memory (MB)
MESI	4	3	0.68	11.5
MOESI	5	3	0.65	23.2
Germanish [11]	6	3	0.68	23.0
German [6]	13	24	4.09	26.7
German with data [6]	15	50	12.05	29.4
Flash [12,14]	73	112	1457.42	169.4

which is symmetric to inv_1 1 2. The generalization of statements, rules, and causal relations can be defined accordingly. Each line in the ground causal relation table (Table 1), is generalized into a parameterized relation, which is the key to generate a proof command to select a proper causal relation to prove.

4   Validation and Conclusion

We implemented paraVerifier in Forte [16] and tested it on a number of cache coherence protocols. The detailed source codes and data can be found in [15]. Each experimental data includes the protocol model, the invariant sets, and the Isabelle proof script. Table 2 summarizes our verification results, recording the resources needed to compute the invariants and generate the proof scripts. Note that our proof of Flash is different from the one of Park et al. [14], where they need to manually construct an abstract transaction model of Flash. Our proof does not require this step and has less human interaction.

Within paraVerifier, our automatic framework for parameterized verification of cache coherence protocol, (1) instead of directly proving the invariants of a protocol by induction, we propose a general proof method based on the consistency lemma to decompose the proof goal into a number of small ones; (2) instead of proving the decomposed subgoals by hand, we automatically generate proofs for them based on the information computed in a small protocol instance.[4]

As we demonstrate in this work, combining theorem proving with automatic proof generation is promising in the field of formal verification of industrial protocols. Theorem proving can guarantee the rigorousness of the verification results, while automatic proof generation can release the burden of human interaction.

Acknowledgment. This work is partially supported by the National Natural Science Foundation of China under Grants No.61170073, No.61170304, No.2011DFG13000, No.61272135, No.61173007, and No.61332009.

---

[4] Technical details of paraVerifier will be made available in a technical report.

References

1. Pnueli, A., Shahar, E.: A platform for combining deductive with algorithmic verification. In: Alur, R., Henzinger, T.A. (eds.) CAV 1996. LNCS, vol. 1102, pp. 0302–9743. Springer, Heidelberg (1996)
2. Björner, N., Browne, A., Manna, Z.: Automatic generation of invariants and intermediate assertions. Theoret. Comput. Sci. **173**(1), 49–87 (1997)
3. Arons, T., Pnueli, A., Ruah, S., Xu, J., Zuck, L.D.: Parameterized verification with automatically computed inductive assertions. In: Berry, G., Comon, H., Finkel, A. (eds.) CAV 2001. LNCS, vol. 2102, pp. 221–234. Springer, Heidelberg (2001)
4. Pnueli, A., Ruah, S., Zuck, L.D.: Automatic deductive verification with invisible invariants. In: Margaria, T., Yi, W. (eds.) TACAS 2001. LNCS, vol. 2031, pp. 82–97. Springer, Heidelberg (2001)
5. Tiwari, A., Rueß, H., Saïdi, H., Shankar, N.: A technique for invariant generation. In: Margaria, T., Yi, W. (eds.) TACAS 2001. LNCS, vol. 2031, pp. 113–127. Springer, Heidelberg (2001)
6. Chou, C.-T., Mannava, P.K., Park, S.: A simple method for parameterized verification of cache coherence protocols. In: Hu, A.J., Martin, A.K. (eds.) FMCAD 2004. LNCS, vol. 3312, pp. 382–398. Springer, Heidelberg (2004)
7. Pang, J., Fokkink, W., Hofman, R., Veldema, R.: Model checking a cache coherence protocol of a java DSM implementation. J. Logic Algebraic Program. **71**(1), 1–43 (2007)
8. Pandav, S., Slind, K., Gopalakrishnan, G.C.: Counterexample guided invariant discovery for parameterized cache coherence verification. In: Borrione, D., Paul, W. (eds.) CHARME 2005. LNCS, vol. 3725, pp. 317–331. Springer, Heidelberg (2005)
9. Lv, Y., Lin, H., Pan, H.: Computing invariants for parameter abstraction. In: Proceedings of the 5th IEEE/ACM Conference on Formal Methods and Models for Codesign (MEMOCODE), pp. 29–38, IEEE CS (2007)
10. Bingham B.: Automatic non-interference lemmas for parameterized model checking. In: Proceedings of the 8th Conference on Formal Methods in Computer-Aided Design (FMCAD), pp.1–8. IEEE CS (2008)
11. Conchon, S., Goel, A., Krstić, S., Mebsout, A., Zaïdi, F.: Cubicle: a parallel smt-based model checker for parameterized systems. In: Madhusudan, P., Seshia, S.A. (eds.) CAV 2012. LNCS, vol. 7358, pp. 718–724. Springer, Heidelberg (2012)
12. McMillan, K.L.: Parameterized verification of the FLASH cache coherence protocol by compositional model checking. In: Margaria, T., Melham, T.F. (eds.) CHARME 2001. LNCS, vol. 2144, pp. 179–195. Springer, Heidelberg (2001)
13. Nipkow, T., Paulson, L.C., Wenzel, M.: Isabelle/HOL - A Proof Assistant for Higher-Order Logic. LNCS, vol. 2283. Springer, Heidelberg (2002)
14. Park, S., Dill, D.L.: Verification of flash cache coherence protocol by aggregation of distributed transactions. In: Proceedings of the 8th Annual ACM Symposium on Parallel Algorithms and Architectures (SPAA), pp. 288–296. ACM (1996)
15. Li, Y.: invFinder: An invariant finder (2014). http://lcs.ios.ac.cn/lyj238/invFinder.html
16. Technical Publications and Training, Intel Corporation: Forte/FL User Guide (2003)

ASSA-PBN: An Approximate Steady-State Analyser of Probabilistic Boolean Networks

Andrzej Mizera$^{(\boxtimes)}$, Jun Pang, and Qixia Yuan

Computer Science and Communications, University of Luxembourg,
Luxembourg, Luxembourg
andrzej.mizera@uni.lu

Abstract. We present ASSA-PBN, a tool for approximate steady-state analysis of large probabilistic Boolean networks (PBNs). ASSA-PBN contains a constructor, a simulator, and an analyser which can approximately compute the steady-state probabilities of PBNs. For large PBNs, such approximate analysis is the only viable way to study their long-run behaviours. Experiments show that ASSA-PBN can handle large PBNs with a few thousands of nodes.

1 Introduction

Probabilistic Boolean networks (PBNs) [1,2], introduced by Shmulevich et al. in 2002 as an extension of Boolean networks, is a modelling framework widely used to model gene regulatory networks (GRNs). Inheriting appealing features of Boolean networks of being simple but effective, PBN additionally is capable to cope with uncertainties both on the data and model selection levels. The dynamics of a PBN with N nodes is governed by a discrete-time Markov chain (DTMC) with exponential in N number of states, i.e., 2^N states. Although qualitative in nature, PBNs provide means for quantifying the influences of genes on other genes and for characterising the long-run behaviour of the system, both based on the steady-state distribution of the associated DTMC. Therefore, the efficient computation of steady-state probabilities is of utter importance. It is well studied how to compute the steady-state distribution of small PBNs with numerical methods [2]. However, due to their computational cost, these methods are not scalable. In the literature, a few statistical methods such as Monte Carlo methods [3], are proposed to deal with large PBNs. A recent study analysed a 96-node PBN of apoptosis using the optPBN tool [4]. However, the existing methods/tools for PBNs are prohibited by the network size. For instance, optPBN can only analyse parts of the 96-node PBN due to its efficiency limits, leaving some properties of the network unconfirmed [4]. Therefore, there is demand for a tool which can handle large PBNs efficiently.

In this work we present ASSA-PBN, a tool which provides the means for efficient analysis of large PBNs. Firstly, it applies the state-of-the-art techniques to the computation of the steady-state probabilities of large PBNs. The current version supports three different statistical methods, i.e., the perfect simulation algorithm [5], the two-state Markov chain approach [6,7], and the Skart method [8].

© Springer International Publishing Switzerland 2015
B. Finkbeiner et al. (Eds.): ATVA 2015, LNCS 9364, pp. 214–220, 2015.
DOI: 10.1007/978-3-319-24953-7_16

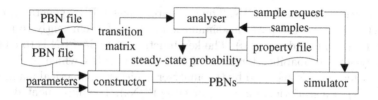

Fig. 1. Structure of ASSA-PBN.

To the best of our knowledge, ASSA-PBN is the first tool to introduce the perfect simulation algorithm and the Skart method to the context of PBNs. Secondly, it contains a fast simulator, which is designed using the alias technique [9]. This makes it capable of handling the steady-state computations that require generation of trajectories consisting of billions of states. Experimental results show that ASSA-PBN can analyse PBNs with thousands of nodes.

2   Architecture and Usage

A PBN models a system such as a GRN with binary-valued nodes. For each node there is a certain number of Boolean functions, known as *predictor functions*, which determine the value of the node at the next time step. The selection of the predictor function is governed by a probability distribution: a probability parameter is associated with each predictor function of the node. Two variants of PBNs are considered: *instantaneous PBNs* and *context-sensitive PBNs*. In the former variant, the selection of a predictor function is performed for each node at each time step. In the latter variant, the PBN evolves in accordance with selected predictor functions and new selection is performed only if indicated by an additional random variable which is updated at each step. Moreover, the so-called PBNs with perturbations, allow the system to transit to the next state due to random perturbations that are governed by a perturbation rate parameter. On top of that *dependent* and *independent PBNs* are considered as well as *synchronous* and *asynchronous* update schemes. The dynamics of a PBN can be viewed as a DTMC. In the case of PBNs with perturbations, the underlying DTMC is *ergodic*, thus having a unique *stationary distribution*, the so-called *steady-state* (or *limiting*) *distribution*, which governs the long-run behaviour of the system. Due to the space limitation, we refer to [10] and [2, page 4] for a formal definition and detailed description of PBNs.

For systems like GRNs, we are often interested in answering the following biological question: what is the probability that a gene or a number of genes will be expressed in the long run? This question can be addressed in the framework of PBNs by determining the steady-state probability for a PBN to be in a certain state or, equivalently, the steady-state probability of a state in the underlying ergodic DTMC. ASSA-PBN is designed to compute the steady-state probabilities for PBNs, especially for large PBNs.

ASSA-PBN contains three major parts (see Fig. 1): a PBN constructor, a PBN simulator, and a PBN analyser. Based on the specified parameters or model file, the constructor can build a PBN. The simulator takes a PBN generated by the constructor as input and performs simulation of the PBN efficiently to produce trajectories (also called samples). The key function of ASSA-PBN is to compute the steady-state probability for a set of states of the PBN which is defined in a property file. This is achieved by the analyser in either a numerical manner (for small PBNs) or a statistical manner (for large PBNs). The implemented numerical methods require the transition matrix of a PBN as input, which is supplied by the constructor; while the implemented statistical methods require simulated trajectories of the PBN as input, which are supplied by the simulator. Simulation is not based on the transition matrix, as a consequence it does not suffer from the state-space explosion problem even for large PBNs. The ASSA-PBN program package can be found at http://satoss.uni.lu/software/ASSA-PBN/.

PBN Constructor. The PBN constructor can either load a PBN from a specification file or generate a random PBN complying with a given parametrisation.

To load a PBN into ASSA-PBN, the user needs to provide a description of the PBN in a specification file. The description consists of four elements: the number of nodes (also known as genes), the definitions of predictor functions of each node, the selection probabilities for the predictor functions of each node, finally the perturbation rate parameter value. The details on the format can be found in the user guide of the program package. ASSA-PBN constructs the PBN based on its loaded specification and stores it in memory in a structure which contains the information from the specification. The stored information is sufficient for performing simulations of the PBN.

For the convenience of experiment and testing, the constructor provides a function for generating a random PBN complying with specified parameters, i.e., the number of nodes in the PBN, the perturbation rate, the maximal number of predictor functions for nodes in the network, and the maximal number of variables of the predictor functions. Given these parameters, the constructor will randomly generate for each node of the PBN the specified number of predictor functions and their selection probabilities. The generated PBN can be saved in a specification file or exported to the optPBN [4] format.

In certain biological experiments, the environmental conditions of cells are kept constant, e.g., sustained activation of cell receptors. Therefore, in ASSA-PBN it is possible to disable the perturbations of certain nodes. This is provided by a filter storing the indices of these nodes that should not undergo perturbations. Note that this does not change the ergodicity of the PBN: since the values of those nodes are kept constant, the state-space of the underlying Markov chain is simply reduced, but it remains ergodic.

Simulator. Statistical approaches are the only viable option for the analysis of PBNs characterised by large state space, e.g., PBNs that arise in the context of realistic biological study of GRNs. However, applications of such methods necessitate generation of trajectories of significant length. Therefore, the efficiency requirement is crucial for enabling analysis of large networks in a reasonable computational time. To achieve this goal, sampling of the consecutive state of the trajectory is performed with the use of an instance of the *alias method*, a class of efficient algorithms for sampling from a discrete probability distribution originally introduced by Walker in [9].

The ASSA-PBN simulator can operate in two modes: (1) the *global alias mode* and (2) the *local alias mode*. In the global mode, a joint probability distribution is considered on all possible combinations of predictor function selections for all the nodes and a single alias table for this distribution is constructed. In the local mode, the independence of the PBN is exploited: individual alias tables are constructed for each node of the PBN. In both cases the consecutive state is generated by updating the value of each node with the predictor function selected for this node. However, in the global mode predictor functions for all nodes are selected simultaneously with the use of only two random numbers, while in the local mode the number of random numbers used is twice the number of nodes. In consequence, the generation of the next state is faster in the global mode, but more expensive in terms of memory usage.

When simulating the next state, the simulator first decides whether perturbations are applied. If yes, the simulator updates the current state accordingly. If no, the simulator chooses the predictor functions for each node and update the current state according to the chosen predictor functions. Notice that the state transition matrix is not needed in the simulation process, which makes ASSA-PBN capable of managing large PBNs.

The simulator is called by the analyser to perform simulation when statistical methods are selected for the analysis of a PBN. We explain the interaction between the simulator and the analyser in the next section.

Analyser. The analyser provides three different classes of methods for the computation of exact/approximate steady-state probabilities. The first class consists of two iterative methods for exact computation of the steady-state distributions: the Jacobi method and the Gauss-Seidel method. However, both of them require the state transition matrix to be constructed by the constructor, which is expensive in terms of memory and time. Therefore, these methods are only suitable for analysing small-size PBNs (the focus of ASSA-PBN is on large PBNs). The two methods are available in probabilistic model checkers, e.g., PRISM [11]. We reimplement them for the comprehensiveness of the tool and the convenience of the user as there is no direct way to handle PBNs in PRISM.

The second class consists of the *perfect simulation algorithm* for sampling the steady-state of DTMCs. It is based on the ingenious idea of the *backward coupling scheme* originally proposed by Propp and Wilson in [12]. The *perfect simulation algorithm* allows to draw independent samples which are distributed exactly in accordance with the steady-state distribution of a DTMC. Thus, it avoids problems related to the speed of convergence to the steady-state distribution or non-zero correlation between consecutive samples. Given a confidence level, the number of required samples used for the approximation of the steady-state probability can be iteratively computed. Due to the uncorrelated, exact samples the use of this sampling method for statistical approximation of steady-state probabilities results in a smaller sample size than the statistical methods from the third class discussed below. The current implementation is in-line with the 'Functional backward-coupling simulation with aliasing' algorithm provided in [5], which highly improves the efficiency. The functional coupling shortens significantly the average coupling time in cases where the aim is to approximate the steady-state probability for a subset of states. In general, larger subsets of interest result in smaller coupling time. Due to the nature of this method, each state of the state space needs to be considered at each step of the coupling scheme. Therefore, this approach is suitable only for medium-size PBNs and is implemented for the comprehensiveness of the tool. Unfortunately, since PBNs with perturbations are non-monotone systems, the very efficient monotone version of perfect simulation [13] in which only a small subset of the state space needs to be considered is of no use in this context.

The third class of available methods consists of two *incremental sampling* methods for approximate computation of the steady-state probabilities, i.e., (1) the Skart method [8] and (2) the two-state Markov chain approach [6]. Both statistical methods operate in accordance with the following scheme. The analyser calls the simulator to generate a trajectory of initial length. The algorithms check whether the trajectory is long enough to compute estimates of average internal statistics, which satisfy a predefined confidence level and precision requirements. If the confidence level and precision are not reached, the simulator will be called again to generate more samples. This process is repeated until the confidence level and precision requirements are met. For a comprehensive description of these methods we refer to [6–8]. They are best suited for large networks which cannot be analysed with the approaches from the previous two classes. Our experiments show that both the Skart method and the two-state Markov chain approach in the current implementations can be used for the approximation of steady-state probabilities for networks consisting of thousands of nodes (see Sect. 3).

3 Comparison, Evaluation and Future Developments

Comparison. Both ASSA-PBN and optPBN are designed for steady-state analysis of PBNs. ASSA-PBN supports three statistical methods for computing the steady-state probabilities of a PBN, while optPBN only prototypically implemented the two-state Markov chain approach in Matlab. We compared our tool with optPBN for the analysis of the 96-node PBN model of apoptosis in [4] using the two-state Markov chain approach. As mentioned in [4], their analysis of the influence of RIP_deubi on complex2 was not handled completely due to the long computational time required by optPBN. With the use of ASSA-PBN, we performed the complete analysis of the influence and presented it in [7]. ASSA-PBN outperforms optPBN in terms of simulation speed. For example, the time cost for simulating 100,000 steps of the 96-node PBN model in optPBN is around 120s, which is almost 100 times more than that in ASSA-PBN.

Our tool is highly related to tools for statistical model checking [14,15]. Existing statistical model checkers are either restricted for bounded properties or cannot directly deal with PBNs. The Skart method and the perfect simulation

Table 1. Approximate steady-state analysis of two large PBNs (confidence level 95 %).

node number	method	the two-state Markov chain			Skart		
	precision	0.01	0.005	0.001	0.01	0.005	0.001
1,000	trajectory size	35,066	133,803	3,402,637	37,999	139,672	3,272,940
	time cost (s)	6.19	23.53	616.26	7.02	24.39	590.26
2,000	trajectory size	64,057	240,662	5,978,309	63,674	273,942	5,936,060
	time cost (s)	20.42	67.60	1722.86	20.65	78.53	1761.05

algorithm have been recently used for statistical model checking of steady state and unbounded until properties [13,16]. To the best of our knowledge, ASSA-PBN is the first tool to introduce those two methods into the context of PBNs.

Evaluation. We have evaluated ASSA-PBN exhaustively on a large number of randomly generated PBNs of different sizes ranging from a few nodes to a few thousands nodes and with different characteristics (network structures being either sparse or dense). We show in Table 1 the trajectory sizes and the time costs for computing steady-state probabilities of two large PBNs using the two-state Markov chain approach and the Skart method for different precision requirements. We have compared the performance of these two methods in computing steady-state probabilities of PBNs on 882 randomly generated PBNs with nodes numbers ranging from 15 to 2,000. We collected 5,263 pairs of results. Based on this complete set of results, i.e., with nodes numbers ranging from 15 to 2,000, the two-state Markov chain approach was faster than the Skart method in most of the compared cases (see [7, Sect. 4] for more details).

Future Developments. One technique to improve the performance of ASSA-PBN is parallel computation. This can be applied to the Jacobi method, the perfect simulation algorithm and the simulation of a PBN. In the future, we plan to implement in ASSA-PBN other algorithms (e.g., see [17]) for approximating steady-state probabilities.

Acknowledgement. Qixia Yuan is supported by the National Research Fund, Luxembourg (grant 7814267).

References

1. Shmulevich, I., Dougherty, E., Zhang, W.: From boolean to probabilistic boolean networks as models of genetic regulatory networks. Proc. IEEE **90**(11), 1778–1792 (2002)
2. Trairatphisan, P., Mizera, A., Pang, J., Tantar, A.A., Schneider, J., Sauter, T.: Recent development and biomedical applications of probabilistic boolean networks. Cell Commun. Signal. **11**, 46 (2013)
3. Shmulevich, I., Gluhovsky, I., Hashimoto, R., Dougherty, E., Zhang, W.: Steady-state analysis of genetic regulatory networks modelled by probabilistic boolean networks. Comp. Funct. Genomics **4**(6), 601–608 (2003)

4. Trairatphisan, P., Mizera, A., Pang, J., Tantar, A.A., Sauter, T.: optPBN: An optimisation toolbox for probabilistic boolean networks. PLOS ONE **9**(7), e98001 (2014)
5. Vincent, J.M., Marchand, C.: On the exact simulation of functionals of stationary Markov chains. Linear Algebra Appl. **385**, 285–310 (2004)
6. Raftery, A., Lewis, S.: How many iterations in the Gibbs sampler? Bayesian Stat. **4**, 763–773 (1992)
7. Mizera, A., Pang, J., Yuan, Q.: Reviving the two-state markov chain approach (technical report) (2015). Accessed on http://arxiv.org/abs/1501.01779
8. Tafazzoli, A., Wilson, J., Lada, E., Steiger, N.: Skart: A skewness-and autoregression-adjusted batch-means procedure for simulation analysis. In: Proceedings of the 2008 Winter Simulation Conference, pp. 387–395 (2008)
9. Walker, A.: An efficient method for generating discrete random variables with general distributions. ACM Trans. Math. Softw. **3**(3), 253–256 (1977)
10. Shmulevich, I., Dougherty, E.R.: Probabilistic Boolean Networks: The Modeling and Control of Gene Regulatory Networks. SIAM Press, Philadelphia (2010)
11. Kwiatkowska, M., Norman, G., Parker, D.: PRISM 4.0: verification of probabilistic real-time systems. In: Gopalakrishnan, G., Qadeer, S. (eds.) CAV 2011. LNCS, vol. 6806, pp. 585–591. Springer, Heidelberg (2011)
12. Propp, J.G., Wilson, D.: Exact sampling with coupled markov chains and applications to statistical mechanics. Random Struct. Algorithms **9**(1), 223–252 (1996)
13. El Rabih, D., Pekergin, N.: Statistical model checking using perfect simulation. In: Liu, Z., Ravn, A.P. (eds.) ATVA 2009. LNCS, vol. 5799, pp. 120–134. Springer, Heidelberg (2009)
14. Younes, H.L.S., Simmons, R.G.: Probabilistic verification of discrete event systems using acceptance sampling. In: Brinksma, E., Larsen, K.G. (eds.) CAV 2002. LNCS, vol. 2404, pp. 223–235. Springer, Heidelberg (2002)
15. Sen, K., Viswanathan, M., Agha, G.: On statistical model checking of stochastic systems. In: Etessami, K., Rajamani, S.K. (eds.) CAV 2005. LNCS, vol. 3576, pp. 266–280. Springer, Heidelberg (2005)
16. Rohr, C.: Simulative model checking of steady state and time-unbounded temporal operators. Trans. Petri Nets Models Concurrency **8**, 142–158 (2013)
17. Gelman, A., Rubin, D.: Inference from iterative simulation using multiple sequences. Stat. Sci. **7**(4), 457–472 (1992)

EviCheck: Digital Evidence for Android

Mohamed Nassim Seghir$^{(\boxtimes)}$ and David Aspinall

University of Edinburgh, Edinburgh, Scotland, UK
mseghir@inf.ed.ac.uk, david.aspinall@ed.ac.uk

Abstract. We present EviCheck, a tool for the verification, certification and generation of lightweight fine-grained security policies for Android. It applies static analysis to check the conformance between an application and a given policy. A distinguishing feature of EviCheck is its ability to generate *digital evidence*: a certificate for the analysis algorithm asserting the conformance between the application and the policy. This certificate can be independently checked by another component (tool) to validate or refute the result of the analysis. The checking process is generally very efficient compared to certificate generation as experiments on 20,000 real-world applications show.

1 Introduction and Related Work

Android security has been recently an active area of investigation and many tools for this purpose have emerged. Some of them rely on dynamic analysis like Aurasium [15], TaintDroid [8] and AppGuard [4]. Other ones are based on static analysis, like FlowDroid [2], ComDroid [6] and Apposcopy [9]. The last family of tools performs an exhaustive exploration of the application behaviour thanks to abstraction (over-approximation), which also leads to some imprecision. We are interested in this category (static analysis) as our aim is to certify the absence of bad behaviour. EviCheck complements these tools as it not only analyses applications but, returns a verifiable certificate attesting the validity of its result. The idea of associating proofs with code was initially proposed by Necula as *Proof-Carrying Code* (PCC) [11]. It has since been generalised to many forms of "certificate", not necessarily representations of proof in a logic. For example, abstract interpretations [1], validating intermediate steps in a compiler [10], etc. It was further used to provide bound guarantees on resource consumption [3,5]. We call the generalised notion "digital evidence". The certificate returned by EviCheck broadens the PCC idea by encompassing lightweight forms of evidence specific to particular properties, e.g., program annotations tracking permissions or resource usage. Digital evidence can be independently checked to validate or refute the result of the analysis. A key point in PCC and related approaches is that the checking process is efficient compared to the generation one, in certain cases it could be 1000 times faster according to our experiments. Thus it may

---

This work was supported by EPSRC under grant number EP/K032666/1 "App Guarden Project".

© Springer International Publishing Switzerland 2015
B. Finkbeiner et al. (Eds.): ATVA 2015, LNCS 9364, pp. 221–227, 2015.
DOI: 10.1007/978-3-319-24953-7_17

ultimately be carried out on the device itself at the point of installation, with the generation process carried out once by the app supplier or app store. To release the user from the burden of writing anti-malware policies, EviCheck offers the option of inferring them automatically using constraint solving.

2 EviCheck's Main Ingredients

EviCheck has several components: policy language, verifier, checker and policy generator. The verification and certification processes are illustrated in Fig. 1.

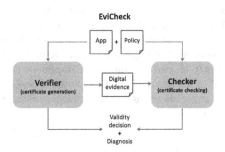

Fig. 1. The architecture of EviCheck and its main components

To illustrate the functionality of the various components of EviCheck, consider the code snippets and the associated graphical interface in Fig. 2, which represent the audio recording app Recorder. The access to the recording device is carried out via object recorder (line 2).

```
1   public class Recorder extends Activity {
2       private MediaRecorder recorder = null;
3       ....
4       public void onCreate (....) {
5           ((Button) findViewById(Start))
6               .setOnClickListener(startClick);
7           ....
8           // startRecording ();
9       }
10
11      private void startRecording() {
12          recorder = new MediaRecorder();
13          recorder.setAudioSource
14          (MediaRecorder.AudioSource.MIC);
15          recorder.setOutputFile(/* file name */);
16          ....
17          recorder.start ();
18      }
19
20      private View.OnClickListener startClick
21          = new View.OnClickListener() {
22      public void onClick(View v) {
23          ....
24          startRecording ();
25      }};
26          ....
27  }
```

Fig. 2. Code snippets and graphical interface of the Recorder app

At the creation phase (onCreate), a callback for a click event is associated with the button Start (line 5). Within the callback onClick, the method startRecording is invoked (line 24) which in turns calls recorder.setAudioSource and recorder.start to set the (on-device) microphone as a source and trigger the recording process. This app requires the permission RECORD_AUDIO which is associated with the API method setAudioSource.

2.1 Policy Language

The policy represents the specification that a user wants to check or a claim that a developer is stating about his app. In EviCheck, a policy consists of a set of rules obeying the grammar:

$$rule := H \ (: | \overset{or}{:}) \ T$$
$$H := method \ | \ (CV|\neg CV)^+$$
$$CV := \text{ENTRY\_POINT} \ | \ \text{ACTIVITY} \ | \ \text{SERVICE} \ | \ \text{RECEIVER}$$
$$| \ \text{ONCLICK\_HANDLER} \ | \ \text{ONTOUCH\_HANDLER} \ | \ LC$$
$$LC := \text{ONCREATE} \ | \ \text{ONSTART} \ | \ \text{ONRESUME} \ | \ ...$$
$$T := (id|\neg id)^*$$

The head H of the rule represents a context in which the tail T should (not) be used. In the grammar, CV represents a context variable specifying the scope for methods to which the rule applies. For example, ENTRY_POINT: all entry points of the app, ACTIVITY: activity methods, ONCLICK_HANDLER: click event handlers, in addition to activity life-cycle callbacks such as ONCREATE, etc. The tail of the rule is a list of (negated) identifiers id's or tags. We use permissions as tags, however tags can be supplied by the user as well. Referring to our running example, we can prohibit recording without user consent via the rule:

$$\text{ENTRY\_POINT}, \neg\text{CLICK\_HANDLER} \ : \ \neg\text{RECORD\_AUDIO} \tag{1}$$

It simply says: *"in all entry points, apart from click event handlers, the permission* RECORD_AUDIO *must not be used"*. It is also possible to rule out another scenario of malicious behaviour, where a service reads the recorded file and sends it to a remote server, via the following rule:

$$\text{SERVICE} \ \overset{or}{:} \ \neg\text{INTERNET}$$
$$\neg\text{READ\_EXTERNAL\_STORAGE}$$

The superscript *or* indicates that this is an or-rule. Its semantics is that either permission INTERNET or READ_EXTERNAL_STORAGE can be used in a service component but not both. By default rules have an and-semantics. Due to space limitations, we do not provide a formal definition of the language semantics.

2.2 The Verifier

As Fig. 1 shows, the verifier (certificate generator) takes an app and a policy as input and answers whether the policy is satisfied by the app and eventually outputs a certificate (digital evidence). If the policy is violated a diagnosis pointing to the violated rules is returned. The verification algorithm consists of a reachability analysis which computes the transitive closure of the call graph with respect to permission usage. Referring to our running example, we start with the map below on the left side as we initially only know that the API method recorder.setAudioSource requires the RECORD_AUDIO permission as implemented by the Android framework. The analysis, which consists of a backward propagation, returns the map on the right side. In this case rule (1) is valid as the only entry points (underlined) we have are onClick and onCreate. If we uncomment line 8 in Fig. 2, RECORD_AUDIO will be reachable from onCreate, hence violating the rule. The final map represents the certificate for the analysis.

setAudioSource : RECORD_AUDIO

setAudioSource : RECORD_AUDIO
<u>onClick</u> : RECORD_AUDIO
<u>onCreate</u> :
startRecording : RECORD_AUDIO

2.3   The Checker

The checker takes as input a certificate (computed map), a policy and an app, and checks whether the certificate is valid (see Fig. 1). It also checks whether the certificate entails the policy. If the certificate is invalid, a message referring to its first inconsistent entry is returned. Certificate checking is lighter than certificate generation as we do not need to compute a fix point (backward propagation). It suffices to go through each method and locally check if the associated set of tags includes all the tags associated with the functions it calls. This procedure has a linear complexity in the number of map entries (functions). It also has a constant space complexity as we are just performing checks without generating any information which needs to be stored.

2.4   Policy Generator

EviCheck is able to automatically infer anti-malware policies using constraint solving. To this end, we need a training set of malware and benign applications where each application is described by a set of properties (p's). For example p_i could be SERVICE :SEND_SMS, meaning that the permission SEND_SMS is used within a service component. A policy P excludes an application A if P contains a rule $\neg p_i$ and p_i belongs to the description of A. We want to find the properties $p_1, \ldots, p_k$ such that the policy composed of $\neg p_1, \ldots, \neg p_k$ allows a maximum of benign applications and excludes a maximum of malware. We use a pseudo-Boolean solver, such as **Sat4j**[1], to solve this kind of optimisation problems where variable values are either 0 or 1 (true or false).

2.5   Technical Discussion

The call graph is the key representation on which our analysis relies. It is therefore essential that the generated call graph is as complete as possible. Java and

---

[1] http://www.sat4j.org/.

object oriented languages in general have many features, such as method overriding, which makes the construction of an exact call graph (statically) at compile time undecidable. Therefore we over-approximate it using the *class hierarchy* approach [13] which permits to conservatively estimate the run-time types of the receiver objects.

Other Issues. Reflection is also a known issue for static analysis. A simple and conservative solution for this problem is to associate a tag t_{ref} with methods of the class java/lang/reflect/Method. We then use the tag t_{ref} to make the policy reflection-aware, e.g., $c : \neg t_{ref}$ to express that reflection should not be used in the context c. A similar solution is applicable for dynamic code loading by associating a tag t_{dyn} with methods of the class dalvik/system/DexClassLoader. Another framework-related challenge consists of modelling event handler callbacks. While the order of callback invocations can be over-approximated via a non-deterministic model, a more precise solution has been proposed in the literature [16]. However, adopting such an approach for EviCheck could incur an additional cost exceeding the one of the core analysis itself.

3   Implementation and Experiments

EviCheck is written in Python ($\sim$ 6000 lines) [12]. It uses Androguard [7] as back-end for parsing Android apps and has also an interface to Soot [14].

As mentioned previously, EviCheck has an option for the automatic generation of policies. In our experiments, we have first automatically generated a policy composed of 22 rules. An example of a rule is RECEIVER : ¬CAMERA, expressing that the camera should not be used in a broadcast receiver component. We then verified the generated policy against a representative set of more than **20,000** apps, from the Google Play store and Android observatory[2], ranging over different domains: games, social, etc. A snapshot of the results obtained with a typical desktop computer is illustrated in Fig. 3.

In the table, symbol ✗ indicates that the policy is violated. Policy violation does not necessarily mean malicious behaviour; it can be used as an alarm trigger in a triage phase to filter out safe apps and to advise more careful scrutiny of the remaining ones. EviCheck can provide a detailed view pointing to the violated rule itself. The diagram on the right shows for each rule the number of apps violating it. The selected rules are numbered according to their appearance in the generated policy.

The checking time is less than 1 s for most of the apps and the ratio between the certificate generation and checking time is on average 70 but can in some cases reach 1000. This is encouraging as our aim is to carry out the checking process on the phone device, which is quite limited in terms of performance.

---

[2] https://androidobservatory.org/.

App	G.T	C.T	#M	Policy
amazon	14.15	0.07	30498	
facebook	32.09	0.08	37106	
whatsapp	25.3	0.08	34143	✗
skype	11.9	0.06	25247	
twitter	17.4	0.07	32807	
...	...	...	...	...

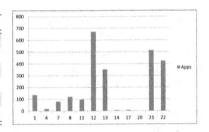

Fig. 3. In the table, G.T is the certificate generation time in seconds, C.T is the checking time and #M is the number of methods in an app. The symbol ✗ means that the policy is violated. The diagram on the right gives for each rule from the policy, identified by its number, the number of apps violating it from a set of 20,000 apps.

References

1. Albert, E., Puebla, G., Hermenegildo, M.V.: Abstraction-carrying code. In: Baader, F., Voronkov, A. (eds.) LPAR 2004. LNCS (LNAI), vol. 3452, pp. 380–397. Springer, Heidelberg (2005)
2. Arzt, S., Rasthofer, S., Fritz, C., Bodden, E., Bartel, A., Klein, J., Traon, Y.L., Octeau, D., McDaniel, P.: Flowdroid: precise context, flow, field, object-sensitive and lifecycle-aware taint analysis for Android apps. In: PLDI, p. 29 (2014)
3. Aspinall, D., MacKenzie, K.: Mobile resource guarantees and policies. In: Barthe, G., Grégoire, B., Huisman, M., Lanet, J.-L. (eds.) CASSIS 2005. LNCS, vol. 3956, pp. 16–36. Springer, Heidelberg (2006)
4. Backes, M., Gerling, S., Hammer, C., Maffei, M., von Styp-Rekowsky, P.: App-Guard – enforcing user requirements on android apps. In: Piterman, N., Smolka, S.A. (eds.) TACAS 2013 (ETAPS 2013). LNCS, vol. 7795, pp. 543–548. Springer, Heidelberg (2013)
5. Barthe, G., Crégut, P., Grégoire, B., Jensen, T., Pichardie, D.: The MOBIUS proof carrying code infrastructure. In: de Boer, F.S., Bonsangue, M.M., Graf, S., de Roever, W.-P. (eds.) FMCO 2007. LNCS, vol. 5382, pp. 1–24. Springer, Heidelberg (2008)
6. Chin, E., Felt, A.P., Greenwood, K., Wagner, D.: Analyzing inter-application communication in Android. In: MobiSys, pp. 239–252 (2011)
7. Desnos, A.: Androguard. http://code.google.com/p/androguard/
8. Enck, W., Gilbert, P., gon Chun, B., Cox, L.P., Jung, J., McDaniel, P., Sheth, A.: Taintdroid: An information-flow tracking system for realtime privacy monitoring on smartphones. In: OSDI, pp. 393–407 (2010)
9. Feng, Y., Anand, S., Dillig, I., Aiken, A.: Apposcopy: semantics-based detection of Android malware through static analysis. In: FSE (2014) (to appear)
10. Leroy, X.: Formal certification of a compiler back-end or: programming a compiler with a proof assistant. In: POPL, pp. 42–54 (2006)
11. Necula, G.C.: Proof-carrying code. In: POPL, pp. 106–119 (1997)
12. Seghir, M.N.: Evicheck. http://groups.inf.ed.ac.uk/security/appguarden/tools/EviCheck/
13. Sundaresan, V., Hendren, L.J., Razafimahefa, C., Vallée-Rai, R., Lam, P., Gagnon, E., Godin, C.: Practical virtual method call resolution for java. In: OOPSLA, pp. 264–280 (2000)

14. Vallée-Rai, R., Gagnon, E.M., Hendren, L., Lam, P., Pominville, P., Sundaresan, V.: Optimizing java bytecode using the soot framework: is it feasible? In: Watt, D.A. (ed.) CC 2000. LNCS, vol. 1781, pp. 18–34. Springer, Heidelberg (2000)
15. Xu, R., Saïdi, H., Anderson, R.: Aurasium: practical policy enforcement for android applications. In: Presented as part of the 21st USENIX Security Symposium, pp. 539–552. USENIX, Berkeley, CA (2012)
16. Yang, S., Yan, D., Wu, H., Wang, Y., Rountev, A.: Static control-flow analysis of user-driven callbacks in Android applications. In: ICSE (2015)

Lazy-CSeq-SP: Boosting Sequentialization-Based Verification of Multi-threaded C Programs via Symbolic Pruning of Redundant Schedules

Vladimir Herdt[1]($\boxtimes$), Hoang M. Le[1], Daniel Große[1], and Rolf Drechsler[1,2]

[1] Group of Computer Architecture, University of Bremen, 28359 Bremen, Germany
{vherdt,hle,dgrosse,drechsle}@cs.uni-bremen.de
[2] Cyber-Physical Systems, DFKI GmbH, 28359 Bremen, Germany

Abstract. Sequentialization has been shown to be an effective symbolic verification technique for concurrent C programs using POSIX threads. Lazy-CSeq, a tool that applies a lazy sequentialization scheme, has won the Concurrency division of the last two editions of the Competition on Software Verification. The tool encodes all thread schedules up to a given bound into a single non-deterministic sequential C program and then invokes a C model checker. This paper presents a novel optimized implementation of lazy sequentialization, which integrates symbolic pruning of redundant schedules into the encoding. Experimental evaluation shows that our tool outperforms Lazy-CSeq significantly on many benchmarks.

Keywords: Formal verification · Concurrency · Sequentialization

1 Introduction

Verifying concurrent programs is a difficult problem, due to the large state space caused by all possible thread schedules. Context-bounded analysis (CBA) [12,13] in combination with sequentialization [10,11,14], especially the lazy sequentialization scheme employed by Lazy-CSeq [8,9], has been shown to be a particular effective symbolic verification technique for concurrent C programs using POSIX threads. Lazy-CSeq has won the Concurrency division of the last two editions of the Competition of Software Verification (SV-COMP) [4,5]. Essentially, Lazy-CSeq works as follows: It transforms the multi-threaded program into an unrolled form, by inlining functions, unwinding loops and cloning instantiated threads into thread functions. The existing *main()* function becomes a thread and is replaced by a new *main()* function, which contains a round-robin scheduler. In each round, each enabled thread is executed for a non-deterministic

This work was supported in part the German Federal Ministry of Education and Research (BMBF) within the project EffektiV under contract no. 01IS13022E and by the German Research Foundation (DFG) within the Reinhart Koselleck project DR 287/23-1.

© Springer International Publishing Switzerland 2015
B. Finkbeiner et al. (Eds.): ATVA 2015, LNCS 9364, pp. 228–233, 2015.
DOI: 10.1007/978-3-319-24953-7_18

number of steps. For this execution, context switch logic is placed inside the thread functions. It allows to preempt a thread execution at statements that can interfere with other threads and therefore ensures that all relevant behaviors will be explored. The local state of the threads is preserved across function calls by making local variables static and initializing them to non-deterministic values to preserve the original semantics. Finally, the scheduler is bounded to execute a fixed number of rounds to create a single non-deterministic bounded sequential C program, which is then verified using a sequential C model checker. More details can be found in [8].

This paper presents a novel optimized round-robin scheduler encoding that incorporates symbolic pruning of redundant schedules and is used as replacement for the Lazy-CSeq scheduler. Furthermore, an extensive static analysis is employed to reduce the number of context switches placed within the threads, by detecting interfering statements more accurately. Experimental evaluation shows that both techniques can boost the performance of lazy sequentialization significantly.

2 Optimized Scheduler Encoding

Basic Round-Robin Scheduler Encoding. A round-robin scheduler, as employed by Lazy-CSeq, encodes a fixed number of thread execution rounds, thus effectively implements a variant of CBA. In every round all enabled threads are executed in a representative total order, each one for a non-deterministic number of steps. This non-determinism models the preemptive semantics of POSIX threads where a thread execution can be arbitrarily preempted by another thread. Thus, in each round, there are three possibilities for a thread: *1.* It is skipped (zero execution step); *2.* It is executed to completion (in this case, the thread becomes disabled and will not be executed in the next rounds); *3.* It is executed up to a point where its execution can be resumed in the next round; In the following the number of threads is denoted as m. Every thread is assigned a unique index $i \in \{1, .., m\}$ according to the representative execution order, and we define $t_i < t_j$ iff $i < j$. A schedule is denoted as a sequence of thread executions with the symbol | as round delimiter. Skipped threads in each round will be omitted for convenience.

Encoding Symbolic Pruning of Redundant Schedules. The main idea of the encoding is based on *round merging*. Consider $m = 3$ and the schedule $t_3 \mid \mid t_2$ (all threads are skipped in the second round). The three rounds can be merged to $t_3 \mid t_2$, but $t_3 \mid t_2$ cannot be merged further, because it is not possible to execute t_3 before t_2 in the same round. Another schedule $t_1 t_2 \mid t_2 t_3$ can be merged into a single round $t_1 t_2 t_3$, because in the second round, t_2 resumes at the point where it stopped before. For every mergeable schedule, there exists an equivalent unmergeable schedule. Thus mergeable schedules are redundant and our encoding aims to prune them. The key observation is the scheduler is only required to maintain a very simple invariant to do so: before t_j is considered, the last executed thread (with non-zero steps) must not be t_j. This invariant ensures that no more than $m - 1$ subsequent thread executions are skipped. Thus, it eliminates all empty rounds and ensures that a new round starts with a thread $t_j < t_i$ which ended the last round, as they could otherwise be merged. This enables a very lightweight encoding of round merging, which only introduces a single new variable to keep track of the last executed thread, and a set of assumptions. Fig. 1 shows a comparison of a single execution of a thread t_j for a non-deterministic number of steps in Lazy-CSeq (left side) and Lazy-CSeq-SP (right side). The functions *guess_pc* and *NC(j)* return a non-deterministic non-negative value and the number of context switches in t_j, respectively. The variables *pc[j]* and *pc_cs* store the current location in t_j and the location of the next context switch, respectively.

```
thread_index = j;                      thread_index = j;
if (active_thread[j] == 1) {           assume (j != last_thread_index);
    pc_cs = pc[j] + guess_pc();        if (active_thread[j] == 1) {
    assume (pc_cs >= 0 &&                  pc_cs = guess_pc();
            pc_cs <= NC(j));               assume (pc_cs <= NC(j));
    thread_j (threadargs[j]);              if (pc_cs > pc[j]) {
    pc[j] = pc_cs;                             thread_j (threadargs[j]);
}                                              pc[j] = pc_cs;
                                               last_thread_index = j;
                                           }
                                       }
```

Fig. 1. Execution of a single thread in Lazy-CSeq (left) and Lazy-CSeq-SP (right)

3   Implementation Details

We have implemented our tool Lazy-CSeq-SP in Python (version 3.4). A web-interface is available at www.systemc-verification.org/LazyCSeqSP for evaluation. An architecture overview is shown in Fig. 2. It expects a C program sequentialized by Lazy-CSeq, which is then further processed in two steps as shown in the lower part of Fig. 2, to produce an optimized C program. In the first step the context switch logic inside the threads, the main function with the scheduler encoding and some other auxiliary definitions generated by Lazy-CSeq are removed by using some simple scripts with regular expression matching. Essentially this results in a program, where all functions (except those marked atomic) have been inlined, loops unwound, and all threads cloned the number of times they are instantiated (the number of *pthread_create* statements is statically known due to the inlining and unwinding performed by Lazy-CSeq). In the second step a static analysis is applied to collect informations, which are then used to compute locations for the context switches. Our analysis is more accurate than Lazy-CSeq and often generates a smaller number of context switches, which also reduces the state space.

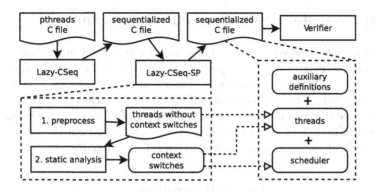

Fig. 2. Tool implementation overview

Reducing Context Switches by Static Analysis. Essentially, the static analysis works as follows: First, the *pycparser* library is used to parse the preprocessed sequentialized file into an AST, which is then transformed and annotated in subsequent phases. This includes a declaration analysis (binding names to declarations), a simple type analysis, a pointer analysis [3,7] and an escape analysis. The collected informations are then used to compute the following sets of data (called *effects*) for every statement: reads, writes, assumptions and *pthread_join* calls. Based on these statement effects a context switch is placed before a statement s if one of the following conditions holds:

1. s has a read-write dependency with any statement from another thread, i.e. both access the same variable with at least one of them writing;
2. s contains a *pthread_join* call or an assumption;
3. s is the initial statement of a thread.

The first condition can be efficiently checked by first combining all statement effects for every thread separately. The third condition ensures that initial non-interfering statements of a thread are not re-executed, when the thread resumes its execution. As an optimization, no context switches are placed due to condition (1) or (2) in the main function thread until a *pthread_create* statement is reached, since initially only the main function thread is enabled. Please note that no context switches are placed before any *pthread_create* statement at all, since creating a new thread does not interfere with the execution of the already available threads. The reason is that enabling another thread can only add additional behaviors, not limit existing ones. Furthermore, only a single context switch is placed before a group of multiple consecutive *pthread_join* calls. Once every created thread has been joined, no more context switches will be placed. Other (*pthread*) library calls are naturally handled with the first condition, e.g. a *pthread_mutex_lock* call is modeled to have a write access to the mutex argument. Finally no context switches are placed before (loop unwinding) assumptions, can be proven to be satisfiable (and have no other dependencies), since they cannot terminate the program execution.

4   Experimental Evaluation and Conclusion

We have evaluated Lazy-CSeq-SP on benchmarks from the Concurrency division of the SV-COMP 2015 [2]. All experiments are performed on a 3.4 GHz AMD machine running Linux. The time and memory limits are set to 600 seconds and 4GB, respectively. The abbreviation T.O. denotes that the time limit has been exceeded. The runtime results in seconds for a set of representative benchmarks are shown in Table 1. A table including results for a larger set of benchmarks is also available at www.systemc-verification.org/LazyCSeqSP.

Table 1. Benchmark results

Benchmark	Lazy-CSeq	+SA	Lazy-CSeq-SP
fib_bench_longest_false.c.r11.u11	278.157	166.388	**12.061**
fkp2013_false.c.r2.u50	4.265	**3.934**	4.298
qw2004_false.c.r1.u1	0.250	**0.238**	0.240
sigma_false.c.r1.u16	7.523	**4.087**	4.244
fib_bench_longest_true.c.r11.u11	243.630	221.486	**15.621**
fk2012_true.c.r3.u8	T.O	**54.875**	56.358
fkp2013_true.c.r3.u48	529.447	**1.895**	2.206
fkp2014_true.c.r5.u5	31.913	12.884	**12.599**
queue_ok_true.c.r4.u20	337.787	278.580	**65.224**
queue_ok_true.c.r5.u20	T.O	T.O	**97.408**
read_write_lock_true.c.r30.u1	311.012	159.506	**5.415**
sssc12_true.c.r3.u7	123.239	76.220	**71.479**
stack_true.c.r5.u5	67.071	21.541	**10.529**

The table shows three different configurations: the original Lazy-CSeq (version 2.0beta), our implementation with optimized context switch placement by static analysis (+SA), and additionally with symbolic pruning of redundant schedules (Lazy-CSeq-SP). To ensure a fair comparison, we patched Lazy-CSeq to place context switches before (potentially unsatisfiable) *while-loop* unwinding assumptions. Otherwise the Lazy-CSeq unwinding would effectively be reduced by one, since the last execution of the loop body would not be considered. The table is divided into two halves. The upper (lower) half shows the results on the unsafe (safe) benchmarks. The number of rounds and the unwinding are encoded into the benchmark name. CBMC version 5.0 is used as backend [1,6]. Only the CBMC runtimes are reported, since the time required to generate the sequentialized file is comparatively negligible.

On the presented benchmarks, clear improvements can be observed for the configuration +SA compared to Lazy-CSeq. Lazy-CSeq-SP improves the results further with some exceptions, where +SA shows better results. These are due to the simpler encoding of +SA, but the runtime differences are not significant. The results clearly show the advantages of symbolic pruning of redundant schedules and encourage further research in this direction. For future work we plan to investigate more aggressive pruning, e.g. symbolic Partial Order Reduction [15].

References

1. CBMC 5.0. http://www.cprover.org/cbmc/download/cbmc-5-0-linux-64.tgz
2. SV-COMP (2015). http://sv-comp.sosy-lab.org/2015/
3. Andersen, L.O.: Program Analysis and Specialization for the C Programming Language. Ph.D. thesis, University of Copenhagen (1994)
4. Beyer, D.: Status report on software verification. In: Ábrahám, E., Havelund, K. (eds.) TACAS 2014 (ETAPS). LNCS, vol. 8413, pp. 373–388. Springer, Heidelberg (2014)
5. Beyer, D.: Software verification and verifiable witnesses. In: Baier, C., Tinelli, C. (eds.) TACAS 2015. LNCS, vol. 9035, pp. 401–416. Springer, Heidelberg (2015)
6. Clarke, E., Kroning, D., Lerda, F.: A tool for checking ANSI-C programs. In: Jensen, K., Podelski, A. (eds.) TACAS 2004. LNCS, vol. 2988, pp. 168–176. Springer, Heidelberg (2004)
7. Hardekopf, B., Lin, C.: The ant and the grasshopper: fast and accurate pointer analysis for millions of lines of code. In: Proceedings of the 2007 ACM SIGPLAN Conference on Programming Language Design and Implementation (PLDI 2007), pp. 290–299. ACM, New York (2007)
8. Inverso, O., Tomasco, E., Fischer, B., La Torre, S., Parlato, G.: Bounded model checking of multi-threaded C programs via lazy sequentialization. In: Biere, A., Bloem, R. (eds.) CAV 2014. LNCS, vol. 8559, pp. 585–602. Springer, Heidelberg (2014)
9. Inverso, O., Tomasco, E., Fischer, B., Torre, S.L., Parlat, G.: Lazy-CSeq 0.6c: An Improved Lazy Sequentialization Tool for C. University of Southampton, Southampton (2014)
10. La Torre, S., Madhusudan, P., Parlato, G.: Reducing context-bounded concurrent reachability to sequential reachability. In: Bouajjani, A., Maler, O. (eds.) CAV 2009. LNCS, vol. 5643, pp. 477–492. Springer, Heidelberg (2009)
11. Lal, A., Reps, T.: Reducing concurrent analysis under a context bound to sequential analysis. Form. Methods Syst. Des. **35**(1), 73–97 (2009)
12. Musuvathi, M., Qadeer, S.: Iterative context bounding for systematic testing of multithreaded programs. In: Proceedings of the 2007 ACM SIGPLAN Conference on Programming Language Design and Implementation (PLDI 2007), pp. 446–455. ACM, New York (2007)
13. Qadeer, S., Rehof, J.: Context-bounded model checking of concurrent software. In: Halbwachs, N., Zuck, L.D. (eds.) TACAS 2005. LNCS, vol. 3440, pp. 93–107. Springer, Heidelberg (2005)
14. Qadeer, S., Wu, D.: Kiss: keep it simple and sequential. In: Proceedings of the ACM SIGPLAN 2004 Conference on Programming Language Design and Implementation (PLDI 2004), pp. 14–24. ACM, New York (2004)
15. Wang, C., Yang, Z.-J., Kahlon, V., Gupta, A.: Peephole partial order reduction. In: Ramakrishnan, C.R., Rehof, J. (eds.) TACAS 2008. LNCS, vol. 4963, pp. 382–396. Springer, Heidelberg (2008)

A Contextual Equivalence Checker for IMJ*

Andrzej S. Murawski[1], Steven J. Ramsay[1]([✉]), and Nikos Tzevelekos[2]

[1] University of Warwick, Coventry, UK
s.ramsay@warwick.ac.uk
[2] Queen Mary University of London, London, UK

Abstract. We present CONEQCT: a contextual equivalence checking tool for terms of IMJ*, a fragment of Interface Middleweight Java for which the problem is decidable. Given two, possibly open (containing free identifiers), terms of the language, the contextual equivalence problem asks if the terms can be distinguished by any possible IMJ context. Although there has been a lot of prior work describing methods for constructing proofs of equivalence by hand, ours is the first tool to decide equivalences for a non-trivial, object-oriented language, completely automatically. This is achieved by reducing the equivalence problem to the emptiness problem for fresh-register pushdown automata. An evaluation demonstrates that our tool works well on examples taken from the literature.

A dedicated webpage for the tool is: http://bitbucket.org/sjr/coneqct.

1 Introduction

Two phrases of a programming language are *contextually equivalent* if occurrences of the first phrase in any program can be replaced by the second phrase without affecting the result of the program. The notion plays a fundamental role in a variety of verification tasks: it can be used to support proofs of correctness for program transformations, code optimisations, refactoring and updates. However, due to quantification over all possible contexts in which a phrase can be inserted ("in any program"), contextual equivalences are notoriously difficult to establish directly. Over the years, both semantic (e.g. domain theory) and operational (e.g. traces, bisimulations, logical relations) methods have been used to provide techniques to overcome the problem, yet decidability results have been scarce. Our tool, which targets a fragment of Middleweight Java augmented with interfaces, capitalises on recent progress in game semantics as well as automata theory over infinite alphabets.

In recent years game semantics has led to the construction of fully abstract models for a whole range of programming languages. Although originating from the tradition of denotational semantics, they have a concrete flavour, which makes them suitable for representations as formal languages. The particular model for Java [10], that we take advantage of in this paper, is built over an infinite set of names (used to model object references), suggesting the use of automata over infinite alphabets as a framework for representing the denotations. Indeed, in the companion research paper [8], we have identified a fragment

© Springer International Publishing Switzerland 2015
B. Finkbeiner et al. (Eds.): ATVA 2015, LNCS 9364, pp. 234–240, 2015.
DOI: 10.1007/978-3-319-24953-7_19

of Java, called IMJ*, whose game semantics can be captured using (visibly) push-down register automata over infinite alphabets with fresh-symbol generation [9]. The automata are equipped with a *finite* set of registers for storing elements of the *infinite* alphabet as well as a pushdown store. In the present tool paper we present the implementation of the associated decision procedure.

Our input language IMJ* is a fragment of Interface Middleweight Java (IMJ) [10]. It is a stripped down version of Middleweight Java (MJ) [4], designed to expose the interactions of MJ-style objects with the environment through the addition of interfaces.

Example 1 ([12]). Consider the interfaces $\mathsf{IntRef} = \{\mathsf{val} : \mathsf{int}\}$, $I = \{m : \mathsf{IntRef} \to \mathsf{IntRef}\}$ and terms $\{\mathsf{IntRef}, I\} \mid \emptyset \vdash M_1, M_2 : I$ given below. Note that a and b are declared locally, i.e. they play the role of private fields. As both are unknown to the environment, the first call to m in any computational scenario will make the if-condition fail and a will be exposed to the environment as a result. Consequently, it can be recorded by the context and used in subsequent interactions with the terms. For M_1, this makes it possible to satisfy the branching condition, which will reveal the second private name b. In contrast, M_2 will never reveal b, however many times the object is used. Hence, the terms are not contextually equivalent. This example appears as inp11.imj in Table 1.

$M_1 \equiv$
  let $a = $ new $\{\_:\mathsf{IntRef};\}$ in
  let $b = $ new $\{\_:\mathsf{IntRef};\}$ in
  new $\{\_:I;\ m:\ \lambda c.\ \text{if } c = a \text{ then } b \text{ else } a\}$

$M_2 \equiv$
  let $a = $ new $\{\_:\mathsf{IntRef};\}$ in
  let $b = $ new $\{\_:\mathsf{IntRef};\}$ in
  new $\{\_:I;\ m:\ \lambda c.\ \text{if } c = b \text{ then } b \text{ else } a\}$

2   Tool Architecture

The tool decides contextual equivalence by compiling the pair of input terms to their game semantics and checking that they are assigned the same meaning. This is a complete method for deciding equivalence due to the full abstraction result in [10], which states that two terms are observationally equivalent iff they are assigned the same sets of (complete) plays by the game model.

The plays are sequences of moves that trace out the possible interactions of a term with its environment. For example, the program may play a move call $a.m(v)^\Sigma$, which represents a call with argument v to method m of an object named a in the environment, at a point in the execution where the externally observable part of the heap is described by Σ. A play can be viewed as a word over an alphabet, but the alphabet is infinite since there is no bound on the number of objects that can be created (and hence the set of objects names a). In IMJ, objects names can only be tested for equality, and in [8], it is shown that a special kind of visibly pushdown register automaton, called an IMJ Automaton (IMJA) suffices to exactly characterise the set of plays assigned to an IMJ* term by its game semantics. In this representation, the move above will have shape

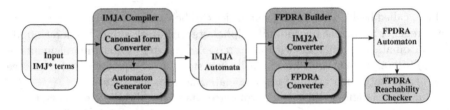

Fig. 1. Overview of tool architecture.

call $r.m(w)^S$, where r is the index of a register of the automaton which contains the name of the object a, w is a symbolic representation of v and S of Σ. Even though Σ may be unbounded, IMJ* terms modify only bounded fragments of the heap, represented by S. Checking that two sets of plays are equal is then reduced to checking IMJA language equivalence (strictly speaking, up to saturation of stores S to their full size corresponding to Σ).

Checking language equivalence of IMJA proceeds through a series of intermediate constructions, ultimately concluding with a fresh-register pushdown automaton (FPDRA). Due to the properties of the translation, the two IMJA are language equivalent iff the FPDRA is (language) empty. An overview is shown in Fig. 1. The tool reports the main characteristics of each of the intermediate constructions (e.g. number of states, number of registers) and the time taken to construct them.

From IMJ* Terms to IMJA. The first transformation is from the pair input terms to a pair of IMJA. This translation is extensively documented in [8] and our implementation is faithful to that description, so we shall not discuss it further here. As soon as the IMJA are produced, we remove states that are not graph-reachable from the initial state or backwards-graph-unreachable from an accepting state (by graph-reachable we mean reachable in the finite transition graph of the IMJA).

From IMJA to IMJ2A. The strategy for checking language equivalence of IMJA is to construct a kind of symmetric difference automaton, which accepts exactly those words that are in one of the two IMJA but not in the other, which is called an IMJ2 Automaton (IMJ2A) in [8]. This is possible, because IMJA operate over a visibly pushdown alphabet [2] and, hence, their stacks can be synchronised. Overall, the translation in *ibid.* ensures that the pair of IMJA represent the same interactions (plays) iff their IMJ2A translate is empty.

From IMJ2A to FPDRA. IMJ2A are defined in terms of the underlying transitions of the two constituent IMJA. Because they refer to two sets of registers, emptiness checking is not straightforward: in order for the automata to synchronise, matching names have to be used as labels. The following is an example of an IMJA2 transition:

$$(q_1, q_2) \xrightarrow{\text{call } r_1.m()^{S_1}, \text{call } r_2.m()^{S_2}} (q_1', q_2')$$

This transition describes how if the two underlying IMJA have reached states q_1 and q_2 respectively and, moreover, the same object name is contained in register r_1 of the first IMJA and register r_2 of the second IMJA and there is a correspondence between the names contained in the registers of the two IMJA which makes S_1 and S_2 correspond, then they will both consume this call move and step into states q_1' and q_2' respectively.

The tool compiles away such special transitions by tracking register correspondences. These are pairs of maps which describe how registers from the two constituent IMJA are represented by registers from the FPDRA under construction. This is achieved by a least fixed point computation: the two initial states are extended with the identity correspondence (representing the fact that initially both IMJA have the same register assignment) and transitions are simulated to obtain a register correspondence at the end of the transition given one at the start. A transition such as the one above can then be compiled into a set of simpler transitions that do not have a semantics that is specialized to representing plays of IMJ* terms. For example, if a correspondence has r_1 from the first IMJA and r_2 from the second being represented by the same register of the new FPDRA and, lifted to stores, makes S_1 and S_2 correspond, then the above transition degenerates to $(q_1, \sigma, q_2) \overset{\epsilon}{\to} (q_1', \sigma, q_2')$. Since we are only interested in emptiness of the IMJ2A, i.e. the impossibility of reaching a final state, the particular letter that is read is irrelevant, which explains why the degenerate transition is an epsilon transition. The result of this fixed point computation is a fresh pushdown-register automaton (FPDRA) [9], that is, a register automaton [11] (RA) with global-fresh transitions and a pushdown stack.

FPDRA Reachability Check via Saturation. Finally we decide the emptiness of the FPDRA by using an extension (to handle global freshness and empty registers) of the saturation algorithm described in [7]. This procedure constructs an RA that represents all the possible configurations of the FPRDA that can reach accepting states. In relation to [7], the main addition is the use of a tagging technique for specifying elements of the registers and the stack that are required to be globally fresh, which allows us to simulate global freshness via local freshness for reachability purposes (cf. [9]). Consequently, equivalence of the two terms is reduced to checking whether an initial configuration of the FPDRA is accepted by the RA, which is solved by graph reachability.

3   Evaluation

We evaluated CONEQCT on examples drawn from the literature around contextual equivalence for high-level languages [1,3,5,6,8,12,13], adapted to IMJ* syntax. (The website of the tool contains a more detailed listing.) For equivalences, the papers contain manually constructed proofs based on logical relations or environmental bisimulations. Their full automation would be challenging, because they require witness relations that have to be guessed. In contrast, CONEQCT is automated and also detects inequivalences.

The tool is written in F# and we evaluated it on Microsoft's .NET Framework 4.5.2, running on a machine with an Intel Core i7 1.8GHz processor and 8 GB

Table 1. Results of the evaluation

Input	Eq?	IMJA 1	IMJA 2	FPDRS	RA	Regs	Time (ms)
inp1.imj	Y	26	82	1688	0	7	1833 ± 11
inp2.imj	Y	1	1	0	0	0	$253 + 10$
inp3.imj	Y	32	32	428	0	6	355 ± 11
inp4.imj	Y	21	22	61	0	2	292 ± 10
inp4b.imj	N	21	12	76	41	2	301 ± 10
inp5.imj	Y	18	3	5	0	4	293 ± 9
inp6.imj	Y	26	26	292	0	4	322 ± 12
inp7.imj	Y	76	16	1078	972	4	445 ± 13
inp7b.imj	N	76	11	418	404	4	373 ± 11
inp8.imj	Y	17	11	124	0	4	289 ± 1
inp9.imj	Y	33	11	287	141	4	326 ± 1
inp9b.imj	N	17	11	138	134	4	320 ± 2
inp10.imj	Y	96	96	1528	0	4	1344 ± 9
inp10b.imj	N	42	96	2476	2468	4	1256 ± 30
inp11.imj	N	92	32	796	796	7	584 ± 4
inp12.imj	Y	11	9	26	0	2	266 ± 1
inp13.imj	Y	13	13	111	0	4	299 ± 1
inp14.imj	Y	13	13	37	0	2	21908 ± 291
inp15.imj	Y	34	242	8714	0	7	3647 ± 49
inp15b.imj	N	34	242	10725	10725	7	4095 ± 44
inp16.imj	Y	272	137	17888	0	8	16499 ± 155
inp16b.imj	N	56	137	11833	11833	8	4731 ± 123

of RAM. The results of the evaluation are shown in Table 1. The first column gives the file name of the input and the second states whether the input is an equivalence (Y) or an inequivalence (N). The next four columns give the number of states in the intermediate constructions. The number of states in the IMJ2A is omitted since it is always a simple function of the number of states in the two constituent IMJA automata. Column seven gives the number of registers in the FPDRA and hence RA, and column eight gives the total time for processing the input in milliseconds (mean $\pm$ s.e.; $n = 10$).

A couple of interesting observations can be made regarding the results. First, in many instances of equivalence, the number of states in the RA is 0. This indicates that the corresponding FPDRA has no accepting states. This happens if, as a result of the fixed point computation, the exploration of register correspondences reveals that it is not possible for the IMJ2A to accept a word. For example, this will be the case when the compilation of the two terms happens to yield identical IMJA.

A second observation regards the time taken. One of the most time expensive examples is input 14, yet the various intermediate constructions are all relatively small. Further investigation reveals that the vast majority of the time is spent constructing the two IMJA. Although the two IMJA that are constructed are ultimately small, as part of their construction far larger automata are built but then later restricted and have many unreachable states pruned away. It will be interesting future work to understand how to ensure that time is not wasted producing such expensive yet transient constructions.

Further Directions. Whilst we have shown that the tool performs well on the kinds of examples seen in the literature, we see further directions which would make this line of work more generally applicable. We aim to optimise the handling of time-intensive automata constructions, and to empower CONEQCT with predicate abstraction, allowing it to reason symbolically not only about object names but also basic data values.

Acknowledgements. Research supported by the Engineering and Physical Sciences Research Council (EP/J019577/1) and the Royal Academy of Engineering (RF: Tzevelekos).

References

1. Ahmed, A., Dreyer, D., Rossberg, A.: State-dependent representation independence. In: Proceedings of POPL, pp. 340–353. ACM (2009)
2. Alur, R., Madhusudan, P.: Visibly pushdown languages. In: Proceedings of STOC 2004, pp. 202–211 (2004)
3. Benton, N., Leperchey, B.: Relational reasoning in a nominal semantics for storage. In: Urzyczyn, P. (ed.) TLCA 2005. LNCS, vol. 3461, pp. 86–101. Springer, Heidelberg (2005)
4. Bierman, G., Parkinson, M., Pitts, A.: MJ: an imperative core calculus for Java and Java with effects. Technical report 563, Computer Laboratory, University of Cambridge (2002)
5. Dreyer, D., Neis, G., Birkedal, L.: The impact of higher-order state and control effects on local relational reasoning. In: Proceedings of ICFP, pp. 143–156. ACM (2010)
6. Koutavas, V., Wand, M.: Small bisimulations for reasoning about higher-order imperative programs. In: Proceedings of POPL, pp. 141–152. ACM (2006)
7. Murawski, A.S., Ramsay, S.J., Tzevelekos, N.: Reachability in pushdown register automata. In: Csuhaj-Varjú, E., Dietzfelbinger, M., Ésik, Z. (eds.) MFCS 2014, Part I. LNCS, vol. 8634, pp. 464–473. Springer, Heidelberg (2014)
8. Murawski, A.S., Ramsay, S.J., Tzevelekos, N.: Game semantic analysis of equivalence in IMJ. In: Finkbeiner, B., Pu, G., Zhang, L. (eds.) ATVA 2015. LNCS, pp. 411–428. Springer, Heidelberg (2015). http://bitbucket.org/sjr/coneqct/src
9. Murawski, A.S., Tzevelekos, N.: Algorithmic games for full ground references. In: Czumaj, A., Mehlhorn, K., Pitts, A., Wattenhofer, R. (eds.) ICALP 2012, Part II. LNCS, vol. 7392, pp. 312–324. Springer, Heidelberg (2012)
10. Murawski, A.S., Tzevelekos, N.: Game semantics for Interface Middleweight Java. In: POPL, pp. 517–528 (2014)

11. Neven, F., Schwentick, T., Vianu, V.: Finite state machines for strings over infinite alphabets. ACM Trans. Comput. Log. **5**(3), 403–435 (2004)
12. Pitts, A.M., Stark, I.D.B.: Operational reasoning for functions with local state. In: Gordon, A.D., Pitts, A.M. (eds.) Higher-Order Operational Techniques in Semantics, pp. 227–273. Cambridge University Press, Cambridge (1998)
13. Welsch, Y., Poetzsch-Heffter, A.: A fully abstract trace-based semantics for reasoning about backward compatibility of class libraries. Sci. Comput. Program. **92**, 129–161 (2014)

Trace Diagnostics Using Temporal Implicants

Thomas Ferrère[1], Oded Maler[1], and Dejan Ničković[2][(✉)]

[1] Verimag, University of Grenoble/CNRS, Grenoble, France
[2] AIT Austrian Institute of Technology, Vienna, Austria
dejan.nickovic@ait.ac.at

Abstract. Runtime verification and model checking are two important methods for assessing correctness of systems. In both techniques,
detecting an error is witnessed by an *execution* that violates the system
specification. However, a faulty execution on its own may not provide
sufficiently precise insight to the causes of the reported violation. Additional, often manual effort is required to properly diagnose the system.
In this paper we present a method for analyzing such causes. The specifications we consider are expressed in LTL (Linear Temporal Logic) and
MTL (Metric Temporal Logic), and the execution models are taken as
ultimately-periodic words, and *finite variability* continuous signals respectively. The *diagnostics* problem is defined for the propositional case as
the search for a small *implicant* of a formula which is satisfied by a given
valuation, or equivalently a subset of that valuation sufficient to render
the formula true. We propose a suitable notion of implicants in the temporal case, that are semantically based on signal subsets, and guarantee
the existence of *prime* implicants for arbitrary temporal properties. An
inductive procedure for finding temporal implicants is obtained by the
introduction of selection functions that appear in a process equivalent
to Skolemization in first order logic. Through the model restrictions we
impose for LTL and MTL we are able to generate concise implicants of
a property, describing a small fragment of the input signal that causes
violation of a formula.

1 Introduction

Our work is concerned with the problem of temporal *monitoring*: given a *single*
behavior w, either in discrete or dense time, and a temporal property φ check
whether $w \models \varphi$. This problem is known as *runtime verification* in software and
assertion checking in hardware. In addition to the yes/no answer, we would
like to produce an informative *diagnostics*, a small fragment of the behavior
which provides a sufficient condition for the violation of φ by w. This additional
information helps localizing and explaining the causes of the fault. We solve the
diagnostics problem for MTL [9], for which we assume that the input signal w
has bounded variability. We further extend our results to LTL [15] under the
assumption of an ultimately periodic input sequence. This makes our technique
applicable to the analysis of counter-example executions as produced by a *model
checking* procedure.

© Springer International Publishing Switzerland 2015
B. Finkbeiner et al. (Eds.): ATVA 2015, LNCS 9364, pp. 241–258, 2015.
DOI: 10.1007/978-3-319-24953-7_20

Consider the temporal logic formula $\Box(p \rightarrow \Diamond_{[1,2]} q)$. It requires that for any instant in time where p holds, there exists another instant within 1 to 2 time units where q holds. The behavior depicted in Fig. 1 violates this temporal property – the violation can be explained by the fact that p holds at time 1 and q does not hold throughout [2,3]. Such a concise piece of information, compared to w which can be a very long signal, will increase our confidence in monitoring and model-checking procedures, and promote their further acceptance in various application domains.

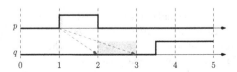

Fig. 1. A behavior that violates $\Box(p \rightarrow \Diamond_{[1,2]} q)$. Grey-shaded area gives one possible explanation.

Finding an explanatory sub-model in the propositional case, is strongly related to the concept of prime implicants of a formula. The problem that we pose in this paper, finding explanatory temporal sub-models, is novel and in order to solve it we had to overcome numerous issues that come from the infinitude of the temporal models. Our main result is an inductive explanation generation scheme for MTL which produces focused dense time sub-signals sufficient to explain violation. A crucial ingredient of the procedure is the elimination of disjunctive operations by the introduction of selection functions similar in spirit to Skolem functions used to eliminate existential quantification. Under a finite variability assumption we can show that explanations can be taken as finitely variable. For LTL, we show similarly that infinite ultimately-periodic sequences admit ultimately-periodic explanatory sub-models.

Related Work. The problem of understanding a counter-example by finding the reason for the failure of a temporal logic formula in the trace itself was studied in [1]. This work differs from ours in several aspects. It adopts a different notion of failures based on Halpern and Pearl causality [6] and considers only LTL but not dense-time temporal logics. The explanations of ultimately periodic sequences are handled by unfolding the trace. Finally, the authors are interested in the detection of the first failure in a trace. In our work we provide more flexibility by means of selection functions, which allow to choose between several different failures. In [13], the authors propose a procedure that provides a minimal debugging window for traces that violate an MTL formula. The result can be seen as a coarse-grain diagnostic, providing a small segment of the input trace yet not discriminating signals and time intervals causing the violation.

There have been various studies on obtaining additional debugging information from counter-examples in LTL model checking. Tight automata [10] were introduced to find shortest finite counter-examples for safety properties, and extended in [17] to infinite words and full LTL. Comparing erroneous and correct traces with distance metrics in order to localize errors has been studied in the context of software checking in [5]. The problem of finding and repairing violations of LTL properties by sequential circuits was studied in [8], where a repair solution based on a game-oriented approach is proposed. A related problem is that of computing unsatisfiable cores for LTL, i.e. finding smaller unsatisfiable sub-formulas, as studied in [7,14,16]. At the syntactic level minimal unsatisfiable cores bear some similarity with prime implicants; they primarily address formal verification concerns.

2   Propositional Foundations

Consider the problem of explaining why a formula φ is *violated* by a given execution w of some system, seen as finding the part of the execution w that causes φ to be violated. Note that through negation this is equivalent to solving the dual problem of explaining why some formula is *satisfied*. We first introduce and study the problem in the simple setting of propositional logic.

2.1   Problem Statement

Let $\mathbb{P}$ be a *finite* set of propositional variables. A valuation w is taken to be a function $P \to \mathbb{B}$ with $P \subseteq \mathbb{P}$ its domain and $\mathbb{B} := \{0, 1\}$ the set of Boolean values. We define propositional formulas over $\mathbb{P}$ and the constant true the usual way. The set of models of a formula φ is noted $[\![\varphi]\!]$. For φ and ψ two formulas we write $\psi \Rightarrow \varphi$ when $[\![\psi]\!] \subseteq [\![\varphi]\!]$, and $\psi \Leftrightarrow \varphi$ when $[\![\psi]\!] = [\![\varphi]\!]$. Note that implication $(\Rightarrow)$ induces a partial order over classes of equivalent $(\Leftrightarrow)$ formulas.

Definition 1 (Terms, Implicants and Prime Implicants). *A* term γ *is defined as a conjunction of literals. If $\gamma \Rightarrow \varphi$ then the term γ is an* implicant *of formula φ. If moreover γ is maximal with respect to $\Rightarrow$ we talk of* prime implicant.

We say that γ *explains* the satisfaction of φ by w, if γ is an implicant of φ and w is a model of γ. Note that the least general explanation of φ relative to w is a term representing the truth status of every variable in w. It is intuitively clear, however that we opt for explanations that are smaller and more general, omitting "don't care" variables. We aim at providing explanations that use small subsets of "do care" variables. The most general explanations are in particular the prime implicants of φ satisfied by w.

Problem ((Minimal) Diagnostics). *Given a valuation w and a formula φ, find a (prime) implicant γ of φ such that $w \models \gamma$.*

2.2   Syntactic and Semantic Formulations

Take φ a formula, w a model of φ and γ a solution to the corresponding diagnostics problem. As $\gamma \Rightarrow \varphi$, there exists a proof of φ under hypothesis γ; a correct algorithm producing the diagnostics is implicitly constructing that proof. The more general the implicant is, the more complex the associated proof can be.

Example 1. Take formula $\varphi := (p \wedge q) \vee (p \wedge \neg q)$ and valuation $w := \{p \mapsto 1, q \mapsto 0, r \mapsto 0\}$. The formulas $\alpha := p$ and $\beta := p \wedge \neg q$ are both implicants of φ, and satisfied by w with α a prime implicant of φ. In sequent calculus the proof $\beta \vdash \varphi$ is direct through a right disjunction rule, while the proof $\alpha \vdash \varphi$ requires the application of several rules, and uses non-intuitionistic reasoning.

We now sketch the semantic counter-parts of implicants, beginning with a refinement relation $\sqsubseteq$ between valuations.

Definition 2. *For two valuations $u : P \to \mathbb{B}$ and $v : Q \to \mathbb{B}$ we have $u \sqsubseteq v$ if and only if $P \subseteq Q$ and $u(p) = v(p)$ for all $p \in P$.*

The space of valuations is a semi-lattice with respect to $\sqsubseteq$ with meet operation $\sqcap$ and least element $\bot$. Let u and v be some valuations with domain P and Q respectively. The valuation $u \sqcap v$ has domain $\{p \in P \cap Q : u(p) = v(p)\}$ and value $u \sqcap v (p) = u(p)$ where defined. The least element $\bot$ is the nowhere-defined valuation with domain $\emptyset$.

One can think of a valuation v over $P \subseteq \mathbb{P}$ as a compact representation for all valuations w over $\mathbb{P}$ such that $v \sqsubseteq w$. A valuation v corresponds to a term γ_v, the conjunction of literals true according to v, and reciprocally any satisfiable term γ corresponds to a valuation v_γ, that assigns a value to variables according to the literals in γ.

Definition 3 (Sub-Model). *A valuation v is a sub-model of φ if for all valuations w over $\mathbb{P}$ such that $v \sqsubseteq w$ we have $w \models \varphi$; if moreover v is minimal with respect to $\sqsubseteq$ we talk of minimal sub-model.*

A valuation v is a sub-model of φ if and only if γ_v is an implicant of φ. The (minimal) diagnostics problem for φ relative to w can thus be formulated equivalently as the problem of finding a (minimal) sub-model of φ contained in w.

2.3   Practical Solution

Note that the minimal diagnostics problem is at least as hard as a satisfiability query, since tautologies can be recognized by their unique prime implicant, the empty term true. However by relaxing the minimality assumption, knowing the truth value of each sub-formula of φ on w allows to construct implicants γ such that $w \models \gamma$ in a simple, top-down fashion. For every formula we take for implicant a combination of implicants for its sub-formulas that are satisfied by w, or violated by w when in the context of a negation. Accordingly we define an operator E (and its dual F) that for a given formula φ returns an implicant of φ (respectively of $\neg\varphi$) which under suitable assumptions is satisfied by w. The explanation of φ is then defined as

$$\mathrm{Exp}(\varphi) = \begin{cases} E(\varphi) & \text{if } w \models \varphi \\ F(\varphi) & \text{otherwise} \end{cases}$$

with

$$E(p) = p \qquad\qquad F(p) = \neg p$$
$$E(\neg\varphi) = F(\varphi) \qquad\qquad F(\neg\varphi) = E(\varphi)$$
$$E(\varphi_1 \vee \varphi_2) = E(\xi(\varphi_1 \vee \varphi_2)) \qquad F(\varphi_1 \vee \varphi_2) = F(\varphi_1) \wedge F(\varphi_2)$$

where ξ is a *selection function* satisfying $\xi(\varphi_1 \vee \varphi_2) \in \{\varphi_1, \varphi_2\}$. When for any formula $\varphi_1 \vee \varphi_2$ such that $w \models \varphi_1 \vee \varphi_2$ it holds $w \models \xi(\varphi_1 \vee \varphi_2)$, we say that ξ is *correct* with respect to w. We can take for example

$$\xi : \varphi_1 \vee \varphi_2 \mapsto \begin{cases} \varphi_1 & \text{if } w \models \varphi_1 \\ \varphi_2 & \text{otherwise} \end{cases}$$

This gives priority to the left disjunct. Under the assumption that ξ is correct with respect to w, the formula $\mathrm{Exp}(\varphi)$ is a solution to the diagnostics problem associated to φ and w. In the case of Example 1, applying the procedure on φ and w yields the explanation β.

3 Temporal Issues

We introduce the temporal logics LTL [15] and MTL [9] in a unified framework. Temporal formulas will be given by the grammar

$$\varphi := p \mid \neg\varphi \mid \varphi \vee \varphi \mid \varphi \mathcal{U}_I \varphi$$

where I is a real interval with integer endpoints. Other temporal connectives are introduced through the abbreviations $\varphi_1 \mathcal{U}\varphi_2 := \varphi_1 \mathcal{U}_{(0,+\infty)}\varphi_2$ for *strict until*, $\bigcirc\varphi := \mathrm{false}\,\mathcal{U}\,\varphi$ for *next*, $\varphi_1 \tilde{\mathcal{U}}\varphi_2 := \varphi_2 \vee (\varphi_1 \wedge \varphi_1 \mathcal{U}\varphi_2)$ for *non-strict until*, $\Diamond\varphi := \mathrm{true}\,\tilde{\mathcal{U}}\,\varphi$ for *eventually*, $\Box\varphi := \neg(\Diamond\neg\varphi)$ for *always* and $\Diamond_I\varphi := \mathrm{true}\,\mathcal{U}_I\varphi$, $\Box_I\varphi := \neg\Diamond_I\neg\varphi$ for their timed versions. LTL formulas are then constructed using temporal connectives $\bigcirc$ and $\tilde{\mathcal{U}}$, while MTL formulas are constructed using temporal connectives $\Diamond_I$ and $\mathcal{U}$.

A temporal behavior is defined as a function $\mathbb{T} \times P \to \mathbb{B}$, for $P \subseteq \mathbb{P}$ a set of propositional variables and $\mathbb{T}$ a linearly-ordered time domain. Given a behavior w we note $w[t]$ its value at time $t \in \mathbb{T}$ taken to be a vector of Boolean values, and w_p the behavior $\mathbb{T} \to \mathbb{B}$ that is the projection of w on the component $p \in \mathbb{P}$. The models for both logics are defined over infinite time domains, $\mathbb{N}$ and $[0, d)$ respectively. In the following, we use the term *signal* to refer both to discrete continuous time behaviors.

We write $I \oplus J = \{t + t' \in \mathbb{T} \ : \ t \in I \text{ and } t' \in J\}$ and $I \ominus J = \{t - t' \in \mathbb{T} \ : \ t \in I \text{ and } t' \in J\}$ the Minkowski sum and difference of two intervals I and J, that we may simply note $t \oplus J$ and $t \ominus J$ when $I = [t, t]$. The semantics of a temporal logic formula φ with respect to a signal $w : \mathbb{T} \times \mathbb{P} \to \mathbb{B}$ and time $t \in \mathbb{T}$ are given as follows:

$$(w,t) \models p \qquad\qquad \leftrightarrow \quad w_p[t] = 1$$
$$(w,t) \models \neg\varphi \qquad\qquad \leftrightarrow \quad (w,t) \not\models \varphi$$
$$(w,t) \models \varphi_1 \vee \varphi_2 \qquad \leftrightarrow \quad (w,t) \models \varphi_1 \text{ or } (w,t) \models \varphi_2$$
$$(w,t) \models \varphi_1 \mathcal{U}_I \varphi_2 \quad \leftrightarrow \quad \exists t' \in t \oplus I, \ (w,t') \models \varphi_2 \text{ and } \forall t'' \in (t,t'), \ (w,t'') \models \varphi_1$$

We say that w is a model of φ and write $w \models \varphi$ when $(w,0) \models \varphi$. A signal can be "projected" for any formula φ to its *satisfaction signal* $w_\varphi : \mathbb{T} \to \mathbb{B}$ such that $w_\varphi[t] = 1$ if and only if $(w,t) \models \varphi$. We extend the notion of satisfaction signal w_φ to sets of formulas Ψ by letting $w_\Psi : \mathbb{T} \times \Psi \to \mathbb{B}$ be a multi-dimensional signal featuring the corresponding $|\Psi|$ satisfaction signals w_ψ for $\psi \in \Psi$. The satisfaction signals of φ and of all its sub-formulas ψ are given as the result of applying a monitoring procedure such as the one from [11] to w and φ.

3.1 Syntactic Rewritings

The fragment of temporal logic based on operators $\neg, \vee, \Diamond_I$ and $\mathcal{U}$ as introduced, has the same expressiveness as the fragment $\neg, \vee$ and $\mathcal{U}_I$, often taken as primitive MTL operators. This equivalence is based on the observation that the timed until operator admits a decomposition into a timing part, and a sequential part [4]. For instance we have $\varphi \mathcal{U}_{(a,b)} \psi \Leftrightarrow \Box_{[0,a]}(\varphi \mathcal{U} \psi) \wedge \Diamond_{(a,b)} \psi$, and similar decompositions in the case of semi-opened and closed timing intervals.

For the purpose of handling the negation of an until formula we introduce its dual operation *release*, with non-strict and strict versions as follows.

$$\varphi \tilde{\mathcal{R}} \psi := \psi \tilde{\mathcal{U}}(\psi \wedge \varphi) \vee \Box \psi$$
$$\varphi \mathcal{R} \psi := \varphi \mathcal{U} \text{ true} \vee \psi \mathcal{U}(\psi \wedge \varphi) \vee \psi \mathcal{U}(\psi \wedge \varphi \mathcal{U} \text{ true}) \vee \Box_{(0,\infty)} \psi$$

In discrete time $\neg(\varphi \tilde{\mathcal{U}} \psi) \Leftrightarrow \neg\varphi \tilde{\mathcal{R}} \neg\psi$, while in continuous time $\neg(\varphi \mathcal{U} \psi) \Leftrightarrow \neg\varphi \mathcal{R} \neg\psi$. We explain the MTL negation of an until as follows: $\varphi \mathcal{U} \psi$ does not hold if φ is immediately false, or if φ becomes false before (or immediately when) ψ becomes true, or if ψ never holds in the future.

3.2 Semantic Restrictions

We now introduce some definitions allowing us to place restrictions on the kind of signals we consider. Given a some constant in $\mathbb{T}$ we note $w^{a\cdots}$ the shifted sequence such that $w^{a\cdots}[t] = w[t + a]$ for all $t \in \mathbb{T}$. For a and b constants in $\mathbb{T}$ we say that some sequence w is *ultimately periodic* with *period* a and *prefix* b if $w^{a+b\cdots} = w^{b\cdots}$ holds. Some real interval I is said to be *uniform* with respect to signal w when $w[t] = w[t']$ for all t and t' in I; if moreover I is maximal with respect to $\subseteq$ we talk of a *maximally uniform* interval. The *variability* of a signal is taken to be the largest number of maximally uniform intervals in any unit length segment of that signal.

In what follows on one hand we assume that all continuous signals have finite variability, that is *MTL finite variability semantics*. On the other hand we consider arbitrary discrete signals, that is *LTL unrestricted semantics*. However we will always assume that the input signal to the LTL diagnostic is ultimately-periodic.

3.3   Sub-models of a Formula

We define, similarly to the propositional case, *sub-signals* with domain $T \subseteq \mathbb{T} \times \mathbb{P}$ and partially ordered $\sqsubseteq$. Sub-signals u and v with respective domains R and S verify $u \sqsubseteq v$ if and only if $R \subseteq S$ and $u_p[t] = v_p[t]$ for all $(t, p) \in R$. Given formula φ and sub-signal v, we say that v is a *sub-model* of φ if $w \models \varphi$ for all signals $w \sqsupseteq v$.

To ensure finite representation we introduce corresponding semantic restrictions (ultimate periodicity, finite variability) on sub-signals. The notions of uniform segment and shifting operation extend to sub-signals in a natural way. A finite variability sub-signal has a domain $\bigcup_{p \in P} T_p \times \{p\}$, where $T_p \subseteq \mathbb{T}$ is the domain of p, such that the number of intervals in the intersection of each T_p with a unit interval admits a maximum. An ultimately-periodic signal v with period a and prefix b has a domain T such that $(t + b, p) \in T$ if and only if $(t + b + a, p) \in T$.

In the discrete case, a relative ultimate-periodicity hypothesis does not guarantee the existence of a minimal sub-model.

Example 2 (LTL). The formula $\varphi := \Diamond \Box p$ has no minimal ultimately-periodic sub-model over the discrete time domain $\mathbb{N}$. Consider the monotone sequence (v_i) of ultimately-periodic sub-models of φ with period 1 and prefix i, and domain $[i, \infty) \times \{p\}$. The sub-signal $\bigsqcap_{i \in \mathbb{N}} v_i = \bot$ is not a sub-model of φ.

We thus fix the period a and prefix b as given by the input signal, and restrict our analysis to sub-models with corresponding ultimate periodicity. For representation convenience we define the domain $\mathbb{T}_{a,b} = \{0, 1, \ldots, b - 1, b^\infty, (b+1)^\infty, \ldots, (a + b - 1)^\infty\}$ featuring *recurrent time* symbols t^∞ for $t = b, b + 1, \ldots, a + b - 1$. For an arbitrary signal w and element $t^\infty \in \mathbb{T}_{a,b}$, we define $w[t^\infty]$ with $w[t^\infty] = 1$ iff $w[t + a \, n] = 1$ for all $n \in \mathbb{N}$. Any ultimately-periodic signal over $\mathbb{T} = \mathbb{N}$ with corresponding period and prefix may be seen without loss of generality as a signal over $\mathbb{T}_{a,b}$.

In the continuous case, uniformly bounding the variability does not even guarantee the existence of a minimal sub-model.

Example 3 (MTL). The formula $\varphi = p\,\mathcal{U}\,\mathrm{true}$ has no minimal sub-model over the dense time domain $[0, 1)$. Consider the monotone sequence (v_i) of sub-models of φ with variability 1, and domain $(0, \frac{1}{i+1}] \times \{p\}$. The sub-signal $\bigsqcap_{i \in \mathbb{N}} v_i = \bot$ is not a sub-model of φ.

To overcome limit problems we extend the temporal domain $\mathbb{T} = [0, d)$ to non-standard reals taken in $\mathbb{T}^+ = \{t^+ : t \in \mathbb{T}\}$ and $\mathbb{T}^- = \{t^- : t \in (0, d]\}$, with $\mathbb{T}^* = \mathbb{T} \cup \mathbb{T}^+ \cup \mathbb{T}^-$. We note $w[t^+]$ the right limit of some signal w at time t and $w[t^-]$ its left limit. Any finite variability signal over $\mathbb{T} = [0, d)$ may be extended this way to a signal over $\mathbb{T}^*$.

3.4   Temporal Implicants

We now introduce sentences based on (possibly infinite) conjunctions of unary predicates $p[t]$ and their negation $\neg p[t]$ for t in some domain $\mathbb{D}$, that we will take to be $\mathbb{T}_{a,b}$ or $\mathbb{T}^*$.

Definition 4 (Terms, Implicants and Prime Implicants). *Temporal terms are are defined using the grammar*

$$\gamma := p[t] \mid \neg p[t] \mid \gamma \wedge \gamma \mid \bigwedge_{t \in D} \theta[t]$$

where $p \in \mathbb{P}$ is a propositional variable, t is a time in $\mathbb{D}$, D is a subset of $\mathbb{D}$, and θ a function from $\mathbb{D}$ to temporal terms. The semantics $\models$ of temporal terms relative to a signal w are as expected for predicates and binary conjunctions, and for the case of general conjunctions are given by

$$w \models \bigwedge_{t \in D} \theta[t] \ \leftrightarrow \ \forall t \in D, w \models \theta[t]$$

An implicant *of some temporal formula φ is a temporal term γ such that $\gamma \Rightarrow \varphi$. We talk of* prime implicant *when γ is maximal with respect to $\Rightarrow$.*

The above definition of temporal terms is very general, allowing arbitrary functions θ under infinite conjunctions. However temporal terms can always be written in a simpler normal form as follows, which is straightforward to prove by structural induction.

Proposition 1 (Normal Form). *For every temporal term there exists an equivalent temporal term of the form $\bigwedge_{\ell \in L} \bigwedge_{t \in T_\ell} \ell[t]$, where L is the set of propositional literals over $\mathbb{P}$. Assuming L is ordered this normal form is unique.*

For any term γ we will write $\bigwedge_{\ell \in L} \bigwedge_{t \in V_\ell^\gamma} \ell[t]$ its normal form. Then given arbitrary terms α and β, it holds $\alpha \Rightarrow \beta$ if and only if $V_\ell^\beta \subseteq V_\ell^\alpha$ for all $\ell \in L$. Notably $\Rightarrow$ defines a partial order over normal form terms.

It is clear that normal form temporal terms are analogous to sub-signals over $\mathbb{D}$. By considering such terms over domains $\mathbb{D} = \mathbb{T}_{a,b}$ and $\mathbb{D} = \mathbb{T}^*$ we obtain the existence of at least one prime implicant for every satisfiable LTL and MTL formula respectively. Recall that we use full discrete semantics over $\mathbb{T} = \mathbb{N}$, and finite variability continuous semantics over $\mathbb{T} = [0, d)$.

Proposition 2 (Existence of Prime Implicants). *For any LTL formula φ and sequence w with period a and prefix b such that $w \models \varphi$ there exists a prime implicant γ of φ over $\mathbb{T}_{a,b}$ such that $w \models \gamma$. For any MTL formula φ and signal w such that $w \models \varphi$ there exists a prime implicant γ of φ over $\mathbb{T}^*$ such that $w \models \gamma$.*

Proof. Let us note Γ the set of implicants γ of φ such that $w \models \gamma$, that we may assume in normal form. In both discrete and continuous cases, w seen as a temporal term is itself an implicant of φ. This gives us $\Gamma \neq \emptyset$.

- In the discrete case Γ is finite, so that there exists of a maximal element of Γ relative to $\Rightarrow$, which proves our proposition.
- In the continuous case, we demonstrate the existence of a maximal element of Γ relative to $\Rightarrow$ by direct application of Zorn's Lemma as follows.

Consider Δ an arbitrary totally ordered subset of Γ. First we can see that Δ is bounded by the temporal term $\alpha = \bigwedge_{\ell \in L} \bigwedge_{t \in U_\ell} \ell[t]$, where each $U_\ell = \bigcap_{\gamma \in \Delta} \overline{V_\ell^\gamma}$ is the intersection over all $\gamma \in \Delta$ of the closure of V_ℓ^γ in $\mathbb{T}^*$. This does not pose any difficulty. We then show that moreover $\alpha \in \Gamma$ so that γ is indeed an upper bound of Δ in Γ. For that we need to show $w \models \alpha$ which is trivial, and to show $\alpha \Rightarrow \varphi$. To demonstrate the latter fact we take w' an arbitrary model of α and prove the existence of some $\gamma \in \Delta$ such that $w' \models \gamma$. As $\Delta \subseteq \Gamma$ we will then have $w' \models \varphi$ by definition of Γ.

Assume, in search of a contradiction that $w' \not\models \gamma$ for all $\gamma \in \Delta$. For each $\gamma \in \Delta$ there exists $\ell \in L$ and $t \in V_\ell^\gamma$ such that $w'_\ell[t] = 0$. We may construct a sequence (γ_i, ℓ_i, t_i) of $\Delta \times L \times \mathbb{T}^*$ such that $t_i \in V_{\ell_i}^{\gamma}$ and $w'_{\ell_i}[t_i] = 0$ for all $i \in \mathbb{N}$, and such that (γ_i) is monotone and diverging, that is $\gamma_i \Rightarrow \gamma_j$ if $i \leq j$, and for all $\gamma \in \Delta$ there exists $i \in \mathbb{N}$ such that $\gamma \Rightarrow \gamma_i$. We take $s_i \in \mathbb{T}$ the standard part of t_i, that is $t_i \in \{s_i^+, s_i^-, s_i\}$. As L is finite, we can safely assume that the sequence (ℓ_i) is constant. As $\mathbb{T}$ is bounded, by Bolzano-Weierstrass Theorem we may in turn assume that the sequence (s_i) is monotone and convergent, an assumption that we extend to (t_i). Let us note ℓ the value of (ℓ_i), and t the limit of (t_i). As (γ_i) is monotone, the subsequence of times $(t_j)_{j \geq i}$ has all its values in $V_\ell^{\gamma_i}$, so that $t \in \overline{V_\ell^{\gamma_i}}$. In particular $t \in \bigcap_{i \in \mathbb{N}} \overline{V_\ell^{\gamma_i}} = \bigcap_{\gamma \in \Delta} \overline{V_\ell^\gamma} = U_\ell$ given that (γ_i) is diverging. Then $t \in U_\ell$ yields $w'_\ell[t] = 1$. By finite variability of w', as (t_i) converges to t there exists i such that $w'_\ell[t_i] = 1$. Yet $w'[t_i] = 0$ by hypothesis. Contradiction! Therefore there exists $\gamma \in \Delta$ such that $w' \models \gamma$.

4   MTL Diagnostics

In this section, we propose an effective procedure to compute implicants of an MTL formula φ relative to a multi-dimensional signal $w : [0, d) \times \mathbb{P} \to \mathbb{B}$ of length d. First, note that the satisfaction signal w_φ of a given formula φ relative to a finite variability signals w has itself finite variability, the variability of satisfaction signals growing at most quadratically with the size of the formula. Like satisfaction, an explanation for a temporal formula is *time dependent* and should be a function from the time domain to formulas that explain satisfaction or violation at some time t. Analogously to the notion of satisfaction signal $w_\varphi : \mathbb{T} \to \mathbb{B}$ we define the notion of *explanation signal* noted $E(\varphi)$ such that $E(\varphi)[t]$ explains the satisfaction of φ by w at time $t \in \mathbb{T}$. We then construct explanations through definitions of $E(\varphi)[t]$ and its dual $F(\varphi)[t]$, which are inductive on the structure of formula φ, and on the times t at which explanations of its sub-formulas are required. We are able to guarantee finite representation by producing finite variability explanation signals. We use selection functions ξ_φ to relate the truth of some formula φ at time t with the truth of its sub-formulas at some time $\xi_\varphi[t]$. Arbitrary selection functions may yet lead to explanations which are almost as large as the signal itself, however we can find selection functions that allow best "explanation sharing". For instance given a non-singular interval I the same t' may belong to $t \oplus I$ for every t in some interval T. Hence a selection function satisfying $\xi_\varphi[t] = t'$ for every $t \in T$ will use only one point to witness the satisfaction of $\varphi = \Diamond_I \psi$ throughout T.

4.1 Non-Standard MTL Semantics

The relation $<$ over the reals of $\mathbb{T}$ naturally extends to $\mathbb{T}^*$ with $t^- < t < t^+$. We then define over $\mathbb{T}^*$ the relation $\ll$ with $t \ll t'$ if and only if $t < t'$ or $t = t' \notin \mathbb{R}$. Interval notations using angled parentheses are introduced with $\langle t, t' \rangle = \{t'' : t \ll t'' \ll t'\}$ and $[t, t') = \{t'' : t \leq t'' \ll t'\}$. The sum of symbolic limit t^+, respectively t^-, and a real number a is taken as $(t + a)^+$, respectively $(t + a)^-$. The sum $t \boxplus I$ of some $t \in \mathbb{T}^*$ and a real interval I is then defined as the closure in $\mathbb{T}^*$ of $t \oplus I$, and the difference $t \boxminus I$ is defined similarly.

We extend the satisfaction relation for temporal formulas to non-standard reals by writing $(w, t) \models \varphi$ if $w_\varphi[t] = 1$. Now conditions induced by timed eventually, and until operators can be expressed in terms of closed intervals of $\mathbb{T}^*$.

Lemma 1. *For any formula φ, ψ, (finite variability) signal w, and time or symbolic limit $t \in \mathbb{T}^*$ we have*

- *$(w, t) \models \Diamond_I \varphi$ if and only if there exists t' in $t \boxplus I$ such that $(w, t') \models \varphi$;*
- *$(w, t) \models \varphi \mathcal{U} \psi$ if and only if there exists $t' \gg t$ such that $(w, t') \models \psi$ and for all $t'' \in \langle t, t' \rangle$ it holds $(w, t'') \models \varphi$.*

4.2 Explanation Operators

We may now formally define operators $E(\varphi)[t]$ and $F(\varphi)[t]$ providing explanations of φ, or $\neg\varphi$ relative to signal w at time $t \in \mathbb{T}^*$ in the form of temporal terms. The explanation of a formula φ relative to a signal w is then given by the application of E or F at time 0 as follows. We let

$$\text{Exp}(\varphi) = \begin{cases} E(\varphi)[0] & \text{if } (w, 0) \models \varphi \\ F(\varphi)[0] & \text{otherwise} \end{cases}$$

with

$$E(p)[t] = p[t]$$
$$E(\neg\varphi)[t] = F(\varphi)[t]$$
$$E(\varphi \vee \psi)[t] = E(\xi_{\varphi \vee \psi}[t])[t]$$
$$E(\Diamond_I \varphi)[t] = \begin{cases} E(\varphi)[t + a] & \text{if } I = [a, a] \\ E(\varphi)[\xi_{\Diamond_I \varphi}[t]] & \text{otherwise} \end{cases}$$
$$E(\varphi \mathcal{U} \psi)[t] = E(\psi)[\xi_{\varphi \mathcal{U} \psi}[t]] \wedge \bigwedge_{\substack{t' \in \\ \langle t, \xi_{\varphi \mathcal{U} \psi}[t] \rangle}} E(\varphi)[t']$$

$$F(p)[t] = \neg p[t]$$
$$F(\neg\varphi)[t] = E(\varphi)[t]$$
$$F(\varphi \vee \psi)[t] = F(\varphi)[t] \wedge F(\psi)[t]$$
$$F(\Diamond_I \varphi)[t] = \bigwedge_{t' \in t \boxplus I} F(\varphi)[t']$$
$$F(\varphi \mathcal{U} \psi)[t] = E(\neg\varphi \mathcal{R} \neg\psi)[t]$$

where $\xi_{\varphi \vee \psi}$ from $\mathbb{T}^*$ to formulas, $\xi_{\Diamond_I \varphi}$ and $\xi_{\varphi \mathcal{U} \psi}$ from $\mathbb{T}^*$ to $\mathbb{T}^*$ are *selection functions* such that for all $t \in \mathbb{T}^*$, it holds $\xi_{\varphi \vee \psi}[t] \in \{\varphi, \psi\}$, $\xi_{\Diamond_I \varphi}[t] \in t \boxplus I$ and $\xi_{\varphi \mathcal{U} \psi}[t] \gg t$.

We say that a selection function ξ_φ is correct with respect to w if for all $t \in \mathbb{T}^*$ such that $(w, t) \models \varphi$ we have

- $(w, t) \models \xi_\varphi[t]$ when φ is of the form $\varphi_1 \vee \varphi_2$;
- $(w, \xi_\varphi[t]) \models \psi$ when φ is of the form $\Diamond_I \psi$;
- $(w, \xi_\varphi[t]) \models \varphi_2$ and $\forall t' \in \langle t, \xi[t] \rangle$, $(w, t') \models \varphi_1$ when φ is of the form $\varphi_1 \mathcal{U} \varphi_2$.

The following result is straightforward to prove from Lemma 1.

Theorem 1 (Soundness). *A term $Exp(\varphi)$, correct with respect to signal w is a solution to the diagnostics problem of φ with respect to w.*

Moreover, given finite variability selection functions our explanations can be effectively represented.

Proposition 3 (Finite Representation). *Assuming all selection functions are finitely variable, the term $Exp(\varphi)$ has a normal form $\bigwedge_{\ell \in L} \bigwedge_{t' \in T_\ell} \ell[t']$ such that each T_ℓ is a finite union of intervals of $\mathbb{T}^*$.*

4.3 Computation of Selection Functions

We describe procedures that define explicit instances of selection functions, and satisfying the correctness and finite variability criteria. The explanation operators can be made constructive when the normalization of the terms they produce is interleaved with the instantiation of selection functions over intervals appearing in the normalization process. It is indeed sufficient to define selection functions piecewise on closed intervals T of $\mathbb{T}^*$. Furthermore we can assume that for such intervals T, formula φ holds for all $t \in T$ as the correctness assumption is void outside such intervals, with the finite variability assumption then trivial to match.

Disjunction. Consider the formula $\varphi \vee \psi$ and the signal w. A finitely variable selection function $\xi_{\varphi \vee \psi}$ and correct with respect to w can be constructed as follows. By finite variability hypothesis on w, the satisfaction signal $w_{\varphi,\psi} : \mathbb{T} \to \mathbb{B}$ has finite variability over any interval T where $\varphi \vee \psi$ holds. We partition T in k maximally uniform intervals T_i, and take $\xi_{\varphi \vee \psi}[t] = \varphi$ over intervals T_i where $(w, t) \models \varphi$, and $\xi_{\varphi \vee \psi}[t] = \psi$ over other intervals. The function $\xi_{\varphi \vee \psi}$ is uniform over all T_i, so has finite variability.

Timed Eventually. Now consider the formula $\Diamond_I \varphi$ for I non-singular and the signal w, and assume that the formula is satisfied over some interval T. We build a procedure that generates a small set of witnesses of φ accounting for the satisfaction of $\Diamond_I \varphi$ by w over T. The satisfaction of $\Diamond_I \varphi$ over T can be explained by the satisfaction of φ at some time points within the interval $T \boxplus I = \bigcup_{t \in T} t \boxplus I$, and in particular the satisfaction of φ at some $s \in T \boxplus I$ provides a sufficient explanation for the satisfaction of $\Diamond_I \varphi$ for all $t \in (s \boxminus I) \cap T$. We use these two observations to generate a piecewise constant selection function $\xi_{\Diamond_I \varphi}$ defined over T and correct relative to a signal w.

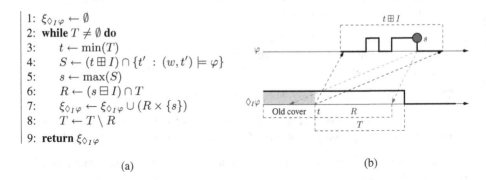

```
1:  ξ◊ᵢφ ← ∅
2:  while T ≠ ∅ do
3:      t ← min(T)
4:      S ← (t ⊞ I) ∩ {t' : (w, t') ⊨ φ}
5:      s ← max(S)
6:      R ← (s ⊟ I) ∩ T
7:      ξ◊ᵢφ ← ξ◊ᵢφ ∪ (R × {s})
8:      T ← T \ R
9:  return ξ◊ᵢφ
```

(a)   (b)

Fig. 2. (a) Algorithm to find a correct instance of $\xi_{\Diamond_I \varphi}$ over T relative to signal w; (b) Example of R and s computation for $\Diamond_I \varphi$.

We present the procedure in Fig. 2-(a); it works as follows. The selection function is initialized (line 1) as nowhere defined. In every iteration of the main while loop (line 2), we find a time domain $S = (t \boxplus I) \cap \{t' : (w, t') \models \varphi\}$ such that φ is satisfied inside S and any point in S provides a sufficient (Lemma 1) explanation for the satisfaction of $\Diamond_I \varphi$ at t taken as the earliest time of T. Such set S is obtained directly from the satisfaction signal w_φ, that we suppose already computed by the monitoring procedure. We then take s the latest time of S, which constitutes a minimal subset of S sufficient to explain the satisfaction of $\Diamond_I \varphi$ throughout the domain $s \boxminus I$; when intersected with T it gives R, a prefix of T. At the end of the iteration, the definition of $\xi_{\Diamond_I \varphi}$ over the interval R is taken as s, which we may write $R \times \{s\}$ identifying selection functions with subsets of $\mathbb{T}^* \times \mathbb{T}^*$ (line 7). The covered prefix R can be removed from T (line 8). The procedure terminates when T the domain remaining to cover becomes empty.

Untimed Until. Consider the formula $\varphi \mathcal{U} \psi$ and the signal w and assume that the formula is satisfied over T, taken without loss of generality to be a closed interval of $\mathbb{T}^*$. For $t \in \mathbb{T}^*$, similarly to the case of timed eventually a single witness $t' \gg t$ of ψ along with a uniform interval $\langle t, t' \rangle$ where φ holds is sufficient to explain the satisfaction of $\varphi \mathcal{U} \psi$ over the whole interval $[t, t']$. With such observations we generate a piecewise constant selection function $\xi_{\varphi \mathcal{U} \psi}$ correct with respect to some signal w and defined over T. We make use of a subroutine $W(\varphi, \psi, t)$ that returns the set of witnesses of ψ in signal w that are sufficient to explain $\varphi \mathcal{U} \psi$ at time $t \in \mathbb{T}^*$ where $\varphi \mathcal{U} \psi$ holds. Thanks to Lemma 1 we have $W(\varphi, \psi, t) = \{t' \gg t : (w, t') \models \psi \text{ and } \forall t'' \in \langle t, t' \rangle, (w, t'') \models \varphi\}$. Assuming the satisfaction signals w_φ and w_ψ given by the monitoring algorithm, the procedure $W(\varphi, \psi, t)$ can be realized as follows. First decompose the domain

$\{t' \in \mathbb{T}^* \ : \ t' \gg t\}$ as a finite partition into uniform intervals of $\mathbb{T}^*$ with respect to $w_{\varphi,\psi}$ that we can assume of the form $[t_i, t_i]$ and (t_i, t_{i+1}) with $(t_i)_{i \leq n}$ an ordered sequence of times. Start from the interval containing $t_0 = t$ and iterate through intervals, accumulating intervals where ψ holds, until φ stops holding at $[t_i, t_i]$ or (t_i, t_{i+1}), or we reach the interval containing $t_n = d^-$ marking the end of the time domain.

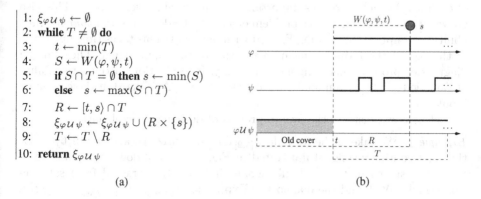

```
1:  ξφ𝒰ψ ← ∅
2:  while T ≠ ∅ do
3:      t ← min(T)
4:      S ← W(φ, ψ, t)
5:      if S ∩ T = ∅ then s ← min(S)
6:      else      s ← max(S ∩ T)
7:      R ← [t, s) ∩ T
8:      ξφ𝒰ψ ← ξφ𝒰ψ ∪ (R × {s})
9:      T ← T \ R
10: return ξφ𝒰ψ
```

(a)   (b)

Fig. 3. (a) Algorithm to find a correct instance of $\xi_{\varphi\,\mathcal{U}\,\psi}$ over T relative to signal w; (b) Example of R and s computation for $\varphi\,\mathcal{U}\,\psi$.

We present the main procedure to compute the selection function in Fig. 3-(a). The procedure first assigns $\xi_{\varphi\,\mathcal{U}\,\psi}$ the empty function $\emptyset$ (line 1). In every iteration of the while loop, we compute an interval S whose elements s are witnesses of ψ providing sufficient explanation for the satisfaction of the $\varphi\,\mathcal{U}\,\psi$ throughout $[t, s)$. When S lies entirely outside T we take s to be the earliest suitable witness of ψ, so as not to impose a condition on φ beyond it (line 5). When S intersects with T on the contrary we look for the latest suitable witness of ψ in their intersection (line 6). As a direct corollary of Lemma 1 the interval $R = [t, s) \cap T$ is now accounted for, hence we define $\xi_{\varphi\,\mathcal{U}\,\psi}$ as taking the value s over interval R (line 8). Eventually R can be removed from T for the next iteration (line 9), and the procedure terminates when T becomes empty.

4.4   Discussion

Our procedure does not guarantee minimality, with for instance propositional tautologies not being recognized. However we obtain some form of temporal minimality through the proposed construction for selection functions. Intuitively each time a witness is required we select the furthest away, which maximizes the interval over which that witness is valid. Let φ be an *eventually* or *until* formula, w a trace such that φ holds for w on some domain T. We claim that selection functions ξ_φ constructed by our algorithms choose a set of witnesses $\xi_\varphi[T] = \{\xi_\varphi[t] \ : \ t \in T\}$ that is minimal relative to w.

The main advantage of our explanation principle is its hierarchical character: every sub-formula has its own explanation, which is then used in turn to account for the satisfaction or violation of its super-formulas. This makes the process of fault-finding transparent: if the fault lies in the specification then it can be localized syntactically, otherwise it lies in the system in which case the explanation of each sub-formula provides important insight on what went wrong. This also allows to solve the diagnostics problem efficiently. Under a uniform *bounded* variability assumption, computing $\text{Exp}(\varphi)$ with our algorithms takes time quadratic in the size of the formula, linear in the size of the input signal. The minimal diagnostics problem has a higher complexity. By reduction to the satisfiability of Bounded-MTL [3], minimal diagnostics is EXPSPACE-hard in the combined input size.

Let us now illustrate the overall process of deriving an explanation.

Example 4. We take φ the formula $\Diamond_{[1,2]} \Box(p \rightarrow \neg(q \,\mathcal{U}\, r))$, and $w : [0,6) \rightarrow \mathbb{B}^3$ the right-continuous signal illustrated in Fig. 4. The top-down computation of $\text{Exp}(\varphi)$ is shown in terms of sub-signals, inductively extracted from satisfaction signals. We found the diagnostics $\text{Exp}(\varphi) \Leftrightarrow \bigwedge_{t \in (2,3]} \neg r[t] \wedge \bigwedge_{t \in [3,3]} \neg q[t] \wedge \bigwedge_{t \in [3,6)} \neg p[t]$. It reads as follows: r is false between 2 and 3, q is false at time 3 and p is false from 3 onwards.

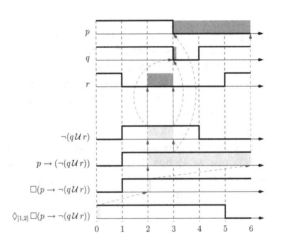

Fig. 4. Computing $\text{Exp}(\varphi)$, for $\varphi = \Diamond_{[1,2]} \Box(p \rightarrow \neg(q \,\mathcal{U}\, r))$.

5 LTL Ultimately-Periodic Diagnostics

Our explanation scheme for LTL formulas solves the diagnostics problem with respect to an ultimately-periodic sequence w with period a and prefix b.

The first remark we make is that the satisfaction sequence w_φ of any LTL formula φ is then also ultimately-periodic. Let us say that a property φ is *future* if for any sequence w and time constant a it holds $(w, a) \models \varphi$ iff $w^{a \cdots} \models \varphi$. It is trivial to check that given an ultimately periodic sequence, future properties have a satisfaction sequence that preserves the prefix and period. Following this remark we may assume that we dispose of the satisfaction sequences for each sub-formula. We refer the reader to [12] for the monitoring of ultimately-periodic sequences.

5.1 Recurrent LTL Semantics

We equip $\mathbb{T}_{a,b}$ with a pseudo-successor function $\widetilde{+}\,1$ that we define by

$$t \,\widetilde{+}\, 1 = t + 1 \qquad\qquad \text{for } t < b - 1$$
$$t^\infty \,\widetilde{+}\, 1 = (t+1)^\infty \qquad\qquad \text{for } b \leq t < a + b - 1$$
$$(b-1) \,\widetilde{+}\, 1 = (a+b-1)^\infty \,\widetilde{+}\, 1 = b^\infty$$

The nth successor of a symbolic time $t \in \mathbb{T}_{a,b}$ is then given by

$$t \,\widetilde{+}\, 0 = t$$
$$t \,\widetilde{+}\, n = (t \,\widetilde{+}\, 1) \,\widetilde{+}\, (n-1) \qquad\qquad \text{for } n \geq 1$$

We further define on $\mathbb{T}_{a,b}$ a preorder relation $\preceq$ such that $t \preceq t'$ if and only if there exists $n \geq 0$ such that $t' = t \,\widetilde{+}\, n$. The usual interval notations $[t, t')$ are extend to arbitrary $t, t' \in \mathbb{T}_{a,b}$ by letting $[t, t') = \{t'' : \exists n \geq 0, t'' = t \,\widetilde{+}\, n \text{ and } \forall k \leq n, t \,\widetilde{+}\, k \neq t'\}$. The semantics of LTL are extended to recurrent times by writing $(w, t^\infty) \models \varphi$ if $(w, t + an) \models \varphi$ for all $n \in \mathbb{N}$. We then have the following implications.

Lemma 2. *For any formula φ, ψ, sequence w, and symbolic time $t \in \mathbb{T}_{a,b}$ we have*

- $(w, t) \models \bigcirc\varphi$ *if* $(w, t \,\widetilde{+}\, 1) \models \varphi$;
- $(w, t) \models \varphi \mathcal{U} \psi$ *if there exists $t' \succeq t$ such that $(w, t') \models \psi$ and $(w, t'') \models \varphi$ for all $t'' \in [t, t')$.*

Note that when w is ultimately-periodic with period a and prefix b, the preceding formulas are satisfied *if and only if* the corresponding conditions hold.

5.2 Explanation Operators

The explanation scheme for LTL is also derived from the propositional one by making operators E and F time dependent. Such operators take a formula φ and a symbolic time $t \in \mathbb{T}_{a,b}$, and return propositional terms over unary predicates $p[t']$ with $p \in \mathbb{P}$ and $t' \in \mathbb{T}_{a,b}$. The explanation Exp is then given by E or F at time 0 as follows. We let

$$\text{Exp}(\varphi) = \begin{cases} E(\varphi)[0] & \text{if } w \models \varphi \\ F(\varphi)[0] & \text{otherwise} \end{cases}$$

with

$$E(p)[t] = p[t]$$
$$E(\neg\varphi)[t] = F(\varphi)[t]$$
$$E(\bigcirc\varphi)[t] = E(\varphi)[t\tilde{+}1]$$
$$E(\varphi \vee \psi)[t] = E(\xi_{\varphi\vee\psi}[t])[t]$$
$$E(\square\,\varphi)[t] = \bigwedge_{t'\succeq t} E(\varphi)[t']$$

$$F(p)[t] = \neg p[t]$$
$$F(\neg\varphi)[t] = E(\varphi)[t]$$
$$F(\bigcirc\varphi)[t] = F(\varphi)[t\tilde{+}1]$$
$$F(\varphi \vee \psi)[t] = F(\varphi)[t] \wedge F(\psi)[t]$$

$$E(\varphi\,\tilde{\mathcal{U}}\,\psi)[t] = E(\psi)[\xi_{\varphi\,\tilde{\mathcal{U}}\,\psi}[t]] \wedge \bigwedge_{t'\in[t,\xi_{\varphi\,\tilde{\mathcal{U}}\,\psi}[t])} E(\varphi)[t'] \qquad F(\varphi\,\tilde{\mathcal{U}}\,\psi)[t] = E(\neg\varphi\,\tilde{\mathcal{R}}\,\neg\psi)[t]$$

where $\xi_{\varphi\vee\psi}$ from $\mathbb{T}_{a,b}$ to formulas, and $\xi_{\varphi\,\tilde{\mathcal{U}}\,\psi}$ from $\mathbb{T}_{a,b}$ to $\mathbb{T}_{a,b}$ are *selection functions* such that for all $t \in \mathbb{T}_{a,b}$, it holds $\xi_{\varphi\vee\psi}[t] \in \{\varphi,\psi\}$ and $\xi_{\varphi\,\tilde{\mathcal{U}}\,\psi}[t] \succeq t$.

We say that a selection function ξ_φ is correct with respect to w if for all $t \in \mathbb{T}_{a,b}$ such that $(w,t) \models \varphi$ we have

- $(w,t) \models \xi_\varphi[t]$ when φ is of the form $\varphi_1 \vee \varphi_2$,
- $(w,\xi_\varphi[t]) \models \varphi_2$ and $\forall t' \in [t,\xi[t]),\ (w,t') \models \varphi_1$ when φ is of the form $\varphi_1\,\tilde{\mathcal{U}}\,\varphi_2$.

Correct selection functions can easily be constructed, knowing that the domain $\mathbb{T}_{a,b}$ is finite. The following result is straightforward to prove from Lemma 2.

Theorem 2 (Soundness). *Under the assumption that selection functions are correct with respect to w, $Exp(\varphi)$ is a solution to the diagnostic problem of φ and w.*

We now give an example of diagnostic produced by our explanation principle.

Example 5. Let φ be the formula $r \rightarrow \bigcirc\square(p\,\tilde{\mathcal{U}}\,\neg q)$ and $w : \mathbb{N} \rightarrow \mathbb{B}^3$ be the sequence with period 4 and prefix 2 defined by the following ω-regular expression:

$$p\,q\,r \cdot p\,q\,r \cdot (\overline{p}\,\overline{q}\,\overline{r} \cdot p\,q\,\overline{r} \cdot \overline{p}\,\overline{q}\,r \cdot p\,q\,r)^\omega$$

We find $Exp(\varphi) = p[1] \wedge \neg q[2^\infty] \wedge p[3^\infty] \wedge \neg q[4^\infty] \wedge p[5^\infty]$, which may be written as the ω-regular language $\text{true} \cdot p \cdot (\overline{q} \cdot p \cdot \overline{q} \cdot p)^\omega$.

6   Conclusion and Perspectives

We have enriched MTL monitoring, and LTL model checking techniques with a focused analysis of the causes of satisfaction/violation of such a specification by a given temporal behavior. For monitoring applications we plan to develop an online version of our algorithms, which may then be integrated in the monitoring procedure to allow fault analysis on a simulation, or even a real execution without having to save all of the monitored signals. Looking more generally at temporal implicants it would be interesting to study alternative formulations, based on the desiderata of [2] that list atomicity of literals, closure under intersection, duality with implicates, etc. Our approach to diagnosis may then transfer to other problems, such as fault localization where a system model is assumed to be available.

Acknowledgements. This work was supported by ANR project CADMIDIA, and the MISTRAL project A-1341-RT-GP coordinated by the European Defence Agency (EDA) and funded by 8 contributing Members (France, Germany, Italy, Poland, Austria, Sweden, Netherland and Luxenbourg) in the framework of the Joint Investment Programme on Second Innovative Concepts and Emerging Technologies (JIP-ICET 2) and the IKT der Zukunft of Austrian FFG project HARMONIA (nr. 845631).

References

1. Beer, I., Ben-David, S., Chockler, H., Orni, A., Trefler, R.: Explaining counterexamples using causality. In: Bouajjani, A., Maler, O. (eds.) CAV 2009. LNCS, vol. 5643, pp. 94–108. Springer, Heidelberg (2009)
2. Bienvenu, M.: Prime implicates and prime implicants: from propositional to modal logic. J. Artif. Intell. Res. **36**(1), 71–128 (2009)
3. Bouyer, P., Markey, N., Ouaknine, J., Worrell, J.B.: On expressiveness and complexity in real-time model checking. In: Aceto, L., Damgård, I., Goldberg, L.A., Halldórsson, M.M., Ingólfsdóttir, A., Walukiewicz, I. (eds.) ICALP 2008, Part II. LNCS, vol. 5126, pp. 124–135. Springer, Heidelberg (2008)
4. D'Souza, D., Tabareau, N.: On timed automata with input-determined guards. In: Lakhnech, Y., Yovine, S. (eds.) FORMATS 2004 and FTRTFT 2004. LNCS, vol. 3253, pp. 68–83. Springer, Heidelberg (2004)
5. Groce, A.: Error explanation with distance metrics. In: Jensen, K., Podelski, A. (eds.) TACAS 2004. LNCS, vol. 2988, pp. 108–122. Springer, Heidelberg (2004)
6. Halpern, J.Y., Pearl, J.: Causes and explanations: a structural-model approach: Part 1: Causes. In: Uncertainty in Artificial Intelligence, pp. 194–202 (2001)
7. Hantry, F., Hacid, M.-S.: Handling conflicts in depth-first search for LTL tableau to debug compliance based languages. In: Formal Languages and Analysis of Contract-Oriented Software, pp. 39–53 (2011)
8. Jobstmann, B., Staber, S., Griesmayer, A., Bloem, R.: Finding and fixing faults. J. Comput. Syst. Sci. **78**(2), 441–460 (2012)
9. Koymans, R.: Specifying real-time properties with metric temporal logic. Real-Time Syst. **2**(4), 255–299 (1990)
10. Kupferman, O., Vardi, M.Y.: Model checking of safety properties. Formal Methods Syst. Des. **19**(3), 291–314 (2001)
11. Maler, O., Nickovic, D.: Monitoring properties of analog and mixed-signal circuits. STTT **15**(3), 247–268 (2013)
12. Markey, N., Raskin, J.-F.: Model checking restricted sets of timed paths. In: Gardner, P., Yoshida, N. (eds.) CONCUR 2004. LNCS, vol. 3170, pp. 432–447. Springer, Heidelberg (2004)
13. Mukherjee, S., Dasgupta, P.: Computing minimal debugging windows in failure traces of AMS assertions. IEEE Trans. CAD Integr. Circ. Syst. **31**(11), 1776–1781 (2012)
14. Pill, I., Semprini, S., Cavada, R., Roveri, M., Bloem, R., Cimatti, A.: Formal analysis of hardware requirements. In: Design Automation Conference, pp. 821–826 (2006)
15. Pnueli, A.: The temporal logic of programs. In: Foundations of Computer Science, pp. 46–57. IEEE (1977)

16. Schuppan, V.: Towards a notion of unsatisfiable and unrealizable cores for LTL. Sci. Comput. Program. **77**(7–8), 908–939 (2012)
17. Schuppan, V., Biere, A.: Shortest counterexamples for symbolic model checking of LTL with past. In: Halbwachs, N., Zuck, L.D. (eds.) TACAS 2005. LNCS, vol. 3440, pp. 493–509. Springer, Heidelberg (2005)

Test Case Generation of Actor Systems

Elvira Albert, Puri Arenas[(✉)], and Miguel Gómez-Zamalloa

DSIC, Complutense University of Madrid, Madrid, Spain
puri@sip.ucm.es

Abstract. Testing is a vital part of the software development process. It is even more so in the context of concurrent languages, since due to undesired task interleavings and to unexpected behaviours of the underlying task scheduler, errors can go easily undetected. Test case generation (TCG) is the process of automatically generating *test inputs* for interesting *coverage criteria*, which are then applied to the system under test. This paper presents a TCG framework for *actor systems*, which consists of three main elements, which are the original contributions of this work: (1) a symbolic execution calculus, which allows symbolically executing the program (i.e., executing the program for unknown input data), (2) improved techniques to avoid performing redundant computations during symbolic execution, (3) new termination and coverage criteria, which ensure the termination of symbolic execution and guarantee that the test cases provide the desired degree of code coverage. Finally, our framework has been implemented and evaluated within the aPET system.

1 Introduction

Concurrent programs are becoming increasingly important as multicore and networked computing systems are omnipresent. Writing correct concurrent programs is more difficult than writing sequential ones, because with concurrency come additional hazards not present in sequential programs such as race conditions, deadlocks, and livelocks. Therefore, software validation techniques urge especially in the context of concurrent programming. Testing is the most widely-used methodology for software validation in industry. It typically requires at least half of the total cost of a software project. *Test Case Generation* (TCG) is a key component to automate testing. It consists in generating *test inputs* for interesting *coverage criteria*, which are then applied to the system under test. Examples of coverage criteria for sequential code are: *statement coverage*, which requires that each instruction of the code is executed; *path coverage*, which requires that each possible path of the execution is tried; etc.

We consider actor systems [2,14], a model of concurrent programming that has been gaining popularity and that is being used in many systems (such as ActorFoundry, Asynchronous Agents, Charm++, E, ABS, Erlang, and Scala). Actor programs consist of computing entities called actors, each with its own local state and thread of control, that communicate by exchanging messages asynchronously. An actor configuration consists of the local state of the actors

© Springer International Publishing Switzerland 2015
B. Finkbeiner et al. (Eds.): ATVA 2015, LNCS 9364, pp. 259–275, 2015.
DOI: 10.1007/978-3-319-24953-7_21

and a set of pending *tasks*. In response to receiving a message, an actor can update its local state, send messages, or create new actors. At each step in the computation of an actor system, firstly an actor and secondly a process of its pending tasks are scheduled.

The aim of this work is to develop a framework for TCG of actor systems. A standard approach to generating test cases statically is to perform a *symbolic execution* of the program [6–8, 12, 17, 19, 20], where the contents of variables are expressions rather than concrete values. Symbolic execution produces a system of constraints over the input variables and the actor's fields containing the conditions to execute the different paths. The conjunction of these constraints represents the equivalence class of inputs that would take this path. This produces, by construction, a (possibly infinite) set of test cases, which satisfy the path-coverage criterion. Briefly, the TCG framework that we propose has three main components, which are the contributions of this work: (1) in Sect. 3, we leverage the semantics used for testing in [3] to the more general setting of symbolic execution; (2) in Sect. 4, we extend and improve the techniques to avoid redundant computation of [3] to eliminate redundancies in symbolic execution and; (3) in Sect. 5, we propose novel termination and coverage criteria, which guarantee termination of the process. We have implemented our framework in aPET [4], a TCG tool for concurrent objects. Our experiments demonstrate the usefulness, impact and effectiveness of the proposed techniques.

2   The Language

We consider a distributed message-passing programming model in which each actor represents a processor, which is equipped with a procedure stack and an unordered buffer of pending tasks. Initially all actors are idle. When an idle actor's task buffer is non-empty, some task is removed, and the task is executed to completion. Each task besides accessing its own actor's global storage, can post tasks to the buffers of any actor, including its own. When a task does complete, its processor becomes idle and chooses a next pending task to execute.

Actors are materialized in the language syntax by means of objects. An actor sends a message to another actor x by means of an asynchronous method call, written $x\ !\ m(\bar{z})$, being $\bar{z}$ parameters of the message or call. In response to a received message, an actor then spawns the corresponding method with the received parameters $\bar{z}$. The number of actors does not have to be known a priory, thus in the language actors can be dynamically created using the instruction new. Tasks from different actors execute in parallel. As in the object-oriented paradigm, a class C denotes a type of actors and it is defined as a set of fields $\mathcal{F}(C)$ and methods void $m(\bar{T}\ \bar{x})\{s;\}$. The grammar for an instruction s is:

$$s ::= s\ ;\ s\ |\ x = e\ |\ \text{while } b \text{ do } s\ |\ \text{if } b \text{ then } s \text{ else } s\ |$$
$$\text{this}.f = y\ |\ x = \text{this}.f\ |\ x = \text{new } C\ |\ x\ !\ m(\bar{z})$$

where x, y, z denote variables names and f a field name. For any entity A, the notation $\bar{A}$ is used as a shorthand for $A_1, ..., A_n$. We use the special actor identifier this to denote the current actor. For the sake of generality, the syntax

$$\text{(mstep)} \quad \frac{selectA(S) = \mathsf{ac}(\mathbf{r}, \bot, h, Q), Q \neq \emptyset, selectT(\mathbf{r}) = t, S \overset{\mathbf{r} \cdot t}{\leadsto}{}^* S'}{S \xrightarrow{\mathbf{r} \cdot t} S'}$$

$$\text{(setf)} \quad \frac{t = tk(t, m, l, \mathsf{this}.f = y; s)}{\mathsf{ac}(\mathbf{r}, t, h, Q \cup \{t\}) \leadsto \mathsf{ac}(\mathbf{r}, t, h[f \mapsto l(y)], Q \cup \{tk(t, m, l, s)\})}$$

$$\text{(getf)} \quad \frac{t = tk(t, m, l, x = \mathsf{this}.f; s)}{\mathsf{ac}(\mathbf{r}, t, h, Q \cup \{t\}) \leadsto \mathsf{ac}(\mathbf{r}, t, h, Q \cup \{tk(t, m, l[x \mapsto h(f)], s)\})}$$

$$\text{(new)} \quad \frac{t = tk(t, m, l, x = \mathsf{new}\ D; s), n = fresh(), h' = newheap(D), l' = l[x \rightarrow \mathbf{r}_n^D]}{\mathsf{ac}(\mathbf{r}, t, h, Q \cup \{t\}) \leadsto \mathsf{ac}(\mathbf{r}, t, h, Q \cup \{tk(t, m, l', s)\}) \cdot \mathsf{ac}(\mathbf{r}_n^D, \bot, h', \{\})}$$

$$\text{(asy)} \quad \frac{t = tk(t, m, l, x\ !\ m_1(\bar{z}); s), l(x) = \mathbf{r}_1, t_1 = fresh(), \mathbf{r} \neq \mathbf{r}_1, l_1 = newlocals(\bar{z}, m_1, l)}{\mathsf{ac}(\mathbf{r}, t, h, Q \cup \{t\}) \cdot \mathsf{ac}(\mathbf{r}_1, t', h', Q') \leadsto}$$
$$\mathsf{ac}(\mathbf{r}, t, h, Q \cup \{tk(t, m, l, s)\}) \cdot \mathsf{ac}(\mathbf{r}_1, t', h', Q' \cup \{tk(t_1, m_1, l_1, bd(m_1))\})$$

$$\text{(return)} \quad \frac{t = tk(t, m, l, \epsilon)}{\mathsf{ac}(\mathbf{r}, t, h, Q \cup \{t\}) \leadsto \mathsf{ac}(\mathbf{r}, \bot, h, Q)}$$

Fig. 1. Summarized semantics for distributed and concurrent execution

of expressions e, boolean conditions b and types T is not specified. We assume that there are no fields with the same name and different type. As usual in the actor model [2,14,22], we suppose that a method does not return a value, but rather that its computation modifies the actor state. The language is simple to explain the contributions of the paper in a clear way, as done in [3,22].

An *actor* is a term $\mathsf{ac}(\mathbf{r}_n^C, t, h, Q)$ where $\mathbf{r}$ stands for reference, n is the actor identifier, C is the class name, t is the identifier of the *active task* that holds the actor's lock or $\bot$ if the actor's lock is free, h is its local heap and Q is the set of tasks in the actor. A *heap* h is a mapping $h : \mathcal{F}(C) \mapsto \mathbb{V}$, where $\mathbb{V} = \mathbb{Z} \cup Ref \cup \{\mathsf{null}\}$ and Ref stands for the set of references of the form $\mathbf{r}_n^C$. Whenever it is clear from the context, we will omit n and C from actor identifiers by using only $\mathbf{r}$. A *task* is a term $tk(t, m, l, s)$ where t is a unique task identifier, m is the method name executing in the task, l is a mapping from local variables to $\mathbb{V}$, and s is the sequence of instructions to be executed. Sometimes we use the identifier t to refer to entire task and we use ϵ to denote an empty sequence of instructions. A *state* S has the form $\mathbf{r}_0 \cdot \mathbf{r}_1 \cdot \ldots \cdot \mathbf{r}_n$, where $\mathbf{r}_i$ is used to refer to the whole actor $\mathsf{ac}(\mathbf{r}_i^{C_i}, t_i, h_i, Q_i)$ and $\mathbf{r}_i \neq \mathbf{r}_j$, $1 \leq i, j \leq n, i \neq j$.

Figure 1 presents the semantics of the actor model. As actors do not share their states, the semantics can be presented as a macro-step semantics [21] (defined by means of the transition "$\longrightarrow$") in which the evaluation of all statements of a task takes place serially (without interleaving with any other task) until it gets the end of the method. In this case, we apply rule (mstep) to select an available task from an actor, namely we apply the function $selectA(S)$ to select non-deterministically one *active* actor in the state (i.e., an actor with a non-empty queue) and $selectT(\mathbf{r})$ to select non-deterministically one task of $\mathbf{r}$'s queue. The transition $\leadsto$ defines the evaluation within a given actor. We sometimes label transitions with $\mathbf{r} \cdot t$, the name of the actor $\mathbf{r}$ and task t selected in (mstep) The rules (getf) and (setf) read and write resp. an actor's field.

void ft(int n) {
  if (n > this.mx) {
    this ! wk(n,this.mx);
    this ! dg(n-this.mx);
  } else {
    this ! wk(n,n);
    this ! rp(1);
  }
}
	void wk(int n,int h) {
	  while (h > 0){
	    this.r = this.r * n;
	    n = n - 1;
	    h = h - 1;
	  }
	}
		void dg(int n) {
		  Fact wkr = new Fact(this,this.mx);
		  wkr ! ft(n);
		}
		void rp(int x) {
		  this.r = this.r * x;
		  if (this.b != null) this.b ! rp(this.r);
		}

Fig. 2. Running example with **class**Fact(Factb, intmx){intr = 1; ...}

The notation $h[f \mapsto l(y)]$ (resp. $l[x \mapsto h(f)]$) stands for the result of storing $l(y)$ in the field f (resp. $h(f)$ in variable x). The remaining sequential instructions are standard and thus omitted. In (new), an active task t in actor $\mathbf{r}$ creates an actor $\mathbf{r}_n^D$ of class D with a fresh identifier $n = \text{fresh}()$, which is introduced to the state with a free lock. Here $h' = newheap(D)$ stands for a default initialization on the fields of class D. (asy) spawns a new task (the initial state is created by *newlocals*) with a fresh task identifier $t_1 = \text{fresh}()$. We assume $\mathbf{r} \neq \mathbf{r}_1$, but the case $\mathbf{r} = \mathbf{r}_1$ is analogous, the new task t_1 is added to Q of $\mathbf{r}$. In what follows, a *derivation* E is a sequence $S_0 \longrightarrow \cdots \longrightarrow S_k$ of macro-steps (applications of (mstep)) starting from an initial state $\text{ac}(\mathbf{r}_0^C, \perp, l, \{tk(0, m, l, bd(m))\})$, where l (resp. h) maps parameters (resp. fields) to elements in $\mathbb{V}$ and $bd(m)$ is the sequence of instructions in the body of m. The derivation is *complete* if all actors in S_k are of the form $\text{ac}(\mathbf{r}, \perp, h, \{\})$. Since the execution is non-deterministic in the selection of actor and task, multiple derivations are possible from a state.

Example 1. Consider the class Fact in Fig. 2, which contains three fields Fact b, int mx and int r. Fields b and mx can be initialized in the constructor Fact(Fact b, int mx) whereas r is always initialized to 1. Let us suppose an actor a is asked to compute the factorial of n (by means of call a ! ft(n)). Actor a computes n∗(n−1)∗...∗(n−a.mx+1) by means of task wk(n, a.mx), and *delegates* to another actor the rest of the computation, by means of task dg(n−a.mx). When an actor is asked to compute the factorial of an n, which is smaller than its mx, then the call this ! wk(n, n) computes directly the factorial of n and the result is *reported* to its caller by means of task rp. The result is then reported back to the initial actor in a chain of rp tasks using field b, which stores the caller actor. The computed result of each actor is stored in field r. The program has a bug, which is only exploited in a concrete sequence of interleavings when at least three actors are involved. Let us consider two derivations that may arise among others from the initial state $S_0 = \text{ac}(\mathbf{r}_0, \perp, h_0, \{tk(0, \text{ft}, l_0, bd(\text{ft}))\})$, where $h_0(\mathbf{r}) = 1$, $h_0(\mathbf{b}) = \mathbf{null}$, $h_0(\text{mx}) = 2$ and $l_0(n) = 5$, i.e., we want to compute factorial of 5 with this.mx equals 2. Arrows are labeled with the identifier of the task(s) selected and it is executed entirely. The contents of the heap and local variables are showed when it is relevant or updated (we only show the new updates). We use h_i, l_i to denote the heap of actor $\mathbf{r}_i$ and the local variables of task t_i respectively.

(a) $S_0 \xrightarrow{0} ac(\mathbf{r}_0, 0, h_0, \{tk(1, \mathsf{wk}, [\mathsf{n}\mapsto 5, \mathsf{h}\mapsto 2], bd(\mathsf{wk})), tk(2, \mathsf{dg}, [\mathsf{n}\mapsto 3], bd(\mathsf{dg}))\}) \xrightarrow{(1,2)^*}$

(b) $ac(\mathbf{r}_0, \bot, [\mathsf{r}\mapsto 5*4], \{\}) \cdot ac(\mathbf{r}_1, \bot, [\mathsf{r}\mapsto 1, \mathsf{b}\mapsto \mathbf{r}_0], \{tk(3, \mathsf{ft}, [\mathsf{n}\mapsto 3], bd(\mathsf{ft}))\}) \xrightarrow{(3)^*}$

(c) $\begin{aligned} &ac(\mathbf{r}_0, \bot, h_0, \{\}) \cdot ac(\mathbf{r}_1, \bot, h_1, \{\}) \cdot ac(\mathbf{r}_2, \bot, h_2, \{tk(4, \mathsf{ft}, l_4, bd(\mathsf{ft}))\}) \\ &\quad h_1(\mathsf{r})=3*2, l_4(n)=1, h_2(\mathsf{r})=1, h_2(\mathsf{b})=\mathbf{r}_1 \end{aligned} \left.\begin{aligned}\\\\\end{aligned}\right\} \xrightarrow{(4)^*}$

(d) $ac(\mathbf{r}_0, \bot, h_0, \{\}) \cdot ac(\mathbf{r}_1, \bot, h_1, \{tk(5, \mathsf{rp}, [\mathsf{x}\mapsto 1], bd(\mathsf{rp}))\}) \cdot ac(\mathbf{r}_2, \bot, h_2, \{\}) \xrightarrow{(5)^*}$

(e) $ac(\mathbf{r}_0, \bot, [\mathsf{r} = 5*4*3*2], \{\}) \cdot ac(\mathbf{r}_1, \bot, h_1, \{\}) \cdot ac(\mathbf{r}_2, \bot, h_2, \{\})$

Note that after executing task 5 we compute the final state (e), where h_0 stores in the field r the value of factorial of 5. Suppose now that, in the above trace, from (b), we first select method dg but we do not execute method wk, and all calls to method rp are executed before method wk. Then:

(c) $\left\{\begin{aligned} &ac(\mathbf{r}_0, \bot, h_0, \{\}) \cdot ac(\mathbf{r}_1, \bot, h_1, \{tk(4, \mathsf{wk}, l_4, bd(\mathsf{wk}))\}) \cdot \\ &ac(\mathbf{r}_2, \bot, [\mathsf{b}\mapsto \mathbf{r}_1], \{tk(5, \mathsf{ft}, [\mathsf{n}\mapsto 1], bd(\mathsf{ft}))\}) \end{aligned}\right\} \xrightarrow{(5)^*}$

(d) $\left\{\begin{aligned} &ac(\mathbf{r}_0, \bot, h_0, \{\}) \cdot ac(\mathbf{r}_1, \bot, h_1, \{tk(4, \mathsf{wk}, l_4, bd(\mathsf{wk}))\}) \cdot \\ &ac(\mathbf{r}_2, \bot, [\mathsf{b}\mapsto \mathbf{r}_1], \{tk(6, \mathsf{wk}, l_6, bd(\mathsf{wk})), tk(7, \mathsf{rp}, l_7, bd(\mathsf{rp}))\}) \end{aligned}\right\} \xrightarrow{(7)^*}$

(e) $\left\{\begin{aligned} &ac(\mathbf{r}_0, \bot, h_0, \{\}) \cdot ac(\mathbf{r}_1, \bot, h_1, \{tk(4, \mathsf{wk}, l_4, bd(\mathsf{wk})), tk(8, \mathsf{rp}, l_8, bd(\mathsf{rp}))\}) \cdot \\ &ac(\mathbf{r}_2, \bot, h_2, \{tk(6, \mathsf{wk}, l_6, bd(\mathsf{wk}))\}) \end{aligned}\right\} \xrightarrow{(8)^*}$

(f) $\left\{\begin{aligned} &ac(\mathbf{r}_0, \bot, h_0, \{tk(9, \mathsf{rp}, l_9, bd(\mathsf{rp}))\}) \cdot ac(\mathbf{r}_1, \bot, h_1, \{tk(4, \mathsf{wk}, l_4, bd(\mathsf{wk}))\}) \cdot \\ &ac(\mathbf{r}_2, \bot, h_2, \{tk(6, \mathsf{wk}, l_6, bd(\mathsf{wk}))\}) \end{aligned}\right\} \xrightarrow{(9)^*}$

(g) $ac(\mathbf{r}_0, \bot, [\mathsf{r}\mapsto 5*4], \{\}) \cdot ac(\mathbf{r}_1, \bot, [\mathsf{r}\mapsto 3*2], \{\}) \cdot ac(\mathbf{r}_2, \bot, [\mathsf{r}\mapsto 1], \{\})\}$

In the last step we have computed $h_0(\mathsf{r})=5*4$, which is an incorrect result, hence exploiting the above-mentioned bug. Although the execution at this point is not finished, none of the pending tasks will modify the value of field r in $\mathbf{r}_0$.   □

3   Symbolic Execution

The main component of our TCG framework is *symbolic execution* [12,17,19, 20,23], whereby instead of on actual values, programs are executed on symbolic values, represented as *constraint variables*. The outcome is a set of equivalence classes of inputs, each of them consisting of the *constraints* that characterize a set of feasible concrete executions of a program that takes the same path and, optionally constraints, which characterize the output of the execution. For instance, consider method int abs(int x){if (x<0) return -x; else return x;}. The outcome is the set $\{\langle \mathsf{X}<0, \mathsf{Y}\doteq -\mathsf{X}\rangle, \langle \mathsf{X}\geq 0, \mathsf{Y}\doteq \mathsf{X}\rangle\}$ where Y refers to the return value. Essentially, there are two elements in the set which will lead to two *test inputs*, the first one captures the execution of the then branch, with the constraint X<0 on the input and Y=−X on the output. The second element captures the execution of the else branch. Symbolic execution thus produces a set of test cases satisfying the path coverage criterion. We use uppercase characters to syntactically distinguish constraint variables from ordinary program variables. In our simplified language, we consider two types of equality and inequality constraints, those that involve integer values and those that involve references (the latter refer to aliasing conditions between references). The constraint variables can represent field or variable names. Given an infinite set of constraint variable names $X, Y, F, G, \ldots \in \mathcal{V}$, an *atomic constraint* φ is of the form:

$$\varphi ::= X \doteq n \mid X \doteq Y \mid X > Y \mid X \doteq ref$$

$$(\text{mstep})_\Phi \ \frac{selectA(\mathcal{S}) = ac(ref, \bot, \_, \mathcal{Q}, \_), \mathcal{Q} \neq \emptyset, selectT(ref) = t, S\square\mathcal{I} \overset{ref \cdot t}{\leadsto}{}^*_\Phi S'\square\mathcal{I}'}{S\square\mathcal{I} \overset{ref \cdot t}{\longrightarrow}_\Phi S'\square\mathcal{I}'}$$

$$(\text{setf})_\Phi \ \frac{t = tk(t, m, \rho, \mathsf{this}.f = y; s), \theta' = \theta[f \mapsto F], \varphi = \{F \dot{=} \rho(y)\}}{ac(ref, t, \theta, \mathcal{Q} \cup \{t\}, \Phi) \leadsto_\Phi ac(ref, t, \theta', \mathcal{Q} \cup \{t'\}, \Phi \cup \varphi)}$$

$$(\text{getf})_\Phi \ \frac{t = tk(t, m, \rho, x = \mathsf{this}.f; s), \rho_1 = \rho[x \mapsto X], \varphi = \{X \dot{=} \theta(f)\}}{ac(ref, t, \theta, \mathcal{Q} \cup \{t\}, \Phi) \leadsto_\Phi ac(ref, t, \theta, \mathcal{Q} \cup \{tk(t, m, \rho_1, s)\}, \Phi \cup \varphi)}$$

$$(\text{new})_\Phi \ \frac{t = tk(t, m, \rho, x = \mathsf{new}\ D; s), n{=}\mathsf{fresh}(), \rho_1 {=} \rho[x \mapsto X], \Phi_1 {=} init(D), \varphi {=} \{X \dot{=} \mathsf{r}_n^D\}}{ac(ref, t, \theta, \mathcal{Q} \cup \{t\}, \Phi) \leadsto_\Phi}$$
$$ac(ref, t, \theta, \mathcal{Q} \cup \{tk(t, m, \rho_1, s)\}, \Phi \cup \varphi) \cdot ac(\mathsf{r}_n^D, \bot, \theta_\mathsf{s}, \{\}, \Phi_1)$$

$$(\text{asy})_{\Phi_1} \ \frac{\begin{array}{c} t = tk(t, m, \rho, x\ !\ m_1(\bar{z}); s), \rho(x)\ \text{is object-bounded in}\ \Phi \\ \Phi \models \rho(x) \dot{=} ref', t_1 {=} \mathsf{fresh}(), \mathsf{fresh}(m_1(\bar{w})\{s_1;\}), \Phi' {=} \Pi_{\rho(\bar{z})} \Phi \cup \{\rho_\mathsf{s}(\bar{w}) \dot{=} \rho(\bar{z})\} \end{array}}{\begin{array}{c} ac(ref, t, \theta, \mathcal{Q} \cup \{t\}, \Phi) \cdot ac(ref', \_, \theta', \mathcal{Q}_1, \Phi_1) \leadsto_\Phi \\ ac(ref, t, \theta, \mathcal{Q} \cup \{t'\}, \Phi) \cdot ac(ref', \_, \theta', \mathcal{Q}_1 \cup \{tk(t_1, m_1, \rho_\mathsf{s}, s_1)\}, \Phi_1 \cup \Phi') \end{array}}$$

$$(\text{asy})_{\Phi_2} \ \frac{\begin{array}{c} t = tk(t, m, \rho, x\ !\ m_1(\bar{z}); s), class(x) {=} D, \rho(x)\ \text{is not object-bounded in}\ \Phi \\ t_1 {=} \mathsf{fresh}(), \mathsf{fresh}(m_1(\bar{w})\{s_1;\}), \Phi' {=} \Pi_{\rho(\bar{z})} \Phi \cup \{\rho_\mathsf{s}(\bar{w}) \dot{=} \rho(\bar{z})\} \end{array}}{\begin{array}{c} ac(ref, t, \theta, \mathcal{Q} \cup \{t\}, \Phi) \cdot ac(\mathsf{s}_n^D, \_, \theta', \mathcal{Q}_1, \Phi_1) \leadsto_\Phi \\ ac(ref, t, \theta, \mathcal{Q} \cup \{t'\}, \Phi \cup \{\rho(x) \dot{=} \mathsf{s}_n^D\}) \cdot ac(\mathsf{s}_n^D, \_, \theta', \mathcal{Q}_1 \cup \{tk(t_1, m_1, \rho_\mathsf{s}, s_1)\}, \Phi_1 \cup \Phi') \end{array}}$$

$$(\text{asy})_{\Phi_3} \ \frac{\begin{array}{c} t = tk(t, m, \rho, x\ !\ m_1(\bar{z}); s), class(x) {=} D, \rho(x)\ \text{is not object-bounded in}\ \Phi, n{=}\mathsf{fresh}() \\ t_1 {=} \mathsf{fresh}(), \mathsf{fresh}(m_1(\bar{w})\{s_1;\}), \Phi' {=} \{\theta_\mathsf{s}(\mathsf{this}) \dot{=} \mathsf{s}_n^D\} \cup \Pi_{\rho(\bar{z})} \Phi \cup \{\rho_\mathsf{s}(\bar{w}) \dot{=} \rho(\bar{z})\} \end{array}}{\begin{array}{c} ac(ref, t, \theta, \mathcal{Q} \cup \{t\}, \Phi)\square\mathcal{I} \leadsto_\Phi ac(ref, t, \theta, \mathcal{Q} \cup \{t'\}, \Phi \cup \{\rho(x) \dot{=} \mathsf{s}_n^D\}) \cdot \\ ac(\mathsf{s}_n^D, \bot, \theta_\mathsf{s}, \{tk(t_1, m_1, \rho_\mathsf{s}, s_1)\}, \Phi')\square\mathcal{I} \cup \{\langle \mathsf{s}_n^D, \theta_\mathsf{s}\rangle\} \end{array}}$$

$$(\text{return})_\Phi \ \frac{t = tk(t, m, \rho, \epsilon)}{ac(ref, t, \theta, \mathcal{Q} \cup \{t\}, \Phi) \leadsto_\Phi ac(ref, \bot, \theta, \mathcal{Q}, \Phi)}$$

Fig. 3. Symbolic execution calculus. t' stands for $tk(t, m, \rho, s)$

where $ref \in Ref^*$ can be either r_n^C or s_n^C, $n \in \mathbb{N}$ and C is a class name. Each element of the form r_n^C stands for a reference of class C created by using a **new** instruction. References of the form s_n^C refer to actors not created with **new** but arising from asynchronous calls in which the calling actor is unknown at the time of the call. We denote by Φ a conjunction of atomic constraints. We use simply r (resp. s) instead of r_n^C (resp. s_n^C) when the values of C and n are irrelevant. We use ref to refer either to r or s and sometimes set notations to refer to Φ.

Figure 3 presents the operational semantics of symbolic execution for the concurrent instructions (the sequential ones are standard). A *symbolic state* has the form $\mathcal{S}\square\mathcal{I}$, where $\mathcal{S}$ is a collection of *symbolic actors* and $\mathcal{I}$ is a set of actors required to know the actors that must be in the initial state to get to the final state, and thus be able to build the test cases in Sect. 5.2. For simplicity, we omit $\mathcal{I}$ in all rules except for $(\text{asy})_{\Phi_3}$, since it is the only rule that modifies $\mathcal{I}$. A *symbolic actor* is represented as $ac(ref, t, \theta, \mathcal{Q}, \Phi)$, where $ref \in Ref^*$ is the actor identifier, t is the identifier of the active task, $\mathcal{Q}$ is the queue of symbolic pending tasks, Φ is a set of constraints involving the fields of the actor and the variables of its tasks, and $\theta : \mathcal{F}(C) \cup \{\mathsf{this}\} \mapsto \mathcal{V}$ is called the *field renaming* that maps fields of class C and the this actor to $\mathcal{V}$. In particular, if f is a field of class C, then

$\theta(f)$ is the current constraint variable F representing f in Φ. A *symbolic task* $tk(t, m, \rho, s)$ of a method m in a class C contains the sequence of instructions s to be executed together with the current renaming $\rho : vars(bd(m)) \mapsto \mathcal{V}$ of those variables in m, where $vars(A)$ stands for the set of variables occurring at any entity A. The constraints associated to these variables are stored in the actor in Φ. As for fields, the renaming is required to build correctly the set of atomic constraints Φ and keep the relation between these constraints and the original variables of method m. An initial state to symbolically execute $m(\bar{x})$ on $\mathbf{s}_n^C$ has the form $\mathcal{S}_0 \Box \mathcal{I}_0$, where $\mathcal{S}_0 = \mathrm{ac}(\mathbf{s}_0^C, \bot, \theta_s, \{tk(0, m, \rho_s, bd(m))\}, \{\theta_s(\mathrm{this}) \doteq \mathbf{s}_0^C\})$, θ_s (resp. ρ_s) is a starting fresh mapping, i.e., $\theta_s(f)$ (resp. $\rho_s(x)$) are mapped to fresh variables and $\mathcal{I}_0 = \langle \mathbf{s}_0^C, m(\bar{x}), \theta_s, \rho_s \rangle$.

The different rules of the symbolic semantics in Fig. 3 extend those in Fig. 1 with constraint handling as follows. As notation, $\rho_1 = \rho[x \mapsto X]$ maps in ρ variable x to the fresh variable X. Rule $(\mathsf{setf})_\Phi$ updates the field mapping θ with the fresh variable F, and stores the new constraint $F \doteq \rho(y)$ in Φ. Since a field is modified, the mapping θ in the actor must be updated. However, in rule $(\mathsf{getf})_\Phi$, the field f is read and thus, it is not required to update θ but ρ. Rule $(\mathsf{new})_\Phi$ adds the constraint $X \doteq \mathbf{r}_n^D$ to Φ and updates ρ. The function $\Phi_1 = init(D)$ initializes Φ_1 with the corresponding initialization of the fields in D and the this actor, i.e., $\theta_s(\mathrm{this}) \doteq \mathbf{r}_n^D \in \Phi_1$ and if a field f in D is initialized to a value v, then $\theta_s(f) \doteq v$ will be in Φ_1. Rule $(\mathsf{return})_\Phi$ allows us to apply rule $(\mathsf{mstep})_\Phi$. A main aspect is the treatment of asynchronous calls $x\ !\ m_1(\bar{z})$, which distinguishes three cases:

1. $(\mathsf{asy})_{\Phi_1}$: *Object x exists in the store.* This condition is checked by seeing if x is bounded in Φ. Formally we say that x is *object-bounded* in Φ if $\rho(x) \in vars(\Phi)$ and $\Phi \models \rho(x) \doteq ref'$, for some actor ref'. In this case, the task m_1 is introduced in the queue of actor ref'. Here $\mathrm{fresh}(m_1(\bar{w})\{s_1;\})$ is a fresh renaming of the variables in m_1. We use $\Pi_{\rho(\bar{z})}\Phi$ to denote the projection of Φ on the variables $\rho(\bar{z})$, i.e., the constraints in Φ involving the input parameters $\bar{z}$. Note that the constraint Φ' is added to Φ_1 in actor ref' in order to store the relation between the formal and actual parameters of method m_1.

2. $(\mathsf{asy})_{\Phi_2}$: *Object x is compatible with objects in the state but $\rho(x)$ is not bounded in Φ.* If $\rho(x)$ is not bounded in Φ, this means either that $\rho(x) \notin vars(\Phi)$, or that $\Phi \not\models \rho(x) \doteq ref'$. Then we need to consider all possible aliasings with actors of compatible type that are in $\mathcal{S}$ whose actor identifiers have not been created using **new**, i.e., those whose actor identifier has the form $\mathbf{s}^D$. For example, for the instructions $\mathsf{y} = \mathbf{new}\ D; \mathsf{x}\ !\ m_1(\bar{z})$ and assuming that x is not bounded, it is incorrect to bound variable x to y, as x must be a different reference. Then if $\mathcal{S}$ contains some actor of class D not created with **new**, then we can assume that $\rho(x)$ and such actor are aliased, and thus store the call in the queue of $\mathbf{s}_n^D$ and $\rho(x) \doteq \mathbf{s}_n^D$ in Φ. Function $class(x)$ returns the class of actor x.

3. $(\mathsf{asy})_{\Phi_3}$: *Actor x corresponds to an actor not yet created.* Then, a new actor is created, forcing $\rho(x)$ to be equals to it. Importantly, this situation requires that an actor of class D be in the initial state. Hence, a new identifier $\mathbf{s}_n^D$ corresponding to an actor not created with **new**, must be introduced in the

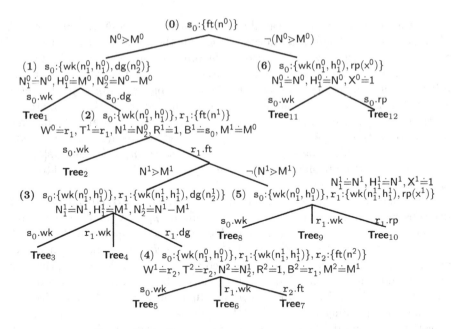

Fig. 4. Symbolic execution for the running example

set $\mathcal{I}$ in order to be able to reconstruct the initial state at the end of the computation. Note that rules $(\mathsf{asy})_{\Phi_2}$ and $(\mathsf{asy})_{\Phi_3}$ are both applicable under the same conditions what generates non-determinism in symbolic execution.

Example 2. Figure 4 shows an excerpt of the symbolic execution tree of method ft. We write **Tree**$_i$, $1 \leq i \leq 12$, to denote partial execution trees, which are not shown due to space limitations. The nodes contain the actor identifiers and their queues of tasks in braces. A superscript in a variable corresponds to the identifier of the actor to which it belongs, e.g., R^2 refers to field r of actor s_2. Subscripts are used to generate fresh variables consecutively. The initial field renaming in the root node is $\theta_s^0 = \{\mathsf{this} \mapsto T^0, r \mapsto R^0, mx \mapsto M^0, b \mapsto B^0\}$, the constraint attached to s_0 is $\Phi^0 = \{T^0 \doteq s_0\}$ and the initial renaming for local variables in $\mathsf{ft}(n^0)$ is $\rho_s^0 = \{n^0 \mapsto N^0\}$. The left branch from node **(0)** corresponds to the **if** instruction for the call $\mathsf{ft}(n^0)$. The condition $n^0 > \mathsf{this.mx}$ produces the constraint $\rho_s^0(n^0) > \theta_s^0(mx)$, i.e., $N^0 > M^0$. Since $\Phi^0 \models \theta_s^0(\mathsf{this}) \doteq s_0$ holds, rule $(\mathsf{asy})_{\Phi_1}$ can be applied to both asynchronous calls (the applications of $(\mathsf{asy})_{\Phi_2}$ and $(\mathsf{asy})_{\Phi_3}$ will be illustrated in the tree in Fig. 5). For the call $\mathsf{this} \,!\, \mathsf{wk}(n^0, \mathsf{this.mx})$, we generate $\mathsf{wk}(n_1^0, h_1^0)$ as fresh renaming for the method, together with the initial renaming $\rho_1^0 = \{n_1^0 \mapsto N_1^0, h_1^0 \mapsto H_1^0\}$. Hence, the constraints $N_1^0 \doteq N^0$ and $H_1^0 \doteq M^0$ are added to the constraints for s_0. Similarly, the constraint $N_2^0 \doteq N^0 - M^0$ originates from using $\mathsf{dg}(n_2^0)$ as renaming for $\mathsf{dg}(n - \mathsf{this.mx})$. The right branch of node **(0)** is associated to the **else** of method ft. In this case, the renaming ρ_1^0 associated to task $s_0.\mathsf{wk}$ maps n_1^0 (resp. h_1^0) to N_1^0 (resp. H_1^0). Similarly, the initial renaming ρ_2^0 for task $s_0.\mathsf{rp}$ maps x^0 to

X^0. Since in (1) we have two tasks, a new branching is required to try the two reorderings. The branch s_0.dg executes the call to dg and thus, after applying rules (new)$_\Phi$ and (asy)$_{\Phi_1}$, a new actor r_1 appears in (2) with a corresponding call to ft in its queue. The constraint $W^0 \doteq r_1$ is added to the constraints of actor s_0, where W^0 is the fresh renaming for variable wkr. From (2), if we execute r_1.ft, branches (3) and (5) are generated. From (3) the execution of r_1.dg creates a new actor r_2 (node (4)) as in (2). □

4 Less Redundant Exploration in Symbolic Execution

Already in the context of dynamic execution, a naïve exploration of the search space to reach all possible system configurations does not scale. The problem is exacerbated in the context of symbolic execution due to the additional non-determinism introduced by the use of constraint variables instead of concrete values. There has been intensive work to avoid the exploration of redundant states, which lead to the same configuration. Partial-order reduction (POR) [9,11] is a general theory that helps mitigate the problem by exploring the subset of all possible interleavings, which lead to a different configuration. Concrete algorithms have been proposed in [3,10,22] for dynamic testing.

In this section, we adapt to the context of symbolic execution and improve the notion of temporal stability of an actor introduced in [3] to avoid redundant exploration. This notion states that, at a given state, if we first select a *temporarily stable actor*, i.e., an actor to which no other actors will post tasks, unless it executes, it is guaranteed that it is not necessary to try executions in which the other actors in the state execute before this one, thus, avoiding such redundant explorations. Note that a temporarily stable actor at a state, might become non-stable in a subsequent state if tasks are added to it after it executes again, hence the temporal nature of the property. This notion is of general applicability and can be used within the algorithms of [10,22]. The original notion of [3] is here extended to consider symbolic states and strengthened to allow the case in which an actor receives a task, which is *independent* of those in the queue of the actor. As it is well-known in concurrent programming [5], tasks t and t' are *independent* if t does not write in the shared locations that t' accesses, and viceversa. We say that t is independent of $\mathcal{Q}$, denoted as $indep(t, \mathcal{Q})$, if t and t' are independent for all $t' \in \mathcal{Q}$.

Definition 1 (temporarily stable actor). $ac(ref, t, \theta, \mathcal{Q}, \Phi)$ *is temporarily stable in* $\mathcal{S}_0$ *iff, for any* $\mathcal{E}$ *starting from* $\mathcal{S}_0$ *and for any subtrace* $\mathcal{S}_0 \xrightarrow{*}_\Phi \mathcal{S}_n \in \mathcal{E}$ *in which the actor ref is not selected, we have* $ac(ref, t, \theta, \mathcal{Q}', \Phi) \in \mathcal{S}_n$ *and for all* $t' \in \mathcal{Q}' - \mathcal{Q}$ *it holds that* $indep(t', \mathcal{Q})$.

Our goal is to define sufficient conditions that ensure actors stability and can be computed during symbolic execution. To this end, given a method m_1 of class C_1, we define $Ch(C_1{:}m_1)$ as the set of all chains of method calls of the form $C_1{:}m_1 \rightarrow C_2{:}m_2 \rightarrow \cdots \rightarrow C_k{:}m_k$, with $k \geq 2$, s.t. $C_i{:}m_i \neq C_j{:}m_j$, $2 \leq i \leq k-1$, $i \neq j$ and there exists a call within $bd(C_i{:}m_i)$ to method $C_{i+1}{:}m_{i+1}$, $1 \leq i < k$. This captures all paths $C_2{:}m_2 \to C_{k-1}{:}m_{k-1}$, without cycles, that go from $C_1{:}m_1$ to $C_k{:}m_k$. The set $Ch(C_1{:}m_1)$ can be computed statically for all methods.

Theorem 1 (sufficient conditions for temporal stability). $ac(ref^{C_n}, \text{-}, \text{-}, Q, \text{-}) \in \mathcal{S}$, *is temporarily stable in* $\mathcal{S}$, *if for every* $ac(ref^{C_1}, \text{-}, \text{-}, Q_1, \text{-}) \in \mathcal{S}$, $ref^{C_n} \neq ref^{C_1}$ *and for every* $tk(\text{-}, m_1, \text{-}, \text{-}) \in Q_1$, *one of the following conditions holds:*

1. *There is no chain* $C_1{:}m_1 \to \cdots \to C_n{:}m_n \in Ch(C_1{:}m_1)$; *or*
2. *For all chains* $C_1{:}m_1 \to \cdots \to C_n{:}m_n \in Ch(C_1{:}m_1)$, m_n *is independent of* Q; *or*
3. *For all chains* $C_1{:}m_1 \to \cdots \to C_n{:}m_n \in Ch(C_1{:}m_1)$, *for all* $ac(ref^{C_i}, \text{-}, \theta, Q_2, \Phi) \in \mathcal{S}$, $1 \leq i \leq n-1$, *and for all* $tk(\text{-}, \text{-}, \rho, \text{-}) \in Q_2$, *it holds that* $\Phi \cup \theta(f) \dot{=} r^{C_n}$ *is unsatisfiable, for all* $f \in \mathcal{F}(C_i)$ *and* $\Phi \cup \rho(x) \dot{=} r^{C_n}$ *is unsatisfiable, for all* x *occurring in* $vars(\Phi) - \mathcal{F}(C_i)$.

Intuitively, the theorem above ensures that no ref^{C_1} can modify the queue of ref^{C_n}. This is because (1) there is no transitive call from m_1 to any method of class C_n, or (2) if there is, the call is independent of those in ref^{C_n}, or (3) there are transitive (non-independent) calls from m_1 to some method of class C_n, but no reference to actor ref^{C_n} can be found.

Example 3. Node (**2**) has two actors and the initial mapping for r_1 contains $\theta_s^1(b)=B^1$. Points 1 and 2 of Theorem 1 does not hold, since from ft (in the queue of r_1) there exists a call to rp and rp and wk are not independent. Besides, $B^1 \dot{=} s_0$ occurs as constraint in (**2**) and thus Point 3 of Theorem 1 neither holds. Hence, actor s_0 is not temporarily stable. However, actor r_1 is temporarily stable in (**2**), since task wk in the queue of s_0 does not call any method of class Fact. This means that **Tree$_2$** in Fig. 4 is redundant and hence not expanded. A similar reasoning allows us to conclude that trees **Tree$_3$**, **Tree$_5$**, **Tree$_6$** and **Tree$_8$** are redundant. To illustrate the need of condition 2, consider a state with two actors r_0, r_1, with task dg resp. ft in the queue of r_0 resp. r_1 and no associated constraints. Then, for both actors neither condition 1 nor 3 in Theorem 1 hold. However, since method dg is independent of the remaining methods of class Fact, condition 2 holds and both actors are temporarily stable. Finally note that, as explained in [3], **Tree$_1$** and **Tree$_4$** are detected redundant, since tasks wk and dg are independent. □

5   Generation of Test Cases

An important problem for the generation of test cases for a given method (without knowledge on the input values) is that the execution tree to be traversed by symbolically executing the method is in general infinite. Hence, it is required to fix a *coverage and termination criterion* (CTC) to guarantee that the number of paths traversed remains finite, while at the same time an interesting set of test-cases is generated.

5.1   Coverage and Termination Criteria for Actor Systems

Given a task executing on an actor, we can ensure its local termination by using existing CTC developed in the sequential setting. For instance, we can use the loop-count criteria [15], which limits the number of times we iterate on loops (and the number of recursive calls) to a threshold k_l. Other existing criteria defined for sequential programs would be valid as well. Unfortunately, the application of these CTC criteria to all tasks of a state does not guarantee termination of the whole TCG process. There are two factors that threaten termination: (1) we can switch from one task to another an infinite number of times, (2) we can create an unbounded number of actors. The following example shows the first factor, a program for which the loop-k criterion does not guarantee termination unless we limit the number of task switches per actor.

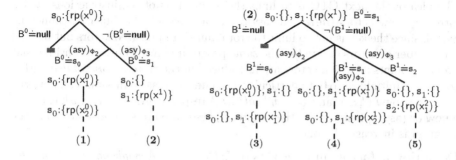

Fig. 5. Task-level and object-number CTC criteria

Example 4. The execution tree for rp(x) in showed in two fragments in Fig. 5 (the right part corresponds to the execution from node (**2**) in the left part). The branch marked with (**1**) is infinite due to the task rp is continuously introduced and extracted from the queue of s_0. By limiting the number of task switches per actor it is possible to prune branch (**1**) and to continue the execution by exploring the branch corresponding to $B^0 \doteq s_1$.   □

In our symbolic semantics, we can easily track the number of task switches per actor *ref* by counting the number of applications of rule (mstep)$_\phi$ on *ref*.

Definition 2 (task-level CTC). *Let* $k \in \mathbb{N}^+$. *A symbolic execution* $\mathcal{E} \equiv \mathcal{S}_0 \Box \mathcal{I}_0 \longrightarrow_\phi^* \mathcal{S}_n \Box \mathcal{I}_n$ *satisfies the task-level CTC iff for all actor ref* $\in \mathcal{S}_n$, *it holds that ref has been selected at most* k *times in* $\mathcal{E}$ *by rule* (mstep)$_\phi$.

Even by limiting the number of task switches per actor, a second factor for non-termination arises when we create an unbounded number of actors for which, the number of task switches does not exceed the limit allowed. New actors arise when applying either (new)$_\phi$ or (asy)$_{\phi_3}$ in Fig. 3. Next example illustrates it.

Example 5. Using the task-level CTC, the branch marked with (**2**) in Fig. 5 can be explored. Such branch comes from the application of rule (asy)$_{\Phi_3}$, which generates a new actor s_1 when executing the asynchronous call this.b ! rp(this.r). The continuation of the branch is detailed in Fig. 5 (right). Branch (**3**) will be pruned by using the task-level CTC because field b in actor s_0 points to s_1 ($B^0 \doteq s_1$) and viceversa, such field points to s_0 in actor s_1 ($B^1 \doteq s_0$). Similarly, branch (**4**) is pruned by the task-level criteria, since the field b in actor s_1 points to s_1 ($B^1 \doteq s_1$). Branch (**5**) behaves differently to the others, since the application of rule (asy)$_{\Phi_3}$ generates a new actor in each execution step and thus the number of new actors grows infinitely. By annotating the instruction this.b ! rp(this.r) in method rp with a counter initialized to 0, it is possible to count the number of times that such instruction is executed. When such counter exceeds a fixed limit, the branch can be pruned.   □

The idea of the next CTC is to limit the application of the instructions, which introduce new actors (**new** and (asy)$_{\Phi_3}$) to a threshold k_o. Such k_o cannot be global, since the key is not to limit the total number of created actors but instead the number of actors created at the same program point. Thus, we consider that program points at which actors are introduced in the state are *annotated* with a counter c_o initialized to 0. In particular, each **new** and asynchronous call have the form $\langle x = \textbf{new } C, c_o \rangle$, and $\langle x = y \mathbin! m(\bar{z}), c_o \rangle$ respectively. When a task executes a **new** or (asy)$_{\Phi_3}$ instruction, the counter c_o associated to such instruction in the program is increased by one.

Definition 3 (actor-number CTC). *Let $k_o \in \mathbb{N}^+$. A symbolic execution $\mathcal{E}$ for an annotated program P satisfies the* actor-number CTC *iff for all instructions $\langle \_, c_o \rangle$ in P it holds that $c_o \leq k_o$.*

5.2   Test Cases for Actor Systems

The generation of *test cases* for a method $m(\bar{x})$ using the above CTC is as follows. We start the symbolic execution of $m(\bar{x})$ using the rules in Fig. 3 such that each derivation is expanded until (a) it is *complete* (i.e., all actors are idle and have empty queues) or (b) one of the CTC in Sect. 5.1 is not satisfied. In case (a), we produce a test case associated to the complete derivation, which defines the initial and final states of such execution. In the context of actor systems, the state is given by the constraints gathered along symbolic execution on the fields of the different actors, denoted as fields(ref, Φ, θ), where ref is the reference of the actor, Φ are the constraints for its field values and θ is the renaming relating constraint variables in Φ with fields. Besides, in the initial state we want to obtain also the constraints gathered for the arguments $\bar{x}$ of the method $m(\bar{x})$. We use the notation args($m(\bar{x}), \Phi, \rho$) to denote the constraints Φ imposed on $\bar{x}$, together with the initial renaming ρ, which keeps the association between $\bar{x}$ and Φ. Due to the non-determinism in symbolic execution, the execution of $m(\bar{x})$ produces a symbolic tree such that a test case is obtained from each of its complete derivations (or branches). The following definition presents the notion of test case associated to a given complete derivation.

Definition 4 (test case). *Let* $\mathcal{E} \equiv S_0 \square \mathcal{I}_0 \xrightarrow{*}_\Phi S_n \square \mathcal{I}_n$ *be a complete symbolic execution such that* $S_0 \square \mathcal{I}_0$ *is an initial state, where* $\mathcal{I}_0 = \{\langle s_0^C, m(\bar{x}), \theta_s, \rho_s \rangle\}$. *The test case for* $\mathcal{E}$ *is defined as the tuple* $\langle \mathcal{A}_I, \mathcal{A}_O \rangle$, *where:*

$$
\begin{aligned}
\mathcal{A}_I = \ &\{\mathsf{args}(m(\bar{x}), \Phi_I, \rho_s) \mid \mathsf{ac}(s_0^C, \_, \_, \_, \Phi) \in S_n, \Phi_I = \Pi_{\rho_s(\bar{x})} \Phi\} \cup \\
&\{\mathsf{fields}(s_0^C, \Phi_I, \theta_s) \mid \mathsf{ac}(s_0^C, \_, \_, \_, \Phi) \in S_n, \Phi_I = \Pi_{\theta_s(\mathcal{F}(C))} \Phi\} \cup \\
&\{\mathsf{fields}(s_k^D, \Phi_I, \theta_s') \mid \mathsf{ac}(s_k^D, \_, \_, \_, \Phi) \in S_n, \langle s_k^D, \theta_s' \rangle \in \mathcal{I}_n, \Phi_I = \Pi_{\theta_s'(\mathcal{F}(D))} \Phi\} \\
\mathcal{A}_O = \ &\{\mathsf{fields}(\mathit{ref}_k^D, \Phi_O, \theta) \mid \mathsf{ac}(\mathit{ref}_k^D, \_, \theta, \_, \Phi) \in S_n, \Phi_O = \Pi_{\theta(\mathcal{F}(C))} \Phi\}
\end{aligned}
$$

In the above definition, we can observe that the test cases are given in terms of the constraints in Φ. An essential aspect is that the renamings ρ_s and θ_s allow us to establish the relation between the names for fields and variables in the program and their corresponding constraint ones in order to generate a correct test case. In particular, the initial state of the test case $\mathcal{A}_I$ contains two types of information: (1) in args we store the information about the constraints gathered for the method arguments $\bar{x}$ that is obtained by projecting the constraints Φ on the original names for the input arguments that were stored in ρ_s, (2) in fields the constraints for the actor fields that are obtained by projecting Φ on the initial names for the actor fields that are stored in θ_s. The final state contains the constraints for the fields gathered in the final state of the computation and applying the renamings that have been computed in θ until the last state.

Example 6. Let us consider the TCG of method $\mathsf{ft}(n^0)$ with limits 1, 5 and 2 resp. for the constants k in criteria loop-k, task-level and actor-number. The following two test cases $\mathcal{A}_1 = \langle \mathcal{A}_I, \mathcal{A}_O \rangle$ and $\mathcal{A}_2 = \langle \mathcal{A}_I, \mathcal{A}_O' \rangle$, are generated from two of the derivations in **Tree$_7$** of Fig. 4, where:

$$
\begin{aligned}
\mathcal{A}_I = \ &\{\mathsf{args}(\mathsf{ft}(n^0), \{N^0 \dot{=} 3\}, \rho_s^0), \mathsf{fields}(s_0^{\mathsf{Fact}}, \{M^0 \dot{=} 1, B^0 \dot{=} \mathbf{null}\}, \theta_s^0)\} \\
\mathcal{A}_O = \ &\{\mathsf{fields}(s_0^{\mathsf{Fact}}, \{M_a^0 \dot{=} 1, B_b^0 \dot{=} \mathbf{null}, R_c^0 \dot{=} R^0 * 3 * 2 * 1\}, \theta_f^0), \ \mathsf{fields}(s_1^{\mathsf{Fact}}, \{M_d^1 \dot{=} 1, \\
&B_e^1 \dot{=} s_0^{\mathsf{Fact}}, R_f^1 \dot{=} 2\}, \theta_f^1), \mathsf{fields}(s_2^{\mathsf{Fact}}, \{M_g^2 \dot{=} 1, B_h^2 \dot{=} s_1^{\mathsf{Fact}}, R_i^2 \dot{=} 1\}, \theta_f^2)\}
\end{aligned}
$$

being $\mathcal{A}_O'$ as $\mathcal{A}_O$ but replacing the first entry for s_0^{Fact} by $\mathsf{fields}(s_0^{\mathsf{Fact}}, \{M_a^0 \dot{=} 1, B_b^0 \dot{=} \mathbf{null}, R_c^0 \dot{=} R^0 * 3 * 1 * 1\}, \theta_f^0)$. The renamings θ_s^0 and ρ_s^0 are defined in Example 2 and the remaining ones are defined as $\theta_f^i(\mathsf{mx}) = M_{\_}^i$, $\theta_f^i(\mathsf{b}) = B_{\_}^i$, $\theta_f^i(\mathsf{r}) = R_{\_}^i$, where $1 \le i \le 2$ and "$\_$" refers to the corresponding subindex. Note that test case $\mathcal{A}_2$ reveals the bug in the program, which is only observable when an intermediate actor in the chain of involved actors (in this case actor s_1^{Fact}), executes task rp before task wk, hence sending to its caller a partial result. $\qquad\square$

From the constraints in the test cases, it is possible to produce actual values by relying on standard *labeling* mechanisms. It is also straightforward to automatically generate xUnit unit tests [4].

Example 7. The following concrete test case is obtained from $\mathcal{A}_1$:

$$
\begin{aligned}
\mathcal{T}_I = \ &\{\mathsf{args}(\mathsf{ft}(n^0), \{n^0 \dot{=} 3\}), \mathsf{fields}(s_0^{\mathsf{Fact}}, \{\mathsf{mx} \dot{=} 1, \mathsf{b} \dot{=} \mathbf{null}, \mathsf{r} \dot{=} 1\})\} \\
\mathcal{T}_O = \ &\{\mathsf{fields}(s_0^{\mathsf{Fact}}, \{\mathsf{mx} \dot{=} 1, \mathsf{b} \dot{=} \mathbf{null}, \mathsf{r} \dot{=} 3 * 2 * 1\}), \\
&\mathsf{fields}(s_1^{\mathsf{Fact}}, \{\mathsf{mx} \dot{=} 1, \mathsf{b} \dot{=} s_0^{\mathsf{Fact}}, \mathsf{r} \dot{=} 2\}), \mathsf{fields}(s_2^{\mathsf{Fact}}, \{\mathsf{mx} \dot{=} 1, \mathsf{b} \dot{=} s_1^{\mathsf{Fact}}, \mathsf{r} \dot{=} 1\})\}
\end{aligned}
$$

In this case, only field r of actor s_0^{Fact} has been labeled (with value 1). $\qquad\square$

6   Implementation and Experimental Evaluation

We have implemented all the techniques presented in the paper within the tool aPET [4], a test case generator for ABS programs, which is available at http://costa.ls.fi.upm.es/apet. ABS [16] is a concurrent, object-oriented, language based on the *concurrent objects* model, an extension of the actors model, which includes *future variables* and synchronization operations. Handling those features within our techniques does not pose any technical complication. This section reports on experimental results, which aim at demonstrating the applicability, effectiveness and impact of the proposed techniques during symbolic execution. The experiments have been performed using as benchmarks: (i) a set of classical actor programs borrowed from [18,21,22] and rewritten in ABS from ActorFoundry, and, (ii) some ABS models of typical concurrent systems. Specifically, *QSort* is a distributed version of the Quicksort algorithm, *PSort* is a modified version of the sorting algorithm used in the dCUTE study [21], *RSim* is a server registration simulation, *DHT* is a distributed hash table, *Mail* is an email client-server simulation, *Cons* resp. *Prod* is the *consume* resp. *produce* method in the classical producer-consumer protocol, and, *Fact* is the distributed factorial in Fig. 2. All sources are available at the above website.

Table 1 shows the results of our experimental evaluation. For each benchmark, we perform the symbolic execution and TCG of its most relevant method(s) with different values for k of the criteria in Sect. 5.1 (resp. loop-k, task-level and actor-number), shown in parenthesis right after the benchmark name. We consider combinations so that we can observe the impact of each criterion in the overall process. E.g., for *QSort*, the impact of look-k is observed comparing executions with parameters $(2, \_, 1)$ and $(3, \_, 1)$; and the impact of actor-number comparing executions with parameters $(2, \_, 1)$ and $(2, \_, 2)$. An underscore indicates that it does not affect the computation, provided it is above a certain minimum (typically 1 or 2). Also, for each benchmark and combination, we perform the TCG both ignoring and exploiting the independency information among tasks. After the name and criteria parameters, the first (resp. second) set of columns show the results ignoring (resp. exploiting) task independency information. For each run, we measure: the number of obtained test cases (column *Tests*); the total time taken and number of states generated by the whole exploration (columns *Time* and *States*); and the number of explorations, which have been cut resp. by criteria loop-k, task-level and actor-number (column $L/T/O$).

A relevant point, which is not shown in the table, is that our sufficient condition for temporal stability is able to determine a stable actor in all states of all benchmarks except for some states in benchmark *PSort*. This demonstrates that our sufficient condition for stability is very effective also in symbolic execution. Another important point to observe is the huge pruning of redundant executions performed when the task independency information is exploited. Last two columns show the reduction in number of tests and TCG time obtained when exploiting task independency information. In general, the more complex the programs and the deeper the exploration, the bigger is the reduction.

Table 1. Experimental evaluation (times in ms on an Intel Core i5 at 3.2GHz, 4GB)

Benchm.	Ignoring task indep. info				Exploiting task indep. info				Reduction	
	Tests	Time	States	L/T/O	Tests	Time	States	L/T/O	Tests	Time
QSort(2,_,1)	236	1934	2688	332/0/1052	236	1934	2688	332/0/1052	1.0x	1.0x
QSort(3,_,1)	1728	39084	44895	4719/0/20524	1728	39084	44895	4719/0/20524	1.0x	1.0x
QSort(2,_,2)	1017	21708	19300	3455/0/7928	1017	21825	19300	3455/0/7928	1.0x	1.0x
PSort(1,_,1)	478	696	1637	2/0/172	239	347	821	2/0/86	2.0x	2.0x
PSort(2,_,1)	3423	>200s	470087	0/0/182550	3425	>200s	470451	1/0/182649	1.0x	1.0x
PSort(1,_,2)	13678	19072	43341	2/0/4148	6839	9508	21673	2/0/2074	2.0x	2.0x
RSim(1,_,1)	9	8	25	1/0/2	4	5	14	1/0/2	2.2x	1.6x
RSim(2,_,1)	441	333	1350	1/0/12	14	20	80	1/0/8	31.5x	16.6x
RSim(2,_,2)	4111	3101	11841	1/0/12	59	82	340	1/0/8	69.7x	37.8x
DHT(1,4,1)	35	665	3179	733/1730/8	21	124	555	125/98/8	1.7x	5.4x
DHT(2,4,1)	97	8171	19018	2977/12639/24	55	2864	2332	349/651/24	1.8x	2.9x
DHT(1,5,1)	35	6425	30231	7065/17090/10	21	343	1623	369/226/10	1.7x	18.7x
DHT(1,5,2)	53	21092	98117	23119/57504/0	39	2615	12613	2879/3632/0	1.4x	8.1x
Mail(2,4,2)	161	1033	4540	654/5184/6	58	236	944	157/648/6	2.8x	4.4x
Mail(3,4,2)	400	12321	46760	2100/72090/24	232	1029	4310	291/3994/24	1.7x	12.0x
Mail(2,5,2)	161	4226	13756	654/9216/582	58	641	2096	157/1152/78	2.8x	6.6x
Mail(2,5,3)	161	4495	14908	660/10368/0	58	665	2240	163/1296/0	2.8x	6.8x
Cons(2,_,_)	15	10	30	1/0/0	9	7	19	1/0/0	1.7x	1.4x
Cons(3,_,_)	159	118	334	1/0/0	33	26	75	1/0/0	4.8x	4.5x
Cons(4,_,_)	3039	2562	6639	1/0/0	153	138	351	1/0/0	19.9x	18.6x
Prod(2,_,_)	29	30	52	10/0/0	17	16	31	6/0/0	1.7x	1.9x
Prod(3,_,_)	398	745	819	100/0/0	82	140	169	21/0/0	4.9x	5.3x
Prod(4,_,_)	9155	30268	20679	1636/0/0	465	1393	1041	85/0/0	19.7x	21.7x
Fact(2,4,2)	720	944	2430	59/0/278	270	451	1128	41/0/128	2.7x	2.1x
Fact(3,4,2)	1104	1425	3576	52/0/395	432	665	1664	38/0/171	2.6x	2.1x
Fact(2,3,2)	72	286	720	59/204/98	54	222	564	41/120/80	1.3x	1.3x
Fact(3,4,3)	3416	4704	11938	63/0/896	960	1668	4094	49/0/282	3.6x	2.8x

7 Related Work and Conclusions

We have presented a novel approach to automate TCG for actor systems, which ensures *completeness* of the test cases w.r.t. several interesting criteria. In order to ensure completeness in a concurrent setting, the symbolic execution tree must consider all possible task interleavings that could happen in an actual execution. The coverage criteria prune the tree in several dimensions: (1) limiting the number of iterations of loops at the level of tasks, (2) limiting the number of task switches allowed in each concurrency unit and (3) limiting the number of concurrency units created. Besides, our TCG framework tries to avoid redundant computations in the exploration of different orderings among tasks. This is done by leveraging and improving existing techniques to further reduce explorations in dynamic testing actor systems to the more general setting of static testing. Most related work is developed in the context of dynamic testing. The stream of papers devoted to further reduce the search space [1,10,18,22] is compatible with our work and the TCG framework can use the same algorithms and techniques, as we showed for the actor's stability of [3]. Dynamic symbolic execution consists in computing in parallel with symbolic execution a concrete test run. In [13] a dynamic symbolic execution framework is presented, however, there is no calculus for symbolic execution. In particular, the difficulties of handling asynchronous calls and the constraints over the field data are not considered.

Acknowledgments. This work was funded partially by the EU project FP7-ICT-610582 ENVISAGE: Engineering Virtualized Services (http://www.envisage-project.eu), by the Spanish MINECO project TIN2012-38137, and by the CM project S2013/ICE-3006.

References

1. Abdulla, P., Aronis, S., Jonsson, B., Sagonas, K.F.: Optimal dynamic partial order reduction. In: Proceedings of the POPL 2014, pp. 373–384. ACM (2014)
2. Agha, G.: Actors: A Model of Concurrent Computation in Distributed Systems. MIT Press, Cambridge (1986)
3. Albert, E., Arenas, P., Gómez-Zamalloa, M.: Actor- and task-selection strategies for pruning redundant state-exploration in testing. In: Ábrahám, E., Palamidessi, C. (eds.) FORTE 2014. LNCS, vol. 8461, pp. 49–65. Springer, Heidelberg (2014)
4. Albert, E., Arenas, P., Gómez-Zamalloa, M., Wong, P.Y.H.: aPET: a test case generation tool for concurrent objects. In: Proceedings of the ESEC/FSE 2013, pp. 595–598. ACM (2013)
5. Andrews, G.R.: Concurrent Programming: Principles and Practice. Benjamin/Cummings, Redwood (1991)
6. Clarke, L.A.: A system to generate test data and symbolically execute programs. IEEE Trans. Softw. Eng. **2**(3), 215–222 (1976)
7. Degrave, F., Schrijvers, T., Vanhoof, W.: Towards a framework for constraint-based test case generation. In: De Schreye, D. (ed.) LOPSTR 2009. LNCS, vol. 6037, pp. 128–142. Springer, Heidelberg (2010)
8. Engel, C., Hähnle, R.: Generating unit tests from formal proofs. In: Gurevich, Y., Meyer, B. (eds.) TAP 2007. LNCS, vol. 4454, pp. 169–188. Springer, Heidelberg (2007)
9. Esparza, J.: Model checking using net unfoldings. SCP **23**(2–3), 151–195 (1994)
10. Flanagan, C., Godefroid, P.: Dynamic partial-order reduction for model checking software. In: Proceedings of the POPL 2005, pp. 110–121. ACM (2005)
11. Godefroid, P.: Using partial orders to improve automatic verification methods. In: Clarke, E., Kurshan, R.P. (eds.) CAV 1990. LNCS, vol. 531, pp. 176–185. Springer, Heidelberg (1991)
12. Gotlieb, A., Botella, B., Rueher, M.: A CLP framework for computing structural test data. In: Palamidessi, C., Moniz Pereira, L., Lloyd, J.W., Dahl, V., Furbach, U., Kerber, M., Lau, K.-K., Sagiv, Y., Stuckey, P.J. (eds.) CL 2000. LNCS (LNAI), vol. 1861, p. 399. Springer, Heidelberg (2000)
13. Griesmayer, A., Aichernig, B., Johnsen, E.B., Schlatte, R.: Dynamic symbolic execution of distributed concurrent objects. In: Lee, D., Lopes, A., Poetzsch-Heffter, A. (eds.) FMOODS 2009. LNCS, vol. 5522, pp. 225–230. Springer, Heidelberg (2009)
14. Haller, P., Odersky, M.: Scala actors: unifying thread-based and event-based programming. Theor. Comput. Sci. **410**(2–3), 202–220 (2009)

15. Howden, W.E.: Symbolic testing and the DISSECT symbolic evaluation system. IEEE Trans. Soft. Eng. **3**(4), 266–278 (1977)
16. Johnsen, E.B., Hähnle, R., Schäfer, J., Schlatte, R., Steffen, M.: ABS: a core language for abstract behavioral specification. In: Aichernig, B.K., de Boer, F.S., Bonsangue, M.M. (eds.) Formal Methods for Components and Objects. LNCS, vol. 6957, pp. 142–164. Springer, Heidelberg (2011)
17. King, J.C.: Symbolic execution and program testing. Commun. ACM **19**(7), 385–394 (1976)
18. Lauterburg, S., Karmani, R.K., Marinov, D., Agha, G.: Evaluating ordering heuristics for dynamic partial-order reduction techniques. In: Rosenblum, D.S., Taentzer, G. (eds.) FASE 2010. LNCS, vol. 6013, pp. 308–322. Springer, Heidelberg (2010)
19. Meudec, C.: ATGen: automatic test data generation using constraint logic programming and symbolic execution. STVR **11**(2), 81–96 (2001)
20. Müller, R.A., Lembeck, C., Kuchen, H.: A symbolic java virtual machine for test case generation. In: Proceedings of the IASTEDSE 2004, pp. 365–371. ACTA Press (2004)
21. Sen, K., Agha, G.: Automated systematic testing of open distributed programs. In: Baresi, L., Heckel, R. (eds.) FASE 2006. LNCS, vol. 3922, pp. 339–356. Springer, Heidelberg (2006)
22. Tasharofi, S., Karmani, R.K., Lauterburg, S., Legay, A., Marinov, D., Agha, G.: TransDPOR: a novel dynamic partial-order reduction technique for testing actor programs. In: Giese, H., Rosu, G. (eds.) FORTE 2012 and FMOODS 2012. LNCS, vol. 7273, pp. 219–234. Springer, Heidelberg (2012)
23. Tillmann, N., de Halleux, J.: Pex–white box test generation for.NET. In: Beckert, B., Hähnle, R. (eds.) TAP 2008. LNCS, vol. 4966, pp. 134–153. Springer, Heidelberg (2008)

Lattice-Based Semantics for Combinatorial Model Evolution

Rachel Tzoref-Brill[1,2]([✉]) and Shahar Maoz[1]

[1] School of Computer Science, Tel Aviv University, Tel Aviv, Israel
maoz@cs.tau.ac.il
[2] IBM, Haifa Research Lab, Haifa, Israel
rachelt@il.ibm.com

Abstract. Combinatorial test design (CTD) is an effective test design technique, considered to be a testing best practice. CTD provides automatic test plan generation, but it requires a manual definition of the test space in the form of a combinatorial model. As the system under test evolves, e.g., due to iterative development processes and bug fixing, so does the test space, and thus, in the context of CTD, evolution translates into frequent manual model definition updates.

In this work, we show that the Boolean semantics currently in use by CTD tools to interpret the model is inadequate for combinatorial model evolution, and propose to replace it with a new lattice-based semantics that (1) provides a consistent interpretation of atomic changes to the model via Galois connections, and (2) exposes which additional parts of the model must change following an atomic change, in order to restore validity. We further use the new lattice-based semantics to define new higher-level atomic operations for combinatorial model evolution. Finally, we identify recurring abstraction and refinement patterns in the evolution of 42 real-world industrial models, and use the new lattice-based semantics to define new higher-level atomic constructs that encapsulate these patterns.

The proposed lattice-based semantics and related new modeling constructs advance the state-of-the-art in CTD with a new foundation for model evolution and with better tools for change comprehension and management.

1 Introduction

Combinatorial test design (CTD) is an effective technique for coping with the verification challenge of increasingly complex software systems, and is considered a testing best practice [1, 2, 5, 8, 26]. In CTD, the test space is manually modeled

This research was done under the terms of a joint study agreement between IBM Corporation Inc (via the IBM Research Lab - Haifa) and Tel Aviv University. Additionally, part of the research leading to these results has received funding from the European Community's Seventh Framework Programme (FP7/2007–2013) under grant agreement no. 610802.

© Springer International Publishing Switzerland 2015
B. Finkbeiner et al. (Eds.): ATVA 2015, LNCS 9364, pp. 276–292, 2015.
DOI: 10.1007/978-3-319-24953-7_22

by a set of parameters, their respective values, and constraints on the value combinations. The aggregate of parameters, values, and constraints is called a *combinatorial model*. We refer to the parameters and their values as the *model domain*. A valid test in the test space is defined to be an assignment of one value to each parameter without violating the constraints. A subset of the space is automatically constructed so that it covers all valid value combinations of every t parameters, where t is usually a user input. This systematic selection of tests is based on empirical data that shows that in most cases, the appearance of a bug depends on the interaction between a small number of features of the system under test [5, 12, 24].

An under-explored challenge for wide deployment of CTD in industry is the manual process for modeling and maintaining the test space. A recent survey by Nie et al. [16] reveals that only around 5 % of the publications on CTD explore the crucial modeling process. The topic of model maintenance is not even mentioned in [16]. However, in practice, model maintenance is of significant importance, since creating a CTD model is not a one time effort. Models must be maintained during the evolution of the system under test, and this need is significantly strengthened by the move to agile methodology and to continuous delivery mode. As software development cycles are getting ever shorter, with monthly and weekly deliveries, test design needs to frequently adjust to changes, which in the context of CTD means frequent model definition updates. While in these settings technologies for handling model changes are increasingly necessary, we are unaware of any work that reasons about the evolution process of combinatorial models or provides tool support for it. Close to 40 CTD tools are listed in [18], for example PICT [4] and ACTS [21]. However, to the best of our knowledge, none of the existing tools provides indication on the effect of change operations on the model, i.e., what is the relation between the original model and the new one, and how they differ. The practitioner is "left in the dark" as to whether the performed change will result in the intended effect, and what other changes are required. This problem exacerbates when a series of such change operations is performed, as is typically the case.

To start examining the evolution of combinatorial models in practice, as a preliminary study, we have gathered information about the evolution of 42 real-world industrial combinatorial models, which have been created over the last 7 years, each with 2–5 versions.[1] The number of parameters in a model version ranged from 4 to 109 (arithmetic mean 18.3); the number of constraints ranged from 0 to 381 (arithmetic mean 32.2). A total of 107 artifacts and 65 version commits were examined. The models originate from various domains and were written by different CTD practitioners. When analyzing the semantic changes applied to the models, we observed 6 recurring patterns, 4 of which are abstraction and refinement patterns. The frequency of occurrence of the latter patterns in real-world model evolution motivated us to try and interpret the evolution

---

[1] Unfortunately, all models are confidential and cannot be shared since they were created for IBM or for its clients. We are in the process of checking the option of sharing most of them after obfuscation.

process using abstraction and refinement techniques. In fact, abstraction and/or refinement patterns were observed in all models, and in 90 % of commits. The first two patterns we identified are *contraction* (in 38 % of the commits) and *extension* (in 52 % of the commits), where parts are either removed from or added to the model to describe the test space with less or more detail. The next two abstraction and refinement patterns we identified are merge and split. These patterns replace existing parts of the model with new parts that describe the original parts with less or more detail. Neither merge nor split are currently directly supported in existing CTD tools, though we detected split in 26 % of the version commits and merge in 14 % of them, implicitly implemented as a series of atomic operations. The last two change pattens we observed were refactoring and correction, both observed in 26 % of the commits.

In this work, we explore the evolution process of combinatorial test space modeling. We show that the Boolean semantics currently in use by CTD tools is inconsistent and inadequate for combinatorial model evolution, and extend it to a lattice-based semantics that provides a consistent interpretation of model changes via Galois connections. A Galois connection establishes the connection between the elements in an abstract domain and those in a concrete domain, via abstraction and concretization functions. We use these functions to uniquely define the validity of tests when moving from a certain test space domain to a more concrete or more abstract domain via an operation on the model domain. The reasoning behind the abstraction and refinement interpretation is that in the inherently incremental and forward fashion evolution process, each change is interpreted in isolation, without knowing the larger context and what changes will follow. In such settings, abstraction and refinement are natural interpretations of model domain changes, since each such change either hides details from the model or adds details to it.

We first address atomic change operations, e.g., adding or removing a parameter and its values, and use the new semantics to present their formal interpretation as either abstractions or refinements. We also use the new semantics as a means to mark the tests whose validity is defined as unknown following such changes in the model, and thus expose the fact that some changes in the model require additional changes to follow.

We further propose two higher-level change operations, which we call merge and split, that capture the merge and split change patterns observed in real-world model evolution. We use our lattice-based semantics to extend the CTD modeling language with constructs that encapsulate these change patterns and enable their safe and consistent application.

It is important to note that in this work we focus on the evolution at the model level, and do not address the evolution of the test plans generated from the model. Furthermore, our work is completely independent of the criteria and algorithm used to generate test plans. Reasoning about co-evolution of models and the test plans derived from them is part of our future work plans.

We implemented the new semantics and related constructs in our industrial-strength commercial CTD tool IBM Functional Coverage Unified Solution (IBM FOCUS) [10, 22]. For scalability, the implementation is symbolic and is based on

Table 1. Example on-line shopping model

Parameter	Values
ItemStatus (IS)	InStock, OutOfStock, NoSuchProduct
OrderShipping (OS)	Air, Ground
DeliveryTimeframe (DT)	Immediate, OneWeek, OneMonth

Constraints
DT = Immediate → OS = Air
DT = OneMonth → OS = Ground

Binary Decision Diagrams. The proposed semantics and related new modeling constructs advance the state-of-the-art in CTD with a new foundation for model evolution and with better tools for change comprehension and management.

2   Running Example and Overview

We start off with an example and overview of our work. The presentation in this section is semi-formal. Formal definitions appear in Sects. 3 to 6.

Table 1 depicts the parameters, values, and constraints of a combinatorial model for an on-line shopping system, which we use as a running example.

The model defines the test space and which tests in it are valid. For example, the test (IS = InStock, OS = Air, DT = Immediate) is valid, while the test (IS = InStock, OS = Ground, DT = Immediate) is invalid.

Example 1: Adding a Value to an Existing Parameter. Following the addition of a new feature to the system, a practitioner added the value Sea to the parameter OrderShipping. Using the Boolean semantics, as is the case in all existing CTD tools, we get that the question whether the test (IS = InStock, OS = Sea, DT = Immediate) is valid is inconsistently answered, depending on the syntactic representation of the test space. If the constraints are written as in Table 1, then this test is invalid. In contrast, if the first constraint was instead written DT = Immediate → OS ≠ Ground, then the same test is valid. Thus, although the two original models have equal semantics (they induce the same set of valid tests), adding the value Sea to the parameter OS results in two different new models. Moreover, the practitioner is not informed of this inconsistency and of what further input is required to resolve it. As a result, tests in the new model might not be assigned with their intended validity.

Our work addresses this problem. With our new, lattice-based semantics, the test in question is assigned with an "unknown" validity, regardless of the syntax in which the original constraints were specified. Intuitively, its validity depends on the order shipping value, for which the practitioner has yet to provide validity information, and is thus defined as unknown. In contrast, the test (IS = InStock, OS = Sea, DT = OneWeek) will be valid in our semantics, because its validity is determined regardless of the order shipping value. Moreover, our tool identifies and marks the tests that have an unknown validity following the addition of the Sea value, namely all tests that contain the combinations (OS = Sea, DT = Immediate) or (OS = Sea, DT = OneMonth), and presents them in a concise form to the practitioner for further validity specification. Thus, our semantics enables exposing to the practitioner what additional changes are required following the addition of the value to the model.

Example 2: Splitting a Value. After further inquiries, the practitioner realized that delivery time frame of one month actually consists of two different values, 6To10WorkingDays and Over10WorkingDays, which represent two separate logical paths of the application under test. To change the model accordingly using existing CTD tools, the practitioner needs to remove the OneMonth value, add the two new values, and change the constraints to consider the split values, without any indication from the tool regarding the effect of each step and the required consequent steps.

We call this type of change a split. Using our semantics, a split is formally presented as a refinement of the model domain, where the split values refine the original value. According to our semantics, a test containing a 6To10WorkingDays or Over10WorkingDays value automatically inherits the validity of the same test with the OneMonth value, which is no longer in the model. Our tool offers a *split* operation that incorporates the above three steps, based on our semantics.

Note that in all existing tools, the practitioner can perform the split only as a sequence of separate steps; after the first two steps, the validity of the different tests in Boolean semantics depends on the syntax in which the original constraints were written, and might differ from the same tests containing the original value. Following the removal of OneMonth and the addition of 6To10WorkingDays and Over10WorkingDays, the set of valid tests will contain the pair (OS = Air, DT = 6To10WorkingDays), while it will not contain the pair (OS = Air, DT = OneMonth). However, this new pair could also be excluded from the set of valid tests if the syntax of the original constraints were different, e.g., DT ≠ Immediate ∧ DT ≠ OneWeek → OS = Ground. Furthermore, as in the case of adding the Sea value, there would be no indication that the constraints should change in order to be consistent with the original model, and thus the practitioner might neglect changing them. The required changes may be easy to manually identify when there are only two constraints in the model, but they are much more challenging when the model contains dozens of parameters and constraints, as is typically the case in real-world industrial models.

Alternative Solutions. One may suggest alternative solutions to overcome the inconsistent constraints interpretation following extensions to the model domain, and the incomplete interpretation following removals from the model domain. For example, to handle the former problem, one may suggest to remove the negation operator from the constraint language made available to the practitioner. While this will resolve the inconsistent interpretation, it will extremely limit the flexibility of the practitioner to specify constraints in a concise manner,

and is thus infeasible in practice. To handle the latter problem, one may suggest
to use propositional semantics, where each partial parameter assignment maps
each constraint to a new constraint. Such a solution will result in numerous versions of the constraints, which the practitioner needs to reason about following
each single removal from the model. In contrast to these alternatives, our proposed lattice-based semantics handles both problems at once, without limiting
the constraints specification language and without requiring the practitioner to
deal with overly complex information.

3   Preliminaries

We provide formal definitions for the mathematical constructs that will be used
throughout this work, the combinatorial model, which defines a test space, and
lattices and Galois connections, which we use as a basis for the new semantics.

Combinatorial Models. A combinatorial model is defined as follows. Let $P =
\{p_1, \ldots, p_n\}$ be an ordered set of parameters, $V = \{V_1, \ldots, V_n\}$ an ordered set
of finite value sets, where V_i is the set of values for p_i, and C a set of Boolean
propositional constraints over P. A test $(v_1, \ldots, v_n)$, where $\forall_i$, $v_i \in V_i$, is a tuple
of assignments to the parameters in P.

The current semantics used in practice by CTD tools [18] is Boolean semantics. In this semantics, a valid test is a test that satisfies all constraints in C.
The semantics of the model is the set of all its valid tests, denoted by $S(P, V, C)$.

Complete Lattices and Galois Connections. A *lattice* is a tuple $L = \langle D,
\sqsubseteq, \sqcup, \sqcap, \bot, \top \rangle$, where D is a set of elements, $\sqsubseteq$ is a partial order on D, $\sqcup$ is the
join operator that defines a least upper bound for every finite set of elements in
D, $\sqcap$ is the meet operator that defines a greatest lower bound for every finite
set of elements in D, $\bot$ is the bottom element in D, defined as $\sqcup \emptyset$, and $\top$ is the
top element in D, defined as $\sqcup D$. L is a *complete lattice* if the meet and join
operators are defined for arbitrary sets in D, rather than only for finite ones.

Given two complete lattices $C = \langle D^C, \sqsubseteq^C, \sqcup^C, \sqcap^C, \bot^C, \top^C \rangle$ and $A =
\langle D^A, \sqsubseteq^A, \sqcup^A, \sqcap^A \bot^A, \top^A \rangle$, representing the concrete domain and the abstract
domain, respectively, a *Galois connection* is a quadruple (C, α, γ, A) that relates
C and A via a monotone abstraction function $\alpha : D^C \to D^A$ and a monotone
concretization function $\gamma : D^A \to D^C$. It must hold that $\forall c \in D^C, c \sqsubseteq \gamma(\alpha(c))$
and $\forall a \in D^A, \alpha(\gamma(a)) \sqsubseteq a$. A *Galois insertion* is a Galois connection for which
$\forall a \in D^A, \alpha(\gamma(a)) = a$. Specifically in our work, c represents a set of tests in the
concrete domain, and a represents a test in the abstract domain. The concrete
domain is derived from the abstract domain by an atomic operation such as
the addition of a value to a parameter. The abstract domain is derived from the
concrete domain by the reverse operation, e.g., the removal of the value from
the parameter. α maps c to a test which is its most precise abstraction in the
abstract domain, and γ maps a to a set of tests which is its most general concretization in the concrete domain. A mathematical introduction to lattices and
Galois connections can be found in [7].

Finally, given a set V, a complete lattice L, and a function $\beta : V \to L$, termed an *extraction function*, the following quadruple $(2^V, \alpha, \gamma, L)$ is a Galois connection between 2^V and L, where $\alpha(X) = \sqcup\{\beta(v) \mid v \in X\}$ for any $X \subseteq V$, and $\gamma(a) = \{v \in V \mid \beta(v) \sqsubseteq a\}$ [17].

4   Lattice-Based Semantics for Combinatorial Model Evolution

We are now ready to present the main contribution of our work, a lattice-based semantics for combinatorial model evolution. We define the new semantics to be consistent with Boolean semantics for a single version of the model, yet to provide a consistent definition of the model following each atomic change in the domain of the model and to mark the assignments whose validity is unknown following such changes.

Our lattice-based semantics for combinatorial models consists of two lattices: an *information lattice*, which captures the parameter assignments, and is by itself a Cartesian product of lattices per parameters, and a *validity lattice*, which captures the validity information for the parameter assignments.

Formally, let $P = \{p_1, \ldots, p_n\}$ be a set of parameters, and $V = \{V_1, \ldots, V_n\}$ a set of finite value sets, where $V_i = \{v_{i1}, \ldots, v_{im_i}\}$ is the set of values for p_i. Let V_{i*} be the set $V_i \bigcup \{\top, \bot\}$. For each parameter p_i we define a complete lattice of possible assignments $L_i = \langle V_{i*}, \sqsubseteq, \sqcup, \sqcap, \bot, \top \rangle$, where $\sqsubseteq$ is a partial order on V_{i*} in which the elements of V_i are not ordered, $\top$ represents the unknown value which contains the least information about the assignment to p_i and therefore is the top element of L_i, and $\bot$ represents a contradicting assignment to p_i and is therefore the bottom element of L_i.

The information lattice is built as the Cartesian product of the lattices defined above: $L_{cart} = \langle V_{1*} \times V_{2*} \times \ldots \times V_{n*}, \sqsubseteq_{cart}, \sqcup_{cart}, \sqcap_{cart}, \bot_{cart}, \top_{cart} \rangle$, where $\sqsubseteq_{cart}$ is the point-wise application of $\sqsubseteq$, and $\sqcup_{cart}$ and $\sqcap_{cart}$ are the point-wise application of $\sqcup$ and $\sqcap$, respectively. $\bot_{cart}$ and $\top_{cart}$ are the elements resulting from the assignment of $\bot$ and $\top$ to all parameters in P, respectively. For simplicity, we merge all tests that contain a $\bot$ value into the $\bot_{cart}$ element. As will become clear in the sequel, the implications of this are minor, as all of these tests map to the empty set of concrete tests, whether valid or not.

Validity is given using a second complete lattice $L_{valid} = \langle \{0, 1, \bot_{valid}, \top_{valid}\}, \sqsubseteq_{valid}, \sqcup_{valid}, \sqcap_{valid}, \bot_{valid}, \top_{valid} \rangle$, where 0 stands for invalid, 1 stands for valid, $\top_{valid}$ stands for unknown validity, and $\bot_{valid}$ stands for contradicting validity. $\sqsubseteq_{valid}$ is a partial order on $\{0, 1, \bot_{valid}, \top_{valid}\}$ in which 0 and 1 are not ordered. Figure 1 depicts the information lattice of our on-line shopping example as well as the validity lattice.

We further define a validity function $F_{valid} : L_{cart} \to L_{valid}$ that maps each element in the Cartesian product to its validity information. A test is an element $t \in L_{cart}$. We denote the value of a parameter $p \in P$ in a test $t \in L_{cart}$ by $t(p)$. A test is a complete test if $\forall p \in P, t(p) \neq \top$. Otherwise it is a partial test. The set

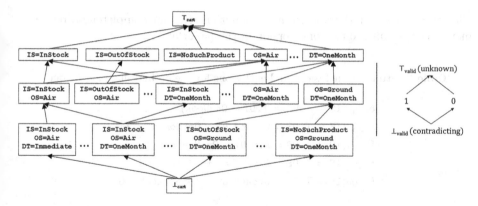

Fig. 1. On the left, part of the information lattice L_{cart} of our on-line shopping example. Parameters that do not appear in a square are assigned with the $\top$ (unknown) value. On the right, the validity lattice L_{valid}.

of valid tests consists of all complete tests $t \in L_{cart}$ such that $F_{valid}(t) = 1$. The set of invalid tests consists of all complete tests $t \in L_{cart}$ such that $F_{valid}(t) = 0$.

We impose the following requirements on F_{valid}, to make it consistent with Boolean propositional constraints, as will be shown by Lemma 2:

1. **Monotonicity.** $\forall t_1, t_2 \in L_{cart}$, if $t_1 \sqsubseteq t_2$ then $F_{valid}(t_1) \sqsubseteq F_{valid}(t_2)$. That is, the more information is given on the parameter assignment, the more information is deduced on the validity of the assignment.
2. **Consistency.** $F_{valid}(t) = \perp_{valid}$ iff $t = \perp_{cart}$.
3. **Completeness.** For a single version of the model, we require that for every complete test t, $F_{valid}(t) \neq \top_{valid}$. This will no longer be a requirement during the evolution of the model.

F_{valid} induces two dual properties: *strongest exclusions* and *strongest inclusions*. A test $t \in L_{cart}$ is a strongest exclusion if $F_{valid}(t) = 0$ and $\forall t', t \sqsubset t' \rightarrow F_{valid}(t') = \top_{valid}$. In other words, a strongest exclusion contains the least assignment information needed to deduce its invalidity. A test $t \in L_{cart}$ is a strongest inclusion if $F_{valid}(t) = 1$ and $\forall t', t \sqsubset t' \rightarrow F_{valid}(t') = \top_{valid}$. In other words, a strongest inclusion contains the least assignment information needed to deduce its validity.

These properties are important as they will allow us to describe F_{valid} and the changes that occur to it uniquely and succinctly. The validity of the other tests is directly determined by the validity of the strongest exclusions and strongest inclusions. Going back to our on-line shopping model, Table 2 presents its F_{valid} function via its strongest exclusions and strongest inclusions.

Lemma 1. *For a single version of a model, (a) the set of strongest exclusions T_{ex} uniquely determines F_{valid}, and (b) the set of strongest inclusions T_{inc} uniquely determines F_{valid}.*

The proof relies on the consistency, monotonicity, and completeness requirements. For details see the long version of the paper at [25].

Table 2. Strongest inclusions and exclusions for the on-line shopping model

$F_{valid}(\text{IS} = \top, \text{OS} = \top, \text{DT} = \text{OneWeek}) = 1$
$F_{valid}(\text{IS} = \top, \text{OS} = \text{Ground}, \text{DT} = \text{OneMonth}) = 1$
$F_{valid}(\text{IS} = \top, \text{OS} = \text{Air}, \text{DT} = \text{OneMonth}) = 0$
$F_{valid}(\text{IS} = \top, \text{OS} = \text{Air}, \text{DT} = \text{Immediate}) = 1$
$F_{valid}(\text{IS} = \top, \text{OS} = \text{Ground}, \text{DT} = \text{Immediate}) = 0$

Lemma 2. *For a single version of a model, lattice-based semantics is consistent with Boolean semantics.*

To prove Lemma 2, we show that a model in Boolean semantics $S(P, V, C)$ can be represented in lattice-based semantics by creating an F_{valid} function that is consistent with the set of valid tests captured by $S(P, V, C)$. Similarly, given a model in lattice-based semantics (P_L, V_L, F_{valid}), we can create a model in Boolean semantics $S(P_L, V_L, C)$ whose set of valid tests is $\{t \in L_{cart} \mid F_{valid}(t) = 1\}$. The full proof appears in [25].

5   Atomic Operations on Combinatorial Models

We observe the following atomic operations that are performed by practitioners on combinatorial models: adding a parameter and its values, removing a parameter and its values, adding a value to an existing parameter, removing a value from an existing parameter, and adding, removing, or changing a constraint.

In the following, we provide semantics for atomic operations on combinatorial models. We interpret each atomic change in the domain of the model as either an abstraction or a refinement via a Galois connection. Abstraction and refinement are natural interpretations of an atomic domain change when viewing it in isolation, without knowing what consequent changes will occur. The Galois connection is a means to automatically provide a consistent definition of the validity of the entire model following a domain change, via its abstraction and concretization functions. We interpret an atomic change in the validity function as an abstraction, refinement, refactoring, correction, or as a mixture of these change types. Higher-level semantic changes are discussed in Sect. 6.

5.1   Adding or Removing a Parameter and Its Values

Adding a parameter p_i with a set of values $V_{i*} = V_i \cup \{\top, \bot\}$ to the model results in a new domain L'_{cart} defined over the set of parameters $P' = P \cup \{p_i\}$ and values $V' = V \cup V_{i*}$. This domain is a refinement of the original domain L_{cart}.

Similarly, removing a parameter p_i and its values V_{i*} from the model results in a new domain which is an abstraction of the original one. The connection between the two domains can be described as a Galois connection $(2^{L'_{cart}}, \alpha, \gamma, L_{cart})$ via an extraction function as follows.

Definition 1 (Galois connection for adding or removing a parameter).
Let $\beta : L'_{cart} \to L_{cart}$ *be an extraction function, where* $\forall t \in L'_{cart}, \beta(t) = t \setminus p_i$. *Then* β *uniquely defines* α *and* γ *functions as follows:* $\forall T \subseteq L'_{cart}, \alpha(T) = \sqcup_{cart}\{\beta(t) \mid t \in T\}$, *and* $\forall t \in L_{cart}, \gamma(t) = \cup\{t' \in L'_{cart} \mid \beta(t') \sqsubseteq_{cart} t\}$.

The intuition behind this reasoning is that the additional parameter adds more details to the domain and to each test derived from this domain, and therefore is a form of refinement. Going back to our on-line shopping model from Sect. 2, adding the parameter ExportControl with values true, false, refines the test space by describing in each test whether or not export control is required. Similarly, removing a parameter hides the information it represents, and is therefore a form of abstraction. For example, removing the parameter IS from the model eliminates from each test the information about the status of the item to be purchased.

Theorem 1. $(2^{L'_{cart}}, \alpha, \gamma, L_{cart})$ *is a Galois insertion.*

The proof follows directly from the definitions of α, β, and γ. For details see [25].

Though the addition or removal of a parameter does not directly change the validity function, it implicitly influences it. As demonstrated in Sect. 2, such changes might result in an inconsistent or inadequate interpretation of the model when Boolean semantics is considered. For example, if a removed parameter appears in the constraints, they can no longer be interpreted with Boolean semantics in the new model due to the missing information.

In contrast, the lattice-based semantics provides a consistent and unique definition of the validity function following a change in the model domain, via the Galois connection. Let $F_{valid} : L_{cart} \to L_{valid}$ be the validity function in the domain without the additional parameter p_i, and $F'_{valid} : L'_{cart} \to L_{valid}$ be the validity function in the domain that includes it. Then the validity functions are defined as follows.

Definition 2 (Validity function following the addition or removal of a parameter). $\forall t \in L'_{cart}, F'_{valid}(t) = F_{valid}(\alpha(\{t\})) = F_{valid}(\beta(t)); \forall t \in L_{cart}, F_{valid}(t) = \sqcup_{valid}\{F'_{valid}(t') \mid t' \in \gamma(t)\}$.

Lemma 3. F_{valid} *and* F'_{valid} *preserve monotonicity and consistency.*

For proof refer to [25].

Note that Definition 2 does not depend on the syntax of the constraints, but rather on Definition 1, i.e., on the Galois connection relating the two domains. According to Definition 2, when a parameter p_i is added to the model, L'_{cart} "inherits" the validity of L_{cart}. That is, $\forall (t, p_i = v) \in L'_{cart}, F'_{valid}((t, p_i = v)) = F_{valid}(\beta((t, p_i = v))) = F_{valid}(t)$. This is indeed the extension of F_{valid}

to F'_{valid} that CTD tools implicitly use. For example, when the parameter
ExportControl is added to the on-line shopping model, the validity of all tests is
determined regardless of the export control information, although they contain
it. Further refinement of the validity information based on the added parameter
can be performed by the practitioner in subsequent steps.

When a parameter is removed from the model, existing CTD tools mark the
constraints in which it appears as erroneous, and the validity function becomes
undefined until the constraints are corrected. For example, if the OS parameter
is removed from the on-line shopping model, the validity information cannot be
computed anymore in Boolean semantics.

In contrast, using Definition 2, we get the following: $\forall t \in L_{cart}, F_{valid}(t) = \sqcup_{valid}\{F'_{valid}(t') \mid t' \in \gamma(t)\} = \sqcup_{valid}\{F'_{valid}(t') \mid t' \in L'_{cart} \wedge \beta(t') \sqsubseteq_{cart} t\} = \sqcup_{valid}\{F'_{valid}((t'', p_i = v)) \mid t'' \sqsubseteq_{cart} t, v \in V_{i*}\} = F'_{valid}(\sqcup_{cart'}\{(t'', p_i = v) \mid t'' \sqsubseteq_{cart} t, v \in V_{i*}\}) = F'_{valid}((t, p_i = \top)).$

That is, the validity of each test in the more abstract model is determined
by assigning the removed parameter with the unknown ($\top$) value. If the validity can still be determined, it is derived from the refined model. If it cannot
be determined, it becomes unknown ($\top_{valid}$). The advantage of our semantics
is that it pinpoints the exact parameter assignments for which the removal
of p_i leads to an unknown validity, and therefore may need to be refined. In
our example, though OS was removed from the model, the validity of the partial test (IS = $\top$, DT = OneWeek) is 1, while the validity of the partial tests
(IS = $\top$, DT = Immediate) and (IS = $\top$, DT = OneMonth) is $\top_{valid}$. This again
demonstrates how the lattice-based semantics provides the practitioner with
more refined information about which parts of the model lost validity information and require further input, and which parts maintained complete validity
information following the change and can be kept as is.

5.2   Adding or Removing a Value from an Existing Parameter

Adding a value v_{ik} to a parameter p_i results in a new domain L'_{cart} defined
over P and the set of values V^*, where $V^*(p_i) = V(p_i) \cup \{v_{ik}\}$. This domain is
a refinement of the previous domain L_{cart}. Similarly, removing a value v_{ik} from
a parameter p_i results in a new domain which is an abstraction of the previous
one. Note that $L_{cart} \subset L'_{cart}$. The connection between the two domains can be
described as a Galois connection $(2^{L'_{cart}}, \alpha', \gamma', L_{cart})$ via an extraction function
as follows.

Definition 3 (Galois connection for adding or removing a value). *Let
$\beta' : L'_{cart} \to L_{cart}$ be an extraction function, where $\forall t \in L'_{cart}, \beta'(t) = t[v_{ik}/\top]$.
Then β' uniquely defines α' and γ' functions as follows: $\forall T \subseteq L'_{cart}, \alpha'(T) = \sqcup_{cart}\{\beta'(t) \mid t \in T\}$, and $\forall t \in L_{cart}, \gamma'(t) = \cup\{t' \in L'_{cart} \mid \beta'(t') \sqsubseteq_{cart} t\}.$*

Similarly to the previous case, the intuition behind this reasoning is that the
additional value adds more details to the domain, this time with respect to the
specific parameter it is being added to, and therefore is a form of refinement.

Adding the value Sea to the OS parameter refines the information about the available shipping methods. Similarly, removing a value from a parameter hides the information it represents for the parameter, and is therefore a form of abstraction. For example, removing the value NoSuchProduct from the parameter IS hides the information of whether the item requested to be purchased actually exists.

Theorem 2. $(2^{L'_{cart}}, \alpha', \gamma', L_{cart})$ *is a Galois insertion.*

The proof follows directly from the definitions of α', β', and γ'. For details see [25].

As in the previous case, though the validity is not explicitly changed by the atomic operation, it is implicitly influenced by it. Again, the Galois connection provides a consistent and unique definition of the validity function, which exposes the exact cases in which the validity becomes unknown due to the domain change, and therefore requires further information from the practitioner.

Definition 4 (Validity function following the addition or removal of a value). $\forall t \in L'_{cart}, F'_{valid}(t) = F_{valid}(\alpha'(\{t\})) = F_{valid}(\beta'(t)); \forall t \in L_{cart}, F_{valid}(t) = \sqcup_{valid}\{F'_{valid}(t') \mid t' \in \gamma'(t)\}.$

Lemma 3 applies to Definition 4 as well. For details see [25].

When a value is added to the model, according to the definition of β', we get that if $t(p_i) \neq v_{ik}$ then $F'_{valid}(t) = F_{valid}(t)$. Otherwise $F'_{valid}(t) = F_{valid}(t')$, where $t'(p_i) = \top \wedge \forall j \neq i, t'(p_j) = t(p_j)$.

That is, the new value is treated as unknown when interpreting the validity of an assignment in which it participates. If the validity can be determined regardless of the value of the parameter p_i, then it remains determined. Otherwise, it is defined as unknown, making the validity function for this assignment under-specified and forcing the practitioner to explicitly define it. As shown in Sect. 2, using Definition 4 we are able to deduce that the validity of (IS = $\top$, OS = Sea, DT = Immediate) is $\top_{valid}$, because the validity of (IS = $\top$, OS = $\top$, DT = Immediate) is also $\top_{valid}$, regardless of the syntax of the original constraints. In contrast, in Boolean semantics, the test is assigned with conflicting 0 and 1 validity in this case, depending on the syntax of the constraints.

When removing a value v_{ik} of a parameter p_i from the model, we get that $F_{valid}(t) = \sqcup_{valid}\{F'_{valid}(t') \mid t' \in \gamma'(t)\} = \sqcup_{valid}\{F'_{valid}(t') \mid t' \in L'_{cart} \wedge \beta'(t') \sqsubseteq_{cart} t\} = \sqcup_{valid}\{F'_{valid}(t') \mid t' \in L'_{cart} \wedge t'[v_{ik}/\top] \sqsubseteq_{cart} t\} = F'_{valid}(\sqcup_{cart'}\{t' \in L'_{cart} \mid t' \sqsubseteq_{cart'} t\}) = F'_{valid}(t).$ In this case, since $L_{cart} \subset L'_{cart}$, we simply get that the validity of t is inherited from the refined model.

5.3   Adding, Removing, or Changing a Constraint

As opposed to a change in the domain of the model that implicitly changes its validity function, an addition, removal, or change in a constraint does not implicitly change the domain of the model. Therefore, it does not require guaranteeing a consistent interpretation of an implicit change. Instead, we reason about the different semantics of changes in the constraints, such as abstraction, refinement, refactoring, and correction, by analyzing their effect on the strongest exclusions and strongest inclusions. Since this analysis is an extension of our proposed semantics that is not required for the understanding of the main contribution of this work, we opt for describing it in [25].

6   Split and Merge Operations on Combinatorial Models

We now move from analyzing each atomic operation in isolation, to examining higher-level operations that stand for a semantic change. Specifically, we focus on two such changes which we call *merge* and *split*. These changes replace existing parts of the model with new parts that describe the original parts with less or more detail. We provide formal definitions for split and merge using our lattice-based semantics, and offer high-level operations for them.

Formally, a *split* operation on a value v_{ik} of a parameter p_i to a set of values $\{v_{ik1}, \ldots, v_{ikm}\}$ results in a new domain L'_{cart} defined over P and the set of values V^*, where $V^*(p_i) = V(p_i) \setminus \{v_{ik}\} \cup \{v_{ik1}, \ldots, v_{ikm}\}$. This domain is a refinement of the previous domain L_{cart}. Similarly, a *merge* operation on a set of values $\{v_{ik1}, \ldots, v_{ikm}\}$ of a parameter p_i to a single value v_{ik} results in a new domain which is an abstraction of the previous one. The connection between the two domains can be described as a Galois connection $(2^{L'_{cart}}, \alpha', \gamma', L_{cart})$ via an extraction function as follows.

Definition 5 (Galois connection for splitting or merging values). *Let* $\beta_{ms} : L'_{cart} \to L_{cart}$ *be an extraction function, where* $\forall t \in L'_{cart}, \beta_{ms}(t) = t[v_{ik1}/v_{ik}] \ldots [v_{ikm}/v_{ik}]$. *Then* β_{ms} *uniquely defines* α_{ms} *and* γ_{ms} *functions as follows:* $\forall T \subseteq L'_{cart}, \alpha_{ms}(T) = \sqcup_{cart}\{\beta_{ms}(t) \mid t \in T\}$, *and* $\forall t \in L_{cart}, \gamma_{ms}(t) = \cup\{t' \in L'_{cart} \mid \beta_{ms}(t') \sqsubseteq_{cart} t\}$.

Theorem 3. $(2^{L'_{cart}}, \alpha_{ms}, \gamma_{ms}, L_{cart})$ *is a Galois insertion.*

The proof follows directly from the definitions of α_{ms}, β_{ms}, and γ_{ms}. For details see [25].

Similarly to the cases described in Sect. 5, the Galois connection is a means to consistently define the new validity function following the domain change, and to expose which new parts of the test space have an unknown validity:

Definition 6 (Validity function following the split or merge of values). $\forall t \in L'_{cart}, F'_{valid}(t) = F_{valid}(\alpha_{ms}(\{t\})) = F_{valid}(\beta_{ms}(t)); \forall t \in L_{cart}, F_{valid}(t) = \sqcup_{valid}\{F'_{valid}(t') \mid t' \in \gamma_{ms}(t)\}$.

Lemma 3 applies to Definition 6 as well. For details see [25].

In case of a split, according to β_{ms} definition, we get that if $t(p_i) \notin \{v_{ik1}, \ldots, v_{ikm}\}$ then $F'_{valid}(t) = F_{valid}(t)$. Otherwise, $F'_{valid}(t) = F_{valid}(t')$, where $\forall j \neq i, t'(p_j) = t(p_j)$, and $t'(p_i) = v_{ik}$. That is, the validity of a test with the split values is inherited from the validity of the same test with the original value.

In case of a merge, we get that $F_{valid}(t) = \sqcup_{valid}\{F'_{valid}(t') \mid t' \in \gamma_{ms}(t)\} = \sqcup_{valid}\{F'_{valid}(t') \mid t' \in L'_{cart} \wedge \beta_{ms}(t') \sqsubseteq_{cart} t\} = \sqcup_{valid}\{F'_{valid}(t') \mid t' \in L'_{cart} \wedge t'[v_{ik1}/v_{ik}]\ldots[v_{ikm}/v_{ik}] \sqsubseteq_{cart} t\}$.

If $t(p_i) \neq v_{ik}$ then we get that $F_{valid}(t) = F'_{valid}(t)$, because in this case t is also in L'_{cart} and the same tests are smaller than t in both domains. Otherwise, $F_{valid}(t) = \sqcup_{valid}\{F'_{valid}(t') \mid \forall j \neq i, t'(p_j) = t(p_j) \wedge t'(p_i) \in \{v_{ik1}, \ldots, v_{ikm}\}\}$. That is, if all split values agree on the validity, the merged value will inherit it. Otherwise, it will be assigned with the $\top_{valid}$ value, forcing the practitioner to explicitly determine it.

In our example from Sect. 2, a split of OneMonth into 6To10WorkingDays and Over10WorkingDays will result in the following additions to F_{valid}:

- $F_{valid}(\text{IS} = \top, \text{OS} = \text{Ground}, \text{DT} = \text{6To10WorkingDays}) = 1$
- $F_{valid}(\text{IS} = \top, \text{OS} = \text{Ground}, \text{DT} = \text{Over10WorkingDays}) = 1$
- $F_{valid}(\text{IS} = \top, \text{OS} = \text{Air}, \text{DT} = \text{6To10WorkingDays}) = 0$
- $F_{valid}(\text{IS} = \top, \text{OS} = \text{Air}, \text{DT} = \text{Over10WorkingDays}) = 0$

As previously noted, in our semantics, a test containing a split value (in our example 6To10WorkingDays or Over10WorkingDays), automatically inherits the validity of the same test with the original value (in our example, OneMonth), whereas in Boolean semantics, its validity is ambiguous, and depends on the syntactic representation of the constraints.

Now assume the practitioner realized that OneWeek and 6To10WorkingDays are functionally equivalent, and should be merged into a single value named UpTo10WorkingDays. As a result of performing the merge as a composite operation in lattice-based semantics, the partial test (IS $= \top$, OS $=$ Air, DT $=$ UpTo10WorkingDays) will be assigned with $\top_{valid}$ validity ("unknown"), since the corresponding strongest exclusions and inclusions in the split model "disagree" on its validity. Similarly to the case of adding a value to the model, we suggest to extend the merge operation to include determination of validity for such merged tests, to result in a validity function that satisfies the completeness requirement, i.e., every complete test has a known validity. The practitioner can assign a 0 or 1 validity to the merged test, which is an abstraction of the split strongest exclusions and inclusions in the merged model. Alternatively, the practitioner can decide to keep the unknown validity, and instead specify a 0 or 1 validity for a set of tests T so that the merged test in question is their least upper bound. For example, a 0 validity can be assigned in this case if the item is out of stock, and a 1 validity can be assigned otherwise.

In contrast, in Boolean semantics, after replacing the split values with the merged one, the question whether the combination of values (OS $=$ Air, DT $=$ UpTo10WorkingDays) appears in the valid set of tests depends entirely on the syntax of the constraints, and there is no indication about the conflicting validity of the split tests with respect to the merged one.

Similarly to split and merge of values, we define corresponding operations for split and merge of parameters. For lack of space, we do not include here the formal definition of these operations, however it is similar in nature to that of split and merge of values for a single parameter.

7   Related Work

There is a large body of work on various aspects of combinatorial testing. To the best of our knowledge, none of it addresses the problem of combinatorial model evolution. Nie et al. [16] survey 93 academic papers on combinatorial testing, and categorize them into 8 different research areas, but do not mention model evolution. There are also many existing CTD tools [4,18,21], which to the best of our knowledge, provide no support for model evolution, though from our practical experience, managing and comprehending changes in models is a challenge encountered frequently by CTD practitioners in their routine tasks.

Qu et al. [20] examine the effectiveness of combinatorial test prioritization and re-generation strategies on regression testing in evolving programs with multiple versions. However, the work ignores the modeling aspects of the evolution.

Much work has been published on the evolution of other kinds of models, from a semantic and syntactic point of view. For example, Maoz et al. presented semantic model differencing for class and activity diagrams [13,14], where the difference between two models is given as a set of diff witnesses, instances of one model that are not instances of the other. We are unaware of any work on model evolution that uses a lattice-based semantics.

Lattices and Galois connections have been widely used in program analysis and verification, based on the abstract interpretation framework [3]. The framework has numerous applications, including for example, in reactive systems [6] and more recently in semantic differencing of programs [19]. Another notable application of lattices is for multi-valued model checking [9,11,15,23]. We are unaware of any use of lattices in the context of model evolution.

8   Summary and Future Work

In this work, we demonstrate the shortcomings of the Boolean semantics currently used by CTD tools for reasoning about model evolution, and extend it with a new lattice-based semantics. The new semantics provides a consistent interpretation of changes in the model, and constitutes a new foundation for better comprehension and management of changes in combinatorial models. We further define higher-level atomic operations for combinatorial model evolution using our lattice-based semantics. An analysis of the evolution of 42 real-world industrial models reveals that these operations are indeed recurring evolution patterns, and serves as preliminary evidence for the strength of our semantics.

This work is a first step in a larger research agenda involving different aspects of combinatorial model evolution. We already implemented the new semantics and higher-level constructs in our CTD tool IBM FOCUS. We plan to perform a thorough evaluation of these enhancements and assess the degree to which they help CTD practitioners manage changes in real-world models.

We also plan to extend our analysis of the evolution of real-world models, and identify additional recurring evolution patterns. The current analysis was mostly performed manually, with only lightweight tool support. We plan to further extend the tool support for semantic differencing between combinatorial models.

Another research direction we are pursuing is the co-evolution of models and the test plans derived from them. We plan to use our lattice-based semantics to establish the connection between the interaction coverage requirements in different versions of a model, and determine what changes are required in the test plan to match the evolved model and coverage requirements.

Finally, our work is part of a more general plan to explore the benefits of lattice-based semantics for supporting the evolution of other kinds of models, for example relational models and transition systems.

References

1. Burroughs, K., Jain, A., Erickson, R.L.: Improved quality of protocol testing through techniques of experimental design. In: SUPERCOMM/ICC (1994)
2. Cohen, M.B., Snyder, J., Rothermel, G.: Testing across configurations: implications for combinatorial testing. SIGSOFT Softw. Eng. Notes 31(6), 1–9 (2006)
3. Cousot, P., Cousot, R.: Abstract interpretation: a unified lattice model for static analysis of programs by construction or approximation of fixpoints. In: POPL (1977)
4. Czerwonka, J.: Pairwise Testing in Real World. In: PNSQC (2006)
5. Dalal, S.R., Jain, A., Karunanithi, N., Leaton, J.M., Lott, C.M., Patton, G.C., Horowitz, B.M.: Model-based testing in practice. In: ICSE (1999)
6. Dams, D., Gerth, R., Grumberg, O.: Abstract interpretation of reactive systems. ACM Trans. Program. Lang. Syst. 19(2), 253–291 (1997)
7. Davey, B.A., Priestley, H.A.: Introduction To Lattices and Order. Cambridge University Press, Cambridge (1990)
8. Grindal, M., Lindström, B., Offutt, J., Andler, S.F.: An evaluation of combination strategies for test case selection. Softw. Eng. Empirical 11(4), 583–611 (2006)
9. Grumberg, O., Lange, M., Leucker, M., Shoham, S.: *Don't know* in the μ-Calculus. In: Cousot, R. (ed.) VMCAI 2005. LNCS, vol. 3385, pp. 233–249. Springer, Heidelberg (2005)
10. IBM Functional Coverage Unified Solution (IBM FOCUS). http://researcher. watson.ibm.com/researcher/view_project.php?id=1871
11. Katoen, J.-P., Klink, D., Leucker, M., Wolf, V.: Three-valued abstraction for probabilistic systems. In: JLAP (2012)
12. Kuhn, D.R., Wallace, D.R., Gallo, A.M.: Software fault interactions and implications for software testing. IEEE Trans. Softw. Eng. 30(6), 418–421 (2004)
13. Maoz, S., Ringert, J.O., Rumpe, B.: ADDiff: semantic differencing for activity diagrams. In: ESEC/FSE (2011)
14. Maoz, S., Ringert, J.O., Rumpe, B.: CDDiff: semantic differencing for class diagrams. In: Mezini, M. (ed.) ECOOP 2011. LNCS, vol. 6813, pp. 230–254. Springer, Heidelberg (2011)
15. Meller, Y., Grumberg, O., Shoham, S.: A framework for compositional verification of multi-valued systems via abstraction-refinement. In: Liu, Z., Ravn, A.P. (eds.) ATVA 2009. LNCS, vol. 5799, pp. 271–288. Springer, Heidelberg (2009)

16. Nie, C., Leung, H.: A survey of combinatorial testing. ACM Comput. Surv. **43**(2), 11 (2011)
17. Nielson, F., Nielson, H.R., Hankin, C.: Principles of Program Analysis. Springer, New York (1999)
18. Pairwise testing website. http://www.pairwise.org/tools.asp
19. Partush, N., Yahav, E.: Abstract semantic differencing via speculative correlation. In: OOPSLA (2014)
20. Qu, X., Cohen, M.B., Woolf, K.M.: Combinatorial interaction regression testing: a study of test case generation and prioritization. In: ICSM (2007)
21. Lei, Y., Kuhn, R., Kacker, R.: Practical combinatorial testing beyond pairwise. IT Prof. **10**(3), 19–23 (2008)
22. Segall, I., Tzoref-Brill, R., Farchi, E.: Using binary decision diagrams for combinatorial test design. In: ISSTA (2011)
23. Shoham, S., Grumberg, O.: 3-valued abstraction: more precision at less cost. Inf. Comput. **206**(11), 1313–1333 (2008)
24. Tai, K.C., Lie, Y.: A test generation strategy for pairwise testing. IEEE Trans. Softw. Eng. **1**, 109–111 (2002)
25. Tzoref-Brill, R., Maoz, S.: Lattice-based semantics for combinatorial model evolution. Technical report H-0323, IBM Research (2015)
26. Wojciak, P., Tzoref-Brill, R.: System level combinatorial testing in practice - the concurrent maintenance case study. In: ICST (2014)

Effective Verification of Replicated Data Types Using Later Appearance Records (LAR)

Madhavan Mukund[✉], Gautham Shenoy R., and S.P. Suresh

Chennai Mathematical Institute, Chennai, India
{madhavan,gautshen,spsuresh}@cmi.ac.in

Abstract. Replicated data types store copies of identical data across multiple servers in a distributed system. For the replicas to satisfy strong eventual consistency, these data types should be designed to guarantee conflict free convergence of all copies in the presence of concurrent updates. This requires maintaining history related metadata that, in principle, is unbounded.

While earlier work such as [2] and [9] has concentrated on declarative frameworks for formally specifying *Conflict-free Replicated Data Types* (CRDTs) and conditions that guarantee the existence of finite-state (*distributed*) reference implementations, there has not been a systematic attempt so far to use the declarative specifications for effective verification of CRDTs.

In this work, we propose a simple *global* reference implementation for CRDTs specified declaratively, and simple conditions under which this is guaranteed to be finite. Our implementation uses the technique of *Later Appearance Record* (LAR). We also outline a methodology for effective verification of CRDT implementations using CEGAR.

1 Introduction

Replicated data types are used by web services that maintain multiple copies of the same data across different servers to provide better availability and fault tolerance. Clients can access and update data at any copy. Replicated data types cover a wide class of data stores that include distributed databases and DNS servers, as well as NoSQL stores such as Redis and memcached. The CAP theorem [4] shows that it is impossible for replicated data types to provide both strong consistency and high availability in the presence of network and node failures. Hence, web services that aim to be highly available in the presence of faults opt for a weaker notion of consistency known as *eventual consistency*. Eventual consistency allows copies to be inconsistent for a finite period of time. However, the web service must ensure that conflicts arising due to concurrent updates across multiple copies are resolved to guarantee that all the copies eventually agree. *Conflict-free Replicated Data Types (CRDTs)*, introduced in [11,12], are a subclass of replicated data types that are eventually consistent and conflict free.

An abstract specification of a data type describes its properties independent of any implementation. Such a specification plays a crucial role in formal

© Springer International Publishing Switzerland 2015
B. Finkbeiner et al. (Eds.): ATVA 2015, LNCS 9364, pp. 293–308, 2015.
DOI: 10.1007/978-3-319-24953-7_23

verification of the correctness of any implementation of the data type. Most of the early work on CRDTs described these data types through implementations [1,8,11,12]. Recently, a comprehensive framework has been proposed in [2] to provide declarative specifications for a wide variety of replicated data types, along with a methodology to prove the correctness of an implementation via replication aware simulations. Unfortunately this strategy does not lend itself to effective formal verification of the implementations.

In [9], we describe a bounded reference implementation of a CRDT generated from a declarative specification. This construction produces a distributed implementation where each replica only has a local view of the overall computation, obtained through the messages that it receives. This requires an intricate distributed timestamping protocol [7,10] to reuse timestamps in order to bound the implementation. Moreover, strong assumptions about the underlying operating environment have to be directly incorporated into the reference implementation.

The main aim of generating a reference implementation is to come up with an effective verification procedure for generic CRDT implementations. The key observation of this paper is that a *global* reference implementation is sufficient for this purpose. In a global reference implementation, we can directly keep track of causality between update events without exchanging additional information between replicas. In fact, we show that we can maintain a local sequential history for each replica in terms of a later appearance record (LAR) [5], from which we can faithfully reconstruct the causality relation. This greatly simplifies the construction. Moreover, the LAR-based construction is independent of any assumptions on the environment required to bound the size of the reference implementation.

The paper is organized as follows. In the next section, we define CRDTs and introduce declarative specifications. Section 3 describes how the construction of a reference implementation. In the next section, we describe an effective technique for CRDTs using CEGAR [3]. We conclude with a summary and a discussion of future research directions.

2   CRDTs, Traces and Specifications

We consider distributed systems consisting of a set $\mathcal{R}$ of N replicas, denoted $[1..N]$. We use p, q, r, s and their primed variants to range over $\mathcal{R}$. These replicas are interconnected through an asynchronous network. We assume that replicas can crash and recover infinitely often. However, when a replica recovers from a crash it is expected to resume operation from some safe state that it was in before the crash. We are interested in replicated data types that are implemented on top of such distributed systems.

A replicated data type exposes a set of side-effect-free operations known as *queries* for clients to obtain information contained in the data type. It makes available a set of state-modifying operations known as *updates* to allow clients to update the contents of the data type. For example, in a replicated set, *contains* is a query method, while *add* and *delete* are update methods.

At any point, a client can interact with any one of the N replicas. The replica that services a query (respectively, update) request from the client is said to be the *source replica* for that query (respectively, update). The source replica uses its local information to process the query. On receiving an update request from the client, the source replica modifies its local state appropriately.

In this paper, we restrict our attention to a class of replicated data types called *Conflict-free Replicated Data Types (CRDTs)*, introduced in [11]. In these data types, each time a replica receives an update request from a client, it applies the update locally and broadcasts to all the other replicas a message containing the data that they require to apply this update. On receiving this broadcast, each replica performs a local update using the data sent by the source replica. We now define some terminology from [11,12] to reason about these data types.

A CRDT $\mathcal{D}$ is a tuple $(\mathcal{V}, \mathcal{Q}, \mathcal{U}, \mathsf{Ret})$ where:

- $\mathcal{V}$ is the underlying set of values stored in the datatype and is called the *universe* of a replicated datatype. For instance, the universe of a replicated read-write register is the set of integers that the register can hold.
- $\mathcal{Q}$ denotes the set of query methods exposed by the replicated data type.
- $\mathcal{U}$ denotes the set of update methods.
- Ret is the set of all return values for queries.

We assume that $\perp$ is a designated "empty value", belonging to both $\mathcal{V}$ and Ret.

Definition 1 (Operations). *An operation of a CRDT $\mathcal{D} = (\mathcal{V}, \mathcal{Q}, \mathcal{U}, \mathsf{Ret})$ is a tuple $o = (m, r, args, ret)$ where $m \in \mathcal{Q} \cup \mathcal{U} \cup \{\mathbf{receive}\}$ is the action, $r \in \mathcal{R}$ is the source replica, args is a tuple of arguments from $\mathcal{V}$, and $ret \in \mathsf{Ret}$ is the return value, satisfying the following conditions:*

- *if $m \in \mathcal{U}$, $ret = \perp$.*
- *if $m = \mathbf{receive}$, $args = ret = \perp$.*

For an operation $o = (m, r, args, ret)$, we define $Op(o) = m$, $Args(o) = args$, $Rep(o) = r$, and $Ret(o) = ret$. We call o a query operation if $m \in \mathcal{Q}$, an update operation if $m \in \mathcal{U}$ and a receive operation if $m = \mathbf{receive}$.
We denote the set of operations of $\mathcal{D}$ by $\Sigma(\mathcal{D})$.

Definition 2 (Run). *A run of a replicated data type is a pair (ρ, φ) where*

- *ρ is a sequence $o_1 o_2 \ldots o_n$ of operations from $\Sigma(\mathcal{D})$.*
- *φ is a partial function from $[1..n]$ to $[1..n]$ such that*
  - *$dom(\varphi) = \{i \leq n \mid o_i$ is a receive operation$\}$.*
  - *if $\varphi(i) = j$ then $j < i$, o_j is an update operation and $Rep(o_i) \neq Rep(o_j)$.*

For a sequence $\rho = o_1 o_2 \cdots o_n$, we denote by $\rho[i]$ the operation o_i, and we denote by $\rho[i : j]$ the subsequence $o_i o_{i+1} \cdots o_j$.

Definition 3. *Let (ρ, φ) be a run with $\rho = o_1 \cdots o_n$. An update operation o_i is said to be delivered if $(\forall r \in \mathcal{R})[r \neq Rep(\rho[i]) \implies (\exists j)[r = Rep(\rho[j]) \wedge \varphi(j) = i]]$.*

Definition 4 (Events). *Let* (ρ, φ) *be a run of a replicated data type. We associate an event with each update and receive operation performed in* ρ*. Formally, the set* $\mathcal{E}_\rho$ *is a set of* events *associated with the operations in* ρ *given by*

$$\mathcal{E}_\rho = \{e_i \mid 1 \le i \le |\rho|, Op(\rho[i]) \in \mathcal{U} \cup \{\mathbf{receive}\}\}.$$

Each $e_i \in \mathcal{E}_\rho$ *corresponds to the operation* $\rho[i]$ *in* ρ*. We define* $Rep(e_i)$*,* $Op(e_i)$ *and* $Args(e_i)$ *to be* $Rep(\rho[i])$*,* $Op(\rho[i])$ *and* $Args(\rho[i])$*.*

We extend φ *to* $\mathcal{E}_\rho$ *as follows. For* $e_i \in \mathcal{E}_\rho$*, let* $\rho[i]$ *be the corresponding event in* ρ*. Then,* $\varphi(e_i) = e_j$ *if* $\varphi(\rho[i]) = j$*.*

Definition 5 (Happened before). *For a run* (ρ, φ) *and a replica* r*, we denote by* $\mathcal{E}_\rho^r$ *the set of* r*-events* $\{e \in \mathcal{E}_\rho \mid Rep(e) = r\}$*. The total order* $\{(e_i, e_j) \mid e_i, e_j \in \mathcal{E}_\rho^r, i < j\}$ *is denoted by* $\le_\rho^r$*. We denote by* $\le_\rho^{\mathbf{receive}}$ *the relation* $\{(\varphi(e), e) \mid e \in \mathcal{E}_\rho, Op(e) = \mathbf{receive}\}$*.*

The happened before *relation on* (ρ, φ)*, denoted* $\preceq_\rho$*, is defined by*

$$\bigcup_{r \in \mathcal{R}} (\le_\rho^{\mathbf{receive}} \cup \le_\rho^r)^+$$

For a pair of update events e, e' *we say that* e has *happened before* e' *if* $e \preceq_\rho e'$*. We say that a pair of events* $e, e' \in \mathcal{E}$ *are* concurrent *(denoted by* $e \parallel_\rho e'$*) when neither* $e \preceq_\rho e'$ *nor* $e' \preceq_\rho e$ *holds.*

The definition of $\preceq_\rho$ is subtle. If a replica r receives information about an update at r', r continues to know about this update even after it performs more local actions. But r does not necessarily know about events at r' prior to this update. Hence, $\preceq_\rho$ is not transitive, though it is always acyclic. If we have a strong delivery criterion like *causal delivery* along with the assumption that each update is broadcast to every replica, then one can show that $\preceq_\rho$ is transitive.

We now define the trace associated with a run.

Definition 6 (Trace). *The* trace *associated with a run* (ρ, φ) *is the triple* $(\mathcal{E}_\rho, \varphi, \preceq_\rho)$*. (The term* trace *is borrowed from Mazurkiewicz trace theory [6]).* *We denote the trace of a run* (ρ, φ) *by* $trace(\rho, \varphi)$*. The set of all traces is denoted by* $\mathcal{T}$*.*

Given a trace $(\mathcal{E}, \varphi, \preceq)$ *and a subset of events* $X \subseteq \mathcal{E}$*, the subtrace induced by* X *is given by* $(X, \varphi_X, \preceq_X)$*, where* φ_X *and* $\preceq_X$ *are the obvious restrictions of* φ *and* $\preceq$ *to the set* X*.*

Definition 7 (View). *Let* $t = (\mathcal{E}, \varphi, \preceq)$ *be a trace. For a replica* $r \in \mathcal{R}$*, the* maximal r-event *in* t *is denoted by* $max_r(t)$*. The* view *of* r *in* t*, denoted* $\partial_r(t)$*, is the subtrace induced by the subset* $\mathcal{E}' = \{e' \in \mathcal{E} \mid e' \preceq max_r(t)\}$*.*

Definition 8 (Declarative Specification and Permitted Runs). *Let* $\mathcal{D} = (\mathcal{V}, \mathcal{Q}, \mathcal{U}, \mathsf{Ret})$ *be a CRDT. A declarative specification of* $\mathcal{D}$ *is a function* $f : \mathcal{T} \times \mathcal{Q} \times \mathcal{V}^* \to \mathsf{Ret}$ *that determines the return value of any query* $q \in \mathcal{Q}$ *with arguments* $args \in \mathcal{V}^*$ *in a trace* t*.*

If f is a declarative specification of $\mathcal{D}$, the set of permitted runs of $\mathcal{D}$, denoted $Runs(\mathcal{D}, f)$, consists of all $\mathcal{D}$-runs (ρ, φ) such that for all query operations $\rho[i] = (q, r, args, ret)$, $ret = f(\partial_r(trace(\rho[i], \varphi)), q, args)$.

If a CRDT is specified declaratively, all responses to queries are determined by the trace generated by a run, and not the specific interleaving of operations in the run. Even this is an overkill—typically, the response to a query is determined not by the entire trace but by the subtrace generated by a set of relevant events whose size is bounded, independent of the length of the trace. Further, this set can usually be computed easily. We now formalize this intuition.

Definition 9 (Computable specification). *Let $\mathcal{D}$ be a CRDT and f be a declarative specification of $\mathcal{D}$. f is said to be computable if there exist computable functions $g : \mathcal{T} \times \mathcal{Q} \times \mathcal{V}^* \to \mathcal{T}$ and $h : \mathcal{T} \times \mathcal{Q} \times \mathcal{V}^* \to Ret$ such that:*

- *$g(t, q, args)$ is a subtrace of t containing only update events.*
- *$f(t, q, args) = h(g(t, q, args), q, args)$.*
- *If $g(t, q, args) \subseteq t' \subseteq t$ then $g(t', q, args) = g(t, q, args)$.*
- *If t and t' are isomorphic, $h(t, q, args) = h(t', q, args)$.*

In such a situation, we say that f is computable via g and h.

The subtrace $g(t, q, args)$ can be thought of as the relevant information needed to compute $f(t, q, args)$. The function h computes the desired value of f using the subtrace identified by g. The third condition captures a monotonicity constraint: information that has become irrelevant now will never reappear as relevant information later.

Example 10. OR-Set [1, 8, 11] is a CRDT implementation of sets. The operations are given by $\mathcal{D}_{OR-Set} = (\mathcal{V}, \{\textbf{contains}\}, \{\textbf{add}, \textbf{delete}\}, \{True, False\})$.

The main issue is resolving concurrent $\textbf{add}$ and $\textbf{delete}$ operations. In OR sets, $\textbf{add}$ wins in such a situation, so $\textbf{contains}$ returns true.

The declarative specification f capturing this behaviour, given via computable functions g and h, is defined as follows:

- *$(\forall x \in \mathcal{V})(\forall t \in \mathcal{T})\ g(t, \textbf{contains}, x)$ is the set of maximal events in the subtrace t_x of t where $t_x = \{e \mid Op(e) \in \{\textbf{add}, \textbf{delete}\} \land Args(e) = x\}$.*
- *$(\forall x \in \mathcal{V})(\forall t \in \mathcal{T})\ h(t, \textbf{contains}, x)$ is True iff there is a maximal event e of t with $Op(e) = \textbf{add}$ and $Args(e) = x$.*

Definition 11 (Bounded specification). *If a specification function f is computable via g and h and there is a bound K such that $|g(t, q, args)| \leq K$ for all t, q and $args$, we say that f is a bounded specification (with bound K).*

Example 12. The specification of OR-Sets provided in Example 10 is bounded with a bound $N = |\mathcal{R}|$ since $g(t, \textbf{contains}, x)$ contains the maximal x-events and there can be at most one maximal x-event in $g(t, \textbf{contains}, x)$ per replica.

3   CRDT Implementation

Recall that a run is a pair (ρ, φ) where ρ is a sequence of operations of $\mathcal{D}$ and φ is a function that identifies the update (at a remote replica) corresponding to each receive operation in ρ. When we consider an implementation of a CRDT, its runs will typically be just sequences of operations. The function φ is not provided along with the run, but it is reasonable to assume that the implementation has enough extra information to identify the update operation corresponding to each receive event. One way to model this abstractly is to timestamp each operation by a natural number and assign the same timestamp to a receive and its matching update. Since we are interested in finite-state CRDT implementations also, we would like to use a bounded linearly ordered set ID of identifiers as timestamps. It is simplest to assume that $ID \subseteq \mathbb{N}$.

For a time-stamped operation $o' = (o, id) \in \Sigma(\mathcal{D}) \times ID$, we define $Id(o') = id$ and $\psi(o') = \psi(o)$ for $\psi() \in \{Rep(), Op(), Ret(), Args()\}$.

We say that a timestamped run $\rho' \in (\Sigma(\mathcal{D}) \times ID)^*$ is *well-formed* if timestamps are assigned sensibly, as follows.

– for every receive operation $\rho'[j]$, there is $i < j$ such that $Id(\rho'[i]) = Id(\rho'[j])$, $Op(\rho'[i]) \in \mathcal{U}$ and for all $k \in [i+1..j-1]$,

$$Op(\rho'[k]) = \textbf{receive} \implies Rep(\rho'[k]) \neq Rep(\rho'[j]) \vee Id(\rho'[k]) \neq Id(\rho'[j]).$$

– For $i < j$, if $\rho'[i]$ and $\rho'[j]$ are update operations and $Id(\rho'[i]) = Id(\rho'[j])$, then for every replica $r \neq Rep(\rho'[i])$, there is a $k \in [i+1..j-1]$ such that $Op(\rho'[k]) = \textbf{receive}$, $Rep(\rho'[k]) = r$ and $Id(\rho'[k]) = Id(\rho'[i])$.

The first condition captures the fact that timestamps unambiguously match receive events to update operations. The second condition prevents a timestamp from being reused before it has been received by all replicas.

The run associated with a well-formed timestamped run $\rho' = ((o_1, \ell_1), (o_2, \ell_2), \ldots, (o_m, \ell_m))$ is a pair (ρ, φ) such that $\rho = o_1 o_2 \cdots o_m$ and for any $i \leq |\rho'|$, if o_i is a receive operation, $\varphi(i) = \max\{j < i \mid \ell_j = \ell_i$ and $Op(o_j) \in \mathcal{U}\}$.

In what follows, we consider only well-formed timestamped runs.

Lemma 13. *For every run (ρ, φ) of $\mathcal{D}$, we can identify a set ID such that there is a well-formed timestamped run $\rho' \in (\Sigma(\mathcal{D}) \times ID)^*$ whose associated run is (ρ, φ).*

Proof. All query operations can be labelled with a fixed identifier (say 0, for concreteness). Each update operation $\rho[i]$ is labelled with the smallest identifier in ID that does not label any undelivered update operation in $\rho[1 : i-1]$. Every receive operation $\rho[i]$ is labelled by the same identifier that labels $\rho[j]$, where $\varphi(i) = j$.

Definition 14 (CRDT Implementation and its runs). *An implementation of a CRDT $\mathcal{D}$ is a tuple $\mathcal{D}_I = (S, s^0, ID, \rightarrow)$ where:*

- S is set the global states.
- $s^0 \in S$ is the initial state.
- $ID \subseteq \mathbb{N}$ is the set of identifiers, which serve as timestamps.
- $\rightarrow \subseteq S \times (\Sigma(\mathcal{D}) \times ID) \times S$ is the transition relation.

A timestamped run $\rho' = o_1' \cdots o_n'$ is accepted by $\mathcal{D}_I$ if there exists a sequence of states $s_0 s_1 \cdots s_n$ such that $s_0 = s^0$, and for every $i \leq n$, $s_{i-1} \xrightarrow{o_i'} s_i$. (ρ, φ) is a run of $\mathcal{D}_I$ if it is the run associated with a well-formed timestamped run ρ' accepted by $\mathcal{D}_I$. We denote the set of all runs of $\mathcal{D}_I$ by $Runs(\mathcal{D}_I)$.

Definition 15 (Correctness of a CRDT Implementation). *Let $\mathcal{D}$ be a CRDT with declarative specification f. An implementation of CRDT $\mathcal{D}_I$ is correct if $Runs(\mathcal{D}_I) \subseteq Runs(\mathcal{D}, f)$.*

We now present a canonical implementation of a CRDT $\mathcal{D} = (\mathcal{V}, \mathcal{U}, \mathcal{Q}, \mathsf{Ret})$ with a declarative specification f. The canonical implementation, denoted $\mathcal{D}_{ref}$, satisfies the property that $Runs(\mathcal{D}_{ref}) = Runs(\mathcal{D}, f)$.

3.1 Reference Implementation

Before we describe the reference implementation, we present the ingredients needed. The aim is to maintain as little information as possible to respond to each query. The key observation is that the reference implementation is *global*— it can pool together information stored at all replicas without paying the cost of synchronization. If we have a declarative specification f of $\mathcal{D}$ that is computable via g and h, then each replica needs to maintain $\bigcup_{q,args} g(t, q, args)$, where t is the view of r at any point in time. The important ingredient in g is the precedence relation between events, and hence the reference implementation needs to store enough information to recover this. The implementation also needs to intelligently discard information that will no longer prove useful.

The most direct implementation would store (as part of the "state" of each replica) the relevant suffix of the trace—the upward closure of the events in $\bigcup_{q,args} g(t, q, args)$. But we choose a more compact representation called *Later Appearance Records* (LARs), from which the information needed to answer queries can be recovered. An LAR is a set of sequences rather than a partial order, and hence easier to manipulate.

Let $\mathcal{L}$ be a (potentially infinite) set of labels, equipped with a total order $\leq$. We use labels to distinguish between multiple occurrences of the same update method at the same replica with the same arguments. Operations equipped with labels are called nodes.

Definition 16 (Node). *A node is a tuple $(u, r, args, l) \in \mathcal{U} \times \mathcal{R} \times \mathcal{V}^* \times \mathcal{L}$. For $v = (u, r, args, l)$, we define $Op(v) = u$, $Rep(v) = r$, $Args(v) = args$ and $Label(v) = l$. The set of all nodes is denoted by $\mathcal{N}$.*

Definition 17 (Later Appearance Record). *A Later Appearance Record (LAR) is a sequence of distinct nodes. For a node v and an LAR A, we write $v \in A$ to denote that v appears in the sequence of nodes in A.*

For nodes $v_1, v_2 \in A$, $v_1 \leq_A v_2$ if v_1 occurs earlier than v_2 in A. If A is an LAR and V is a set of nodes then $A - V$ is the subsequence of A consisting of nodes not in V. The set of all LARs is denoted by $\mathcal{A}$.

Each replica uses the LAR to record the order in which it has seen updates, originating locally as well as remotely. In an actual implementation, updates are generated at replicas, and information about them is passed to other replicas by the network, whose behaviour is not under the control of the implementation. But it is assumed that when a replica receives information about an update, it can determine which update is being mentioned. The network might sometimes provide additional guarantees about message delivery (such as *causal delivery* or *FIFO delivery*), and we can sometimes make use of these facts to simplify the implementation. Here we present the general case, without any assumptions about the network.

When information about an update has been passed to all other replicas, we would like to be able to discard this information from every replica. For this, it becomes important to record the set of replicas to which information about an update has been communicated. This is modelled using a *network node*. Recall that a node is an update operation along with an identifying label. A network node attaches to a node a timestamp as well information about the state of replicas that have received the update.

Definition 18 (Network node). *A network node is a member of $\mathcal{N} \times ID \times 2^{\mathcal{R}}$. The set of all network nodes is denoted by $\mathcal{N}_{net}$. For a network node $v_{net} = (v, id, R)$ we define $Node(v_{net})$ to mean v, $Id(v_{net})$ to mean id and define $Rep(v_{net})$, $Id(v_{net})$, $Args(v_{net})$ and $Label(v_{net})$ to be the corresponding functions applied on v. We use $Delivered(v_{net})$ to denote R.*

A configuration consists of the LAR of each replica along with the network nodes pertaining to undelivered updates. The aim is to try to purge nodes from LARs whenever possible. A *consistent configuration* is one where these purges have been done safely. Specifically, replica r does not purge a node pertaining to a local update so long as it is present in the LAR of some other replica. Also, if information about a local update has not yet been communicated to all other replicas, r does not purge the corresponding node.

Definition 19 (Configuration). *A configuration C is a member of $\mathcal{A}^{\mathcal{R}} \times 2^{\mathcal{N}_{net}}$. For any configuration $C = ((A_1, A_2, \ldots, A_N), V_{net})$, we denote by $C[r]$ the LAR A_r. We shall denote by C_{net} the set of network nodes V_{net}.*

We say that a configuration C is consistent iff

- *$\forall r, r'$ if there exists $v \in C[r]$ such that $Rep(v) = r'$ then $v \in C[r']$.*
- *$\forall v_{net} \in C_{net}$ if $r \in Delivered(v_{net})$ then $Node(v_{net}) \in C[r]$.*

The trivial configuration denoted by C^0 is one where $\forall r \in \mathcal{R} : C^0[r]$ is the empty LAR and $C^0_{net} = \emptyset$. We denote the set of all consistent configurations by $\mathcal{C}$.

Using the LARs of all the replicas, we can reconstruct the happened before relation for all events that are mentioned in a configuration. Suppose r sees two updates u' and u'' originating at r' and r''. Since updates are seen at the originating replica first before being seen by others, the relation between u' and u'' can be determined by their relative order of appearances in the LARs of r' and r''. Here we crucially use the fact that our implementation is *global*.

Definition 20 (Precedence and Concurrency). *Let C be a consistent configuration. Let r be a replica and $v_i, v_j \in C[r]$ with $Rep(v_i) = r'$ and $Rep(v_j) = r''$. We say that v_i precedes v_j in C, denoted by $v_i \leq_C v_j$, if $(v_i \in C[r''] \land v_i \leq_{C[r'']} v_j) \land (v_j \in C[r'] \implies v_i \leq_{C[r']} v_j)$. (In other words, both r' and r'' locally see v_i before v_j.)*

If neither $v_i \leq_C v_j$ nor $v_j \leq_C v_i$ for any $v_i, v_j \in C[r]$, then we say that v_i and v_j are concurrent in C, denoted by $v_i \parallel_C v_j$.

For a consistent configuration C and replica r, the view of r in C, denoted by $\partial_r(C)$, is the trace $(C[r], \leq_C)$.

If a node in a trace t contains information about an update that is in $g(t, q, args)$ for a query $q(args)$, then that node cannot be purged—otherwise the response to that query would be inaccurate. This is formalized below.

Definition 21 (Relevant node). *Let f be a specification of $\mathcal{D}$ computable via g and h. We say that a node v in a consistent configuration C is relevant with respect to f if there exists a replica r, query $q \in \mathcal{Q}$ and args $\in \mathcal{V}^*$, such that $v \in g(\partial_r(C), q, args)$.*

3.2   Details of the Reference Implementation

The reference implementation is formally presented below. Each replica maintains an LAR to which it appends information pertaining to each local update. On receiving information about a remote update, it again appends this to the LAR, and also seeks to purge from all LARs nodes that have ceased to become relevant and have been seen by all replicas. This enables the reuse of labels. Since at any trace t the relevant nodes subsume all subtraces of the form $g(t, q, args)$, it follows that the implementation never purges information that is needed to answer a query.

Let f be a specification of a CRDT $\mathcal{D}$ computable via g and h. Its reference implementation is defined to be $\mathcal{D}_{ref} = (\mathcal{C}, C_0, ID, \rightarrow_{ref})$ where $ID = \mathbb{N}$ and $\rightarrow_{ref}$ is defined as follows.

Let $C, C' \in \mathcal{C}$ and let $o = ((m, r, args, ret), id) \in \Sigma(D) \times ID$. Then $C \xrightarrow{o}_{ref} C'$ iff one of the following holds:

- $m \in \mathcal{Q}$ and $ret = f(\partial_r(C), m, args)$ and $C' = C$.
- $m \in \mathcal{U}$, $\forall v_{net} \in C_{net} : Id(v_{net}) \neq id$, and C' is defined as follows:
  - $\forall r' \in \mathcal{R} : r' \neq r \implies C'[r'] = C[r']$.
  - $C'[r] = C[r].v$, with $v = (m, r, args, l)$ where l is a label such that $\forall v' \in C[r] : Label(v') \neq l$.

- $C'_{net} = C_{net} \cup \{(v, id, \{r\})\}$.
- $m = \mathbf{receive}$ and there exists a node v and $R \subseteq \mathcal{R}$ such that $(v, id, R) \in C_{net}$ and $r \notin R$, and C' is defined as follows:
  Let C'' be a configuration given by
  - $\forall r' \neq r : C''[r'] = C[r']$.
  - $C''[r] = C[r].v$.
  - $C''_{net} = C_{net} \cup \{(v, id, R \cup \{r\})\} \setminus \{(v, id, R)\}$.

  If $R \cup \{r\} \neq \mathcal{R}$ then $C' = C''$ else
  - $\forall r' \in \mathcal{R} : C'[r'] = C''[r'] - V$, where

$$V = \{v \in \bigcap_{r' \in \mathcal{R}} C''[r'] \mid v \text{ is not relevant in } C''\}.$$

  - $C'_{net} = C''_{net} \setminus \{(v, id, R \cup \{r\})\}$.

3.3 Correctness of the Reference Implementation

Lemma 22. *Every reachable configuration C of $\mathcal{D}_{ref}$ is consistent.*

Proof. The initial configuration is trivially consistent, and each transition purges only those nodes that are no longer relevant and are delivered to every replica. This proves the lemma.

Lemma 23. *Suppose $\rho' \in (\Sigma(\mathcal{D}) \times ID)^*$ is accepted by $\mathcal{D}_{ref}$ and that $C_0 \xrightarrow{\rho'}_{ref} C$. Let (ρ, φ) be the run associated with ρ' and $t = trace(\rho, \varphi)$. Then, for all r, q and args, $g(\partial_r(t), q, args)$ is isomorphic to $g(\partial_r(C), q, args)$.*

Proof. The proof is by induction on the length of ρ'. The case when $\rho' = \varepsilon$ is trivial. So let $\rho' = \sigma'.o$. Let C' be a configuration such that $C_0 \xrightarrow{\sigma'}_{ref} C' \xrightarrow{o}_{ref} C$. Let (σ, φ) be the run corresponding to σ' and let $t' = trace(\sigma, \varphi)$. We assume by the induction hypothesis that for all r, q and args, $g(\partial_r(t'), q, args)$ is isomorphic to $g(\partial_r(C'), q, args)$. There are three cases to be considered.

o **is a query operation:** In this case $C = C'$ and $t = t'$, so the lemma follows.

o **is an update operation:** Suppose $Rep(o) = r$. For $r' \neq r$, it is clear from the transition rules that $C[r'] = C'[r']$. It is also the case that $\partial_{r'}(t) = \partial_{r'}(t')$, so the lemma still holds for queries at replicas other than r.

On the other hand, $C[r] = C'[r].v$ where v is a node with a fresh id, corresponding to o. Since v is the latest node in $C[r]$ and $v \notin C[r']$ for any other r', it is clear that $v' \leq_C v$ iff $v' \in C[r]$. But $v' \in C[r]$ iff v' corresponds to an update received by r or originating in r. Thus $\partial_r(C) = \partial_r(C') \cup \{v\}$, with v as the largest element. It is easy to see that the maximal r-event in the trace t is greater than all other events in $\partial_r(t')$. Thus $g(\partial_r(C), q, args)$ is isomorphic to $g(\partial_r(t), q, args)$.

o **is a receive operation:** Suppose $Rep(o) = r$. We add a node at the end of $C[r]$, but also purge all the LARs of some irrelevant nodes (those that are received by every replica). Since irrelevant nodes do not feature in $g(\partial_{r'}(t), q, args)$ for any r' and $q(args)$, all we need to show is that the order among relevant nodes is captured correctly. But the order between update events does not change at the point of time of a receive. It can be checked that $\leq_C \; = \; \leq_{C'}$, and thus the lemma follows.

Lemma 24. *Suppose a well-formed timestamped run $\rho' \in (\Sigma(\mathcal{D}) \times ID)^*$ is accepted by $\mathcal{D}_{ref}$. Let (ρ, φ) be the run associated with ρ'. Then $(\rho, \varphi) \in Runs(\mathcal{D}, f)$.*

Proof. Suppose $C_0 \xrightarrow{\rho'}_{ref} C$. Let $t = trace(\rho, \varphi)$. Since $g(\partial_r(C), q, args)$ is isomorphic to $g(t, q, args)$ and since h returns the same values on isomorphic traces, it easily follows that for all query operations $\rho[i] = (q, r, args, ret)$, $ret = f(\partial_r(trace(\rho[i], \varphi)), q, args)$. Thus $(\rho, \varphi) \in Runs(\mathcal{D}, f)$.

Lemma 25. *Suppose $(\rho, \varphi) \in Runs(\mathcal{D}, f)$. Let $\rho' \in (\Sigma(\mathcal{D}) \times ID)^*$ be a well-formed timestamped run whose associated run is (ρ, φ). Then ρ' is accepted by $\mathcal{D}_{ref}$.*

Proof. We prove the lemma for $\rho'[1 : i]$, by induction on i. The base case, when $i = 0$ is trivial. So let $i > 0$. Suppose $\rho'[1 : i - 1]$ is accepted by $\mathcal{D}_{ref}$ by an execution ending in configuration C. Let (σ, φ) and (σ', φ) be the runs associated with $\rho'[1 : i - 1]$ and $\rho'[1 : i]$ respectively. Let $t = trace(\sigma, \varphi)$ and $t' = trace(\sigma', \varphi)$. Let $o = \rho'[i] = ((m, r, args, ret), id)$. There are three cases to consider.

$m \in \mathcal{Q}$: In this case $t = t'$. We know that $ret = f(\partial_r(t'), m, args) = f(\partial_r(t), m, args)$. But we also know that $g(\partial_r(C), m, args)$ is isomorphic to $g(\partial_r(t), m, args)$. Thus it follows that $ret = f(\partial_r(C), m, args)$. Hence $C \xrightarrow{o} C$ and $\rho'[1 : i]$ is accepted by $\mathcal{D}_{ref}$.

$m \in \mathcal{U}$: Since $\rho'[1 : i]$ is well-formed, it has to be the case that either id is not used in $\rho'[1 : i - 1]$, or if it is used in an update operation $\rho'[j]$, every replica has received that update in $\rho'[j+1 : i-1]$. Thus, there is no node $v_{net} \in C_{net}$ with $Id(v_{net}) = id$. So, o is enabled at C and $\rho[1 : i]$ is accepted by $\mathcal{D}_{ref}$.

$m =$ **receive:** Since $\rho'[1 : i]$ is well-formed, it has to be the case that there is an earlier update at some other replica with the same identifier that has not yet been communicated to r. Thus there exists a node v and $R \subseteq \mathcal{R}$ such that $(v, id, R) \in C_{net}$ and $r \notin R$. It follows that o is enabled at C and $\rho'[1 : i]$ is accepted by $\mathcal{D}_{ref}$.

From the previous two lemmas we can conclude the following:

Theorem 26. $Runs(\mathcal{D}_{ref}) = Runs(\mathcal{D}, f)$

3.4   Bounding the Reference Implementation

For effective verification, we need to ensure that the set of traces of the CRDT has a finite representation. The reference implementation constructed in the previous section is not necessarily finite-state. The unboundedness arises due to several reasons.

- If the size of the universe is not bounded, the number of nodes, and hence the number of configurations, will not be bounded.
- If there is no bound on the number of undelivered messages, then the number of network states would be unbounded, and therefore the size of C_{net} of any configuration C is unbounded.
- If the specification of the CRDT itself is not finite, then the number of relevant nodes in the configuration is unbounded, even when the universe V is finite.

With some reasonable assumptions, we can ensure that the reference implementation is finite-state.

1. **Universe Size:** We assume that the size of the universe is bounded by a parameter m. This is a reasonable assumption since most CRDT implementations treat the elements of the universe in a uniform manner. Hence for the purpose of verification, it suffices to consider a universe whose size is bounded.
2. **Delivery Constraints:** We assume that the number of undelivered messages in the network is bounded by the parameter b. Again, this is a reasonable assumption since most practical implementations of strong eventual consistency also requires that messages are reliably delivered to all the replicas. We can pick a sufficiently large b that correctly characterizes the network guarantee of the actual implementation.
3. **Bounded Specification:** We assume that the specification function f computable via g and h comes with a bound K. Let k be the maximum arity of any $q \in \mathcal{Q}$. If the universe if bounded, the number of query instances is bounded by $|\mathcal{Q}| \times m^k$. Since the specification function has a bound K, the size of the relevant nodes in a configuration is bounded by $\ell = K \times |\mathcal{Q}| \times m^k$. For example, in case of OR-sets, to answer the query **contains**(x) it suffices to keep track of the maximal x-events. Since the number of replicas $\mathcal{R}$ is bounded by N the number of maximal x-events is bounded by N. Hence if the universe is bounded by m then the number of relevant nodes in a configuration is no more than $m \cdot N$.

We now prove that, with these assumptions, the size of the reference implementation is bounded. Each configuration of $\mathcal{D}_{ref}$ consists of an LAR for each replica, and a set of network nodes. As is clear from the transition rules, the only network nodes we retain are those that are still undelivered to some replicas. Thus, if there is a bound on the number of undelivered messages, there is also a bound on the number of network nodes present in each configuration. But the set of network nodes that occur in all configurations might still be unbounded. To bound this, we need to bound the set of all nodes and the set ID. The size of the set ID can be bounded by b, the number of undelivered messages, as explained below.

Let C be a reachable configuration of $\mathcal{D}_{ref}$ and o an update operation enabled at C. Now it has to be the case that only if there are at most $b-1$ network nodes in C_{net} (otherwise, there would be more than b undelivered messages in the run upto and including o). Thus as long ID has b elements, the reference implementation can always attach a fresh timestamp to o. (Formally this means that we can map any timestamped run of $\mathcal{D}_{ref}$ to an equivalent run which uses at most b timestamps.)

We now turn to bounding the set of all nodes. The only unbounded component in this is the set $\mathcal{L}$ of labels.

Lemma 27. *If the number of undelivered messages is bounded by b and the number of relevant events is bounded by ℓ then it is sufficient to have a label set $\mathcal{L}$ of size $b + \ell$.*

Proof. Let $\rho = \rho'.o$ be any run of the reference implementation such that the number of undelivered messages in ρ is bounded by b. Let o be an update operation at replica r. Let C' be the configuration of the reference implementation at the end of ρ'.

Note that the number of undelivered update operations in ρ' is strictly less than b; otherwise, ρ would have more than b undelivered messages. It follows that the number of undelivered nodes in C' is at most $b-1$. (A node v is undelivered in C' if $(v, R) \in C'_{net}$ for some $R \subseteq \mathcal{R}$.) A node v is present in some LAR $C'[r']$ if v is undelivered or v is relevant. Thus the number of distinct nodes in C' is at most $b + \ell - 1$. Thus if $|\mathcal{L}| = b + \ell$, there is at least one free label in $\mathcal{L}$ to label the new node $C[r] \setminus C'[r]$. Thus, it is sufficient to have a label set $\mathcal{L}$ of size $b + \ell$.

From the above, we can conclude that the number of nodes in $\mathcal{N}$ is bounded by $|\mathcal{U}| \times N \times m^{k'} \times (b + \ell)$ (where, as before, k' is the maximum arity of any $u \in \mathcal{U}$).

Since the set ID is also bounded (by b, as already explained), the set of network nodes is bounded (by $|\mathcal{N}| \times |ID| \times 2^N$).

From Lemma 27 it is clear that the number of distinct nodes in any configuration cannot exceed $b + \ell$. Since the number of undelivered messages are bounded by b, the number of network nodes is bounded by b. Thus, the set of all configurations $\mathcal{C}$ is bounded as follows:

$$|\mathcal{C}| \le |\mathcal{N}|^{(b+\ell)} \times |\mathcal{N}_{net}|^b.$$

Theorem 28. *If the number of undelivered messages and the size of the universe are bounded and we have a bounded specification for the CRDT, then the reference implementation is bounded.*

4 Effective Verification Using Bounded Reference Implementation via CEGAR

Verifying CRDT implementations is a challenging task. For instance, consider an implementation that uses a bounded set of timestamps as we have proposed, except that the size of this set is too small. Under certain circumstances, a replica may be forced to reuse a timestamp even when a previous update with the same timestamp has not been delivered. To detect such an error, we have to explore a run that exceeds the bound in the implementation. Unfortunately, we typically do not have access to the internal details of the implementation, so this bound is not known in advance. This results in an unbounded verification task.

Alternatively, we have seen that by making reasonable restrictions on the universe of the datatype and the behaviour of the underlying messasge delivery system, we can generate a bounded reference implementation. Once we have such a bounded reference implementation, we can use Counter Example Guided Abstract Refinement (CEGAR) [3] to effectively verify a given CRDT implementation with respect to the assumptions made on the environment.

More formally, given a implementation of a CRDT with bounded specification, let us assume suitable bounds on the size of the universe, m, and the number of undelivered messages, b. We fix the bounded set of timestamps ID accordingly. We assume the existence of an abstraction function that provides a finite state abstraction $\mathcal{D}_I = (S_I, s^0, ID, \rightarrow_I)$ of the implementation, whose runs are in $(\Sigma(D) \times ID)^*$.

We then construct the synchronous product $\mathcal{M}_{sync} = ((S_I \times C) \cup \{s_{err}\}, (s^0, C^0), ID, \rightarrow_{sync})$, where $\rightarrow_{sync}$ is defined as follows:

- The action $o \in \Sigma(\mathcal{D}) \times ID$ is enabled at the product state (s, C) iff o is enabled at s in $\mathcal{D}_I$. If o is enabled then we define
  - $(s, C) \xrightarrow{o}_{sync} s_{err}$, if o is not enabled at C in $\mathcal{D}_{ref}$
  - $(s, C) \xrightarrow{o}_{sync} (s', C')$, if $s \xrightarrow{o}_I s'$ and $C \xrightarrow{o}_{ref} C'$.
- $\forall o \in \Sigma_{\mathcal{D}} : o$ is not enabled at s_{err}

Lemma 29. *If ρ is a run of $\mathcal{M}_{sync}$ resulting in the state s_{err} starting from the initial state (s^0, C^0), then $\rho \in Runs(\mathcal{D}_I) \setminus Runs(\mathcal{D}, f)$.*

Thus any run ρ leading to the state s_{err} in the synchronous product is a potential counter example. As usual, we can use the finite abstraction to try trace an actual run in original implementation corresponding to ρ. If we succeed in finding such a run, we have found a bug in the original implementation. If the abstract counterexample turns out to be infeasible, then we refine our abstraction using the feedback obtained from our failure to construct a valid run. We repeat this process until a bug is found or we are satisfied with the level of abstraction to which we have verified the system.

5   Conclusion

In this paper, we have shown how to construct a reference implementation for a CRDT that is described using a bounded declarative specification. By imposing reasonable constraints on the universe of the datatype and the underlying message delivery subsystem, the reference implementation can be made finite-state. This can be exploited to verify any given implementation using CEGAR.

The key observation in this paper is that a global reference implementation suffices for verification. This greatly simplifies the construction compared to the distributed reference implementation described in [9], which requires an intricate distributed timestamping procedure due to the local nature of the information available at each replica.

The other interesting feature of our reference implementation is that the basic construction using LARs is independent of the assumptions that we make on the set of data values and the nature of message delivery in order to bound the set of timestamps used. Thus, the reference implementation relies only on the declarative specificaton of the CRDT. We can then separately reason about the size of this implementation under various constraints on the operating environment.

In future work, we would like to explore further benefits of declarative specifications for replicated data types. In particular, one challenging problem is to develop a theory in which we can compose such specifications to derive complex replicated data types by combining simpler ones.

References

1. Bieniusa, A., Zawirski, M., Preguiça, N.M., Shapiro, M., Baquero, C., Balegas, V., Duarte, S.: An optimized conflict-free replicated set. CoRR, abs/1210.3368 (2012)
2. Burkhardt, S., Gotsman, A., Yang, H., Zawirski, M.: Replicated data types: specification, verification, optimality. In: The 41st Annual ACM SIGPLAN-SIGACT Symposium on Principles of Programming Languages, POPL 2014, 20–21 January, 2014, San Diego, CA, USA, pp. 271–284 (2014)
3. Clarke, E.M., Grumberg, O., Jha, S., Lu, Y., Veith, H.: Counterexample-guided abstraction refinement for symbolic model checking. J. ACM 50(5), 752–794 (2003)
4. Gilbert, S., Lynch, N.A.: Brewer's conjecture and the feasibility of consistent, available, partition-tolerant web services. SIGACT News 33(2), 51–59 (2002)
5. Gurevich, Y., Harrington, L.: Trees, automata, and games. In: Proceedings of the Fourteenth Annual ACM Symposium on Theory of Computing, STOC 1982, pp. 60–65. ACM, New York (1982)
6. Mazurkiewicz, A.: Trace theory. In: Brauer, W., Reisig, W., Rozenberg, G. (eds.) Advances in Petri Nets 1986. LNCS, vol. 255, pp. 278–324. Springer, Heidelberg (1987)
7. Mukund, M., Kumar, K.N., Sohoni, M.A.: Bounded time-stamping in message-passing systems. Theor. Comput. Sci. 290(1), 221–239 (2003)
8. Mukund, M., Shenoy R., G., Suresh, S.P.: Optimized OR-sets without ordering constraints. In: Chatterjee, M., Cao, J., Kothapalli, K., Rajsbaum, S. (eds.) ICDCN 2014. LNCS, vol. 8314, pp. 227–241. Springer, Heidelberg (2014)
9. Mukund, M., Shenoy R., G., Suresh, S.P.: Bounded implementations of replicated data types. In: D'Souza, D., Lal, A., Larsen, K.G. (eds.) VMCAI 2015. LNCS, vol. 8931, pp. 355–372. Springer, Heidelberg (2015)
10. Mukund, M., Sohoni, M.A.: Keeping track of the latest gossip in a distributed system. Distributed Comput. 10(3), 137–148 (1997)

11. Shapiro, M., Preguiça, N., Baquero, C., Zawirski, M.: A comprehensive study of Convergent and Commutative Replicated Data Types. Rapport de recherche RR-7506, INRIA (2011). http://hal.inria.fr/inria-00555588/PDF/techreport.pdf
12. Shapiro, M., Preguiça, N., Baquero, C., Zawirski, M.: Conflict-free replicated data types. In: Défago, X., Petit, F., Villain, V. (eds.) SSS 2011. LNCS, vol. 6976, pp. 386–400. Springer, Heidelberg (2011)

TSO-to-TSO Linearizability Is Undecidable

Chao Wang[1,2]($\boxtimes$), Yi Lv[1], and Peng Wu[1]

[1] State Key Laboratory of Computer Science, Institute of Software,
Chinese Academy of Sciences, Beijing, China
wangch@ios.ac.cn
[2] University of Chinese Academy of Sciences, Beijing, China

Abstract. *TSO-to-TSO linearizability* is a variant of linearizability for concurrent libraries on the Total Store Order (TSO) memory model. It is proved in this paper that TSO-to-TSO linearizability for a bounded number of processes is undecidable. We first show that the trace inclusion problem of a classic-lossy single-channel system, which is known undecidable, can be reduced to the history inclusion problem of specific libraries on the TSO memory model. Based on the equivalence between history inclusion and extended history inclusion for these libraries, we then prove that the extended history inclusion problem of libraries is undecidable on the TSO memory model. By means of extended history inclusion as an equivalent characterization of TSO-to-TSO linearizability, we finally prove that TSO-to-TSO linearizability is undecidable for a bounded number of processes.

1 Introduction

Libraries of high performance concurrent data structures have been widely used in concurrent programs to take advantage of multi-core architectures, such as *java.util.concurrent* for Java and *std::thread* for C++11. It is important but notoriously difficult to ensure that concurrent libraries are designed and implemented correctly. *Linearizability* [10] is accepted as a *de facto* correctness condition for a concurrent library with respect to its sequential specification on the sequential consistency (SC) memory model [11]. It is well known that on the SC memory model linearizability of a concurrent library is decidable for a bounded number of processes [1], but undecidable for an unbounded number of processes [5].

However, modern multiprocessors (e.g., x86 [14], POWER [15]) and programming languages (e.g., C/C++ [4], Java [13]) do not comply with the SC memory model. As a matter of fact, they provide *relaxed memory models*, which allow subtle behaviors due to hardware or compiler optimization. For instance, in a multiprocessor system implementing the total store order (TSO) memory model [14], each processor is equipped with an FIFO store buffer. Any write operation

---

This work is partially supported by the National Natural Science Foundation of China under Grants No.60721061, No.60833001, No.61272135, No.61700073, No.61100069, No.61472405, and No.61161130530.

B. Finkbeiner et al. (Eds.): ATVA 2015, LNCS 9364, pp. 309–325, 2015.
DOI: 10.1007/978-3-319-24953-7_24

performed by a processor is put into its local store buffer first and can then be flushed into the main memory at any time.

The notion of linearizability has been extended for relaxed memory models, e.g., *TSO-to-TSO linearizability* [7] and *TSO-to-SC linearizability* [9] for the TSO memory model and two variants of linearizability [3] for the C++ memory model. These notions generalize the original one by relating concurrent libraries with their abstract implementations, in the way as shown in [8] for the SC memory model. It is worth mentioning that these notions of linearizability satisfy the abstraction theorem [3,7,9]: if a library is linearizable with respect to its abstract implementation, every observable behavior of any client program using the former can be observed when the program uses the latter instead. Concurrent software developer can benefit from this correspondence in that the library can be safely replaced with its abstract implementation for the sake of optimization or the ease of verification of the client program.

The decision problems for linearizability on relaxed memory models become more complicated. Because of the hierarchy of memory models, it is rather trivial to see that linearizability on relaxed memory models is undecidable for an unbounded number of processes, based on the known undecidability result on the SC memory model [5]. But the decision problem of linearizability on relaxed memory models remains open for a bounded number of processes.

In this paper we mainly study the decision problem for the TSO-to-TSO linearizability of concurrent libraries within a bounded number of processes. TSO-to-TSO linearizability is the first definition of linearizability on relaxed memory models. It relates a library running on the TSO memory model to its abstract implementation running also on the TSO memory model. Histories of method invocations/responses are typically concerned by the standard notion of linearizability. For TSO-to-TSO linearizability, such histories have to be extended to reflect the interactions between concurrent libraries and processor-local store buffers.

The main result of this paper is that TSO-to-TSO linearizability is undecidable for a bounded number of processes. We first show that the extended history inclusion is an equivalent characterization of TSO-to-TSO linearizability. Then, we prove our undecidability result by reducing the trace inclusion problem between any two configurations of a classic-lossy single-channel system to the extended history inclusion problem between two specific libraries. Recall that the trace inclusion problem between configurations of a classic-lossy single-channel system is undecidable [16]. The reduction is achieved by using as a bridge the history inclusion between these two specific libraries.

Technically, we present a library template that can be instantiated as a specific library for a configuration of a classic-lossy single-channel system. The library is designed with three methods M_i for $1 \leq i \leq 3$. We use two processes P_1 and P_2, calling methods M_1 and M_2, respectively, to simulate the traces of the classic-lossy single-channel system starting from the given configuration. This is based on the observation that on the TSO memory model, a process may miss updates by other processes because multiple flush operations may occur between consecutive read operations of the process [2]. But a channel system accesses the content of a channel always in an FIFO manner; while on the contrary, a process on the TSO memory model always reads the latest updates in its local store buffer (whenever possible). Herein, processes P_1 and P_2 alternatively update their own store buffers, while read only from each other's store buffer. In this way, the labeled transitions of the classic-lossy single-channel system can be reproduced through the interactions between processes P_1 and P_2. Furthermore, we use the third process P_3, calling method M_3 repeatedly, to return each fired transition label repeatedly, so that the traces of the classic-lossy single-channel system starting from a given configuration can be mimicked by the histories of the library exactly. Specially, methods M_1 and M_2 never return, while method M_3 just uses an atomic write operation to return labels in order not to touch process P_3's store buffer. Consequently, we can easily establish the equivalence between the history inclusion and the extended history inclusion between the specific libraries.

By constructing two specific libraries based on the above library template, we show that the trace inclusion problem between any two configurations of a classic-lossy single-channel system can be reduced to the history inclusion problem between the corresponding two concurrent libraries, while the history inclusion relation and the extended history inclusion relation are equivalent between these two libraries. Then, the undecidability result of TSO-to-TSO linearizability for a bounded number of processes follows from its equivalent characterization and the undecidability result of classic-lossy single-channel system. To our best knowledge, this is the first result on the decidability of linearizability of concurrent libraries on relaxed memory models.

Related Work. Efforts have been devoted on the decidability and model checking of linearizability on the SC memory model [1,5,6,12,17]. The principle of our equivalent characterization for TSO-to-TSO linearizability is similar to that of the characterization given by Bouajjani et al. in [6], where history inclusion is proved to be an equivalent characterization of linearizability. Alur et al. proved that for a bounded number of processes, checking whether a regular set of histories is linearizable with respect to its regular sequential specification can be reduced to a history inclusion problem, and hence is decidable [1]. Bouajjani et al. proved that the problem of whether a library is linearizable with respect to its regular sequential specification for a unbounded number of processes is undecidable, by a reduction from the reachability problem of a counter machine (which is known to be undecidable) [5].

On the other hand, the decidability of linearizability on relaxed memory models is still open for a bounded number of processes. The closest work to ours is [2] by Atig et al., where a lossy channel system is simulated by a concurrent program on the TSO memory model. Our approach of using methods M_1 and M_2 to simulate a classic-lossy single-channel system is inspired by their work. However, in [2], it was the decidable reachability problem of the channel system that was reduced to the reachability problem of the concurrent program on the TSO memory model. Hence, only the start and end configurations of the channel system are needed in their reduction. In this paper, we reduce the trace inclusion problem between any two configurations of a classic-lossy single-channel system, which is undecidable, to the TSO-to-TSO linearizability problem. Our reduction needs to show exactly each step of transitions in the channel system.

2   TSO Concurrent Systems

In this section, we first present the notations of libraries, the most general clients and TSO concurrent systems. Then, we introduce their operational semantics on the TSO memory model.

2.1   Notations

In general, a finite sequence on an alphabet Σ is denoted $l = \alpha_1 \cdot \alpha_2 \cdot \ldots \cdot \alpha_k$, where $\cdot$ is the concatenation symbol and $\alpha_i \in \Sigma$ for each $1 \leq i \leq k$. Let $|l|$ denote the length of l, i.e., $|l| = k$, and $l(i)$ denote the i-th element of l for $1 \leq i \leq k$, i.e., $l(i) = \alpha_i$. For an alphabet Σ', let $l \uparrow_{\Sigma'}$ denote the projection of l to Σ'. Given a function f, let $f[x : y]$ be the function that shares the same value as f everywhere, except for x, where it has the value y. We use _ for an item, of which the value is irrelevant.

A *labelled transition system* (*LTS*) is a tuple $\mathcal{A} = (Q, \Sigma, \rightarrow, q_0)$, where Q is a set of states, Σ is a set of transition labels, $\rightarrow \subseteq Q \times \Sigma \times Q$ is a transition relation and q_0 is the initial state. A state of the LTS $\mathcal{A}$ may be referred to as a *configuration* in the rest of the paper.

A path of $\mathcal{A}$ is a finite transition sequence $q_1 \xrightarrow{\beta_1} q_2 \xrightarrow{\beta_2} \ldots \xrightarrow{\beta_k} q_{k+1}$ for $k \geq 0$. A trace of $\mathcal{A}$ is a finite sequence $t = \beta_1 \cdot \beta_2 \cdot \ldots \cdot \beta_k$, where $k \geq 0$ if there exists a path $q_1 \xrightarrow{\beta_1} q_2 \xrightarrow{\beta_2} \ldots \xrightarrow{\beta_k} q_{k+1}$ of $\mathcal{A}$. Let $path(\mathcal{A}, q)$ and $trace(\mathcal{A}, q)$ denote all the paths and traces of $\mathcal{A}$ that start from q, respectively. We write $path(\mathcal{A})$ and $trace(\mathcal{A})$ for short if $q = q_0$.

2.2   Libraries and the Most General Clients

A library implementing a concurrent data structure provides a set of methods for external users to access the data structure. It may contain private memory locations for its own use. A client program is a program that interacts with libraries. For simplicity, we assume that each method has just one parameter and one return value if it returns. Furthermore, all the parameters and the return values are passed via a special register r_f.

For a library, let $\mathcal{X}$ be a finite set of its memory locations, $\mathcal{M}$ be a finite set of its method names, $\mathcal{D}$ be its finite data domain, $\mathcal{R}$ be a finite set of its register names and $\mathcal{RE}$ be a finite set of its register expressions over $\mathcal{R}$. Then, a set $PCom$ of primitive commands considered in this paper includes:

- Register assign commands in the form of $r = re$;
- Register reset commands in the form of $havoc$;
- Read commands in the form of $read(x, r)$;
- Write commands in the form of $write(r, x)$;

- *Cas* commands in the form of $r_1 = cas(x, r_2, r_3)$;
- Assume commands in the form of $assume(r)$;
- Call commands in the form of $call(m)$;

where $r, r_1, r_2, r_3 \in \mathcal{R}, re \in \mathcal{RE}, x \in \mathcal{X}$. Herein, the notations of registers and register expressions are similar to those used in [7].

A *cas* command compresses a read and a write commands into a single one, which is meant to be executed atomically. It is often implemented with the compare-and-swap or load-linked/store-conditional primitive at the level of multiprocessors. This type of commands is widely used in concurrent libraries. A *havoc* command [7] assigns arbitrary values to all registers in $\mathcal{R}$.

A control-flow graph is a tuple $CFG = (N, L, T, q_i, q_f)$, where N is a finite set of program positions, L is a set of primitive commands, $T \subseteq N \times L \times N$ is a control-flow transition relation, q_i is the initial position and q_f is the final position.

A library $\mathcal{L}$ can then be defined as a tuple $\mathcal{L} = (Q_\mathcal{L}, \rightarrow_\mathcal{L}, InitV_\mathcal{L})$, such that $Q_\mathcal{L} = \bigcup_{m \in \mathcal{M}} Q_m$ is a finite set of program positions, where Q_m is the program positions of a method m of this library; $\rightarrow_\mathcal{L} = \bigcup_{m \in \mathcal{M}} \rightarrow_m$ is a control-flow transition relation, where for each $m \in \mathcal{M}$, $(Q_m, PCom, \rightarrow_m, i_m, f_m)$ is a control-flow graph with a unique initial position i_m and a unique final position f_m; $InitV_\mathcal{L} : \mathcal{X} \rightarrow \mathcal{D}$ is an initial valuation for its memory locations.

The most general client of a library is a special client program that is used to exhibit all possible behaviors of the library. Formally, the most general client $\mathcal{MGC}$ of library $\mathcal{L}$ is defined as a tuple $(\{q_c, q_c'\}, \rightarrow_c)$, where q_c and q_c' are two program positions, $\rightarrow_c = \{(q_c, havoc, q_c')\} \cup \{(q_c', call(m), q_c) | m \in \mathcal{M}\}$ is a control-flow transition relation and $(\{q_c, q_c'\}, PCom, \rightarrow_c, q_c, q_c)$ is a control-flow graph. Intuitively, the most general client repeatedly calls an arbitrary method with an arbitrary argument for arbitrarily many times.

2.3   TSO Operational Semantics

Assume a concurrent system consists of n processes, each of which runs the most general client program of a library on a separate processor. Then, the operational semantics of a library can be defined in the context of the concurrent system.

For a library $\mathcal{L} = (Q_\mathcal{L}, \rightarrow_\mathcal{L}, InitV_\mathcal{L})$, its operational semantics on the TSO memory model is defined as an LTS $[\![\mathcal{L}, n]\!]_{te}^1 = (Conf_{te}, \Sigma_{te}, \rightarrow_{te}, InitConf_{te})$, where $Conf_{te}, \Sigma_{te}, \rightarrow_{te}, InitConf_{te}$ are defined as follows.

Each configuration of $Conf_{te}$ is a tuple (p, d, u, r), where

- $p : \{1, \ldots, n\} \rightarrow \{q_c, q_c'\} \cup Q_\mathcal{L}$ represents control states of each process;
- $d : \mathcal{X} \rightarrow \mathcal{D}$ represents values at each memory location;
- $u : \{1, \ldots, n\} \rightarrow (\{(x, a) | x \in \mathcal{X}, a \in \mathcal{D}\} \cup \{call(m, a) | m \in \mathcal{M}, a \in \mathcal{D}\} \cup \{return(m, a) | m \in \mathcal{M}, a \in \mathcal{D}\})^*$ represents contents of each processor-local store buffer; each processor-local store buffer may contain a finite sequence of pending write, pending call or pending return operations;

---

[1] "*t*" represents TSO memory model. "*e*" represents that the operational semantics in this paper extends standard TSO operational semantics [14] similarly as [7].

- $r : \{1, \ldots, n\} \to (\mathcal{R} \to \mathcal{D})$ represents values of the registers of each process.

Σ_{te} consists of the following subsets of operations as transition labels.

- Internal operations: $\{\tau(i)|1 \leq i \leq n\}$;
- Read operations: $\{read(i, x, a)|1 \leq i \leq n, x \in \mathcal{X}, a \in \mathcal{D}\}$;
- Write operations: $\{write(i, x, a)|1 \leq i \leq n, x \in \mathcal{X}, a \in \mathcal{D}\}$;
- *Cas* operations: $\{cas(i, x, a, b)| \ 1 \leq i \leq n, x \in \mathcal{X}, a, b \in \mathcal{D}\}$;
- Flush operations: $\{flush(i, \ x, a)| \ 1 \leq i \leq n, x \in \mathcal{X}, a \in \mathcal{D}\}$;
- Call operations: $\Sigma_{cal} = \{call(i, m, a)|1 \leq i \leq n, m \in \mathcal{M}, a \in \mathcal{D}\}$;
- Return operations: $\Sigma_{ret} = \{return(i, m, a)|1 \leq i \leq n, m \in \mathcal{M}, a \in \mathcal{D}\}$;
- Flush call operations: $\Sigma_{fcal} = \{flushCall(i, m, a)|1 \leq i \leq n, m \in \mathcal{M}, a \in \mathcal{D}\}$;
- Flush return operations: $\Sigma_{fret} = \{flushReturn(i, m, a)|1 \leq i \leq n, m \in \mathcal{M}, a \in \mathcal{D}\}$.

The initial configuration $InitConf_{te} \in Conf_{te}$ is a tuple $(p_{init}, InitV_{\mathcal{L}}, u_{init}, r_{init})$, where $p_{init}(i) = q_c$, $u_{init}(i) = \epsilon$ (representing an empty buffer) and $r_{init}(i)(r) = regV_{init}$ (a special initial value of a register) for $1 \leq i \leq n, r \in \mathcal{R}$;

The transition relation $\to_{te}$ is the least relation satisfying the transition rules shown in Fig. 1. Our operational semantics for the internal, read, write, flush, call, return, flush call and flush return operations are similar to the one presented in [7], except that the xlock and xunlock operations in [7] are replaced with the *cas* operations here.

- *Register-Assign* rule: A function $f_{re} : (\mathcal{R} \to \mathcal{D}) \times \mathcal{RE} \to \mathcal{D}$ is used to evaluate register expression *re* under register valuation *rv* of current process, and its value is assigned to register r_1.
- *Library-Havoc* and *MGC-Havoc* rules: *havoc* commands are executed for libraries and the most general clients respectively.
- *Assume* rule: If the value of register r_1 is *true*, current process can execute *assume* command. Otherwise, it must wait.
- *Read* rule: A function $lookup(u, d, i, x)$ is used to search for the latest value of x from its processor-local store buffer or the main memory, i.e.,

$$lookup(u, d, i, x) = \begin{cases} a & \text{if } u(i) \uparrow_{\Sigma_x} = (x, a) \cdot l, \ \textit{for some } l \in \Sigma_x^* \\ d(x) & \text{otherwise} \end{cases}$$

where $\Sigma_x = \{(x, a)|a \in \mathcal{D}\}$ is the set of pending write operations for x.
A read operation will take the latest value of x from its processor-local store buffer if possible, otherwise, it looks up the value in memory.
- *Write* rule: A write operation will insert a pair of a location and a value to the tail of its processor-local store buffer.
- *Cas-Success* and *Cas-Fail* rules: A *cas* command can only be executed when the processor-local store buffer is empty and thus forces current process to clear its store buffer in advance. A successful *cas* command will change the value of memory location x immediately. The result of whether this *cas* command succeeds is stored in register r_1.
- *Flush* rule: The memory system may decide to flush the entry at the head of a processor-local store buffer to memory at any time.

$$\frac{p(i) = q_1, q_1 \xrightarrow{r_1 = re}_{\mathcal{L}} q_2, r(i) = rv, f_{re}(rv, re) = a}{(p, d, u, r) \xrightarrow{\tau(i)}_{te} (p[i:q_2], d, u, r[i:rv[r_1:a]])} \textit{Register-Assign}$$

$$\frac{p(i) = q_1, q_1 \xrightarrow{havoc}_{\mathcal{L}} q_2, rv \in \mathcal{R} \to \mathcal{D}}{(p, d, u, r) \xrightarrow{\tau(i)}_{te} (p[i:q_2], d, u, r[i:rv])} \textit{Library-Havoc}$$

$$\frac{p(i) = q_c, rv \in \mathcal{R} \to \mathcal{D}}{(p, d, u, r) \xrightarrow{\tau(i)}_{te} (p[i:q_c'], d, u, r[i:rv])} \textit{MGC-Havoc}$$

$$\frac{p(i) = q_1, q_1 \xrightarrow{assume(r_1)}_{\mathcal{L}} q_2, r(i)(r_1) = true}{(p, d, u, r) \xrightarrow{\tau(i)}_{te} (p[i:q_2], d, u, r)} \textit{Assume}$$

$$\frac{p(i) = q_1, q_1 \xrightarrow{read(x,r_1)}_{\mathcal{L}} q_2, r(i) = rv, lookup(u, d, i, x) = a}{(p, d, u, r) \xrightarrow{read(i,x,a)}_{te} (p[i:q_2], d, u, r[i:rv[r_1:a]])} \textit{Read}$$

$$\frac{p(i) = q_1, q_1 \xrightarrow{write(r_1,x)}_{\mathcal{L}} q_2, r(i)(r_1) = a, u(i) = l}{(p, d, u, r) \xrightarrow{write(i,x,a)}_{te} (p[i:q_2], d, u[i:(x,a) \cdot l], r)} \textit{Write}$$

$$\frac{p(i) = q_1, q_1 \xrightarrow{r_1 = cas(x,r_2,r_3)}_{\mathcal{L}} q_2, r(i) = rv, rv(r_2) = d(x) = a, rv(r_3) = b, u(i) = \epsilon}{(p, d, u, r) \xrightarrow{cas(i,x,a,b)}_{te} (p[i:q_2], d[x:b], u, r[i:rv[r_1:true]])} \textit{Cas-Success}$$

$$\frac{p(i) = q_1, q_1 \xrightarrow{r_1 = cas(x,r_2,r_3)}_{\mathcal{L}} q_2, r(i) = rv, rv(r_2) = a, rv(r_3) = b, rv(r_2) \neq d(x), u(i) = \epsilon}{(p, d, u, r) \xrightarrow{cas(i,x,a,b)}_{te} (p[i:q_2], d, u, r[i:rv[r_1:false]])} \textit{Cas-Fail}$$

$$\frac{u(i) = l \cdot (x, a)}{(p, d, u, r) \xrightarrow{flush(i,x,a)}_{te} (p, d[x:a], u[i:l], r)} \textit{Flush}$$

$$\frac{p(i) = q_c', r(i)(r_f) = a, u(i) = l}{(p, d, u, r) \xrightarrow{call(i,m,a)}_{te} (p[i:i_m], d, u[i:call(m, a) \cdot l], r)} \textit{Call}$$

$$\frac{p(i) = f_m, r(i)(r_f) = a, u(i) = l}{(p, d, u, r) \xrightarrow{return(i,m,a)}_{te} (p[i:q_c], d, u[i:return(m, a) \cdot l], r)} \textit{Return}$$

$$\frac{u(i) = l \cdot call(m, a)}{(p, d, u, r) \xrightarrow{flushCall(i,m,a)}_{te} (p, d, u[i:l], r)} \textit{Flush-Call}$$

$$\frac{u(i) = l \cdot return(m, a)}{(p, d, u, r) \xrightarrow{flushReturn(i,m,a)}_{te} (p, d, u[i:l], r)} \textit{Flush-Return}$$

Fig. 1. Transition Rules of $\to_{te}$

- *Call* and *Return* rules: To deal with *call* command, a call marker is added into the tail of processor-local store buffer and current process starts to execute the initial position of method m. When the process comes to the final position of method m it can launch a *return* operation, add a return marker to the tail of processor-local store buffer and start to execute the most general client.

– *Flush-Call* and *Flush-Return* rules: The call and return marker can be discarded when they are at the head of processor-local store buffer. Such operations are used to define TSO-to-TSO linearizability only.

3   TSO-to-TSO Linearizability and Equivalent Characterization

3.1   TSO-to-TSO Linearizability

The behavior of a library is typically represented by histories of interactions between the library and the clients calling it (through call and return operations). A finite sequence $h \in (\Sigma_{cal} \cup \Sigma_{ret})^*$ is a history of an LTS $\mathcal{A}$ if there exists a trace t of $\mathcal{A}$ such that $t \uparrow_{(\Sigma_{cal} \cup \Sigma_{ret})} = h$. Let $history(\mathcal{A})$ denote all the histories of $\mathcal{A}$.

TSO-to-TSO linearizability is a variant of linearizability on the TSO memory model. It additionally concerns the behavior of a library in the context of processor-local store buffers, i.e., the interactions between the library and store buffers through flush call and flush return operations. A finite sequence $eh \in (\Sigma_{cal} \cup \Sigma_{ret} \cup \Sigma_{fcal} \cup \Sigma_{fret})^*$ is an extended history of an LTS $\mathcal{A}$ if there exists a trace t of $\mathcal{A}$ such that $t \uparrow_{(\Sigma_{cal} \cup \Sigma_{ret} \cup \Sigma_{fcal} \cup \Sigma_{fret})} = eh$. Let $ehistory(\mathcal{A})$ denote all the extended histories of $\mathcal{A}$, and $eh|_i$ the projection of eh to the operations of the i-th process. Two extended history eh_1 and eh_2 are equivalent, if for each $1 \leq i \leq n$, $eh_1|_i = eh_2|_i$.

Definition 1 (*TSO-to-TSO linearizability* [7]). *For any two extended histories eh_1 and eh_2 of libraries, eh_1 is TSO-to-TSO linearizable to eh_2, if*

– *eh_1 and eh_2 are equivalent;*
– *there is a bijection $\pi : \{1, \ldots, |eh_1|\} \to \{1, \ldots, |eh_2|\}$ such that for any $1 \leq i \leq |eh_1|$, $eh_1(i) = eh_2(\pi(i))$;*
– *for any $1 \leq i < j \leq |eh_1|$, if $(eh_1(i) \in \Sigma_{ret} \cup \Sigma_{fret}) \wedge (eh_1(j) \in \Sigma_{cal} \cup \Sigma_{fcal})$, then $\pi(i) < \pi(j)$.*

For two libraries $\mathcal{L}_1$ and $\mathcal{L}_2$, we say that $\mathcal{L}_2$ TSO-to-TSO linearizes $\mathcal{L}_1$, if for any $eh_1 \in ehistory(\llbracket \mathcal{L}_1, n \rrbracket_{te})$, there exists $eh_2 \in ehistory(\llbracket \mathcal{L}_2, n \rrbracket_{te})$, such that eh_1 is TSO-to-TSO linearizable to eh_2.

Informally speaking, if eh_1 is *TSO-to-TSO Linearizable* to eh_2, then eh_2 keeps all the non-overlapping pairs of call/flush call and return/flush return operations in eh_1 in the same order.

3.2   Equivalence Characterization

To handle the decision problem of TSO-to-TSO linearizability, we show that the extended history inclusion is an equivalent characterization of TSO-to-TSO linearizability. This is presented formally as the following lemma.

Lemma 1. *For any two libraries $\mathcal{L}_1$ and $\mathcal{L}_2$, $\mathcal{L}_2$ TSO-to-TSO linearizes $\mathcal{L}_1$ if and only if $ehistory(\llbracket \mathcal{L}_1, n \rrbracket_{te}) \subseteq ehistory(\llbracket \mathcal{L}_2, n \rrbracket_{te})$.*

Proof (Sketch). The *if* direction is obvious by the definition of TSO-to-TSO linearizability (Definition 1).

The *only if* direction can be proved with a transformation relation $\Rightarrow_{ER}$ and a distance function $eWitSum$ we define upon extended histories. Given extended histories eh_1 and eh_2, we say eh_1 can be transformed in one step to eh_2, written $eh_1 \Rightarrow_{ER} eh_2$, if eh_2 can be obtained by swapping two adjacent elements of eh_1 and eh_1 is TSO-to-TSO linearizable to eh_2. The non-negative distance function $eWitSum(eh_1, eh_2)$ for two equivalent extended histories eh_1 and eh_2 is used to measure the difference between eh_1 and eh_2. Through the well-defined transformation relation and distance function, we can first show that if an extended history eh_1 is TSO-to-TSO linearizable to another extended history eh_2 and $eh_1 \neq eh_2$, then there exists a third extended history eh_3, such that

- eh_1 is TSO-to-TSO linearizable to eh_3;
- $eh_3 \Rightarrow_{ER} eh_2$;
- eh_3 is TSO-to-TSO linearizable to eh_2;
- the distance between eh_1 and eh_3 is strictly less than the one between eh_1 and eh_2.

In this way, if an extended history $eh_1 \in ehistory(\llbracket \mathcal{L}_1, n \rrbracket_{te})$ is TSO-to-TSO linearizable to an extended history $eh_2 \in ehistory(\llbracket \mathcal{L}_2, n \rrbracket_{te})$, then eh_1 can be transformed to eh_2 by a finite number of $\Rightarrow_{ER}$ transformations. We further show that eh_1, eh_2 and all the intermediate extended histories along the transformations are indeed the extended histories of $\llbracket \mathcal{L}_2, n \rrbracket_{te}$. □

4 Undecidability of TSO-to-TSO Linearizability

As the main result of this paper, we present in this section that the TSO-to-TSO linearizability of concurrent libraries is undecidable for a bounded number of processes. We first reduce the trace inclusion problem between any two configurations of a classic-lossy single-channel system to the history inclusion problem between two specific concurrent libraries. Then, our main undecidability result follows from the equivalence between the history inclusion and the extended history inclusion for these two libraries. Recall that the latter is equivalent to TSO-to-TSO linearizability between the two libraries based on the above Lemma 1.

4.1 Classic-Lossy Single-Channel Systems

A classic-lossy single-channel system [16] is a tuple $\mathcal{S} = (Q_{cs}, \Sigma_{cs}, \{c_{cs}\}, \Gamma_{cs}, \Delta_{cs})$, where Q_{cs} is a finite set of control states, Σ_{cs} is a finite alphabet of messages, c_{cs} is the name of the single channel, Γ_{cs} is a finite set of transition labels and $\Delta_{cs} \subseteq Q_{cs} \times \Sigma_{cs}^* \times \Gamma_{cs} \times Q_{cs} \times \Sigma_{cs}^*$ is a transition relation.

Given two finite sequences $l_1 = \alpha_1 \cdot \alpha_2 \cdot \ldots \cdot \alpha_u$ and $l_2 = \beta_1 \cdot \beta_2 \cdot \ldots \cdot \beta_v$, we say that l_1 is a *subword* of l_2, denoted $l_1 \sqsubseteq l_2$, if there exists $1 \leq i_1 < \ldots < i_u \leq v$ such that for any $1 \leq j \leq u$, $\alpha_j = \beta_{i_j}$. Then, the operational semantics of $\mathcal{S}$ is given by an LTS $\mathcal{CL}(\mathcal{S}) = (Conf_{cs}, \Gamma_{cs}, \rightarrow_{cs}, initConf_{cs})$, where

$Conf_{cs} = Q_{cs} \times \Sigma_{cs}^*$ is a set of configurations with $initConf_{cs} \in Conf_{cs}$ as the initial configuration. The transition relation $\rightarrow_{cs}$ is defined as follows: (q_1, W_1) $\xrightarrow{\alpha}_{cs} (q_2, W_2)$ if there exists $(q_1, U, \alpha, q_2, V) \in \Delta_{cs}$ and $W' \in \Sigma_{cs}^*$ such that $U \cdot W' \sqsubseteq W_1$ and $W_2 \sqsubseteq W' \cdot V$.

It is known that for two configurations $(q_1, W_1), (q_2, W_2) \in Conf_{cs}$ of a classic-lossy single-channel system $\mathcal{S}$, the trace inclusion between (q_1, W_1) and (q_2, W_2) is undecidable [16].

4.2   Simulation on the TSO Memory Model

On the TSO memory model flush operations are launched nondeterministically by the memory system. Therefore, between two consecutive $read(x, \_)$ operations, more than one flush operations to x may happen. The second read operation can only read the latest flush operation to x, while missing the intermediate ones. These missing flush operations are similar to the missing messages that may happen in a classic-lossy single-channel system. This makes it possible to simulate a classic-lossy single-channel system with a concurrent program running on the TSO memory model. We implement such simulation through a library $\mathcal{L}_{\mathcal{S},q,W}$ specifically constructed based on a classic-lossy single-channel system $\mathcal{S}$ and a given configuration $(q, W) \in Conf_{cs}$.

For a classic-lossy single-channel system $\mathcal{S} = (Q_{cs}, \Sigma_{cs}, \{c_{cs}\}, \Gamma_{cs}, \Delta_{cs})$, assume the finite data domain $\mathcal{D}_{cs} = Q_{cs} \cup \Sigma_{cs} \cup \Delta_{cs} \cup \{\sharp, start, end, \perp, true, false,$ $regV_{init}, rule_f\}$, where $Q_{cs} \cap \Sigma_{cs} = \emptyset$, $Q_{cs} \cap \Delta_{cs} = \emptyset$, $\Sigma_{cs} \cap \Delta_{cs} = \emptyset$, and the symbols $\sharp, start, end, \perp, true, false, regV_{init}$ and $rule_f$ do not exist in $Q_{cs} \cup \Sigma_{cs} \cup \Delta_{cs}$. Given a configuration $(q, W) \in Conf_{cs}$ of $\mathcal{S}$, the library $\mathcal{L}_{\mathcal{S},q,W}$ is constructed with three methods M_1, M_2 and M_3, and three private memory locations x, y and z. x is used to transmit the channel contents from M_2 to M_1, while y is used to transmit the channel contents from M_1 to M_2. z is used to transmit the transition labels of $\mathcal{CL}(\mathcal{S})$ from M_2 to M_3. It is also used to synchronize M_2 and M_3. The symbol $\sharp$ is used as the delimiter to ensure that one element will not be read twice. The symbols $start$ and end represent the start and the end of the channel contents, respectively. $\perp$ is the initial value of x, y and z. The symbol $rule_f$ is an additional transition rule that is used to indicate the end of a simulation.

We now present the three methods in the pseudo-code, shown in Methods 1, 2 and 3. The if and $while$ statements used in the pseudo-code can be easily implemented by the $assume$ commands as well as other commands in our formation of a library. For the sake of brevity, the following macro notations are used. For sequence $l = a_1 \cdot \ldots \cdot a_m$, let $writeSeq(x,l)$ denote the commands of writing $a_1, \sharp, \ldots, a_m, \sharp$ to x in sequence, and $readSeq(x,l)$ denote the commands of reading $a_1, \sharp, \ldots, a_m, \sharp$ from x in sequence. We use $v := readOne(x)$ to represent the commands of reading $e, \sharp$ from x in sequence for some $e \neq \sharp$ and then assigning e to v. If $readSeq(x,l)$ or $readOne(x)$ fails to read the specified content, then the calling process will no long proceed. We use $writeOne(x, reg)$ to represent the commands of writing a, $\sharp$ to x in sequence where a is the current value of register reg. In the pseudo-code, r is a register in $\mathcal{R}$.

The pseudo-code of method M_1 is shown in Method 1. M_1 contains an infinite loop that never returns (Lines 1-3). At each round of the loop, it reads a new update from x and writes it to y.

The pseudo-code of method M_2 is shown in Method 2. M_2 first guesses a transition rule $rule_1$, puts $rule_1$ and W into the processor-local store buffer by writing them to x (Lines 1-2). Then, it begins an infinite loop that never returns (Lines 3-16). At each round of the loop, it reads the current transition rule $rule_2 \in \Delta_{cs}$ of S (Line 4) and guesses a transition rule $rule_3 \in \Delta_{cs} \cup \{rule_f\}$ (Line 5). If M_2 guesses the rule $rule_f$ in Line 5, then in the next round of this loop it will be blocked at Line 4 and the simulation terminates. M_2 does not confirm $rule_2$ until it reads $start \cdot U_1$ from y at Line 6 (intermediate values of y may be lost). At Line 7, it writes $rule_3 \cdot start$ to y. Then, it reads the remaining contents of method M_1's processor-local store buffer (intermediate values of y may be lost) and writes them and V_1 to x (Lines 8-13). In Lines 14-16, it transmits the transition label α_1 to method M_3.

The pseudo-code of method M_3 is shown in Method 3. M_3 first waits for M_2 to transmit transition label to it though z by a non $\perp$ value (Lines 1-4). Then it acknowledges M_2 at Line 5 and returns this transition label z at Line 6. M_3

Method 1. M_1

Input: an arbitrary argument
```
1  while true do
2      r := readOne(x);
3      writeOne(y, r);
```

Method 2. M_2

Input: an arbitrary argument
```
1   guess a transition rule rule₁ = (q, -, -, -, -) ∈ Δcs ∪ {rulef};
2   writeSeq(x, rule₁ · start · W · end);
3   while true do
4       r := readOne(y) for some rule rule₂ = (q₁, U₁, α₁, q₂, V₁) ∈ Δcs;
5       guess a transition rule rule₃ that is either some (q₂, -, -, -, -) ∈ Δcs or rulef;
6       readSeq(y, start · U₁);
7       writeSeq(x, rule₃ · start);
8       while true do
9           r := readOne(y);
10          if r = end then
11              break;
12          writeSeq(x, r);
13      writeSeq(x, V₁ · end);
14      z := α₁;
15      while z ≠ ⊥ do
16          ;
```

Method 3. M_3

Input: an arbitrary argument
Output: transition label for one step in $CL(S)$
1 **while** *true* **do**
2 | $r := z$;
3 | **if** $r \neq \perp$ **then**
4 | | **break**;
5 $cas(z, r, \perp)$;
6 **return** v;

---

uses a *cas* command to communicate with M_2. It never puts a pending write operation to its processor-local store buffer.

4.3 Undecidability of History Inclusion

In this subsection we show that given a classic-lossy single-channel system S and a configuration $(q, W) \in Conf_{cs}$, the histories of library $\mathcal{L}_{S,q,W}$ simulate exactly the paths of S starting from (q, W).

A path $p_S = (q_1, W_1) \xrightarrow{\alpha_1}_{cs} (q_2, W_2) \xrightarrow{\alpha_2}_{cs} \ldots \xrightarrow{\alpha_k}_{cs} (q_{k+1}, W_{k+1}) \in path(\mathcal{CL}$ $(S), (q_1, W_1))$ is *conservative*, if the following two conditions hold: (1) it contains at least one transition, (2) assume the *i-th* step uses rule $r_i = (q_i, U_i, \alpha_i, q_{i+1}, V_i)$ for each $1 \leq i \leq k$, then for each $1 \leq i \leq k$, there exists $W_i', W_i'' \in \Sigma_{cs}^*$ such that $U_i \cdot W_i' \sqsubseteq W_i$, $W_i'' \sqsubseteq W_i'$ and $W_{i+1} = W_i'' \cdot V_i$. Intuitively, each *i-th* step of a conservative path does not lose any element in V_i.

A trace $t_{\mathcal{L}} \in trace([\![\mathcal{L}_{S,q,W}, 3]\!]_{te})$ is *effective*, if $t_{\mathcal{L}}$ contains at least one operation $return(\_, M_3, \_)$. Otherwise, it is *ineffective*.

There is actually a close connection between the conservative paths of $CL(S)$ and the effective traces of $[\![\mathcal{L}_{S,q,W}, 3]\!]_{te}$. An effective trace $t_{\mathcal{L}} \in trace([\![\mathcal{L}_{S,q,W}, 3]\!]_{te})$ and a conservative path $p_S \in path(\mathcal{CL}(S), (q, W))$ *correspond*, if the sequence of return values of M_3 in $t_{\mathcal{L}}$ is the same as the sequence of transition labels of p_S.

Figure 2 shows an example of generating a corresponding effective trace of $[\![\mathcal{L}_{S,q,W}, 3]\!]_{te}$ from a conservative path of $CL(S)$. Note that many possible executions of $[\![\mathcal{L}_{S,q,W}, 3]\!]_{te}$ can get into deadlock due to the operational semantics and the pseudo-code of each method. Herein, we consider only the executions where M_3 always manages to output return labels accordingly. In Fig. 2, contents of a store buffer are written from left to right, while the time progresses from left to right, too. Assume $(q, W) = (q_1, a \cdot a)$ and there is a conservative path $p_S = (q_1, a \cdot a) \xrightarrow{\alpha_1}_{cs} (q_2, b \cdot c) \xrightarrow{\alpha_2}_{cs} (q_3, a)$, where the first step uses rule $rule_1 = (q_1, a, \alpha_1, q_2, b \cdot c)$ (loses a in the channel), and the second one uses rule $rule_2 = (q_2, b, \alpha_2, q_3, a)$ (loses c in the channel). For this path, we can get a corresponding effective trace of $t_{\mathcal{L}}$ as follows:

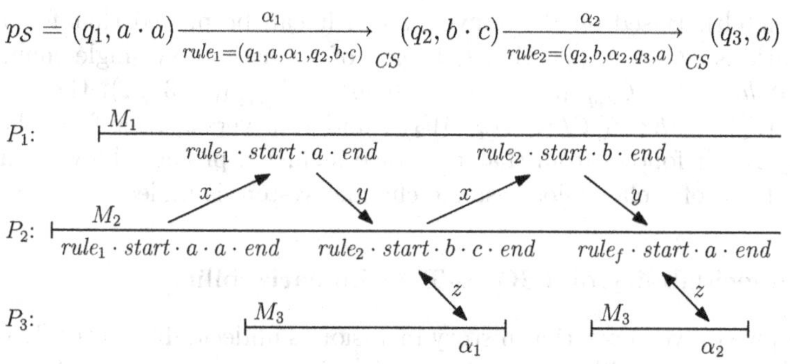

$$p_S = (q_1, a \cdot a) \xrightarrow[rule_1=(q_1,a,\alpha_1,q_2,b\cdot c)]{\alpha_1} (q_2, b \cdot c) \xrightarrow[rule_2=(q_2,b,\alpha_2,q_3,a)]{\alpha_2} (q_3, a)$$

P_1: M_1
  $rule_1 \cdot start \cdot a \cdot end$ $rule_2 \cdot start \cdot b \cdot end$

P_2: M_2
  $rule_1 \cdot start \cdot a \cdot a \cdot end$ $rule_2 \cdot start \cdot b \cdot c \cdot end$ $rule_f \cdot start \cdot a \cdot end$

P_3: M_3 M_3
  α_1 α_2

Fig. 2. A Conservative Path and its Corresponding Effective Trace

1. Run M_1, M_2 and M_3 in processes P_1, P_2 and P_3 respectively. Recall that M_1 and M_2 never return, while each invocation of M_3 is associated with an interval shown in Fig. 2.
2. At Line 2 of Method 2, M_2 puts $(x, rule_1)$, $(x, \sharp)$, $(x, start)$, $(x, \sharp)$, (x, a), $(x, \sharp)$, (x, a), $(x, \sharp)$, (x, end), $(x, \sharp)$ into the store buffer of process P_2.
3. By several loops between Lines 1-3, M_1 captures the updates of x in a lossy manner, and puts $(y, rule_1)$, $(y, \sharp)$, $(y, start)$, $(y, \sharp)$, (y, a), $(y, \sharp)$, (y, end), $(y, \sharp)$ into the store buffer of process P_1.
4. At Line 4 of Method 2, M_2 captures the updates of y in a lossy manner. M_2 guesses an applicable transition rule $rule_2$, and then puts $(x, rule_2)$, $(x, \sharp)$, $(x, start)$, $(x, \sharp)$, (x, b), $(x, \sharp)$, (x, c), $(x, \sharp)$, (x, end), $(x, \sharp)$ into the store buffer of process P_2, according to transition rule $rule_1$.
5. M_2 sends the transition label α_1 to M_3 at Line 14 of Method 2. Then, M_3 returns α_1 and we finish simulating the first transition in p_S.
6. By several loops between Lines 1-3, M_1 captures the updates of x in a lossy manner, and puts $(y, rule_2)$, $(y, \sharp)$, $(y, start)$, $(y, \sharp)$, (y, b), $(y, \sharp)$, (y, end), $(y, \sharp)$ into the store buffer of process P_1.
7. At Line 4 of Method 2, M_2 captures the updates of y. Then, M_2 decides to terminate the simulation and puts $(x, rule_f)$, $(x, \sharp)$, $(x, start)$, $(x, \sharp)$, (x, a), $(x, \sharp)$, (x, end), $(x, \sharp)$ into the store buffer of process P_2, according to transition rule $rule_2$.
8. M_2 sends the transition label α_2 to M_3 at Line 14 of Method 2. Then, M_3 returns α_2 and we finish simulating the second transition in p_S.

It can be seen that $t_{\mathcal{L}}$ and p_S correspond in this example. We further prove the claim in the technical report version of this paper [18] that for any conservative path $p_S \in path(\mathcal{CL}(S), (q, W))$, there exists an effective trace $t_{\mathcal{L}} \in trace(\llbracket \mathcal{L}_{S,q,W}, 3 \rrbracket_{te})$ such that $t_{\mathcal{L}}$ and p_S correspond, and vice versa.

The following lemma shows that the history inclusion between concurrent libraries is undecidable on the TSO memory model.

Lemma 2. *For any two libraries $\mathcal{L}_1$ and $\mathcal{L}_2$, it is undecidable whether history $(\llbracket \mathcal{L}_1, 3 \rrbracket_{te}) \subseteq history(\llbracket \mathcal{L}_2, 3 \rrbracket_{te})$.*

Proof (Sketch). Based on the above claim , it can be proved that for any two configurations (q_1, W_1), $(q_2,\ W_2) \in Conf_{cs}$ of a classic-lossy single-channel system $\mathcal{S}$, if $history(\llbracket\ \mathcal{L}_{\mathcal{S},q_1,W_1}, 3 \rrbracket_{te}) \subseteq history\ (\llbracket \mathcal{L}_{\mathcal{S},q_2,W_2},\ 3\ \rrbracket_{te})$, then $trace(\mathcal{CL}$ $(\mathcal{S}),\ (q_1, W_1)) \subseteq trace(\ \mathcal{CL}(\mathcal{S}), (q_2, W_2))$, and vice versa. Therefore, the undecidability result follows from that the trace inclusion problem between any two configurations of a classic-lossy single-channel system is undecidable [16].   □

4.4   Undecidability of TSO-to-TSO Linearizability

Although we prove above that history inclusion is undecidable on the TSO memory model, there is still a gap between the history inclusion and the extended history inclusion between concurrent libraries. Obviously there exist libraries $\mathcal{L}_1$ and $\mathcal{L}_2$ such that $history(\llbracket\mathcal{L}_1, n\rrbracket_{te}) \subseteq history(\llbracket\mathcal{L}_2, n\rrbracket_{te})$ but $ehistory(\llbracket\mathcal{L}_1, n\rrbracket_{te}) \not\subseteq ehistory(\llbracket\mathcal{L}_2, n\rrbracket_{te})$. We show in this subsection that for the two libraries $\mathcal{L}_{\mathcal{S},q_1,W_1}$ and $\mathcal{L}_{\mathcal{S},q_2,W_2}$, corresponding to the configurations (q_1, W_1) and (q_2, W_2) of a classic-lossy single-channel system, respectively, the history inclusion and the extended history inclusion between $\mathcal{L}_{\mathcal{S},q_1,W_1}$ and $\mathcal{L}_{\mathcal{S},q_2,W_2}$ coincides on the TSO memory model.

Without loss of generality, assume M_1 and M_2 of $\mathcal{L}_{\mathcal{S},q,W}$ are called by processes P_1, P_2, respectively; while M_3 of $\mathcal{L}_{\mathcal{S},q,W}$ is repeatedly called by process P_3. Then, an extended history $eh \in ehistory(\llbracket\mathcal{L}_{\mathcal{S},q,W}, 3\rrbracket_{te})$ that contains at least one return operation of M_3 is in the following form:

- The first six operations of eh are always call and corresponding flush call operations of M_1, M_2 and M_3, while these operations may occur in any order.
- The projection of eh on P_i is exactly $call(i, M_i, \_) \cdot flushCall(i, M_i, \_)$ for $i \in \{1, 2\}$.
- Figure 3 shows the possible positions of flush call (*fcal*) and flush return (*fret*) operations in eh. Since M_3 always executes a *cas* command before it returns, during each round of a call to M_3 in P_3, the flush call operation must occur before the *cas* operation (see the dashed vertical lines in Fig. 3); hence it can only occur before the return operation of M_3.

  During each round of a call to M_3 in P_3, the flush return operation may occur alternatively at two positions: the first position is after the return operation of M_3 and before the next round of a call operation of M_3, as shown by the position of $fret_1$ in Fig. 3 (*a*); while the second one is after the next round of a call operation of M_3 and before the consequent flush call operation, as shown by the position of $fret_1$ in Fig. 3 (*b*).

To prove that the history inclusion and the extended history inclusion coincide between libraries $\mathcal{L}_{\mathcal{S},q_1,W_1}$ and $\mathcal{L}_{\mathcal{S},q_2,W_2}$, we need to show that for an extended history eh_1 of $\llbracket\mathcal{L}_{\mathcal{S},q_1,W_1}, 3\rrbracket_{te}$, if eh_1 contains a return operation in P_3 and $eh_1 \uparrow_{(\Sigma_{cal}\cup\Sigma_{ret})} \in history(\llbracket\mathcal{L}_{\mathcal{S},q_2,W_2}, 3\rrbracket_{te})$, then $eh_1 \in ehistory(\llbracket\mathcal{L}_{\mathcal{S},q_2,W_2}, 3\rrbracket_{te})$. Because $eh_1 \uparrow_{(\Sigma_{cal}\cup\Sigma_{ret})}$ is a history of $\llbracket\mathcal{L}_{\mathcal{S},q_2,W_2}, 3\rrbracket_{te}$, there exists a path $p'_{\mathcal{L}}$ of $\llbracket\mathcal{L}_{\mathcal{S},q_2,W_2}, 3\rrbracket_{te}$ corresponding to eh_1. From $p'_{\mathcal{L}}$ we can generate another path $p_{\mathcal{L}}$ of $\llbracket\mathcal{L}_{\mathcal{S},q_2,W_2}, 3\rrbracket_{te}$ such that the extended history along $p_{\mathcal{L}}$ is exactly eh_1.

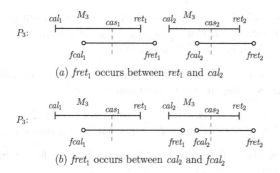

(a) *fret*₁ occurs between *ret*₁ and *cal*₂

(b) *fret*₁ occurs between *cal*₂ and *fcal*₂

Fig. 3. Possible positions of flush call and flush return operations

The path $p_{\mathcal{L}}$ is generated from $p'_{\mathcal{L}}$ by changing the positions of the flush return operations. Recall that during each round of a call to M_3, the flush return operation may occur alternatively at two positions only. Since M_3 does not insert any pending write operation into the process P_3's store buffer, $p'_{\mathcal{L}}$ can be transformed into $p_{\mathcal{L}}$ by swapping each flush return operation in $p'_{\mathcal{L}}$ from its current position to the other possible one (if necessary).

An extended history is *effective* if it contains at least one $return(\_, M_3, \_)$ operation. Otherwise, it is *ineffective*. The following lemma formalizes the idea describe above.

Lemma 3. *For a classic-lossy single-channel system $\mathcal{S}$ and two configurations* (q_1, W_1), $(q_2, W_2) \in Conf_{cs}$, *if $eh_1 \in ehistory([\![\mathcal{L}_{\mathcal{S},q_1,W_1}, 3]\!]_{te})$ is an effective extended history and $eh_1 \upharpoonright_{(\Sigma_{cal} \cup \Sigma_{ret})} \in history([\![\mathcal{L}_{\mathcal{S},q_2,W_2}, 3]\!]_{te})$, then $eh_1 \in ehistory([\![\mathcal{L}_{\mathcal{S},q_2,W_2}, 3]\!]_{te})$.*

With the help of Lemma 3, we can prove that the history inclusion and the extended history inclusion between the specific libraries coincide on the TSO memory model.

Lemma 4. *For two configurations $(q_1, W_1), (q_2, W_2)$ of a classic-lossy single-channel system $\mathcal{S}$, $history([\![\mathcal{L}_{\mathcal{S},q_1,W_1}, 3]\!]_{te}) \subseteq history([\![\mathcal{L}_{\mathcal{S},q_2,W_2}, 3]\!]_{te})$ if and only if $ehistory ([\![\mathcal{L}_{\mathcal{S},q_1,W_1}, 3]\!]_{te}) \subseteq ehistory([\![\mathcal{L}_{\mathcal{S},q_2,W_2}, 3]\!]_{te})$.*

Proof. The *if* direction is obvious.

The *only if* direction can be proved by contradiction. Assume there is an extended history eh_1 such that $eh_1 \in ehistory([\![\mathcal{L}_{\mathcal{S},q_1,W_1}, 3]\!]_{te})$ but $eh_1 \notin ehistory([\![\mathcal{L}_{\mathcal{S},q_2,W_2}, 3]\!]_{te})$.

It can be seen that the sets of the ineffective extended histories of $\mathcal{L}_{\mathcal{S},q_1,W_1}$ and $\mathcal{L}_{\mathcal{S},q_2,W_2}$ are the same. By assumption, eh_1 is not an ineffective extended history of $\mathcal{L}_{\mathcal{S},q_2,W_2}$, thus it is not an ineffective extended history of $\mathcal{L}_{\mathcal{S},q_1,W_1}$. However, eh_1 is an extended history of $\mathcal{L}_{\mathcal{S},q_1,W_1}$, so eh_1 must be an effective extended history of $\mathcal{L}_{\mathcal{S},q_1,W_1}$.

Let history $h = eh_1 \uparrow_{(\Sigma_{cal} \cup \Sigma_{ret})}$. It is obvious that $h \in history([\![\mathcal{L}_{\mathcal{S},q_1,W_1},3]\!]_{te})$. Then, by assumption, $h \in history([\![\mathcal{L}_{\mathcal{S},q_2,W_2},3]\!]_{te})$. By Lemma 3, $eh_1 \in ehistory($ $[\![\mathcal{L}_{\mathcal{S},q_2,W_2},3]\!]_{te})$, which contradicts the assumption.   □

The undecidability of TSO-to-TSO linearizability for a bounded number of processes is a direct consequence of Lemmas 1, 2 and 4.

Theorem 1. *For any two concurrent libraries $\mathcal{L}_1$ and $\mathcal{L}_2$, it is undecidable whether $\mathcal{L}_2$ TSO-to-TSO linearizes $\mathcal{L}_1$ for a bounded number of processes.*

The proof details of Lemmas 1, 2, 3 and 4 can be found in the technical report version of the paper [18].

5   Conclusion and Future Work

We have shown that the decision problem of TSO-to-TSO linearizability is undecidable for a bounded number of processes. The proof method is essentially by a reduction from a known undecidable problem, the trace inclusion problem of a classic-lossy single-channel system. To facilitate such a reduction, we introduced an intermediate notion of history inclusion between concurrent libraries on the TSO memory model. We then demonstrated that a configuration (q, W) of a classic-lossy single-channel system $\mathcal{S}$ can be simulated by a specific library $\mathcal{L}_{\mathcal{S},q,W}$, interacting with three specific processes on the TSO memory model. Although history inclusion does not coincide with extended history inclusion in general, they do coincide on a restricted class of libraries. We prove that $\mathcal{L}_{\mathcal{S},q,W}$ lies within such class. Finally, our undecidability result follows from the equivalence between extended history inclusion and TSO-to-TSO linearizability.

The problem of the linearizability between libraries on the SC memory model [8] can be shown to be decidable for a bounded number of processes. This is due to the provable equivalence between history inclusion and linearizability on the SC memory model, while the former is decidable. Thus, our work states clearly a boundary of decidability for linearizability of concurrent libraries on various memory models. In fact, as a by-product of this work, if the notion of TSO-to-TSO linearizability is weaken to the one without concerning flush call and flush return operations, the problem of this weaker notion is already undecidable on the TSO memory model. Both results have been proved in the technical report version of this paper [18].

Other relaxed memory models, such as the memory models of POWER and ARM, are much weaker than the TSO memory model. We conjecture that variants of linearizability on these relaxed memory models may also be reduced to some new forms of extended history inclusion, similar to the variants of linearizability for C/C++ memory model in [3], and these variants should also be undecidable. However, we find no clue to the decision problem of TSO-to-SC linearizability for a bounded number of processes, since TSO-to-SC linearizability is between linearizability on the SC memory model and TSO-to-TSO linearizability. As future work, we would like to investigate the decidability of TSO-to-SC linearizability and other variants of linearizability for relaxed memory models.

References

1. Alur, R., McMillan, K., Peled, D.: Model-checking of correctness conditions for concurrent objects. In: LICS 1996, pp. 219–228. IEEE Computer Society (1996)
2. Atig, M.F., Bouajjani, A., Burckhardt, S., Musuvathi, M.: On the verification problem for weak memory models. In: Hermenegildo, M.V., Palsberg, J. (eds.) POPL 2010, pp. 7–18. ACM (2010)
3. Batty, M., Dodds, M., Gotsman, A.: Library abstraction for C/C++ concurrency. In: Giacobazzi, R., Cousot, R. (eds.) POPL 2013, pp. 235–248. ACM (2013)
4. Batty, M., Owens, S., Sarkar, S., Sewell, P., Weber, T.: Mathematizing C++ concurrency. In: Ball, T., Sagiv, M. (eds.) POPL 2011, pp. 55–66. ACM (2011)
5. Bouajjani, A., Emmi, M., Enea, C., Hamza, J.: Verifying concurrent programs against sequential specifications. In: Felleisen, M., Gardner, P. (eds.) ESOP 2013. LNCS, vol. 7792, pp. 290–309. Springer, Heidelberg (2013)
6. Bouajjani, A., Emmi, M., Enea, C., Hamza, J.: Tractable refinement checking for concurrent objects. In: Rajamani, S.K., Walker, D. (eds.) POPL 2015, pp. 651–662. ACM (2015)
7. Burckhardt, S., Gotsman, A., Musuvathi, M., Yang, H.: Concurrent library correctness on the TSO memory model. In: Seidl, H. (ed.) Programming Languages and Systems. LNCS, vol. 7211, pp. 87–107. Springer, Heidelberg (2012)
8. Filipović, I., O'Hearn, P., Rinetzky, N., Yang, H.: Abstraction for concurrent objects. In: Castagna, G. (ed.) ESOP 2009. LNCS, vol. 5502, pp. 252–266. Springer, Heidelberg (2009)
9. Gotsman, A., Musuvathi, M., Yang, H.: Show no weakness: sequentially consistent specifications of TSO libraries. In: Aguilera, M.K. (ed.) DISC 2012. LNCS, vol. 7611, pp. 31–45. Springer, Heidelberg (2012)
10. Herlihy, M.P., Wing, J.M.: Linearizability: a correctness condition for concurrent objects. ACM Trans. Program. Lang. Syst. $12(3)$, 463–492 (1990)
11. Lamport, L.: How to make a multiprocessor computer that correctly executes multiprocess program. IEEE Trans. Comput. $28(9)$, 690–691 (1979)
12. Liu, Y., Chen, W., Liu, Y.A., Sun, J., Zhang, S.J., Dong, J.S.: Verifying linearizability via optimized refinement checking. IEEE Trans. Software Eng. $39(7)$, 1018–1039 (2013)
13. Manson, J., Pugh, W., Adve, S.V.: The Java memory model. In: Palsberg, J., Abadi, M. (eds.) POPL 2005, pp. 378–391. ACM (2005)
14. Owens, S., Sarkar, S., Sewell, P.: A better x86 memory model: x86-TSO. In: Berghofer, S., Nipkow, T., Urban, C., Wenzel, M. (eds.) TPHOLs 2009. LNCS, vol. 5674, pp. 391–407. Springer, Heidelberg (2009)
15. Sarkar, S., Sewell, P., Alglave, J., Maranget, L., Williams, D.: Understanding POWER multiprocessors. In: Hall, M.W., Padua, D.A. (eds.) PLDI 2011, pp. 175–186. ACM (2011)
16. Schnoebelen, P.: Bisimulation and other undecidable equivalences for lossy channel systems. In: Kobayashi, N., Babu, C.S. (eds.) TACS 2001. LNCS, vol. 2215, pp. 385–399. Springer, Heidelberg (2001)
17. Vechev, M., Yahav, E., Yorsh, G.: Experience with model checking linearizability. In: Păsăreanu, C.S. (ed.) Model Checking Software. LNCS, vol. 5578, pp. 261–278. Springer, Heidelberg (2009)
18. Wang, C., Lv, Y., Wu, P.: TSO-to-TSO Linearizability is Undecidable. Technical report ISCAS-SKLCS-15-03, State Key Laboratory of Computer Science, ISCAS, CAS (2015). http://lcs.ios.ac.cn/~lvyi/files/ISCAS-SKLCS-15-03.pdf

Formal Verification of Infinite-State BIP Models

Simon Bliudze[1], Alessandro Cimatti[2], Mohamad Jaber[3], Sergio Mover[2],
Marco Roveri[2], Wajeb Saab[1], and Qiang Wang[1](✉)

[1] École Polytechnique Fédérale de Lausanne, Lausanne, Switzerland
qiang.wang@epfl.ch
[2] Fondazione Bruno Kessler, Trento, Italy
[3] American University of Beirut, Beirut, Lebanon

Abstract. We propose two expressive and complementary techniques
for the verification of safety properties of infinite-state BIP models. Both
our techniques deal with the full BIP specification, while the existing
approaches impose considerable restrictions: they either verify finite-
state systems or they do not handle the transfer of data on the interactions and priorities.

Firstly, we propose an instantiation of the ESST (Explicit Scheduler
Symbolic Thread) framework to verify BIP models. The key insight is to
apply symbolic reasoning to analyze the behavior of the system described
by the BIP components, and an explicit-state search to analyze the
behavior of the system induced by the BIP interactions and priorities.
The combination of symbolic and explicit exploration techniques allow
to benefit from abstraction, useful when reasoning about data, and from
partial order reduction, useful to mitigate the state space explosion due
to concurrency.

Secondly, we propose an encoding from a BIP model into a symbolic,
infinite-state transition system. This technique allows us to leverage the
state of the art verification algorithms for the analysis of infinite-state
systems.

We implemented both techniques and we evaluated their performance
against the existing approaches. The results show the effectiveness of our
approaches with respect to the state of the art, and their complementar-
ity for the analysis of safe and unsafe BIP models.

1 Introduction

BIP [2,4] is a framework for the component-based design of complex concurrent systems that is being actively used in many industrial settings [3,5]. The
verification of BIP plays a crucial role in the *Rigorous System Design* methodology [28], where a correct implementation of the system is obtained by a series
of transformations from its high-level model; proving that a property holds in
the model will ensure that it holds in the implementation.

This work was carried out within the D-MILS project, which is partially funded
under the European Commission's Seventh Framework Programme (FP7).

© Springer International Publishing Switzerland 2015
B. Finkbeiner et al. (Eds.): ATVA 2015, LNCS 9364, pp. 326–343, 2015.
DOI: 10.1007/978-3-319-24953-7_25

Despite the importance of verifying BIP models, the existing approaches (e.g. implemented in tools like DFINDER [7],VCS [20] and BIP2UPPAAL [29]) impose considerable restrictions on the models that can be analyzed. In particular, only DFINDER verifies models with infinite-state data variables. However, DFINDER does not consider the data transfer on interactions, an essential feature to express that data is exchanged among the components (consider that in BIP the components cannot share variables), and the priorities among interactions.

In this paper, we focus on the safety property verification of infinite-state BIP models, and we propose two techniques that are: (i) expressive enough to capture *all* the features of infinite-state BIP models (e.g. data transfer, priorities); (ii) complementary, with respect to the performance, for verifying safe and unsafe models.

The first solution is a novel verification algorithm based on the *Explicit Scheduler, Symbolic Threads* (ESST) framework [16]. The ESST extends lazy predicate abstraction and refinement [21, 22] to verify concurrent programs formed by a set of cooperative threads and a non-preemptive scheduler; the main characteristic of the approach is to use lazy predicate abstraction to explore threads and explicit-state techniques to explore the scheduler. The choice of ESST is motivated by the clear separation of computations and coordination in the BIP language, which is similar to the separation of threads and scheduler in the ESST, and by the ESST efficiency, since the ESST outperforms the verification techniques based on sequentialization (e.g. in the context of SystemC and Fair Threads programs [16]). In our work, we show an *efficient* instantiation of the ESST framework in an algorithm that verifies BIP models (ESST$_{BIP}$). The instantiation is not trivial, and consists of defining a suitable interaction model between the threads and the scheduler, the consequent mapping of BIP components into threads, and of implementing the scheduler. Moreover, we improve the performance of our approach with several optimizations, which are justified by the BIP semantic.

In our second solution we explore a conceptually simple, but still novel, encoding of a BIP model into an infinite-state transition system. This alternative flow is motivated by the recent advancements in the verification of infinite-state systems (e.g. see [14, 23]). Also this technique supports all the BIP features, like priorities and data transfer on interactions.

We provide an implementation of both approaches: the ESST$_{BIP}$ is implemented in the KRATOS [13] software model checker; the translational approach is performed using the BIP framework and then verified with the NUXMV [12] model checker. We performed a thorough experimental evaluation comparing the performance of the two techniques and of DFINDER (in this case, only on the models without data transfers). The results show that the proposed approaches always perform better than DFINDER, and that ESST$_{BIP}$ and the translational approach using NUXMV are complementary, with ESST$_{BIP}$ being more efficient in finding counterexamples for unsafe models, while the translational approach using NUXMV is more efficient in proving correctness of safe models.

This paper is structured as follows. We first provide the background of the BIP language in Sect. 2. Then in Sect. 3 we describe the ESST$_{\text{BIP}}$ algorithm, as well as its optimizations. In Sect. 4 we show the encoding of BIP into a symbolic transition system. Then, in Sect. 5 we review the related work and in Sect. 6 we present the experimental evaluation. Finally, in Sect. 7 we draw some conclusions and outline directions for future work.

2   The BIP Model

We denote by Var a set of variables with domain $\mathbb{Z}^1$, (i.e. for all $x \in Var$, $Dom(x) = \mathbb{Z}$). An *assignment* is of the form $x := exp$, where $x \in Var$ and exp is a linear expression over Var. An *assumption* is of the form $[bexp]$, where $bexp$ is a Boolean combination of predicates over Var. Let $BExp(Var)$ be the set of assumptions and $Exp(Var)$ be the set of assignments. Let $Ops(Var) = BExp(Var) \cup Exp(Var) \cup \{skip\}$ be the set of edge operations, where $skip$ denotes an operation without effects on Var. A *state* $s : Var \to \mathbb{Z}$ is a mapping from variables to their valuations; we use $State$ to denote the set of all possible states. We define an evaluation function $[\![\cdot]\!]_\mathcal{E} : exp \to (State \to \mathbb{Z})$ for assignments and $[\![\cdot]\!]_\mathcal{B} : bexp \to (State \to \{true, false\})$ for assumptions. We refer to [16] for the definition of $[\![\cdot]\!]_\mathcal{E}$ and $[\![\cdot]\!]_\mathcal{B}$. We denote by $s[x := e]$ the substitution of x by e in expression s.

The BIP Syntax. An *atomic component* is a tuple $B_i = \langle Var_i, Q_i, P_i, E_i, l_{0_i} \rangle$ where Var_i is a set of variables, Q_i is a set of locations, P_i is a set of ports, $E_i \subseteq Q_i \times P_i \times BExp(Var_i) \times Exp(Var_i) \times Q_i'$ is a set of edges extended with guards and operations and $l_{0_i} \in Q_i$ is the initial location.

We assume that, for each location, every pair of outgoing edges labeled with the same port has disjoint guards. This can be achieved by simply renaming the ports and imposes no restrictions on the BIP expressiveness. We also identify a set of *error locations*, $Q_{err_i} \subseteq Q_i$ to encode the safety property[2].

Let $\mathcal{B} = \{B_1, \ldots, B_n\}$ be a set of atomic components. An *interaction* γ for $\mathcal{B}$ is a tuple $\langle Act, g, op \rangle$ such that: $Act \subseteq \bigcup_{i=1}^n P_i$, $Act \neq \emptyset$, and for all $i \in [1, n]$, $|Act \cap P_i| \leq 1$, $g \in BExp(\bigcup_{Bj \in \gamma_\mathcal{B}} Var_j)$ and $op \in Exp(\bigcup_{Bj \in \gamma_\mathcal{B}} Var_j)$, where $\gamma_\mathcal{B} = \{Bj | Bj \in \mathcal{B}, Act \cap P_j \neq \emptyset\}$.

We assume that the sets of ports of the components in a BIP model and the sets of local variables are disjoint (i.e. for all $i \neq j$, $P_i \cap P_j = \emptyset$ and $Var_i \cap Var_j = \emptyset$). For a port $\alpha \in P_i$, we identify with $id(\alpha)$ the index i of the component B_i.

Let Γ be a set of interactions, a *priority model* π of Γ is a strict partial order of Γ. For $\gamma_1, \gamma_2 \in \Gamma$, γ_1 has a lower priority than γ_2 if and only if $(\gamma_1, \gamma_2) \in \pi$. For simplicity, we write $\gamma_1 < \gamma_2$ in this case.

---

[1] We also consider finite domain variables (e.g. Boolean), which can be easily encoded in $\mathbb{Z}$.

[2] We can express any safety property using additional edges, interactions and error locations.

A BIP *model* $\mathcal{P}_{\text{BIP}}$ is a tuple $\langle \mathcal{B}, \Gamma, \pi \rangle$, where $\mathcal{B} = \langle B_1, \ldots, B_n \rangle$ is a set of atomic components, Γ is a set of interactions over $\mathcal{B}$ and π is a priority model for Γ.

We assume that each component B_i of $\mathcal{P}_{\text{BIP}}$ has at most an error location, without outgoing edges and such that the port of all its incoming edges is $error_i$; each $error_i$ appears in a unique singleton interaction and all such interactions have the highest priority in $\mathcal{P}_{\text{BIP}}$. Any BIP model can be put into such form (see [10]).

The BIP Semantics. A *configuration* c of a BIP model $\mathcal{P}_{\text{BIP}}$ is a tuple $\langle \langle l_1, s_1 \rangle, \ldots, \langle l_n, s_n \rangle \rangle$ such that for all $i \in [1,n]$, $l_i \in Q_i$ and $s_i : Var_i \to \mathbb{Z}$ is a state of B_i. Let $\mathcal{P}_{\text{BIP}} = \langle \mathcal{B}, \Gamma, \pi \rangle$ be a BIP model and $c = \langle \langle l_1, s_1 \rangle, \ldots, \langle l_n, s_n \rangle \rangle$ be a configuration. The interaction $\gamma = \langle Act, g, op \rangle \in \Gamma$ is *enabled* in c if, for all the components $B_i \in \mathcal{B}$ such that $Act \cap P_i \neq \emptyset$, there exists an edge $\langle l_i, Act \cap P_i, g_i, op_i, l_i' \rangle \in E_i$ and $[\![g_i]\!]_{\mathcal{B}}(s_i) = true$, and $[\![g]\!]_{\mathcal{B}}(s_1, \ldots, s_n) = true$.

A BIP model $\mathcal{P}_{\text{BIP}} = \langle \mathcal{B}, \Gamma, \pi \rangle$ can take an edge from the configuration $c = \langle \langle l_1, s_1 \rangle, \ldots, \langle l_n, s_n \rangle \rangle$ to the configuration $c' = \langle \langle l_1', s_1' \rangle, \ldots, \langle l_n', s_n' \rangle \rangle$ if there exists an interaction $\gamma = \langle Act, g, op \rangle$ such that: (i) γ is enabled in c; (ii) there does not exist an enabled interaction $\gamma' \in \Gamma$ in c such that $\gamma' > \gamma$; (iii) for all $B_i \in \mathcal{B}$ such that $Act \cap P_i \neq \emptyset$, there exists $\langle l_i, Act \cap P_i, g_i, op_i, l_i' \rangle \in E_i$ and if $op = x := exp$, $op_i = y := exp_i$ then $s_i'' = s_i[x := [\![exp]\!]_{\mathcal{E}}(s_i)]$, $s_i' = s_i''[y := [\![exp_i]\!]_{\mathcal{E}}(s_i'')]$; (iv) for all $B_i \in \mathcal{B}$ such that $Act \cap P_i = \emptyset$, $l_i' = l_i$ and $s_i' = s_i$.

We use the notation $c \xrightarrow{\gamma} c'$ to denote that there exists an edge from the configuration c to the configuration c' on the interaction γ. A configuration $c_0 = \langle \langle l_1, s_1 \rangle, \ldots, \langle l_n, s_n \rangle \rangle$ is an *initial configuration* if, for some $i \in [1,n]$, $l_i = l_{0_i}$ and, for all $i \in [1,n]$, s_i is a valuation for Var_i[3]. A configuration c is *reachable* if and only if there exists a sequence of configurations $c_0 \xrightarrow{\gamma_1} c_1 \xrightarrow{\gamma_2} \ldots \xrightarrow{\gamma_k} c_k$, such that c_0 is an initial configuration and $c_k = c$. A BIP model is *safe* if no error locations are reachable.

3   ESST for BIP (ESST$_{\text{BIP}}$)

3.1   The ESST Framework

In this subsection we provide the necessary background on the ESST framework, following the presentation of [16,17].

Programming Model. The ESST framework analyzes a multi-threaded program $\mathcal{P} = \langle \mathcal{T}, \text{SCHED} \rangle$, consisting of a set of *cooperative threads* $\mathcal{T} = \langle T_1, \ldots, T_n \rangle$ and a *non-preemptive scheduler* SCHED. A non-preemptive scheduler cannot interrupt the execution of a thread, while a cooperative thread is responsible for suspending its execution and releasing the control to the scheduler.

---

[3] While we did not add initial predicates for Var_i, this can be encoded with an additional initial location and an edge that has as guard the initial predicates.

A *thread* $T_i = \langle G_i, LVar_i \rangle$ is a sequential program with a set of local variables $LVar_i$ and is represented by a control-flow graph (CFG) $G_i = (L_i, E_i, l_{0_i}, L_{err_i})$, where: (i) L_i is the set of locations; (ii) $E_i \subseteq L_i \times Ops(LVar_i) \times L_i$ is the set of edges; (iii) $l_{0_i} \in L_i$ is the entry location; (iv) $L_{err_i} \subseteq L_i$ is the set of *error locations*.

A *scheduler* SCHED $= \langle SVar, F_S \rangle$ has a set of variables $SVar$ and a scheduling function F_S. For each thread T_i, the scheduler maintains a variable $st_{T_i} \in SVar$ to keep track of its status (i.e. *Running, Runnable, Waiting*). A *scheduler state* $\mathbb{S}$ is an assignment to all the variables $SVar$. Given a scheduler state $\mathbb{S}$ where no thread is *Running*, $F_S(\mathbb{S})$ generates the set of scheduler states that describes the next thread to be run. We denote by *SState* the set of all possible scheduler states, and by $SState_{One}$ the set of scheduler states, where only one thread is *Running*. A thread can change the scheduler state by calling a *primitive function*. For example, the call to a primitive function can change the thread status from *Running* to *Waiting* to release the control to the scheduler.

The intuitive semantics of a multi-threaded program is the following: the program executes the thread in the *Running* status (note that there is at most one running thread); the running thread T_i can suspend its execution, setting the variable st_{T_i} to a value different from *Running*, by calling an appropriate primitive function; when there are no running threads, the scheduler executes its scheduling function to generate a set of running threads. The next thread to run is picked non-deterministically. See [10] for a formal definition of the semantic.

The ESST Algorithm. The ESST algorithm [16,17] performs a reachability analysis of a multi-threaded program $\mathcal{P} = \langle \mathcal{T}, F_S \rangle$ using explicit-state techniques to explore the possible executions of the scheduler and lazy predicate abstraction [22] to explore the executions of the threads. In the following, we rely on the extended version of the ESST where the scheduler execution is semi-symbolic [17], since we will need a scheduler that reads and writes the local state of the threads. We provide a concise description of the reachability analysis algorithm, and refer to [16,17] for the details.

The ESST constructs an *abstract reachability forest* (ARF) to represent the reachable states. An *ARF node* is a tuple $\langle\langle l_1, \varphi_1 \rangle, \ldots, \langle l_n, \varphi_n \rangle, \varphi, \mathbb{S}\rangle$, where for all $i \in [1, n]$, $l_i \in L_i$ is a location of T_i and φ_i is a local region (a formula over $LVar_i$), φ is a global region[4] (a formula over $\bigcup_{i \in [1,n]} LVar_i$) and $\mathbb{S}$ is a scheduler state. The ARF is constructed by expanding the ARF nodes. An ARF node can be expanded as long as it is not *covered* (no other nodes in the ARF include the set of states denoted by this node) or if it is not an error node (the node does not contain any error location). If ESST terminates and all the nodes in the ARF are covered then $\mathcal{P}$ is *safe*. If the expansion of the ARF reaches an error node, the ESST builds an abstract counterexample (a path in the ARF from the initial node to the error node), which is simulated in the concrete program;

---

[4] Whereas in the general ESST framework the global region is used to track both local and global variables, we use it to only track the relations among the local variables due to the data transfer on interactions.

if the simulation succeeds, we find a real counter-example and the program is *unsafe*. Otherwise the counter-example is spurious, the ESST refines the current abstraction, and restarts the expansion (see [16] for details).

The node expansion uses three basic operations: the symbolic execution of a thread (based on the *abstract strongest post-condition*), the execution of a primitive function, and the semi-symbolic execution of the scheduling function F_S. The *abstract strongest post-condition* $SP_{op}^{\delta}(\varphi)$ is the *predicate abstraction* of the set of states reachable from any of the states in the region φ after executing the operation op, using the set of predicates δ. ESST associates a set of predicates to thread locations ($\delta_{l_i'}$), as well as to the global region (δ). The primitive functions are executed by the primitive executor SEXEC : $(SState \times PrimitiveCall) \rightarrow (\mathbb{Z} \times SState)$ to update the scheduler state. The scheduler function F_S is implemented by a function $F_S : ARFNodes \rightarrow (2^{SState_{One} \times LFProg})$, where $SState_{One}$ is the set of scheduler states with only one running thread, $ARFNodes$ is the set of *ARF* nodes and *LFProg* is the set of loop-free programs (programs that contains assignments and conditional statements, but not loops) over the variables of $\mathcal{P}^5$. A ARF node $\eta = (\langle l_1, \varphi_1 \rangle, \ldots, \langle l_n, \varphi_n \rangle, \varphi, \mathbb{S})$ is expanded by the following two rules:

E1. If $\mathbb{S}(st_{T_i}) = Running$ and there exists an edge $(l_i, op, l_i') \in E_i$, create a successor node $(\langle l_1, \varphi_1' \rangle, \ldots, \langle l_i', \varphi_i' \rangle, \ldots, \langle l_n, \varphi_n' \rangle, \varphi', \mathbb{S}')$, where:

  - $\langle \mathbb{S}', \hat{op} \rangle = \begin{cases} \langle \mathbb{S}, op \rangle & \text{if } op \text{ is not a primitive function call} \\ \langle \mathbb{S}'', x := v \rangle & \text{if } op \text{ is } x := f(\boldsymbol{y}) \text{ and } (v, \mathbb{S}'') = \text{SEXEC}(\mathbb{S}, f(\boldsymbol{y})) \end{cases}$

  - $\varphi_i' = SP_{\hat{op}}^{\delta_{l_i'}}(\varphi_i \wedge \varphi)$, $\varphi_j' = \varphi_j$, for $i \neq j$, and $\varphi' = SP_{\hat{op}}^{\delta}(\varphi)$.
    ($\delta_{l_i'}$ and δ are the precisions associated to the location l_i and to the global region respectively).

E2. If there are no running threads, for each $\langle \mathbb{S}', P^{lf} \rangle \in F_S(\eta)$ create a successor node
    $(\langle l_1, \varphi_1' \rangle, \ldots, \langle l_n, \varphi_n' \rangle, \varphi', \mathbb{S}')$, where $\varphi_j' = SP_{P^{lf}}^{\delta_{l_j'}}(\varphi_j \wedge \varphi)$, for $j \in [1, n]$ and $\varphi' = SP_{P^{lf}}^{\delta}(\varphi)$.

The rule E1 expands the ARF node by unfolding the CFG edge $\langle l, op, l' \rangle$ of the running thread T_i. If the operation op is not a primitive function, then the scheduler state is unchanged (i.e. $\mathbb{S}' = \mathbb{S}$). Otherwise, if the operation op is a primitive function, (e.g. $x := f(\boldsymbol{y})$), the algorithm executes the primitive executor SEXEC to change the scheduler state and collect the return value of the function (i.e. $(v, \mathbb{S}'') = \text{SEXEC}(\mathbb{S}, f(\boldsymbol{y}))$). In both cases, the state of the running thread and the global region are updated by computing the abstract strongest post condition. The rule E2 executes the scheduling function to create a new ARF node for each output state of the scheduling function when all the threads are not running. A detailed illustration of the execution of scheduling function will be give in Sect. 3.2.

3.2   Instantiation of ESST for BIP

To instantiate ESST for BIP, there are two naïve approaches. One is to translate a BIP model to a SystemC program, hence relying on the SystemC primitive functions and the SystemC scheduler (i.e. the existing instantiation of
ESST [16]). This approach is inefficient, since one has to encode the BIP semantics with additional threads. Another approach is to reuse the SystemC primitive
functions as in [16,17], modifying the scheduler to mimic the BIP semantics. This
approach is not efficient either, since the primitive functions in SystemC only
allow threads to notify and wait for events. This has the effect of introducing
additional variables in the scheduler to keep track of the sent and received events,
which considerably increases the state space to be explored.

   In this paper, we provide a novel instantiation of the ESST framework to
analyze BIP models, it consists of: (i) a mapping from BIP to multi-threaded
programs and the definition of a new primitive function $wait()$ used by threads
to interact with the scheduler; (ii) a new semi-symbolic scheduler that respects
the BIP operational semantics and preserves the reachability of error locations.

   We use the ESST version with a semi-symbolic scheduler, instead of using
a purely explicit one, allowing the scheduler to read and write the state of the
threads. This feature is important to analyse BIP models because, in BIP, interaction guards and effects are expressed over the global state of the system.
Moreover, the semi-symbolic scheduler is also needed to correctly enforce the
BIP priorities.

   In each scheduling loop, the scheduler performs two tasks: (i) it computes
the set of possible interactions and chooses one to be run; (ii) it schedules the
execution of each thread that participates in the chosen interaction. When all
the threads are in the $Waiting$ state, the scheduler computes the set of possible
interactions and chooses one interaction to be run by setting the status of the
participating threads to $Runnable$, and by setting the value of a local variable in
the thread. The variable is used in the guards of the thread edges and encode the
BIP ports. Moreover, the scheduler is also responsible for executing the global
effects of the interaction. Whithin each scheduling cycle, the scheduler picks the
$Runnable$ threads one by one, until no such threads are available.

Primitive Functions and Threads. In our BIP instantiation of ESST we
introduce a primitive function $wait()$, which suspends the execution of the calling
thread and releases the control back to the scheduler (thus, we have only one
primitive function). The function does not change the state of the thread, but
changes the status of the thread in the scheduler state to $Waiting$. Since the
return value of $wait()$ is of no interest, we will write $wait()$ instead of $x := wait()$.
Formally, the semantics of $wait()$ is defined by the primitive executor SEXEC,
that is $[\![wait()]\!]_{\mathcal{E}}(s, \mathbb{S}) = \text{SEXEC}(\langle \mathbb{S}, wait() \rangle) = \langle *, \mathbb{S}' \rangle$, where $*$ denotes a dummy
return value, s is the state of T_i, and $\mathbb{S}' = \mathbb{S}[st_{T_i} := Waiting]$, if T_i is the caller
of $wait()$.

   Given an $atomic\ component$ $B_i = \langle Var_i, Q_i, E_i, l_{0_i}, Q_{err_i} \rangle$ of $\mathcal{P}_{\text{BIP}}$, we define
the $thread$ $T_i = \langle G_i, LVar_i \rangle$, where $LVar_i = Var_i \cup \{evt^i\}$, $Dom(evt^i) = \mathbb{Z}$ and
$G_i = (L_i, E_i, l'_{0_i}, L_{err_i})$, where:

$$L_i = \{l, l_{wait} | l \in Q_i\} \cup \{l_e | e \in E_i, e = \langle l, \alpha, g, op, l' \rangle\};$$

$$E_i = \{\langle l, wait(), l_{wait} \rangle | l \in Q_i\} \cup$$

$$\{\langle l_{wait}, evt^i = \alpha, l_e \rangle, \langle l_e, op, l' \rangle | e \in E_i, e = \langle l, \alpha, g, op, l' \rangle\};$$

$$l'_{0_i} = l_{0_i};$$

$$L_{err_i} = Q_{err_i}.$$

We introduce an additional integer variable evt^i for each thread and we associate every port α to a distinct integer value; for clarity, we use the notation $evt^i = \alpha$ instead of $evt^i = i$, where $i \in \mathbb{Z}$ is the value we associated to the port α. The CFG G_i of the thread is obtained from a transformation of the BIP atomic component B_i: (i) adding a location l_{wait} and an edge from l to l_{wait} for each $l \in Q_i$; (ii) for each edge $e = \langle l, \alpha, g, op, l' \rangle \in E_i$, add an intermediate location l_e, and an edge from l_{wait} to l_e, labelled with $evt^i = \alpha$, and an edge from l_e to l', labelled with op[6].

The edge to the location l_{wait} labelled by the primitive function $wait()$ ensures that the thread releases the control to the scheduler, waiting that the scheduler chooses an interaction to be run. The subsequent edge labelled by $evt^i = \alpha$ ensures that the thread only executes the edge chosen by the scheduler and constrained by the value of the variable evt^i. Notice that the edge guard will be taken into account by the BIP scheduler.

Semi-symbolic BIP Scheduler. For analyzing BIP models, we design the semi-symbolic BIP scheduler $\text{SCHED}(\mathcal{P}_{BIP}) = \langle F_S, SVar \rangle$, where $SVar = \{st_{T_1}, \dots, st_{T_n}\}$, and F_S is the scheduling function that respects the BIP semantics. As required by the ESST, the scheduler keeps the status of each thread T_i in a variable st_{T_i}, with values $\{Running, Runnable, Waiting\}$. Initially all st_{T_i} are $Runnable$.

Given an ARF node $\eta = \langle\langle l_1, \varphi_1 \rangle, \dots, \langle l_n, \varphi_n \rangle, \varphi, \mathbb{S}\rangle$, we say that an interaction $\gamma = \langle\{\alpha_1, \dots, \alpha_k\}, g, op\rangle$ is $enabled$ if there exists a set of edges $\{t_{\alpha_1}, \dots, t_{\alpha_k}\}$ such that, for all $i \in [1, k]$, $t_{\alpha_i} \in E_{id(\alpha_i)}$, $t_{\alpha_i} = \langle l_{id(\alpha_i)}, \alpha_i, g_{t_{\alpha_i}}, op_{t_{\alpha_i}}, l'_{t_{\alpha_i}} \rangle$. In that case, we write $enabled(\eta, \gamma)$ and we denote with $EnabledSet(\eta)$ the set of all the enabled interactions in η. Notice that the concept of enabled interaction on an ARF node is different from the one we had on a BIP configuration: we do not check the satisfiability of the guards in the ARF node to determine the set of enabled interactions. Instead, interaction guards and effects are accounted for by the symbolic execution of the scheduling function.

F_S alternates two different phases: (i) scheduling of new interactions; (ii) execution of edges participating in the chosen interaction. Given an ARF node $\eta = \langle\langle l_1, \varphi_1 \rangle, \dots, \langle l_n, \varphi_n \rangle, \varphi, \mathbb{S}\rangle$, $F_S(\eta)$ is defined as follows:

F1. If for all $st_{T_i} \in SVar$, such that $\mathbb{S}(st_{T_i}) = Waiting$ and $EnabledSet(\eta) = \{\gamma_1, \dots, \gamma_k\}$, $F_S(\eta) = \{\langle\mathbb{S}_1, P_1^{lf}\rangle, \dots, \langle\mathbb{S}_k, P_k^{lf}\rangle\}$, where for all $i \in [1, k]$:

---

[6] Note that, while the formal presentation introduces intermediate locations and edges, in practice these are collapsed in a single edge since we use the *large block encoding* [8].

$-\ \gamma_i = \langle \{\alpha_i^1, \ldots, \alpha_i^l\}, g_i, op_i \rangle;$

$-\ \mathbb{S}_i = \mathbb{S}[st_{T_{id(\alpha_i^1)}} := Runnable, \ldots, st_{T_{id(\alpha_i^l)}} := Runnable];$

$-\ P_i^{lf} = p; g_i; g_e; op_i; evt_{id(\alpha_i^1)}^1 := \alpha_i^1; \ldots; evt_{id(\alpha_i^l)}^l := \alpha_i^l,$ where

$p = \bigwedge_{\langle \gamma_i, \gamma' \rangle \in \pi, \alpha \in \gamma'} \bigwedge_{\langle l, \alpha, g_\alpha, op_\alpha, l' \rangle \in E_{id(\alpha)}} \neg g_\alpha$

and $g_e = \bigwedge_{\alpha \in \gamma_i} \bigvee_{\langle l, \alpha, g_\alpha, op_\alpha, l' \rangle \in E_{id(\alpha)}} g_\alpha.$

F2. If there exists a thread T_i, such that $\mathbb{S}(st_{T_i}) = Runnable$, then $F_S(\eta) = \{\langle \mathbb{S}[st_{T_i} := Running], skip \rangle\}.$

In rule F1, the formula p encodes the priority constraints (there are no enabled interactions with a higher priority than γ_i), and the formula g_e imposes that, in each thread that participates in the interaction, there is at least one enabled edge labeled with the corresponding interaction port. Thus, the loop free program P_i^{lf} ensures that the interaction γ_i will be scheduled, according to the BIP semantics, and also imposes the correct ports that must be executed by the threads. The rule F2 just picks the next thread to be run.

Correctness of ESST$_{\mathrm{BIP}}$.

Theorem 1. *Let* $\mathcal{P}_{\mathrm{BIP}} = \langle \mathcal{B}, \Gamma, \pi \rangle$ *be a BIP model and* $\mathcal{P} = \langle \mathcal{T}, \mathrm{SCHED}(\mathcal{P}_{\mathrm{BIP}}) \rangle$ *be the corresponding multi-threaded program with semi-symbolic BIP scheduler* $\mathrm{SCHED}(\mathcal{P}_{\mathrm{BIP}})$. *If the* ESST$_{\mathrm{BIP}}$ *algorithm terminates on* $\mathcal{P}$, *then the* ESST$_{\mathrm{BIP}}$ *returns* safe *iff the BIP model* $\mathcal{P}_{\mathrm{BIP}}$ *is safe.*

For lack of space, we provide the proofs in the extended technical report [10].

3.3   Optimizations

In this section we present some optimizations aiming to reduce the number of the ARF nodes that must be explored during the reachability analysis.

Partial Order Reduction for BIP. The application of POR to the ESST$_{\mathrm{BIP}}$ is based on the following idea: when the ESST$_{\mathrm{BIP}}$ executes the scheduling function F_S on a node η, it creates the successor nodes only for a representative subset of the set of all the enabled interactions $EnabledSet(\eta)$. To compute the independence relation between interactions, we define the following *valid dependence relation* [16] for BIP models: two interactions are *dependent* if they share a common component. This valid dependent relation can be computed statically from the BIP model. We have implemented both persistent set and sleep set POR approaches. The use of POR in ESST$_{\mathrm{BIP}}$ is correct since the application of POR to the general ESST framework is sound, provided a valid dependence relation [16].

Simultaneous Execution of the Edges Participating in an Interaction.
In the basic ESST$_{\text{BIP}}$, we serialize the edges participating in the same interaction since we use a scheduling function that allows only one thread to run at a time. Consider an ARF node $\eta = \langle \langle l_1, \varphi_1 \rangle, \ldots, \langle l_n, \varphi_n \rangle, \varphi, \mathbb{S} \rangle$, and an interaction $\gamma = \langle \{\alpha_1, \ldots, \alpha_k\}, g, op \rangle$ enabled in η. Let $\{t_{\alpha_1}, \ldots, t_{\alpha_k}\}$ be the set of participating edges in γ and $op_{\alpha_1}, \ldots, op_{\alpha_k}$ be their respective effects. When we expand η, we will create the following sequence of successor nodes:

$$\eta \xrightarrow{E2} \eta_1 \xrightarrow{E2} \eta_2 \xrightarrow{\alpha_1} \eta_3 \xrightarrow{op_{\alpha_1}} \eta_4 \xrightarrow{wait()} \eta_5 \xrightarrow{E2} \eta_6 \xrightarrow{\alpha_2} \ldots \xrightarrow{wait()} \eta_{2+4k}$$

where the label E2 denotes the execution of the ESST$_{\text{BIP}}$ scheduler function. The intermediate nodes $\eta_1, \ldots, \eta_{2+4k-1}$ are due to the sequentialization of the execution of the edges participating in the interaction. These intermediate nodes increase the complexity of the reachability analysis. They do not correspond to any state reachable in the BIP model, where all the edges involved in an interaction are executed simultaneously, and are an artefact of the encoding of the BIP model into the ESST framework. We can modify the search discussed in Sect. 3 in order to avoid the generation of these intermediate states by (i) extending the primitive execution function SEXEC to simultaneously evaluate a sequence of primitive functions, (ii) changing the node expansion rule E1 of ESST as follows:

E1'. If $\mathbb{S}(st_{T_i}) = Running$, let $T_R = \{T_i \in T | \mathbb{S}(st_{T_i}) \neq Waiting\}$ be the set of threads not in the $Waiting$ state. Let $op = op_1; \ldots; op_k$ be a sequential composition (in arbitrary order) of the operations labeling the outgoing edges $(l_i, op_i, l'_i) \in E_i$, for $T_i \in T_R$[7]. The successor node is$(\langle l'_1, \varphi'_1 \rangle, \ldots, \langle l'_n, \varphi'_n \rangle, \varphi', \mathbb{S}')$, where:

$$- \langle \mathbb{S}', \hat{op} \rangle = \begin{cases} \langle \mathbb{S}, op \rangle & \text{if none of the } op_i \text{ in } op \text{ is a call to } wait() \\ \langle \mathbb{S}'', skip \rangle & \text{if all } op_i \text{ in } op \text{ is a } wait() \text{ and} (*, \mathbb{S}'') = \text{SEXEC}(\mathbb{S}, op) \end{cases}$$

$- \varphi'_i = SP^{\delta_{l'_i}}_{\hat{op}_i}(\varphi_i \wedge \varphi)$ for each thread $T_i \in T_R$, $\varphi'_j = \varphi_j$ and $l'_j = l_j$ for each thread $T_j \notin T_R$, and $\varphi' = SP^{\delta}_{\hat{op}}(\varphi)$, where $\hat{op}_i$ is the projection of $\hat{op}$ on the instructions of thread T_i.

We remark that, in BIP, we do not have shared variables. Thus, all the op_i are local to the corresponding components, and executing a sequence of op_i altogether will not create any conflict. The correctness of this optimization can be easily justified since it respects BIP operational semantics.

Implicit Primitive Functions. The previous optimization does not remove all the intermediate ARF nodes $\eta_1, \ldots, \eta_{2+4k-1}$ visited by the ESST$_{\text{BIP}}$ that do not have a corresponding configurations in the BIP operational semantics. In particular, we can avoid the creation of the intermediate ARF nodes created

---

[7] Note that there is no non-determinism on the outgoing edge to be executed by each thread T_i after the scheduling of the interaction γ.

by calls to *wait()* noting that: (i) *wait()* is always executed immediately after the execution of some edge t_{α_i} labeled by α_i, i.e. $\eta \xrightarrow{\alpha_i} \eta' \xrightarrow{wait()} \eta''$ (see the description of the sequence of the ARF nodes visited after the scheduling of an interaction in the previous optimization); (ii) *wait()* only modifies the scheduler states of an ARF node. Thus, we can combine the execution of *wait()* with the execution of its preceding edge t_{α_i}. This optimization can be integrated in the ESST$_{\mathrm{BIP}}$ framework by modifying rule E1 as follows.

E1". If $\mathbb{S}(st_{T_i}) = Running$, and $\{(l_i, op, l_i^1), (l_i^1, wait(), l_i')\} \subseteq E_i$, then the successor node is $(\langle l_1, \varphi_1' \rangle, \ldots, \langle l_n, \varphi_n' \rangle, \varphi', \mathbb{S}')$, where:

- $\langle \mathbb{S}', \hat{op} \rangle = \langle \mathbb{S}'', op; skip \rangle$ if op is not $wait()$ and $(*, \mathbb{S}'') = \textsc{Sexec}(\mathbb{S}, wait())$
- $\varphi' = SP_{\hat{op}}^{\delta}(\varphi)$, $\varphi_i' = SP_{\hat{op}}^{\delta l_i'}(\varphi_i \wedge \varphi)$, and $\varphi_j' = \varphi_j$, for $i \neq j$,

This optimization is correct with respect to BIP semantics since ESST$_{\mathrm{BIP}}$ will still visit all the reachable states of the original BIP model $\mathcal{P}_{\mathrm{BIP}}$. To see this, notice that there are no interactions to be scheduled in the intermediate sequence of ARF nodes created while executing an interaction, and after the execution of the edge t_{α_i} the thread T_i will always stop its execution.

We remark that the optimization for the implicit execution of primitive functions and the optimization for the simultaneous execution of the edges of an interaction can be combined together, to further reduce the search space of the basic ESST$_{\mathrm{BIP}}$.

4 Encoding BIP into Transition System

In this section, we show how to encode a BIP model into a Symbolic Transition System, thus enabling a direct application of state-of-the-art model checkers for infinite state systems, such as the NUXMV [12] symbolic model checker.

A *Symbolic Transition System* (STS) is a tuple $S = \langle V, I, Tr \rangle$, where: (i) V is a finite set of variables, (ii) I is a first-order formula over V (called *initial condition*), and (iii) Tr is a first-order formula over $V \cup V'$ (called *transition condition*[8]). The semantic of an STS can be given in terms of an explicit transition systems (see for example [26]).

The encoding of a BIP model $\mathcal{P}_{\mathrm{BIP}} = \langle \mathcal{B}, \Gamma, \pi \rangle$ as an STS $S_{\mathcal{P}_{\mathrm{BIP}}} = \langle V, I, Tr \rangle$ is the following. The set of variables is defined as:

$$V = \bigcup_{i=1}^n \{loc_i\} \cup \bigcup_{i=1}^n \{x | x \in Var_i\} \cup \bigcup_{i=1}^n \{v_\alpha | \alpha \in P_i\} \cup \{v_\Gamma\}$$

where for all $i \in [1, n]$, we preserve the domain of each var $x \in Var_i$, $Dom(loc_i) = Q_i$; for all $\alpha \in P_i$, $Dom(v_\alpha) = \{true, false\}$; and $Dom(v_\Gamma) = \Gamma$.

The initial condition is $I = \bigwedge_i^n (loc_i = l_{0_i})$, since we do not have initial predicates in $\mathcal{P}_{\mathrm{BIP}}$. The transition condition is $Tr = (\bigwedge_{i=1}^n (Tr_{e_i} \wedge Tr_{p_i}) \wedge Tr_\Gamma \wedge Tr_\pi$, where Tr_{e_i} encodes the edges of the component B_i, Tr_{p_i} determines when

---

[8] Hereby and below, we denote with $V' = \{x' | x \in V\}$ the set of primed variables of V.

the variable v_α for port α is true, Tr_Γ encodes when an interaction is enabled, and Tr_π encodes the priorities.

In the following, let $\Gamma_{B_i} = \{\langle Act, g, op \rangle | Act \cap P_i \neq \emptyset \}$ be the set of all the interactions on which B_i participates and $\Gamma_e = \{\langle Act, g, op \rangle | e = \langle l_i, \alpha, g_e, op_e, l_i' \rangle,$ $\alpha \in Act\}$, with $e \in E_i$, be the set of interactions that contain the port that labels e.

The encoding of an edge e of a component B_i is defined as:

$$Tr_{e_i} = \bigvee_{e = \langle l_i, Act \cap P_i, g_e, op_e, l_i' \rangle \in E_i} loc_i = l_i \wedge loc_i' = l_i' \wedge g_e \wedge \bigvee_{\gamma \in \Gamma_{B_i}} v_\Gamma = \gamma \wedge$$

$$\bigwedge_{\gamma \in \Gamma_{B_i}} \left(v_\Gamma = \gamma \rightarrow \bigwedge_{x \in Var_i} x' = update(x, e, \gamma) \right) \wedge \bigwedge_{\gamma \notin \Gamma_{B_i}} \left(v_\Gamma = \gamma \rightarrow \bigwedge_{x \in Var_i} x' = x \right)$$

$$update(x, e, \gamma) = \begin{cases} replace(e, \gamma) & \text{if } op_e = x := e \\ replace(x, \gamma) & \text{otherwise} \end{cases}$$

and $replace(e, \gamma)$ is a function that replaces all the occurrences of a variables y in e with e_γ, if $op_\gamma = y := e_\gamma$ and $\gamma = \langle Act, g_\gamma, op_\gamma \rangle$[9]. Tr_{p_i} is defined as $\bigwedge_{\alpha \in \Gamma} \left(v_\alpha \leftrightarrow \bigvee_{\langle l_i, \alpha, g_e, op_e, l_i' \rangle \in E_i} (loc_i = l_i \wedge g_e) \right)$. Finally, the conditions that constraint the interactions to their ports and the priorities among the interactions are defined as:

$$Tr_\Gamma = \bigwedge_{\gamma = \langle Act_\gamma, g_\gamma, op_\gamma \rangle \in \Gamma} \bigwedge_{\alpha \in Act_\gamma} v_\Gamma = \gamma \rightarrow (v_\alpha \wedge g_\gamma)$$

$$Tr_\pi = \bigwedge_{(\gamma_1, \gamma_2) \in \Gamma, \gamma_1 = \langle Act_{\gamma_1}, g_{\gamma_1}, op_{\gamma_1} \rangle} \left(g_{\gamma_1} \wedge \bigwedge_{\alpha \in Act_{\gamma_1}} v_\alpha \right) \rightarrow v_\Gamma \neq \gamma_2$$

Theorem 2. *The transition system $S_{P_{BIP}}$ for a BIP model $\mathcal{P}_{\mathrm{BIP}}$ preserves reachability of any configuration of the BIP model.*

The proof relies on the fact that the state space of the BIP model is preserved. The initial configuration is preserved by formula I, where loc_i is constrained to the initial locations of the corresponding component. The transition relation is also preserved, since the variable v_Γ can be assigned to the value representing an interaction γ, enabling the corresponding edges, if and only if γ is enabled in the corresponding state of the BIP model. The valuations of the additional variables v_α and v_Γ do not alter the state space: their valuations are constrained by formula the Tr to reflect the BIP semantics.

5   Related Work

Several approaches to the verification of BIP models have been explored in the literature. DFINDER [7] is a verification tool for BIP models that relies on compositional reasoning for identifying deadlocks and verifying safety properties.

---

[9] Note that, while in our definition op_γ is a single assignment, the approach can be easily generalized to sequential programs applying a *single-static assignment (SSA)* transformation [18].

The tool has several limitations: it is unsound in the presence of data transfers among components (it assumes that the involved variables do not exchange values); its refinement procedure is not effective for infinite-state systems, since it consists only in removing the found unreachable deadlock states from the next round of the algorithm; finally, it can only handle BIP models with finite domain variables or integers. Our approaches instead are sound in the presence of data transfer, they exploit standard refinement mechanisms (e.g. refinement based on interpolation) and can handle BIP models with real variables.

The VCS [20] tool supports the verification of BIP models with data transfer among components, using specialized BDD- and SAT-based model checking algorithms for BIP. Differently from our approach, VCS is only able to deal with finite domain variables, and priority is ignored.

Our encoding in transition system is related to works in [25,29]. In [29], a timed BIP model is translated into Timed Automata and then verified with UPPAAL [6]. The translation handles data transfers, but it is limited to BIP models with finite domain data variables and without priorities. In [25], the authors show an encoding of a BIP models into Horn Clauses. They do not handle data transfers on interactions and do not describe how to handle priorities. We remark that, any transition system can be encoded into Horn Clauses and then verified with tools such as Z3 [23] or ELDARICA [24].

With respect to the verification of multi-threaded programs, the works most related to ours are [16,17,30]. In [16,17], the authors present the ESST framework, instantiating it for SystemC [27] and FairThreads [11]. They neither consider instantaneous synchronizations nor priorities among interactions. Instead, in this work we instantiate the ESST framework for the analysis of BIP models, which encompasses instantaneous synchronizations and priorities. The semi-symbolic scheduler in [17] is also different from ours: while they use the semi-symbolic scheduler to handle parameters of the primitive functions, we use it to change the status of the local threads. We also apply and adapt several optimizations sound w.r.t. the BIP operational semantics. The work in [30] combines lazy abstraction and POR for the verification of generic multi-threaded programs with pointers. They do not leverage on the separation between coordination and computation which is the core of our ESST$_{BIP}$ approach. Moreover, because of the pointers, they rely on a dynamic dependence relation for applying POR.

6   Experimental Evaluation

We implemented ESST$_{BIP}$ extending the KRATOS [13] software model checker. We implemented the encoding from BIP to transition system in a tool based on the BIP framework [2]. Our tool generates models in the input language of NUXMV, allowing us to reuse its model checking algorithms.

In the experimental evaluation, we used several benchmarks taken and adapted from the literature, including the temperature control system model and ATM transaction model used in [7], the train gate control system model used in [25], and several other consensus and voting algorithm models. Every

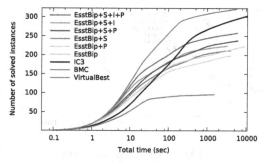

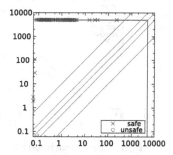

Fig. 1. Cumulative plot for all the benchmarks

Fig. 2. Run time (sec.) DFINDER (y axes) Ic3 (x axes)

benchmark is scalable with respect to the number of components. In total, we created 379 instances of both safe and unsafe models, and verified different invariant properties. All the benchmarks are infinite-state, due to integer variables, and some of them feature data transfer on interaction. Due to lack of space, we do not provide the details of each benchmark, but refer to our webpage[10] for more information.

We run several configurations of $ESST_{BIP}$: ESSTBIP, ESSTBIP+P, ESSTBIP+S, ESSTBIP+S+P, ESSTBIP+S+I and ESSTBIP+S+I+P, where ESSTBIP is the base version without any optimization, P denotes the use of partial order reduction, S denotes the use of the simultaneous execution of the interaction edges and I denotes the implicit execution of the primitives functions. After the encoding into transition systems, we run two algorithms implemented in NUXMV: (IC3) an implementation of the *IC3* algorithm integrated with predicate abstraction [14]; (BMC) an implementation of *Bounded Model Checking* [9] via SMT [1] solving. For the benchmarks that do not exhibit data transfer, we also compared our approaches against DFINDER (version 2) [7].

All the experiments have been performed on a cluster of 64-bit Linux machines with a 2.7 Ghz Intel Xeon X5650 CPU, with a memory limit set to 8 Gb and a time limit of 900 s. The tools and benchmarks used in the experiments are available in our webpage.

Comparison with DFINDER. We first compare on the subset of the benchmarks (100 instances) that DFINDER can handle (these benchmarks do not have data transfer and are safe). We compare DFINDER and Ic3 in the scatter plot of Fig. 2: DFINDER is able to solve only 4 of our instances, while Ic3 solves all the 100 instances. The best configuration of $ESST_{BIP}$ (ESSTBIP+S+I+P) shows a similar trend (solving 75 instances). For lack of space we do not show the respective plot. DFINDER requires about 142 s to solve the four benchmarks, while both Ic3 and ESSTBIP+S+I+P solve all of them in a fraction of a second. The main explanations for these results are: (i) DFINDER cannot prove 60

---

[10] https://es.fbk.eu/people/mover/atva15-kratos.tar.bz2.

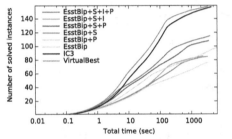
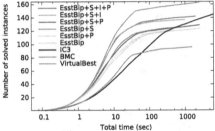

Fig. 3. Safe benchmarks   **Fig. 4.** Unsafe benchmarks

instances since it cannot find strong enough invariants to prove the property; (ii) it exceeds the memory limits for the remaining 36 instances.

Comparison of NUXMV and ESST$_{BIP}$. We show the results of the comparison among our approaches on the full set of instances in Fig. 1, where we plot the cumulative time to solve an increasing number of instances. Ic3 clearly outperforms all the other approaches, while the version of ESST$_{BIP}$ with all the optimization outperforms all the other ESST$_{BIP}$ configurations. In Fig. 3 we focus only on the safe instances: the plot shows that Ic3 is more efficient than ESST$_{BIP}$. Ic3 is much more effective than ESST$_{BIP}$ on a subset of the instances, where Ic3 can easily find an inductive invariant (for this subset, the number of frames needed by Ic3 to prove the property does not increase when increasing the number of components in each benchmark). In these cases instead, ESST$_{BIP}$ still has to visit several nodes before succeeding in the coverage check. In Fig. 4, we focus on the unsafe properties. Both all the ESST$_{BIP}$ approaches that enable the implicit primitive function execution and Ic3 outperform BMC. The main reason is that BMC is not effective on long counterexamples, while in our benchmarks the length of the counterexamples grows with the number of components. We also observe that, for the unsafe cases, the approach EsstBip+S+I+P is faster than Ic3. Thus, the experiments show that Ic3 and ESST$_{BIP}$ are complementary, with Ic3 being more efficient in the safe case, and ESST$_{BIP}$ being more efficient for the unsafe ones. This can be also seen in Fig. 1, where we plot the virtual best configuration (VIRTUALBEST) (i.e. the configuration obtained taking the lower run time for each benchmark), which shows the results that we would obtain running all our approaches in parallel (in a portfolio approach).

Evaluation of the ESST$_{BIP}$ Optimization. In Fig. 5a and b we show two scatter plots to compare the results obtained with and without partial order reduction. The plot 5a shows how POR improves the performance when applied to EsstBip (for EsstBip+S we get similar results), while the plot 5b shows the same for EsstBip+S+I. The plots show that POR is effective on almost all benchmarks, even if in some cases the POR bookkeeping introduces some overhead. In Fig. 5c and d we show the results of applying the simultaneous execution

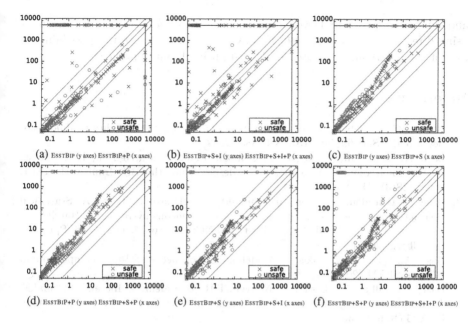

Fig. 5. Scatter plots of run times (sec.) for the $ESST_{BIP}$ optimizations

of the edges participating in an interaction to the basic configuration with and without partial order reduction enabled (ESSTBIP and ESSTBIP+P). In both cases, the improvements to the run times brought by the concurrent execution of edges is consistent, since the run times are always lower and the number of solved instances higher. Finally, in Fig. 5e and f we show the plots that compares ESSTBIP+S with ESSTBIP+S+I and ESSTBIP+S+P with ESSTBIP+S+I+P. In both cases the implicit execution of the primitives functions always brings a performance improvement.

7   Conclusions and Future Work

In this paper, we described two complementary approaches for the verification of infinite-state BIP models that, contrary to the existing techniques, consider all the features of BIP such as the global effects on the interactions and priorities. First, we instantiated for BIP the ESST framework and we integrated several optimization sound w.r.t. the BIP semantics. Second, we provided an encoding of BIP models into symbolic transition systems, enabling us to exploit the existing state of the art verification algorithms. Finally, we implemented the proposed techniques and performed an experimental evaluation on several benchmarks. The results show that our approaches are complementary, and that they outperform DFINDER w.r.t performance and also w.r.t. the coverage of the BIP features. As future work we would like extend the proposed techniques to support timed BIP [4] (e.g. the symbolic encoding could be extended to HYDI [15]) and, in the case of ESST we would improve its performance in finding bugs using direct model checking [19]. Finally, we will investigate the possibility to exploit the invariants computed by DFINDER in all our approaches.

References

1. Barrett, C.W., Sebastiani, R., Seshia, S.A., Tinelli, C.: Satisfiability modulo theories. Handb. Satisfiability **185**, 825–885 (2009)
2. Basu, A., Bensalem, S., Bozga, M., Combaz, J., Jaber, M., Nguyen, T.H., Sifakis, J.: Rigorous component-based system design using the BIP framework. IEEE Softw. **28**(3), 41–48 (2011)
3. Basu, A., Bensalem, S., Bozga, M., Caillaud, B., Delahaye, B., Legay, A.: Statistical abstraction and model-checking of large heterogeneous systems. In: Hatcliff, J., Zucca, E. (eds.) FMOODS 2010, Part II. LNCS, vol. 6117, pp. 32–46. Springer, Heidelberg (2010)
4. Basu, A., Bozga, M., Sifakis, J.: Modeling heterogeneous real-time components in BIP. In: SEFM (2006)
5. Basu, A., Gallien, M., Lesire, C., Nguyen, T.H., Bensalem, S., Ingrand, F., Sifakis, J.: Incremental component-based construction and verification of a robotic system. ECAI **178**, 631–635 (2008)
6. Behrmann, G., David, A., Larsen, K.G., Håkansson, J., Pettersson, P., Yi, W., Hendriks, M.: UPPAAL 4.0. In: QEST (2006)
7. Bensalem, S., Bozga, M., Nguyen, T.-H., Sifakis, J.: D-Finder: a tool for compositional deadlock detection and verification. In: Bouajjani, A., Maler, O. (eds.) CAV 2009. LNCS, vol. 5643, pp. 614–619. Springer, Heidelberg (2009)
8. Beyer, D., Cimatti, A., Griggio, A., Keremoglu, M.E., Sebastiani, R.: Software model checking via large-block encoding. In: FMCAD (2009)
9. Biere, A., Cimatti, A., Clarke, E., Zhu, Y.: Symbolic model checking without BDDs. In: Cleaveland, W.R. (ed.) TACAS 1999. LNCS, vol. 1579, p. 193. Springer, Heidelberg (1999)
10. Bliudze, S., Cimatti, A., Jaber, M., Mover, S., Roveri, M., Saab, W., Wang, Q.: Formal verification of infinite-state bip models. Technical report. https://es-static.fbk.eu/people/mover/paper/fvbip.pdf
11. Boussinot, F.: FairThreads: mixing cooperative and preemptive threads in C. Concurrency Comput. Pract. Experience **18**(5), 445–469 (2006)
12. Cavada, R., Cimatti, A., Dorigatti, M., Griggio, A., Mariotti, A., Micheli, A., Mover, S., Roveri, M., Tonetta, S.: The nuXmv Symbolic Model Checker. In: Biere, A., Bloem, R. (eds.) CAV 2014. LNCS, vol. 8559, pp. 334–342. Springer, Heidelberg (2014)
13. Cimatti, A., Griggio, A., Micheli, A., Narasamdya, I., Roveri, M.: KRATOS – a software model checker for systemC. In: Gopalakrishnan, G., Qadeer, S. (eds.) CAV 2011. LNCS, vol. 6806, pp. 310–316. Springer, Heidelberg (2011)
14. Cimatti, A., Griggio, A., Mover, S., Tonetta, S.: IC3 modulo theories via implicit predicate abstraction. In: Ábrahám, E., Havelund, K. (eds.) TACAS 2014 (ETAPS). LNCS, vol. 8413, pp. 46–61. Springer, Heidelberg (2014)
15. Cimatti, A., Mover, S., Tonetta, S.: HyDI: a language for symbolic hybrid systems with discrete interaction. In: SEAA (2011)
16. Cimatti, A., Narasamdya, I., Roveri, M.: Software model checking with explicit scheduler and symbolic threads. Log. Methods Comput. Sci. **8**(2), 1–42 (2012)

17. Cimatti, A., Narasamdya, I., Roveri, M.: Verification of parametric system designs. In: FMCAD (2012)
18. Cytron, R., Ferrante, J., Rosen, B.K., Wegman, M.N., Zadeck, F.K.: Efficiently computing static single assignment form and the control dependence graph. ACM Trans. Program. Lang. Syst. 13(4), 451–490 (1991)
19. Edelkamp, S., Schuppan, V., Bošnački, D., Wijs, A., Fehnker, A., Aljazzar, H.: Survey on directed model checking. In: Peled, D.A., Wooldridge, M.J. (eds.) MoChArt 2008. LNCS, vol. 5348, pp. 65–89. Springer, Heidelberg (2009)
20. He, F., Yin, L., Wang, B.-Y., Zhang, L., Mu, G., Meng, W.: VCS: a verifier for component-based systems. In: Van Hung, D., Ogawa, M. (eds.) ATVA 2013. LNCS, vol. 8172, pp. 478–481. Springer, Heidelberg (2013)
21. Henzinger, T.A., Jhala, R., Majumdar, R., McMillan, K.L.: Abstractions from proofs. ACM SIGPLAN Not. 39, 232–244 (2004). ACM
22. Henzinger, T.A., Jhala, R., Majumdar, R., Sutre, G.: Lazy abstraction. In: POPL (2002)
23. Hoder, K., Bjørner, N.: Generalized property directed reachability. In: Cimatti, A., Sebastiani, R. (eds.) SAT 2012. LNCS, vol. 7317, pp. 157–171. Springer, Heidelberg (2012)
24. Hojjat, H., Konečný, F., Garnier, F., Iosif, R., Kuncak, V., Rümmer, P.: A verification toolkit for numerical transition systems. In: Giannakopoulou, D., Méry, D. (eds.) FM 2012. LNCS, vol. 7436, pp. 247–251. Springer, Heidelberg (2012)
25. Hojjat, H., Rümmer, P., Subotic, P., Yi, W.: Horn clauses for communicating timed systems. In: HCVS (2014)
26. Manna, Z., Pnueli, A.: The Temporal Logic of Reactive and Concurrent Systems: Specification. Springer, New York (1992)
27. IEEE 1666: SystemC language Reference Manual (2005)
28. Sifakis, J.: Rigorous system design. Found. Trends Electron. Des. Autom. 6(4), 293–362 (2013)
29. Su, C., Zhou, M., Yin, L., Wan, H., Gu, M.: Modeling and verification of component-based systems with data passing using BIP. In: ICECCS (2013)
30. Wachter, B., Kroening, D., Ouaknine, J.: Verifying multi-threaded software with Impact. In: FMCAD (2013)

PBMC: Symbolic Slicing for the Verification of Concurrent Programs

Habib Saissi[(✉)], Péter Bokor, and Neeraj Suri

Technische Univeristät Darmstadt, Darmstadt, Germany
{saissi,pbokor,suri}@deeds.informatik.tu-darmstadt.de

Abstract. This paper proposes a novel optimization of bounded model checking (BMC) for better run-time efficiency. Specifically, we define *projections*, an adaptation of dynamic program slices, and instruct the bounded model checker to check projections only. Given state properties over a subset of the program's variables, we prove the soundness of the proposed optimization.

We propose a symbolic encoding of projections and implement it for a prototype language of concurrent programs. We have developed a tool called PBMC to evaluate the efficiency of the proposed approach. Our evaluation with various concurrent programs justifies the potential of projections to efficient verification.

1 Introduction

Automated verification of complex programs is known to be a hard problem. The complexity of the task grows exponentially when the considered programs exhibit concurrent behavior [28]. Bounded model checking (BMC) [8] is a widely used verification technique, e.g., [12]. In BMC, a formula encoding the behavior of the program is computed and passed to an SMT/SAT solver along with the negation of the property. The solver then checks whether there exists an execution leading to a state violating the property. Thanks to the recent advances in the field of SAT solving, bounded model checking is becoming a problem solution for verification of concurrent programs [1,2,6]. The efficiency can be greatly improved by constraining the search space depending on the property of interest. Concretely, the encoding of the program is constrained by excluding behavior that is irrelevant or redundant with respect to the property. For example, the solver can be instructed to partially order (instead of totally order) transitions of the program, e.g., [6].

In this paper, we propose *projections* to constrain the search space of a bounded model checker. Conceptually, projections are slices of a program with respect to a set of variables. They are especially useful for the analysis of concurrent programs. For example, a projection with respect to the local state of a process may exclude transitions of other non-interfering processes. As a result, the interleavings of the excluded transitions (exponential in the number of transitions) do not have to be considered by the solver. Intuitively, projections consist

© Springer International Publishing Switzerland 2015
B. Finkbeiner et al. (Eds.): ATVA 2015, LNCS 9364, pp. 344–360, 2015.
DOI: 10.1007/978-3-319-24953-7_26

of executions which only contain transitions directly or indirectly affecting the variables of interest.

Contributions. Our first contribution is that we introduce projections, an adaptation of program slices to general transition systems, and show that they preserve the relevant safety properties of a program. The idea of projections is a general one and is independent of how the program states are explored. Our second contribution is that we present a symbolic encoding of projections for concurrent programs; we call the encoding PBMC (projection-based BMC) because it can be used for efficient bounded model checking. Note that although we concentrate on concurrent programs our result equally holds for single-threaded programs. Interestingly, PBMC can be seen as a form of *dynamic program slicing* [5]. In contrast to existing program analysis approaches where static program slicing is applied prior to the actual analysis, e.g. [12,14,26] , PBMC enumerates slices on-the-fly. The resulting slices are as precise as the dynamic ones because they are calculated based on feasible executions. To the best of our knowledge, PBMC is the first application of dynamic program slicing with BMC. Our final contribution is that we implement a prototype of PBMC and use it to verify simplified versions of a set of concurrent programs where program slicing in its traditional form fails to reduce the size of the program. The experiments show substantial verification time reductions compared to traditional BMC.

The paper is organized as follows. Sections 2 and 3 provide a motivating example and discusses the related work. In Sect. 4, we formalize and prove the correctness of projections. Section 5 describes the symbolic encoding of projections and Sect. 6 shows our evaluation results.

2   Motivating Example

We motivate our approach using a simple example. Consider the program shown in Fig. 1a consisting of three concurrent and sequential processes sharing different variables and an array B. We label the instructions on the different program locations l_1, l_2, l_3 and l_4. Assume that we are verifying a property which involves only the variable y. That is, we are interested in the values that y can take in any possible run of the program. There are 12 possible interleavings of the instructions. Assuming that initially $a = 0, b = 1, x = 0$ and $B[k] = 10 + k$ for every k-th position in the array, we list in Fig. 1 the possible runs which may be relevant. Every transition in the runs corresponds to a concrete execution of an instruction. For instance, t_5 and t_2 are two different transitions, but correspond to the same instruction l_4. When analyzing the program statically[1], one can only reason in terms of instructions. By doing that, it is clear that the program contains three *"dependencies"*: The execution of l_3 always *depends on* that of l_1 because l_1 always writes to variable a which l_3 reads from. For the same reason, the execution of l_4 depends on l_3. More interestingly, the execution of l_3 depends on l_2 only if $a = b$. This corresponds in Fig. 1 to the sequence σ_3, as transition

---

[1] Ignoring our assumption about the initial values of the variables.

H. Saissi et al.

t_3 writes in a position in B that t_7 reads from. We refer to σ_1, σ_2 and σ_3 as *projections* of the program on the set of variables $\{y\}$. Intuitively, in order to preserve all the possible values that y can take, it is enough to consider sequences where every transition t either writes to y, or there is another transition after it which also writes to y and transitively depends on t. For example in σ_3, transition t_3 is included because it influences t_7 which in turn influences t_8. Transition t_8 is kept in the projection since it writes to y. In general, projecting a run on a set of variables F means that we keep every transition that writes to variables in F or affects another transition after it already included in the projection.

$P_1\{$ $P_2\{$ $P_3\{$

     $l_1 : a = 1;$ $l_2 : B[b] = 5;$ $l_3 : x = B[a];$

        $\}$ $\}$ $l_4 : y = x + 7;$

                                                       $\}$

(a) An example concurrent program.

$t_1 : x = 10$	$t_3 : a = 1$	$t_3 : a = 1$
$t_2 : y = 17$	$t_4 : x = 11$	$t_6 : B[1] = 5$
	$t_5 : y = 18$	$t_7 : x = 5$
		$t_8 : y = 12$
σ_1	σ_2	σ_3

(b) 3 projections on y out of 12 possible runs.

Fig. 1. A motivating example

Given that the safety property of interest involves a subset of variables, the verification time of such programs can be greatly reduced if we constrain the exploration to projected executions. We use BMC to symbolically describe the behavior of the program and add constraints that characterize projections. By doing so, we constrain the search space of the model checker but still preserve all possible values that the variables in the property can take. If a state violating the property is reachable, a projection is returned. Furthermore, as projections contain only relevant instructions, they are easier to interpret and analyze.

Note that static program slicing techniques [30] applied to this program would not help in the reduction of the search space as it will return a copy of the whole program. This is due to the conditional dependencies of instructions accessing arrays and the concurrency, in which case it's not clear before execution whether an instruction affecting a variable of interest v will be actually executed before another instruction assigning a value to v. For instance, it's not clear whether l_1 will be executed before l_3. Besides, if the values of a and b depend on some nondeterministic behavior, e.g., concurrency or user input, it might not be possible to predict whether $a = b$. In this case, static program slicing conservatively over-approximate the slices.

3   Related Work

Program Slicing. PBMC is the first approach to combine dynamic slicing and BMC. Our approach e is based on a notion similar to program slicing [30]. Static program slicing has been used to reduce the size of programs under verification, e.g., [12,14,26] where a slice of the program is computed and passed to the model checker. However, the returned slice is an over-approximation of the instructions that are in fact relevant to the slicing criterion. This is due to the fact that inferring dependencies statically, a prerequisite for deriving slices, is hard with the presence of concurrency [21,26]. In PBMC, formulas describing precisely when dependencies occur are generated passed to a solver along with the verification formula. In dynamic slicing [5], the program is run with concrete input and the slicing is done directly on the execution path. Although the slices returned by dynamic slicing techniques are accurate, they only concern the considered execution path. To use dynamic slicing with verification, one would have to enumerate all paths which contradicts the purpose of using slicing for reducing the number of explored paths. The slicing in PBMC is dynamic since only reachable, and therefore feasible, paths are sliced.

Partial-Order Reduction. A common technique against state space explosion is partial-order reduction (POR) [17]. Whereas POR's reduction comes from executing commutative transitions in one representative order, in PBMC it is based on the notion of conflicting read/write operations. Existing POR semantics, however, do not subsume projections. Widely-known POR semantics such as stubborn sets [9,28], persistent sets [17], and ample sets [13] guarantee preserving all deadlocks of the program. In some cases [17], the preservation of deadlocks also entails that of local states. On the other hand, projections do not necessary preserve all deadlocks nor all local states. Existing POR techniques include [4,9,15,18,20,29] among others.

BMC. An interesting way of combining slicing with BMC is described in [16]. Tunneling and slicing based reduction makes use of slicing to decompose a BMC formula into disjoint smaller instances covering subsets of the program. These formulas are constructed such that the original formula is satisfiable only if at least one of the smaller instances can be satisfied. Nevertheless, the used slicing is static and therefore is imprecise.

Our approach for reduction is similar to MPOR [20], where constraints are added to the BMC formula to guide the search. The constraints used in this approach are based on Mazurkiewicz's traces [23], the underlying semantics for most POR theories. Our symbolic encoding of the transition system enhances the encoding used in MPOR. Furthermore, POR and projections are orthogonal techniques that can be used in combination for better reductions as demonstrated in [14]. This is the case because the definition of path projections alone still allows for two Mazurkiewicz equivalent paths to be considered in the search. We argue that our encoding can be augmented by the constraints of MPOR for better performance. To see this, consider two executions t_4, t_1, t_2, t_3 and t_2, t_1, t_4, t_3 such that t_3 depends on both t_1 and t_2. From both executions we can derive projections t_1, t_2, t_3 and t_2, t_1, t_3, respectively. Since there is no dependency between t_2

and t_1, both projected executions are Mazurkiewicz equivalent. It follows then that it is sufficient to consider one of the projections.

Encodings. We adapted the encoding used in [20] which does not require unwinding of loops as in [10,12] or [27]. Yet, unwinding loops may be beneficial and allow different encoding, e.g., using single static assignment form to reduce the number of variables in the formula. The idea behind projections is independent of the used encoding and therefore can be adapted for use with other BMC formulas. For instance in CBMC [6], transitions are associated with clock variables that reflect how they are (partially-)ordered. Intuitively, a path corresponds to a partial order over transitions where only dependent ones are strictly ordered. Thus, constraints are used to enforce a total order on the dependent transitions. Using such an encoding, the model checker might still explore some partial orders which are not relevant to the property. Hence, two dependent transitions will still have to be ordered although they might not have any influence on the property. Given a subset of variables, we argue that projection constraints can be added to such an encoding to further reduce the number of interleavings of dependent transitions. This can be done by constraining the used read-from relation according to the definition of projections.

Other Symbolic Approaches. Another possibility is to use slicing on-demand to refine the search for assertion violations. For instance, Path slicing [19] is a technique that has been implemented within the Blast model checker [7] which makes use of counterexample guided refinement techniques [11]. In Blast, slicing is used to simplify the counterexample analysis phase that serves the purpose of refining the search. Our approach is different from path slicing in the sense that the search for bugs is constrained from the beginning using projections to guide the solver toward feasible counterexamples. PBMC, and BMC based approaches in general, are fundamentally different from Blast, and other tools such as [22,24,25,29], where the verification formulas are generated and refined incrementally with the help of the solver. In BMC, a single formula describing the whole program is computed statically and the exploration work is deferred to the SMT solver. A comprehensive discussion of the advantages and disadvantages of incremental generation and refinement of the verification formula over BMC approaches is beyond the scope of this work.

4   Property Preservation with Projections

4.1   System Model

We abstract programs by general transition systems, where a transition may read and/or write a set of variables.

General Transition Systems. Formally, the system is defined as a tuple $TS = (S, S_0, T)$ where S, $S_0 \subseteq S$, and $T = \{t | t : S \rightharpoonup S\}$ are the set of states, initial states, and the set of *transitions*, respectively. In the rest of paper, we will always write s_0 to refer to an initial state.

A program defines a set of atomic instructions (e.g., lines of code). In every state a (possibly empty) set of transitions is eligible for execution. For example, transitions may correspond to instructions of different processes. If the set of transitions is non-empty, one of them is executed moving the program to a unique successor state. Formally, a transition $t \in T$ is a partial function such that $t(s) = s'$ iff t can be executed in s and it leads to state s'.[2] In that case, we say that t is enabled in s. For convenience, we also write $s \xrightarrow{t} s'$ if $t(s) = s'$.

A finite path σ in the transition system TS is a sequence $s_0 \xrightarrow{t_1} s_2 \xrightarrow{t_2} \ldots \xrightarrow{t_n} s_n$, also written as $s_0 \xrightarrow{t_1, t_2, \ldots, t_n} s_n$, such that $t_{i+1}(s_i) = s_{i+1}$ for all $0 \le i < n$. In that case, we write $\sigma \in TS$.

In addition, we assume that every state s assigns a value $s(v)$ to every $v \in V$, where V is the set of variables. Given a set $F \subseteq V$, we refer to the values assigned by s to variables $v \in F$ by $s(F)$. We write $s(F) = s'(F)$ for two states s and s', if for all $v \in F$, $s(v) = s'(v)$.

Dependency Relation. The execution of a transition involves reading from and writing to a subset of variables. We assign to every transition t a *read/write set* of variables [17,28], denoted as $r(t)/w(t) \subseteq V$ respectively. A transition t is said to read from (write to) a variable v if $v \in r(t)$ ($v \in w(t)$). The read set of a transition contains all variables that may have an influence on whether a transition is enabled and the outcome of its execution. On the other hand, the write set of a transition consist of the variables that it might modify.

Formally, $w(t)$ is defined such that for every $v \in V$, $v \in w(t)$ iff there are $s, s' \in S$ such that $s \xrightarrow{t} s'$ and $s(v) \ne s'(v)$. Note that the write set of a transition does not include a variable it never modifies. We define the read set $r(t)$ as the smallest set such that for every $s, s' \in S$, if $s(v) = s'(v)$ for every $v \in r(t)$, then

- t is enabled in s iff t is enabled in s', and
- if t is enabled in s, then for every $v' \in w(t)$, $t(s)(v') = t(s')(v')$.

We define a *dependency* relation $D \subseteq T \times T$ to model any interference between transitions. A transition t depends on a transition t' if t reads from a variable that t' writes to. In that case, we also say that t influences t' and write $(t, t') \in D$.

Definition 1 (Dependency Relation). *Given two transitions t and $t' \in T$, we say that t' depends on t and write $(t, t') \in D$ iff $r(t') \cap w(t) \ne \emptyset$.*

Note that two transitions only writing to the same variable are not considered to be dependent as the execution of one of them before the other does not influence the behavior of latter.

4.2   Projections

In this section, we propose the projection semantics and present a theorem that guarantees that preserving projections on a set of variables is a sufficient condition for preserving properties defined over those variables.

---

[2] For simplicity we focus on deterministic systems, although our results equally hold for non-deterministic programs.

First, we give a formal definition of path projections on a set of variables. Intuitively, a projection of a path σ on a set of variables F is a sequence of transitions containing every transition t that either writes into a variable in F, or there is a transition t' after it such that t' depends on t and t' is also in the projection.

Definition 2 (Projection). *Given a set of variables $F \subseteq V$ and a path $\sigma = s_0 \xrightarrow{t_1,\dots,t_n} s_n$, $\sigma|_F = t_{j_1}, t_{j_2}, \dots, t_{j_k}$ is said to be a projection of σ on F, if $1 \le j_1 < j_2 < \dots < j_k \le n$ and for all $1 \le i \le n$, $i \in \{j_1, j_2, \dots, j_k\}$ iff:*

(a) $w(t_i) \cap F \ne \emptyset$, or
(b) there exists $j \in \{j_2, j_3, \dots, j_k\}$ such that $i < j$ and $(t_i, t_j) \in D$.

Property Preservation. Our main result is that projections can be used to constraint the search space of a model checker. For that purpose we must guarantee that projections on a set of variables preserve the properties of those variables. Assume two transition systems TS, TS' and a set of variables $F \subseteq V$. If for every path $\sigma = s_0 \xrightarrow{t_1, t_2, \dots, t_n} s_n \in TS$, there exists a path $\sigma' = s_0 \xrightarrow{t'_1, t'_2, \dots, t'_m} s'_m \in TS'$ such that $s_n(F) = s'_m(F)$, we say that TS' *preserves the properties* of F in TS. Furthermore, we say that TS' *preserves the projections* of F in TS, if for every path $\sigma = s_0 \xrightarrow{t_1, t_2, \dots, t_n} s_n \in TS$, there exists a path $\sigma' = s_0 \xrightarrow{t'_1, t'_2, \dots, t'_m} s'_m \in TS'$ such that $\sigma|_F = t'_1, t'_2, \dots, t'_m$.

Theorem 1 (Property Preservation). *Let TS and TS' be two transition systems and $F \subseteq V$ a set of variables. If TS' preserves the projections of F in TS then it also preserves the properties of F in TS.*

We prove Theorem 1 via a series of lemmas. First, we introduce the following auxiliary definitions: Let t_i, t_j be two transitions, $\alpha = t_1 t_2 \dots t_n$ a sequence of transitions, and $\sigma = s_0 \xrightarrow{\alpha} s_n$ be the resulting path. For convenience, we will write $t_i \in \sigma$ and $t_i \in \alpha$ if $i \in \{1, 2, \dots, n\}$. Furthermore, if $j \in \{i+1, \dots, n\}$, we write $t_i <_\sigma t_j$ or $t_j >_\sigma t_i$.

First, we show that between two successive transitions in a projection $\sigma|_F$, the values assigned to variables in F and the ones read by any transition in $\sigma|_F$ after the second transition remain unmodified by all transitions outside the projection.

Lemma 1. *Let $\sigma = s_0 \xrightarrow{t_1, t_2, \dots, t_n} s_n$ be a path, $F \subseteq V$ a set of variables and t_k, $t_{k'}$ two transitions such that $t_k <_\sigma t_{k'}$ and for every $t_{k-1} <_\sigma t_i <_\sigma t_{k'+1}$ $t_i \notin \sigma|_F$. For every $t_{k-1} <_\sigma t_j <_\sigma t_{k'+1}$, $t_q >_\sigma t_{k'}$ such that $t_q \in \sigma|_F$ and $v \in r(t_q)$, $s_j(F) = s_{k-1}(F)$ and $s_j(v) = s_{k-1}(v)$.*

Proof. Let σ be a path, $\sigma|_F$ its projection on a variable set $F \subseteq V$, and two transitions t_k and $t_{k'}$ as described above. We know that for all $t_{k-1} <_\sigma t_j <_\sigma t_{k'+1}$, $w(t_j) \cap F = \emptyset$. Otherwise, t_j would be included in $\sigma|_F$ between t_k and $t_{k'}$ (Definition 2). This means that $s_{j-1}(F) = s_j(F) = s_{k-1}(F)$. Given a transition

$t_q \in \sigma|_F$ such that $t_q >_\sigma t_{k'}$, we assume that there is a variable $v \in r(t_q)$ such that for a $j \in \{k, \ldots, k'\}$, $s_j(v) \neq s_{k-1}(v)$. Let j be the first such an index. This implies that $s_{k-1}(v) = s_{j-1}(v) \neq s_j(v)$. We then have $v \in w(t_j)$ and therefore $r(t_q) \cap w(t_j) \neq \emptyset$. From Definition 1 it follows that $(t_j, t_q) \in D$. Consequently, t_j should also be included in $\sigma|_F$. This contradicts our initial assumption. □

With the help of Lemma 1 we show that every projection is also a path and that it reaches a state where the assigned values to variables in F are the same as in the original path.

Lemma 2. *Let* $\sigma = s_0 \xrightarrow{t_1,t_2,\ldots,t_n} s_n$ *be a path and* $\sigma|_F = t_{j_1}, t_{j_2}, \ldots, t_{j_k}$ *its projection on variable set* $F \subseteq V$. *Then there exists a path* $\sigma' = s_0 \xrightarrow{t_{j_1},t_{j_2}\ldots,t_{j_k}} s'_k$ *such that* $s_n(F) = s'_k(F)$.

Proof. We separately consider the case where $\sigma|_F$ is empty, i.e. contains no transition. In this case, we have for every $t_i \in \sigma$, $t_i \notin \sigma|_F$. From Lemma 1, it follows that $s_0(F) = s_n(F)$ and σ' exists as an empty path.

Now we assume that $\sigma|_F$ contains at least one transition. We start by proving, for every $1 \leq q \leq k$, the existence of the path that consists of the first q transitions of $\sigma|_F$, that $s'_q(F) = s_{j_q}(F)$ and that for every $v \in r(t_j)$ such that $t_j >_\sigma t_{j_q}$ and $t_j \in \sigma|_F$, $s'_q(v) = s_{j_q}(v)$. The proof is an induction on the number of the first q transitions in the projection. Consider the case of the first transition t_{j_1} in the projection. Since $\forall i \in \{1, \ldots, j_1 - 1\}$ $t_i \notin \sigma|_F$, we know that $s_0(F) = s_{j_1-1}(F)$, and that for every $v \in r(t_{j_1})$, $s_0(v) = s_{j_1-1}(v)$ (Lemma 1). Thus, since t_{j_1} is enabled in s_{j_1-1}, it is also enabled in s_0, and there is a state s'_1 such that $s_0 \xrightarrow{t_{j_1}} s'_1$ and $s'_1(v) = s_{j_1}(v)$ for every $v \in w(t_{j_1})$ (read set definition). Since for every $v \in F$ such that $s_0(v) \neq s'_1(v)$ is in $w(t)$ (write set definition), it follows that $s'_1(F) = s_{j_1-1}(F)$. We assume now that the property holds for the first q transitions and prove it after considering the $q+1$-th transition $t_{j_{q+1}}$. From Lemma 1 it follows then that $s_{j_q}(F) = s_{j_{q+1}-1}(F)$ and $s_{j_q}(v) = s_{j_{q+1}-1}(v)$ for every $v \in r(t_j)$ such that $t_j > t_{j_q}$ and $t_j \in \sigma|_F$. Using the induction assumption it follows then that $s'_q(F) = s_{j_{q+1}-1}(F)$ and $s'_q(v) = s_{j_{q+1}-1}(v)$. Consequently, t_{q+1} is enabled in s'_q and there exists a state s'_{q+1} such that $s'_q \xrightarrow{t_{q+1}} s'_{q+1}$, $s'_{q+1}(F) = s_{j_{q+1}}(F)$ and $\forall v \in w(t_{j_{q+1}})$, $s'_{q+1}(v) = s_{j_{q+1}}(v)$ (read/write set definitions). Let $v \in r(t_j)$ such that $s'_{q+1}(v) \neq s_{j_{q+1}}(v)$. This means that there is a variable $v' \in w(t_{j_{q+1}})$ such that $s'_{q+1}(v') \neq s_{j_{q+1}}(v')$ which is a contradiction.

Now that we have proved the property, we know that for $q = k$ we have $s'_k(F) = s_{j_k}(F)$ and that the path σ' exists. We know that for every $i \in \{j_k + 1, \ldots, n\}$ we have $t_i \notin \sigma|_F$ and $w(t_i) \cap F = \emptyset$ since otherwise t_i would be included in the projection (Definition 2). It implies then that $s_n(F) = s_{j_k}(F) = s'_k(F)$. □

Lemma 2 also implies that, given a transition system TS, a projection preserving transition system TS' always exists. This is true because from a path in TS one can always construct a valid projection path from it. Proving Theorem 1 is now straightforward.

Proof. Let $\sigma = s_0 \xrightarrow{t_1, t_2, \ldots, t_n} s_n$ be a path in TS and F a set of variables. The projection preservation implies that there exists a path $\sigma' = s_0 \xrightarrow{t'_1, t'_2 \ldots t'_m} s'_m$ in TS' such that $\sigma|_F = \sigma'$. From Lemma 2 follows that $s_n(F) = s'_m(F)$.   □

We have just proved that every reachable combination of values that the variables in F can take, is also reachable through a projection. In other words, Theorem 1 allows us to safely narrow down the search space of a model checker to projections, while still preserving all possible paths of a program.

5   PBMC: A Symbolic Implementation

In this section, we show how we implemented projections semantics for process-based concurrent programs in PBMC.

5.1   Process-Based Concurrent Programs

First, we informally describe how general concurrent programs can be expressed as a transition system. We assume a general shared memory model where a set of *processes* communicate via *shared variables*. In the corresponding transition system, a state consists of variables, and every transition is associated with a process. Processes are *sequential*. This means that two transitions that are enabled in a state must be from different processes. Hence, for every state s, a process has at most one enabled transition. Sequential processes can be modeled using an auxiliary variable for every process, called program counter. The program counter variable of a process can only be accessed by the process itself and designates the instruction that can be executed next.

5.2   Projection Encoding

Given a concurrent program, a property, and a fixed depth k, bounded model checking encodes a formula that an SMT/SAT solver can check for satisfiability. The property is true for some path iff the formula is satisfiable. More precisely, the formula is of the form $\Phi = \rho \wedge \Psi$ where ρ denotes the property formula and Ψ encodes a path of length k. The formula Φ is satisfiable iff there exists a path of at most k steps that satisfies ρ. To check whether the property ρ is valid for every possible path of a maximal length k, it suffices to replace it with its negation in Φ and prove the unsatisfiability of the resulting formula.

In the following, we explain how we encode Ψ to implement projections. The basic (unprojected) encoding adapts the structure used in [20]. Let F be the set of variables which appears in the property formula. To model the changes affecting the state of the program throughout the path we create for every $v \in V$ and $0 \leq i \leq k$ a variable v^i to represent the content of v in the i-th state of the path.

Core Formula. A path is only valid if it starts from an initial state. We add a constraint I to encode this fact.

$$I := \bigwedge_{v \in V} \left(v^0 = s_0(v) \right)$$

Let L be the set of all the instructions in the program. For every transition $t \in T$, we refer to the instruction it corresponds to, with $inst(t) \in L$. Given an instruction $l \in L$, let $trans(l)$ be the set of transitions that are mapped to it. In every step $0 \le i \le k - 1$, we model the possible selection of an instruction l using a formula denoted as T_l^i. If no instruction is selected for a step i, for instance because the length of the returned path is smaller than k, an additional constraint M makes sure that the variables remain unmodified for that step. To guide the solver to only consider projections on F, we add a constraint C_F. Setting C_F to *true* results in the solver considering every possible path. To encode all possible projections on set F, we obtain the following formula:

$$\Psi := I \wedge M \wedge C_F \wedge \bigwedge_{i=0}^{k-1} \bigwedge_{l \in L} T_l^i$$

Transition Encoding. For each instruction $l \in L$, we add an instruction constraint l^i that represents the changes that occur when l is executed at step i. We introduce variables sel^i that encode the instruction choice in every step: $sel^i = l$ iff instruction l was selected for execution in step i. Not that, due to process sequentiality, the selection of an instruction l implies the execution of a corresponding unique transition $t \in trans(l)$ given by the variables v^i. To describe the selection of instructions at different steps we make use of the sel^i variables and the instruction constraints:

$$T_l^i := sel^i = l \implies l^i$$

If an instruction l is selected for execution at step i, then l^i should hold, i.e., the variables should be updated accordingly. Otherwise, if no instruction is selected at step i, every variable in the system remains unchanged:

$$M := \bigwedge_{i=0}^{k-1} \left(\bigwedge_{l \in L} sel^i \ne l \implies \bigwedge_{v \in V} v^{i+1} = v^i \right)$$

If the depth value k is larger than the length of the path satisfying Ψ, some steps are filled with "dummy" instructions[3]. In this case, the solver will spend some time trying to figure out in which position to place the dummy instructions. We found it more efficient to force the solver to place those instructions at the beginning of the path such that there are no gaps, i.e., no dummy instruction is

---

[3] More precisely, the solver will assign a value to sel^i which does not correspond to any of the instructions.

chosen after a "non-dummy" instruction has been selected. We do this by adding a formula that further constrains the assignment of the sel^i variables. We omit the formula as it is an optimization not necessary for the correctness of Ψ.

Projection Encoding. We describe how the projection constraint C_F is generated for a set of variables F. The dependency relation D is encoded using variables d_{ij} which are true iff there is a transition t_1 which is executed at step i and a transition t_2 executed at j such that $(t_1, t_2) \in D$. Specifically, we have:

$$d_{ij} := \bigvee_{t_1 \in T} \left(sel^i = inst(t_1) \wedge \bigvee_{t_2 \in \{t | (t_1, t) \in D\}} sel^j = inst(t_2) \right)$$

C_F directly translates the definition of projections (Definition 2):

$$C_F := \bigwedge_{i=0}^{k-1} \left(\bigvee_{t \in \{t' | w(t') \cap F \neq \emptyset\}} sel^i = inst(t) \vee \bigvee_{j=i+1}^{k-1} d_{ij} \vee \bigwedge_{l \in L} sel^i \neq l \right)$$

Informally, for every selected transition t_i either it writes into a variable included in F or there is a transition t_j in the projection after it such that $(t_i, t_j) \in D$. The last clause allows dummy instructions to be selected without rendering the formula unsatisfiable.

Examples. We show how we encode instructions based on the examples of simple assignments and if statements in our process-based concurrent system model. To model process sequentiality, we define program counter variables $pc_p \in V$ for every process p.

Let l be an *assignment* $x := e$ at a process moving the program counter from loc_1 to loc_2, then $l^i :=$

$$pc_p^i = loc_1 \wedge pc_p^{i+1} = loc_2 \wedge x^{i+1} = e^i \wedge \bigwedge_{v \in V \setminus \{x, pc_p\}} v^{i+1} = v^i$$

Considering an *if statement* $if(c)$ that moves the program counter from loc_1 to location loc_2 if c evaluates to true and to loc_3 otherwise, we have $t^i :=$

$$pc_p^i = loc_1 \wedge \left((c \wedge pc_p^{i+1} = loc_2) \vee (\neg c \wedge pc_p^{i+1} = loc_3) \right) \wedge \bigwedge_{v \in V \setminus \{pc_p\}} v^{i+1} = v^i$$

Dependency Encoding. To illustrate how the dependency relation is encoded, we consider the motivating example in Sect. 2. Because of conflicting read/write accesses, we have three potential dependencies: l_3 depends on l_1, l_4 depends on l_3 and l_3 depends on l_2. The first two dependencies hold for any two transitions associated with the instructions. For instance, every transition corresponding to l_3 depends on every transition associated with l_1. On the other hand, the third dependency holds only if $a = b$. To encode d_{ij}, we must consider every possible dependency. First, there is a dependency if $sel^i = l_1$ and $sel^j = l_3$ or

$sel^i = l_3$ and $sel^j = l_4$. For the dependency between l_3 and l_2, we must include the condition $a = b$. Concretely, the following should hold: $sel^i = l_2$, $b^i = a^j$ and $sel^j = l_3$. In summary, to have a dependency between step i and j the following formula should hold:

$$d_{ij} := (sel^i = l_1 \wedge sel^j = l_3) \vee (sel^i = l_3 \wedge sel^j = l_4) \vee (sel^i = l_2 \wedge (b^i = a^j \wedge sel^j = l_3))$$

The size of a dependency formula depends on the number of potentially dependent instructions and not on the transitions.

Implementation. We implemented PBMC using the above encoding in the Python language. The prototype is based on the Z3 SMT solver and makes use of its Python API [3]. We developed a simplified language that provides basic programming constructs such as assignments, if statements and while loops. The tool supports arrays in addition to boolean and integer variables through the efficient implementation of their respective theories in Z3. Every program contains a header with declarations of variables, the number of processes in the program, an optional initial state assignment and a list of properties to be verified. The body of the program lists the instructions of every process separately in the style of the example shown in Fig. 1a.

We now explain the workflow of PBMC. First, the program is parsed and per instruction read/write summaries are created. For instructions accessing an integer or boolean variables the read/write sets are the same for every matching transition. In the case of instructions involving arrays, we also take note of the accessed index. The dependencies are then inferred based on the gathered summaries. For every two instructions l_1, l_2, we add a dependency for the corresponding transitions if l_1 writes to a variable v that l_2 reads from. If v is an array, we add the condition that the indexes are equal. Next, the tool translates the parsed program into a Z3 formula as previously shown. Subsequently, the found dependencies are used to construct the projection constraints which are added to the formula along with the negated property to be checked and the optional initial state formula. Then, the solver is called to check the satisfiability of the whole formula. Finally, the output of the solver is interpreted and a counter example path, if existing, is reconstructed. The returned path is a projection that leads to a state where the property is violated. The tool can be started with parameters to set up the length of paths to be considered and whether projection should be applied.

6 Experiments and Evaluation

In this section, we present preliminary experiments and evaluation of PBMC. We challenge our approach by choosing four benchmarks where static program slicing would return a mere copy of the program, and therefore be ineffective, to demonstrate the potential of using projections in program verification.

Next, we present the used benchmarks:

- **Litmus Tests (Litmus):** In our first benchmark, we generate random instructions accessing shared and local variables. The property we check in this example is whether variables assume certain values. For this case, we use 5 configurations ranging from 4 to 8 processes.

- **Indexer:** Our second benchmark is the indexer program taken from [15], where a shared hash table is accessed concurrently by different processes. Every process attempts to insert data into a location of the hash table. If it is already occupied, the process calculates a new hash value and retries again. This operation is repeated until an empty location is found. In the indexer program, dependencies between variable accesses result from writing to and reading from the same hash table location. The property we consider for this example is whether a hash value collisions can occur, which is known to be false for the configurations we consider in our setup [18]. We use two configurations with 2 and 4 processes.

- **File System (FSys):** This example was also adapted from [15]. In this benchmark, files are associated with inode data structures which point to memory locations where informations about files are stored. For every memory location there is a busy bit indicating whether it has been allocated to an inode. Each inode and busy bit is guarded by a distinct lock to avoid race conditions. When a process picks an inode and no memory was yet allocated for it, it tries to allocate a free memory location. Here dependencies are hard to detect statically because it is not clear in advance in which order inodes will be assigned by the processes. We check for buffer overflow errors in this benchmark and use one configuration which consist of 5 processes.

- **Dining Philosophers (DPhil):** We implemented the dining philosophers algorithm in our prototype language. The version we use is deadlock and livelock free. While every philosopher (process) maintains a local state, they share an array of chopsticks. To check for the availability of chopsticks, philosophers access the shared array. For simplicity, since collisions can only occur between neighboring processes, we ignore dependencies involving non-neighboring processes. A mutex is used to guarantee atomicity of operations on the shared array elements. The property we are interested in is whether two neighbor philosophers can be eating at the same time. To challenge our tool we inject a bug in the program and evaluate its capacity of finding counter example paths. The injected bug misuses the shared mutex and thus violates the mutual exclusion property. We set the unrolling depth large enough such that the counter example can be found. For this example we use seven different configurations ranging from 5 to 15 processes.

For every example we use two setups: BMC and PBMC. In general, we observed a trade-off between the complexity of the generated constraints and the amount of reduction achieved during the actual solving. In Fig. 2, we show the amount of time spent by PBMC and BMC to verify an unsatisfiable property for the litmus test example with 5 processes with different path depths. The fluctuations of the performance are explained by the fact that SMT solvers make extensive use of heuristics to explore the search space. For small path depth values, the overhead of creating the constraints and handling them by the SMT solver outperforms the reduction that is achieved by using PBMC. Only after

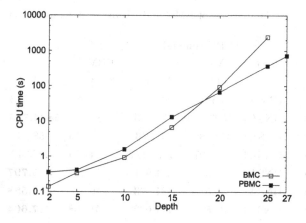

Fig. 2. Comparing the total verification time of BMC and PBMC with different path depths for Litmus 5 and an unsatisfiable property.

reaching a threshold path depth of 20, we observed a clear improvement over BMC. Since the creation of the constraints can be done separately, one can efficiently reduce that threshold by parallelizing the constraint generation process. Moreover, after reaching depth 27 BMC runs out of memory (after two hours) while PBMC finishes the verification within approximately 13 min.

In Table 1, we measure the improvement brought by our approach over BMC in terms of CPU time in different setups. In the name column, we append the number of processes to the name of the used benchmark. For every experiment we specify the unrolling depth used and whether the property was satisfiable. For satisfiable properties we write SAT and UNSAT otherwise. The solving time column shows the amount of time spent by the solver to return an answer excluding the initial analysis and formula building steps. On the other hand, total time includes all the steps. In the reduction column, we give the reduction percentage, in terms of total time, of PBMC in comparison with BMC. From comparing the total and solving times in the table, one can see that as the program complexity increases, the time required for the two initial steps in PBMC's workflow becomes insignificant. This means that for small configurations PBMC brings no improvement in the performance, as the total time is dominated by the time spent on analyzing the program and constructing the formula. On the other hand, PBMC clearly outperforms BMC for larger configurations due to substantial reductions in solving time which becomes more significant. In summary, the results in the table confirms the global trend that was shown in Fig. 2. The relatively small reduction in the dining philosopher example can be explained by the extensive use of the globally shared mutex. In that example, all the transitions depend on the ones manipulating the mutex. This results in a large number of dependencies involving all the variables, including those in the property. In general, the larger the setting is with fewer dependencies involving the variables in the property of interest, the better is the reduction of PBMC.

Table 1. Comparison of BMC and PBMC in different settings.

Configuration			CPU time (s)				Time red.
Name	Depth	Prop.	BMC		PBMC		
			Solv.	Total	Solv.	Total	
Indexer 2	10	UNSAT	19.531	20.116	5.088	**5.773**	71.30 %
Indexer 4	15	UNSAT	15979.298	15981.531	5881.442	**5884.755**	63.18 %
FSys 5	30	UNSAT	37.058	**47.376**	1.825	58.139	—
FSys 5	60	UNSAT	206.297	**227.427**	14.879	227.942	—
FSys 5	70	UNSAT	627.547	651.991	40.469	**325.797**	50 %
FSys 5	90	UNSAT	949.518	981.573	10.478	**467.558**	52.37 %
FSys 5	100	UNSAT	735.898	771.039	51.768	**617.664**	19.90 %
DPhil 5	10	SAT	5.921	**8.830**	7.671	12.665	—
DPhil 7	10	SAT	14.391	**19.162**	14.945	22.585	—
DPhil 10	10	SAT	51.229	59.460	39.607	**52.139**	12.31 %
DPhil 12	10	SAT	77.121	88.028	66.544	**82.618**	6.14 %
DPhil 15	10	SAT	219.824	235.581	182.689	**204.752**	13.08 %
Litmus 4	20	SAT	10.649	**11.348**	13.988	15.819	—
Litmus 5	20	SAT	605.336	**606.475**	654.573	657.102	—
Litmus 6	20	SAT	3888.401	3889.363	908.573	**911.550**	76.56
Litmus 7	20	SAT	2611.024	2612.562	349.708	**353.544**	86.46 %
Litmus 8	20	SAT	>2 h	>2 h	59.738	**64.031**	Infeasible w/o proj.

7   Conclusion

We have presented projections, an enhanced dynamic slicing notion that can be combined with BMC and proved its correctness. Also, we have implemented PBMC, a bounded model checker that incorporates projections using a novel BMC encoding. By augmenting the BMC formula with projections, PBMC restrains the search space of the model checker and significantly improves on the efficiency over traditional BMC. Our evaluation with examples of concurrent programs has shown major reductions in terms of verification time compared to traditional BMC encoding, even in cases where static slicing proves ineffective.

Acknowledgment. Research supported by TUD Cased & EC-SPRIDE.

References

1. ESBMC. http://www.esbmc.org/. Accessed 4 October 2015
2. LLBMC. http://llbmc.org/. Accessed 4 October 2015

3. Z3. http://z3.codeplex.com/. Accessed 4 October2015
4. Abdulla, P., Aronis, S., Jonsson, B., Sagonas, K.: Optimal dynamic partial order reduction. In: POPL, pp. 373–384. ACM Press (2014)
5. Agrawal, H., Horgan, J.R.: Dynamic program slicing. In: PLDI, pp. 246–256. ACM Press (1990)
6. Alglave, J., Kroening, D., Tautschnig, M.: Partial orders for efficient bounded model checking of concurrent software. In: Sharygina, N., Veith, H. (eds.) CAV 2013. LNCS, vol. 8044, pp. 141–157. Springer, Heidelberg (2013)
7. Beyer, D., Henzinger, T.A., Jhala, R., Majumdar, R.: The software model checker Blast. Int. J. Softw. Tools Technol. Transf. 9(5–6), 505–525 (2007)
8. Biere, A., Cimatti, A., Clarke, E., Zhu, Y.: Symbolic model checking without BDDs. In: Cleaveland, W.R. (ed.) TACAS 1999. LNCS, vol. 1579, pp. 193–207. Springer, Heidelberg (1999)
9. Bokor, P., Kinder, J., Serafini, M., Suri, N.: Supporting domain-specific state space reductions through local partial-order reduction. In: ASE, pp. 113–122. IEEE Press (2011)
10. Burckhardt, S., Alur, R., Martin, M.M.: Checkfence: checking consistency of concurrent data types on relaxed memory models. In: PLDI, pp. 12–21. ACM Press (2007)
11. Clarke, E., Grumberg, O., Jha, S., Lu, Y., Veith, H.: Counterexample-guided abstraction refinement. In: Emerson, E.A., Sistla, A.P. (eds.) CAV 2000. LNCS, vol. 1855, pp. 154–169. Springer, Heidelberg (2000)
12. Clarke, E., Kroning, D., Lerda, F.: A tool for checking ANSI-C programs. In: Jensen, K., Podelski, A. (eds.) TACAS 2004. LNCS, vol. 2988, pp. 168–176. Springer, Heidelberg (2004)
13. Clarke, E.M., Grumberg, O., Peled, D.: Model Checking. MIT Press, Cambridge (1999)
14. Dwyer, M.B., Hatcliff, J., Hoosier, M., Ranganath, V.P., Wallentine, T.: Evaluating the effectiveness of slicing for model reduction of concurrent object-oriented programs. In: Hermanns, H., Palsberg, J. (eds.) TACAS 2006. LNCS, vol. 3920, pp. 73–89. Springer, Heidelberg (2006)
15. Flanagan, C., Godefroid, P.: Dynamic partial-order reduction for model checking software. In: POPL, pp. 110–121. ACM Press (2005)
16. Ganai, M., Gupta, A.: Tunneling and slicing: towards scalable BMC. In: DAC, pp. 137–142. IEEE Press (2008)
17. Godefroid, P., van Leeuwen, J., Hartmanis, J., Goos, G., Wolper, P.: Partial-Order Methods for the Verification of Concurrent Systems. LNCS, vol. 1032. Springer, Heidelberg (1996)
18. Gueta, G., Flanagan, C., Yahav, E., Sagiv, M.: Cartesian partial-order reduction. In: Bošnački, D., Edelkamp, S. (eds.) SPIN 2007. LNCS, vol. 4595, pp. 95–112. Springer, Heidelberg (2007)
19. Jhala, R., Majumdar, R.: Path slicing. In: PLDI, pp. 38–47. ACM Press (2005)
20. Kahlon, V., Wang, C., Gupta, A.: Monotonic partial order reduction: an optimal symbolic partial order reduction technique. In: Bouajjani, A., Maler, O. (eds.) CAV 2009. LNCS, vol. 5643, pp. 398–413. Springer, Heidelberg (2009)
21. Krinke, J.: Advanced slicing of sequential and concurrent programs. In: International Conference on Software Maintenance, pp. 464–468. IEEE Press (2004)
22. Lal, A., Qadeer, S., Lahiri, S.K.: A solver for reachability modulo theories. In: Madhusudan, P., Seshia, S.A. (eds.) CAV 2012. LNCS, vol. 7358, pp. 427–443. Springer, Heidelberg (2012)

23. Mazurkiewicz, A.: Trace theory. In: Brauer, W., Reisig, W., Rozenberg, G. (eds.) Advances in Petri Nets 1986. LNCS, vol. 255, pp. 278–324. Springer, Heidelberg (1987)

24. McMillan, K.L.: Lazy abstraction with interpolants. In: Ball, T., Jones, R.B. (eds.) CAV 2006. LNCS, vol. 4144, pp. 123–136. Springer, Heidelberg (2006)

25. Păsăreanu, C.S., Visser, W., Bushnell, D., Geldenhuys, J., Mehlitz, P., Rungta, N.: Symbolic pathfinder: integrating symbolic execution with model checking for java bytecode analysis. Autom. Softw. Eng. **20**(3), 391–425 (2013)

26. Ranganath, V.P., Hatcliff, J.: Slicing concurrent java programs using Indus and Kaveri. Int. J. Softw. Tools Technol. Transfer **9**(5–6), 489–504 (2007)

27. Sinha, N., Wang, C.: On interference abstractions. In: POPL, pp. 423–434. ACM Press (2011)

28. Valmari, A.: The state explosion problem. In: Reisig, W., Rozenberg, G. (eds.) APN 1998. LNCS, vol. 1491, pp. 429–528. Springer, Heidelberg (1998)

29. Wachter, B., Kroening, D., Ouaknine, J.: Verifying multi-threaded software with Impact. In: FMCAD, pp. 210–217. IEEE Press (2013)

30. Weiser, M.: Program slicing. In: ICSE, pp. 439–449. IEEE Press (1981)

On the Complexity of Model-Checking Branching and Alternating-Time Temporal Logics in One-Counter Systems

Steen Vester[(✉)]

Technical University of Denmark, Kongens Lyngby, Denmark
stve@dtu.dk

Abstract. We study the complexity of the model-checking problem for the branching-time logic CTL* and the alternating-time temporal logics ATL/ATL* in one-counter processes and one-counter games respectively. The complexity is determined for all three logics when integer weights are input in unary (non-succinct) and binary (succinct) as well as when the input formula is fixed and is a parameter. Further, we show that deciding the winner in one-counter games with LTL objectives is 2EXPSPACE-complete for both succinct and non-succinct games. We show that all the problems considered stay in the same complexity classes when we add quantitative constraints that can compare the current value of the counter with a constant.

1 Introduction

The branching-time temporal logics CTL* [11] and CTL [8] and the linear-time temporal logic LTL [19] are some of the most widely applied logics for auto-mated verification. In particular, model-checking of these logics has been a very succesful approach [10]. The alternating-time temporal logics ATL and ATL* [1] extend these logics making it possible to reason about settings where several entities interact. The model-checking problem for alternating-time temporal log-ics subsumes the realizability problem for LTL [20,21] which is the problem of deciding whether there exists a program satisfying a given LTL specification no matter how the environment behaves. This is closely related to the synthesis problem which consists of generating a program meeting such a specification. The model-checking problems have been studied quite extensively for finite-state systems, but for infinite-state systems there are still many interesting open problems.

In this work we focus on the model-checking problem for some of the simplest infinite-state systems one can construct, namely finite-state systems combined with an unbounded counter that can hold a non-negative integer value. The complexity of model-checking such systems has been determined for LTL [9,12] and CTL [12,13] but not yet for CTL*, ATL and ATL* which is the main purpose of this paper. Another focus of this paper is to consider generalizations of the logics capable of expressing combined qualitative and quantitative properties of

© Springer International Publishing Switzerland 2015
B. Finkbeiner et al. (Eds.): ATVA 2015, LNCS 9364, pp. 361–377, 2015.
DOI: 10.1007/978-3-319-24953-7_27

systems. This is done by extending to subsets of the quantitative alternating-time temporal logics QATL and QATL* [7] making it possible to compare the counter value with constants. This extension lets us express many interesting properties of systems in a simple way. As an example, consider deciding the winner in an energy game [2] modelling systems in which a controller needs to keep an energy level positive. This can be done by model-checking the QATL formula $\langle\langle \texttt{Ctrl}\rangle\rangle \mathbf{G}(r > 0)$ where r is used to denote the current value of the counter.

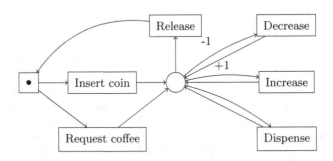

Fig. 1. Model of interaction between a vending machine controller and an environment.

Let us give another example of a QATL specification. Consider the game in Fig. 1 modelling the interaction between the controller of a vending machine and an environment. The environment controls the rectangular states and the controller controls the circular state. Initially, the environment can insert a coin or request coffee. Upon either input the controller can decrease or increase the balance, dispense coffee or release control to the environment again. Some examples of specifications in QATL* using this model are

- $\langle\langle\{\texttt{Ctrl}\}\rangle\rangle \mathbf{G}(\text{Request} \wedge (r < 3) \rightarrow \mathbf{XX}\text{Release})$: The controller can make sure that control is released immediately whenever coffee is requested and the balance is less than 3.
- $\langle\langle\{\texttt{Ctrl}\}\rangle\rangle \mathbf{G}(\text{Request} \wedge (r \geq 3) \rightarrow \mathbf{F}\text{Dispense})$: The controller can make sure that whenever coffee is requested and the balance is at least 3 then eventually a cup of coffee is dispensed.

It is indeed quite natural to model systems with a resource (e.g. battery level, time, money) using a counter where production and consumption correspond to increasing and decreasing the counter respectively. Extending to several counters would be meaningful, but as reachability games are already undecidable for games with two counters [6] the restriction to a single counter is very important.

1.1   Contribution

The contribution of this paper is to present algorithms and complexity results for model-checking of CTL*, ATL and ATL* in one-counter systems. The complexity is investigated both in terms of whether only edge weights in $\{-1, 0, +1\}$ can be used (non-succinct systems) or if we allow any integer weights encoded in binary (succinct systems). We also distinguish between data complexity and combined complexity. In data complexity, the formula is assumed to be fixed whereas in combined complexity both the formula and the game are parameters.

We characterize the complexity of all the model-checking problems that arise from these distinctions. For CTL* the results on data complexity follow directly from results in [12,13,22] even though this is not mentioned explicitly. We also show that the logics considered can be extended with quantitative constraints without a jump in complexity and that deciding the winner in a one-counter game with LTL objectives is 2ExpSpace-complete as for ATL* model-checking in one-counter games in all cases considered. This closes a gap between 2ExpTime-completeness in finite-state games with LTL objectives and 3ExpTime-completeness in pushdown games with LTL objectives [17]. The results are presented below together with related results from the literature (Tables 1 and 2).

Table 1. Complexity of model-checking. All results are completeness results.

	Non-succinct		Succinct	
	Data	Combined	Data	Combined
CTL	PSPACE [13,22]	PSPACE [13,22]	ExpSpace [12]	ExpSpace [12]
CTL*	PSPACE [13,22]	ExpSpace	ExpSpace [12]	ExpSpace
μ-calculus	PSPACE [14,15,22]	PSPACE [14,15,22]	ExpSpace [12]	ExpSpace [12]
ATL	PSPACE	PSPACE	ExpSpace	ExpSpace
ATL*	PSPACE	2ExpSpace	ExpSpace	2ExpSpace

Table 2. Complexity of deciding the winner in one-counter games with LTL objectives. All results are completeness results.

Non-succinct		Succinct	
Data	Combined	Data	Combined
PSPACE	2ExpSpace	ExpSpace	2ExpSpace

1.2 Outline

In Sect. 2 we introduce the setting of the paper. In Sect. 3 model-checking algorithms based on model-checking games are presented. In Sect. 4 we provide lower bounds matching the complexity of the algorithms from Sect. 4. Section 5 provides concluding remarks.

2 Preliminaries

In this section we introduce the models, logics and problems considered.

2.1 One-Counter Games

A *one-counter game* (OCG) is a particular kind of finitely representable infinite-state game. Such a game is represented by a finite game graph where each transition is labelled with an integer from the set $\{-1, 0, 1\}$ as well as a counter that can hold any non-negative value. When a transition labelled v is taken and the current counter value is c, the counter value changes to $c + v$. We require that transitions are only applicable when $c + v \geq 0$.

Definition 1. *A one-counter game is a tuple* $\mathcal{G} = (S, \Pi, (S_j)_{j \in \Pi}, R, \mathrm{AP}, L)$ *where S is a finite set of states, Π is a finite set of players, $\bigcup_{j \in \Pi} S_j$ partitions S, $R \subseteq S \times \{-1, 0, 1\} \times S$ is a transition relation, AP is a finite set of propositions and $L : S \to 2^{\mathrm{AP}}$ is a labelling function.*

An OCG is played by placing a token in an initial state s_0 and then moving the token between states for an infinite number of rounds. The transitions must respect the transition relation and the intuition is that player j controls the successor state when the token is placed on a state in S_j. At any point of the game, the current counter value is given by the sum of the initial value $v_0 \in \mathbb{N}$ and all edge weights encountered so far.

More formally, an element $c \in S \times \mathbb{N}$ is called a *configuration* of the game. For a sequence $\rho = c_0 c_1 ...$ of configurations we define $\rho_i = c_i$, $\rho_{\leq i} = c_0 ... c_i$ and $\rho_{\geq i} = c_i c_{i+1} ....$. A *play* is a maximal sequence $\rho = (s_0, v_0)(s_1, v_1)...$ of configurations such that for all $i \geq 0$ we have $(s_i, v_{i+1} - v_i, s_{i+1}) \in R$ and $v_i \geq 0$. A *history* is a proper prefix of a play. The set of plays and histories in an OCG $\mathcal{G}$ are denoted by $\mathrm{Play}_{\mathcal{G}}$ and $\mathrm{Hist}_{\mathcal{G}}$ respectively.

A *strategy* for player $j \in \Pi$ in $\mathcal{G}$ is a partial function $\sigma : \mathrm{Hist}_{\mathcal{G}} \to S \times \mathbb{N}$ defined for all histories $h = (s_0, v_0)...(s_\ell, v_\ell)$ s.t. $s_\ell \in S_j$ requiring that if $\sigma(h) = (s, v)$ then $(s_\ell, v - v_\ell, s) \in R$. A play (resp. history) $\rho = c_0 c_1 ...$ (resp. $\rho = c_0 ... c_\ell$) is compatible with a strategy σ_j for player $j \in \Pi$ if $\sigma_j(\rho_{\leq i}) = \rho_{i+1}$ for all $i \geq 0$ (resp. $0 \leq i < \ell$) such that $\rho_i \in S_j \times \mathbb{N}$. For a coalition $A \subseteq \Pi$ of players a collective strategy $\sigma = (\sigma_j)_{j \in A}$ is a tuple of strategies, one for each player in A. We denote by $\mathrm{Strat}_{\mathcal{G}}^A$ the set of collective strategies of coalition A. For an initial configuration c_0 and collective strategy $\sigma = (\sigma_j)_{j \in A}$ we denote by $\mathrm{Play}_{\mathcal{G}}(c_0, \sigma)$ the plays with initial configuration c_0 compatible with σ_j for every $j \in A$.

We extend one-counter games so arbitrary integer weights are allowed and such that transitions are still disabled if they would make the counter go negative. Such games are called *succinct one-counter games* (SOCGs). The special cases of OCGs and SOCGs where $|\Pi| = 1$ are called *one-counter processes* (OCPs) and *succinct one-counter processes* (SOCPs) respectively. In these cases we omit Π and $(S_j)_{j \in \Pi}$ from the definition.

By a *one-counter parity game* (OCPG) we mean a one-counter game with two players and a parity winning condition. It was shown in [22] that the winner can be determined in an OCPG in PSPACE by reducing to the emptiness problem for alternating two-way parity automata [24].

Proposition 1. *Determining the winner in OCPGs is in* PSPACE.

2.2 Temporal Logics

The logics considered are fragments of alternating-time temporal logic ATL* [1] interpreted in one-counter games. The formulas of ATL* are defined by

$$\Phi ::= p \mid \neg\Phi_1 \mid \Phi_1 \vee \Phi_2 \mid \mathbf{X}\Phi_1 \mid \Phi_1\mathbf{U}\Phi_2 \mid \langle\!\langle A \rangle\!\rangle\Phi_1$$

where $p \in$ AP, $A \subseteq \Pi$ and Φ_1, Φ_2 are ATL* formulas. We define the syntactic fragment ATL of ATL* by the grammar

$$\varphi ::= p \mid \neg\varphi_1 \mid \varphi_1 \vee \varphi_2 \mid \langle\!\langle A \rangle\!\rangle\mathbf{X}\varphi_1 \mid \langle\!\langle A \rangle\!\rangle\mathbf{G}\varphi_1 \mid \langle\!\langle A \rangle\!\rangle\varphi_1\mathbf{U}\varphi_2$$

where $p \in$ AP, $A \subseteq \Pi$ and φ_1, φ_2 are ATL formulas. The branching-time logics CTL [8] and CTL* [11] are the fragments of ATL and ATL* respectively such that $|\Pi| = 1$. In this case the universal and existential path quantifiers are defined by $\mathbf{A} = \langle\!\langle \emptyset \rangle\!\rangle$ and $\mathbf{E} = \langle\!\langle \{I\} \rangle\!\rangle$ where $\Pi = \{I\}$. LTL [19] is the fragment of CTL* with no path quantifiers. We interpret formulas of ATL* in OCGs. In ATL* we have state formulas and path formulas which are interpreted in configurations and plays of the OCG respectively. For definitions of state and path formulas, see [1]. The semantics of a formula is defined with respect to a given OCG $\mathcal{M} = (S, \Pi, (S_j)_{j\in\Pi}, R, \text{AP}, L)$. For all states $s \in S$, plays $\rho \in \text{Play}_{\mathcal{M}}$, $p \in$ AP, $i \in \mathbb{N}$, $A \subseteq \Pi$, ATL* state formulas Φ_1, Φ_2 and ATL* path formulas Ψ_1, Ψ_2 define

$$
\begin{aligned}
&\mathcal{M}, s, i \models p && \text{iff } p \in L(s) \\
&\mathcal{M}, s, i \models \neg\Phi_1 && \text{iff } \mathcal{M}, s, i \not\models \Phi_1 \\
&\mathcal{M}, s, i \models \Phi_1 \vee \Phi_2 && \text{iff } \mathcal{M}, s, i \models \Phi_1 \text{ or } \mathcal{M}, s, i \models \Phi_2 \\
&\mathcal{M}, s, i \models \langle\!\langle A \rangle\!\rangle\Psi_1 && \text{iff } \exists\sigma \in \text{Strat}_{\mathcal{M}}^{A}.\forall\pi \in \text{Play}_{\mathcal{M}}((s,i),\sigma).\mathcal{M},\pi \models \Psi_1 \\
&\mathcal{M}, \rho \models \Phi_1 && \text{iff } \mathcal{M}, \rho_0 \models \Phi_1 \\
&\mathcal{M}, \rho \models \neg\Psi_1 && \text{iff } \mathcal{M}, \rho \not\models \Psi_1 \\
&\mathcal{M}, \rho \models \Psi_1 \vee \Psi_2 && \text{iff } \mathcal{M}, \rho \models \Psi_1 \text{ or } \mathcal{M}, \rho \models \Psi_2 \\
&\mathcal{M}, \rho \models \mathbf{X}\Psi_1 && \text{iff } \mathcal{M}, \rho_{\geq 1} \models \Psi_1 \\
&\mathcal{M}, \rho \models \Psi_1\mathbf{U}\Psi_2 && \text{iff } \exists k \geq 0.\mathcal{M}, \rho_{\geq k} \models \Psi_2 \text{ and } \forall 0 \leq j < k.\mathcal{M}, \rho_{\geq j} \models \Psi_1
\end{aligned}
$$

The semantics is extended in the natural way to SOCGs. In LTL, CTL and CTL* the formulas are interpreted in OCPs and SOCPs as defined above.

As an extension, we consider fragments of the quantitative alternating-time temporal logics QATL and QATL* [7]. These logics extend ATL and ATL* with state formulas of the form $r \bowtie c$ where $c \in \mathbb{Z}$, $\bowtie \in \{\leq, <, =, >, \geq, \equiv_k\}$ and $k \in \mathbb{N}$. This type of formula is called a counter constraint and is interpreted such that e.g. $r \leq 5$ is true if the current counter value is at most 5 whereas $r \equiv_4 3$ is true if the current counter value is equivalent to 3 modulo 4. Formally, the semantics is given by $\mathcal{M}, s, i \models r \bowtie c$ iff $i \bowtie c$. The extension of $\mathcal{L} \in \{\text{LTL}, \text{CTL}, \text{CTL}^*\}$ with counter constraints is called $Q\mathcal{L}$ as for QATL*.

In this paper we focus on the model-checking problem. That is to decide, given an OCG/SOCG $\mathcal{M}$, a state s in $\mathcal{M}$, a natural number i and a state formula φ whether $\mathcal{M}, s, i \models \varphi$. When model-checking non-succinct models, the initial counter value, edge weights and integers in the formula are assumed to be input in unary. For succinct models they are input in binary.

3   Model-Checking Algorithms

When model-checking branching and alternating-time temporal logics in finite-state systems, the standard approach is to process the state subformulas from the innermost to the outermost, at each step labelling states where the subformula is true. This approach does not work directly in our setting since the state space is infinite. We therefore take a different route and develop a model-checking game in which we can avoid explicitly labelling the configurations in which a subformula is true. This approach gives us optimal complexity in all cases considered and also allows us to extend to quantitative constraints in a natural way. We first present the approach for ATL and afterwards adapt it to ATL* and CTL* by combining it with automata on infinite words. Finally it is shown how to handle counter constraints.

3.1   A Model-Checking Game for ATL

We convert the model-checking problem asking whether $\mathcal{M}, s_0, i \models \varphi$ for an ATL formula φ and OCG $\mathcal{M} = (S, \Pi, (S_j)_{j \in \Pi}, R, \mathrm{AP}, L)$ to a model-checking game $\mathcal{G}_{\mathcal{M}, s_0, i}(\varphi)$ between two players Verifier and Falsifier that are trying to respectively verify and falsify the formula. The construction is done so Verifier has a winning strategy in $\mathcal{G}_{\mathcal{M}, s_0, i}(\varphi)$ if and only if $\mathcal{M}, s_0, i \models \varphi$ and is done inductively on the structure of φ. For a given ATL formula, a given OCG $\mathcal{M}$ and a given state s in $\mathcal{M}$ we define a characteristic OCG $\mathcal{G}_{\mathcal{M}, s}(\varphi)$. Note that the initial counter value is not present in the construction yet. When illustrating the games, the circle states are controlled by Verifier, square states are controlled by Falsifier and diamond states can be both depending on the game. States with color 1 are filled and states with color 0 are not. Verifier wins the game if the least color that appears infinitely often during the play is even, otherwise Falsifier wins the game. The edges are labelled with counter updates, but 0-labels are omitted. The construction is done as follows.

- $\mathcal{G}_{\mathcal{M}, s}(p)$: There are two cases which are illustrated in Fig. 2 to the left.
- $\mathcal{G}_{\mathcal{M}, s}(\varphi_1 \vee \varphi_2)$: The game is shown in Fig. 2 in the middle.
- $\mathcal{G}_{\mathcal{M}, s}(\neg \varphi_1)$: The game is constructed from $\mathcal{G}_{\mathcal{M}, s}(\varphi_1)$ by interchanging circle states and square states and either adding or subtracting 1 to/from all colors.
- $\mathcal{G}_{\mathcal{M}, s}(\langle\!\langle A \rangle\!\rangle \mathbf{X} \varphi_1)$: Let $R(s) = \{(s, v, s') \in R\} = \{(s, v_1, s_1), ..., (s, v_m, s_m)\}$. There are two cases to consider. One when $s \in S_j$ for some $j \in A$ and one when $s \notin S_j$ for all $j \in A$. Both are illustrated in Fig. 2 to the right.

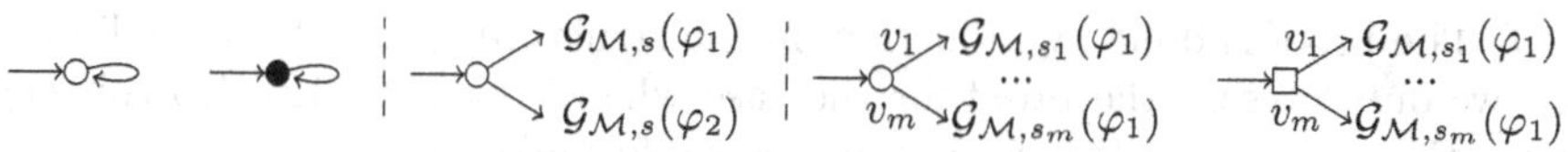

Fig. 2. $\mathcal{G}_{M,s}(p)$ to the left for $p \in L(s)$ and $p \notin L(s)$. $\mathcal{G}_{M,s}(\varphi_1 \vee \varphi_2)$ is in the middle. $\mathcal{G}_{M,s}(\langle\!\langle A \rangle\!\rangle \mathbf{X} \varphi_1)$ to the right in the cases where $s \in \bigcup_{j \in A} S_j$ and where $s \notin \bigcup_{j \in A} S_j$.

- $\mathcal{G}_{M,s}(\langle\!\langle A \rangle\!\rangle \mathbf{G} \varphi_1)$: We let $\mathcal{G}_{M,s}(\langle\!\langle A \rangle\!\rangle \mathbf{G} \varphi_1)$ have the same structure as M, but with a few differences. Verifier controls all states that are in $\bigcup_{j \in A} S_j$ and Falsifier controls the rest. Further, for each transition $t = (s', v, s'') \in R$ we add a state s_t controlled by Falsifier between s' and s''. If the player controlling s' chooses transition t the play is taken to the state s_t from which Falsifier can either choose to continue to s'' or to $\mathcal{G}_{M,s''}(\varphi_1)$. Every state in $\mathcal{G}_{M,s}(\langle\!\langle A \rangle\!\rangle \mathbf{G} \varphi_1)$ which is not part of $\mathcal{G}_{M,s''}(\varphi_1)$ has color 0. It is illustrated in Fig. 3. The intuition is that Falsifier can challenge and claim that φ_1 is not true in the current configuration. If he does so, Verifier must be able show that it is in fact true in order to win. In addition, such a module is added before the initial state s so Falsifier can challenge the truth of φ_1 already in the initial state.

- $\mathcal{G}_{M,s}(\langle\!\langle A \rangle\!\rangle \varphi_1 \mathbf{U} \varphi_2)$: The game is similar to the case of $\langle\!\langle A \rangle\!\rangle \mathbf{G}$. The differences are that every state is colored 1 and for each transition $t = (s', v, s'') \in R$ we add two states s_t and s'_t controlled by Verifier and Falsifier respectively with transitions to $\mathcal{G}_{M,s''}(\varphi_2)$ and $\mathcal{G}_{M,s''}(\varphi_1)$ respectively. It is illustrated in Fig. 3. The intuition is similar, but here Verifier loses unless he can claim φ_2 is true at some point (and subsequently show this). In addition φ_1 cannot become false before this point, because then Falsifier can claim φ_1 is false and win. As for the previous case, such a module is added before the initial state as well.

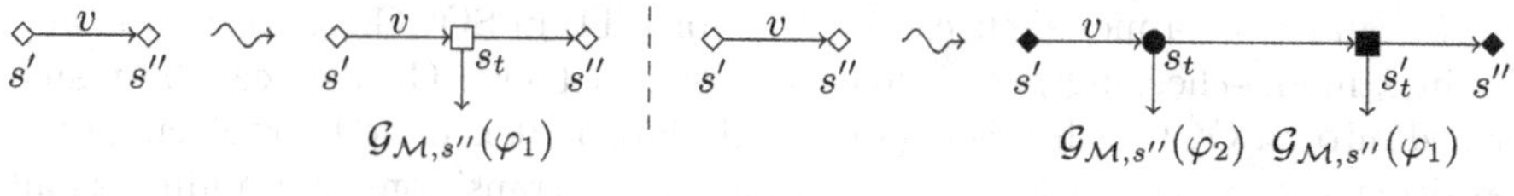

Fig. 3. $\mathcal{G}_{M,s}(\langle\!\langle A \rangle\!\rangle \mathbf{G} \varphi_1)$ and $\mathcal{G}_{M,s}(\langle\!\langle A \rangle\!\rangle \varphi_1 \mathbf{U} \varphi_2)$ are obtained by updating each transition in M as shown to the left and right respectively.

Finally, we define the game $\mathcal{G}_{M,s,i}(\varphi)$ from $\mathcal{G}_{M,s}(\varphi)$ and $i \in \mathbb{N}$ by adding an initial module such that the counter is increased to i before entering $\mathcal{G}_{M,s}(\varphi)$. We can now show the following by induction on the structure of the ATL formula.

Proposition 2. *For every OCG M, state s in M, $i \in \mathbb{N}$ and $\varphi \in ATL$*

$$M, s, i \models \varphi \text{ if and only if Verifier has a winning strategy in } \mathcal{G}_{M,s,i}(\varphi)$$

Proof. The proof is done by induction on the structure φ. Due to space limitations we only present the proof for the case where $\varphi = \langle\!\langle A \rangle\!\rangle \mathbf{G} \varphi_1$. To this end assume that the proposition is true for the subformula φ_1.

The intuition of the construction is that Verifier controls the players in A and Falsifier controls the players in $\Pi \setminus A$. At each configuration $(s', v) \in S \times \mathbb{N}$ of the game Falsifier can challenge the truth value of φ_1 by going to $\mathcal{G}_{\mathcal{M}, s', v}(\varphi_1)$ in which Falsifier has a winning strategy if and only if φ_1 is indeed false in $\mathcal{M}, s', v$ by the induction hypothesis. If Falsifier challenges at the wrong time or never challenges then Verifier can make sure to win.

More precisely, suppose Verifier has a winning strategy σ in $\mathcal{G}_{\mathcal{M}, s, i}(\langle\!\langle A \rangle\!\rangle \mathbf{G} \varphi_1)$ then every possible play when Verifier plays according to σ either never goes into one of the modules $\mathcal{G}_{\mathcal{M}, s'}(\varphi_1)$ or the play goes into one of the modules at some point and never returns. Since σ is a winning strategy for Verifier, we have by the induction hypothesis that every pair $(s', v) \in S \times \mathbb{N}$ reachable when Verifier plays according to σ is such that $\mathcal{M}, s', v \models \varphi_1$, because otherwise σ would not be a winning strategy for Verifier. If coalition A follows the same strategy σ adapted to $\mathcal{M}$ then the same state, value pairs are reachable. Since for all these reachable pairs (s', v) we have $\mathcal{M}, s', v \models \varphi_1$ this strategy is a witness that $\mathcal{M}, s, i \models \langle\!\langle A \rangle\!\rangle \mathbf{G} \varphi_1$.

On the other hand, suppose that coalition A can ensure $\mathbf{G} \varphi_1$ from (s, i) using strategy σ. Then in every reachable configuration (s', v) we have $\mathcal{M}, s', v \models \varphi_1$. From this we can generate a winning strategy for Verifier in $\mathcal{G}_{\mathcal{M}, s, i}(\langle\!\langle A \rangle\!\rangle \mathbf{G} \varphi_1)$ that plays in the same way until (if ever) Falsifier challenges and takes a transition to a module $\mathcal{G}_{\mathcal{M}, s', v}(\varphi_1)$ for some (s', v). Since the same configurations can be reached before a challenge as when A plays according to σ, this means that Verifier can make sure to win in $\mathcal{G}_{\mathcal{M}, s', v}(\varphi_1)$ by the induction hypothesis. Thus, if Falsifier challenges Verifier can make sure to win and if Falsifier never challenges Verifier also wins since all states reached have color 0. Thus, Verifier has a winning strategy in $\mathcal{G}_{\mathcal{M}, s, i}(\langle\!\langle A \rangle\!\rangle \mathbf{G} \varphi_1)$. □

We can create a model-checking game for ATL in SOCGs as for OCGs and obtain a model-checking game which is a succinct OCPG. This can be transformed into an OCPG that is exponentially larger. It is done by replacing each transition with weight v with a path that has $|v|$ transitions and adding small gadgets so a player loses if he takes a transition with value $-w$ for $w \in \mathbb{N}$ when the current counter value $r < w$. The exponential blowup is due to weights being input in binary. By Proposition 1 this gives upper bounds for ATL model-checking. Matching lower bounds follow from PSPACE-hardness [13] and EXPSPACE-hardness [12] of data complexity of CTL in OCPs and SOCPs respectively.

Theorem 1. *The data complexity and combined complexity of model-checking ATL are* PSPACE-*complete for OCGs and* EXPSPACE-*complete for SOCGs.*

3.2 Adapting the Construction to ATL*

As for ATL we rely on the approach of a model-checking game when model-checking ATL*. However, due to the extended possibilities of nesting we do not handle temporal operators directly as for ATL. Instead, we resort to translation of LTL formulas into deterministic parity automata (DPA) which are combined with the model-checking games. This gives us model-checking games which are one-counter parity games as for ATL, but with a doubly-exponential blowup.

Let $\mathcal{M} = (S, \Pi, (S_j)_{j \in \Pi}, R, AP, L)$ be an OCG, $s_0 \in S$, $i \in \mathbb{N}$ and φ be an ATL* state formula. The algorithm to decide whether $\mathcal{M}, s_0, i \models \varphi$ follows along the same lines as our algorithm for ATL. That is, we construct a model-checking game $\mathcal{G}_{\mathcal{M}, s_0, i}(\varphi)$ between Verifier and Falsifier such that Verifier has a winning strategy in $\mathcal{G}_{\mathcal{M}, s_0, i}(\varphi)$ if and only if $\mathcal{M}, s_0, i \models \varphi$. The construction is done inductively on the structure of φ. For each state $s \in S$ and state formula φ we define a characteristic OCG $\mathcal{G}_{\mathcal{M}, s}(\varphi)$.

For formulas of the form $p, \neg\varphi_1$ and $\varphi_1 \vee \varphi_2$ the construction is as for ATL assuming in the inductive cases that $\mathcal{G}_{\mathcal{M}, s}(\varphi_1)$ and $\mathcal{G}_{\mathcal{M}, s}(\varphi_2)$ have already been defined. The interesting case is $\varphi = \langle\!\langle A \rangle\!\rangle \varphi_1$. Here, let $\psi_1, ..., \psi_m$ be the outermost proper state subformulas of φ_1. Let $P = \{p_1, ..., p_m\}$ be fresh propositions and let $f(\varphi_1) = \varphi_1[\psi_1 \mapsto p_1, ..., \psi_m \mapsto p_m]$ be the formula obtained from φ_1 by replacing the outermost proper state subformulas with the corresponding fresh propositions. Let $AP' = AP \cup P$. Now, $f(\varphi_1)$ is an LTL formula over AP'. We can therefore construct a DPA $\mathcal{A}_{f(\varphi_1)}$ with input alphabet $2^{AP'}$ such that the language $L(\mathcal{A}_{f(\varphi_1)})$ of the automaton is exactly the set of linear models of $f(\varphi_1)$. The number of states of the DPA can be bounded by $2^{2^{O(|f(\varphi_1)|)}}$ and the number of colors of the DPA can be bounded by $2^{O(|f(\varphi_1)|)}$ [18].

The game $\mathcal{G}_{\mathcal{M}, s}(\varphi)$ is now constructed with the same structure as $\mathcal{M}$, where Verifier controls the states for players in A and Falsifier controls the states for players in $\Pi \setminus A$. However, we need to deal with truth values of the formulas $\psi_1, ..., \psi_m$ which can in general not be labelled to states in $\mathcal{M}$ since they depend both on the current state and counter value. Therefore we change the structure to obtain $\mathcal{G}_{\mathcal{M}, s}(\varphi)$: For each transition $(s, v, t) \in R$ we embed a module as shown in Fig. 4. Here, $2^{AP'} = \{\Phi_0, ..., \Phi_\ell\}$ and for each $0 \leq j \leq \ell$ we let $\{\psi_{j0}, ..., \psi_{jk_j}\} = \{\psi_i \mid p_i \in \Phi_j\} \cup \{\neg\psi_i \mid p_i \notin \Phi_j\}$. Such a module is added before the initial state as well.

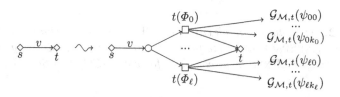

Fig. 4. $\mathcal{G}_{\mathcal{M}, s}(\langle\!\langle A \rangle\!\rangle \varphi)$ is obtained by updating each transition as shown in the figure.

The idea is that when a transition is taken from (s, w) to $(t, w + v)$, Verifier must specify which of the propositions $p_1, ..., p_m$ are true in $(t, w + v)$, this is done by picking one of the subsets Φ_j (which is the set of propositions that are true in state $t(\Phi_j)$). Then, to make sure that Verifier does not cheat, Falsifier has the opportunity to challenge any of the truth values of the propositions specified by Verifier. If Falsifier challenges, the play never returns again. Thus, if Falsifier challenges incorrectly, Verifier can make sure to win the game. However, if Falsifier challenges correctly then Falsifier can be sure to win the game. If Verifier has a winning strategy, then it consists in choosing the correct values of the propositions at each step. If Verifier does choose correctly and Falsifier never challenges, the winner of the game should be determined based on whether the LTL property specified by $f(\varphi_1)$ is satisfied during the play. We handle this by labelling $t(\Phi_j)$ with the propositions in Φ_j. Further, since every step of the game is divided into three steps (the original step, the specification by Verifier and the challenge opportunity for Falsifier) we alter $\mathcal{A}_{f(\varphi_1)}$ such that it only takes a transition every third step. This simply increases its size by a factor 3. We then perform a product of the game with the updated parity automaton to obtain the parity game $\mathcal{G}_{\mathcal{M},s}(\langle\!\langle A \rangle\!\rangle \varphi_1)$. It is important to note that the product with the automaton is not performed on the challenge modules (which are already colored), but only with states in the main module. This keeps the size of the game doubly-exponential in the size of the formula. It is possible to prove the following by induction on the structure of the formula. All cases except for $\langle\!\langle A \rangle\!\rangle \varphi$ are as for ATL. In the last case the proof follows the intuition outlined above.

Proposition 3. *For every OCG $\mathcal{M}$, state s in $\mathcal{M}$, $i \in \mathbb{N}$ and $\varphi \in$ ATLs*

$$\mathcal{M}, s, i \models \varphi \text{ if and only if Verifier has a winning strategy in } \mathcal{G}_{\mathcal{M},s,i}(\varphi)$$

The size of the model-checking game is doubly-exponential in the size of the formula for both OCGs and SOCGs. Indeed, we extend the technique to SOCGs as in the case of ATL. However, with respect to complexity, the blowup caused by the binary representation of edge weights only matters when the formula is fixed since the game is already doubly-exponential when the input formula is a parameter. Using Proposition 1 we get upper bounds on complexity of model-checking ATL*. For data complexity the lower bounds follow from data complexity of CTL. 2ExpSpace-hardness for combined complexity is proved in Sect. 4.

Theorem 2. *The data complexity for ATL* model-checking is PSpace-complete and ExpSpace-complete for OCGs and SOCGs respectively. The combined complexity is 2ExpSpace-complete for both OCGs and SOCGs.*

3.3 Adapting the Construction to CTL*

While the model-checking game for ATL* works immediately for CTL*, the doubly-exponential size can improved. The reason is that when the model is not alternating, we can use non-deterministic Büchi automata (NBAs) for path subformulas instead of DPAs. To handle a formula of the form $\varphi = \mathbf{E}\varphi_1$ we do as for $\langle\!\langle A \rangle\!\rangle \varphi_1$ in the previous section except that the automaton $\mathcal{A}_{f(\varphi)}$ is now an NBA with $2^{O(|f(\varphi)|)}$ states [25]. Further, we need to handle the fact that the automaton is non-deterministic and therefore can have several legal transitions.

The game is simply adjusted by letting Verifier choose the transitions in the original system as well as of the automaton in each step of the main module in $\mathcal{G}_{\mathcal{M},s}(\varphi)$. This works as he just needs to show that there exists a path in the OCP along with an accepting run of the automaton in order to be sure to win. If one such exists he can show it by playing this path as well as playing the corresponding run of the automaton. The only power that Falsifier has in the main module is the possibility to challenge the values for subformulas proposed by Verifier. Thus, if Verifier proposes an incorrect valuation or plays a path that is not accepting then Falsifier can make sure to win.

Note that this construction makes the model-checking game exponential in the size of the formula. Again, Proposition 1 provides us with upper bounds. A matching EXPSPACE lower bounds for combined complexity of model-checking CTL* in OCPs is shown in Sect. 4.

Theorem 3. *The combined complexity of model-checking* CTL* *is* EXPSPACE-*complete for both OCPs and SOCPs.*

The PSPACE-completeness and EXPSPACE-completeness of data complexity of CTL* model-checking in OCPs and SOCPs follow immediately from results in the literature. Indeed, lower bounds are inherited from CTL model-checking results [12,13] and upper bounds can be derived from μ-calculus results [22] as for every CTL* formula there is an equivalent μ-calculus formula. However, note that in these cases our construction above provides the matching upper bounds as well without resorting to a translation from CTL* formulas to μ-calculus formulas.

3.4   Adding Counter Constraints

The model-checking game can be extended to handle counter constraints by creating characteristic games $\mathcal{G}_{\mathcal{M},s}(r \bowtie c)$ for atomic formulas of the form $r \bowtie c$ with $\bowtie \in \{\leq, <, =, >, \geq, \equiv_k\}$ where $k \in \mathbb{N}$ and $c \in \mathbb{Z}$. As examples, see $\mathcal{G}_{\mathcal{M},s}(r \leq c)$ and $\mathcal{G}_{\mathcal{M},s}(r \equiv_k c)$ illustrated in Fig. 5. Using similar constructions we can handle the other cases as well. Note that adding these constraints to the logics does not increase the complexity of the algorithms in any of the cases considered.

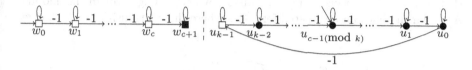

Fig. 5. $\mathcal{G}_{\mathcal{M},s}(r \leq c)$ to the left and $\mathcal{G}_{\mathcal{M},s}(r \equiv_k c)$ to the right.

Having added counter constraints it is quite easy to see that model-checking of CTL* in one-counter processes with zero-tests can be done without increasing the complexity. This can be accomplished by updating the CTL* formula to only consider paths that are legal according to the zero-tests. By reusing a technique from [3] we can also handle systems where the counter value is allowed to be negative. Similar constructions can be made for ATL and ATL* model-checking by using alternation between players to check that no player can choose a transition that he is not allowed to choose without losing.

4   Lower Bounds

For the combined complexity of CTL* in OCPs an ExpSpace lower bound does not follow immediately since the combined complexity of CTL is PSpace-complete in OCPs. To show this lower bound we do a reduction from the data complexity of CTL in SOCPs which requires a bit more work.

Proposition 4. *The combined complexity of model-checking* CTLs *in OCPs is* ExpSpace-*hard.*

Proof. We do the proof by a reduction from the model-checking problem for a fixed CTL formula in an SOCP. That is, given a CTL formula φ, an SOCP $\mathcal{M} = (S, R, \mathrm{AP}, L)$, an initial state s_0 and value $v \in \mathbb{N}$ we want to construct a CTL* formula φ' and an OCP $\mathcal{M}' = (S', R', \mathrm{AP}', L')$ such that

$$\mathcal{M}, s_0, 0 \models \varphi \text{ if and only if } \mathcal{M}', s_0, 0 \models \varphi'$$

The challenge of the construction is that $\mathcal{M}'$ can only have transitions with weights in $\{-1, 0, 1\}$. In order to accomplish this without blowing up the state space exponentially we add a module for each transition $(s, v, s') \in R$ designed to simulate adding v to the counter value. We explain the construction for $v \geq 0$ first. Let $c \in \mathbb{N}$ be the smallest number such that $2^c > w$ for every integer w that is the label of a transition in $\mathcal{M}$. Then every edge weight can be represented using c bits. Now, to obtain $\mathcal{M}'$ we do as follows. For every transition $t = (s, v, s') \in R$ with $v \geq 0$ we replace t with a module $\mathcal{M}'_t$ as shown in Fig. 6.

   In this module it is possible to increase the counter by any non-negative value before completing the transition from s to s'. It is even possible to stay in the module between s and s' forever (unlike in $\mathcal{M}$). Note also that v does not appear in the module at all. We will use the CTL* formula to focus on paths that behave as the transition (s, v, s') in $\mathcal{M}$ when passing through this module. A similar module can be created for $v < 0$ where the +1 transitions are changed

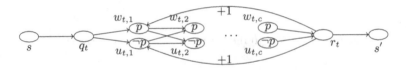

Fig. 6. Module $\mathcal{M}'_t$ for transition $t = (s, v, s')$ with $v \geq 0$.

to -1 transitions. We suppose that all new states in $\mathcal{M}'$ are labelled with the proposition up and all states from $\mathcal{M}$ are not. Further, for each state s in $\mathcal{M}'$ there is a special proposition s which is true exactly in that state.

Observe that the resulting structure $\mathcal{M}'$ is an OCP since there are only transition weights in $\{-1, 0, 1\}$ and further, the reduction is polynomial in the number of bits used to represent the integer weights in $\mathcal{M}$. We next propose a function f mapping CTL formulas to CTL* formulas such that $\mathcal{M}, s_0, 0 \models \varphi$ if and only if $\mathcal{M}', s_0, 0 \models f(\varphi)$ for every CTL formula φ. First, let

$$\psi_{count} = \bigwedge_{t=(s,v,s') \in R} \mathbf{G}(\psi_1(t) \wedge \psi_2(t) \wedge \psi_3(t) \wedge \psi_4(t))$$

The intuition is that the path formula ψ_{count} is true along a path in $\mathcal{M}'$ if every subpath through a module $\mathcal{M}'_t$ with $t = (s, v, s')$ updates the counter by adding exactly v before reaching s'. Thus, the formula is true along a path ρ' in $\mathcal{M}'$ if and only if ρ' corresponds to a path in $\mathcal{M}$ (where each counter update of value v takes $(|v| + 1) \cdot (c + 1) + 2$ steps in ρ'). The reason that we need to enforce counter updates in this way is to not blow up the size of the OCP $\mathcal{M}'$. This is important since edge weights are exponentially large in the input in $\mathcal{M}$.

The truth value of proposition p is used as the bit-representation of the value that the counter has already been updated with where the least significant bit occurs first. The intuitive meaning of the subformulas are as follows for each transition $t = (s, a, s')$.

- $\psi_1(t)$: When the module $\mathcal{M}'_t$ is entered, the path goes through only $\neg p$ states until r_t since the counter has initially been updated with 0.
- $\psi_2(t)$: The counter value must be updated by one every time r_t is reached except the last time before the module is left.
- $\psi_3(t)$: The path must exit the module before the counter has been updated 2^c times.
- $\psi_4(t)$: If the path exits the module, the counter must have been updated exactly $|v|$ times.

The subformulas are defined in LTL as below, where $\mathbf{X}^j$ is defined inductively by $\mathbf{X}^1 = \mathbf{X}$ and $\mathbf{X}^j = \mathbf{X}^{j-1}\mathbf{X}$ for $j > 1$.

$$\psi_1(t) = q_t \rightarrow \left(\bigwedge_{i=1}^{c} \mathbf{X}^i \neg p \right)$$

$$\psi_2(t) = \left[(q_t \vee r_t) \rightarrow \bigwedge_{i=1}^{c} \left(\bigwedge_{j=1}^{i-1} \mathbf{X}^j p \leftrightarrow (\mathbf{X}^{i+c+1} p \leftrightarrow \mathbf{X}^i \neg p) \right) \right] \mathbf{U}$$
$$\mathbf{X}(\neg r_t \mathbf{U}(r_t \wedge \mathbf{X} s'))$$

$$\psi_3(t) = r_t \rightarrow \left(\bigvee_{i=1}^{c} \mathbf{X}^i p \right) \mathbf{U} \mathbf{X} s'$$

Finally, for each transition $t = (s, v, s')$ let $v' = |v|$ and let $b_1, ..., b_c$ be the c-bit representation of v' where b_1 is the least significant bit. Let B_t be the set of indices j such that $b_j = 1$ and C_t be the set of indices j such that $b_j = 0$. Now, define

$$\psi_4(t) = (q_t \vee r_t) \wedge \mathbf{X}(\neg r_t \mathbf{U}(r_t \wedge \mathbf{X}s')) \rightarrow \bigwedge_{j \in B_t} \mathbf{X}^j p \wedge \bigwedge_{j \in C_t} \mathbf{X}^j \neg p$$

We next define f inductively on the structure of a CTL formula. Thus, for every proposition q from the labelling of $\mathcal{M}$ and all CTL formulas φ_1, φ_2

$$f(q) = q$$

$$f(\varphi_1 \vee \varphi_2) = f(\varphi_1) \vee f(\varphi_2)$$

$$f(\neg \varphi_1) = \neg f(\varphi_1)$$

$$f(\mathbf{EG}\varphi_1) = \mathbf{E}(\psi_{count} \wedge \mathbf{G}(up \vee (\neg up \wedge f(\varphi_1))))$$

$$f(\mathbf{E}\varphi_1 \mathbf{U}\varphi_2) = \mathbf{E}(\psi_{count} \wedge (up \vee (\neg up \wedge f(\varphi_1)))\mathbf{U}(\neg up \wedge f(\varphi_2)))$$

$$f(\mathbf{EX}\varphi_1) = \mathbf{E}(\psi_{count} \wedge (\mathbf{X}up\mathbf{UX}(\neg up \wedge f(\varphi_1))))$$

It is now possible to show by a simple induction on the structure of the CTL formula φ that for every state $s_0 \in S$ and every $v \in \mathbb{N}$ we have $\mathcal{M}, s_0, v \models \varphi$ if and only if $\mathcal{M}', s_0, v \models f(\varphi)$. □

For combined complexity of ATL* we can show that 2ExpSpace is a tight lower bound by a reduction from the word acceptance problem of a doubly-exponential space deterministic Turing machine.

Proposition 5. *The combined complexity of model-checking* ATLs *is* 2ExpSpace-*hard in both OCPs and SOCPs.*

Proof (Sketch). In [15] the emptiness problem for alternating finite automata with a one-letter alphabet (1L-AFA) is shown to be PSpace-complete by a reduction from the word acceptance problem of a polynomial space deterministic Turing machine. Another way to interpret the emptiness problem of 1L-AFAs is the problem of determining the winner in a one-counter game with two players Verifier and Falsifier where Verifier has a reachability condition and Falsifier has a safety condition. As a first step in our proof we do a similar reduction, but do it from a doubly-exponential space deterministic Turing machine $\mathcal{T}$ and an input word w to a one-counter reachability game $\mathcal{G}$ with a number of states that is doubly-exponential in the size $|w|$ of w and polynomial in the size $|\mathcal{T}|$ of $\mathcal{T}$.

In order to shrink the size of the game, we use a similar trick as in the proof of Proposition 4 to implement a counter by using an LTL objective for Verifier rather than a reachability objective. But whereas in the proof of Proposition 4 we only needed a c-bit counter capable of counting from 0 to $2^c - 1$ we now need a $2^{|w|^k}$-bit counter capable of counting from 0 to $2^{2^{|w|^k}} - 1$ where k is a constant. In order to accomplish this we can use alternation between the players, such that Falsifier can perform tests that Verifier updates the counter appropriately during the play. The details are similar to an idea from [4,5,16].

In total we end up with a one-counter game $\mathcal{M}$ and an LTL objective φ both of size polynomial in $|\mathcal{T}|$ and $|w|$ such that $\mathcal{T}$ accepts w if and only if the initial state of the $\mathcal{M}$ satisfies the ATL* formula $\langle\!\langle\{\text{Verifier}\}\rangle\!\rangle\varphi$ where $\varphi \in$ LTL. Note that the intermediate step with a doubly-exponential sized game is not needed but it makes the intuition and the proof much simpler. The game $\mathcal{M}$ and the LTL objective φ can be constructed directly from $\mathcal{T}$ and w in polynomial time.   □

Since our lower bound is for formulas of the form $\langle\!\langle\{I\}\rangle\!\rangle\varphi$ where φ is an LTL formula and I is a player this means that the complexity of deciding the winner in one-counter games with LTL objectives is 2ExpSpace-complete both in the succinct and non-succinct case. With a fixed formula the complexity of this problem is PSpace-complete in OCGs due to PSpace-hardness of model-checking LTL in finite-state systems [23]. For SOCGs the model-checking game from Sect. 3 provides a reduction from data complexity of model-checking CTL in SOCPs to deciding the winner in succinct OCPGs with a fixed number of colors. Such a parity condition can be expressed by a fixed LTL objective.

Corollary 1. *Deciding the winner in two-player OCGs and SOCGs with LTL objectives are both* 2ExpSpace-*complete. For a fixed LTL formula, these problems are* PSpace-*complete and* ExpSpace-*complete respectively.*

5   Concluding Remarks

Model-checking of quantitative extensions of branching and alternating-time temporal logics in one-counter systems is a very natural approach to verification and synthesis of systems with combined qualitative and quantitative objectives. In this paper we have provided complexity results for important basic problems which can help guide the direction for further research in this area.

I want to thank Valentin Goranko and Michael Reichhardt Hansen for discussions and helpful comments.

References

1. Alur, R., Henzinger, T.A., Kupferman, O.: Alternating-time temporal logic. J. ACM **49**(5), 672–713 (2002)
2. Bouyer, P., Fahrenberg, U., Larsen, K.G., Markey, N., Srba, J.: Infinite runs in weighted timed automata with energy constraints. In: Cassez, F., Jard, C. (eds.) FORMATS 2008. LNCS, vol. 5215, pp. 33–47. Springer, Heidelberg (2008)

3. Bouyer, P., Gardy, P., Markey, N.: Quantitative verification of weighted kripke structures. In: Cassez, F., Raskin, J.-F. (eds.) ATVA 2014. LNCS, vol. 8837, pp. 64–80. Springer, Heidelberg (2014)
4. Bozzelli, L.: Complexity results on branching-time pushdown model checking. Theoret. Comput. Sci. **379**(1–2), 286–297 (2007)
5. Bozzelli, L., Murano, A., Peron, A.: Pushdown module checking. Form. Methods Syst. Des. **36**(1), 65–95 (2010)
6. Brázdil, T., Jančar, P., Kučera, A.: Reachability games on extended vector addition systems with states. In: Abramsky, S., Gavoille, C., Kirchner, C., Meyer auf der Heide, F., Spirakis, P.G. (eds.) ICALP 2010. LNCS, vol. 6199, pp. 478–489. Springer, Heidelberg (2010)
7. Bulling, N., Goranko, V.: How to be both rich and happy: combining quantitative and qualitative strategic reasoning about multi-player games (extended abstract). In: SR, pp. 33–41 (2013)
8. Clarke, E.M., Emerson, E.A.: Design and synthesis of synchronization skeletons using branching time temporal logic. In: Kozen, D. (ed.) Logic of Programs 1981. LNCS, vol. 131, pp. 52–71. Springer, Heidelberg (1982)
9. Demri, S., Gascon, R.: The effects of bounding syntactic resources on presburger LTL. J. Log. Comput. **19**(6), 1541–1575 (2009)
10. Emerson, E.A.: The beginning of model checking: a personal perspective. In: Grumberg, O., Veith, H. (eds.) 25 Years of Model Checking. LNCS, vol. 5000, pp. 27–45. Springer, Heidelberg (2008)
11. Emerson, E.A., Halpern, J.Y.: "sometimes" and "not never" revisited: on branching versus linear time temporal logic. J. ACM **33**(1), 151–178 (1986)
12. Göller, S., Haase, C., Ouaknine, J., Worrell, J.: Model checking succinct and parametric one-counter automata. In: Abramsky, S., Gavoille, C., Kirchner, C., Meyer auf der Heide, F., Spirakis, P.G. (eds.) ICALP 2010. LNCS, vol. 6199, pp. 575–586. Springer, Heidelberg (2010)
13. Göller, S., Lohrey, M.: Branching-time model checking of one-counter processes and timed automata. SIAM J. Comput. **42**(3), 884–923 (2013)
14. Holzer, M.: On emptiness and counting for alternating finite automata. In: Developments in Language Theory, pp. 88–97 (1995)
15. Jancar, P., Sawa, Z.: A note on emptiness for alternating finite automata with a one-letter alphabet. Inf. Process. Lett. **104**(5), 164–167 (2007)
16. Kupferman, O., Madhusudan, P., Thiagarajan, P.S., Vardi, M.Y.: Open systems in reactive environments: control and synthesis. In: Palamidessi, C. (ed.) CONCUR 2000. LNCS, vol. 1877, pp. 92–107. Springer, Heidelberg (2000)
17. Löding, C., Madhusudan, P., Serre, O.: Visibly pushdown games. In: Lodaya, K., Mahajan, M. (eds.) FSTTCS 2004. LNCS, vol. 3328, pp. 408–420. Springer, Heidelberg (2004)
18. Piterman, N.: From nondeterministic büchi and streett automata to deterministic parity automata. In: Logical Methods in Computer Science, 3(3) (2007)
19. Pnueli, A.: The temporal logic of programs. In: FOCS, pp. 46–57 (1977)
20. Pnueli, A., Rosner, R.: On the synthesis of a reactive module. In: POPL, pp. 179–190 (1989)
21. Pnueli, A., Rosner, R.: On the synthesis of an asynchronous reactive module. In: Ausiello, G., Dezani-Ciancaglini, M., Rocca, S.R.D. (eds.) ICALP 1989. LNCS, vol. 372, pp. 652–671. Springer, Heidelberg (1989)
22. Serre, O.: Parity games played on transition graphs of one-counter processes. In: Aceto, L., Ingólfsdóttir, A. (eds.) FOSSACS 2006. LNCS, vol. 3921, pp. 337–351. Springer, Heidelberg (2006)

23. Sistla, A.P., Clarke, E.M.: The complexity of propositional linear temporal logics. J. ACM **32**(3), 733–749 (1985)
24. Vardi, M.Y.: Reasoning about the past with two-way automata. In: Larsen, K.G., Skyum, S., Winskel, G. (eds.) ICALP 1998. LNCS, vol. 1443, pp. 628–641. Springer, Heidelberg (1998)
25. Wolper, P., Vardi, M.Y., Sistla, P.V.: Reasoning about infinite computation paths (extended abstract). In: FOCS, pp. 185–194 (1983)

Hierarchical Information Patterns and Distributed Strategy Synthesis

Dietmar Berwanger[1]([✉]), Anup Basil Mathew[1,2],
and Marie van den Bogaard[1]

[1] LSV, CNRS & Université Paris-Saclay, Paris, France
dwb@lsv.fr
[2] IMSC, Chennai, India

Abstract. Infinite games with imperfect information are deemed to be undecidable unless the information flow is severely restricted. One fundamental decidable case occurs when there is a total ordering among players, such that each player has access to all the information that the following ones receive.

In this paper we consider variations of this hierarchy principle for synchronous games with perfect recall, and identify new decidable classes for which the distributed synthesis problem is solvable with finite-state strategies. In particular, we show that decidability is maintained when the information hierarchy may change along the play, or when transient phases without hierarchical information are allowed.

1 Introduction

Realising systems that are correct by design is a persistent ambition of computing science. The stake is particularly high for systems that interact with an unpredictable environment over indeterminate time. Pioneering results in the area of synthesis, due to Büchi and Landweber [3], and Rabin [17], show that the task can be automatised for the case of a monolithic design, with correctness conditions specified by automata over infinite objects — words or trees representing computations. A most natural framework for representing the problem setting and its solution is in terms of infinite games with perfect information over finite graphs, as described by Pnueli and Rosner in [15], and by Thomas in [18].

For distributed systems in which several components interact towards satisfying a global specification, the game-theoretical formulation of the synthesis problem leads to games with imperfect information and the question of whether there exists a winning strategy that can be distributed among several players. Unfortunately, such games are much less amenable to automated solutions: as pointed out by Peterson and Reif in [14], it is generally undecidable whether a solution, that is, a distributed winning strategy, exists for a finitely presented game for two players against Nature (or the environment); furthermore, Janin [8] showed that, even if a solution exists, it may not be implementable by a finite-state device. As there is no hope for solving the distributed synthesis problem

© Springer International Publishing Switzerland 2015
B. Finkbeiner et al. (Eds.): ATVA 2015, LNCS 9364, pp. 378–393, 2015.
DOI: 10.1007/978-3-319-24953-7_28

uniformly, it remains to look out for classes that allow for an algorithmic treatment. For surveys on results in this direction, see e.g., the article [5] of Gastin, Sznajder, and Zeitoun, and the thesis of Puchala [16].

One fundamental case in which the distributed synthesis problem becomes decidable is that of hierarchical systems: these correspond to games where there is a total order among the players such that, informally speaking, each player has access to the information received by the players that come later in the order. Peterson and Reif [14] showed that for games in this setting, it is decidable — although, with nonelementary complexity — whether distributed winning strategies exist and if so, finite-state winning strategies can be effectively synthesised. The result was extended by Pnueli and Rosner [15] to the framework of distributed systems over fixed linear architectures where information can flow only in one direction. Later, Kupferman and Vardi developed a fundamental automata-theoretic approach [12] that allows to extend the decidability result from linear-time to branching-time specifications, and also removes some of the syntactic restrictions imposed by the fixed-architecture setting of Pnueli and Rosner. Finally, Finkbeiner and Schewe [4] give an effective characterisation of communication architectures on which distributed synthesis is decidable. The criterion requires absence of information forks, which implies a hierarchical order in which processes, or players, have access to the observations provided by the environment.

The setting of games is more liberal than that of architectures with fixed communication channels. For instance, Muscholl and Walukiewicz [13] present a decidable class of synthesis problems under different assumptions on the communication between processes that are not subsumed by information-fork free architectures. A rather general, though non-effective condition for games to admit finite-state distributed winning strategies is given in [2], based on epistemic models representing the knowledge acquired by players in a game with perfect recall. This condition suggests that, beyond the fork-free architecture classification there may be further natural classes of games for which the distributed synthesis problem is decidable.

In this paper, we study a relaxation of the hierarchical information pattern underlying the basic decidability results on games with imperfect information. Firstly, we extend the assumption of hierarchical observation, that is *positional* information, by incorporating perfect recall. Rather than requiring that a player *observes* the signal received by a less-informed player, we will require that he can *deduce* it from his observation of the play history. It can easily be seen that this gives rise to a decidable class, and it is likely that previous authors had a perfect-recall interpretation in mind when describing hierarchical systems, even if the formal definitions in the relevant literature generally refer to observations.

Secondly, we investigate the case when the hierarchical information order is not fixed, but may change dynamically along the play. This allows to model situations where the schedule of the interaction allows a less-informed player to become more informed than others, or where the players may coordinate on designating one to receive certain signals, and thus become more informed than others. We show that this condition of dynamic hierarchical observation also leads to a decidable class of the distributed synthesis problem.

As a third extension, we consider the case where the condition of hierarchical information (based on perfect recall) is intermittent. That is, along every play, it occurs infinitely often that the information sets of players are totally ordered; nevertheless, there may be histories at which incomparable information sets arise, as it is otherwise typical of information forks. We show that, at least for the case of winning conditions over attributes observable by all players, this condition of recurring hierarchical observation is already sufficient for the decidability of the synthesis problem, and that finite-state winning strategies exist for all solvable instances.

For all the three conditions of hierarchical information, it is decidable with relatively low complexity whether they hold for a given game. However, the complexity of solving a game is nonelementary in all cases, as they are more general than the condition of hierarchical observation, known to admit no elementary lower bound [15].

2   Preliminaries

2.1   Games on Graphs

We use the standard model of concurrent games with imperfect information, following the notation from [2]. There is a set $N = \{1, \ldots, n\}$ of players and a distinguished agent called Nature. A list of elements $x = (x^i)_{i \in N}$, one for each player, is a *profile*. For each player i, we fix a set A^i of *actions* and a set B^i of *observations*; these are finite sets.

A *game graph* $G = (V, E, (\beta^i)_{i \in N})$ consists of a finite set V of nodes called *positions*, an edge relation $E \subseteq V \times A \times V$ representing simultaneous *moves* labelled by action profiles, and a profile of *observation* functions $\beta^i : V \to B^i$ that label every position with an observation, for each player. We assume that the graph has no dead ends, that is, for every position $v \in V$ and every action profile $a \in A$, there exists an outgoing move $(v, a, w) \in E$.

Plays start at a designated initial position $v_0 \in V$ and proceed in rounds. In a round at position v, each player i chooses simultaneously and independently an action $a^i \in A^i$, then Nature chooses a successor position v' reachable along a move $(v, a, v') \in E$. Now, each player i receives the observation $\beta^i(v')$, and the play continues from position v'. Thus, a *play* is an infinite sequence $\pi = v_0, v_1, v_2, \ldots$ of positions, such that for all $\ell \geq 0$, there exists a move $(v_\ell, a, v_{\ell+1}) \in E$. A *history* is a nonempty prefix $\pi = v_0, v_1, \ldots, v_\ell$ of a play; we refer to ℓ as the *length* of the history, and we denote by $\mathrm{Hist}(G)$ the set of all histories on the game graph G. The observation function extends from positions to histories[1] and plays as $\beta^i(\pi) = \beta^i(v_1), \beta^i(v_2), \ldots$, and we write $\mathrm{Hist}^i(G) := \{\beta^i(\pi) \mid \pi \in \mathrm{Hist}(G)\}$ for the set of *observation histories* of player i. We say that two histories π, π' are *indistinguishable* to player i, and write $\pi \sim^i \pi'$, if $\beta^i(\pi) = \beta^i(\pi')$. This is an equivalence relation, and its classes

---

[1] Note that we discard the observation at the initial position; this will be technically convenient and does not restrict the model.

are called the *information sets*. The information set of player i at history π is $P^i(\pi) := \{\pi' \in \text{Hist}(G) \mid \pi' \sim^i \pi\}$. Accordingly, our model is *synchronous* and we assume *perfect recall*.

A *strategy* for player i is a mapping $s^i : V^* \to A^i$ from histories to actions such that $s^i(\pi) = s^i(\pi')$, for any pair $\pi \sim^i \pi'$ of indistinguishable histories. We denote the set of all strategies of player i with S^i and the set of all strategy profiles by S. A history or play $\pi = v_0, v_1, \ldots$ *follows* the strategy $s^i \in S^i$ if, for every $\ell > 0$, we have $(v_\ell, a, v_{\ell+1}) \in E$ for some action profile a with $a^i = s^i(v_0, v_1, \ldots, v_\ell)$. The play π follows a strategy profile $s \in S$ if it follows all strategies s^i. The set of possible *outcomes* of a strategy profile s is the set of plays that follow s.

A *winning condition* over a game graph G is a set $W \subseteq V^\omega$ of plays. A *distributed game* $\mathcal{G} = (G, W)$ is described by a game graph and a winning condition. We say that a play π is winning in $\mathcal{G}$ if $\pi \in W$. A strategy profile s is winning in $\mathcal{G}$ if all its possible outcomes are so. In this case, we refer to s as a *distributed winning strategy*. *Solving* a game means to determine whether a distributed winning strategy exists, and if so, to construct one.

Automata. Our focus is on finitely-represented games, where the game graphs are finite and the winning conditions described by finite-state automata. Specifically, winning conditions are given by a colouring function $\gamma : V \to C$ and an ω-regular set $W \subseteq C^\omega$ describing the set of plays $v_0, v_1, \ldots$ with $\gamma(v_0), \gamma(v_1), \cdots \in W$. In certain cases, we assume that the colouring is *observable* to each player i, that is, $\beta^i(v) \neq \beta^i(v')$ whenever $\gamma(v) \neq \gamma(v')$. For general background on automata for games, we refer to the survey [7].

Strategies shall also be represented as finite-state machines. A *Moore* machine over an input alphabet Σ and an output alphabet Γ is described by a tuple (M, m_0, μ, ν) consisting of a finite set M of *memory states* with an initial state m_0, a memory *update* function $\mu : M \times \Sigma \to M$ and an *output* function $\nu : M \to \Gamma$ defined on memory states. Intuitively, the machine starts in the initial memory state m_0, and proceeds as follows: in state m, upon reading an input symbol $x \in \Sigma$, updates its memory state to $m' := \mu(m, x)$ and then outputs the letter $\nu(m)$. Formally, the update function μ is extended to input words in Σ^* by setting, $\mu(\varepsilon) := m_0$, for the empty word, and by setting, $\mu(x_0 \ldots x_{\ell-1} x_\ell) := \mu(\mu(x_0 \ldots x_{\ell-1}), x_\ell)$, for all nontrivial words $x_0 \ldots x_{\ell-1} x_\ell$. This gives rise to the function $M : \Sigma^* \to \Gamma^*$ *implemented* by M, defined by $(x_0, \ldots, x_\ell) := \nu(\mu(x_0 \ldots x_\ell))$. A *strategy automaton* for player i on a game G, is a Moore machine M with input alphabet B^i and output alphabet A^i. The strategy implemented by M is defined as $s^i(v_0, \ldots, v_{\ell-1}) := M(\beta^i(v_0 \ldots v_{\ell-1}))$. A *finite-state strategy* is one implemented by a strategy automaton.

Sometimes it is convenient to refer to Mealy machines rather than Moore machines. These are finite-state machines of similar format, with the only difference that the output function $\nu : M \times \Sigma \to \Gamma$ refers to transitions rather than their target state.

In the following we will speak of several classes $\mathcal{C}$ of finite games, always assuming that winning conditions are given as ω-regular languages. We say that the *synthesis problem for $\mathcal{C}$ is finite-state solvable* if

(i) it is decidable whether a given game $\mathcal{G} \in \mathcal{C}$ admits a distributed winning strategy, and

(ii) if yes, we can effectively construct a profile of finite-state machines that implements a distributed winning strategy for $\mathcal{G}$.

3   Static Information Hierarchies

3.1   Hierarchical Observation

We set out from the basic pattern of hierarchical information underlying the decidability results cited in the introduction [12,14,15]. These results rely on a positional interpretation of information, i.e., on observations.

Definition 1. A game graph yields *hierarchical observation* if there exists a total order $\preceq$ among the players such that whenever $i \preceq j$, then for all pairs v, v' of positions, $\beta^i(v) = \beta^i(v')$ implies $\beta^j(v) = \beta^j(v')$.

In other words, if $i \preceq j$, then the observation of player i determines the observation of player j.

Kupferman and Vardi present an automata-theoretic construction [12] for solving the distributed synthesis problem for such games. The key operation is that of *widening* – a finite-state interpretation of strategies for a less-informed player j within the strategies of a more-informed player $i \preceq j$. This allows to first solve a game as if all the moves were performed by the most-informed player, which comes first in the order $\preceq$, and successively discard solutions that cannot be implemented by the less-informed players, i.e., those which involve strategies that are not in the image of the widening interpretation.

Theorem 2 [12]. For games with hierarchical observation, the synthesis problem is finite-state solvable.

3.2   Incorporating Perfect Recall

In a first step, we extend the notion of hierarchical information to incorporate the power of perfect recall that players have. While maintaining the requirement of a fixed order, we now ask that the *information set* of a player determines the information sets of those who follow in the order.

Definition 3. A game graph yields *(static) hierarchical information* if there exists a total order $\preceq$ among the players such that, for all histories π, if $i \preceq j$, then $P^i(\pi) \subseteq P^j(\pi)$.

The following lemma provides an operational characterisation of the condition. We detail the proof, as its elements will be used later.

Lemma 4. *A game graph G yields static hierarchical information if, and only if, for every pair $i \preceq j$ of players, there exists a Moore machine that outputs $\beta^j(\pi)$ on input $\beta^i(\pi)$, for every history π in G.*

Proof. For an arbitrary game graph G, let us denote the relation between the observations of two players i and j along the histories of G by

$$T^{ij} := \{(\beta^i(\pi), \beta^j(\pi)) \in (B^i \times B^j)^* \mid \pi \in \mathrm{Hist}(G)\}.$$

This is a regular relation, recognised by the game graph G when viewed as a finite-word automaton A_G^{ij} over the alphabet of observation pairs $B^i \times B^j$. Concretely, $A_G^{ij} := (V, B^i \times B^j, v_0, \Delta, V)$ is a nondeterministic automaton on states corresponding to positions of G, with transitions $(v, (b^i, b^j), v') \in \Delta$ if there exists a move $(v, a, v') \in E$ such that $\beta^i(v') = b^i$ and $\beta^j(v') = b^j$; all states are accepting.

($\Leftarrow$) If there exists a Moore machine that recognises T^{ij}, then T^{ij} is actually a function. Thus, $\pi \sim^i \pi'$ implies $\beta^j(\pi) = T^{ij}(\beta^i(\pi)) = T^{ij}(\beta^i(\pi')) = \beta^j(\pi')$, and therefore $\pi \sim^j \pi'$.

($\Rightarrow$) Assuming that G yields static hierarchical information, consider the automaton M^{ij} obtained by determinising A_G^{ij} and trimming the result, that is, removing all states that do not lead to an accepting state. As G yields hierarchical information, the relation T^{ij} recognised by M^{ij} is functional, and hence M^{ij} is deterministic in the input component i: for any state v there exists precisely one outgoing transition along each observation $b^i \in B^i$. In other words, M^{ij} is a Mealy machine, which we can transform into an equivalent Moore machine, as desired. $\qquad\qquad\qquad\qquad\qquad\qquad\qquad\qquad\qquad\qquad\qquad\qquad\square$

Theorem 5. *For games with static hierarchical information, the synthesis problem is finite-state solvable.*

Proof. Intuitively, we transform an arbitrary game graph $G = (V, E, \beta)$ with static hierarchical *information* into one with hierarchical *observation*, by taking the synchronised product of G with automata that signal to each player i the observations of all players $j \succeq i$. We shall see that this preserves the solutions to the distributed synthesis problem, for any winning condition on G.

To make the construction precise, let us fix a pair $i \preceq j$ of players, and consider the Moore machine $M^{ij} = (M, m_0, \mu, \nu)$ from the proof of Lemma 4, which translates the observations $\beta^i(\pi)$ into $\beta^j(\pi)$, for every history π in G. We define the product $G \times M^{ij}$ as a new game graph with the same sets of actions as G, and the same observation alphabets $(B^k)_{k \neq i}$, except for player i, for which we expand the alphabet to $B^i \times B^j$ to also include observations of player j. The new game is over positions in $V \times M$ with moves $((v, m), a, (v', m'))$ if $(v, a, v') \in E$ and $\mu(m, \beta^i(v)) = m'$. The observations for player i are given by $\beta^i(v, m) = (\beta^i(v), \nu(m))$, whereas they remain unchanged for all other players $\beta^k(v, m) = \beta^k(v)$, for all $k \neq i$.

The obtained product graph is equivalent to the original game graph G, in the sense that they have the same tree unravelling, and the additional components in the observations of player i (representing observations of player j, given by the Moore machine M^{ij}) are already determined by his own observation history, so player i cannot distinguish any pair of histories in the new game that he could not distinguish in the original game. Accordingly, the strategies on the expanded game graph $G \times M^{ij}$ correspond to strategies on G, such that the outcomes of any distributed strategy are preserved. In particular, for any winning condition over G, a distributed strategy is winning in the original game if, and only if, it is winning in the expanded game $G \times M^{ij}$. On the other hand, the (positional) observations of Player i in the expanded game determine the observations of Player j.

By applying the transformation for each pair $i \preceq j$ of players successively, we obtain a game graph that is equivalent to G under every winning condition, and which additionally yields hierarchical observation. Due to Theorem 2, we can thus conclude that, under ω-regular winning condition, the synthesis problem is finite-state solvable for games with static hierarchical information.   □

To decide whether a given game graph yields static hierarchical information, the collection of Moore machines according to Lemma 4, for all players i, j, may be used as a witness. However, this yields an inefficient procedure, as the determinisation of a functional transducer involves an exponential blowup; precise bounds for such translations are given by Weber and Klemm in [19]. More directly, one could verify that each of the transductions A_G^{ij} relating observation histories of Players i, j, as defined in the proof of Lemma 4, is functional. This can be done in polynomial time using, e.g., the procedure described by Béal et al. in [1].

We can give a precise bound in terms of nondeterministic complexity.

Lemma 6. *The problem of deciding whether a game yields static hierarchical information is* NLogSpace-*complete.*

Proof. The complement problem — of deciding whether for a given game there exists a pair of players i, j that cannot be ordered in either way — is solved by the following nondeterministic procedure: Guess a pair i, j of players, then check that $i \not\preceq j$, by following nondeterministically a pair of histories $\pi \sim^i \pi'$, such that $\pi \not\sim^j \pi'$; symmetrically, check that $j \not\preceq i$. The procedure requires only logarithmic space for maintaining pointers to four positions while tracking the histories. Accordingly, the complement problem is in NLogSpace, and since the complexity class is closed under complement, our decision problem of whether a game yields static hierarchical information also belongs to NLogSpace.

For hardness, we reduce the emptiness problem for nondeterministic finite automata, known to be NLogSpace-hard [10], to the problem of deciding whether the following game for two players playing on the graph of the automaton yields hierarchical information: Nature chooses a run in the automaton, the players can only observe the input letters, unless an accepting state is reached; if this happens, Nature sends to each player privately one bit, which violates the condition of hierarchical information. Thus, the game has hierarchical information if, and only if, no input word is accepted.   □

3.3   Signals and Game Transformations

Functions that return information about the current history, such as those constructed in the proof of Lemma 4 will be a useful tool in our exposition, especially when the information can be made observable to some players.

Given a game graph G, a *signal* is a function defined on the set of histories in G, or on the set of observation histories of some player i. We say that a signal $f : \mathrm{Hist}(G) \to C$ is *information-consistent* for player i if any two histories that are indistinguishable to player i have the same image under f. A finite-state signal is one implemented by a Moore machine. Any finite-state signal $f : \mathrm{Hist}(G) \to C$ can also be implemented by a Moore machine M^i over the observation alphabet B^i, such that $M(\pi) = M^i(\beta^i(\pi))$ for every history π. The *synchronisation* of G with a finite-state signal f is the expanded game graph (G, f) obtained by taking the synchronised product $G \times M$, as described in the proof of Lemma 4. In case f is information-consistent for player i, it can be made *positionally observable* to this player, without changing the game essentially. The result is a game graph (G, f^i) that expands (G, f) with an additional observation component $f^i(v)$ for player i at every position v, such that $f(\pi) = f^i(v)$ for each history π that ends at v. Under any winning strategy, the game (G, f^i) is finite-state equivalent to G, in the sense that winning strategies of the original game can be transformed into winning strategies of the synchronised game via standard finite-state operations. In particular, the transformation preserves solutions to the finite-state synthesis problem.

4 Dynamic Hierarchies

In this section, we maintain the requirement on the information sets of players to be totally ordered at every history. However, in contrast to the case of static hierarchical information, we allow the order to depend on the history and to change dynamically along a play.

Definition 7. We say that a history π yields *hierarchical information* if the information sets $\{P^i(\pi) \mid i \in N\}$ are totally ordered by inclusion. A game graph G yields *dynamic* hierarchical information if every history yields hierarchical information.

In other words, a game has dynamic hierarchical information if there is no history at which the information sets of two players are incomparable. To decide whether this is the case, we can use a nondeterministic procedure similar to the one in Lemma 6, to guess two players i, j and three histories $\pi \sim^i \pi'$ and $\pi'' \sim^j \pi$, such that $\pi' \not\prec^i \pi''$ and $\pi' \not\prec^j \pi''$. Since, for a history π, witnesses π', π'' can be guessed and verified by a nondeterministic automaton, it also follows that, for every finite game, the set of histories that yield hierarchical information is regular.

Lemma 8. *(i) For every finite game, we can construct a deterministic finite automaton that recognises the set of histories that yield hierarchical information.*

(ii) The problem of deciding whether a game yields dynamic hierarchical information is NLogSpace-*complete.*

In the remainder of the section, we show that, under this more liberal condition, distributed games are still decidable.

Theorem 9. *For games with dynamic hierarchical information, the synthesis problem is finite-state solvable.*

For the proof, we transform an arbitrary game $\mathcal{G}$ with dynamic hierarchical information into one with static hierarchical information, among a different set of n *shadow* players $1', \ldots, n'$, where each shadow player i' plays the role of the i-most informed player in the original game, in a sense that we will make precise soon. The information sets of the shadow players follow their nominal order, that is, if $i < j$ then $P^{i'}(\pi) \subseteq P^{j'}(\pi)$. The resulting shadow game inherits the graph structure of the orginal game, and we will ensure that, for every history π,

(i) each shadow player i' has the same information (set) as the i-most informed actual player, and
(ii) each shadow player i' has the same choice of actions as the i-most informed actual player.

This shall guarantee that the shadow game preserves the winning status of the original game.

The construction proceeds in two phases. Firstly, we expand the game graph G so that the correspondence between actual and shadow players does not depend on the history, but only on the current position. This is done by synchronising G with a finite-state machine that signals to each player his rank in the information hierarchy at the current history. Secondly, we modify the game graph, where the shadow-player correspondence is recorded as a positional attribute, such that the observation of each player is received by his shadow player, at every position; similarly, the actions of each player are transferred to his shadow player. Finally, we show how finite-state winning strategies for the shadow game can be re-distributed to the actual players to yield a winning profile of finite-state winning strategies for the original game.

4.1   Information Rank Signals

For the following, let us fix a game $\mathcal{G}$ with dynamic hierarchical information with the usual notation. For a history π, we write $\preceq_\pi$ for the total order among players induced by the inclusions between their information sets at π. To formalise the notion of an i-most informed player, we use the shortcut $i \approx_\pi j$ for $i \preceq_\pi j$ and $j \preceq_\pi i$; likewise, we write $i \prec_\pi j$ for $i \preceq_\pi j$ and not $j \preceq_\pi i$.

Then, the *information rank* of player i over the game graph G is a signal $\mathrm{rank}^i : \mathrm{Hist}(G) \to N$ defined by

$$\mathrm{rank}^i(\pi) := |\{j \in N \mid j \prec_\pi i \text{ or } (j < i \text{ and } j \approx_\pi i)\}|.$$

Likewise, we define the *order* of player i *relative* to player j as a signal $\preceq_j^i$: $\mathrm{Hist}(G) \to \{0, 1\}$ with $\preceq_j^i(\pi) = 1$ if, and only if, $i \preceq_\pi j$.

Lemma 10. *The information rank of each player i and his order relative to any player j are finite-state signals that are information-consistent to player i.*

Proof. We detail the argument for the rank, the case of relative order is similar and simpler.

Given a game $\mathcal{G}$ as in the statement, let us verify that the signal rank^i is information-consistent, for each player i. Towards this, consider two histories $\pi \sim^i \pi'$ in G, and suppose that some player j does not count for the rank of i at π, in the sense that either $i \prec_\pi j$ or $(i \approx_\pi j$ and $i < j)$ — in both cases, it follows that $\pi \sim^j \pi'$, hence $P^j(\pi) = P^j(\pi')$, which implies that j does not count for the rank of i at π' either. Hence, the set of players that count for the rank of player i is the same at π and at π', which means that $\text{rank}^i(\pi) = \text{rank}^i(\pi')$.

To see that the signal rank^i can be implemented by a finite-state machine, we first build, for every pair i, j of players, a nondeterministic automaton A_i^j that accepts the histories π where $j \prec_\pi i$, by guessing a history $\pi' \sim^i \pi$ and verifying that $\pi' \not\sim^j \pi$. To accept the histories that satisfy $i \approx_\pi j$, we take the product of the automata A_i^j and A_j^i for $i \preceq_\pi j$ and $j \preceq_\pi i$ and accept if both accept. Combining the two constructions allows us to describe, for every player j, an automaton A_j to recognise the set of histories at which j counts for $\text{rank}^i(\pi)$.

Next, we determinise each of the automata A_j and take appropriate Boolean combinations to obtain a Moore machine M^i with input alphabet V and output alphabet $\mathcal{P}(N)$, which upon reading a history π in G, outputs the set of players that count for $\text{rank}^i(\pi)$. Finally we replace each set in the output of M^i by its size to obtain a Moore machine that returns on input $\pi \in V^*$, the rank of player i at the actual history π in G.

As we showed that rank^i is an information-consistent signal, we can conclude that there exists a Moore machine that inputs observation histories $\beta^i(\pi)$ of player i and outputs $\text{rank}^i(\pi)$. $\square$

One consequence of this construction is that we can view the signals rank^i and $\preceq_j^i$ as attributes of positions rather than properties of histories. Accordingly, we can assume without loss of generality that the observations of each player i have an extra rank component taking values in N and that the symbol j is observed at history π in this component if, and only if, $\text{rank}^i(\pi) = j$. When referring to the positional attribute $\preceq_j^i$ at v, it is more convenient to write $i \preceq_v j$ rather than $\preceq_j^i$.

4.2 Smooth Overtaking

As we suggested in the proof outline, each player i and his shadow player, identified by the observable signal rank^i, should be equally informed. To achieve this, we will let the observation of player i be received by his shadow, in every round of a play. However, since the rank of players, and hence the identity of the shadow, changes with the history, an information loss can occur when the information order between two players, say $1 \prec 2$ along a move is swapped to become $2 \prec 1$ in the next round. Intuitively, the observation received by player 2 after this move contains one piece of information that allows him to catch up with player 1, and another piece of information to overtake player 1. Due to their rank change along the move, the players would now also change shadows. Consequently, the shadow of 1 at the target position, who was previously as (little) informed as player 2, just receives the new observation of player 1, but he may miss the piece of information that allowed player 2 to catch up (and which player 1 had).

We describe a transformation to smoothen the switches in the information order, such that this artefact does no longer occur. Formally, for a play π in a game, we say that Player i and j cross at stage ℓ if $P^i(\pi_\ell) \subsetneq P^j(\pi_\ell)$ and $P^j(\pi_{\ell+1}) \subsetneq P^i(\pi_{\ell+1})$. We say that a game with dynamic hierarchical information is *cross-free* if there are no crossing players in any play.

Lemma 11. *Every game with dynamic hierarchical information is finite-state equivalent to a game that is cross-free.*

Proof (sketch). We define a signal for each pair of players i, j that represents the knowledge that player j has about the current observation of player i. If this signal is made observable to Player i only at histories π at which $i \preceq_\pi j$, the game remains essentially unchanged, as players only receive information from less-informed players, which they could hence deduce from their observation. Concretely, we define the signal $\lambda_j^i : V^* \to \mathcal{P}(B^i)$ by

$$\lambda_j^i(\pi) := \{\beta^i(v') \ : \ v' \text{ is the last state of some history } \pi' \in P^j(\pi)\}.$$

Clearly, this is a finite-state signal.

Now we look at the synchronised product of G with the signals $(\lambda_j^i)_{i,j \in N}$ and the relative-order signal $\preceq_j^i$ constructed in the proof of Lemma 10. In the resulting game graph, we add to every move (v, a, w) an intermediary position u, at which we assign, for every player i the observation $\{\lambda_j^i(w) \ : \ i \preceq_w j\}$. Intuitively, this can be viewed as a half-step lookahed signal that player i receives from player j who may have been more informed at the source position v – thus the signal is not necessarily information-consistent for player i. Still, adding the signal leaves the game essentially unchanged, as the players cannot react to the received observation before reaching the target w, at which point the information is no longer relevant. On the other hand, along moves at which the information order between players switches, the intermediary position ensures that the players attain equal information.

To adjust the ω-regular winning conditions for $\mathcal{G}$ to the new game, and to turn any finite-state distributed winning strategy for the new game corresponds into one for the original game, we may just ignore the added intermediary positions. In summary, the construction yields a game graph with no crossings that is finite-state equivalent to the original game graph. □

4.3   Shadow Players

We are now ready to describe the construction of the shadow game associated to a game $\mathcal{G} = (V, E, \beta, W)$ with dynamic hierarchical information. Without loss of generality, we can assume that every position in G is marked with the attributes $\text{rank}^i(v)$ and $\sim^i_j$, for all players i, j according to Lemma 10 and that the game graph is cross-free, according to Lemma 11.

The shadow game $\mathcal{G}' = (V \cup \{\ominus\}, E', \beta', W)$ is also played by n players and has the same winning condition as $\mathcal{G}$. The action and the observation alphabet of each shadow player consists of the union of the action and observation alphabets of all actual players. The game graph G' has the same positions as G, plus one sink $\ominus$ that absorbs all moves along unused action profiles. The moves of G' are obtained from G by assigning the actions of each player i to his shadow player $j = \text{rank}^i(v)$ as follows: for every move $(v, a, v') \in E$, there is a move $(v, x, v') \in E'$ labelled with the action profile x obtained by a permutation of a corresponding to the rank order, that is, $a^i = x^j$ for $j = \text{rank}^i(v)$, for all players i. Finally, at every position $v \in V$, the observation of any player i in the original game G is assigned to his shadow player, that is $\beta'^j(v) := \beta^i(v)$, for $j = \text{rank}^i(v)$.

By construction, the shadow game yields static hierarchical information, according to the nominal order of the players. We can verify, by induction on the length of histories, that for every history π, the information set of player i at π in G is the same as the one of his shadow player $\text{rank}^i(\pi)$ in G'.

Finally, we show that the distributed synthesis problem for G reduces to the one on G', and vice versa. To see that $\mathcal{G}'$ admits a winning strategy if $\mathcal{G}$ does, let us fix a distributed strategy s for the actual players in $\mathcal{G}$. We define a signal $\sigma^j : \text{Hist}(G') \to A$ for each player in $\mathcal{G}'$, by setting $\sigma^j(\pi) := s^i(\pi)$ if $j = \text{rank}^i(\pi)$, for each history π. This signal is information-consistent for player j, since, at any history π, his information set is the same as for the actual player i with $\text{rank}^i(\pi) = j$, and because the strategy of the actual player i is information-consistent for himself. Hence, σ^j is a strategy for player j in G'. Furthermore, at every history, the action taken by the shadow player $j = \text{rank}^i(\pi)$ has the same outcome as if it was taken by the actual player i in G. Hence, the set of play outcomes of the profiles s and σ are the same and we can conclude that, if there exists a distributed winning strategy for G, then there also exists one for G'. Notice that this implication holds under any winning condition, without assuming ω-regularity.

For the converse implication, let us suppose that the shadow game $\mathcal{G}'$ admits a winning profile σ of finite-state strategies. We consider, for each actual player i of G, the signal $s^i : \text{Hist}(G) \to A^i$ that maps every history π to the action $s^i(\pi) := \sigma^j(\pi)$ of the shadow player $j = \text{rank}^i(\pi)$. This is a finite-state signal, as we can implement it by synchronising G with rank^i, the observations on the shadow players, and the winning strategies σ^j, for all shadow players j. Moreover, s^i is information-consistent to the actual player i, because all histories $\pi \in P^i(\pi)$, have the same value $\text{rank}^i(\pi) =: j$, and, since s^j is information-consistent for player j, the actions prescribed by $s^j(\pi)$ must be the same, for all $\pi \in P^j(\pi) = P^i(\pi)$. In conclusion, the signal s^i represents a finite-state strategy for player i. The profile s has the same set of play outcomes outcome as σ, so s is indeed a distributed finite-state strategy, as desired.

In summary, we have shown that any game G with dynamic hierarchical information admits a winning strategy if, and only if, the associated shadow game with static hierarchical observation admits a finite-state winning strategy. The latter question is decidable according to Theorem 5. We showed that for every positive instance G', we can construct a finite-state distributed strategy for G. This concludes the proof of Theorem 9.

5   Transient Perturbations

As a third pattern of hierarchical information, we consider the case where incomparable information sets may occur at some histories along a play, but it is guaranteed that a total order will be re-established in a finite number of rounds.

Definition 12. A play yields *recurring hierarchical information* if there are infinitely many histories that yield hierarchical information. A game yields *recurring hierarchical information* if all its plays do so.

Given a play π, we call a *gap* any interval $[t, t + \ell]$ of rounds such that the players do not have hierarchical information at any round in $[t, t + \ell]$; the length of the gap is $\ell + 1$. A game has *gap size* m if the length of all gaps in its plays are uniformly bounded by m. One important insight is that, in finite games with recurring hierarchical information, only gaps of uniformly bounded size can arise.

Lemma 13. *If a game yields recurring hierarchical information, then its gap size is finite.*

Proof. Let G be an arbitrary finite game graph. As we pointed out in Lemma 8, a history π does not yield hierarchical information if there exist two players i, j with incomparable information sets; the set of histories at which this occurs can be recognised by a deterministic word automaton. Let $\mathcal{A}$ be a deterministic automaton for the complement language intersected with $\mathrm{Hist}(G)$, that is, $\mathcal{A}$ accepts all histories with hierarchical information. If we now view $\mathcal{A}$ as a Büchi automaton, which accepts all words with infinitely many prefixes accepted by $\mathcal{A}$, we obtain a deterministic ω-word automaton that recognises the set of plays with recurring hierarchical information in G. Applying a standard pumping argument, we can conclude that, if the graph G at the outset yields recurring hierarchical information, its gap size is bounded by the number of states in the automaton $\mathcal{A}$. $\square$

To determine whether a game yields recurring hierarchical information, it is sufficient to check whether the automaton constructed in the proof of Lemma 13 accepts every play.

Corollary 14. *It is decidable whether a game yields recurring hierarchical information.*

We can show that the synthesis problem for this class of games is finite state-solvable, by using the information tracking construction from [2].

Theorem 15. *For games with recurring hierarchical information and observable ω-regular winning conditions, the synthesis problem is finite-state solvable.*

Proof. The tracking construction of [2] reduces the problem of solving a distributed game with imperfect information for n players to that of solving a zero-sum game with perfect information for two players. This is done by unravelling the given game graph G and labelling every history with the *epistemic model* that represents the current knowledge of players, that is, a structure over $\text{Hist}(G)$ equipped with the indistinguishability relations $\sim^i$ and an attribute designating the last state the history; for the epistemic model at a history π, only histories accessible from π via a sequence of $\sim^i$-relations matter. The unravelling generates a game on an infinite tree with perfect information, from which winning strategies can be translated back and forth to the original game.

The main result of [2] shows that, whenever two nodes of the unravelling tree carry homomorphically equivalent labels, they can be identified without changing the solution of the game, at least for observable ω-regular winning conditions. Consequently, the strategy synthesis problem is decidable for a class of games, whenever the unravelling process of any game in the class is guaranteed to generate only finitely many epistemic models, up to homomorphic equivalence.

Games graphs with recurring hierarchical information satisfy this condition. Firstly, for a fixed game, there exist only finitely many epistemic models, up to homomorphic equivalence, where the $\sim^i$-relations are totally ordered by inclusion [2, Sect. 5]. In other words, epistemic models of bounded size are sufficient to describe all histories with hierarchical information. Secondly, by Lemma 13, from any history with hierarchical information, the (finitely branching) tree of continuation histories with incomparable information is of bounded depth, hence only finitely many epistemic models can occur in the unravelling. Overall, this implies that every game with recurring hierarchical information and observable winning condition has a finite quotient under homomorphic equivalence. According to [2], we can conclude that the distributed strategy problem for the class is finite-state solvable.   □

6   Discussion

The bottom-line message of our investigation is that the principle of ordered information flow can afford some flexibility. Still, this may not open floodgates for natural applications to automated synthesis under imperfect information. Rather than expecting information in a real-world system to respect a total order, we see applications in high-level synthesis towards systems on which hierarchical information patterns are enforced to allow for further refinement.

One possible scenario is inspired from multi-level synthesis as proposed in [9] for program repair. Here, the objective is to synthesise a system in several steps: firstly, construct a high-level strategy for a system prototype, in which only a subset of actions is controllable or/and not all observations are reliable, and subsequently refine this strategy to fulfil further specifications, by controlling more actions or relying on more observations.

For our concrete setting, the first-level synthesis problem can be formulated as follows: given an arbitrary distributed game, determine whether it admits a distributed finite-state winning strategy such that the synchronised product with the original game yields a residual game graph with hierarchical information; if possible, construct one. For the next level, the residual game graph can then be equipped with another winning condition, and the actions or observations may be refined. In either case, the condition of hierarchical information enforced by the first-level procedure is in place and guarantees decidability of the synthesis problem, for each subsequent level.

It can be easily seen that for any arbitrary graph game, the set of strategies that maintain dynamic hierarchical information is regular. In this case, the multi-level synthesis approach can hence be combined with existing automata-theoretic methods. Unfortunately, this would not work out when the objective is to synthesise a graph with recurring hierarchical information; already the problem of eventually attaining dynamic hierarchical information is undecidable.

Finally, a promising approach towards handling coordination problems under imperfect information is proposed in recent work of Genest, Katz, Peled and Schewe [6,11], in which strategies are viewed by separating the control and communication layers. The shadow game in our reduction of dynamic to static hierarchical information can be understood as an instance of this idea, with the scheduling of shadow players corresponding to a communication layer, and the actual execution of their strategy (as in the static hierarchical game), to the control layer.

Acknowledgement. This work was supported by the European Union Seventh Framework Programme under Grant Agreement 601148 (CASSTING) and by the Indo-French Formal Methods Lab (LIA Informel).

References

1. Béal, M.-P., Carton, O., Prieur, C., Sakarovitch, J.: Squaring transducers: an efficient procedure for deciding functionality and sequentiality of transducers. In: Gonnet, G.H., Viola, A. (eds.) LATIN 2000. LNCS, vol. 1776, pp. 397–406. Springer, Heidelberg (2000)
2. Berwanger, D., Kaiser, L., Puchala, B.: A perfect-information construction for coordination in games. In: Chakraborty, S., Kumar, A. (eds.) FSTTCS 2011, LIPiCS, Leibniz-Zentrum für Informatik, **13**, pp. 387–398 (2011)
3. Büchi, J.R., Landweber, L.H.: Solving sequential conditions by finite-state strategies. Trans. Am. Math. Soc. **138**, 295–311 (1969)
4. Finkbeiner, B., Schewe, S.: Uniform distributed synthesis. In: Panagaden, P. (ed.) LICS 2005, pp. 321–330. IEEE (2005)
5. Gastin, P., Sznajder, N., Zeitoun, M.: Distributed synthesis for well-connected architectures. Formal Methods Sys. Des. **34**, 215–237 (2009)
6. Genest, B., Peled, D., Schewe, S.: Knowledge = observation + memory + computation. In: Pitts, A. (ed.) FOSSACS 2015. LNCS, vol. 9034, pp. 215–229. Springer, Heidelberg (2015)
7. Grädel, E., Thomas, W., Wilke, T. (eds.): Automata, Logics, and Infinite Games. LNCS, vol. 2500. Springer, Heidelberg (2002)

8. Janin, D.: On the (high) undecidability of distributed synthesis problems. In: van Leeuwen, J., Italiano, G.F., van der Hoek, W., Meinel, C., Sack, H., Plášil, F. (eds.) SOFSEM 2007. LNCS, vol. 4362, pp. 320–329. Springer, Heidelberg (2007)

9. Jobstmann, B., Griesmayer, A., Bloem, R.: Program repair as a game. In: Etessami, K., Rajamani, S.K. (eds.) CAV 2005. LNCS, vol. 3576, pp. 226–238. Springer, Heidelberg (2005)

10. Jones, N.D.: Space-bounded reducibility among combinatorial problems. J. Comput. Syst. Sci. **11**, 68–85 (1975)

11. Katz, G., Peled, D., Schewe, S.: Synthesis of distributed control through knowledge accumulation. In: Gopalakrishnan, G., Qadeer, S. (eds.) CAV 2011. LNCS, vol. 6806, pp. 510–525. Springer, Heidelberg (2011)

12. Kupferman, O., Vardi, M.Y.: Synthesizing distributed systems. In: Halpern, J. (ed.) LICS 2001, pp. 389–398. IEEE Computer Society Press, June 2001

13. Muscholl, A., Walukiewicz, I.: Distributed synthesis for acyclic architectures. In: Raman, V., Suresh, S. P. (eds.) FSTTCS, LIPIcs. Schloss Dagstuhl - Leibniz-Zentrum fuer Informatik, **29**, pp. 639–651 (2014)

14. Peterson, G.L., Reif, J.H.: Multiple-person alternation. In: FOCS 1979, pp. 348–363. IEEE (1979)

15. Pnueli, A., Rosner, R.: Distributed reactive systems are hard to synthesize. In: FOCS 1990, pp. 746–757. IEEE Computer Society Press (1990)

16. Puchala, B.: Synthesis of Winning Strategies for Interaction under Partial Information, P.hD. thesis, RWTH Aachen University (2013)

17. Rabin, M.O.: Automata on infinite objects and Church's thesis, no. 13 in Regional Conference Series in Mathematics, American Mathematical Society (1972)

18. Thomas, W.: On the synthesis of strategies in infinite games. In: Mayr, E. W., Puech, C. (eds.) STACS 1995, pp. 1–13 (1995)

19. Weber, A., Klemm, R.: Economy of description for single-valued transducers. Inf. Comput. **118**, 327–340 (1995)

Cooperative Reactive Synthesis

Roderick Bloem[1], Rüdiger Ehlers[2]([✉]), and Robert Könighofer[1]

[1] IAIK, Graz University of Technology, Graz, Austria
ruediger.ehlers@uni-bremen.de
[2] University of Bremen and DFKI GmbH, Bremen, Germany

Abstract. A modern approach to engineering correct-by-construction systems is to synthesize them automatically from formal specifications. Oftentimes, a system can only satisfy its guarantees if certain environment assumptions hold, which motivates their inclusion in the system specification. Experience with modern synthesis approaches shows that synthesized systems tend to satisfy their specifications by actively working towards the violation of the assumptions rather than satisfying assumptions and guarantees together. Such uncooperative behavior is undesirable because it violates the aim of synthesis: the system should try to satisfy its guarantees and use the assumptions only when needed. Also, the assumptions often describe the valid behavior of other components in a bigger system, which should not be obstructed unnecessarily.

In this paper, we present a hierarchy of *cooperation levels* between system and environment. Each level describes how well the system enforces both the assumptions and guarantees. We show how to synthesize systems that achieve the highest possible cooperation level for a given specification in Linear Temporal Logic (LTL). The synthesized systems can also exploit cooperative environment behavior during operation to reach a higher cooperation level that is not enforceable by the system initially. The worst-case time complexity of our synthesis procedure is doubly-exponential, which matches the complexity of standard LTL synthesis.

1 Introduction

When synthesizing reactive systems from their formal specifications, we typically start with a set of guarantees that the system should fulfill and a set of assumptions about the environment. A synthesis tool then computes an implementation that satisfies the guarantees in all environments that satisfy the assumptions. In many specifications, the system can influence whether the assumptions are satisfied; in particular, the system can actively force the environment to violate the assumptions. The resulting implementation is correct: it fulfills its guarantees if the assumptions are fulfilled. However, it does so in an undesirable way.

This work was supported in part by the Austrian Science Fund (FWF) through the research network RiSE (S11406-N23), by the European Commission through the projects STANCE (317753) and IMMORTAL (644905), and by the Institutional Strategy of the University of Bremen, funded by the German Excellence Initiative.

© Springer International Publishing Switzerland 2015
B. Finkbeiner et al. (Eds.): ATVA 2015, LNCS 9364, pp. 394–410, 2015.
DOI: 10.1007/978-3-319-24953-7_29

Take for example a flight stabilization system that adds small forces to choices of forces issued by the pilot. The system guarantees state that there is little jitter in the absolute forces applied. This can only work for "well-behaved" evolutions of the manually selected force values, which in turn depend on the forces currently applied. Without the well-behavedness assumption, the system has no way to stabilize the flight. However, if the system has the opportunity to add forces that make the pilot violate this assumption, it can do so without violating its overall specification (namely that the guarantees must hold whenever the assumptions hold). Clearly, such behavior is not covered by the specifier's intent.

This observation leads to the question of how we can synthesize systems that cooperate with the environment whenever possible. Our main idea is that, at any point in time, the system should try to be as cooperative as possible while still ensuring correctness. Depending on the concrete situation, several levels of cooperation may be possible. Some examples are:

1. The system can enforce both the assumptions and guarantees to hold.
2. The system can enforce the guarantees if the assumptions hold and the system can give the environment the opportunity to satisfy the assumptions at the same time.
3. The system can neither enforce the assumptions nor the guarantees, but environment and system together can satisfy both.

The first of these levels is most beneficial: there is no need to rely on the environment, not even for satisfying the assumptions. On the second level we can satisfy the correctness objective even without allowing the system to enforce an assumption violation. From states of the third level, the system cannot enforce correctness. However, instead of resigning and behaving arbitrarily, the system still offers some executions along which both the assumptions and guarantees are fulfilled, thereby optimistically assuming that the environment is helpful.

In this paper, we perform a rigorous analysis of cooperation between the system and its environment in the setting of reactive synthesis. We generalize the three levels of cooperation from above to a fine-grained *cooperation hierarchy* that allows us to reason about how cooperative a controller for a given specification can be. A level in our hierarchy describes what objectives (in terms of assumptions and guarantees) the controller can achieve on its own and for what objectives it has to rely on the environment.

As a second contribution, we present a synthesis procedure to construct a controller that always picks the highest possible cooperation level in our hierarchy for a given linear-time temporal logic (LTL) specification. The synthesized controllers do not only enforce the highest possible level statically, but also exploit environment behavior that enables reaching a higher level that cannot be enforced initially. Thus, implementations synthesized with our approach are *maximally cooperative*, without any need to declare cooperation in the specification explicitly by enumerating scenarios in which a system can operate in a cooperative way. Our *maximally cooperative synthesis procedure* takes at most doubly-exponential time, which matches the complexity of standard LTL synthesis. Our techniques are applicable to all ω-regular word languages. For specifications given as deterministic Rabin word automata, the complexity is polynomial in the number of states and exponential in the number of acceptance condition pairs.

Outline. The presentation of this paper is structured as follows. Section 2 reviews related work and Sect. 3 introduces background and notation. Section 4 then presents our hierarchy of cooperation levels, while Sect. 5 describes our synthesis approach for obtaining cooperative systems. We conclude in Sect. 6. An extended version [7] of this paper contains extensions and more examples.

2   Related Work

In earlier work [6], we already pointed out that existing synthesis approaches handle environment assumptions in an unsatisfactory way. We postulated that synthesized systems should (1) *be correct*, (2) *not be lazy* by satisfying guarantees even if assumptions are violated, (3) *never give up* by working towards the satisfaction of the guarantees even if this is not possible in the worst case, and (4) *cooperate* by helping the environment to satisfy the assumptions that we made about it [6]. Our current work addresses all of these challenges.

Besides correctness, our main focus is on cooperation, which is also addressed by Assume-Guarantee Synthesis [12] and synthesis under rationality assumptions [3,10,11,18]. These approaches do not distinguish between system and environment, but synthesize implementations for both. Each component works under certain assumptions about the other components not deviating from their synthesized implementations arbitrarily. In contrast, our work handles the system and its environment asymmetrically: we prefer the guarantees over the assumptions and prioritize correctness over supporting the environment.

Similar to existing work on synthesis of robust [4] and error-resilient [16] systems, our synthesis approach is also *not lazy* [6] in satisfying guarantees. The reason is that satisfying guarantees is more preferable in our cooperation hierarchy than satisfying guarantees only if the assumptions are satisfied. In contrast to the existing work, we do not only consider the worst case environment behavior for satisfying guarantees (even if assumptions are violated), but also the scenario where guarantees can only be satisfied with the help of the environment.

Like [17], we also address the *never give up* challenge [6] because our cooperation hierarchy also includes levels on which the system cannot enforce the guarantees any more. Still, our synthesis approach lets the system satisfy the guarantees for *some* environment behavior whenever that is possible.

In contrast to quantitative synthesis [1,5] where the synthesized system maximizes a certain pay-off, our approach is purely qualitative: a certain level of the hierarchy is either achieved or not. In this way, we not only avoid the computational blow-up induced by operating with numerical data, but also remove the need to assign meaningful quantities (such as probabilities) to the specifications.

Finally, [15] presents an extension of a synthesis algorithm for so-called GR(1) specifications [8] to produce mission plans for robots that always offer some execution on which both assumptions and guarantees are satisfied. Hence, [15] gives a solution for one level in our hierarchy, implemented for a subset of LTL.

3   Preliminaries

We denote the Boolean domain by $\mathbb{B} = \{\mathsf{false}, \mathsf{true}\}$ and the set of natural numbers (including 0) by $\mathbb{N}$.

Words: We consider synthesis of reactive systems with a finite set $I = \{i_1, \ldots, i_m\}$ of Boolean input signals and a finite set $O = \{o_1, \ldots, o_n\}$ of Boolean outputs. The input alphabet is $\mathcal{I} = 2^I$, the output alphabet is $\mathcal{O} = 2^O$, and $\Sigma = \mathcal{I} \times \mathcal{O}$. The set of finite (infinite) words over Σ is denoted by Σ^* (Σ^ω), where ϵ is the word of length 0. A set $L \subseteq \Sigma^\omega$ of infinite words is called a *(word) language.*

Specifications: A specification φ over Σ defines a language $L(\varphi)$ of allowed words. In this paper, specifications consist of two parts, the *environment assumptions* $\mathcal{A}$ and the *system guarantees* $\mathcal{G}$. These parts can be combined by logical operators. For example, we write $\mathcal{A} \to \mathcal{G}$ to specify that the guarantees (only) need to hold if the assumptions are satisfied. We say that some finite word $w \in \Sigma^*$ is a *bad prefix* for φ if there does not exist a word $w' \in \Sigma^\omega$ such that $ww' \in L(\varphi)$. The set of infinite words that have no bad prefixes of φ will be called the *safety hull* of φ.

Reactive Systems: A reactive system interacts with its environment in a synchronous way. In every time step j, the system first provides an output letter $y_j \in \mathcal{O}$, after which the environment responds with an input letter $x_j \in \mathcal{I}$. This is repeated in an infinite execution to produce the *trace* $w = (x_0, y_0)(x_1, y_1) \ldots \in \Sigma^\omega$.

We can represent the complete behavior of a reactive system by a *computation tree* $\langle T, \tau \rangle$, where T is the set of nodes and a subset of $\mathcal{I}^*$, and τ assigns labels to the tree nodes. In such a tree, we have $\tau : T \to \mathcal{O}$, i.e., the tree nodes are labeled by the last output of the system. We call trees $\langle T, \tau \rangle$ with $T = \mathcal{I}^*$ *full trees* and consider only these henceforth, unless otherwise stated. We say that some trace $w = (x_0, y_0)(x_1, y_1) \ldots \in \Sigma^\omega$ is *included* in $\langle T, \tau \rangle$ if for all $i \in \mathbb{N}$, $y_i = \tau(x_0 \ldots x_{i-1})$. In such a case, we also say that w is a *branch* of $\langle T, \tau \rangle$.

We say that some specification φ is *realizable* if there exists a computation tree for the system all of whose traces are in $L(\varphi)$. The set of traces of $\langle T, \tau \rangle$ is denoted by $L(\langle T, \tau \rangle)$ and called the *word language* of $\langle T, \tau \rangle$. The set of all computation trees over $\mathcal{I}$ and $\mathcal{O}$ is denoted by $\mathcal{S}$. Since a computation tree represents the full behavior of a reactive system, we use these two terms interchangeably.

Rabin Word and Tree Automata: In order to represent specifications over Σ in a finitary way, we employ *Rabin automata*. For word languages, we use deterministic Rabin word automata, which are defined as tuples $\mathcal{R} = (Q, \Sigma, \delta, q_0, \mathcal{F})$, where Q is the finite set of *states*, Σ is the finite alphabet, $\delta : Q \times \Sigma \to Q$ is the *transition function*, $q_0 \in Q$ is the initial state of $\mathcal{R}$, and $\mathcal{F} \subseteq 2^Q \times 2^Q$ is the *acceptance condition* of $\mathcal{R}$. Given a word $w \in \Sigma^\omega$, $\mathcal{R}$ induces a *run* $\pi = \pi_0 \pi_1 \pi_2 \ldots \in Q^\omega$, where $\pi_0 = q_0$ and for every $i \in \mathbb{N}$, we have $\pi_{i+1} = \delta(\pi_i, w_i)$. The run π is *accepting* if there exists some *acceptance condition pair* $(F, G) \in \mathcal{F}$ such that $\inf(\pi) \cap F = \emptyset$, and $\inf(\pi) \cap G \neq \emptyset$, where $\inf$ maps a sequence to the set of elements that appear infinitely often in the sequence. We say that w is accepted by $\mathcal{R}$ if there exists a run for w that is accepting. The language of $\mathcal{R}$, denoted as

$L(\mathcal{R})$, is defined to be the set of words accepted by $\mathcal{R}$. The language of a state $q \in Q$ is defined to be the language of the automaton $\mathcal{R}_q = (Q, \Sigma, \delta, q, \mathcal{F})$, which differs from $\mathcal{R}$ only by its initial state. Without loss of generality, we assume that every Rabin automaton has a designated state $\top$ that has the full language, i.e., for which $L(\mathcal{R}_\top) = \Sigma^\omega$.

In addition to deterministic Rabin word automata, we will later also need non-deterministic Rabin tree automata. A non-deterministic Rabin tree automaton $\mathcal{R} = (Q, \mathcal{I}, \mathcal{O}, \delta, q_0, \mathcal{F})$ is defined similarly to a word automaton, except that δ has a different structure, and we now have two alphabets, namely a *branching alphabet* $\mathcal{I}$ and a *label alphabet* $\mathcal{O}$. The transition function δ is defined as $\delta : Q \times \mathcal{O} \to 2^{\mathcal{I} \to Q}$. A tree automaton accepts or rejects computation trees instead of words. Given a computation tree $\langle T, \tau \rangle$, we say that some tree $\langle T', \tau' \rangle$ is a run tree of $\mathcal{R}$ for $\langle T, \tau \rangle$ if $T' = T$, $\tau' : T' \to Q$, $\tau'(\epsilon) = q_0$, and for all $t' \in T'$, there exists a function $f \in \delta(\tau'(t'), \tau(t'))$ such that for all $i \in \mathcal{I}$, $f(i) = \tau'(t'i)$. We say that $\langle T', \tau' \rangle$ is *accepting* if every branch of $\langle T', \tau' \rangle$ is accepting, i.e., its sequence of labellings satisfies the Rabin acceptance condition $\mathcal{F}$. We say that a tree automaton accepts a computation tree if it has a corresponding accepting run tree.

Given a Rabin word automaton $\mathcal{R}$ as specification over the alphabet $\Sigma = \mathcal{I} \times \mathcal{O}$, we can check if there exists a tree with branching alphabet $\mathcal{I}$ and label alphabet $\mathcal{O}$ all of whose traces are in the language of $\mathcal{R}$. It has been shown that this operation can be performed in time exponential in $|\mathcal{F}|$ and polynomial in $|Q|$ by first translating the Rabin word automaton to a non-deterministic Rabin tree automaton with the same set of states and the same acceptance condition (in linear time), and then checking the tree automaton's language for emptiness [19]. This approach gives rise to a reactive synthesis procedure for specifications in *linear temporal logic* (LTL) [19]: we can first translate the LTL specification to a deterministic Rabin word automaton with a number of states that is doubly-exponential in the length of the specification, and a number of acceptance condition pairs that is exponential in the length of the specification. Overall, this gives a doubly-exponential time procedure for LTL reactive synthesis, which matches the known complexity of the problem.

4   A Hierarchy of Cooperation Levels

In this section, we develop a hierarchy of cooperation levels that a system may achieve. We use a special logic to specify desired properties of the system to be synthesized. The syntax of a formula Φ in this logic is defined as

$$\Phi ::= \varphi \mid \langle E \rangle \varphi \mid \mathsf{G}\langle E \rangle \varphi \mid \Phi \wedge \Phi, \tag{1}$$

where φ is a linear-time specification (e.g., an LTL formula) over an alphabet Σ. The Boolean connective $\wedge$ has its expected semantics. The formula $\langle E \rangle \varphi$ is satisfied for a system $\langle T, \tau \rangle$ if there exists some trace of $\langle T, \tau \rangle$ on which φ holds. Similarly, the formula $\mathsf{G}\langle E \rangle \varphi$ is satisfied if, from any point in a reactive system's trace that has been seen so far, there exists some suffix trace of the system such that φ holds. We call an instance of the grammar in Formula 1 a *cooperation level specification*. Our logic ranges over computation trees and has similarities to *strategy logic* [13] as well as *alternating-time temporal logic* (ATL) [2]. Yet, its semantics, to be given below, is very different. In particular, linear-time specifications φ are seen as atomic and even within the scope of a G operator, φ is only evaluated on *complete traces* of a system, always starting at the root of a computation tree.

More formally, we define the semantics as follows. Formulas are interpreted over a computation tree $\langle T, \tau \rangle \in \mathcal{S}$ using the following rules:

$$
\begin{aligned}
\langle T,\tau \rangle &\models \varphi & &\text{iff}\quad \forall w \in L(\langle T,\tau \rangle) : w \in L(\varphi) \\
\langle T,\tau \rangle &\models \langle E \rangle \varphi & &\text{iff}\quad \exists w \in L(\langle T,\tau \rangle) : w \in L(\varphi) \\
\langle T,\tau \rangle &\models \mathsf{G}\langle E \rangle \varphi & &\text{iff}\quad \forall w \in L(\langle T,\tau \rangle), i \in \mathbb{N}.\, \exists w' \in L(\langle T,\tau \rangle) \cap L(\varphi). \\
& & & \qquad\quad w_0 \ldots w_{i-1} = w'_0 \ldots w'_{i-1} \\
\langle T,\tau \rangle &\models \Phi_1 \wedge \Phi_2 & &\text{iff}\quad (\langle T,\tau \rangle \models \Phi_1) \wedge (\langle T,\tau \rangle \models \Phi_2)
\end{aligned}
$$

Most cases are straightforward, but $\mathsf{G}\langle E \rangle \varphi$ requires some attention. We follow an arbitrary trace of $\langle T, \tau \rangle$ up to step $i-1$. At step $i-1$, there must be some continuation of the trace that satisfies φ and that is part of the system's computation tree. If such a continuation exists in every step i, then $\mathsf{G}\langle E \rangle \varphi$ is satisfied.

4.1 Defining the Interesting Levels of Cooperation

We start with the linear-time specification $\mathcal{A}$, which represents the assumptions about the environment, and $\mathcal{G}$, which represents the guarantees. We can combine them to the linear-time properties $\mathcal{A} \to \mathcal{G}$ and $\mathcal{A} \wedge \mathcal{G}$. The first of these represents the classical correctness requirement for reactive synthesis, while the latter represents the optimistic linear-time property that both assumptions and guarantees hold along a trace of the system. As generators for cooperation level specifications, we consider all rules from the grammar in Eq. 1 except for the second one, as it is rather weak, and only considers what can happen from the initial state of a system onwards. Additionally, leaving out the conjuncts of the form $\langle E \rangle \varphi$ strengthens the semantic foundation for our *maximally cooperative synthesis* approach in Sect. 5.2. However, we discuss the consideration of conjuncts of the form $\langle E \rangle \varphi$ in Sect. 4.3.

Combining all four linear-time properties with the two chosen ways of lifting a linear-time property to our logic gives the following different conjuncts for cooperation level specifications:

$$
D = \{\mathcal{A} \to \mathcal{G}, \mathcal{G}, \mathcal{A}, \mathsf{G}\langle E \rangle (\mathcal{A} \wedge \mathcal{G}), \mathsf{G}\langle E \rangle \mathcal{G}, \mathsf{G}\langle E \rangle \mathcal{A}, \mathsf{G}\langle E \rangle (\mathcal{A} \to \mathcal{G})\} \tag{2}
$$

A *cooperation level specification* is a conjunction between elements from this set. So there are $2^7 = 128$ possible cooperation levels in this setting. Note that we removed the linear-time property $\mathcal{A} \wedge \mathcal{G}$ from D, as it can be simulated by a conjunction between $\mathcal{A}$ and $\mathcal{G}$ on the level of cooperation level specifications.

We can reduce the 128 possible cooperation levels substantially by using our knowledge of the semantics of cooperation level specifications, which can be expressed in *reduction rules*. For example, if in a cooperation level specification, for some linear-time property $\varphi \in \{\mathcal{A}, \mathcal{G}, \mathcal{A} \to \mathcal{G}, \mathcal{A} \wedge \mathcal{G}\}$, φ is a conjunct along with $\mathsf{G}\langle E\rangle\varphi$, then we can remove the latter from the cooperation level specification as that conjunct is implied by the former. This is because if along every trace of a computation tree, φ holds, then for every node in the tree, we can find a trace containing the node along with φ holds. In a similar fashion, we can observe

- that $\mathcal{G}$ implies $\mathcal{A} \to \mathcal{G}$,
- that $\mathsf{G}\langle E\rangle(\mathcal{A} \wedge \mathcal{G})$ implies $\mathsf{G}\langle E\rangle\mathcal{A}$ and $\mathsf{G}\langle E\rangle\mathcal{G}$,
- that $\mathsf{G}\langle E\rangle\mathcal{G}$ implies $\mathsf{G}\langle E\rangle(\mathcal{A} \to \mathcal{G})$,
- that $\mathcal{A} \to \mathcal{G}$ and $\mathcal{A}$ together imply $\mathcal{G}$, and
- that $\mathcal{A} \to \mathcal{G}$ and $\mathsf{G}\langle E\rangle\mathcal{A}$ together imply $\mathsf{G}\langle E\rangle(\mathcal{A} \wedge \mathcal{G})$,
- that $\mathcal{A}$ and $\mathsf{G}\langle E\rangle\mathcal{G}$ together imply $\mathsf{G}\langle E\rangle(\mathcal{A} \wedge \mathcal{G})$,
- that $\mathsf{G}\langle E\rangle(\mathcal{A} \to \mathcal{G})$ and $\mathcal{A}$ together imply $\mathsf{G}\langle E\rangle(\mathcal{G})$.

Only in the last three of these *rules*, conjuncts of the forms $\mathsf{G}\langle E\rangle\varphi$ and φ interact. For example, if $\mathcal{A} \to \mathcal{G}$ holds along all traces of a computation tree, and we know that through every node in the tree, there is a trace on which $\mathcal{A}$ holds, then along this trace, $\mathcal{A} \wedge \mathcal{G}$ holds as well. Thus, we also know that the computation tree satisfies $\mathsf{G}\langle E\rangle(\mathcal{A} \wedge \mathcal{G})$. Note that $\mathsf{G}\langle E\rangle(\mathcal{A} \wedge \mathcal{G})$ is not equal to $\mathsf{G}\langle E\rangle(\mathcal{G}) \wedge \mathsf{G}\langle E\rangle(\mathcal{A})$ because there exist computation trees for which a part of their traces satisfy $\mathcal{A} \wedge \neg\mathcal{G}$, the other traces satisfy $\mathcal{G} \wedge \neg\mathcal{A}$, but none of their traces satisfy $\mathcal{A} \wedge \mathcal{G}$.

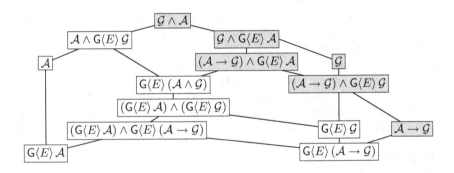

Fig. 1. A Hasse diagram of the hierarchy of cooperation levels.

After reducing the set of distinct cooperation levels by these reduction rules, we obtain only 15 semantically different subsets of D, which form a lattice with its partial order defined by implication. We leave out the **true** element of the lattice in the following (as it is trivially satisfied by all computation trees), and visualize the remaining cooperation levels hierarchically in Fig. 1. For every cooperation level, implied elements of D have also been left out in the vertex labeling.

Every edge in the figure denotes a "stricter than"-relation, with the upper element being the stricter one. Vertices that enforce the traditional correctness criterion $\mathcal{A} \to \mathcal{G}$ are colored in gray.

In the next section, we discuss the different levels of the cooperation hierarchy in an example. After that, we will discuss design decisions that we made when constructing the hierarchy, as well as extensions and alternatives.

4.2   Example

This section presents an example from real life to illustrate some cooperation levels from Fig. 1. A more extensive example is given in the extended version of this paper [7].

An IT provider makes a contract with a customer. The provider promises that whenever the computer breaks, it will eventually deliver a new computer, or one of its technicians will come to the customer to fix the computer while providing some free printing supplies as a bonus. The customer accepts the conditions, mainly because of the possibility of free printing supplies. The contract between the customer and the IT provider contains the following assumptions under which it has to be fullfilled: (1) every traffic blockade on the way to the customer is eventually cleared, and (2) if the road to the customer is clear and the IT provider technician is working on the computer, then it will eventually be fixed. The latter assumption is part of the contract to exclude problems with the customer's software, which is not the responsibility of the IT provider. By simply replacing parts of the computer one-by-one, the problem is eventually fixed. We also have an additional assumption that traffic can be blocked on purpose by the IT provider, which is not written into the contract.

We model the setting with two Boolean input variables c, b and four Boolean output variables t, d, m, n for the IT service provider's behavior. Variable c is true if the computer is currently working, b is true when the traffic is not blocked, $f = $ true indicates that the IT provider's technician is trying to fix the computer, $m = $ true means that free printing supplies are delivered, $n = $ true means that the IT service provider delivers a new computer, and $d = $ true means that the provider currently blocks the traffic on purpose. In LTL syntax[1], the guarantee can be written as $\mathcal{G} = \mathsf{G}\big(\neg c \to \mathsf{F}(n \vee (c \wedge m))\big)$. The assumptions can be formalized as $\mathcal{A} = \mathsf{G}(\mathsf{F}b) \wedge \mathsf{G}\big((b \wedge f) \to \mathsf{F}c\big) \wedge \mathsf{G}(d \to \neg b)$.

The following table summarizes some cooperation levels that can be achieved with different behavior of the IT provider, each expressed as an LTL property whose fulfillment completely determines the valuation of the output variables in all time steps. We focus on levels that enforce $\mathcal{A} \to \mathcal{G}$ (which are colored gray in Fig. 1).

Behavior 1 enforces an assumption violation by blocking the traffic. This is very uncooperative with the customers (and all other drivers on the streets). In this case, $\mathsf{G}\langle E \rangle \mathcal{A}$ does not hold as the environment cannot satisfy $\mathcal{A}$ from any point in any trace because it cannot set b to true at some point without violating

---

[1] In LTL syntax, G means "always" and F means "eventually".

Nr	Behavior	Level in Fig. 1
1	$\mathsf{G}(d \wedge \neg f \wedge \neg m \wedge \neg n)$	$\mathcal{A} \to \mathcal{G}$
2	$\mathsf{G}(d \wedge m \wedge \neg f \wedge \neg n)$	$(\mathcal{A} \to \mathcal{G}) \wedge \mathsf{G}\langle E\rangle\mathcal{G}$
3	$\mathsf{G}(f \wedge m \wedge \neg n \wedge \neg d)$	$(\mathcal{A} \to \mathcal{G}) \wedge \mathsf{G}\langle E\rangle\mathcal{A}$
4	$\mathsf{G}(n \wedge d \wedge \neg f \wedge \neg m)$	$\mathcal{G}$
5	$\mathsf{G}(n \wedge \neg d \wedge \neg f \wedge \neg m)$	$\mathcal{G} \wedge \mathsf{G}\langle E\rangle\mathcal{A}$

$\mathcal{A}$, but not ever doing so violates $\mathcal{A}$ as well. The cooperation level specification part $\mathsf{G}\langle E\rangle\mathcal{G}$ does not hold either because since n and m are both false all of the time, $\mathcal{G}$ is not fulfilled along any trace.

Behavior 2 is better because printing supplies are always delivered. This satisfies $\mathsf{G}\langle E\rangle\mathcal{G}$ because, at any point, the environment can make the computer work again (which occasionally happens with computers). $\mathsf{G}\langle E\rangle\mathcal{A}$ is still not satisfied for the same reason as before.

Behavior 3 is even less destructive. The technician tries to fix the computer ($f = \mathsf{true}$) and brings along free printing supplies ($m = \mathsf{true}$) without blocking traffic. This satisfies the guarantees if the assumptions are satisfied. On top of that, the assumptions can always be satisfied by setting both b and c to true. Since d is always false, the last assumption (which was the problem before) always holds.

Behavior 4 is better than Behavior 2 but incomparable with Behavior 3. By always (or repeatedly) providing a new computer, $\mathcal{G}$ is enforced independent of the assumptions. However, $\mathsf{G}\langle E\rangle\mathcal{A}$ does not hold because, since the traffic is blocked ($d = \mathsf{true}$), the assumptions cannot hold.

Behavior 5 is similar but without enforcing a traffic blockade. It thus satisfies $\mathcal{G}$ and $\mathsf{G}\langle E\rangle\mathcal{A}$ simultaneously. The last two of the four assumptions are even enforced. However, since the first assumption cannot be enforced by any behavior of the IT provider, $\mathcal{G} \wedge \mathcal{A}$ cannot be achieved.

4.3   Discussion

Before solving the *cooperative synthesis* problem in the next section, let us discuss some interesting aspects of our hierarchy of cooperation levels.

Incomparable Levels: As already discussed in the example, our hierarchy of cooperation levels in Fig. 1 contains levels that are incomparable, i.e., where neither of the levels is stricter or clearly more desirable. The relative preferences between such levels may depend on the application. Among the levels that enforce $\mathcal{A} \to \mathcal{G}$ (gray in Fig. 1), there is only one incomparability, namely between $\mathcal{G}$ and $(\mathcal{A} \to \mathcal{G}) \wedge \mathsf{G}\langle E\rangle\mathcal{A}$. The former favors the guarantees, the latter the assumptions. For incomparabilities between a level that enforces $\mathcal{A} \to \mathcal{G}$ and one that does not, we suggest to prefer the former unless there are good reasons not to.

Symmetry in Fig. 1: Our hierarchy is asymmetric because we included $\mathcal{A} \to \mathcal{G}$ but not $\mathcal{G} \to \mathcal{A}$ in D. Including $\mathcal{A} \to \mathcal{G}$ contradicts the philosophy of cooperation to some extend, but is justified by the fact that we always take the point of view of the system in this paper, and try to synthesize a *correct implementation* that also helps the environment to satisfy its assumptions whenever this is reasonable, but without assuming that the environment has its own goals and behaves *rationally* (as in [3,10–12,18]). The guarantees often cannot be enforced unconditionally by the system, so the system has to rely on the assumptions to hold. However, the combination of $\mathcal{A} \to \mathcal{G}$ with $\mathsf{G}\langle E\rangle\mathcal{A}$ (or $\mathsf{G}\langle E\rangle\mathcal{G}$) in a cooperation level specification eliminates the possibility for the system to achieve correctness by simply enforcing a violation of $\mathcal{A}$ (and $\mathcal{G}$).

Additional Operators: We did not include any properties with a plain $\langle E\rangle$-operator in our default hierarchy. The reason is that $\langle E\rangle\varphi$ is quite a weak goal. The system could have exactly one trace on which φ is satisfied. As soon as the environment deviates from the input along this trace, the system can behave arbitrarily. Our default hierarchy also does not contain any occurrences of $\mathcal{A}\vee\mathcal{G}$, but this is mainly to keep the presentation simple. Including $\mathcal{A}\vee\mathcal{G}$ and $\mathsf{G}\langle E\rangle(\mathcal{A}\vee\mathcal{G})$ would extend the hierarchy to 23 levels. Additionally including $\langle E\rangle$ wherever $\mathsf{G}\langle E\rangle$ is applied results in 77 levels. Thus, even with extensions in the applied operators, the size of our hierarchy remains manageable. Details to these refined hierarchies and the reduction rules to obtain them can be found in the appendix of [7].

Fine-Grainedness: Our hierarchy considers two dimensions: the goals (in terms of assumptions and guarantees) to achieve, and the certainty with which the goal can be achieved: enforced, always reachable ($\mathsf{G}\langle E\rangle$), and initially reachable ($\langle E\rangle$, if considered). In contrast, most existing synthesis approaches [4,5,16] (see Sect. 2) that go beyond plain correctness only focus on *enforcing* a maximum in the dimension of goals. Yet, in this dimension they are often more fine-grained, e.g., by considering individual assumptions and guarantees or how often some property is violated. In principle, we could also increase the granularity in our goal dimension. However, this also comes at a price: it would increase the size of the hierarchy and induce more incomparabilities, which makes it more difficult to define the preference between the incomparable levels for a concrete application.

5 Synthesizing Desirable Systems

After defining our hierarchy of cooperation levels, we turn towards the synthesis of implementations that maximize the possible cooperation level. We start by describing how we can synthesize an implementation for a single cooperation level, and then show in Sect. 5.2 how to synthesize *maximally cooperative implementations*, which move upwards in the cooperation level hierarchy whenever possible during the execution.

5.1 Implementing a Single Cooperation Level

The simple reduction of the cooperative synthesis problem for LTL to synthesis from a logic such as *strategy logic* [13] is obstructed by the fact that in our semantics, we always analyze traces from the start when evaluating a subformula of the shape $G\langle E\rangle\varphi$. Strategy logic lacks a *rewind* operator that would allow to jump back to the start of a trace. We could, however, encode a cooperation level specification into CTL* with linear past [9], and use a corresponding synthesis procedure.

Instead of following this route, we give a direct automata-theoretic approach to the synthesis of reactive systems that implement some level of cooperation with the environment on a specification $(\mathcal{A}, \mathcal{G})$. The automata built in our approach keep information about the states of the assumptions and guarantees explicit, which is needed to synthesize maximally cooperative implementations in the next subsection. Also, it makes the synthesis approach applicable to general ω-regular word language specifications.

Starting from the linear-time properties $\mathcal{A}$ and $\mathcal{G}$, we show how to build a non-deterministic Rabin tree automaton that encodes the synthesis problem for some cooperation level specification H. Such a tree automaton can be checked for language emptiness in order to perform synthesis for one level of cooperation.

Let $\mathcal{R}_{\mathcal{A}}$, $\mathcal{R}_{\mathcal{G}}$, $\mathcal{R}_{\mathcal{A}\rightarrow\mathcal{G}}$, and $\mathcal{R}_{\mathcal{A}\wedge\mathcal{G}}$ be deterministic Rabin word automata that encode $\mathcal{A}$, $\mathcal{G}$, $\mathcal{A} \rightarrow \mathcal{G}$, and $\mathcal{A}\wedge\mathcal{G}$. We translate the conjuncts (elements of D from Eq. 2) of some expression H in the grammar from Eq. 1 to non-deterministic Rabin tree automata $\mathcal{T}^D$ individually and then build the product $\mathcal{T}^H$ between these tree automata, which encodes that all elements of H have to be satisfied in a candidate computation tree. As cooperation level specifications have only three types of conjuncts, namely φ, $\langle E\rangle\varphi$, and $G\langle E\rangle\varphi$ for some linear-time property φ, we simply give the translations for these types separately.

Case φ: If φ is a linear-time property, the occurrence of φ in a cooperation level specification indicates that φ should hold on every trace of a synthesized implementation. Translating $\mathcal{R}_\varphi = (Q, \mathcal{I}\times\mathcal{O}, \delta, q_0, \mathcal{F})$ to a Rabin tree automaton $\mathcal{T}^D = (Q, \mathcal{I}, \mathcal{O}, \delta', q_0, \mathcal{F})$ that enforces φ to hold along all traces in the tree is a standard construction, where we set:

$$\forall q \in Q, o \in \mathcal{O} : \delta'(q, o) = \{\{i \mapsto \delta(q, (i, o)) \mid i \in \mathcal{I}\}\}$$

Case $\langle E\rangle\varphi$: Here, we require the synthesized system to offer one path along which φ holds. In the tree automaton, we non-deterministically choose this path. Starting with $\mathcal{R}_\varphi = (Q, \mathcal{I}\times\mathcal{O}, \delta, q_0, \mathcal{F})$, we obtain $\mathcal{T}^D = (Q, \mathcal{I}, \mathcal{O}, \delta', q_0, \mathcal{F})$ with:

$$\forall q \in Q, o \in \mathcal{O} : \delta'(q, o) = \bigcup_{i\in\mathcal{I}}\{\{i \mapsto \delta(q, (i, o))\} \cup \{i' \mapsto \top \mid i' \in \mathcal{I}, i' \neq i\}\}$$

Case $G\langle E\rangle\varphi$: In this case, for every node in a computation tree, we require the synthesized system to have a path on which φ holds that includes the selected node. Given $\mathcal{R}_\varphi = (Q, \mathcal{I} \times \mathcal{O}, \delta, q_0, \mathcal{F})$, we can implement this requirement as a non-deterministic Rabin tree automaton $\mathcal{T}^D = (Q', \mathcal{I}, \mathcal{O}, \delta', q_0', \mathcal{F}')$ with:

$$Q' = Q \times \mathbb{B}$$

$$\forall (q,b) \in Q', o \in \mathcal{O} : \delta'((q,b),o) = \bigcup_{i \in \mathcal{I}} \{\{i \mapsto (\delta(q,(i,o)), \text{true})\}$$

$$\cup \{i' \mapsto (\delta(q,(i',o)), \text{false}) \mid i' \in \mathcal{I}, i' \neq i\}\}$$

$$q_0' = (q_0, \text{true})$$

$$\mathcal{F}' = \{(F \times \{\text{true}\}, G \times \{\text{true}\}) \mid (F,G) \in \mathcal{F}\}$$

$$\cup \{(\emptyset, Q \times \{\text{false}\})\}$$

The automaton augments the states in Q by a Boolean flag. From every node in a computation tree accepted by $\mathcal{T}^D$, regardless of whether it is flagged by true or false, there must exist a branch consisting only of true-labeled nodes. The original acceptance condition $\mathcal{F}$ must hold along this branch. However, not all branches of a tree accepted by $\mathcal{T}^D$ have to satisfy φ, as those branches along which the flag is false infinitely often are trivially accepting. Intuitively, $\mathcal{T}^D$ also enforces the safety hull of φ along all branches in the computation tree as once a bad prefix has been seen on the way to a computation tree node, there cannot exist a branch containing the node along which φ holds, which is enforced by the (required) successor branch that is always labeled by true.

In order to obtain a non-deterministic Rabin tree automaton $\mathcal{T}^H$ for a complete cooperation level specification H, we can compute a product automaton from the Rabin tree automata $\mathcal{T}^D$ for the individual conjuncts. Computing such a product automaton is a standard operation in automata theory. Given a set $\{(Q_1, \mathcal{I}, \mathcal{O}, \delta_1, q_{0,1}, \mathcal{F}_1), \ldots, (Q_n, \mathcal{I}, \mathcal{O}, \delta_n, q_{0,n}, \mathcal{F}_n)\}$ of non-deterministic Rabin tree automata, their product is defined as the non-deterministic Rabin tree automaton $\mathcal{T}^H = (Q, \mathcal{I}, \mathcal{O}, \delta, q_0, \mathcal{F})$ with:

$$Q = Q_1 \times \ldots \times Q_n$$

$$\delta((q_1, \ldots, q_n), o) = \bigotimes_{i \in \{1, \ldots, n\}} \delta_i(q_i, o)$$

$$q_0 = (q_{0,1}, \ldots, q_{0,n})$$

$$\mathcal{F} = \{(F_1 \times \ldots \times F_n, G_1 \times \ldots \times G_n) \mid$$

$$(F_1, G_1) \in \mathcal{F}_1, \ldots, (F_n, G_n) \in \mathcal{F}_n\}$$

The second line of this equation holds for all $(q_1, \ldots, q_n) \in Q$ and $o \in \mathcal{O}$. Also, we used the special operator $\bigotimes$ that maps sets $\{M_i \subseteq 2^{Q_i \to \mathcal{I}}\}_{j \in \{1, \ldots, n\}}$ to the set

$$\{\{((q_1, \ldots, q_n), i) \in Q \times \mathcal{I} \mid \bigwedge_{j \in \{1, \ldots, n\}} f_j(i) = q_j\} \mid f_1 \in M_1, \ldots, f_n \in M_n\}$$

By performing reactive synthesis using the product Rabin tree automaton as specification, we can obtain an implementation that falls into the chosen cooperation level.

5.2 Maximally Cooperative Synthesis

For linear-time specifications $\mathcal{A}$ and $\mathcal{G}$, there are typically some cooperation level specifications that are not realizable (such as $\mathcal{A} \wedge \mathcal{G}$) and some that are realizable (such as $G\langle E\rangle(\mathcal{A} \to \mathcal{G})$). By iterating over all cooperation level specifications and applying reactive synthesis for the product Rabin tree automata T' computed by the construction from above, we can check which is the highest cooperation level that can be realized and compute a respective implementation.

In some cases, there may however be the possibility to switch to a higher level of cooperation during the system's execution. Take for example the case that initially, the cooperation level $G\langle E\rangle\mathcal{A} \wedge (\mathcal{A} \to \mathcal{G})$ is not realizable, but $(\mathcal{A} \to \mathcal{G})$ is. This may be the case if $\mathcal{A}$ represents the constraint that the environment has to perform a certain finite sequence of actions in reaction to the system's output, which is representable as a safety property. If the actions are triggered by the system, then the system cannot ensure that the environment succeeds with performing them correctly, hence violating $\mathcal{A}$. If $\mathcal{A} \to \mathcal{G}$ can only be realized by the system by triggering these actions at least once, then after these actions have been performed by the environment, the cooperation level specification $G\langle E\rangle\mathcal{A} \wedge (\mathcal{A} \to \mathcal{G})$ can however be enforced by the system by not triggering them again.

This observation motivates the search for *maximally cooperative implementations*, which at any point in time realize the highest possible cooperation level. Before describing how to synthesize such implementations, let us first formally define what this means.

When determining the cooperation level during the execution of a system, we only look at the part of its computation tree that is consistent with the input obtained from the environment so far. Given a computation tree $\langle T, \tau\rangle$ and the input part of a prefix trace $w^{\mathcal{I}} = w_0^{\mathcal{I}} w_1^{\mathcal{I}} \ldots w_n^{\mathcal{I}} \in \mathcal{I}^*$, we define the *bobble tree* [14] of $\langle T, \tau\rangle$ for $w^{\mathcal{I}}$ to be the tree $\langle T', \tau'\rangle$, where $T' = \{\epsilon\} \cup \{w_0^{\mathcal{I}} w_1^{\mathcal{I}} \ldots w_k^{\mathcal{I}} \mid k \leq n\} \cup \{w^{\mathcal{I}} t \mid t \in \mathcal{I}^*\}$, and $\tau'(t) = \tau(t)$ for all $t \in T'$. We call $w^{\mathcal{I}}$ the split node of $\langle T', \tau'\rangle$ and $(\tau(\epsilon), w_0^{\mathcal{I}})(\tau(w_0^{\mathcal{I}}), w_1^{\mathcal{I}}) \ldots (\tau(w_0^{\mathcal{I}} \ldots w_{n-1}^{\mathcal{I}}), w_n^{\mathcal{I}})$ the *split word* of $\langle T', \tau'\rangle$. Intuitively, the bobble tree has a single path to the split node $w^{\mathcal{I}}$ and is full from that point onwards. Cutting a full computation tree into a bobble tree does not reduce the cooperation level that the tree fulfills for the specification types in the classes that we can built from the conjuncts in D (from Eq. 2):

Lemma 1. *Let $\langle T, \tau\rangle$ be a computation tree and $\langle T', \tau'\rangle$ be a bobble tree built from $\langle T, \tau\rangle$. If for some cooperation level specification H consisting of conjuncts in D, we have that $\langle T, \tau\rangle$ fulfills H, then $\langle T', \tau'\rangle$ also fulfills H.*

Proof. Proof by induction over the structure of H, using the semantics given on page 5. All conjuncts in D have an outermost universal quantification over the elements in $L(\langle T, \tau\rangle)$. Reducing the number of elements in $L(\langle T, \tau\rangle)$ does not make these constraints harder to fulfill.

Bobble trees provide us with a semantical basis for switching between cooperation levels: if a reactive system $\langle T, \tau\rangle$ for a cooperation level H executes, and after some prefix trace w, there exists a bobble tree with split word w that allows a strictly higher cooperation level H', then it makes sense to continue the execution of the system according to cooperation level H'. We thus define:

Definition 1. *Let* $(\mathcal{A}, \mathcal{G})$ *be a linear-time specification. We call a computation tree* $\langle T, \tau \rangle$ *maximally cooperative if for every split node* $t \in T$*, the bobble tree induced by* t *and* $\langle T, \tau \rangle$ *implements a highest possible cooperation level for* $\mathcal{A}$ *and* $\mathcal{G}$ *among the bobble trees with the same split word.*

Note that since for some bobble tree, there may be multiple highest cooperation levels, it makes sense to define a preference order for the cooperation level specifications, so that when synthesizing an implementation, the implementation can always pick the most desired one when the possibility to move up in the hierarchy arises.

In order to synthesize maximally cooperative implementations, we first need a way to check, for every split word, for the existence of a bobble tree for cooperation level specifications. The special structure of the tree automata $\mathcal{T}^H$ built according to the construction in Sect. 5.1 offers such a way.

Definition 2. *Let* $\mathcal{T}^H = (Q, \mathcal{I}, \mathcal{O}, \delta, q_0, \mathcal{F})$ *be a non-deterministic tree automaton for a cooperation level specification built according to the (product) construction from Sect. 5.1. We have that* Q *is of the shape* $C_1 \times \ldots \times C_n$*, where for every* $i \in \{1, \ldots, n\}$*, we either have* $C_i = Q'$ *or* $C_i = Q' \times \mathbb{B}$ *for some Rabin word automaton state set* Q'*. For a state* $q = (c_1, \ldots, c_n) \in Q$*, we define* $unpack(q) = unpack(c_1) \cup \ldots \cup unpack(c_n)$*, where we concretize* $unpack(q') = q'$ *and* $unpack((q', b)) = q'$ *for some word automaton state* $q' \in Q'$ *and* $b \in \mathbb{B}$*.*

Lemma 2. *Let* $\mathcal{T}^H$ *be a tree automaton built according to the (product) construction from Sect. 5.1 from a cooperation level specification with conjuncts in* D *over the linear-time specifications* $\mathcal{A}$*,* $\mathcal{G}$*,* $\mathcal{A} \to \mathcal{G}$*, and* $\mathcal{A} \wedge \mathcal{G}$*. Let those linear-time specifications be represented by Rabin word automata with the state sets* $Q_{\mathcal{A}}$*,* $Q_{\mathcal{G}}$*,* $Q_{\mathcal{A} \to \mathcal{G}}$*, and* $Q_{\mathcal{A} \wedge \mathcal{G}}$*, respectively. Without loss of generality, let these state sets be disjoint. We have that:*

1. *For all reachable states* q *in* $\mathcal{T}^H$*, there is at most one state in* $unpack(q)$ *from each of* $Q_{\mathcal{A}}$*,* $Q_{\mathcal{G}}$*,* $Q_{\mathcal{A} \to \mathcal{G}}$*, and* $Q_{\mathcal{A} \wedge \mathcal{G}}$*.*
2. *All states in* $\mathcal{T}^H$ *with the same set* $unpack(q)$ *have the same languages.*

Proof. The first claim follows directly from the constructions from Sect. 5.1: for every state in the individual Rabin tree automata $\mathcal{T}^D$ built from cooperation level specification conjuncts of the shapes $\mathsf{G}\langle E \rangle \varphi$ and φ, the automata always track the state of the corresponding word automata for a branch of the tree.

For the second claim, we decompose the states in $\mathcal{T}^H$ into their factors and prove the claim for each factor individually. For factors originating from cooperation level specifications of the shape φ for some linear-time property φ, this fact is trivial. For factors originating from specification conjuncts of the shape $\mathsf{G}\langle E \rangle \varphi$, the claim follows from the fact that the tree automaton states that only differ in their Boolean flag have the same successor state functions.

Lemma 2 tells us how we can switch between cooperation levels. Assume that we can always read off *all* current states of $Q_{\mathcal{A}}$, $Q_{\mathcal{G}}$, $Q_{\mathcal{A} \to \mathcal{G}}$, and $Q_{\mathcal{A} \wedge \mathcal{G}}$ from $unpack(q)$ for any state q of a product tree automaton $\mathcal{T}^H$. This assumption can be made satisfied by letting T^H be the product of *all* elements in the set of considered cooperation level specification conjuncts D, but only using the ones in the current cooperation level H when building the acceptance condition of T^H. Now consider a second cooperation level specification H' that is higher in the hierarchy than H and its associated tree automaton $T^{H'}$. Let W be the states in T^H with a non-empty language and W' be the states of $T^{H'}$ with a non-empty language. If we find a state q' in $T^{H'}$ for which $unpack(q') = unpack(q)$, and state q' has a non-empty language, then we can simply re-route every transition to q to q' and obtain a new tree automaton with the states in T^H and $T^{H'}$ that enforces a higher cooperation level on a bobble tree along all branches in run trees that lead to q. If we now identify the non-empty tree automaton states for all cooperation level specifications in our hierarchy, and apply this approach to all pairs of the corresponding tree automata and all of their states, we end up with a tree automaton that accepts maximally cooperative computation trees. More formally, this line of reasoning shows the correctness of the following construction:

Definition 3. *Let $H_1, \ldots, H_{14}$ be the cooperation level specifications of our hierarchy, ordered by preference and respecting the hierarchy's partial order $\leq_H$, and let $T_1^H, \ldots, T_{14}^H$ be the non-deterministic Rabin tree automata for them. Let us furthermore rename states q in an automaton T_j^H to (q, j) to make their names unique, and let every tree automaton T_j^H be given as a tuple $(Q_j, \mathcal{I}, \mathcal{O}, \delta_j, q_{0,j}, \mathcal{F}_j)$. Let $W \subseteq \bigcup_j Q_j$ be the states in the tree automata with a non-empty language. We define the Rabin tree automaton $T = (Q', \mathcal{I}, \mathcal{O}, \delta', q_0', \mathcal{F}')$ encoding the maximally cooperative synthesis problem as follows:*

$$Q' = \bigcup_{j \in \{1, \ldots, 14\}} Q_j$$

$$q_0' = q_{0,j} \quad for \quad j = \max\{j \in \{1, \ldots, 14\} \mid q_{0,j} \in W\}$$

$$\mathcal{F}' = \mathcal{F}_1 \cup \ldots \cup \mathcal{F}_{14}$$

$$\delta'((q, j), o) = \{\{i \mapsto (q'', j') \mid j' = \max\{k \in \{1, \ldots, 14\} \mid \exists (q'', k) \in Q_k :$$
$$(q'', k) \in W, unpack(q'') = unpack(f(i)), H_j \leq_H H_k\},$$
$$unpack(q'') = unpack(f(i)),$$
$$((j = j') \rightarrow q'' = f(i))\} \mid f \in \delta_j(q, o)\}$$
$$for \ all \ (q, j) \in Q' \ and \ o \in \mathcal{O}$$

Theorem 1. *A Rabin tree automaton built from linear-time specifications $\mathcal{A}$ and $\mathcal{G}$ according to Definition 3 encodes the maximally cooperative synthesis problem for the specification $(\mathcal{A}, \mathcal{G})$. Building the tree automaton and checking it for emptiness can be performed in doubly-exponential time for specifications in LTL.*

For specifications given as deterministic Rabin word automata, the time complexity is polynomial in the number of states and exponential in the number of acceptance pairs.

Proof. For the correctness, note that the tree automaton can switch between cooperation levels only finitely often, and whenever it switches, it only does so to strictly higher levels of cooperation.

To obtain doubly-exponential time complexity of maximally cooperative synthesis from LTL specifications, we first translate $\mathcal{A}$, $\mathcal{G}$, $\mathcal{A} \rightarrow \mathcal{G}$, and $\mathcal{A} \land \mathcal{G}$ to deterministic Rabin word automata with a doubly-exponential number of states and a singly-exponential number of acceptance condition pairs, which takes doubly-exponential time. The overall sizes of the tree automata build for the cooperation levels are then polynomial in the sizes of the Rabin word automata. We can compute W in time exponential in the number of acceptance pairs and polynomial in the number of tree automaton states, which sums up to doubly-exponential time (in the lengths of $\mathcal{A}$ and $\mathcal{G}$) for LTL. When building $\mathcal{T}$ and computing the accepted computation tree, the same argument applies. If the specification is given in form of deterministic Rabin word automata, then all the product automata computed in the process have a number of states that is polynomial in the number of states of the input automata and a number of acceptance pairs that is polynomial in the number of acceptance pairs of the input automata. By the complexity of checking Rabin tree automata for emptiness and computing W, the second claim follows as well.

Theorem 1 states that synthesizing maximally cooperative implementations from LTL specifications does not have a higher complexity than LTL synthesis in general. Note, however, that both the synthesis time and the size of the resulting systems can increase in practice as the Rabin automata built in cooperative synthesis are larger than in standard LTL synthesis.

Also note that we can extend the theory from this subsection to also include cooperation level specification conjuncts of the shape $\langle E \rangle \varphi$. However, we would need to add flags to the tree automata to keep track of whether the current branch in a computation tree is the one on which φ should hold. As these flags need to be tracked along changes between the cooperation levels, the definitions from this subsection would become substantially more complicated. Thus, we refrained from doing so here.

6   Conclusion

Conventional synthesis algorithms often produce systems that actively work towards violating environment assumptions rather than satisfying assumptions and guarantees together. In this paper, we worked out a fine-grained hierarchy of cooperation levels between the system and the environment for satisfying both guarantees *and* assumptions as far as possible. We also presented a synthesis procedure that maximizes the cooperation level in the hierarchy for linear-time specifications, such as Linear Temporal Logic (LTL). The worst-case complexity of this procedure for LTL is the same as of conventional LTL synthesis. Our approach relieves the user from requiring cooperation in the specification explicitly, which helps to keep the specification clean and abstract.

In the future, we plan to work out cooperative synthesis procedures for other specification languages, and evaluate the results on industrial applications.

References

1. Almagor, S., Boker, U., Kupferman, O.: Formalizing and reasoning about quality. In: Fomin, F.V., Freivalds, R., Kwiatkowska, M., Peleg, D. (eds.) ICALP 2013, Part II. LNCS, vol. 7966, pp. 15–27. Springer, Heidelberg (2013)
2. Alur, R., Henzinger, T.A., Kupferman, O.: Alternating-time temporal logic. J. ACM **49**(5), 672–713 (2002)
3. Berwanger, D.: Admissibility in infinite games. In: Thomas, W., Weil, P. (eds.) STACS 2007. LNCS, vol. 4393, pp. 188–199. Springer, Heidelberg (2007)
4. Bloem, R., Chatterjee, K., Greimel, K., Henzinger, T.A., Hofferek, G., Jobstmann, B., Könighofer, B., Könighofer, R.: Synthesizing robust systems. Acta Inf. **51**(3–4), 193–220 (2014)
5. Bloem, R., Chatterjee, K., Henzinger, T.A., Jobstmann, B.: Better quality in synthesis through quantitative objectives. In: Bouajjani, A., Maler, O. (eds.) *CAV* 2009. LNCS, vol. 5643, pp. 140–156. Springer, Heidelberg (2009)
6. Bloem, R., Ehlers, R., Jacobs, S., Könighofer, R.: How to handle assumptions in synthesis. In: SYNT, pp. 34–50 (2014)
7. Bloem, R., Ehlers, R., Könighofer, R.: Cooperative reactive synthesis. CoRR, abs/1507.02531 (2015) Accessed on http://arxiv.org/abs/1507.02531
8. Bloem, R., Jobstmann, B., Piterman, N., Pnueli, A., Sa'ar, Y.: Synthesis of reactive(1) designs. J. Comput. Syst. Sci. **78**(3), 911–938 (2012)
9. Droste, M., Quaas, K.: A kleene-schützenberger theorem for weighted timed automata. In: Amadio, R.M. (ed.) FOSSACS 2008. LNCS, vol. 4962, pp. 142–156. Springer, Heidelberg (2008)
10. Brenguier, R., Raskin, J.-F., Sassolas, M.: The complexity of admissibility in omega-regular games. In: CSL-LICS, p. 23 (2014)
11. Chatterjee, K., Doyen, L., Filiot, E., Raskin, J.-F.: Doomsday equilibria for omega-regular games. In: McMillan, K.L., Rival, X. (eds.) VMCAI 2014. LNCS, vol. 8318, pp. 78–97. Springer, Heidelberg (2014)
12. Chatterjee, K., Henzinger, T.A.: Assume-guarantee synthesis. In: Grumberg, O., Huth, M. (eds.) TACAS 2007. LNCS, vol. 4424, pp. 261–275. Springer, Heidelberg (2007)
13. Chatterjee, K., Henzinger, T.A., Piterman, N.: Strategy logic. Inf. Comput. **208**(6), 677–693 (2010)
14. Ehlers, R., Finkbeiner, B.: Monitoring realizability. In: Khurshid, S., Sen, K. (eds.) RV 2011. LNCS, vol. 7186, pp. 427–441. Springer, Heidelberg (2012)
15. Ehlers, R., Könighofer, R., Bloem, R.: Synthesizing cooperative reactive mission plans. In: IROS, IEEE (2015)
16. Ehlers, R., Topcu, U.: Resilience to intermittent assumption violations in reactive synthesis. In: HSCC, pp. 203–212 (2014)
17. Faella, M.: Admissible strategies in infinite games over graphs. In: Královič, R., Niwiński, D. (eds.) MFCS 2009. LNCS, vol. 5734, pp. 307–318. Springer, Heidelberg (2009)
18. Fisman, D., Kupferman, O., Lustig, Y.: Rational synthesis. In: Esparza, J., Majumdar, R. (eds.) TACAS 2010. LNCS, vol. 6015, pp. 190–204. Springer, Heidelberg (2010)
19. Pnueli, A., Rosner, R.: On the synthesis of a reactive module. In: POPL (1989)

Game Semantic Analysis of Equivalence in IMJ

Andrzej S. Murawski[1], Steven J. Ramsay[1], and Nikos Tzevelekos[2]($^{(\boxtimes)}$)

[1] University of Warwick, Coventry, UK
[2] Queen Mary University of London, London, UK
nikos.tzevelekos@qmul.ac.uk

Abstract. Using game semantics, we investigate the problem of verifying contextual equivalences in Interface Middleweight Java (IMJ), an imperative object calculus in which program phrases are typed using interfaces. Working in the setting where data types are non-recursive and restricted to finite domains, we identify the frontier between decidability and undecidability by reference to the structure of interfaces present in typing judgments. In particular, we show how to determine the decidability status of problem instances (over a fixed type signature) by examining the position of methods inside the term type and the types of its free identifiers. Our results build upon the recent fully abstract game semantics of IMJ. Decidability is proved by translation into visibly pushdown register automata over infinite alphabets with fresh-input recognition.

1 Introduction

Contextual equivalence is the problem of determining whether two (possibly open) program phrases behave equivalently when placed into any possible whole-program context. It is regarded as a gold standard for the identification of behaviours in programming language semantics and is a fundamental concern during refactoring and compiler optimisations. For example, it can be used to determine whether two implementations of an interface behave equivalently irrespective of who might interact with them.

In this work, we undertake an algorithmic study of contextual equivalence for Java-style objects through the imperative object calculus Interface Middleweight Java (IMJ). IMJ was introduced in [11] as a setting in which to capture the contextual interactions of code written in Middleweight Java [2]. Our aim is to isolate those features of the language, or collections of features taken together, that are so expressive that contextual equivalence becomes undecidable. By such a determination, not only do we gain insight into the power (or complexity) of the features, but also we are able to design *complementary* fragments for which we have *decision procedures*. The result of our study is the first classification of decidable cases for contextual equivalence in a core fragment of Java and, on the conceptual front, an exposition of the fundamental limits of automated verification in this setting.

We start delineating the decidable cases by eliminating two features that clearly make IMJ Turing-complete, namely, recursive types and infinite data

© Springer International Publishing Switzerland 2015
B. Finkbeiner et al. (Eds.): ATVA 2015, LNCS 9364, pp. 411–428, 2015.
DOI: 10.1007/978-3-319-24953-7_30

domains (e.g. unbounded Integers). Hence, our starting point is a *finitary* restriction of IMJ, in which these two features have been removed. Next we uncover two less obvious features that make termination undecidable (note that termination is a special case of contextual equivalence with **skip**): *storage of method-carrying objects in fields* and *unrestricted recursion*. We show that if either of these resources is available then it is possible to construct a program which simulates a queue machine. In contrast, if the storage of method-carrying objects is banned and recursion discarded in favour of iteration, we obtain a fragment with decidable termination. Consequently, we need to work with the iterative fragment in which storage of method-carrying objects is prohibited.

Returning to the general case of contextual equivalence, recall that it concerns program phrases which are not necessarily closed or of type void, which leads us to analyse the problem in terms of the result type and the kinds of free variables that may occur in the phrase. When we consider the free variables of a phrase, we find that equivalence is undecidable whenever the phrase relies on *a free variable that is an object whose method(s) accept method-carrying objects as parameters*, irrespective of the type of the phrase itself. When we consider the type of a program phrase, we find that undecidability is inevitable whenever the phrase:

1. *is an object whose method(s) return method-carrying objects*, or
2. *is an object whose method(s) require a parameter that is itself an object whose method(s) accept method-carrying objects as parameters*, irrespective of the free variables upon which the phrase depends.

In contrast, we prove that equivalence is decidable for the class of program phrases that avoid the three criteria. This class is constrained but it still remains a non-trivial object-oriented language: fields cannot store method-carrying objects, but objects with methods can be created at will. Inheritance and encapsulation are supported fully.

Both our undecidability and decidability arguments are enabled by the fully abstract game semantics of IMJ [11], which characterises contextual equivalence of IMJ program phrases by means of *strategies* (sets of interaction traces which capture the observable behaviour of a program). For undecidability, we observe that, in each of the three cases mentioned above, the patterns of interaction that arise between the phrase and the contexts with which it can be completed are expressive enough to encode the runs of a queue machine. On the other hand, to prove decidability, we show that (in the relevant cases) the corresponding strategies can be related to context-free languages over *infinite* alphabets. More precisely, we develop a routine which, starting from program phrases, can construct variants of pushdown register automata [12] that represent the associated game semantics. In this way, the problem is ultimately reduced to emptiness testing for this class of automata, which is known to be decidable.

Related Work. We believe we are the first to present a fully automated method for proving contextual equivalences in a Java-like setting, accompanied by a systematic analysis of decidable cases. Contextual equivalence is well known to pose a challenge to automated verification due to quantification over contexts.

The quest for obtaining more direct methods of attack on the problem in the Java setting has underpinned a great deal of semantic research, mainly using operational approaches [1,6–8,15], but this did not lead to decision procedures. In our case, the potential for automation stems from the compositionality of the underlying semantics, which allows for a compositional translation of terms into automata in the decidable cases. Previous work based on games-based verification was mainly concerned with various fragments of ML equipped with storage of ground-type values [5,10]. In contrast, in this paper we tackle richer interactions of objects equipped with methods. Compared with these fragments of ML, IMJ contexts are more discriminating, because objects provide a modicum of higher-order state. This motivates our independent study.

$$Types \ni \theta ::= \text{void} \mid \text{int} \mid I \qquad IDfns \ni \Theta ::= \epsilon \mid (\text{f} : \theta), \Theta \mid (\text{m} : \vec{\theta} \to \theta), \Theta$$

$$MImps \ni \mathcal{M} ::= \epsilon \mid (\text{m} : \lambda \vec{x}.M), \mathcal{M} \qquad ITbls \ni \Delta ::= \epsilon \mid (I \equiv \Theta), \Delta \mid (I\langle I \rangle \equiv \Theta), \Delta$$

$$Terms \ni M ::= x \mid \text{null} \mid a \mid i \mid \text{if } M \text{ then } M \text{ else } M \mid M \oplus M \mid M; M \mid (I)M \mid M = M$$

$$\mid M.\text{f} \mid M.\text{m}(\vec{M}) \mid \text{new}\{x : I; \mathcal{M}\} \mid M.\text{f} := M \mid \text{skip} \mid \text{let } x = M \text{ in } M \mid \text{while } M \text{ do } M$$

$$\frac{}{\Delta | \Gamma \vdash x : \theta} {(x:\theta) \in \Gamma} \qquad \frac{}{\Delta | \Gamma \vdash a : I} {(a:I) \in \Gamma} \qquad \frac{}{\Delta | \Gamma \vdash \text{skip} : \text{void}} \qquad \frac{}{\Delta | \Gamma \vdash \text{null} : I} {I \in \text{dom}(\Delta)}$$

$$\frac{i \in [0, \text{MAXINT}]}{\Delta | \Gamma \vdash i : \text{int}} \qquad \frac{\Delta | \Gamma \vdash M, M' : \text{int}}{\Delta | \Gamma \vdash M \oplus M' : \text{int}} \qquad \frac{\Delta | \Gamma \vdash M : \text{int} \quad \Delta | \Gamma \vdash M' : \text{void}}{\Delta | \Gamma \vdash \text{while } M \text{ do } M' : \text{void}}$$

$$\frac{\Delta | \Gamma \vdash M : \text{int} \quad \Delta | \Gamma \vdash M', M'' : \theta}{\Delta | \Gamma \vdash \text{if } M \text{ then } M' \text{ else } M'' : \theta} \qquad \frac{\bigwedge_{i=1}^{n}(\Delta | \Gamma \uplus \{\vec{x}_i : \vec{\theta}_i\} \vdash M_i : \theta_i)}{\Delta | \Gamma \vdash \mathcal{M} : \{\text{m}_i : \vec{\theta}_i \to \theta_i \mid 1 \le i \le n\}}$$

$$\frac{\Delta | \Gamma \vdash M, M' : I}{\Delta | \Gamma \vdash M = M' : \text{int}} \qquad \frac{\Delta | \Gamma \vdash M : \text{void} \quad \Delta | \Gamma \vdash M' : \theta}{\Delta | \Gamma \vdash M; M' : \theta} \qquad \frac{\Delta | \Gamma \vdash M : I \quad \Delta | \Gamma \vdash M' : \theta}{\Delta | \Gamma \vdash M.\text{f} := M' : \text{void}} {\Delta(I).\text{f} = \theta}$$

$$\frac{\Delta | \Gamma \vdash M : I}{\Delta | \Gamma \vdash M.\text{f} : \theta} {\Delta(I).\text{f} = \theta} \qquad \frac{\Delta | \Gamma \vdash M : I'}{\Delta | \Gamma \vdash (I)M : I} {\substack{\Delta \vdash I \le I' \\ \vee I' \le I}} \qquad \frac{\Delta | \Gamma, x : I \vdash \mathcal{M} : \Theta}{\Delta | \Gamma \vdash \text{new}\{x : I; \mathcal{M}\} : I} {\Delta(I) \upharpoonright Meths = \Theta}$$

$$\frac{\Delta | \Gamma \vdash M : I \quad \bigwedge_{i=1}^{n}(\Delta | \Gamma \vdash M_i : \theta_i)}{\Delta | \Gamma \vdash M.\text{m}(M_1, \cdots, M_n) : \theta} {\Delta(I).\text{m} = \vec{\theta} \to \theta} \qquad \frac{\Delta | \Gamma \vdash M : \theta' \quad \Delta | \Gamma, x : \theta' \vdash M' : \theta}{\Delta | \Gamma \vdash \text{let } x = M \text{ in } M' : \theta}$$

Fig. 1. Definition of IMJ$_f$. Typing rules for terms and method-set implementations.

2 Finitary IMJ

We work on Interface Middleweight Java (IMJ), an imperative object calculus based on Middleweight Java [2] which was introduced and examined game semantically in [11]. Here we examine the finitary restriction of IMJ which excludes recursive datatypes and unbounded integers. We call this fragment IMJ$_f$.

We let $\mathbb{A}$ be a countably infinite set of object **names**, which we range over by a and variants. Names will appear in most syntactic constructs and also in the game model and automata we will consider next. For any construction X

that may contain (finitely many) names, we define the **support** of X, denoted $\nu(X)$, to be the set of names occurring in X. Moreover, for any permutation $\pi : \mathbb{A} \xrightarrow{\cong} \mathbb{A}$, the **application** of π on X, written $\pi \cdot X$, to be the structure we obtain from X by transposing all names inside X according to π. Formally, the above are spelled out in terms of *nominal sets* [4].

For any pair of natural numbers $i \leq j$ we shall write $[i, j]$ for the set $\{i, i+1, \cdots j\}$. To rule out infinite data domains in IMJ_f we let integers range over $[0, \mathrm{MaxInt}]$, where MaxInt is some fixed natural number.

The definition of IMJ_f is given in Fig. 1. In more detail, we have the following components:

Intfs, *Flds* and *Meths* are sets of **interface, field** and **method identifiers** respectively. We range over interfaces by I, over fields by f and over methods by m. The types θ of IMJ_f are selected from *Types*. An **interface definition** Θ is a finite set of typed fields and methods. We require that each identifier f, m can appear at most once in each such definition.

An **interface table** Δ is a finite assignment of interface definitions to interface identifiers. We write $I\langle I' \rangle \equiv \Theta$ for interface extension: interface I extends I' with fields and methods from Θ. We require that each I can be defined at most once in Δ (i.e. there is at most one element of Δ of the form $I : \Theta$ or $I\langle I' \rangle \equiv \Theta$) and if $(I\langle I' \rangle \equiv \Theta) \in \Delta$ then $\mathsf{dom}(\Delta(I')) \cap \mathsf{dom}(\Theta) = \emptyset$. Thus, each Θ can be seen as a finite partial function $\Theta : (\textit{Flds} \cup \textit{Meths}) \rightharpoonup \textit{Types}^*$. We write Θ.f for $\Theta(\mathsf{f})$, and Θ.m for $\Theta(\mathsf{m})$. Similarly, Δ defines a partial function $\Delta : \textit{Intfs} \rightharpoonup \textit{IDfns}$. In IMJ_f there is a **recursive types restriction** by which recursive (and mutually recursive) definitions of interfaces are not allowed.

IMJ_f **terms** form the set *Terms*, where we let x range over a set *Vars* of *variables*. Moreover, "$\oplus$" is selected from some set of binary numeric operations which includes "$=$". Boolean guards are implemented using numbers, with false represented by 0 and true by any other number. $\mathcal{M}$ is a **method-set implementation** (we stipulate that each m appear at most once in each $\mathcal{M}$).

IMJ_f terms are typed in contexts comprising an interface table Δ and a variable context $\Gamma = \{x_1 : \theta_1, \cdots, x_n : \theta_n\} \cup \{a_1 : I_1, \cdots, a_m : I_m\}$ such that any interface in Γ occurs in $\mathsf{dom}(\Delta)$. The typing rules are given in Fig. 1. Here, we write $\Delta(I) \restriction \textit{Meths}$ to denote the interface definition of I according to Δ restricted to method specifiers. We write $I \leq I'$ to assert that I is a subtype of I'. The subtyping relation is induced by the use of interface extension in interface definitions as usual. Note, as in Java, downcasting is typable but terms of this form will not make progress in our operational semantics.

In several places in the sequel we will use **variable interfaces**: for each type θ, we let $\mathsf{Var}_\theta \equiv \{\textit{val} : \theta\}$ be an interface representing a reference of type θ.

Definition 1. We define the sets of **term values, heap configurations** by:

$$\textit{TVals} \ni v ::= \mathsf{skip} \mid i \mid \mathsf{null} \mid a \qquad \textit{HCnfs} \ni V ::= \epsilon \mid (\mathsf{f} : v), V$$

The set of *States* ($\ni S$) is the set of partial functions $\mathbb{A} \rightharpoonup \textit{Intfs} \times (\textit{HCnfs} \times \textit{MImps})$. If $S(a) = (I, (V, \mathcal{M}))$ then we write $S(a) : I$, while $S(a)$.f and $S(a)$.m stand for V.f and $\mathcal{M}$.m respectively, for each f, m. The transition relation is defined on terms within a state, that is, on pairs $(S,M) \in States \times Terms$, and is presented in full in [11].

We now define the central problem of our study. Given $\Delta|\emptyset \vdash M$: void, we say that M **terminates** and write $M \Downarrow$ just if there exists S such that $(\emptyset, M) \to^* (S, \text{skip})$.

Definition 2. Given $\Delta|\Gamma \vdash M_i : \theta$ $(i = 1, 2)$, we shall say that $\Delta|\Gamma \vdash M_1 : \theta$ *contextually approximates* $\Delta|\Gamma \vdash M_2 : \theta$ if, for all $\Delta' \supseteq \Delta$ and all contexts $C[-]$ such that $\Delta'|\emptyset \vdash C[M_i]$: void, if $C[M_1] \Downarrow$ then $C[M_2] \Downarrow$. Two terms are *contextually equivalent* (written $\Delta|\Gamma \vdash M_1 \cong M_2 : \theta$) if they approximate each other.

Let $\mathcal{X}$ range over subsets of IMJ_f. The *equivalence problem* for $\mathcal{X}$ is to decide equivalence of arbitrary $\mathcal{X}$-terms (under general IMJ_f contexts).

$\boxed{\mathcal{X}\text{--EQUIV: Given } \mathcal{X}\text{-terms } \Delta|\Gamma \vdash M_1, M_2 : \theta, \text{ does } \Delta|\Gamma \vdash M_1 \cong M_2 \text{ hold?}}$

Example 3 ([8]). Let $\Delta = \{\mathsf{Empty}, \mathsf{Cell}, \mathsf{Var}_{\mathsf{Empty}}, \mathsf{Var}_{\mathsf{int}}\}$, where Empty is the empty interface (no fields or methods) and $\mathsf{Cell} \equiv \{\mathsf{get} : \mathsf{void} \to \mathsf{Empty}, \mathsf{set} : \mathsf{Empty} \to \mathsf{void}\}$, and consider the terms $\Delta|\emptyset \vdash M_1, M_2 : \mathsf{Cell}$:

$M_1 \equiv$ let $v = $ new $\{ \_: \mathsf{Var}_{\mathsf{Empty}}\}$ in
    new $\{ \_: \mathsf{Cell};$
        $get : \lambda\_.\ v.\,val,$
        $set : \lambda y.$ if y=null then div else $v.val$:=$y \}$

$M_2 \equiv$ let $b = $ new $\{ \_: \mathsf{Var}_{\mathsf{int}}\}$ in
    let $v = $ new $\{ \_: \mathsf{Var}_{\mathsf{Empty}}\}$ in let $w = $ new $\{ \_: \mathsf{Var}_{\mathsf{Empty}}\}$ in
    new $\{ \_: \mathsf{Cell};$
        $get : \lambda\_.$ if $b.val$=1 then $(b.\,val$:=0; $v.\,val)$ else $(b.\,val$:=1; $w.\,val),$
        $set : \lambda y.$ if y=null then div else $v.val$:=$y; w.val$:=$y \}$

Here div stands for while 1 do skip. We saw in [11] that $\Delta|\emptyset \vdash M_1 \cong M_2 : \mathsf{Cell}$, by comparing the game semantics of M_1 and M_2. The equivalence can be verified automatically, as the terms reside in the decidable fragment for equivalence (we revisit these terms in Sect. 6).

3   Preliminary Analysis: Termination

Since termination can be reduced to contextual equivalence, a good starting point for analysing fragments of IMJ_f that have decidable equivalence is to exclude those that have undecidable termination. The restrictions on IMJ_f preclude obvious undecidability arguments based on arithmetic or recursive datatypes such as lists. However, in this section we identify two more subtle causes for undecidability of termination: fields containing objects with methods, and recursion.

Theorem 4. *The termination problem for* IMJ$_f$ *is undecidable. In particular, it is undecidable for terms* $\Delta|\emptyset \vdash M : \mathsf{void}$ *where*

1. *there are no recursive definitions but fields can store objects with methods,*
2. *no field stores a method-carrying object, but there are recursive method definitions.*

Proof (sketch). In both cases it is possible to encode a queue machine. Since there are no recursive types the structure of the queue has to be coded into other language features. For example, in 1, the links are formed by capturing an existing object in a closure which forms part of the definition of a method. □

It follows that any fragment of IMJ$_f$ containing unrestricted recursion or allowing for fields to store method-carrying objects necessarily also has an undecidable equivalence problem. Since IMJ$_f$ already provides a more restricted form of recursion in the while construct, a natural question is to next ask whether termination is still undecidable in the fragment in which fields are restricted to only store objects *without* attached methods and recursion is *disallowed* in favour of iteration.

Definition 5. The ***method dependency graph*** of a term $\Delta|\Gamma \vdash M : \theta$ has as nodes pairs (I, m) of interface $I \in \mathrm{dom}(\Delta)$ and method $m \in \Delta(I)$ and an edge from (I, m) to (J, m') just if there is a subterm of M which has shape $\mathsf{new}\{x : I; \mathcal{M}_1, (m : \lambda\vec{x}. C[P.m'(\vec{N})]), \mathcal{M}_2\}$ with $\Delta|\Gamma' \vdash P : J'$ and $J \leq J'$. That is, such an edge exists just if there is an instance of interface I whose implementation of m depends upon $J.m'$. We say a term $\Delta|\Gamma \vdash M : \theta$ is ***iterative*** just if its dependency graph is acyclic.

We shall henceforth consider the fragment of IMJ$_f$ containing iterative terms $\Delta|\emptyset \vdash M : \mathsf{void}$ in which all fields in Δ have types conforming to the grammar:

$$G ::= \mathsf{void} \mid \mathsf{int} \mid \overrightarrow{f : G}$$

where we write $\overrightarrow{f : G}$ to mean an interface identifier that is declared to contain only some number of fields, whose types again conform to G. We call such types *ground*. For this fragment, termination is decidable.

Theorem 6. *If* $\Delta|\emptyset \vdash M : \mathsf{void}$ *is an iterative term and fields in* Δ *belong to* G *then* $M\Downarrow$ *is decidable.*

Proof (sketch). We define a suitable notion of *visible state* (cf. visible heap of [3]) and show that is has bounded depth. Our definition is more general than that in [3], where the heap consists of objects which may be linked to other objects through pointer fields, since in IMJ$_f$ objects are also equipped with method implementations. □

Next we attack contextual equivalence for the IMJ$_f$ fragment with decidable termination. That is, terms do not use recursion and fields are of ground type.

Our approach utilises the game model of IMJ [11], adapted to finite integers, the main ingredients of which are seen next.[1] The model makes it possible to analyse the observable computational steps of a program phrase and its environment, and plays a crucial role in our decidability and undecidability proofs.

4   The Game Model

Game semantics models computation as an exchange of moves between two players, representing respectively the program (*player P*) and its environment (*player O*). A program phrase is interpreted as a strategy in the game determined by its type, and the patterns of interaction between the players are made concrete in the plays of the game. Given an IMJ term $\Delta|\Gamma \vdash M : \theta$, its game semantics is a *strategy*: a set of formal interactions (called *plays*), each of which consists of a sequence of tokens (called *moves-with-store*) that capture the computational potential of M. Moves, plays and strategies will involve names in their constructions (that is, they shall live within nominal sets [4]).

The moves available for play are very specific and depend upon the typing environment $\Delta|\Gamma \vdash \theta$. For each type θ, we set Val_θ to be the set of *semantic values* of type θ, given by: $Val_{\mathsf{void}} = \{\star\}$, $Val_{\mathsf{int}} = [0, \mathrm{MaxInt}]$ and $Val_I = \mathbb{A} \cup \{\mathsf{nul}\}$. We write Val for the union of all Val_θ's and, for each type sequence $\vec{\theta} = \theta_1, \cdots, \theta_n$, set $Val_{\vec{\theta}} = Val_{\theta_1} \times \cdots \times Val_{\theta_n}$. We let a **stores** Σ be finite partial functions $\Sigma : \mathbb{A} \rightharpoonup Intfs \times (Flds \rightharpoonup Val)$ (from names to object types and field assignments) satisfying two closure conditions. To spell them out, given Σ and $v \in Val$, we first define judgments $\Sigma \vdash v : \theta$ by the following rules.

$$\frac{v \in Val_{\mathsf{void}}}{\Sigma \vdash v : \mathsf{void}} \qquad \frac{v \in Val_{\mathsf{int}}}{\Sigma \vdash v : \mathsf{int}} \qquad \frac{\Sigma(v) : I \vee v = \mathsf{null}}{\Sigma \vdash v : I}$$

Now, whenever $\Sigma(a) = (I, \phi)$, we also stipulate the following conditions.

- $\Delta(I).\mathsf{f} = \theta'$ implies that $\phi(\mathsf{f})$ is defined and $\Sigma \vdash \phi(\mathsf{f}) : \theta$, where $\theta \leq \theta'$.
- $\phi(\mathsf{f}) = v$ implies that $\Delta(I).\mathsf{f}$ is defined and, if $v \in \mathbb{A}$ then $v \in \mathrm{dom}(\Sigma)$.

We let *Sto* be the set of all stores. Note that, for every store Σ, $\nu(\Sigma) \subseteq \mathrm{dom}(\Sigma)$.

Definition 7. Given a typing environment $\Delta|\Gamma \vdash \theta$ with $\Gamma = \{x_1 : \theta_1, \cdots, x_n : \theta_n, a_1 : I_1, \cdots, a_m : I_m\}$, its **moves** are $M_{[\![\Delta|\Gamma \vdash \theta]\!]} = M_{[\![\Gamma]\!]} \cup M_{[\![\theta]\!]} \cup Calls \cup Retns$, where

$$M_{[\![\Gamma]\!]} = \{\pi \cdot (v_1, ..., v_n, a_1, ..., a_m) \mid \vec{v} \in Val_{\vec{\theta}} \wedge \pi : \mathbb{A} \xrightarrow{\cong} \mathbb{A}\}$$
$$Calls = \{\mathsf{call}\ a.\mathsf{m}(\vec{v}) \mid a \in \mathbb{A} \wedge \vec{v} \in Val^*\}$$
$$Retns = \{\mathsf{ret}\ a.\mathsf{m}(v) \mid a \in \mathbb{A} \wedge v \in Val\}$$

and $M_{[\![\theta]\!]} = Val_\theta$. A **move-with-store** is pair of a move and a store, written m^Σ.

---

[1] Since the space we can devote in this paper to the exposition of the game model is limited, we kindly refer the reader to [11] for a thorough account.

A **play** is a sequence of moves-with-store that adheres to the following grammar,

$$P_{[\Delta|\Gamma\vdash\theta]} ::= \epsilon \mid m_\Gamma^\Sigma X \mid m_\Gamma^\Sigma Y m_\theta^\Sigma X \qquad (\textit{Well-Bracketing})$$
$$X ::= Y \mid Y\,(\text{call } a.m(\vec{v}))^\Sigma X$$
$$Y ::= \epsilon \mid YY \mid (\text{call } a.m(\vec{v}))^\Sigma Y\,(\text{ret } a.m(v))^\Sigma$$

where m_Γ and m_θ range over $M_{[\Gamma]}$ and $M_{[\theta]}$ respectively, and satisfies some additional conditions [11]: *Frugality*, *Well-Classing* and *Well-Calling*. A play is called *complete* if it is of the form $m_\Gamma^\Sigma Y m_\theta^\Sigma Y$. We write $P_{[\Delta|\Gamma\vdash\theta]}$ for the set of plays over $\Delta|\Gamma \vdash \theta$. The first move-with-store of a play is played by player O, and from there on players alternate. In particular, the set of plays of length 1 is equal to $P^1_{\Delta|\Gamma} = \{m^\Sigma \mid m \in M_{[\Gamma]} \wedge \Sigma \in Sto \wedge \nu(m) \subseteq \text{dom}(\Sigma)\}$ and its elements called *initial moves-with-store*.

A **strategy** in $[\![\Delta|\Gamma \vdash \theta]\!]$ is an even-prefix-closed set of plays from $P_{[\Delta|\Gamma\vdash\theta]}$ satisfying the combinatorial conditions of *Determinacy*, *Equivariance* and *O-closure* (cf. [11]). We write $\text{comp}(\sigma)$ for the set of complete plays of a strategy σ.

For each table Δ, games yield a category where the morphisms are strategies and the objects are representations of typing environments Γ and types θ. A term-in-context $\Delta|\Gamma \vdash M : \theta$ is translated into a strategy in $[\![\Delta|\Gamma \vdash M : \theta]\!]$ in a compositional manner [11]. We give a flavour of this interpretation in the next example.

Example 8. Consider interfaces $\text{Var}_{\text{int}} = \{val : \text{int}\}, I = \{run : \text{void} \to \text{void}\}$ and terms $f : I \vdash M_i : I$ given below, where div implements divergence, f is a free variable of type I, and assert(*condition*) stands for if *condition* then skip else div. The following terms live in the fragment for which equivalence will be shown decidable.

$$M_1 \equiv \text{let } x = \text{new } \{ \_: \text{Var}_{\text{int}} \} \text{ in}$$

new { _: I;

run : $\lambda\_$. if $x.val=0$ then ($x.val:=1$; $f.run()$; assert $(x.val=2)$)

else (if $x.val=1$ then $x.val:=2$ else div)

}

$$M_2 \equiv \text{new } \{ \_: I; \ run: \lambda\_. \text{ div} \}$$

The two terms are not equivalent, since they can be distinguished by a context that first calls the *run* method of M_1 (thus triggering a call to $f.run()$) and then calls M_1's *run* again from within the *run* method of f. This will engage M_1 in a terminating interaction, while calling M_1's *run*. On the other hand, as soon as M_2's *run* method is called, we obtain divergence. In game semantics, this is witnessed by the (unique) complete play of $[\![M_1]\!]$: $n_f^{\Sigma_0} n^\Sigma \text{call } n.run(\star)^\Sigma \text{ call } n_f.run(\star)^\Sigma \text{ call } n.run(\star)^\Sigma \text{ ret } n.run(\star)^\Sigma \text{ ret } n_f.run(\star)^\Sigma$ $\text{ret } n.run(\star)^\Sigma$, where $\Sigma_0 = \{n_f : I\}$ and $\Sigma = \Sigma_0 \cup \{n : I\}$. Note that the moves in the play correspond exactly to those interactions that happen between the term and its environment (the initial moves $n_f^{\Sigma_0}$ and n^Σ correspond to the environment presenting the object n_f which instantiates the free variable f and the program presenting the object n to which M_1 evaluates). Computation that is local to M_1 is not part of the play. On the other hand, no such play exists in $[\![M_2]\!]$.

Theorem 9 ([11]). *For all* IMJ$_f$ *terms* $\Delta|\Gamma \vdash M_1, M_2 : \theta$, $M_1 \cong M_2$ *if and only if* comp($[\![M_1]\!]$) = comp($[\![M_2]\!]$).

5   Contextual Equivalence is Undecidable

For a start, we identify three undecidable cases. They will inform the design of the decidable fragment in the next section. Each undecidable case is characterised by the presence of a method in a particular place of the typing judgment $\Delta|\Gamma \vdash M : \theta$. To establish undecidability, let $\mathcal{Q} = \{Q, Q_E, Q_D, \delta, q_I, \delta_E, \delta_D\}$, with the Q_E the set of states from which an enqueue transition in δ_E will fire and Q_D the set of states from which a dequeue transition in δ_D will fire. We shall construct IMJ$_f$ terms $\Delta|\Gamma \vdash M_1, M_2 : \theta$ such that $M_1 \cong M_2$ if and only if $\mathcal{Q}$ does not halt. Neither recursion nor iteration will be used in the argument and all fields will belong to G. The terms M_1, M_2 will not simulate queue machines directly, i.e. via termination and constructing a queue. Instead, we shall study the interaction (game) patterns they engage in and find that their geometry closely resembles the queue discipline.

Case 1. In this case the undecidability argument will rely on the interface table $\Delta = \{I_1, I_2, I_3, I_4\}$, where $I_1 \equiv val : \text{int}$, $I_3 \equiv step : \text{void} \to \text{void}$, $I_2 \equiv tmp : I_1$ and $I_4 \equiv run : I_3 \to \text{void}$; and terms $\Delta|x : I_4 \vdash M_1, M_2 : \text{void}$. Note that I_4 occurs in the context and the argument type of one of its methods contains a method. We give the relevant terms M_1, M_2 below, where $N_1 \equiv \text{div}$ and $N_2 \equiv \text{assert}(global.val = \text{halt})$.

```
1    let  global  = new {_:I₁}, aux = new{_:I₂} in
2    aux.tmp := new{_:I₁};
3    x.run( new{ _:I₃;
4             step:  λ_. assert( global.val ∈ Q_E);
5                   let  mine = new{_:I₁}, prev = aux.tmp in
6                   aux.tmp := mine;
7                   mine.val := π₁δ_E(global.val); global.val := π₂δ_E(global.val);
8                   x.run( new{ _:I₃;
9                          step:  λ_. assert( global.val ∈ Q_D);
10                                 assert (prev.val = 0 and mine.val ≠ 0);
11                                 global.val := δ_D(global.val, mine.val);
12                                 mine.val := 0;
13                                 if ( aux.tmp = mine) then globalval := halt });
14                   N_i });
15   N_i
```

The terms M_i are constructed in such a way that any interaction with them results in a call to $x.run$ (line 3). The argument is a new object of type I_3, i.e. it is equipped with a *step* method. Calls to that *step* method are used to mimic each enqueuing: the value is stored in a local variable *mine*, and *global* is used to keep track of the state of the machine. Note that a call to *step* triggers a call to *x.run* whose argument is another new object of type I_3 (line 8) with a different *step* method, which can subsequently be used to interpret the dequeuing of the stored element once it becomes the top of the queue. The queue discipline is enforced thanks to private variables of type I_2, which store references to stored elements as they are added to the queue: once a new value is added a pointer to the previous value is recorded in *prev* (line 5). To make sure that only values at the front of the queue are dequeued we insert assertions that checks if the preceding value was already dequeued (line 10). Other assertions (lines 4, 9) guarantee that we model operations compatible with the state of the machine. Finally, the difference between N_1 and N_2 makes it possible to detect a potential terminating run of the queue.

Theorem 10. *Contextual equivalence is undecidable for terms of the form $\Delta | x : I_4 \vdash M_1, M_2 : \mathsf{void}$, where M_1, M_2 are recursion- and iteration-free.*

Using a similar approach, though with different representation schemes for queue machines, one can show two more cases undecidable. We mention below the interfaces used in each case.

Case 2. $\Delta = \{I_1, I_2, I_3, I_5\}$, where $I_5 \equiv enq : \mathsf{void} \to I_3$. An analogue argument can then be formulated for terms $\Delta | \emptyset \vdash M : I_5$. Note that I_5 is used as a term type and that it features a method whose result type also contains a method.

Case 3. $\Delta = \{I_1, I_2, I_3, I_4, I_6\}$, where $I_6 \equiv enq : I_4 \to \mathsf{void}$. An analogue argument can then be formulated for terms $\Delta | \emptyset \vdash M : I_6$. Note that I_6 is used as a term type and that it contains a method whose argument type has a method.

In the next section we devise a fragment of IMJ_f that forbids each of these cases, which leads to decidability of $\cong$.

6   Equivalence is Decidable for IMJ*

In this section we delineate a fragment of IMJ_f that circumvents the undecidable cases identified in the previous section. In order to avoid Case 1, in the context we shall only allow interfaces conforming to the grammar given below.

$$\mathsf{L} ::= \mathsf{void} \mid \mathsf{int} \mid (\overrightarrow{\mathsf{f} : \mathsf{G}},\ \overrightarrow{\mathsf{m} : \vec{\mathsf{G}} \to \mathsf{L}})$$

Note that this prevents methods from having argument types containing methods. Put otherwise, L interfaces are first-order types.

Similarly, in order to avoid Cases 2 and 3, we restrict term types to those generated by the grammar R on the left below:

$$\mathsf{R} ::= \mathsf{void} \mid \mathsf{int} \mid (\overrightarrow{\mathsf{f} : \mathsf{G}},\ \overrightarrow{\mathsf{m} : \vec{\mathsf{L}} \to \mathsf{G}}) \qquad \mathsf{B} ::= \mathsf{void} \mid \mathsf{int} \mid (\overrightarrow{\mathsf{f} : \mathsf{G}},\ \overrightarrow{\mathsf{m} : \vec{\mathsf{G}} \to \mathsf{G}})$$

Observe that the intersection of L and R is captured by B.

Using the above restrictions, we define IMJ* to be a fragment of IMJ$_f$ consisting of iterative terms $\Delta | \Gamma \vdash M : \theta$ such that $\text{cod}(\Gamma) \subseteq \mathsf{L}$ and $\theta \in \mathsf{R}$. Due to asymmetries between L and R, we do not rely on the standard inductive definition of the syntax and define it by a new grammar, given below. Note that in the grammar below the types of x, y are required to be in L, and the type of M is in R. Sometimes the types of x, y and M have to match (e.g. in let $x = M$ in M'), which enforces them to be in B. We write x^B to say that x must be in B and not only in L.

$$M ::= \text{null} \mid x^\mathsf{B} \mid i \mid \text{skip} \mid \text{new}\{\, x : \mathsf{R} \; ; \overrightarrow{\mathsf{m} : \lambda \vec{x}.M}\,\} \mid x = x' \mid a^\mathsf{B} \mid M; M' \mid M.\mathsf{f}$$
$$\mid \text{if } M \text{ then } M' \text{ else } M'' \mid M.\mathsf{f} := M' \mid M = M' \mid M.\mathsf{m}(\vec{M}) \mid (I)M \mid M \oplus M'$$
$$\mid \text{while } M \text{ do } M' \mid \text{let } x = (I)y \text{ in } M \mid y.\mathsf{f} \mid \text{let } x = y.\mathsf{m}(\vec{M}) \text{ in } M \mid \text{let } x = M \text{ in } M'$$

Our approach for deciding equivalence in IMJ* consists in translating terms into automata that precisely capture their game semantics, and solving the corresponding language equivalence problem for the latter. The automata used for this purpose are a special kind of automata over infinite alphabets, defined in the next section.

6.1 Automata

The automata we consider operate over an infinite alphabet $\mathbb{W}$ containing moves-with-store:

$$\mathbb{W} = \{ m^\Sigma \mid m \in M_{[\![\Delta | \Gamma \vdash \theta]\!]} \wedge \Sigma \text{ a store} \wedge \nu(m) \subseteq \text{dom}(\Sigma) \}$$

for given Γ, Δ, θ. Each automaton will operate on an infinite fragment of $\mathbb{W}$ with stores of bounded size. Thus, the sequences accepted by our automata correspond to representations of plays where the domain of the store has been restricted to a bounded size. Due to bounded visibility, such a representation will be complete.

Even with bounded stores, $\mathbb{W}$ is infinite due to the presence of elements of $\mathbb{A}$ (the set of object names) in it. In order to capture names in a finite manner, our automata use a register mechanism. That is, they come equipped with a finite number of registers where they can store names, compare them with names read from the input, and update them to new values during their operation. Thus, each automaton transition refers to names *symbolically*: via the indices of the registers where they can be found. The automata are also equipped with a visible pushdown stack which can also store names; these names are communicated between the registers and the stack via push/pop operations. They are therefore pushdown extensions of Fresh-Register Automata [10,14].

To spell out formal definitions, let R refer to the number of registers of our automata and let $\mathbb{C}_{\text{st}}$ be a finite set of stack symbols. These will vary between different automata. We set:

$$\mathbb{C} = \{\, \star, \text{nul} \,\} \cup [0, \text{MaxInt}] \qquad \mathbb{C}_\mathbf{r} = \{\, \mathbf{r}_i \mid i \in [1, R] \,\}$$

$\mathbb{C}$ is the set of constant values that can appear in game moves. $\mathbb{C}_\mathbf{r}$ are the constants whose role is to refer to the registers symbolically (e.g. $\mathbf{r}_2$ refers to register number 2).

Definition 11. Given some interface table Δ, we let the set of **symbolic values** be $Val_{\mathsf{S}} = \mathbb{C} \cup \mathbb{C}_{\mathbf{r}}$. The sets of **symbolic moves**, **stores** and **labels** are given by:

$$Mov_{\mathsf{S}} = Val_{\mathsf{S}}^{*} \cup \{\mathsf{call}\,\mathbf{r}_i.\mathsf{m}.(\vec{x}), \mathsf{ret}\,\mathbf{r}_i.\mathsf{m}(x) \mid x\vec{x} \in Val_{\mathsf{S}}^{+}\}$$
$$Sto_{\mathsf{S}} = \mathbb{C}_{\mathbf{r}} \rightharpoonup Intfs \times (Flds \rightharpoonup Val_{\mathsf{S}})$$

and $Lab_{\mathsf{S}} = Mov_{\mathsf{S}} \times Sto_{\mathsf{S}}$. For any $x \in Val_{\mathsf{S}} \cup Mov_{\mathsf{S}} \cup Sto_{\mathsf{S}} \cup Lab_{\mathsf{S}}$, we write $\nu_{\mathbf{r}}(x)$ for the set of registers appearing in x. We range over symbolic values by ℓ and variants, symbolic moves by μ etc., and symbolic stores by S etc. For symbolic labels we may use variants of Φ or, more concretely, μ^{S}.

The semantics of our automata employs assignments of names to registers. Given such an assignment, we can move from symbolic entities to non-symbolic ones.

Definition 12. The set of **register assignments** is $Reg = \{\rho : \mathbb{C}_{\mathbf{r}} \overset{\cong}{\rightharpoonup} \mathbb{A}\}$ and contains all partial injections from registers to names. Given $\rho \in Reg$ and any $x \in Val_{\mathsf{S}} \cup Mov_{\mathsf{S}} \cup Sto_{\mathsf{S}} \cup Lab_{\mathsf{S}}$, we can define the non-symbolic counterpart of x:

$$\rho(x) = x[\rho(\mathbf{r}_1)/\mathbf{r}_1] \cdots [\rho(\mathbf{r}_R)/\mathbf{r}_R]$$

where substitution is defined by induction on the syntax of x. In particular, $\rho(x)$ is undefined if, for some index i, $\mathbf{r}_i \in \nu_{\mathbf{r}}(x)$ but $\rho(\mathbf{r}_i)$ is not defined.

The combination of symbolic labels with register assignments allows us to capture elements of $\mathbb{W}$. That is, whenever an automaton is at a state where a transition with label μ^{S} can be taken and the current register content is ρ, the automaton will perform the transition and accept the letter $\rho(\mu^{S}) \in \mathbb{W}$.

The pushdown stack that we will be using is going to be of the *visible* kind: stack operations will be stipulated by the specific symbolic label of a transition. We thus assume that the set of symbolic moves be partitioned into three parts,[2] which in turn yields a partition of symbolic labels:

$$Mov_{\mathsf{S}} = Mov_{\mathsf{push}} \uplus Mov_{\mathsf{pop}} \uplus Mov_{\mathsf{noop}} \qquad Lab_{\alpha} = \{\mu^{S} \in Lab \mid \mu \in Mov_{\alpha}\}$$

where $\alpha \in \{\mathsf{push}, \mathsf{pop}, \mathsf{noop}\}$. We let $Stk = (\mathbb{C}_{\mathsf{st}} \times Reg)^{*}$ be the set of *stacks*. We shall range over stacks by σ, and over elements of a stack σ by (s, ρ).

Definition 13. The set of **transition labels** is $TL = TL_{\mathsf{push}} \uplus TL_{\mathsf{pop}} \uplus TL_{\mathsf{noop}}$ where, for $\alpha \in \{\mathsf{push}, \mathsf{pop}, \mathsf{noop}\}$:

$$TL_{\alpha} = \{(X, \Phi, \phi) \in \mathcal{P}(\mathbb{C}_{\mathbf{r}}) \times Lab_{\alpha} \times S_{\alpha} \mid X \subseteq \nu_{\mathbf{r}}(\Phi)\}$$

and $S_{\mathsf{push}} = \mathbb{C}_{\mathsf{st}} \times \mathcal{P}(\mathbb{C}_{\mathbf{r}})$, $S_{\mathsf{pop}} = \mathbb{C}_{\mathsf{st}} \times \mathcal{P}(\mathbb{C}_{\mathbf{r}})^{2}$, $S_{\mathsf{noop}} = \{()\}$.

We range over TL by $\nu X.(\Phi, \phi)$, where if $X = \emptyset$ then we may suppress the νX part altogether; if X is some singleton $\{\mathbf{r}_i\}$ then we may shorten $\nu\{\mathbf{r}_i\}$ to $\nu\mathbf{r}_i$. On the other hand, ϕ can either be:

---

[2] The partitioning depends on the type of the move (e.g. only P-calls can be pushes, and only O-returns can be pops) and is made explicit in the automata construction.

- a *push pair* (s, Z), whereby we may denote $\nu X.(\Phi, \phi)$ by $\nu X.\Phi/(s, Z)$;
- a *pop triple* (s, Y, Z), in which case we may write $\nu X.\Phi, (s, Y, Z)$;
- or a *no-op* (), and we may simply write $\nu X.\Phi$.

A transition $\nu X.(\Phi, \phi)$ can thus be seen as doing three things:[3]

- it refreshes the names in registers X (i.e. νX stands for "new X");
- it accepts the letter $\rho(\Phi) \in \mathbb{W}$, where ρ is the "refreshed" assignment;
- it performs the stack operations stipulated by ϕ.

These actions will be described in detail after the following definition.

Definition 14. Given a number of registers R, an ***IMJ-automaton*** is a tuple $\mathcal{A} = \langle Q, q_0, X_0, \delta, F \rangle$ where:

- Q is a finite set of states, partitioned into Q_O (O-states) and Q_P (P-states);
- $q_0 \in Q_P$ is the initial state; $F \subseteq Q_O$ are the final ones;
- $X_0 \subseteq \mathbb{C}_r$ is the set of initially non-empty registers;
- $\delta \subseteq (Q_P \times TL_{PO} \times Q_O) \cup (Q_O \times TL_{OP} \times Q_P) \cup (Q_P \times \mathcal{P}(\mathbb{C}_r) \times Q_P) \cup (Q_O \times (\mathcal{P}(\mathbb{C}_r) \cup (\mathbb{C}_r \xrightarrow{\cong} \mathbb{C}_r)) \times Q_O)$ is the transition relation;

where $TL_{PO} = TL_{\mathsf{noop}} \cup TL_{\mathsf{push}}$, $TL_{OP} = TL_{\mathsf{noop}} \cup TL_{\mathsf{pop}}$.

We next explain the semantics of IMJ-automata. Let $\mathcal{A}$ be as above. A ***configuration*** of $\mathcal{A}$ consists of a quadruple $(q, \rho, \sigma, H) \in Q \times Reg \times Stk \times \mathcal{P}_{\mathsf{fn}}(\mathbb{A})$. By saying that $\mathcal{A}$ is in configuration (q, ρ, σ, H) we mean that, currently: the automaton state is q; the register assignment is ρ; the stack is σ; and all the names that have been encountered so far are those in H (i.e. H stands for the current *history*).

Suppose $\mathcal{A}$ is at a configuration (q, ρ, σ, H). If $q \xrightarrow{\nu X.(\mu^S, \phi)} q'$ then $\mathcal{A}$ will accept an input $m^{\Sigma} \in \mathbb{W}$ and move to state q' if the following steps are successful.

- If $\mu^S \in Lab_{\mathsf{pop}}$ and $\phi = (s, Y, Z)$ then $\mathcal{A}$ will check whether the stack has the form $\sigma = (s, \rho')::\sigma'$ with $\mathsf{dom}(\rho') = Y$ and ρ, ρ' being the same in Z and complementary outside it, that is: $\mathsf{dom}(\rho) \cap \mathsf{dom}(\rho') = Z$ and $\rho \cup \rho'$ is a valid assignment. If that is the case, it will pop the top of the stack into the registers, that is, set $\sigma = \sigma'$ and $\rho = \rho \cup \rho'$.
- $\mathcal{A}$ will update the registers in X with fresh names, that is, it will check whether $\mathsf{dom}(\rho) \cap X = \emptyset$ and, if so, it will set $\rho = \rho[r_{i_1} \mapsto a_1] \cdots [r_{i_m} \mapsto a_m]$, where $i_1, \cdots, i_m$ is an enumeration of X and $a_1, \cdots, a_m$ are distinct names such that:
    - if $q_1 \in Q_O$ then $a_1, \cdots, a_m \notin \mathsf{cod}(\rho)$ (*locally fresh*),
    - if $q_1 \in Q_P$ then $a_1, \cdots, a_m \notin H$ (*globally fresh*).
  In the latter case, $\mathcal{A}$ will set $H = H \cup \{a_1, \cdots, a_m\}$.
- $\mathcal{A}$ will check whether $m^{\Sigma} = \rho(\mu^S)$.

---

[3] As we see next, these actions do not necessarily happen in this order (pops happen first).

424   A.S. Murawski et al.

- If $\mu^S \in Lab_{\mathsf{push}}$ and $\phi = (s, Z)$ then $\mathcal{A}$ will perform a push of all registers in Z, along with the constant s, that is, it will set $\sigma = (s, \rho \restriction Z) :: \sigma$.

Let ρ' be the resulting assignment after the above steps have been taken, and similarly for H'. The semantics of the above transition is the configuration step $(q, \rho, \sigma, H) \xrightarrow{m^\Sigma} (q', \rho', \sigma', H')$.

On the other hand, if $q \xrightarrow{X} q'$ then $\mathcal{A}$ will apply the 'mask' X on the registers, that is, set $\rho' = \rho \restriction X$, and move to q' without reading anything, i.e. $(q, \rho, \sigma, H) \xrightarrow{\epsilon} (q', \rho \restriction X, \sigma, H)$.

Finally, if $q \xrightarrow{\pi} q$ then $\mathcal{A}$ will permute its registers according to π, i.e. it will perfom $(q, \rho, \sigma, H) \xrightarrow{\epsilon} (q', \rho \circ \pi^{-1}, \sigma, H)$.

Given an initial assignment ρ_0 such that $\mathsf{dom}(\rho_0) = X_0$ and taking $H_0 = \mathsf{cod}(\rho_0)$, the **language accepted** by $(\mathcal{A}, \rho_0)$ is

$$\mathcal{L}(\mathcal{A}, \rho_0) = \{w \in \mathbb{W}^* \mid (q_0, \rho_0, \epsilon, H_0) \xrightarrow{w} (q, \rho, \epsilon, H) \wedge q \in F\}.$$

We say that $\mathcal{A}$ is **deterministic** if, from any configuration, there is at most one way to accept each input $x \in \mathbb{W}$.

Let us next look at the two terms from Example 3 and give an automaton which captures their semantics.

Example 15. Consider $\Delta \mid \emptyset \vdash M_1, M_2 : \mathsf{Cell}$ from Example 3. The game semantics of the two terms consists of plays of the shape $\star^\emptyset\, n^{\Sigma_0}\, G_0^*\, L_1\, G_1^* \cdots L_k\, G_k^*$, where:

$G_0 = \mathsf{call}\, n.\mathsf{get}(\star)^{\Sigma_0}\, \mathsf{ret}\, n.\mathsf{get}(\mathsf{nul})^{\Sigma_0}$ $G_i = \mathsf{call}\, n.\mathsf{get}(\star)^{\Sigma_i}\, \mathsf{ret}\, n.\mathsf{get}(n_{i-1})^{\Sigma_i}$ $(i > 0)$
$L_i = \mathsf{call}\, n.\mathsf{set}(n_i)^{\Sigma_i}\, \mathsf{ret}\, n.\mathsf{set}(\star)^{\Sigma_i}$
$\Sigma_i = \{n \mapsto (\mathsf{Cell}, \emptyset)\} \cup \{n_j \mapsto (\mathsf{Empty}, \emptyset) \mid j \in [1, i]\}$

for any $n, n_1, \cdots, n_i \in \mathbb{A}$ with $n \neq n_j$ $(j \in [1, i])$. We construct the following IMJ-automaton with 2 registers and $X_0 = \emptyset$.

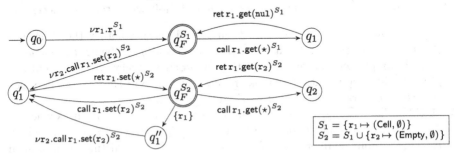

The automaton *represents* plays as above, starting from their second move[4] and matching each Σ_i to a representation $\hat{\Sigma}_i = \Sigma_0 \cup \{n_i \mapsto (\mathsf{Empty}, \emptyset)\}$. The first transition corresponds to the move n^{Σ_0}: the transition label $\nu r_1.r_1^{S_1}$ stipulates

---

[4] This is a technical convenience of the interpretation: as we see next, we translate each canonical term into a family of automata, one per (symbolic) initial move-with-store (here, the unique initial move is $\star^\emptyset$). Initial states take the initial move as given and are therefore P-states.

that the automaton will accept n^{Σ_0}, for some/any fresh name n, and store n in its first register (i.e. register $\mathbf{r}_1$). Observe how the value n, stored in $\mathbf{r}_1$, is invoked in later transitions. For instance, the transition labelled $\mathsf{call}\,\mathbf{r}_1.\mathsf{get}(\star)^{S_1}$ will accept the input $\mathsf{call}\,n.\mathsf{get}(\star)^{\Sigma_0}$. Note also that there are two kinds of transitions involving register $\mathbf{r}_2$. Transitions labelled $\nu\mathbf{r}_2.\mathsf{call}\,\mathbf{r}_1.\mathsf{set}(\mathbf{r}_2)^{S_2}$ set the value of register $\mathbf{r}_2$ to some locally fresh value n'' and accept $\mathsf{call}\,n.\mathsf{set}(n'')^{\Sigma_0 \cup \{n'' \mapsto (\mathsf{Empty},\emptyset)\}}$ (note how, in the transition from $q_F^{S_2}$ to q_1', the automaton first clears the contents of $\mathbf{r}_2$). On the other hand, the transition $\mathsf{call}\,\mathbf{r}_1.\mathsf{set}(\mathbf{r}_2)^{S_2}$ corresponds to accepting $\mathsf{call}\,n.\mathsf{set}(n')^{\Sigma_0 \cup \{n' \mapsto (\mathsf{Empty},\emptyset)\}}$ and n' is the current value of register $\mathbf{r}_2$ (i.e. no register update takes place in this case).

6.2   Automata for IMJ*

The automata of the previous section are expressive enough to capture the semantics of terms in IMJ*, in the following manner. As seen in the previous example, IMJ-automata do not produce the actual plays of the modelled terms but representations thereof. The reason is that the stores in the game semantics accumulate all names that are played, and are therefore unbounded in size, whereas the size of symbolic stores is by definition bounded for each automaton. Our machines represent the actual stores by focussing on the part of the store that the term can access in its current environment (cf. bounded visibility). From a representative "play", where stores are this way bounded, we obtain an actual play by extending stores to their full potential and allowing the values of the added names to be solely determined by O.

Definition 16. Let $s = m_1^{\Sigma_1} \cdots m_k^{\Sigma_k}$ and $t = m_1^{T_1} \cdots m_k^{T_k}$ be a play and a sequence of moves-with-store over $\Delta|\Gamma \vdash \theta$ respectively. We call s an *extension* of t if $T_i \subseteq \Sigma_i$ ($i \in [1,k]$) and, for any $i \in [1, k/2]$, if $a \in \mathsf{dom}(\Sigma_{2i}) \setminus \mathsf{dom}(T_{2i})$ then $\Sigma_{2i}(a) = \Sigma_{2i-1}(a)$. The set of all extensions of t is $\mathsf{ext}(t)$.

We can now state our main translation result. Recall that, for each Δ, Γ, we write $P_{\Delta|\Gamma}^1$ for the set of initial moves-with-store in $[\![\Delta|\Gamma \vdash \theta]\!]$. The set of its *initial symbolic moves-with-store* is the finite set: $(\!|\Delta|\Gamma|\!) = \{ \mu_0^{S_0} \in Lab_{\mathsf{S}} \mid \exists \rho_0.\ \rho_0(\mu_0^{S_0}) \in P_{\Delta|\Gamma}^1 \}$. We say that a triple $(m^{\Sigma}, \Phi, \rho) \in P_{\Delta|\Gamma}^1 \times (\!|\Delta|\Gamma|\!) \times Reg$ is compatible if $m^{\Sigma} = \rho(\Phi)$ and $\mathsf{cod}(\rho) = \mathsf{dom}(\Sigma)$, and let $P_{[\![\Delta|\Gamma\vdash\theta]\!]}^{m,\Sigma}$ be the set of plays over $\Delta|\Gamma \vdash \theta$ starting with m^{Σ}.

Theorem 17. *Let $\Delta|\Gamma \vdash M : \theta$ be an IMJ* term. We can effectively define a family of deterministic IMJ-automata $(\!|M|\!) = \{ (\!|M|\!)_\Phi \mid \Phi \in (\!|\Delta|\Gamma|\!) \}$ such that*

$$\bigcup_{w \in \mathcal{L}((\!|M|\!)_{\Phi,\rho})} \mathsf{ext}(m^{\Sigma} w) = \mathsf{comp}([\![\Delta|\Gamma \vdash M : \theta]\!]) \cap P_{[\![\Delta|\Gamma\vdash\theta]\!]}^{m,\Sigma}$$

for each compatible (m^{Σ}, Φ, ρ).

The construction encompasses two stages: first, a syntactic translation of terms into canonical forms (of an appropriate kind) is applied; the latter is followed by a construction of IMJ-automata for terms in canonical form. Both steps are compositional, defined by induction on the term syntax. Let us revisit Example 15 to demonstrate the whole construction.

Example 18. Recall terms $\Delta|\emptyset \vdash M_i :$ Cell $(i = 1, 2)$ from Examples 3, 15. Applying our translation on M_1 and removing unreachable states we obtain the following automaton with $R = 3$ and $X_0 = \emptyset$.

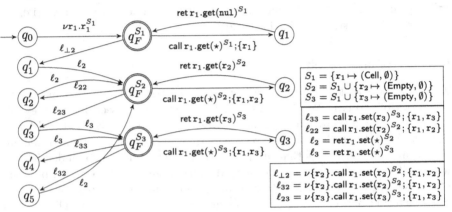

We can observe that the constructed automaton is obfuscated compared to the one we manually constructed in Example 15, which suggests that the translation can be further optimised: e.g. states q_1', q_2' and q_5' can be evidently unified (q_3', q_4' too). There is also a symmetry between $q_F^{S_2}$ and $q_F^{S_3}$.

Let now $\Delta|\Gamma \vdash M_1, M_2 : \theta$ be IMJ* terms. The previous theorem provides us with deterministic IMJ-automata $\mathcal{A}_i = (\!| M_i |\!)_\Phi$ $(i = 1, 2)$ representing the complete plays of $[\![M_i]\!]$ which start with m^Σ, for each compatible triple (m^Σ, Φ, ρ). Thus, since the game model is fully abstract with respect to complete plays (Theorem 9), to decide whether $M_1 \cong M_2$ it suffices to check whether $\mathcal{A}_1$ and $\mathcal{A}_2$ represent the same sets of complete plays, for all compatible (m^Σ, Φ, ρ).

We achieve the latter by constructing a product-like IMJ-automaton $\mathcal{B}$ which jointly simulates the operation of $\mathcal{A}_1$ and $\mathcal{A}_2$, looking for possible discordances in their operation which would signal that there is a complete play which one of them can represent but the other cannot. That is, $\mathcal{B}$ operates in *joint simulation mode* or in *divergence mode*. When in simulation mode, at each configuration and input move-with-store $m'^{\Sigma'}$:

- if $\mathcal{A}_1$ and $\mathcal{A}_2$ both accept $m'^{\Sigma'}$ (modulo extensions) then $\mathcal{B}$ accepts $m'^{\Sigma'}$ and proceeds its joint simulation of $\mathcal{A}_1, \mathcal{A}_2$;
- if, say, $\mathcal{A}_1$ accepts $m'^{\Sigma'}$ but $\mathcal{A}_2$ cannot accept it, then $\mathcal{B}$ enters divergence mode: it proceeds with simulating only $\mathcal{A}_1$ with the target of reaching a final state (dually if $\mathcal{A}_2/\mathcal{A}_1$ accepts/not-accepts $m'^{\Sigma'}$). If the latter is successful, then $\mathcal{B}$ will have found a complete play that can be represented by $\mathcal{A}_1$ but not by $\mathcal{A}_2$.

Because our automata use visibly pushdown stacks and rely on the same partitioning of tags, we can synchronise them using a single stack. In addition, $\mathcal{B}$ needs to keep in its registers the union of the names stored by $\mathcal{A}_1$ and $\mathcal{A}_2$. Inside its states, $\mathcal{B}$ keeps information on: the current states of $\mathcal{A}_1$ and $\mathcal{A}_2$; the way the names of its registers correspond to the names in the registers of $\mathcal{A}_1$ and $\mathcal{A}_2$; the current joint symbolic state (this is for resolving expansions). On the other hand, once in divergence mode, say for $\mathcal{A}_1$, $\mathcal{B}$ operates precisely like $\mathcal{A}_1$. The automaton can only accept in divergence mode, if the simulated automaton (here $\mathcal{A}_1$) accepts.

Theorem 19. *For $\Delta|\Gamma \vdash M_1, M_2 : \theta$ and (m^Σ, Φ, ρ) as above, we can effectively construct an IMJ-automaton $\mathcal{B}$ such that $\mathcal{L}(\mathcal{B}, \rho) = \emptyset$ iff $\mathsf{comp}(\llbracket \Delta|\Gamma \vdash M_1 : \theta \rrbracket) = \mathsf{comp}(\llbracket \Delta|\Gamma \vdash M_2 : \theta \rrbracket)$.*

As variants of *pushdown fresh-register automata*, IMJ-automata have decidable emptiness problem [10]. Moreover, the number of compatible triples (m^Σ, Φ, ρ) is bounded with respect to Γ, Δ modulo name-permutations. This yields the following.

Corollary 20. IMJ*–EQUIV *is decidable.*

7   Conclusion and Further Work

In Sect. 3 we showed that the ability to construct terms using unrestricted recursion leads to undecidable termination. Hence, we subsequently dropped unrestricted recursion in favour of the natural alternative: iteration through IMJ$_f$'s while construct. We conclude by discussing a finer gradation of recursion which allows us to study the algorithmic properties of a larger, if perhaps less natural, class of terms: those using only *first-order* recursion. We show that our bounded-depth visible store argument extends to this new fragment.

Definition 21. We say that a method $I.m$ declared in Δ is ***first-order*** just if $I.m$ has type of shape $(\mathsf{G}, \dots, \mathsf{G}) \to \mathsf{G}$. Otherwise we shall say that it is ***higher-order***. Fix a term $\Delta|\emptyset \vdash P : \mathsf{void}$. We say that P is 1-***recursive*** just if, whenever there is a cycle $(I_1, m_1), \dots, (I_k, m_k)$ in its method dependency graph, then every $I_i.m_i$ is first-order.

For 1-recursive terms, new objects may be created at every frame of an increasingly large stack of recursive calls and then returned back down the chain so as to be visible in all contexts. However, the number of frames in this call stack which are associated with methods that can pass method-carrying objects as parameters is ultimately bounded by the 1-recursion restriction.

Lemma 22. *Let Δ have only G-valued fields and $\Delta|\emptyset \vdash M : \mathsf{void}$ be 1-recursive. Then M has bounded-depth visible state.*

For the equivalence problem, it is unclear whether our argument carries over to the first-order recursion setting. Recall that we rely on an equivalence-like testing procedure for *visibly* pushdown register automata. With recursion we cannot hope to remain in the visible setting [9] and the decidability status of language equivalence for general pushdown register automata over infinite alphabets is currently unknown (it would require extending the celebrated result of Sénizergues [13]).

References

1. Ábrahám, E., Bonsangue, M.M., de Boer, F.S., Grüner, A., Steffen, M.: Observability, connectivity, and replay in a sequential calculus of classes. In: de Boer, F.S., Bonsangue, M.M., Graf, S., de Roever, W.-P. (eds.) FMCO 2004. LNCS, vol. 3657, pp. 296–316. Springer, Heidelberg (2005)
2. Bierman, G., Parkinson, M., Pitts, A.: MJ: An imperative core calculus for Java and Java with effects. Technical report 563, Computer Laboratory, University of Cambridge (2002)
3. Bouajjani, A., Fratani, S., Qadeer, S.: Context-bounded analysis of multithreaded programs with dynamic linked structures. In: Damm, W., Hermanns, H. (eds.) CAV 2007. LNCS, vol. 4590, pp. 207–220. Springer, Heidelberg (2007)
4. Gabbay, M.J., Pitts, A.M.: A new approach to abstract syntax with variable binding. Formal Aspects Comput. **13**, 341–363 (2002)
5. Hopkins, D., Murawski, A.S., Ong, C.-H.L.: A fragment of ML decidable by visibly pushdown automata. In: Aceto, L., Henzinger, M., Sgall, J. (eds.) ICALP 2011, Part II. LNCS, vol. 6756, pp. 149–161. Springer, Heidelberg (2011)
6. Jagadeesan, R., Pitcher, C., Riely, J.: Open bisimulation for aspects. In: AOSD. ACM (2007)
7. Jeffrey, A., Rathke, J.: Java JR: fully abstract trace semantics for a core java language. In: Sagiv, M. (ed.) ESOP 2005. LNCS, vol. 3444, pp. 423–438. Springer, Heidelberg (2005)
8. Koutavas, V., Wand, M.: Reasoning about class behavior. In: FOOL/WOOD (2007)
9. Murawski, A.S., Ong, C.-H.L., Walukiewicz, I.: Idealized algol with ground recursion, and DPDA equivalence. In: Caires, L., Italiano, G.F., Monteiro, L., Palamidessi, C., Yung, M. (eds.) ICALP 2005. LNCS, vol. 3580, pp. 917–929. Springer, Heidelberg (2005)
10. Murawski, A.S., Tzevelekos, N.: Algorithmic games for full ground references. In: Czumaj, A., Mehlhorn, K., Pitts, A., Wattenhofer, R. (eds.) ICALP 2012, Part II. LNCS, vol. 7392, pp. 312–324. Springer, Heidelberg (2012)
11. Murawski, A.S., Tzevelekos, N.: Game semantics for Interface Middleweight Java. In: POPL, pp. 517–528. ACM (2014)
12. Segoufin, L.: Automata and logics for words and trees over an infinite alphabet. In: Ésik, Z. (ed.) CSL 2006. LNCS, vol. 4207, pp. 41–57. Springer, Heidelberg (2006)
13. Sénizergues, G.: L(A)=L(B)? decidability results from complete formal systems. Theor. Comput. Sci. **251**(1–2), 1–166 (2001)
14. Tzevelekos, N.: Fresh-register automata. In: POPL, pp. 295–306 (2011)
15. Welsch, Y., Poetzsch-Heffter, A.: Full abstraction at package boundaries of object-oriented languages. In: Simao, A., Morgan, C. (eds.) SBMF 2011. LNCS, vol. 7021, pp. 28–43. Springer, Heidelberg (2011)

Looking at Mean-Payoff Through Foggy Windows

Paul Hunter, Guillermo A. Pérez$^{(\boxtimes)}$, and Jean-François Raskin

Université Libre de Bruxelles – Brussels, Brussels, Belgium
{phunter,gperezme,jraskin}@ulb.ac.be

Abstract. Mean-payoff games (MPGs) are infinite duration two-player zero-sum games played on weighted graphs. Under the hypothesis of perfect information, they admit memoryless optimal strategies for both players and can be solved in NP∩coNP. MPGs are suitable quantitative models for open reactive systems. However, in this context the assumption of perfect information is not always realistic. For the partial-observation case, the problem that asks if the first player has an observation-based winning strategy that enforces a given threshold on the mean-payoff, is undecidable. In this paper, we study the window mean-payoff objectives introduced recently as an alternative to the classical mean-payoff objectives. We show that, in sharp contrast to the classical mean-payoff objectives, some of the window mean-payoff objectives are decidable in games with partial-observation.

1 Introduction

Mean-payoff games (or MPGs, for short) [13] are infinite duration, two-player, zero-sum games played on weighted graphs, useful for modelling reactive systems with quantitative objectives and designing algorithms to synthesize controllers for such systems [6]. Like other verification games played on graphs, two players move a token around the graph for an infinite number of steps. One of the players selects a label, after which the second chooses an edge with this label. The token is then moved along the selected edge. This infinite interaction between the two players results in an infinite path in the graph. The objective of Player 1 is to maximize the limiting average payoff of the edges (defined by the weights that annotate them) traversed in this infinite path, while Player 2 tries to minimize this average. It has been shown in [3,13] that both players in an MPG can play optimally using memoryless strategies, and as a consequence, those games are known to be solvable in NP∩coNP. The question of whether they can be solved in polynomial-time is an important open question, and although pseudo-polynomial-time algorithms to solve these games are known [5,23], the lack of efficient algorithms clearly limits the development of tools.

In the version of MPG described above, the game is of *perfect information*: both players have complete knowledge of the history of the play up to the current

---

P. Hunter, J.-F. Raskin—Supported by the ERC inVEST (279499) project.

G.A. Pérez—Supported by F.R.S.-FNRS fellowship.

B. Finkbeiner et al. (Eds.): ATVA 2015, LNCS 9364, pp. 429–445, 2015.
DOI: 10.1007/978-3-319-24953-7_31

position of the token. For many applications such as controller synthesis, it is often more natural to assume that players have only partial knowledge of the current state of the game. In practice, players may model processes with private variables that other players (processes) may not see, or controllers that acquire information about their environment using sensors with bounded precision, etc. Unfortunately, it has been shown in [10] that MPGs with *partial-observation* are undecidable.

Window mean-payoff (WMP) objectives were recently introduced in [9] as an alternative to the classical MP objectives. In a WMP objective instead of considering the long-run average along the whole play, payoffs are considered over a local bounded window *sliding* along the play. The objective is then to make sure that the average payoff is at least zero over every window. The WMP objectives enjoy several nice properties. First, in contrast to classical MP objectives, we have a polynomial-time algorithm for determining WMP games. Second, they can be considered as "approximations" of the classical MP objectives in the following sense: (*i*) they are a *strengthening* of the MP objective, i.e. winning for the WMP objective implies winning for the MP objective, (*ii*) if a (finite memory) strategy guarantees an MP with value $\varepsilon > 0$ then that strategy also achieves the WMP objective for a window size that is bounded by a function of ε and the game and strategy memory sizes. We remark that, indeed, this is a very weak type of "approximation". However, one cannot hope for much better considering that in [15] it was shown the existence of a polynomial-time approximation scheme for MP objectives would imply that MPGs are solvable in polynomial time.

From a practical point of view, WMP objectives present several advantages. First, they are algorithmically more tractable: in the setting of perfect information games, WMP games can be solved in polynomial-time while the classical MP objectives are only known to be in NP ∩ coNP. Second, WMP objectives provide stronger guarantees to the system designer: while classical MP objectives only ensure good performances in the *limit* (long run), variants of WMP objectives provide good performance after a *fixed* or *bounded* amount of time. As we show in this paper, these advantages transfer to the setting of games with incomplete information, and this is highly desirable for practical purposes. Indeed, to apply synthesis in practice, our models should be as close as possible to the systems that we want to simulate. As classical MPGs with partial-observation leads to undecidability, it is natural to investigate WMP objectives, and in this respect there are two pieces of good news: first, they lead to decidability, and second, there is a potential of algorithmic support with symbolic implementation.

Contributions. In this paper we consider the extension of WMP objectives to games with partial-observation. We show that, in sharp contrast with classical MP objectives, some of the WMP objectives are decidable for such games. As in [9], we consider several variants of the window MP objectives. For all objectives, we provide complete complexity results and optimal algorithms. More precisely, our main contributions are as follows:

- First, we consider a definition in which the window size is fixed and the sliding window is started at the initial move of the game, this is called the *direct window* objective. For this definition we give an optimal EXP-time algorithm (Theorem 3) in the form of a reduction to a *safety game*. Additionally, we show that this safety game has a nice structure that induces a natural partial order on game positions. In turn this partial order can be used to obtain a *symbolic algorithm* based on the antichain approach [12]. This shows that WMP objectives allow us not only to recover decidability but they also lead to games that have the potential to be solved efficiently in practice. The antichain approach has already been applied and implemented with success for LTL synthesis [4], omega-regular games with partial observation [2], and language inclusion between non-determinisitic Büchi automata [11].
- Second, we consider two natural prefix-independent definitions for the window objectives, the *(uniform) fixed window* objectives. We also give optimal EXP-time algorithms for these two definitions (Theorems 5 and 6), when weights are polynomially bounded in the size of the game arena. For these objectives, we show that the sets of good abstract plays (i.e. observation-action sequences) form regular languages whose complements can be recognized by non-deterministic Büchi automata of pseudo-polynomial size (Propositions 2 and 3). These automata can then be turned into deterministic parity automata that can be used as observers to transform the game of partial-observation into a game of perfect information with a parity objective.
- Finally, we show that, when the size of the window is not fixed but rather left as a parameter, then for all the objectives that we consider the decision problems are undecidable (Theorem 2).

2   Preliminaries

Weighted Game Arenas. A *weighted game arena with partial-observation* (WGA, for brevity) is a tuple $G = \langle Q, q_I, \Sigma, \Delta, w, Obs \rangle$, where Q is a finite set of states, $q_I \in Q$ is the initial state, Σ is a finite set of actions, $\Delta \subseteq Q \times \Sigma \times Q$ is the transition relation, $w : \Delta \to \mathbb{Z}$ is the weight function, and $Obs \in \mathsf{Partition}(Q)$ is a set of observations containing $\{q_I\}$. Let $W = \max\{|w(t)| : t \in \Delta\}$. We assume Δ is total, i.e. for every $(q, \sigma) \in Q \times \Sigma$ there exists $q' \in Q$ such that $(q, \sigma, q') \in \Delta$. If every element of Obs is a singleton, then we say G is a *WGA with perfect information* and if $|Obs| = 1$ we say G is *blind*. For simplicity, we denote by $\mathsf{post}_\sigma(s) = \{q' \in Q \mid \exists q \in s : (q, \sigma, q') \in \Delta\}$ the set of σ-successors of a set of states $s \subseteq Q$.

In this work, unless explicitly stated otherwise, we depict states from a WGA as circles and transitions as arrows labelled by an action-weight pair: $\sigma, x \in \Sigma \times \{-W, \ldots, W\}$. Observations are represented by dashed boxes and colors, where states with the same color correspond to the same observation.

Abstract & Concrete Paths. A *concrete path* in an WGA is a sequence $q_0 \sigma_0 q_1 \sigma_1 \ldots$ where for all $i \geq 0$ we have $q_i \in Q$, $\sigma_i \in \Sigma$ and $(q_i, \sigma_i, q_{i+1}) \in \Delta$. An *abstract path* is a sequence $o_0\sigma_0 o_1\sigma_1\ldots$ where $o_i \in Obs$, $\sigma_i \in \Sigma$ and such that there is a concrete path $q_0\sigma_0 q_1\sigma_1\ldots$ for which $q_i \in o_i$, for all i. Given an abstract path ψ, let $\gamma(\psi)$ be the set of concrete paths that agree with the observation and action sequence. Formally $\gamma(\psi) = \{q_0\sigma_0 q_1\sigma_1\ldots \mid \forall i \geq 0 : q_i \in o_i \text{ and } (q_i, \sigma, q_{i+1}) \in \Delta\}$. Also, given abstract (respectively concrete) path $\rho = o_0\sigma_0\ldots$ and integers k, l we define $\pi[k..l] = o_k\ldots o_l$, $\pi[..k] = \pi[0..k]$, and $\pi[l..] = o_l\sigma_l o_{l+1}\ldots$.

Given a concrete path $\pi = q_0\sigma_0 q_1\sigma_1\ldots$, the *payoff* up to the $(n+1)$-th element is given by

$$w(\pi[..n]) = \sum\nolimits_{i=0}^{n-1} w(q_i, \sigma_i, q_{i+1}).$$

If π is infinite, we define two *mean-payoff* values $\underline{MP}$ and $\overline{MP}$ as:

$$\underline{MP}(\pi) = \liminf_{n\to\infty} \tfrac{1}{n} w(\pi[..n]) \qquad \overline{MP}(\pi) = \limsup_{n\to\infty} \tfrac{1}{n} w(\pi[..n])$$

Plays & Strategies. A play in a WGA G is an infinite abstract path starting at $o_I \in Obs$ where $q_I \in o_I$. Denote by $\mathsf{Plays}(G)$ the set of all plays and by $\mathsf{Prefs}(G)$ the set of all finite prefixes of such plays ending in an observation. Let $\gamma(\mathsf{Plays}(G))$ be the set of concrete paths of all plays in the game, and $\gamma(\mathsf{Prefs}(G))$ be the set of all finite prefixes of all concrete paths.

An *observation-based strategy for Eve* is a function from finite prefixes of plays to actions, i.e. $\lambda_\exists : \mathsf{Prefs}(G) \to \Sigma$. A play $\psi = o_0\sigma_0 o_1\sigma_1\ldots$ is *consistent* with $\lambda_\exists$ if $\sigma_i = \lambda_\exists(\psi[..i])$ for all i. We say an observation-based strategy for Eve $\lambda_\exists$ has *memory* μ if there is a set M with $|M| = \mu$, an element $m_0 \in M$, and functions $\alpha_u : M \times Obs \to M$ and $\alpha_o : M \times Obs \to \Sigma$ such that for any play prefix $\rho = o_0\sigma_0\ldots o_n$ we have $\lambda_\exists(\rho) = \alpha_o(m_n, o_n)$, where m_n is defined inductively by $m_{i+1} = \alpha_u(m_i, o_i)$ for $i \geq 0$.

Objectives. An *objective* for a WGA G is a set V_G of plays, i.e. $V_G \subseteq \mathsf{Plays}(G)$. We say plays in V_G are *winning for Eve*. Conversely, all plays not in V_G are *winning for Adam*. We refer to a WGA with a fixed objective as a game. Having fixed a game, we say a strategy λ is *winning* for a player if all plays consistent with λ are winning for that player. We say a player *wins* a game if (s)he has a winning strategy. We write V instead of V_G if G is clear from the context.

Given WGA G and a threshold $\nu \in \mathbb{Q}$, the *mean-payoff* (MP) objectives $\mathsf{MPSup}_G(\nu) = \{\psi \in \mathsf{Plays}(G) \mid \forall \pi \in \gamma(\psi) : \overline{MP}(\pi) \geq \nu\}$ and $\mathsf{MPInf}_G(\nu) = \{\psi \in \mathsf{Plays}(G) \mid \forall \pi \in \gamma(\psi) : \underline{MP}(\pi) \geq \nu\}$ require the mean-payoff value be at least ν. We omit the subscript in the objective names when the WGA is clear from the context. Let $\nu = \frac{a}{b}$, w' be a weight function mapping $t \in \Delta$ to $b \cdot w(t) - a$, for all such t, and G' be the WGA resulting from replacing w' in G for w. We note that Eve wins the $\mathsf{MPSup}_{G'}(0)$ (respectively, $\mathsf{MPInf}_{G'}(0)$) objective if and only if she wins $\mathsf{MPSup}_G(\nu)$ (resp., $\mathsf{MPInf}_G(\nu)$).

3   Window Mean-Payoff Objectives

In what follows we recall the definitions of the *window mean-payoff* (WMP) objectives introduced in [9] and adapt them to the partial-observation setting.

For the classical MP objectives Eve is required to ensure the long-run average of all concretizations of the play is at least ν. WMP objectives correspond to conditions which are sufficient for this to be the case. All of them use as a main ingredient the concept of concrete paths being "good". Formally, given $i \geq 0$ and *window size bound* $l_{\max} \in \mathbb{N}_0 = \mathbb{N} \setminus \{0\}$, let the set of concrete paths χ with the *good window* property be

$$\mathsf{GW}(\nu, i, l_{\max}) = \{\chi \mid \exists j \leq l_{\max} : w(\chi[i..(i+j)]) \geq \nu \cdot j\}.$$

As in [9], we assume the value of $l_{\max}$ is polynomially bounded by the size of the arena.

For the first of the WMP objectives Eve is required to ensure all suffixes of all concretizations of the play can be split into concrete paths of length at most $l_{\max}$ and average weight at least ν. The MP objectives are known to be prefix-independent, therefore a prefix-independent version of this first objective is a natural objective to consider as well. We study two such candidates. One which asks of Eve that there is some i such that all suffixes – after i – of all concretizations of the play can be split in the same way as before. This is quite restrictive since the i is *uniform* for all concretizations of the play. The second prefix-independent version of the objective we consider allows for non-uniformity.

Formally, the *fixed window mean-payoff* (FWMP) objectives for a given WGA and threshold $\nu \in \mathbb{Q}$ are defined below. For convenience we denote by ψ plays from $\mathsf{Plays}(G)$ and concrete plays by π, i.e. elements of $\gamma(\mathsf{Plays}(G))$.

$$\mathsf{DirFix}(\nu, l_{\max}) = \{\psi \mid \forall \pi \in \gamma(\psi), \forall i \geq 0 : \pi \in \mathsf{GW}(\nu, i, l_{\max})\}$$
$$\mathsf{UFix}(\nu, l_{\max}) = \{\psi \mid \exists i \geq 0, \forall \pi \in \gamma(\psi), \forall j \geq i : \pi \in \mathsf{GW}(\nu, j, l_{\max})\}$$
$$\mathsf{Fix}(\nu, l_{\max}) = \{\psi \mid \forall \pi \in \gamma(\psi), \exists i \geq 0, \forall j \geq i : \pi \in \mathsf{GW}(\nu, j, l_{\max})\}$$

For the FWMP objectives, we consider $l_{\max}$ to be a value that is given as input. Another natural question that arises is whether we can remove this input and consider an even weaker objective in which one asks if there exists an $l_{\max}$. This is captured in the definition of the *bounded window mean-payoff* (BWMP) objectives which are defined for a given threshold $\nu \in \mathbb{Q}$.

$$\mathsf{UDirBnd}(\nu) = \{\psi \mid \exists l_{\max} \in \mathbb{N}_0, \forall \pi \in \gamma(\psi), \forall i \geq 0 : \pi \in \mathsf{GW}(\nu, i, l_{\max})\}$$
$$\mathsf{DirBnd}(\nu) = \{\psi \mid \forall \pi \in \gamma(\psi), \exists l_{\max} \in \mathbb{N}_0, \forall i \geq 0 : \pi \in \mathsf{GW}(\nu, i, l_{\max})\}$$
$$\mathsf{UBnd}(\nu) = \{\psi \mid \exists l_{\max} \in \mathbb{N}_0, \exists i \geq 0, \forall \pi \in \gamma(\psi), \forall j \geq i : \pi \in \mathsf{GW}(\nu, j, l_{\max})\}$$
$$\mathsf{Bnd}(\nu) = \{\psi \mid \forall \pi \in \gamma(\psi), \exists l_{\max} \in \mathbb{N}_0, \exists i \geq 0, \forall j \geq i : \pi \in \mathsf{GW}(\nu, j, l_{\max})\}$$

As with the mean-payoff objectives we can assume, without loss of generality, that $\nu = 0$. Henceforth, we omit ν.

3.1 Relations Among Objectives

Figure 1 gives an overview of the relative strengths of each of the objectives and how they relate to the mean-payoff objective. The strictness, in general, of

Fig. 1. Implications among the objectives

Fig. 2. Blind WGA where, for any $l_{max} \in \mathbb{N}_0$, the only possible abstract play is in $\text{Fix}(l_{max})$ but not in $\text{UFix}(l_{max})$.

Fig. 3. Perfect information WGA where Eve wins both MP objectives but none of the FWMP or BWMP objectives.

most inclusions was established in [9], and Fig. 2 provides an example for the remaining case between Fix and UFix.

In general the mean-payoff objective is not sufficient for the FWMP or BWMP objectives, e.g. see Fig. 3. Our first result shows that if, however, Eve has a *finite memory* winning strategy for a *strictly positive* threshold, then this strategy is also winning for any of the FWMP or BWMP objectives. A specific subcase of this was first observed in Lemma 2 of [9].

Theorem 1. *Given WGA G, if Eve has a finite memory winning strategy for the MPInf(ϵ) (or MPSup(ϵ)) objective, for $\epsilon > 0$, then the same strategy is winning for her in the DirFix(μ)$_G$ game – where μ is bounded by the memory used by the strategy.*

3.2   Lower Bounds

In [9] it was shown that in multiple dimensions, with arbitrary window size, solving games with the (direct) fixed window objective was complete for EXP-time. We now show that in our setting this hardness result holds, even when the window size is a fixed constant and the weight function is given in unary.

Lemma 1. *Let $l_{max} \in \mathbb{N}_0$ be a fixed constant. Given WGA G, determining if Eve has a winning strategy for the DirFix(l_{max}), UFix(l_{max}) or the Fix(l_{max}) objectives is EXP-hard, even for unary weights.*

Proof. We give a reduction from the problem of determining the winner of a safety game with imperfect information, shown in [7] to be EXP-complete.

A safety game with imperfect information is played on a non-weighted game arena with partial-observation $G = \langle Q, q_I, \Sigma, \Delta, Obs \rangle$. A play of G is winning for Eve if and only if it never visits the *unsafe state* set $\mathcal{U} \subseteq Q$. Without loss of generality, we assume unsafe states are *trapping*, i.e. $(u, \sigma, q) \in \Delta$ and $u \in \mathcal{U}$ imply that $u = q$.

Let w be the transition weight function mapping $(u, \sigma, q) \in \Delta$ to -1 if $u \in \mathcal{U}$ and all other $t \in \Delta$ to 0. Denote by G_w the resulting WGA from adding w to G. It should be clear that Eve wins the safety game G if and only if she wins $\mathsf{MPInf}_{G_w}(0)$, $\mathsf{DirFix}_{G_w}(l_{\max})$, $\mathsf{UFix}_{G_w}(l_{\max})$, and $\mathsf{Fix}_{G_w}(l_{\max})$ – for any $l_{\max}$. That is, all objectives are equivalent for G_w.   □

In [9] the authors show that determining if Eve has a winning strategy in the k-dimensional version of the UDirBnd and UBnd objectives with perfect information is non-primitive recursive hard. We show that, in our setting, these decision problems are undecidable.

Theorem 2. *Given WGA G, determining if Eve has a winning strategy for any of the BWMP objectives is undecidable, even if G is blind.*

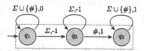

Fig. 4. Gadget which forces Eve to play infinitely many #.

Fig. 5. Gadget which, given that Eve will play # infinitely often, forces her to play # in intervals of bounded length.

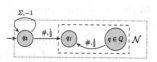

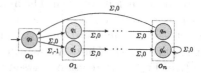

Fig. 6. Blind gadget to simulate the weighted automaton $\mathcal{N}$.

Fig. 7. For $n > l_{\max} + 1$ the abstract path $(o_0 \ldots o_n)^\omega$ is winning for the Fix condition but infinitely often visits an unsafe state in the construction from Sect. 4.

Proof (Sketch). Our proof is by a reduction from the universality problem of weighted finite automata which is undecidable [1]. A *weighted finite automaton* is a tuple $\mathcal{N} = \langle Q, \Sigma, q_I, \Delta, w \rangle$. A *run* of the automaton on a word $x = \sigma_0 \sigma_1 \ldots \sigma_n \in \Sigma^*$ is a sequence $r = q_0 q_1 \ldots q_n \in Q^+$ such that $(q_i, \sigma_i, q_{i+1}) \in \Delta$ for all $0 \le i < n$. The cost of the run r is $w(r) = \sum_{i=0}^{n-1} w(q_i, \sigma_i, q_{i+1})$. If the automaton is non-deterministic, it may have several runs on x. In that case, the *cost of x in $\mathcal{N}$* (denoted by $\mathcal{N}(x)$) is defined as the minimum of the costs of all its accepting runs on x.

The *universality* problem for weighted automata is to decide whether, for a given automaton $\mathcal{N}$, the following holds: $\forall x \in \Sigma^* : \mathcal{N}(x) < 0$. If so, $\mathcal{N}$ is *universal*. Our reduction constructs a blind WGA, $G_{\mathcal{N}}$, so that:

- if $\mathcal{N}$ is not universal, then Eve has a winning strategy for the objective UDirBnd,
- if $\mathcal{N}$ is universal, then Adam has a winning strategy for the complement of the objective Bnd.

As shown in Fig. 1, UDirBnd $\subseteq$ Bnd and all the other BWMP objectives lie in between those two. So, our reduction establishes the undecidability of all BWMP objectives at once.

Our reduction follows the gadgets given in Figs. 4, 5 and 6. When the game starts, Adam chooses to play from one of the three gadgets. As the game is blind for Eve, she does not know what is the choice of Adam and so she must be prepared for all possibilities. Note also that as Eve is blind, her strategy can be formalized by an infinite word $w \in (\Sigma \cup \{\#\})^\omega$. The first two gadgets force Eve to play a word w such that: (C_1) there are infinitely many $\#$ in w, and (C_2) there exists a bound $b \in \mathbb{N}$ such that the distance between two consecutive $\#$ in w is bounded by b. Note that although (C_1) holds under a mean-payoff objective, the Bnd objective is necessary to ensure (C_2).

Now, we assume Eve plays a word $w = \#w_1\#w_2\#w_3\# \ldots \#w_n\# \ldots$ that respects conditions C_1 and C_2, and we consider what happens when Adam plays in the third gadget (Fig. 6). The best strategy for Adam is to simulate the accepting runs of $\mathcal{N}$. If $\mathcal{N}$ is not universal then Eve chooses $w_1 \in \Sigma^*$ such that $\mathcal{N}(w_1) \geq 0$, and then she plays the strategy $(\#w_1)^\omega$ and she wins the objective UDirBnd. Indeed Eve plays a finite memory strategy that forces a mean-payoff which is at least $\frac{0.5}{b} > 0$ as each new $\#$ brings $+\frac{1}{2}$ and we know $\mathcal{N}(w_1) \geq 0$. The result then follows from Theorem 1. If $\mathcal{N}$ is universal, no matter which word w is played by Eve, the mean-payoff of the outcome of the game will be at most $\frac{-0.5}{b}$ as any word $w_1 \in \Sigma^*$ played between two consecutive $\#$ is such that $\mathcal{N}(w_1) \leq -1$. Thus, Adam wins for the complement of the mean-payoff objective. From the relation between the mean-payoff objective and Bnd (see Fig. 1) it follows that Adam wins for the complement of the objective Bnd. $\square$

4   Solving DirFix Games

In this section we establish an upper bound to match our lower bound of Sect. 3.2 for determining the winner of DirFix games. We first observe that for WGAs with perfect information the DirFix($l_{\max}$) objective has the flavor of a safety objective. Intuitively, a play π is winning for Eve if every suffix of π has a prefix of length at most $l_{\max}$ with average weight of at least 0. As soon as the play reaches a point for which this does not hold, Eve loses the play. In WGAs with partial-observation we need to make sure the former holds for all concretizations of an abstract play.

Consider an abstract path ψ and a positive integer n. We say a window of length l is open at $q \in \gamma(\psi[n])$ if there is some concretization χ of $\psi[..n]$ with $q = \chi[n]$ such that $\chi \notin \mathsf{GW}(n - l, l)$.

We construct a non-weighted game arena with perfect information G' from G. Eve's objective in G' will consist in ensuring the play never reaches locations in which there is an open window of length $l_{\max}$, for some state. This corresponds to a safety objective. Whether Eve wins the new game can be determined in time linear w.r.t. the size of the new game (see, e.g. [22]). The game will be played on a set of functions $\mathcal{F}$ which is described in detail below. We then show how to transfer winning strategies of Eve from G' to G and vice versa in Lemmas 5 and 6. Hence, this yields an algorithm to determine if Eve wins the $\mathsf{DirFix}(l_{\max})$ objective which runs in exponential-time.

Theorem 3. *Given WGA G, determining if Eve has a winning strategy for the $\mathsf{DirFix}(l_{max})$ objective is* EXP-*complete.*

Let us define the functions which will be used as the state space of the game. Intuitively, we keep track of the *belief* of Eve as well as the windows with the minimal weight open at every state of the belief.[1]

For the rest of this section let us fix a WGA with partial-observation G and a window size bound $l_{\max} \in \mathbb{N}_0$. We begin by defining the set of functions $\mathcal{F}$ as the set of all functions $f : Q \to (\{1, \ldots, l_{\max}\} \to \{-W \cdot l_{\max}, \ldots, 0\}) \cup \{\bot\}$. Denote by $\mathsf{supp}(f)$ the *support* of f, i.e. the set of states $q \in Q$ such that $f(q) \neq \bot$. For $q \in \mathsf{supp}(f)$, we denote by $f(q)_i$ the value $f(q)(i)$. The function $f_I \in \mathcal{F}$ is such that $f_I(q_I)_l = 0$, for all $1 \leq l \leq l_{\max}$, and $f_I(q) = \bot$ for all $q \in Q \setminus \{q_I\}$. Given $f_1 \in \mathcal{F}$ and $\sigma \in \Sigma$, we say $f_2 \in \mathcal{F}$ is a σ-*successor* of f_1 if

- $\mathsf{supp}(f_2) = \mathsf{post}_\sigma(\mathsf{supp}(f_1)) \cap o$ for some $o \in Obs$;
- for all $q \in \mathsf{supp}(f_2)$ and all $1 \leq j \leq l_{\max}$ we have that $f_2(q)_j$ maps to $\max\{-W \cdot l_{\max}, \min\{0, \zeta(q)\}\}$, where $\zeta(q)$ is defined as follows

$$
\zeta(q) = \begin{cases} \displaystyle\min_{\substack{p \in \mathsf{supp}(f_1) \wedge (p,\sigma,q) \in \Delta, \\ f_1(p)_{j-1} < 0}} f_1(p)_{j-1} + w(p,\sigma,q) & \text{if } j \geq 2 \\[2ex] \displaystyle\min_{p \in \mathsf{supp}(f_1) \wedge (p,\sigma,q) \in \Delta} w(p,\sigma,q) & \text{otherwise.} \end{cases}
$$

Lemma 2. *The number of elements in $\mathcal{F}$ is not greater than $2^{|Q| \cdot l_{max} \cdot \log(W \cdot l_{max})}$.*

We extend the supp operator to finite sequences of functions and actions. In other words, given $\rho' = f_0 \sigma_0 f_1 \sigma_1 \in (\mathcal{F} \cdot \Sigma)^*$, $\mathsf{supp}(\rho') \mapsto s_0 \sigma_0 s_1 \sigma_1 \ldots$ where $s_i = \mathsf{supp}(f_i)$ for all $i \geq 0$. In an abuse of notation, we define the function $\mathsf{supp}^{-1} : (Obs \cdot \Sigma)^* \times \mathcal{F} \to (\mathcal{F} \cdot \Sigma)^*$ which maps abstract paths to function-action sequences. Formally, given $\rho = o_0 \sigma_0 o_1 \sigma_1 \cdots \in \mathsf{Prefs}(G)$ and $\varphi \in \mathcal{F}$ with $\mathsf{supp}(\varphi) \subseteq o_0$, $\mathsf{supp}^{-1}(\rho, \varphi) \mapsto f_0 \sigma_0 f_1 \sigma_1 \ldots$ where $f_0 = \varphi$ and for all $i \geq 0$ we have that f_{i+1} is the σ_i-successor of f_i such that $\mathsf{supp}(f_{i+1}) \subseteq o_{i+1}$. Both supp and supp^{-1} are extended to infinite sequences in the obvious manner.

The following two results enunciate the key properties of sequences of the form $(\mathcal{F} \cdot \Sigma)^*$. Intuitively, the set of all those sequences corresponds to the windowed, weighted unfolding of G with information about reachable states as well as open windows.

---

[1] The terms belief and knowledge are used to denote a state from any variation of the classic "Reif construction" [19] to turn a game with partial-observation into a game with perfect information. Other names for similar constructions include "knowledge-based subset construction" (see e.g. [10]).

Lemma 3. *Let $\rho = o_0\sigma_0 \ldots o_n$ be an abstract path, $\varphi \in \mathcal{F}$ such that $supp(\varphi) \subseteq o_0$ and $supp^{-1}(\rho, \varphi) = f_0\sigma_0 \ldots f_n \in (\mathcal{F} \cdot \Sigma)^*$. A state $q \in Q$ is reachable from some state $q_0 \in supp(\varphi)$ through a concrete path $q_0\sigma_0 \ldots q_n \in \gamma(\rho)$ if and only if $q \in supp(f_n)$.*

Lemma 4. *Let $\rho = o_0\sigma_0 \ldots o_n$ be an abstract path, $\varphi \in \mathcal{F}$ such that $supp(\varphi) \subseteq o_0$ and $supp^{-1}(\rho, \varphi) = f_0\sigma_0 \ldots f_n \in (\mathcal{F} \cdot \Sigma)^*$. Given state $p \in supp(f_n)$ and $1 \leq l \leq l_{max}$ such that $l \leq n$, then there is a window of length l open at p if and only if $f_n(p)_l < 0$.*

Formally, the arena $G' = \langle \mathcal{F}, f_I, \Sigma, \Delta' \rangle$. The transition relation Δ' contains the transition (f_1, σ, f_2) if f_2 is the σ-successor of f_1. Eve, in G', is required to avoid states $\mathcal{U} = \{f \in \mathcal{F} \mid \exists q \in supp(f) : f(q)_{l_{max}} < 0\}$.

Lemma 5. *If Eve wins the safety objective in G', then she also wins the DirFix(l_{max}) objective in G.*

Proof. Assume λ' is a winning strategy for Eve in G'. We define a strategy λ for her in G as follows: $\lambda(\rho) \mapsto \lambda'(supp^{-1}(\rho, f_I))$ for all $\rho \in \mathsf{Prefs}(G)$. We claim that λ is winning for her in G. Towards a contradiction, assume $\psi \in \mathsf{Plays}(G)$ is consistent with λ and that $\psi \notin \mathsf{DirFix}(l_{max})$. Recall that this implies there are $n \in \mathbb{N}, q \in Q$ such that there is a window of length l_{max} open at $q \in \gamma(\psi[n])$. By Lemma 4 we then get that f_n from $supp^{-1}(\psi, f_I) = f_0\sigma_0 f_1\sigma_1 \ldots$ is in $\mathcal{U}$. As $supp^{-1}(\psi, f_I)$ is consistent with λ', this contradicts the assumption that λ' was winning. $\qquad\square$

Lemma 6. *If Eve wins the DirFix(l_{max}) objective in G, then she also wins the safety objective in G'.*

Proof. Assume λ is a winning strategy for Eve in G. We define a strategy λ' for her in G' as follows: $\lambda'(\rho') \mapsto \lambda \circ obs \circ supp(\rho')$ for all $\rho' \in \mathsf{Prefs}(G')$. We claim that λ' is winning for her in G'. Again, towards a contradiction, assume $\psi' \in \mathsf{Plays}(G')$ is consistent with λ' and that ψ' visits some $f \in \mathcal{U}$. This implies, by Lemma 4, that there is a window of length l_{max} open at some $q \in supp(f)$ in $\psi = obs(supp(\psi'))$. As Δ is total, for any $\sigma \in \Sigma$ Eve plays then there is valid σ-successor of q that Adam can choose as the next state. Hence there is some $\chi \in \mathsf{Plays}(G)$ consistent with λ such that χ and ψ have the same prefix up i_q, where $q \in \gamma(\chi[i_q])$, and there is a concretization π of χ such that $\pi[i_q] = q$. As χ is consistent with λ and $\chi \notin \mathsf{DirFix}(l_{max})$, this contradicts the fact that it was a winning strategy. $\qquad\square$

4.1 A Symbolic Algorithm for DirFix Games

We note that the state space of the construction G' presented in Sect. 4 admits an order such that if a state is smaller than another state, according to said order, and Eve has a strategy to win from the latter, then she has a strategy to win from the former. In this section we formalize this notion by defining the order and, in line with [4,8], propose an *antichain*-based algorithm to solve the safety game on G'.

We define the *uncontrollable predecessors* operator $\mathsf{UPre} : \mathcal{P}(\mathcal{F}) \to \mathcal{P}(\mathcal{F})$ as

$$\mathsf{UPre}(S) = \{p' \in \mathcal{F} \mid \forall \sigma \in \Sigma, \exists q' \in S : (p', \sigma, q') \in \Delta'\}.$$

For $S \in \mathcal{P}(\mathcal{F})$, we denote by $\mu X.(S \cup \mathsf{UPre}(X))$, the *least fixpoint* of the function $F : X \to S \cup \mathsf{UPre}(X)$ in the μ-calculus notation (see [14]). Note that F is defined on the powerset lattice, which is finite. The following is a well-known result about the relationship between safety games and the UPre operator (see e.g. [16]).

Proposition 1. *Eve wins a safety game with unsafe state set $\mathcal{U}$ if and only if the initial state of the game is not contained in $\mu X.(\mathcal{U} \cup \mathsf{UPre}(X))$.*

Definition 1 (The partial order). *Given $f', g' \in \mathcal{F}$ we say $f' \preceq g'$ if and only if $\mathsf{supp}(f') \subseteq \mathsf{supp}(g')$ and*

$$\forall q \in \mathsf{supp}(f'), \forall i \in \{1, \ldots, l_{max}\}, \exists j \in \{i, \ldots, l_{max}\} : f'(q)_i \geq g'(q)_j.$$

An *antichain* is a non-empty set $S \in \mathcal{P}(\mathcal{F})$ such that for all $x, y \in S$ we have $x \not\preceq y$. We denote by $\mathfrak{A}$ the set of all antichains. Given $a, b \in \mathfrak{A}$, denote by $a \sqsubseteq b$ the fact that $\forall x \in b, \exists y \in a : y \preceq x$. For $S \in \mathcal{P}(\mathcal{F})$ we denote by $\lfloor S \rfloor$ the set of minimal elements of S, that is $\lfloor S \rfloor = \{x \in S \mid \forall y \in S : y \preceq x \text{ implies } y = x\}$. Clearly $\lfloor S \rfloor$ is an antichain.

Given $S \in \mathcal{P}(\mathcal{F})$ we denote by $S{\uparrow}$ the *upward-closure* of S, that is $S{\uparrow} = \{t \in \mathcal{F} \mid S \preceq t\}$. We say a set $s \in \mathcal{P}(\mathcal{F})$ is *upward-closed* if $S = S{\uparrow}$. Note that $\lfloor S \rfloor{\uparrow} = S{\uparrow}$ and therefore, if S is upward-closed, the antichain $\lfloor S \rfloor$ is a succinct representation of S.

Lemma 7. *The following assertions hold.*

1. *$\mathcal{U}$ is upward-closed.*
2. *If $S, T \in \mathcal{P}(\mathcal{F})$ are two upward-closed sets, then $S \cup T$ is also upward-closed.*

The usual way of showing an antichain algorithm works dictates that we now prove the UPre operator, when applied to upward-closed sets, outputs an upward-closed set as well. Unfortunately, this is not true in our case. The following example illustrates this difficulty.

Example 1. Consider the WGA from Fig. 3 and let $l_{max} = 2$. We note that the function f such that $f(q_0) = \bot$ and $f(q_1)_1 = 1, f(q_1)_2 = 0$ is in $\mathsf{UPre}(\mathcal{U})$. We also have that for the function g such that $g(q_0) = \bot$ and $g(q_1)_1 = 0, g(q_1)_2 = 1$ we get that $f \preceq g$. It is easy to verify $g \notin \mathsf{UPre}(\mathcal{U})$. Hence, $\mathsf{UPre}(\mathcal{U})$ is not upward-closed.

However, we claim that one can circumvent this issue by ignoring elements from $\mathcal{U}$. Thus we are able to prove that, under some conditions, UPre does preserve "upward-closedness".

Lemma 8. *Given upward-closed set* $S \in \mathcal{P}(\mathcal{F})$ *and* $f, g \in \mathcal{F} \setminus \mathcal{U}$, *if* $f \in$ UPre(S) *and* $f \preceq g$, *then* $g \in$ UPre(S).

We define a version of the uncontrollable predecessors' operator which manipulates antichains instead of subsets of $\mathcal{F}$.

$$\lfloor \mathsf{UPre} \rfloor (a) = \lfloor \{p' \in \mathcal{F} \setminus \mathcal{U} \mid \forall \sigma \in \Sigma, \exists q' \in a, \exists r' \in \mathcal{F} : (p', \sigma, r') \in \Delta' \wedge q' \preceq r'\} \rfloor$$

Given $a, b \in \mathfrak{A}$ we denote by $a \sqcup b$ the *least upper bound* of a and b, i.e. $a \sqcup b = \lfloor \{q' \in \mathcal{F} \mid q' \in a \text{ or } q' \in b\} \rfloor$. It is easy to check that $(a \sqcup b)\uparrow = a\uparrow \cup b\uparrow$ for any $a, b \in \mathfrak{A}$.

Theorem 4. *Given WGA G, Eve wins the* DirFix(l_{max}) *objective if and only if* $\{q'_I\} \not\sqsupseteq \mu X.(\lfloor \mathcal{U} \rfloor \sqcup \lfloor \mathsf{UPre} \rfloor (X))$.

5 Solving **Fix** Games

Since Fix games are a prefix-independent version of DirFix games, it seems logical to consider an analogue of the perfect information game from the previous section with a prefix-independent condition. Indeed, the reader might be tempted to extend the approach used to solve DirFix games by replacing the safety objective with a *co-Büchi* objective in order to solve UFix or Fix games. However, we observe that although Eve winning in the resulting game is sufficient for her to win the original Fix game, it is not necessary. Indeed, an abstract play visits states from $\mathcal{U}$ infinitely often if and only if for infinitely many i there is a concretization of the play prefix up to i which violates GW(i, l_{max}). Nevertheless, this does not imply there exists one (infinite) concretization of the play which violates GW(i, l_{max}) for infinitely many i. Figure 7 illustrates this phenomenon.

For the reasons stated above, we propose to solve Fix games in a different way. We first introduce the notion of *observer*. Let $\mathcal{A}$ be a deterministic parity automaton.[2] We say $\mathcal{A}$ is an *observer for the objective* V if the language of $\mathcal{A}$ is V, i.e. $\mathcal{L}(\mathcal{A}) = V$. In [7], the authors show that the synchronized product of G and an observer for V is a parity game of perfect information which is won by Eve if and only if she wins G. Thus, it suffices to find an algorithm to construct an observer for Fix(l_{max}) to be able to solve Fix games.

For convenience, we start by describing a non-deterministic machine that accepts as its language the complement of Fix(l_{max}). Note that all elements of Fix(l_{max}) start with the observation $\{q_I\}$ so it suffices to describe the machine that accepts any word $w \in (\Sigma \cdot Obs)^{\omega}$ such that $\{q_I\} \cdot w \in$ Plays$(G) \setminus$ Fix(l_{max}). The construction is similar to the one used in [7] to make objectives of imperfect information games visible. Intuitively, at each step of the game and after Adam has revealed the next observation we will guess his actual choice of state using non-determinism. Additionally, we shall guess whether or not a violating window starts at the next step. The state space of the automaton will therefore consist

---

[2] We refer the reader who is not familiar with parity automata or games to [22].

of a single state from Q, a negative integer to record the weight of the tracked window, and the length of the current open window.

Formally, let $\mathcal{N}$ be the automaton consisting of the state space $F = Q \times \{1,\ldots,l_{\max}\} \times \{-W \cdot l_{\max},\ldots,-1\} \cup \{\bot\}$; initial state $(q_I, 1, \bot)$; input alphabet $\Sigma' = \Sigma \times Obs$; and $\Delta'' \subseteq F \times \Sigma' \times F$. The transition relation Δ'' has a transition $((p,i,n),(\sigma,o),(q,j,m))$ if $(p,\sigma,q) \in \Delta$, $q \in o$,

$$m = \begin{cases} w(p,\sigma,q) & \text{if } w(p,\sigma,q) < 0 \\ n + w(p,\sigma,q) & \text{if } n \neq \bot \wedge n + w(p,\sigma,q) < 0 \wedge i < l_{\max} \\ \bot & \text{otherwise,} \end{cases}$$

$$j = \begin{cases} i+1 & \text{if } m = n + w(p,\sigma,q) \\ 1 & \text{otherwise.} \end{cases}$$

We say a state $(q,i,n) \in F$ is accepting if $i = l_{\max}$ and $n \neq \bot$. The automaton accepts a word x if and only it has a run $(q_0,i_0,n_0)\,(\sigma_0,o_0)\,(q_1,i_1,n_1)\,(\sigma_1,o_2)\ldots$ on x such that for infinitely many j we have that (q_j,i_j,n_j) is accepting.

Proposition 2. *The non-deterministic Büchi automaton $\mathcal{N}$ accepts a word $\psi \in$ Plays(G) if and only if $\psi \notin$ Fix(l_{max}).*

At this point we determinize $\mathcal{N}$ and complement it to get a deterministic automaton with state space of size exponential in the size of $\mathcal{N}$ yet has parity index polynomial w.r.t. the size of Q (see [18,20,21]). The synchronized product of G and the observer yields a parity game with the same size bounds. The desired result follows from the parity games' algorithm and results of [17].

Theorem 5. *Given WGA G, determining if Eve has a winning strategy for the Fix(l_{max}) objective can be decided in time exponential in W and the size of G.*

Corollary 1. *Given WGA G with unary encoded weights, deciding if Eve has a winning strategy for the Fix(l_{max}) objective is* EXP-*complete.*

6   Solving UFix Games

In order to determine the winner of UFix games, we proceed as in the previous section by finding a non-deterministic Büchi automaton that recognizes the set of bad abstract plays. However, in this case the situation is more complicated because a bad abstract play might arise from a violation in the *uniformity*, rather than because of a concrete path with infinitely many window violations. Figure 2 illustrates this issue. To overcome this, we first provide an alternative characterization of the bad abstract plays for Eve. Consider some $\psi \in$ Plays(G). We say $\pi \in \gamma(\psi)$ *merges with infinitely many violating paths* if for all $i \geq 0$, there are $j \geq i$, $k \geq j + l_{\max}$ and some $\chi \in \gamma(\psi[..k])$ such that $\pi[k] = \chi[k]$ and $\chi \notin$ GW$(j,l_{\max})$. We refer to j as the position of the violation and to k as the position of the merge. Our next result formally states the relationship between concrete plays merging for multiple violations and UFix games.

Lemma 9. *Given WGA G and $\psi \in \text{Plays}(G)$, there is $\pi \in \gamma(\psi)$ merging with infinitely many violating paths if and only if $\psi \notin \text{UFix}(l_{max})$.*

Proof. ($\Rightarrow$) Assume there is a $\pi \in \gamma(\psi)$ merging with infinitely many violating paths. We have that there are two infinite sequences of indices $J = \{j_0, j_1, \dots\}$ and $K = \{k_0, k_1, \dots\}$ such that $j_l < j_{l+1}$ and $j_l + l_{max} \le k_l$, for all $l \ge 0$, and for which we know that there is concrete path $\chi_l \in \gamma(\psi[..k_l])$ such that $\chi[j_l..j_l + l_{max}]$ realizes an open window of length l_{max} and $\chi_l[k_l] = \pi[k_l]$, for all $l \ge 0$. Observe that for all $l \ge 0$ we have that $\chi_l \cdot \pi[k_l..] \in \gamma(\psi)$ and that $\chi_l \cdot \pi[k_l..] \notin \text{GW}(j_l, l_{max})$. In other words, $\forall l \ge 0, \exists \alpha \in \gamma(\psi), \exists m \ge l : \alpha \notin \text{GW}(m, l_{max})$ which implies that $\psi \notin \text{UFix}(l_{max})$.

($\Leftarrow$) Assume $\psi \notin \text{UFix}(l_{max})$. We have that there is a infinite sequence of indices $J = \{j_0, j_1, \dots\}$ such that $j_k < j_{k+1}$, for all $k \ge 0$, and for which we know there is a concrete play $\pi_k \in \gamma(\psi)$ such that $\pi_k \notin \text{GW}(j_k - l_{max}, l_{max})$, for all $k \ge 0$. Observe that for all $i \ge 0$ the set $\gamma(\psi[i])$ is finite and bounded by $|Q|$. Thus, by Pigeonhole Principle we have that, for all $n \ge 0$ there is $\eta_n \in \{\pi_m \mid 1 \le m \le |Q| \cdot n\} \subseteq \gamma(\psi)$ which merges with at least n violating paths. Consider an arbitrary η_1. If η_1 merges with infinitely many violating paths then we are done and the claim holds. Otherwise it only merges with a finite number of violating paths, say a_1. From the previous argument we know there is an $\eta_{a_1'} \in \gamma(\psi)$ that merges with at least $a_1' = a_1 + 1$. Clearly η_1 and $\eta_{a_1'}$ are disjoint at every point after a_1', lest η_1 would merge with a new violating path. We inductively repeat the process, if $\eta_{a_i'}$ merges with infinitely many violating paths then we are done. Otherwise it only merges with some finite number of violating paths, say a_i. In that case we turn our attention to $\eta_{a_{i+1}'}$. Note that since Q is finite this process can only be done a finite number of times. Indeed, after having discarded at most $|Q| - 1$ concrete plays (which are disjoint after some finite point) it must be the case the last remaining possible concrete play has the desired property or we would have a contradiction with our assumptions. Thus, there is some concrete play $\pi \in \gamma(\psi)$ that merges with infinitely many violating paths. □

We now construct the non-deterministic Büchi automaton $\mathcal{N}'$ that recognizes plays which contain a concrete path merging with infinitely many violating paths. The idea is that we non-deterministically keep track of two paths: one that will eventually witness a violation and then merge with the other, which ultimately serves as the witness for the path that merges with infinitely many violating paths. When the two paths merge, the automaton non-deterministically selects a new path to witness the violation. This is achieved by guessing a state in the belief set of Eve, as these states represent the end states of any concrete play consistent with the abstract play so far. To avoid the double exponential associated with taking the Reif construction before determinizing the automaton, we instead compute the belief set on-the-fly using a Moore machine that feeds into our non-deterministic automaton. By transferring the exponential state increase to an exponential increase in the alphabet size, the overall size of the determinized automaton (after composition with the Moore machine) will be at most singly exponential in the size of our game and W.

More specifically, denote by $\mathcal{B}$ the machine that, given $\psi = o_0\sigma_0o_1\sigma_1\cdots \in$ Plays(G) as its input yields the infinite sequence $o_0\sigma_0s_0o_1\sigma_1s_1\cdots \in (Obs \cdot \Sigma \cdot \mathcal{P}(Q))^\omega$ such that $s_0 = \{q_I\}$ and for all $i \geq 0$ we have $s_{i+1} = \text{post}_{\sigma_i}(s_i)$. One can easily give a definition of $\mathcal{B}$ – which closely resembles a subset construction – with a state space at most exponential w.r.t. G. Observe that $\mathcal{B}$ realizes a continuous function, in the sense that every prefix of length i of the input uniquely defines the next s_{i+1} annotation. Thus, the annotation can be done on-the-fly.

Formally, $\mathcal{N}'$ consists of the state space $F' = Q \times Q \times \{1,\ldots,l_{\max}\} \times \{-W \cdot l_{\max},\ldots,-1\} \cup \{\bot,\top\}$; initial state $(q_I, q_I, 1, \bot)$; input alphabet $\Sigma'' = \Sigma \times Obs \times \mathcal{P}(Q)$; and $\Delta''' \subseteq F \times \Sigma'' \times F$. The transition relation Δ''' has a transition $((p,p',i,n),(\sigma,o,s),(q,q',j,m))$ if $(p',\sigma,q') \in \Delta$, $q \in s$, $q' \in o$,

$$m = \begin{cases} w(p,\sigma,q) & \text{if } (p,\sigma,q) \in \Delta \wedge w(p,\sigma,q) < 0 \\ n + w(p,\sigma,q) & \text{if } (p,\sigma,q) \in \Delta \wedge n \neq \bot \wedge n + w(p,\sigma,q) < 0 \wedge i < l_{\max} \\ \top & \text{if } (p,\sigma,q) \in \Delta \wedge (n \neq \top \vee p \neq p') \wedge n \neq \bot \wedge i = l_{\max} \\ \bot & \text{otherwise,} \end{cases}$$

$$j = \begin{cases} l_{\max} & \text{if } m = \top \\ i+1 & \text{if } m = n + w(p,\sigma,q) \\ 1 & \text{otherwise.} \end{cases}$$

We say a state $(q,q',i,n) \in F'$ is accepting if $q = q'$, $n = \top$. $\mathcal{N}'$ accepts a word x if and only it has a run $(q_0,q_0',i_0,n_0)\,(\sigma_0,o_1,s_1)\,(q_1,q_1',i_1,n_1)\,(\sigma_1,o_2,s_2)\ldots$ on x such that for infinitely many j we have that (q_j,q_j',i_j,n_j) is accepting.

Proposition 3. *The non-deterministic Büchi automaton $\mathcal{N}'$ accepts a word $\alpha = \mathcal{B}(\psi)$, where $\psi \in$ Plays(G), if and only if $\psi \notin$ UFix(l_{max}).*

We recall that determinizing $\mathcal{N}'$ and complementing it yields an exponentially bigger deterministic automaton. Its composition with $\mathcal{B}$, itself exponentially bigger, accepts the desired set of plays and is still singly exponential in the size of the original arena and W. Once more, the desired result follows from the algorithm presented in [17].

Theorem 6. *Given WGA G, determining if Eve has a winning strategy for the UFix(l_{max}) objective can be decided in time exponential in W and the size of G.*

Corollary 2. *Given WGA G with unary encoded weights, deciding if Eve has a winning strategy for the UFix(l_{max}) objective is EXP-complete.*

References

1. Almagor, S., Boker, U., Kupferman, O.: What's decidable about weighted automata? In: Bultan, T., Hsiung, P.-A. (eds.) ATVA 2011. LNCS, vol. 6996, pp. 482–491. Springer, Heidelberg (2011)

2. Berwanger, D., Chatterjee, K., De Wulf, M., Doyen, L., Henzinger, T.A.: Alpaga: a tool for solving parity games with imperfect information. In: Kowalewski, S., Philippou, A. (eds.) TACAS 2009. LNCS, vol. 5505, pp. 58–61. Springer, Heidelberg (2009)

3. Björklund, H., Sandberg, S., Vorobyov, S.: Memoryless determinacy of parity and mean payoff games: a simple proof. TCS **310**(1), 365–378 (2004)

4. Bohy, A., Bruyère, V., Filiot, E., Jin, N., Raskin, J.-F.: Acacia+, a tool for LTL synthesis. In: Madhusudan, P., Seshia, S.A. (eds.) CAV 2012. LNCS, vol. 7358, pp. 652–657. Springer, Heidelberg (2012)

5. Brim, L., Chaloupka, J., Doyen, L., Gentilini, R., Raskin, J.-F.: Faster algorithms for mean-payoff games. Formal Methods Syst. Des. **38**(2), 97–118 (2011)

6. Chakrabarti, A., de Alfaro, L., Henzinger, T.A., Stoelinga, M.: Resource interfaces. In: Alur, R., Lee, I. (eds.) EMSOFT 2003. LNCS, vol. 2855, pp. 117–133. Springer, Heidelberg (2003)

7. Chatterjee, K., Doyen, L.: The complexity of partial-observation parity games. In: Fermüller, C.G., Voronkov, A. (eds.) LPAR-17. LNCS, vol. 6397, pp. 1–14. Springer, Heidelberg (2010)

8. Chatterjee, K., Doyen, L., Henzinger, T.A., Raskin, J.-F.: Algorithms for omega-regular games with imperfect information. In: Ésik, Z. (ed.) CSL 2006. LNCS, vol. 4207, pp. 287–302. Springer, Heidelberg (2006)

9. Chatterjee, K., Doyen, L., Randour, M., Raskin, J.-F.: Looking at mean-payoff and total-payoff through windows. In: Van Hung, D., Ogawa, M. (eds.) ATVA 2013. LNCS, vol. 8172, pp. 118–132. Springer, Heidelberg (2013)

10. Degorre, A., Doyen, L., Gentilini, R., Raskin, J.-F., Toruńczyk, S.: Energy and mean-payoff games with imperfect information. In: Dawar, A., Veith, H. (eds.) CSL 2010. LNCS, vol. 6247, pp. 260–274. Springer, Heidelberg (2010)

11. Doyen, L., Raskin, J.-F.: Antichains for the automata-based approach to model-checking. Logical Methods Comput. Sci. **5**(1), 1–20 (2009)

12. Doyen, L., Raskin, J.-F.: Antichain algorithms for finite automata. In: Esparza, J., Majumdar, R. (eds.) TACAS 2010. LNCS, vol. 6015, pp. 2–22. Springer, Heidelberg (2010)

13. Ehrenfeucht, A., Mycielski, J.: Positional strategies for mean payoff games. Int. J. Game Theory **8**, 109–113 (1979)

14. Emerson, E.A., Jutla, C.S.: Tree automata, mu-calculus and determinacy (extended abstract). In: STOCS, pp. 368–377. IEEE (1991)

15. Gentilini, R.: A note on the approximation of mean-payoff games. Inf. Process. Lett. **114**(7), 382–386 (2014)

16. Grädel, E.: Positional determinacy of infinite games. In: Diekert, V., Habib, M. (eds.) STACS 2004. LNCS, vol. 2996, pp. 4–18. Springer, Heidelberg (2004)

17. Jurdziński, M.: Small progress measures for solving parity games. In: Reichel, H., Tison, S. (eds.) STACS 2000. LNCS, vol. 1770, pp. 290–301. Springer, Heidelberg (2000)

18. Piterman, N.: From nondeterministic Büchi and Streett automata to deterministic parity automata. Logical Methods Comput. Sci. **3**(3), 1–21 (2007)

19. Reif, J.H.: The complexity of two-player games of incomplete information. J. Comput. Syst. Sci. **29**(2), 274–301 (1984)

20. Safra, S.: On the complexity of ω-automata. In: Symposium on Foundations of Computer Science, pp. 319–327. IEEE (1988)

21. Safra, S.: Exponential determinization for omega-automata with strong-fairness acceptance condition (extended abstract). In: STOC, pp. 275–282 (1992)

22. Thomas, W.: On the synthesis of strategies in infinite games. In: Mayr, E.W., Puech, C. (eds.) STACS 1995. LNCS, vol. 900, pp. 1–13. Springer, Heidelberg (1995)
23. Zwick, U., Paterson, M.: The complexity of mean payoff games on graphs. TCS **158**(1), 343–359 (1996)

Bounded Verification with On-the-Fly Discrepancy Computation

Chuchu Fan[✉] and Sayan Mitra

Department of Electrical and Computer Engineering,
University of Illinois at Urbana-Champaign, Champaign, USA
{cfan10,mitras}@illinois.edu

Abstract. Simulation-based verification algorithms can provide formal safety guarantees for nonlinear and hybrid systems. The previous algorithms rely on user provided model annotations called discrepancy function, which are crucial for computing reachtubes from simulations. In this paper, we eliminate this requirement by presenting an algorithm for computing piecewise exponential discrepancy functions. The algorithm relies on computing local convergence or divergence rates of trajectories along a simulation using a coarse over-approximation of the reach set and bounding the maximal eigenvalue of the Jacobian over this over-approximation. The resulting discrepancy function preserves the soundness and the relative completeness of the verification algorithm. We also provide a coordinate transformation method to improve the local estimates for the convergence or divergence rates in practical examples. We extend the method to get the input-to-state discrepancy of nonlinear dynamical systems which can be used for compositional analysis. Our experiments show that the approach is effective in terms of running time for several benchmark problems, scales reasonably to larger dimensional systems, and compares favorably with respect to available tools for nonlinear models.

1 Introduction

Verifying and falsifying nonlinear, switched, and hybrid system models using numerical simulations have been studied in detail [4,10,12,17,20]. The bounded time safety verification problem for a given model is parameterized by a time bound, a set of initial states, and a set of unsafe states and it requires one to decide if there exists a behavior of the model that reaches any unsafe set from any initial state. The simulation-based procedure for this problem first generates a set of numerical approximations of the behaviors from a finite sampling of the initial states. Next, by bloating these simulations by an appropriately large factor it computes an over-approximation of the reachable states from the initial set. If this over-approximation proves safety or produces a counter-example, then

The results presented here came about from work supported and funded by the National Science Foundation (NSF CSR 1016791) and the Air Force Office of Scientific Research (AFOSR YIP FA9550-12-1-0336).

B. Finkbeiner et al. (Eds.): ATVA 2015, LNCS 9364, pp. 446–463, 2015.
DOI: 10.1007/978-3-319-24953-7_32

the algorithm decides, otherwise, it draws more samples of initial states and repeats the earlier steps to compute a more precise over-approximation. With post-processing of the reachtube over-approximations this basic procedure can be utilized to verify termporal precedence [13] and richer classes of properties [8].

In order to make this type of procedure sound, the bloating factor should be chosen to be large. Specifically, it should be large enough to make each bloated simulation an over approximation of the reachable states of the system not only from the sampled initial state, but also from a large enough neighborhood of that state so that the union of these neighborhoods cover the entire set of initial states. On the other hand, to make the procedure complete, or at least relatively complete modulo the precision of the machine, it should be possible to make the error due to bloating arbitrarily small for any point in time. These two opposing requirements are captured in the definition of a *discrepancy function* of [12]: For an n-dimensional dynamical system, it is any function $\beta : \mathbb{R}^{2n} \times \mathbb{R}_{\geq 0} \to \mathbb{R}_{\geq 0}$, such that (a) it gives an upper-bound on the distance between any two trajectories $\xi(x,t)$ and $\xi'(x,t)$ of the system $|\xi(x,t) - \xi(x',t)| \leq \beta(x,x',t)$, and (b) it vanishes as x approaches x'. Simply using the Lipschitz constant of the dynamic function gives one such bound, but it grows exponentially with time even for some incrementally stable models [2].

In [12], it is observed that the notion of a contraction metric [23] gives a much tighter bound and it provided heuristics for finding them for some classes of polynomial systems. Sensitivity analysis approaches give strict error bounds for linear systems [10], but for nonlinear models the bounds are less clear. We present a more detailed overview of related work in Sect. 2. This paper fills this gap by providing a subroutine that computes a local version of the discrepancy function which turns out to be adequate and effective for sound and relatively complete simulation-based verification of more general nonlinear systems. This subroutine, *ComputeLDF*, itself uses a Lipschitz constant and the Jacobian of the dynamic function (the right hand side of the differential equation) and simulations of the system. The Lispchitz constant is used to construct a coarse, one-step over-approximation of the reach set of the system along a simulation. Then it computes an upper bound on the maximum eigenvalue of the symmetric part of the Jacobian over this over approximation, using a theorem from matrix perturbation theory. This gives an exponential bound on the distance between two trajectories, but roughly, the exponent is the best it can be as it is close to the maximum eigenvalue of the linear approximation of the system in the neighborhood. A key advantage of this scheme is that it is not necessary for the underlying system to have any special properties (such as incremental stability). In practice, ComputeLDF has been used successfully verify a powertrain control model proposed by Toyota Research group as a challenge problem [11,14], and the model of a neural circuit in a multicellular organism [21] .

In this paper, we also propose two practical extensions of this approach. First, we show that a linear coordinate transformation can bring about exponential improvements in the estimated distance. Secondly, we propose a technique for computing input-to-state discrepancy functions for analyzing composed systems and systems with bounded nondeterministic inputs. We report the results from a number of experiments performed with a prototype implementation of this approach applied to safety verification.

2 Related Work

Most existing techniques for formal verification rely on performing *reachability analysis*, which is a way of computing an overapproximation of the set of states that the system can reach over a given time horizon [16]. In [1] the authors provide an approach by linearizing the nonlinear system locally, and bounding the linearization error by Lagrange remainders. In [7], Taylor model is employed to analyze nonlinear hybrid systems. A pervasive challenge in such techniques is that the analysis can be too conservative, and faces the curse of dimensionality.

Simulation based verification has been studied in several papers recently [1,8,10,22]. Sensitivity analysis [8,10] is a technique to systematically simulate arbitrary continuous systems and nonlinear systems with inputs. The novelty of their approach consist in the use of the *sensitivity matrix* : a matrix that captures the sensitivity of the system to its initial condition x_0. This is then used to give an upper bound on the distance between two system trajectories. In [18] the authors present a convenient implementation of sensitivity analysis in the Simulink software. However, this approach cannot formally prove safety, as a quadratic error term is ignored when computing this upper bound. In [22], the authors provide methods to overapproximate the distance between trajectories; however, these methods are mainly applicable to affine and polynomial systems. In contrast, in Sects. 4 and 5 we have provided a strict over-approximation of Lipschitz continuous systems with respect to uncertainty in the initial conditions and uncertainty in the input signals.

The idea of discrepancy function can be seen as a generalization of the incremental stability [2]. An incremental Lyapunov function-based approach is used in [17]. The authors construct a finite symbolic model that is approximately bisimilar to the original switched system. Also in [26], incremental Lyapunov is used to compute finite sound abstractions of control systems without stability assumption. In this paper, our approach bypasses the incremental stability requirement by focusing on the bounded time verification, and we address on computing a good distance between trajectories.

Contraction in [23] is defined as the region in which the eigenvalues of the symmetric part of the Jacobian is uniformly negative. Contraction metrics introduced in [23] is also used in [12] to perform sound and relative complete analysis of nonlinear systems. We extend this idea of contraction by proving that given a region S, the maximum eigenvalue of the symmetric part of the Jacobian matrix over compact set S provides an exponential bound on the distance between any two trajectories in S.

3 Background

For a vector $x \in \mathbb{R}^n$, $\|x\|$ is the l^2-norm of x and x_i denotes its ith component. For $\delta \geq 0$, $B_\delta(x) = \{x' \in \mathbb{R}^n \mid \|x' - x\| \leq \delta\}$. For a set $S \subseteq \mathbb{R}^n$, $B_\delta(S) = \cup_{x \in S} B_\delta(x)$.

Let $S \oplus B_\delta(0)$ represents the Minkowski sum of S and $B_\delta(0)$. Therefore, $S \oplus B_\delta(0) = B_\delta(S)$. For sets $S_1, S_2 \subseteq \mathbb{R}^n$, $hull(S_1, S_2)$ is their convex hull. The diameter of a compact set S is $dia(S) = \sup_{x_1,x_2 \in S} \|x_1 - x_2\|$.

A continuous function $f : \mathbb{R}^n \to \mathbb{R}$ is *smooth* if all its higher derivatives and partial derivatives exist and are also continuous. It has a Lipschitz constant $L \geq 0$ if for every $x, x' \in \mathbb{R}^n$, $\|f(x) - f(x')\| \leq L\|x - x'\|$. A function $f : \mathbb{R}_{\geq 0} \to \mathbb{R}_{\geq 0}$ is a *class $\mathcal{K}$ function* if it is continuous, strictly increasing, and $f(0) = 0$.

Given a differentiable vector-valued function $f : \mathbb{R}^n \times \mathbb{R}^{\geq 0} \to \mathbb{R}^n$, the Jacobian J_f of f is the matrix-valued function of all the first-order partial derivatives of f. Let $f_i, i = 1 \ldots n : \mathbb{R}^n \to \mathbb{R}_{\geq 0}$ be the scalar components of f. The Jacobian of f is: $(J_f(x))_{ij} = \frac{\partial f_i(x)}{\partial x_j}$. The *symmetric part of the Jacobian of f* matrix is defined as $\frac{1}{2}(J_f(x) + J_f^T(x))$.

For an $n \times n$ matrix A, $\|A\|$ represents the l^2-norm of A: $\|A\| = \sqrt{\lambda_{\max}(A^H A)}$. A^H is the *conjugated transpose* of A, and $\lambda_{\max}(A)$ is the largest eigenvalue of matrix A. When A is a real matrix, we write it as A^T. If $\forall x \in \mathbb{R}^n$, $x^T A x \leq 0$, then we say A is negative-semidefinite, and write $A \preceq 0$. We write $A \preceq B$ if $A - B \preceq 0$.

Safety Verification Problem. Consider an *autonomous dynamical system*:

$$\dot{x} = f(x), \tag{1}$$

where $f : \mathbb{R}^n \to \mathbb{R}^n$ is a Lipschitz continuous function. A *solution or a trajectory* of the system is a function $\xi : \mathbb{R}^n \times \mathbb{R}_{\geq 0} \to \mathbb{R}^n$ such that for any initial point $x_0 \in \mathbb{R}^n$ and at any time $t \geq 0$, $\xi(x_0, t)$ satisfies the differential Eq. (1).

The *bounded-time safety verification problem* is parameterized by: (a) an n-dimensional dynamical system, that is, the function f defining the right hand side of its differential equation, (b) a compact set $\Theta \subseteq \mathbb{R}^n$ of initial states, (c) an open set $\mathbb{U} \subseteq \mathbb{R}^n$ of unsafe states, and (d) a time bound $T > 0$. A state x in $\mathbb{R}^n$ is *reachable from Θ within* a time interval $[t_1, t_2]$ if there exists an initial state $x_0 \in \Theta$ and a time $t \in [t_1, t_2]$ such that $x = \xi(x_0, t)$. The set of all reachable states in the interval $[t_1, t_2]$ is denoted by $\mathsf{Reach}(\Theta, [t_1, t_2])$. If $t_1 = 0$ then we write $\mathsf{Reach}(t_2)$ when set Θ is clear from the context. Given a bounded-time safety verification problem, we would like to design algorithms for deciding if any reachable state is safe, that is, if $\mathsf{Reach}(T) \cap \mathbb{U} = \varnothing$. If there exists some $\epsilon > 0$ such that $B_\epsilon(\mathsf{Reach}(T)) \cap \mathbb{U} = \varnothing$, we say the system is robustly safe. A sequence of papers [10,12,13] presented algorithms for solving this problem for a broad class of nonlinear dynamical, switched, and hybrid systems. In the remainder of this section, we present an overview of this approach (Algorithm 1).

Simulations, Reachtubes and Annotations. The algorithm uses simulation oracles that give sampled numerical simulations of the system from individual initial states.

Definition 1. *A (x_0, τ, ϵ, T)-simulation of the system described in Eq. (1) is a sequence of time-stamped sets $(R_0, t_0), (R_1, t_1) \ldots, (R_n, t_n)$ satisfying:*

(1) Each R_i is a compact set in $\mathbb{R}^n$ with $dia(R_i) \leq \epsilon$.

(2) *The last time $t_n = T$ and for each i, $0 < t_i - t_{i-1} \leq \tau$, where the parameter τ is called the* sampling period.

(3) *For each t_i, the trajectory from x_0 at t_i is in R_i, i.e., $\xi(x_0, t_i) \in R_i$, and for any $t \in [t_{i-1}, t_i]$, the solution $\xi(x_0, t) \in hull(R_{i-1}, R_i)$.*

Simulation engines generate a sequence of states and error bounds using numerical integration. Libraries like CAPD [6] and VNODE-LP [24] compute such simulations for a wide range of nonlinear dynamical system models and the R_i's are represented by some data structure like hyperrectangles.

Closely related to simulations are *reachtubes*. For a set of states $D \subseteq \mathbb{R}^n$, a (D, τ, T)-*reachtube* of (1) is a sequence of time-stamped sets $(R_0, 0), (R_1, t_1) \ldots, (R_n, t_n)$ satisfying:

(1) *Each $R_i \subseteq \mathbb{R}^n$ is a compact set of states.*
(2) *The last time $t_n = T$ and for each i, $0 \leq t_i - t_{i-1} \leq \tau$.*
(3) *For any $x_0 \in D$, and any time $t \in [t_{i-1}, t_i]$, the solution $\xi(x_0, t) \in R_i$.*

A reachtube is analogous to a simulation from a set of states, but they are much harder to compute. In fact, an algorithm for computing exact reachtubes readily solves the safety verification problem.

The algorithms in [12,19] require the user to decorate the model with annotations called *discrepancy functions* for computing reachtubes.

Definition 2. *A continuous function $\beta : \mathbb{R}^n \times \mathbb{R}^n \times \mathbb{R}_{\geq 0} \to \mathbb{R}_{\geq 0}$ is a* discrepancy *function of the system in Eq. (1) if*

(1) *for any $x, x' \in \mathbb{R}^n$, and any time $t > 0$, $\|\xi(x, t) - \xi(x', t)\| \leq \beta(x, x', t)$, and*
(2) *for any t, as $x \to x'$, $\beta(., ., t) \to 0$,*
(3) *$\forall \epsilon > 0, \forall x, x' \in \mathbb{R}^n, \exists \delta$ such that for any time t, $\|x - x'\| < \delta \Rightarrow \beta(x, x', t) < \epsilon$.*

If the function β meets the two conditions for any pair of states x, x' in a compact set K instead of $\mathbb{R}^n$ in both condition (1) and (3), then it is called a K-*local discrepancy function*.

The annotation β gives an upper bound on the distance between two neighboring trajectories as a function of their initial states and time. Unlike incremental stability conditions [2], the second condition on β does not require the trajectories to converge as time goes to infinity, but only as the initial states converge. Obviously, if the function f has a Lipschitz constant L, then $\beta(x, x', t) = \|x - x'\| e^{Lt}$ meets the above criteria. In [12,19] other heuristics have been proposed for finding discrepancy functions. As will be clear from the following discussion, the quality of the discrepancy function strongly influences the performance of the simulation-based verification algorithm. [12,19,20] need user provided discrepancy and simulation engines to give verification of bounded time safety and temporal precedence properties. In this paper, we will present approaches for computing *local discrepancy functions* that unburdens the user from finding these annotations.

3.1   Verification Algorithm

The simulation-based verification algorithm is shown in Algorithm 1. It takes as input some finite description of the parameters of a safety verification problem, namely, the function f, the initial set Θ, the unsafe set $\mathbb{U}$, and the time bound T. It has two main data stuctures: The first, $\mathcal{C}$ returned by function *Partition*, is a collection of triples $\langle \theta, \delta, \epsilon \rangle$ such that the union of all the δ-balls around the θ's completely cover the initial set Θ. The second data structure $\mathcal{R}$ incrementally gets the bounded-time reachtube from Θ.

Initially, $\mathcal{C}$ has a singleton cover $\langle \theta_0, \delta_0, \epsilon_0 \rangle$ such that $\delta_0 = dia(\Theta)$, $\Theta \subseteq B_{\delta_0}(\theta_0)$, and ϵ_0 is a small constant for simulation precision.

In the **while**-loop, this verification algorithm iteratively refines the cover of Θ and for each $\langle \theta, \delta, \epsilon \rangle$ in $\mathcal{C}$, computes over-approximations of the reachtube from $B_\delta(\theta)$. The higher-level structure of the algorithm is familiar: if the reachtube from $B_\delta(\theta)$ proves to be safe, i.e., disjoint from $\mathbb{U}$, then the corresponding triple is removed from $\mathcal{C}$ (Line 10). If part of the simulation from θ overlaps with $\mathbb{U}$, then the system is declared to be unsafe (Line 12). Otherwise, a finer cover of $B_\delta(\theta)$ is created, and the corresponding triples with finer parameters are added to $\mathcal{C}$.

Here we discuss the reachtubes computed from discrepancy and simulations. For each $\langle \theta, \delta, \epsilon \rangle$ in $\mathcal{C}$, a $(\theta, \tau, \epsilon, T)$-simulation ψ, which is a sequence of $\{(R_i, t_i)\}$, is generated. Note that ψ contains the trajectory from θ, $\xi(\theta, t), t \in [0, T]$. Then we bloat each R_i by some factor (Line 7) such that the resulting sequence contains the reachtube from $B_\delta(\theta)$. It is shown that this bloated simulation is guaranteed to be an over-approximation of $\mathsf{Reach}(B_\delta(\theta), T)$ and the union of these bloated simulations is an over-approximation of $\mathsf{Reach}(\Theta, T)$. Therefore, the algorithm is sound. Furthermore, the second property of β ensures that the reach set over-approximations become tighter and tighter as we make δ smaller and smaller. Finally it will return "SAFE" for robustly safe reachtubes or find a counter example and return "UNSAFE". For user defined discrepancy function, the factor is obtained by maximizing $\beta(\theta, \tilde{\theta}, t)$ over $\tilde{\theta} \in B_\delta(\theta)$ and $t \in [t_{i-1}, t_i]$. Indeed this is the approach taken in the algorithm presented in [12]. In this paper, we will analyze in detail the *ComputeLDF* subroutine which computes a local version of discrepancy function automatically. The following results from [12] state two key properties of the algorithm. Although in [12] β was defined globally, it is easy to check that the local version still satisfies them.

Theorem 1. *Algorithm 1 is sound, i.e., if it returns "SAFE" then the system is safe; when it returns "UNSAFE" there exists at least one execution from Θ that is unsafe. It is relatively complete, i.e., if the system is robustly safe, it will terminate and return "SAFE". If any executions from Θ is unsafe, it will terminate and return "UNSAFE".*

4   Local Discrepancy Function

In this section, we present the *ComputeLDF* algorithm and its analysis. This algorithm computes a special type of local discrepancy in terms of time-varying

---

Algorithm 1. Verification Algorithm

Input: $\Theta, \mathbb{U}, T$
1 $\delta \leftarrow dia(\Theta)$; $\epsilon \leftarrow \epsilon_0$; $\mathcal{C} \leftarrow \varnothing$; $\mathcal{R} \leftarrow \varnothing$; // epsilon$_0$ is a small constant
2 $\mathcal{C} \leftarrow \langle Partition(\Theta, \delta), \delta, \epsilon \rangle$
3 **while** $\mathcal{C} \neq \varnothing$ **do**
4 $\quad$ **foreach** $(\theta, \delta, \epsilon) \in \mathcal{C}$ **do**
5 $\quad\quad$ $\psi = \{(R_i, t_i)\}_{i=1}^k \leftarrow Simulate(\theta, \tau, \epsilon, T)$
6 $\quad\quad$ $\beta \leftarrow ComputeLDF(\psi, J_f, L_f, \delta, \epsilon)$
7 $\quad\quad$ $\mathrm{D} \leftarrow \psi \oplus \beta$
8 $\quad\quad$ **if** $D \cap \mathbb{U} = \varnothing$ **then**
9 $\quad\quad\quad$ $\mathcal{C} \leftarrow \mathcal{C} \setminus \{(\theta, \delta, \epsilon)\}$
10 $\quad\quad\quad$ $\mathcal{R} \leftarrow \mathcal{R} \cup D$
11 $\quad\quad$ **else if** $\exists k, R_k \subseteq \mathbb{U}$ **then**
12 $\quad\quad\quad$ **return** (UNSAFE, $\mathcal{R}$)
13 $\quad\quad$ **else**
14 $\quad\quad\quad$ $\mathcal{C} \leftarrow \mathcal{C} \setminus \{(\theta, \delta, \epsilon)\}$
15 $\quad\quad\quad$ $\mathcal{C} \leftarrow \mathcal{C} \cup Partition(\Theta \cap B_\delta(\theta), (\frac{\delta_1}{2}, \ldots, \frac{\delta_N}{2}), \frac{\epsilon}{2})$

16 **return** (SAFE, $\mathcal{R}$)

---

exponential functions that bound from above the distance between two trajectories starting from a compact neighborhood. Roughly speaking, it computes the rate of trajectory convergence or divergence for an interval of time instances.

Definition 3. *Consider a compact set* $C \subseteq \mathbb{R}^n$ *and a sequence of time points* $0 = t_0 < t_1 < t_2 < \ldots < t_k = T$. *For* $\forall x_1, x_2 \in C, \forall t \in [0, T]$, *a piecewise exponential discrepancy function* $\beta : C \times C \times [0, T] \rightarrow \mathbb{R}_{\geq 0}$ *is defined as:*

$$\beta(x_1, x_2, t) = \begin{cases} \|x_1 - x_2\|, & if\ t = t_0, \\ \beta(x_1, x_2, t_{i-1})e^{b[i](t-t_{i-1})}, & if\ t \in (t_{i-1}, t_i], \end{cases} \tag{2}$$

where $b[1], \ldots, b[k]$ *are real constants.*

From the definition, we can immediately get that $\beta(x_1, x_2, t) = \|x_1 - x_2\|$ $e^{b[i](t-t_{i-1})+\sum_{j=1}^{i-1} b[j](t_j - t_{j-1})}$, $i = 1, \ldots, k$, where t_{i-1} is the largest time point in the sequence before t.

4.1   ComputeLDF Algorithm

Algorithm 2 shows the pseudocode for *ComputeLDF* used in Line 6 of the verification algorithm. *ComputeLDF* takes as input a parameter δ, an error bound for simulation ϵ, the Lipschitz constant L_f, the Jacobian matrix J_f of function f, and a $(\theta, \tau, \epsilon, T)$-simulation $\psi = \{(R_i, t_i)\}, i = 0, 1, \ldots, k$. It computes a piecewise exponential local discrepancy function (LDF) for the compact set $B_\delta(R_0)$ and for the time points $t_0, \ldots, t_k$ and returns it as an array of exponential coefficients b.

Algorithm 2. Algorithm *ComputeLDF*.

Input: $\psi = \{(R_i, t_i)\}_{i=1}^k, J_f, L_f, \delta, \epsilon$

1 $\Delta \leftarrow \delta, b \leftarrow$ zeros(k)
2 **for** $i = 1{:}k$ **do**
3 $\quad \tau \leftarrow t_i - t_{i-1}$
4 $\quad d \leftarrow (\Delta + \epsilon)e^{L_f \tau}$
5 $\quad S \leftarrow hull(R_{i-1}, R_i) \oplus B_d(0)$
6 $\quad J \leftarrow J_f(center(S))$
7 $\quad \lambda \leftarrow \max(eig(J + J^T)/2)$
8 $\quad$ error $\leftarrow$ upper $_{x \in S}\|(J_f(x) + J_f^T(x)) - (J + J^T)\|$
9 $\quad b[i] \leftarrow \lambda + \text{error}/2$
10 $\quad \Delta \leftarrow (\Delta + \epsilon)e^{b[i]\tau}$

11 **return** b

The algorithm starts with the initial set $B_\delta(R_0)$ and with $\Delta = \delta$. In each iteration of the **for**-loop it computes exponent $b[i]$ corresponding to the time interval $[t_{i-1}, t_i]$. In the ith iteration, Δ is updated so that $B_\Delta(R_{i-1})$ is an over-approximation of the reachable states from $B_\delta(R_0)$ at t_{i-1} (Lemma 5). In Lines 4–5, a set S is computed by bloating the convex hull $hull(R_{i-1}, R_i)$ by a factor of $d = (\Delta + \epsilon)e^{L_f(t_i - t_{i-1})}$. The set S will later be proved to be a (coarse) over-approximation of the reachtube from $B_\Delta(R_{i-1})$ over the time interval $[t_{i-1}, t_i]$ (Lemma 1). In Lines 6–9 an upper bound on the maximum eigenvalue of the symmetric part of the Jacobian over the set S, is computed as $b[i]$ (Lemma 3). Then Δ is updated as $(\Delta + \epsilon)e^{b[i](t_i - t_{i-1})}$ for the next iteration.

4.2   Analysis of ComputeLDF

In this section, we will prove that $ComputeLDF(\psi, J_f, L_f, \delta, \epsilon)$ returns a piece-wise exponential LDF of the system in Eq. (1), for the compact neighborhood $B_\delta(R_0)$, and the sequence of the time points in the simulation ψ. We establish some lemmas to prove the main theorem. The complete proof of the lemmas can be found in the technical report [15]. First, we show in Lemma 1 that in the ith iteration of the loop, the computed S is an over-approximation of the set of states that can be reached by the system from $B_\Delta(R_{i-1})$ over the time interval $[t_{i-1}, t_i]$.

Lemma 1. *In the ith iteration of ComputeLDF,* Reach$(B_\Delta(R_{i-1}), [t_{i-1}, t_i]) \subseteq S$.

Lemma 1 shows that using Lipschitz constant and Gronwall's inequality we can get an one step over-approximation of the reachtube.

Next, using the generalized mean value theorem (Lemma 2), we get that in the ith iteration, the computed $b[i]$ in Line 9 is the exponential divergence (if positive) or convergence (negative) rate of the distance between any two trajectories starting from $B_\Delta(R_{i-1})$ over time $[t_{i-1}, t_i]$.

Lemma 2. *For any continuously differentiable vector-valued function $f : \mathbb{R}^n \to \mathbb{R}^n$, and $x, r \in \mathbb{R}^n$, $f(x + r) - f(x) = \left(\int_0^1 J_f(x + sr)ds \right) \cdot r$, where the integral is component-wise.*

Next, we will use a well-known theorem that gives bounds on eigenvalues of perturbed symmetric matrices, the proof of which uses the Courant-Fischer minimax theorem.

Theorem 2. *If A and E are $n \times n$ symmetric matrices, then*

$$\lambda_n(E) \le \lambda_k(A + E) - \lambda_k(A) \le \lambda_1(E),$$

where $\lambda_i(\cdot)$ is the ith largest eigenvalue of a matrix.

Corollary 1. *If A and E are $n \times n$ symmetric matrices, then*

$$|\lambda_k(A + E) - \lambda_k(A)| \le \|E\|. \tag{3}$$

Since A is symmetric, $\|A\| = \sqrt{\lambda_{\max}(A^T A)} = \max(|\lambda(A)|)$. From Theorem 2, we have $|\lambda_k(A + E) - \lambda_k(A)| \le \max\{|\lambda_n(E)|, |\lambda_1(E)|\} = \|E\|$. If $E(x)$ is a matrix-valued function: $\mathbb{R}^n \to \mathbb{R}^{n \times n}$ maps a state $x \in \mathbb{R}^n$ to a matrix $E(x)$, and every component of $E(x), e_{ij}(x) : \mathbb{R}^n \to \mathbb{R}$ is continuous over some compact closed set S, then we can get an upper bound of $\|E(x)\|$ over S by compute the upper bound of the absolute value of each term $e_{ij}(x)$, $|e_{ij}(x)|$ over S. Let $\text{upper}_{x \in S}(|e_{ij}(x)|)$ be denoted by $\tilde{e}_{ij}$, then we know $\forall x \in S, \|E(x)\| \le \sqrt{\sum_{i=1}^n \sum_{j=1}^n \tilde{e}_{ij}^2}$. Because we assume the system to be Lipschitz continuous, the upper bound of the symmetric part of the Jacobian matrix in Line 8 always exists. Using Corollary 1, we next show in Lemma 3 that $b[i]$ calculated in Line 9 bounds the eigenvalues of the symmetric part of Jacobian matrix over S.

Lemma 3. *In the ith iteration, for $\forall x \in S : J_f^T(x) + J_f(x) \preceq 2b[i]I$.*

Proof. Let S be the set computed in Line 5 and J be the Jacobian evaluated at the center s_0 of S. Consider any point $x \in S$. We define the perturbation matrix $E(x) \equiv J_f^T(x) + J_f(x) - (J^T + J)$. Since $J_f^T(x) + J_f(x)$ and $J^T + J$ are symmetric matrices, Corollary 1 implies that $\lambda_{max}(J_f^T(x) + J_f(x)) - \lambda_{max}(J^T + J) \le \|E(x)\|$. The *error* term computed in Line 8 is the upperbound on $\|E(x)\|$. Therefore, $\lambda_{max}(J_f^T(x) + J_f(x)) \le \lambda_{max}(J^T + J) + error$. In Line 9 set $b[i]$ equals to $\lambda_{max}((J^T + J)/2) + error/2$. Thus, $\lambda_{max}(J_f^T(x) + J_f(x)) \le 2b[i]$, which immediately indicates that $\forall x \in S : J_f^T(x) + J_f(x) \preceq 2b[i]I$.

By Lemmas 2 and 3, we can prove as in Lemma 4 that $b[i]$ calculated in Line 9 is the exponential rate of divergence or convergence of two trajectories starting from $B_\Delta(R_{i-1})$ over the interval $[t_{i-1}, t_i]$.

Lemma 4. *In the ith iteration, for any two states $x_1, x_2 \in B_\Delta(R_{i-1})$ at time t_{i-1}, and any time $t \in [t_{i-1}, t_i]$, $\|\xi(x_1, t) - \xi(x_2, t)\| \le \|x_1 - x_2\| e^{b[i](t - t_{i-1})}$.*

This lemma can be deduced using Lemma 2.

Up to this point all the lemmas were statements about a single iteration of the for -loop, next we show that in the ith iteration of the loop, $B_\Delta(R_i)$ used in Lemmas 1 and 4 is the reach set from $B_\delta(R_0)$ at time t_i.

Lemma 5. *For* $\forall i = 1, \ldots, k$, $\mathsf{Reach}(B_\delta(R_0), [t_i, t_i]) \subseteq B_{\Delta_i}(R_i)$, *and* $\mathsf{Reach}(B_{\Delta_{i-1}}(R_{i-1}), [t_{i-1}, t_i]) \subseteq hull(R_{i-1}, R_i) \oplus B_{\Delta'_i}(0)$, *where Δ_i is Δ after Line 10 is executed in the ith iteration, and $\Delta'_i = \max\{\Delta_i, \Delta_{i-1} + \epsilon\}$.*

Proof. The lemma is proved by induction on i. First, we know that when $i = 1$, $\mathsf{Reach}(B_\delta(R_0), [t_0, t_0]) = B_\delta(R_0) = B_{\Delta_0}(R_0)$. Then we will prove that

$$\mathsf{Reach}(B_\delta(R_0), [t_0, t_1]) \subseteq hull(R_0, R_1) \oplus B_{\max\{\Delta_1, \Delta_0 + \epsilon\}}(0),$$

using Lemma 4.

Assuming that the lemma holds for $i = m - 1$, we have $\mathsf{Reach}(B_\delta(R_0),$ $[t_{m-1}, t_{m-1}]) \subseteq B_{\Delta_{m-1}}(R_{m-1})$. And we will prove that the lemma holds for $i = m$ as well.

$\cup_{i=1}^k \{hull(R_{i-1}, R_i) \oplus B_{\Delta'_i}(0)\}$ contains the $(B_\delta(R_0), \tau, T)$-reachtube of the system. Line 7 of Algorithm 1 is computed in this way. Now we are ready to prove the main theorem.

Theorem 3. *The items in array b computed by ComputeLDF are the coefficients of a $B_\delta(R_0)$-local piecewise exponential discrepancy function (Definition 3).*

Proof. First of all consider any time $t \in [t_0, t_1]$ and any two states: $x_1, x_2 \in B_\delta(R_0)$. By Lemma 4, $\|\xi(x_1, t) - \xi(x_2, t)\| \le \|x_1 - x_2\|e^{b[1](t-t_0)}$. Then consider $t \in [t_1, t_2]$. By Lemma 5 we know at time t_1, $\xi(x_1, t_1)$ and $\xi(x_2, t_1)$ are all contained in $B_{\Delta_1}(R_1)$, so we can use Lemma 4 such that for any time $t \in [t_1, t_2]$, $\|\xi(x_1, t) - \xi(x_2, t)\| \le \|\xi(x_1, t_1) - \xi(x_2, t_1)\|e^{b[2](t-t_1)} \le \|x_1 - x_2\|e^{b[2](t-t_1)+b[1](t_1-t_0)}$.

The procedure above can be performed iteratively as follows. For any time $t \in [t_{i-1}, t_i]$, by Lemma 5 we know at time t_{i-1}, $\xi(x_1, t_{i-1})$ and $\xi(x_2, t_{i-1})$ are all contained in $B_{\Delta_{i-1}}(R_{i-1})$. By Lemma 4 it follows that

$$\|\xi(x_1, t) - \xi(x_2, t)\| \le \|\xi(x_1, t_{i-1}) - \xi(x_2, t_{i-1})\|e^{b[i](t-t_{i-1})}$$
$$\le \|x_1 - x_2\|e^{b[i](t-t_{i-1})+\sum_{j=1}^{i-1} b[j](t_j-t_{j-1})}.$$

Next we will prove that
$\beta(x_1, x_2, t) \equiv \|x_1 - x_2\|e^{b[i](t-t_{i-1})+\sum_{j=1}^{i-1} b[j](t_j-t_{j-1})}$ is a valid LDF.

In Lines 6–9, because J is a real matrix, the maximum eigenvalue λ of $(J^T + J)/2$ is bounded. Assume that each component of $E(x) = J_f^T(x) + J_f(x) - J^T - J$ is continuous over the closed set S, then we can find the upper bound of $\|E(x)\|$, so the "error" term is also bounded. Therefore, each $b[i]$ is bounded. So $\forall t \in [t_{i-1}, t_i]$, $i = 1, \ldots, k$, $\exists N < \infty$, such that $e^{b[i](t-t_{i-1})+\sum_{j=1}^{i-1} b[j](t_j-t_{j-1})}$ is bounded by N from the above.

As $x_1 \to x_2$, obviously,

$$\|x_1 - x_2\|e^{b[i](t-t_{i-1})+\sum_{j=1}^{i-1} b[j](t_j-t_{j-1})} \to 0.$$

And for any $\epsilon > 0$, $\exists \delta = \epsilon/N > 0$, such that $\forall x_1, x_2 \in B_\delta(R_0)$ and $\|x_1 - x_2\| < \delta$, it follows

$$\|x_1 - x_2\|e^{b[i](t-t_{i-1})+\sum_{j=1}^{i-1} b[j](t_j-t_{j-1})} < \epsilon/N \cdot N = \epsilon.$$

So $\beta(x_1, x_2, t) = \|x_1 - x_2\|e^{b[i](t-t_{i-1})+\sum_{j=1}^{i-1} b[j](t_j-t_{j-1})}$ is a $B_\delta(R_0)$-local piecewise discrepancy function and the array b contains the corresponding coefficients.

4.3   Coordinate Transformation

In this section, we will discuss the issue that the upper bound of the symmetric part of the Jacobian computed in Lines 6–9 may introduce loss in precision. We propose a a strategy to reduce this loss by first performing a coordinate transformation. Consider a simple linear system:

$$\dot{x} = [0 \ \ 3; -1 \ \ 0]x, \tag{4}$$

which has eigenvalues $\pm\sqrt{3}i$ and thus its trajectories oscillate. The symmetric part of the Jacobian is $[0 \ \ 1; 1 \ \ 0]$ with eigenvalues ± 1, which gives the exponentially growing discrepancy with $b = 1$. In what follows, we will see that a tighter bound can be obtained by first taking a linear transformation of x. The following is a coordinate transformed version of Lemma 4. The coordinate transformation matrix P can be any $n \times n$ real invertible matrix, and the condition number of P is $\|P\|\|P^{-1}\|$.

Lemma 6. *In i^{th} iteration of the loop, for any $x_1, x_2 \in B_\Delta(R_{i-1})$, and any $t \in [t_{i-1}, t_i]$,*

$$\|\xi(x_1, t) - \xi(x_2, t)\| \leq K\|x_1 - x_2\|e^{\tilde{\lambda}_{max}(S)(t-t_{i-1})},$$

where $\tilde{\lambda}_{max}(S)$ is the upper bound of $\frac{1}{2}(\widetilde{J_f}^T(x) + \widetilde{J_f}(x))$ over the set S, $\widetilde{J_f}(x) = PJ_f(x)P^{-1}$, and K is the condition number of P.

The proof of Lemma 6 is similar to the proof of Lemma 4 considering the coordinate transformation. This shows that the distance can be bounded in the same way for the transformed system with a (possibly much smaller) $\tilde{\lambda}_{max}(S)$ but with an additional multiplicative cost of $cond(P)$.

To choose the coordinate transformation matrix, one approach that produces good empirical results is making the Jacobian matrix at the center point a real Jordan form. Let S be the set computed in Line 5 and J is the Jacobian evaluated at the center s_0 of S. Let $\tilde{J} = PJP^{-1}$ the real Jordan form and use the matrix P as the coordinate transformation matrix for $J_f(x)$. Contraction matrix [23] introduces more general coordinate transformation. However, there are no general methods to compute it for nonlinear systems. Choosing a constant matrix as transformation is an implementable approach, and Lemma 6 applies to any invertible matrix.

In the previous example (4), the Jacobian matrix is constant, and the discrepancy function without coordinate transformation is:

$$\|\xi(x_1, t) - \xi(x_2, t)\| \leq \|x_1 - x_2\| e^{t - t_1}.$$

If we use $P = [1 \quad 3; -\sqrt{3} \quad \sqrt{3}]$ as the coordinate transformation matrix, $\tilde{J} = PJP^{-1} = [0 \quad \sqrt{3}; -\sqrt{3} \quad 0]$, and the discrepancy function with coordinate transformation is

$$\|\xi(x_1, t) - \xi(x_2, t)\| \leq \sqrt{3} \|x_1 - x_2\|.$$

In practice, the coordinate transformation can be made for longer time interval $[t_{i-k}, t_i]$, where $k > 2$, to reduce the multiplicative error term $\prod cond(P[i])$.

5   Local Input-State Discrepancy

Large and complex models of dynamical system are created by composing smaller modules or subsystems. Consider a dynamical system A consisting of several interacting subsystems $A_1, \ldots, A_N$, that is, the input signals of a subsystem A_i are driven by the outputs (or states) of some another component A_j. Let's say that each A_i is n-dimensional which makes A nN-dimensional. One way of achieving scalable verification of A is to exploit this compositional structure and somehow analyze the component A_i's to infer properties of A.

In [20], the notion of input-to-state (IS) discrepancy was introduced to address the problem of finding annotations for large models. It is shown that if we can find input-to-state (IS) discrepancy functions for the individual component A_i, then we can construct a reduced N-dimensional model M such that the executions of M serve as the discrepancy of the overall system. Thus, from IS-discrepancy for the smaller A_i models and simulations of the N-dimensional system M, we are able to verify A. This has the beneficial side-effect that if the A_i's are rewired in a new topology, then only the reduced model changes [19]. However, [20] still assumes that the user provides the IS-discrepancy for the smaller modules. In this section, we will show the approach used in the previous section can be used to get IS discrepancy function for Lipschitz continuous nonlinear subsystems A_i. Furthermore, it gives an over-approximation of the reachsets with nondeterministic bounded inputs.

5.1   Defining Local IS Discrepancy

Consider a dynamical system with inputs:

$$\dot{x} = f(x, u) \tag{5}$$

where $f : \mathbb{R}^n \times \mathbb{R}^p \to \mathbb{R}^n$ is Lipschitz continuous. For a given input signal which is a integrable function $v : [0, \infty) \to \mathbb{R}^p$, and an initial state $x_0 \in \mathbb{R}^n$, a solution (or trajectory) of the system is a function $\xi : \mathbb{R}^n \times \mathbb{R}_{\geq 0} \to \mathbb{R}^n$ such that $\xi(x_0, 0) = x_0$ and for any time $t \geq 0$, $\dot{\xi}(x, t) = f(\xi(x, t), v(t))$.

First, we give the original definition of IS discrepancy function for the system in [5]. Here $\mathcal{U}$ is the set $\{u | u : [0, \infty) \to \mathbb{R}^p\}$ of all input signals.

Definition 4. *A pair of uniformly continuous functions* $\beta : \mathbb{R}_{\geq 0} \times \mathbb{R}_{\geq 0} \to \mathbb{R}_{\geq 0}$ *and* $\gamma : \mathbb{R}_{\geq 0} \to \mathbb{R}_{\geq 0}$ *is called C-local input-to-state discrepancy if*

(1) β is of class $\mathcal{K}$ with respect to its first argument and γ is also of class $\mathcal{K}$,
(2) for any pair of initial states $x, x' \in C$, any pair of input signals $u, u' \in \mathcal{U}$, and $t \in \mathbb{R}_{\geq 0}$: $\|\xi(x, t) - \xi(x', t)\| \leq \beta(\|x - x'\|, t) + \int_0^t \gamma(\|u(s) - u'(s)\|) ds$.

For a bounded, compact set $\mathcal{I} \subseteq \mathbb{R}^p$. A family of bounded time input signals over $\mathcal{I}$ is the set $\mathcal{U}(\mathcal{I}) = \{u | u : [0, T) \to \mathcal{I}\}$ of integrable functions. We denote $\text{Reach}(K, \mathcal{U}(\mathcal{I}), [t_1, t_2])$ as the reachable states of the system from compact set K with input set $\mathcal{U}(\mathcal{I})$ over $[t_1, t_2]$. Next, we introduce an inductive definition of IS discrepancy for inputs over compact neighborhoods.

Definition 5. *Consider compact sets $K \in \mathbb{R}^n, \mathcal{I} \in \mathbb{R}^p$ and a sequence of time points $0 = t_0 < t_1 < t_2 < \ldots < t_k = T$. For any pair of initial states $x_1, x_2 \in K$, any pair of input signals $u_1, u_2 \in \mathcal{U}(\mathcal{I})$, the $(K, \mathcal{U}(\mathcal{I}))$-local IS discrepancy function $\alpha : K^2 \times \mathcal{U}(\mathcal{I})^2 \times \mathbb{R}_{\geq 0} \to \mathbb{R}_{\geq 0}$ is defined as:*

$$\alpha(x_1, x_2, u_1, u_2, t) = \begin{cases} \|x_1 - x_2\|, & \text{if } t = t_0, \\ \alpha(x_1, x_2, u_1, u_2, t_{i-1}) e^{a[i](t - t_{i-1})} + \\ M[i] e^{a[i](t - t_{i-1})} \int_{t_{i-1}}^t \|u_1(\tau) - u_2(\tau)\| d\tau & \text{if } t \in (t_{i-1}, t_i] \end{cases}$$

where $a[1], \ldots, a[k], M[1], \ldots, M[k]$ are real constants.

5.2   Algorithm for Local IS Discrepancy

The approach to find $(K, \mathcal{U}(\mathcal{I}))$-local IS discrepancy function is similar to *ComputeLDF* algorithm, which also uses a **for** -loop to compute the coefficients $a[i]$ and $M[i]$. The only changes are 1) in Line 5 S should be computed as in Lemma 7, 2) in Line 10 Δ should be updated as in Lemma 9. Next we illustrate this process in more detail. First, we use Lipschitz constant to get a coarse over-approximation of $\text{Reach}(K, \mathcal{U}(\mathcal{I}), [t_{i-1}, t_i])$ parallel to Lemma 1. Let $l = dia(\mathcal{I})$.

Lemma 7. *In i^{th} iteration of the **for** -loop, $\text{Reach}(B_\Delta(R_{i-1}), \mathcal{U}(\mathcal{I}), [t_{i-1}, t_i]) \subseteq S$, where $S = hull(R_{i-1}, R_i) \oplus B_{\Delta'}(R_i)$ and $\Delta' = (\Delta + \epsilon)(e^{L_f \tau_i}) + l L_f e^{L_f \tau_i} \tau_i$, $\tau_i = t_i - t_{i-1}$.*

Two trajectories starting from $x_1, x_2 \in \mathbb{R}^n$ at t_{i-1}, with $u_1, u_2 \in \mathcal{U}(\mathcal{I})$ as inputs respectively, their distance at time t, $\|\xi(x_1, t) - \xi(x_2, t)\| \leq \|x_1 - x_2\|(e^{L_f(t - t_{i-1})}) + L_f e^{L_f(t - t_{i-1})} \cdot \int_{t_{i-1}}^t \|u_1(\tau) - u_2(\tau)\| d\tau$. The lemma directly follows this inequality.

Next we give a one step IS discrepancy function in Lemma 9. Before proving it, we need another generalized form of mean value theorem:

Lemma 8. *For any continuous and differentiable function* $f : \mathbb{R}^n \times \mathbb{R}^p \to \mathbb{R}^n$, $f(x+r, u+w) - f(x,u) = \left(\int_0^1 J_x(x + sr, u + w) ds \right) r + \left(\int_0^1 J_u(x, u + \tau w) d\tau \right) w$, *where* $J_x = \frac{\partial f(x,u)}{\partial x}$ *and* $J_u = \frac{\partial f(x,u)}{\partial u}$ *are the Jacobian matrices of* f *with respect to* x *and* u.

Proof. The lemma follows by writing $f(x + r, u + w) - f(x, u) = f(x + r, u + w)$ $- f(x, u + w) + f(x, u + w) - f(x, u)$ and then invoking Lemma 2.

Lemma 9. *Consider the* i^{th} *iteration of the loop for a dynamic system [5]. Let* $x, x' \in B_\Delta(R_{i-1})$, *and* $\xi(x, t)$, $\xi(x', t)$ *be the trajectories starting from* x *and* x' *with input* $u_1(t), u_2(t) \in \mathcal{U}(\mathcal{I})$ *respectively, where* $t \in [t_{i-1}, t_i]$. *Then,*

$$\|\xi(x, t) - \xi(x', t)\| \leq \|x - x'\| e^{a(t - t_{i-1})} + M e^{a(t - t_{i-1})} \int_{t_{i-1}}^t \|u_1(\tau) - u_2(\tau)\| d\tau, \quad (6)$$

where $a = \lambda_{max}(S) + \frac{1}{2}$, $\lambda_{max}(S)$ *is the upperbound of the eigenvalues of the symmetric part of* J_x *over* S, *and* $M = \max_{u \in \mathcal{U}(\mathcal{I})} (\|J_u(\xi(x, t), u)\|)$.

To prove Lemma 9, we will use Lemma 8 and the detailed proof can be found in [15].

Using Lemma 9 to get the coefficients $a[i]$ and $M[i]$ in each time interval $[t_{i-1}, t_i]$, $i = 1 \ldots, k$, we will have:

Theorem 4. *The items in array* a *and* M *are a coefficients of the* $(K, \mathcal{U}(\mathcal{I}))$-*local IS discrepancy function for the system [5].*

This theorem enables us to compute the $(K, \mathcal{U}(\mathcal{I}))$-local IS discrepancy function for each subsystem A_i. Although in the original definition we assume the IS discrepancy function is valid for any input signals $u_1, u_2 \in \mathcal{U}$, in practice A_i can only take A_j's outputs or states as inputs, which is bounded. Thus, [20] can still use $(K, \mathcal{U}(\mathcal{I}))$-local IS discrepancy function computed by this approach. Furthermore, the $(K, \mathcal{U}(\mathcal{I}))$-local IS discrepancy function here can over-approximate the reachset of the systems in (5) with the input u being chosen nondeterministically in some compact set.

6 Experimental Evaluation

We have implemented the verification Algorithm 1 and the *ComputeLDF* subroutine with coordinate transformations in Matlab. The implementation and the examples are available from [15]. For simulation we use Matlab's built-in ODE solver. The Jacobian matrix, an upper bound of the Lipschitz constant are given as inputs. In addition, the function to do the term-wise maximization of the error matrix is also given as inputs (see Sect. 4.2). We use the absolute error for ODE solver as the error bounds for simulation. The results presented here are based on experiments performed on an Intel Xeon V2 desktop computer.

Comparison with Other Tools. We compare the performance of our algorithm with two other tools, namely, Flow* [7] and HyCreate [5], for safety verification problem of nonlinear dynamical systems. We use seven benchmarks which are shown in Table 1 with time bound $T = 10s$. Flow* uses Taylor models for approximating reachtubes from a set of initial states. Currently, it returns "Safe" or "Unknown", but not "Unsafe". HyCreate uses the face-lifting approach of [9] and provides a intuitive interface for creating models.

Table 1. Safety verification for benchmark examples. dim: dimension of the model; δ: diameter of the initial set; $\mathbb{U}$: unsafe set; #Sim: number of simulations with coordinate transformation; LDF: runtime of our implementation (with coordinate transformation) in secs.

	example	dim	δ	$\mathbb{U}$	#Sim	LDF(s)	flow*(s)	HyCreate(s)
1	Vanderpol	2	0.5	x>2.0	9	0.378	11.2	2.776
2	Brusselator	2	0.5	x>1.3	21	1.01	11.8	1.84
3	Jet Engine	2	0.4	x>2.0	5	0.353	8.74	5.54
4	Robot arm	4	0.5	x>2.5	81	4.66	169	>300
5	CoupledVanderpol	4	0.5	x>2.5	41	2.21	93	49.8
6	Sinusoidal Tracking	6	0.5	x>10	185	13.2	258	>300
7	Lorenz Attractor	3	0.02	x>1e4	570	13.99	53.4	TO
8	Fixed-wing UAV (T=10)	7	3	x> 39	321	20.8	TO	TO
9	Helicopter	28	0.02	x>4	585	67.7	TO	TO
10	Fixed-wing UAV (T=50)	7	3	x> 39	321	99.8	TO	TO
11	Fixed-wing UAV (T=100)	7	3	x> 39	321	196	TO	TO

Vanderpol, CoupledVanderpol, JetEngine, and Brusselator are commonly used, low-dimensional, nonlinear benchmarks. Sinusoidal tracking [25] is a 6 dimensional nonlinear designed as a frequency estimator. The Lorenz Attractor (row 7) is a well known chaotic dynamical system. Robot arm is a 4 dimensional nonlinear system described in [3]. The Helicopter is a high dimension linear model of a helicopter system from [16]. In row 10 and 11, we increase the time bound of the fixed-wing model to $T = 50$ and $T = 100$ respectively and the results show that the algorithm scales reasonably for longer time horizons. Columns (#Sim) and (LDF) are the results of the proposed algorithm *ComputeLDF* with coordinate transformation. More results of the algorithm without coordinate transformation can be found in [15].

Flow* and HyCreate generate a single over-approximation of the reachtube from the initial set independent of the safety property. While our algorithm will refine the initial sets when the reachtube intersects with the unsafe set. In all of these benchmarks, we make the unsafe set close to the reachtubes, to make the models safe yet it needs a lot of refinements to arrive at that conclusion. Overall, the proposed approach with coordinate transformation outperformed others in terms of the running time, especially in high dimensional benchmarks.

The "TO" in the table means the algorithm timed out at 30 min. Of course, our implementation requires the users to give the symbolic expression of the Jacobian matrix and term-wise maximization functions, while Flow* and HyCreate just needs the differential equations. Moreover, our implementation currently handles only nonlinear dynamical systems, and both Flow* and HyCreate can handle hybrid systems.

Properties of LDF. We explore the behavior of the algorithm with respect to changes in the relative positions of the initial set and the unsafe set. We use the nonlinear model of the Robot arm system. We fix the point $[1.5, 1.5, 0, 0]$ as the center of the initial set and $T = 10$ seconds as the time bound, and vary the diameter of the initial set (δ) and the unsafe set ($\mathbb{U} : \theta > c$), where θ is the angle of the arm. The number of simulations used by the algorithm with coordinate transformation (#Sim), the diameter of the reach tube at the final time T (dia), and the total running time (RT) are shown in Table 2.

From the first 4 rows in the Table, we see the expected behavior that for a fixed unsafe set, the diameter of the Reachtube decreases with decreasing δ. This corresponds to the property that the discrepancy function $\beta(x, x', t)$ goes to 0 as the initial points $x \to x'$, and therefore the error in the reachability computation decreases monotonically with the diameter of the initial set. Rows 3 and 5-6 show that if we fix the size of the initial set, then as the unsafe set comes closer to the actual reachtube, the number of simulations increases and therefore the running time increases until the system becomes unsafe. As more refinements are made by the algorithm, the accuracy (measured by the diameter of the reachtube) improves. Similar trend is seen in rows 7-8, the algorithm will need more refinements to find a counter example that shows unsafe behavior, if the unsafe set is close to the boundary of the reachtube.

Next, we explore the behavior of the algorithm (with coordinate transformation) with large initial sets. We use the 7 dimensional model of a fixed-wing UAV. The initial sets are defined as balls with different radii around a center point $[30, 980, 0, 125, 0, 0, 30.4]$ and δ in the first column is the diameter of the

Table 2. Safety verification for a robot arm with different initial states and unsafe sets. safety: safety result returned by verification algorithm;

	δ	$\mathbb{U}$	saftey	#Sim	dia	RT(s)
1	0.6	$\theta > 3$	safe	17	5.6e-3	0.948
2	0.3	$\theta > 3$	safe	9	2.6e-3	0.610
3	0.2	$\theta > 3$	safe	5	1.8e-3	0.444
4	0.1	$\theta > 3$	safe	1	1.5e-3	0.271
5	0.2	$\theta > 2.5$	safe	9	1.7e-3	0.609
6	0.2	$\theta > 2.15$	safe	161	9.2e-4	6.705
7	0.2	$\theta > 2.14$	unsafe	45	N/A	1.997
8	0.2	$\theta > 2.1$	unsafe	1	N/A	0.267

Table 3. Safety verification for a fixed-wing UAV with large initial sets.

	δ	$\mathbb{U}$	#Sim	RT(s)
1	50	$H > 400$	24001	1518
2	46	$H > 400$	6465	415
3	40	$H > 400$	257	16.33
4	36	$H > 400$	129	8.27
5	20	$H > 400$	1	0.237

initial sets. The unsafe set is defined as $H > c$, where H is the thrust of UAV. The time horizon is fixed at $T = 10$ seconds. As shown in Table 3, our algorithm can handle large initial set and high dimension systems. Although it may need many simulations (24001 covers), the algorithm terminates in 30 mins. All the results of this table are safe.

7 Conclusions and Future Work

In this paper, we present an algorithm *ComputeLDF* to compute local discrepancy functions, which is an upperbound of the distance between trajectories starting from an initial set. The algorithm computes the rate of trajectory convergence or divergence for small time intervals and gives the rate as coefficients of a continuous piecewise exponential function. The local discrepancy we compute satisfies the definition of discrepancy function, so the verification algorithm using *ComputeLDF* as a subroutine is sound and relatively complete. We also provide a coordinate transformation method to improve the estimation of rates. Furthermore, we extend the algorithm to compute input-to-state discrepancy functions. *ComputeLDF* has been successfully used to verify several complex nonlinear systems like powertrain control system [11,14]. In the future, we plan on using more rigorous ODE solvers like [6] and embedding the algorithm in verification tools like C2E2 [12] for verification of hybrid systems.

References

1. Althoff, M., Stursberg, O., Buss, M.: Reachability analysis of nonlinear systems with uncertain parameters using conservative linearization. In: CDC, pp. 4042–4048 (2008)
2. Angeli, D.: A lyapunov approach to incremental stability properties. IEEE Trans. Autom. Control **47**(3), 410–421 (2002)
3. Angeli, D., Sontag, E.D., Wang, Y.: A characterization of integral input-to-state stability. IEEE Trans. Autom. Control **45**(6), 1082–1097 (2000)
4. Annpureddy, Y., Liu, C., Fainekos, G., Sankaranarayanan, S.: S-TALIRO: a tool for temporal logic falsification for hybrid systems. In: Abdulla, P.A., Leino, K.R.M. (eds.) TACAS 2011. LNCS, vol. 6605, pp. 254–257. Springer, Heidelberg (2011)
5. Bak, S., Caccamo, M.: Computing reachability for nonlinear systems with hycreate. In: Demo and Poster Session, HSCC (2013)
6. CAPD. Computer assisted proofs in dynamics (2002). http://www.capd.ii.uj.edu.pl/
7. Chen, X., Ábrahám, E., Sankaranarayanan, S.: Flow*: an analyzer for non-linear hybrid systems. In: Sharygina, N., Veith, H. (eds.) CAV 2013. LNCS, vol. 8044, pp. 258–263. Springer, Heidelberg (2013)
8. Dang, T., Donzé, A., Maler, O., Shalev, N.: Sensitive state-space exploration. In: CDC, pp. 4049–4054 (2008)
9. Dang, T., Maler, O.: Reachability analysis via face lifting. In: Henzinger, T.A., Sastry, S.S. (eds.) HSCC 1998. LNCS, vol. 1386, pp. 96–109. Springer, Heidelberg (1998)

10. Donzé, A., Maler, O.: Systematic simulation using sensitivity analysis. In: Bemporad, A., Bicchi, A., Buttazzo, G. (eds.) HSCC 2007. LNCS, vol. 4416, pp. 174–189. Springer, Heidelberg (2007)

11. Duggirala, P.S., Fan, C., Mitra, S., Viswanathan, M.: Meeting a powertrain verification challenge. In: Kroening, D., Păsăreanu, C.S. (eds.) CAV 2015. LNCS, vol. 9206, pp. 536–543. Springer, Heidelberg (2015)

12. Duggirala, P.S., Mitra, S., Viswanathan, M.: Verification of annotated models from executions. In: EMSOFT, pp. 26:1–26:10 (2013)

13. Duggirala, P.S., Wang, L., Mitra, S., Viswanathan, M., Muñoz, C.: Temporal precedence checking for switched models and its application to a parallel landing protocol. In: Jones, C., Pihlajasaari, P., Sun, J. (eds.) FM 2014. LNCS, vol. 8442, pp. 215–229. Springer, Heidelberg (2014)

14. Fan, C., Duggirala, P.S., Mitra, S., Viswanathan, M.: Progress on powertrain verification challenge with C2E2. ARCH (2015)

15. Fan, C., Mitra, S.: Bounded verification with on-the-fly discrepancy computation (full version). http://web.engr.illinois.edu/cfan10/research.html

16. Frehse, G., Le Guernic, C., Donzé, A., Cotton, S., Ray, R., Lebeltel, O., Ripado, R., Girard, A., Dang, T., Maler, O.: SpaceEx: scalable verification of hybrid systems. In: Gopalakrishnan, G., Qadeer, S. (eds.) CAV 2011. LNCS, vol. 6806, pp. 379–395. Springer, Heidelberg (2011)

17. Girard, A., Pola, G., Tabuada, P.: Approximately bisimilar symbolic models for incrementally stable switched systems. IEEE Trans. Autom. Control 55(1), 116–126 (2010)

18. Han, Z., Mosterman, P.J.: Towards sensitivity analysis of hybrid systems using simulink. In: HSCC, pp. 95–100 (2013)

19. Huang, Z., Fan, C., Mereacre, A., Mitra, S., Kwiatkowska, M.: Invariant verification of nonlinear hybrid automata networks of cardiac cells. In: Biere, A., Bloem, R. (eds.) CAV 2014. LNCS, vol. 8559, pp. 373–390. Springer, Heidelberg (2014)

20. Huang, Z., Mitra, S.: Proofs from simulations and modular annotations. In: HSCC, pp. 183–192 (2014)

21. Islam, M., DeFrancisco, R., Fan, C., Grosu, R., Mitra, S., Smolka, S.A., et al.: Model checking tap withdrawal in c. elegans (2015). arXiv preprint arXiv:1503.06480

22. Julius, A.A., Pappas, G.J.: Trajectory based verification using local finite-time invariance. In: Majumdar, R., Tabuada, P. (eds.) HSCC 2009. LNCS, vol. 5469, pp. 223–236. Springer, Heidelberg (2009)

23. Lohmiller, W., Slotine, J.-J.E.: On contraction analysis for non-linear systems. Automatica 34(6), 683–696 (1998)

24. Nedialkov, N.: VNODE-LP: Validated solutions for initial value problem for ODEs. Technical report, McMaster University (2006)

25. Sharma, B.B., Kar, I.N.: Design of asymptotically convergent frequency estimator using contraction theory. IEEE Trans. Autom. Control 53(8), 1932–1937 (2008)

26. Zamani, M., Pola, G., Mazo, M., Tabuada, P.: Symbolic models for nonlinear control systems without stability assumptions. IEEE Trans. Autom. Control 57(7), 1804–1809 (2012)

Formal Verification of Simulink/Stateflow Diagrams

Liang Zou[1], Naijun Zhan[1], Shuling Wang[1($\boxtimes$)], and Martin Fränzle[2]

[1] State Key Laboratory of Computer Science, Institute of Software,
Chinese Academy of Sciences, Beijing, China
wangsl@ios.ac.cn
[2] Department of Computing Science, C. V. Ossietzky Universität Oldenburg,
Oldenburg, Germany

Abstract. Simulink is an industrial de-facto standard for building executable models of control systems and their environments. Stateflow is a toolbox used to model reactive systems via hierarchical statecharts within a Simulink model, extending Simulink's scope to event-driven and hybrid forms of embedded control. In safety-critical control systems, exhaustive coverage of system dynamics by formal verification would be desirable, being based on a formal semantics of combined Simulink/ Stateflow graphical models. In our previous work, we addressed the problem of formal verification of pure Simulink diagrams via an encoding into HCSP, a formal modelling language encoding hybrid system dynamics by means of an extension of CSP. In this paper, we extend the approach to cover Simulink models containing Stateflow components also. The transformation from Simulink/Stateflow to HCSP is fully automatic, and the formal verification of the encoding is supported by a Hybrid Hoare Logic (HHL) prover based on Isabelle/HOL. We demonstrate our approach by a real world case study originating from the Chinese High-speed Train Control System (CTCS-3).

Keywords: Simulink/Stateflow · Formal verification · Hybrid CSP · Hybrid Hoare Logic

1 Introduction

Simulink [1] is an environment for the model-based analysis and design of signal-processing systems. Being based on a large palette of individually simple function blocks and their composition by continuous-time synchronous data-flow, it offers an intuitive graphical modeling language reminiscent of circuit diagrams and thus appealing to the practicing engineer. Stateflow [2] is a toolbox adding facilities for modeling and simulating reactive systems by means of hierarchical statecharts, extending Simulink's scope to event-driven and hybrid forms of embedded control. Modeling, analysis, and design using Simulink/Stateflow have become a de-facto standard in the embedded systems industry, as the circuit analogy of Simulink and the hierarchy mechanisms of Stateflow, which include sequential

© Springer International Publishing Switzerland 2015
B. Finkbeiner et al. (Eds.): ATVA 2015, LNCS 9364, pp. 464–481, 2015.
DOI: 10.1007/978-3-319-24953-7_33

and concurrent state composition, help to comprehend the massively concurrent mixed-signal dynamics arising from the multiple data paths and state-rich reactive components present in modern embedded control systems.

System analysis and design validation within Simulink/Stateflow are based on numerical simulation, rendering it prone to incomplete coverage of open systems and possible unsoundness of analysis results due to numerical error. There are various partial remedies to this problem: Statistical model checking (SMC, cf. e.g. [6]) tries to save the virtues of simulation-based analysis, namely low computational complexity and moderate constraints on the shape of models, while addressing the coverage problem through a rigorous statistical interpretation of simulation results. Yet being a simulation-based procedure that employs the standard simulators, it still is subject to the soundness issue of numerical simulation. Set-based numerical simulation computing enclosures of system trajectories, as pioneered already in the sixties [14], could in principle resolve this problem, but variants handling non-smooth derivatives [16], as omnipresent in Simulink/Stateflow models, do not scale to the system sizes encountered in industrial models. The same applies to state-exploratory methods either computing (an overapproximation of) the reachable state space or (semi-)deciding a symbolic reachability criterion. These require to translate the Simulink model into the input language of a formal verification tool for hybrid discrete-continuous systems, be it an automaton-based language [3] or a symbolic description [9], and employ the corresponding verification engines. These engines pursue an exhaustive search of the state space, thus providing certificates which cover all input stimuli possible in an open system, and do increasingly apply verified arithmetic, rendering them resistant against numerical error. Fully automatic analysis of Simulink/Stateflow models is, however, hampered by Simulink's modeling paradigm of connecting numerous concurrently executing small blocks via continuous-time synchronous dataflow, yielding tightly coupled, fine-granular concurrency in the translated models, which is detrimental to state-exploratory analysis.

In this paper, we do therefore investigate the translation of Simulink/Stateflow into a process calculus with its richer set of composition primitives. We present an encoding of the semantics in terms of HCSP [11], a formal modelling language encoding hybrid system dynamics by means of an extension of CSP [10], thus providing the formal basis for an automatic translation from Simulink/Stateflow to HCSP. As analysis of HCSP models is supported by an interactive Hybrid Hoare Logic (HHL) prover based on Isabelle/HOL, this provides a gateway to mechanized verification, which we demonstrate on a real world case study originating from the Chinese High-speed Train Control System. This research extends our previous work [23] addressing Simulink only.

Related Work. There has been a range of work on translating Simulink into modelling formalisms supported by analysis and verification tools. Tripakis *et al.* [19] present an algorithm for translating discrete-time Simulink models to Lustre, a synchronous language featuring a formal semantics and a number of tools for validation and analysis. Cavalcanti *et al.* [4] put forth a semantics for discrete-time Simulink diagrams using Circus, a combination of Z and CSP. Meenakshi *et al.* [12] propose an algorithm translating a Simulink subset into the input language of the finite-state model checker NuSMV. Chen *et al.* [5] present a translation of Simulink models to the real-time specification language Timed Interval Calculus (TIC), which can accommodate continuous Simulink diagrams directly, and they validate TIC models using an interactive theorem prover. Their translation is confined to continuous blocks whose outputs can be represented explicitly by a closed-form mathematical relation on their inputs. In contrast, our previous work [23] can handle all continuous blocks by using the notions of differential equations and invariants in the HCSP encodings, and the use of a process calculus based language facilitates compositionality in both construction and verification.

Beyond the pure Simulink models considered in the above approaches, models comprising reactive components triggered by and affecting Simulink's dataflow have also been studied recently. Hamon *et al.* [7] propose an operational semantics of Stateflow, which serves as a foundation for developing tools for formal analysis of Stateflow designs. Scaife *et al.* [17] translate a subset of Stateflow into Lustre for formal analysis. Tiwari [18] defines a formal semantics of Simulink/Stateflow using guarded pushdown automata, in which continuous dynamical systems modeled by Simulink are discretized, and he discusses how to verify a guarded sequence via type checking, model checking and theorem proving. Agrawal *et al.* [3] propose a method to translate Simulink/Stateflow models into hybrid automata using graph flattening, and the target models represented by hybrid automata can then be formally analyzed and verified by model checkers for hybrid systems. Their approach induces certain limitations, both for the discrete-continuous interfaces in Simulink/Stateflow models, where the output signals of Stateflow blocks are required to be Boolean and to immediately connect to the selector input of an analog switch block, and for the forms of continuous dynamics, as most model checkers for hybrid systems support only very restricted differential equations. Miller *et al.* [13] propose a method to translate discrete Simulink/Stateflow models into Lustre for formal analysis. In our approach, we relax these constraints and consider how to define a formal semantics for the combination of Simulink/Stateflow in general, including advanced features like *early return logic*, *history junction*, *nontermination* of Stateflow. We gain this flexibility by resorting to interactive theorem proving rather than automatic model checking for discharging the proof obligations.

2   Simulink/Stateflow and Hybrid CSP

In this section, we briefly introduce the source language Simulink/Stateflow, the target language Hybrid CSP (HCSP), the specification language Hybrid Hoare Logic and its prover. We expand only on the most relevant features of Simulink/Stateflow, and the reader is referred to [1,2] for more details.

2.1   Simulink

A Simulink model contains a set of blocks, subsystems, and wires, where blocks and subsystems cooperate by data-flow through the connecting wires. An elementary block receives input signals and computes output signals according to user-defined parameters altering its functionality. One typical parameter is *sample time*, which defines how frequently the computation is performed. Blocks are classified into two types: *continuous blocks* with sample time 0, and *discrete blocks* with positive sample time. Blocks and subsystems in a model receive inputs and compute outputs in parallel.

Figure 1 gives a Simulink model of train movement, comprising four blocks, including continuous integrator blocks v and p and discrete blocks c and acc. Block v outputs the velocity of the train by integrating acceleration acc over time; similarly, p outputs the distance of the train computed by timewise integration of velocity v, and acc computes acceleration from the constant provided by c and distance p.

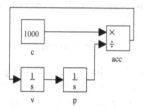

Fig. 1. A simple control system

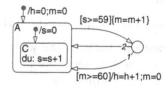

Fig. 2. A timer

2.2   Stateflow

As a toolbox integrated into Simulink, Stateflow offers the modeling capabilities of statecharts for reactive systems. It can be used to construct Simulink blocks, fed with Simulink inputs and producing Simulink outputs. A Stateflow diagram has a hierarchical structure, which can be an *AND diagram*, for which states are arranged in parallel and all of them become active whenever the diagram is activated; or an *OR diagram*, for which states are connected with transitions and only one of them can be active. In the following, we will explain the main ingredients of Stateflow.

Alphabet: The alphabet of a Stateflow diagram consists of a finite set of events and variables. An event can be an input or output of the diagram, or may be local to it. A variable may also be set as input, output, or local, and moreover, it can be associated with an initial value if necessary.

States: States can be hierarchical, containing another Stateflow diagram. Because of hierarchy, transitions originating from a state are classified into two types depending on whether or not their target states are inside the same state:

ingoing and outgoing transitions. All transitions are ordered by a strict priority such that there is no non-determinism in transition selection. A state may be associated with three optional types of actions: An *entry action* executed when the state is activated; a *during action* executed when no transition is enabled; and an *exit action* executed imemdaitely before a transition leaves the state. The actions of Stateflow may be either assignments, or emissions of events, etc.

States in an AND diagram are assigned priorities and their actions are actually executed in sequential order according to that priority.

Transitions: A transition is a connection between states. In Stateflow, it may be a complex transition network, consisting of several transitions joined by junctions. Default transitions with no source states or source junctions are allowed for OR diagrams, and they are used to select the active state when the OR diagram is activated. Each transition is of the form $E[C]\{cAct\}/tAct$, where E is an event, C is the guard condition, $cAct$ the condition action, and $tAct$ the action. All these components are optional. $cAct$ will be executed immediately when event E is triggered and condition C holds, while $tAct$ will is put in a queue first and executed after the corresponding transition is taken.

These syntactic components form the basis of the follwing execution semantics.

Initialization: Initially, the whole system is activated: for an AND diagram, all the parallel states are activated according to the priority order; while for an OR diagram, one of the states is activated by performing the default transition.

Broadcasting and Executing Transition: Each Stateflow diagram is activated at sample times periodically or by trigger events, depending on the diagram's settings. For the second case, as soon as one of the trigger event arrives, called *current event*, it will be broadcasted through the whole diagram. For an AND diagram, the event will be broadcasted sequentially to the parallel states inside the diagram according to the priority order; while for an OR diagram, it will find the active state of the diagram and be broadcasted to it. It will then check the outgoing transitions of the current active state according to the priority order, and if there is one valid transition that is able to reach a state, the transition will be taken; otherwise, check the ingoing transitions in the same way. If there is neither an outgoing nor an ingoing valid transition enabled, the during action of the state will be executed, and then the event is broadcasted recursively to the sub-diagram inside the state.

The transition might connect states at different levels in the hierarchical diagram. When a transition connecting two states is taken, it will first find the common ancestor of the source and target states, i.e. the nearest state that contains both of them inside, then perform the following steps: exit from the source state (including its sub-diagram) step by step and at each step execute the exit action of the corresponding state and set it to be *inactive*, and then enter step by step to the target state (including its sub-diagram), and at each step, set the corresponding state to be *active* and execute the corresponding entry action.

Figure 2 gives an example of Stateflow. States A and C are activated initially, with variables h, m, and s being set to 0. A has a transition network to itself, enabled when s equals to 59. Once the network is enabled, the outgoing transition is executed, and thus m is increased by 1; then it will execute transition 1 due to its higher priority, increasing h by 1 and resetting m to 0 if m equals to 60. If transition 1 is not enabled, 2 is taken.

The combination of Simulink and Stateflow is exemplified by the two examples in Figs. 1 and 2. In order to implement the block acc in Fig. 1, we revise the Stateflow diagram in Fig. 2 as follows: We add a condition action $[True]\{acc = 1000/p + m/100\}$ to transition 2 of the Stateflow diagram, updating the train's acceleration every minute to become $1000/p + m/100$. We then replace blocks acc and c by the modified diagram.

2.3 Hybrid CSP (HCSP)

HCSP [8,20,21] is a formal language for describing hybrid systems. It is an extension of Hoare's Communicating Sequential Processes (CSP) by timing constructs, interrupts, and differential equations modelling continuous evolution. Data exchange among processes is confined to instantaneous synchronous communication, avoiding shared variables as present in Simulink. For a comprehensive introduction to HCSP refer to [20].

The syntax of HCSP is given as follows:

$$P: := \text{skip} \mid x := e \mid ch?x \mid ch!e \mid P;Q \mid B \rightarrow P \mid P \sqcup Q \mid X$$
$$\mid \mu X.P \mid \langle \mathcal{F}(\dot{s}, s) = 0 \& B \rangle \mid \langle \mathcal{F}(\dot{s}, s) = 0 \& B \rangle \trianglerighteq []_{i \in I}(io_i \rightarrow Q_i)$$
$$S: := P \mid S \| S$$

Here, io_i stands for a communication event, i.e., $ch?x$ or $ch!e$, P, Q, Q_i for HCSP processes, x and s for variables, X for process variables, and ch for channel names. B and e are Boolean and arithmetic expressions. The intended meaning of the individual constructs is as follows:

- skip, $x := e$ (assignment), $ch?x$ (input), $ch!e$ (output), X, $P;Q$ (sequential composition), $B \rightarrow P$ (conditional statement), $P \sqcup Q$ (internal choice), $\mu X.P$ (recursion) and $P \| Q$ (parallel composition) are understood as in CSP.
- $\langle \mathcal{F}(\dot{s}, s) = 0 \& B \rangle$ is the continuous evolution statement, where s represents a vector of real variables and $\dot{s}$ their derivatives. It forces s to continuously evolve according to the differential equation $\mathcal{F}(s, \dot{s}) = 0$ as long as condition B holds, and terminates immediately when B turns false.
- $\langle \mathcal{F}(\dot{s}, s) = 0 \& B \rangle \trianglerighteq []_{i \in I}(io_i \rightarrow Q_i)$ behaves like $\langle \mathcal{F}(\dot{s}, s) = 0 \& B \rangle$, except that the continuous evolution is preempted as soon as one of the communications io_i occurs, then being followed by the respective Q_i. If the continuous evolution terminates before any preemption then the overall process terminates directly.

2.4 Hybrid Hoare Logic (HHL)

In [11], we have extended Hoare Logic to hybrid systems by adding history formulas to describe continuous properties that hold throughout the whole execution of HCSP processes. The history formulas are defined within Duration Calculus (DC), which is an extension of Interval Temporal Logic (ITL) [15] for specifying and reasoning about real-time systems. In HHL, each specification for a sequential process P takes the form $\{Pre\}\, P\, \{Post; HF\}$, where $Pre, Post$ are traditional pre-/post-conditions on variables expressed in first-order logic, and HF is a history formula in DC recording the execution history of P, including real-time and continuous properties. The specification for a parallel process is then obtained by assigning to each sequential component an HHL condition $\{Pre_1, Pre_2\}\, P_1 \| P_2\, \{Post_1, Post_2; HF_1, HF_2\}$. Each HCSP construct is axiomatized within HHL by a set of axioms and inference rules. A more comprehensive explanation of HHL can be found at [11,20]. For tool support, we have implemented an interactive theorem prover for HHL based on Isabelle/HOL [20,22]. The tool can be downloaded from https://github.com/submission/Sim2HCSP.

3   From Simulink/Stateflow to HCSP

In previous work [23], we have translated a subset of Simulink into HCSP processes and then applied the HHL prover to the target processes for formal verification. In this section, we will first discuss the translation of Stateflow models into HCSP and then show how this translation can be integrated with our previous work, so that we get a translation from Simulink/Stateflow graphical models into HCSP. We first consider each of the main ingredients of Stateflow, including transition networks, broadcasting, states etc., and then provide a general template for translating a Stateflow diagram.

3.1   Transition Networks

For translating a transition, two main issues should be considered: first, a transition network may consist of several transitions joined by junctions, thus we need to traverse the transition network to find each valid transition path; second, a transition may have super-structure, i.e. the source and target states can be at different levels, so an appropriate ordered sequence of exit and entry actions has to be executed upo transitioning.

Algorithm 1 presents the main recursive algorithm for translating a transition network with source state S and triggering event E to a HCSP process. The boolean variable *done* indicates whether a valid transition that connects S and a destination state has been executed in current transition network. **TTN** adopts depth-first search. In order to deal with possible loops in a transition network N, we introduce a process variable P_J for each junction J in N, and P_{set} to store the process equation corresponding to P_J defined by recursively calling **TTN** starting from $J.\,target$ and $cPath$ represent current location and current

---

Algorithm 1. Translating Transition Networks (**TTN**$(S, E, done)$)

Require: A source state S, a triggering event E, and a boolean variable *done*

Ensure: A HCSP process *proc* representing the transition network starting from S and a set of HCSP processes P_{set} that assist the definition of *proc*

    Vars *cPath, target, proc* = "$ACT_{LOC} = ACT$", $P_{set} = \emptyset$;

  1: **for** ($cPath = 1$; $cPath \leq S.tSize$; $cPath = cPath + 1$) **do**

  2:     $t = S.getTrans(cPath)$; *target* $= t.getTarget()$;

  3:     *proc* = *proc* ⨟ "$(E == t.getEvent()$ & $t.getCond()$ & $\neg done) \rightarrow$

             $(t.getCAction(); ACT := (ACT_{LOC}; t.getTAction()));$";

  4:     **if** *target.isState()* **then**

  5:         Find common father for states S, *target*, and all junctions along the intermediate path;

  6:         *proc* = *proc* ⨟ "$P_{exit}; ACT; P_{entry}; done := True);$";

  7:     **else**

  8:         **if** $\neg P_{set}.contains(P_{target})$ **then**

  9:             $P_{set}.put(P_{target}, \mathbf{TTN}(target, E, done))$;

10:         **end if**

11:         *proc* = *proc* ⨟ P_{target} ⨟ ")";

12:     **end if**

13: **end for**

---

transition being traversed respectively. ACT is a process variable to accumulate the transition actions that have been traversed.

proc is a string that represents the constructed HCSP process, which is put within double quotes in the algorithm. Operator ⨟ is used to concatenate two strings. At the beginning, *proc* is initialized by "$ACT := skip;$", then it is extended by concatenating the process constructed by calling **TTN** $(S, E, done)$. Finally, by solving equations in P_{set}, each occurrence of P_J in *proc* can be replaced by the corresponding solution.

We explain Algorithm 1 now. It starts by initializing ACT_{LOC} by ACT, and P_{set} by $\emptyset$. The **for** loop then translates the transitions of S according to their order:

1. line 2 gets the transition according to the path number *cPath*, assigns it to t, and stores its target in *target*;
2. at line 3, if the event of t is same as E, the condition of t is satisfied, and *done* is *False*, then the condition action is taken, meanwhile the transition action is put in ACT. Whenever the previous branch of current source state or junction failed, the corresponding accumulated actions in ACT will be discarded by recovering ACT to the value stored in ACT_{LOC} at the first entry of this source state or junction. Note that ACT plays the role of a stack here.
3. at lines 4–6, if *target* is a state (rather than a junction), indicating that a valid transition is found, then find the common father of S, *target*, and all junctions along the intermediate path, exit from S step by step (by process P_{exit}), execute the transition actions ACT that are accumulated for S, enter to *target* step by step (by P_{entry}), and set *done* to be *True*, meaning that

no further transition is needed, and *proc* is closed in this loop with right a bracket.

4. otherwise (line 8–11), if *target* is a junction, not traversed yet (i.e., not in P_{set}), then call **TTN** to get the definition of P_{target} (i.e. the HCSP process constructed from **TTN**($target, E, done$)) and store definition equation in P_{set}, finally P_{target} and a right bracket is added at the end of *proc*.

5. at line 12, the current iteration of the **for** loop completes, and the next iteration will start to consider the next transition of S.

Notice that for some transitions, the triggering event (or condition) may not exist. For such case, the guard $E = t.getEvent()$ (or $t.getCond()$) in line 3 will set to $True$. Since the number of junctions is finite, **TTN** is called finitely often. Hence, Algorithm 1 terminates for any finite transition networks, no matter whether it contains loop or not.

Example 1. Figure 3 presents an example of a transition network with a loop. By applying the algorithm, we obtain the process listed below the statechart. In the process, we set a state S to active or inactive by assigning the corresponding Boolean variable a_S to 1 or 0 respectively.

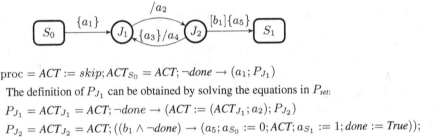

proc $= ACT := skip; ACT_{S_0} = ACT; \neg done \rightarrow (a_1; P_{J_1})$

The definition of P_{J_1} can be obtained by solving the equations in P_{set}:

$P_{J_1} = ACT_{J_1} = ACT; \neg done \rightarrow (ACT := (ACT_{J_1}; a_2); P_{J_2})$

$P_{J_2} = ACT_{J_2} = ACT; ((b_1 \wedge \neg done) \rightarrow (a_5; a_{S_0} := 0; ACT; a_{S_1} := 1; done := True));$
$\quad \neg done \rightarrow (a_3; ACT := (ACT_{J_2}; a_4); P_{J_1})$

Fig. 3. A transition network with a circle

3.2   Broadcasting and Monitor Process

When an event is broadcasted, an OR diagram will broadcast the event to its active state, while an AND diagram will broadcast the event to each of its sub-diagrams according to the priority order. During broadcasting, a new local event may be emitted inside some sub-diagram, interrupting the current execution due to the local event. After the completion of processing the local event, the interrupted execution will be resumed.

We define a monitor process $\mathcal{M}$ in terms of HCSP to coordinate the execution of broadcasted events. The constant n stands for the number of parallel states of the current diagram, E for the current event, *num* for the sub-diagram to which current event is broadcasted. EL and NL are two stacks respectively to store the broadcasted events and the corresponding sub-diagrams to which these events are broadcasted.

$$\mathcal{M} \;\hat{=}\; num := 0; (\mathcal{M}_{main})^*$$
$$\mathcal{M}_{main} \;\hat{=}\; (num == 0) \rightarrow (P_{tri}; CH_{in}?iVar; num := 1; EL := [\,]; NL := [\,];$$
$$\mathbf{push}(EL, E); \mathbf{push}(NL, 1));$$
$$(num == 1) \rightarrow (BC_1!E; VOut_1!sv[\,](BR_1?E; \mathbf{push}(EL, E); \mathbf{push}(NL, 1); num := 1)$$
$$[\,](BO_1?; VIn_1?sv; num := num + 1; \mathbf{pop}(NL); \mathbf{push}(NL, num));$$
$$\cdots$$
$$(num == n) \rightarrow (BC_n!E; VOut_n!sv[\,](BR_n?E; \mathbf{push}(EL, E); \mathbf{push}(NL, 1); num := 1)$$
$$[\,](BO_n?; VIn_n?sv; num := num + 1; \mathbf{pop}(NL); \mathbf{push}(NL, num));$$
$$num == n + 1 \rightarrow (\mathbf{pop}(EL); \mathbf{pop}(NL); \mathbf{isEmpty}(EL) \rightarrow (num := 0; CH_{out}!oVar);$$
$$\neg \mathbf{isEmpty}(EL) \rightarrow (E := \mathbf{top}(EL); num := \mathbf{top}(NL))))$$

As shown above, $\mathcal{M}$ initializes num to 0, and then repeats $\mathcal{M}_{main}$, which specifies how to trigger current diagram by current event as follows:

$\boldsymbol{num}$=0: The monitor waits for a triggering event E from outside first, modelled by P_{tri}, then receives the input data on $iVar$. Afterwards updates num to be 1, initializes both EL and NL to be empty, and then pushes E to stack EL and 1 to stack NL indicating the first sub-diagram to be triggered by E.

$1 \leq \boldsymbol{num} \leq n$: The monitor broadcasts current event to the num-th sub-diagram with the following three options:

1. either it broadcasts current event along channel BC_{num} to the num-th sub-diagram and sends the shared data along channel $VOut_{num}$ to it also;
2. or it receives a local event from the num-th sub-diagram along channel BR_{num}, which will interrupt the broadcasting of current event, then the local event will be broadcasted immediately to the first sub-diagram;
3. or it receives an acknowledgment from the num-th sub-diagram along channel BO_{num} to indicate that the broadcasting of E has been completed and at the same time receives the new shared data along VIn_{num}. Afterwards, it will broadcast the event to the $(num + 1)$-th sub-diagram if it exists.

$\boldsymbol{num} = n + 1$: This indicates that the broadcasting of the current event has been finished. Consequently, the event and the corresponding sub-diagram are removed from the respective stack. If the resulting EL is empty, which indicates that the broadcast on current event E has completed, then sets num to become 0, outputs variable $oVar$, and waits for another triggering event from outside of the diagram. Otherwise, there still is some interrupted broadcast, and for such case, it will retrieve the previous event and its corresponding sub-diagram by reading the new top values from EL and NL and resume the interrupted broadcast event.

Note that if a diagram is triggered by sample time, then P_{tri} is simply defined as a wait statement of HCSP, i.e. **wait** T for sample time T.

3.3 Stateflow Diagrams

Finally, a Stateflow diagram can be defined as a process template $\mathcal{D}$, which is a parallel composition of the monitor process $\mathcal{M}$ and the parallel states $\mathcal{S}_1, \cdots, \mathcal{S}_n$ of the diagram. Especially, when the diagram is an OR diagram, n will be 1, and the only state $\mathcal{S}_1$ corresponds to the virtual state that contains the diagram, which has no (entry/during/exit) action nor transitions associated to it.

$\mathcal{S}_i$ first initializes the local variables of the state and activates the state by executing the entry action, defined by P_{init} and P_{entry} respectively; then it is triggered whenever an event E is emitted by the monitor. and performs the following actions: first, initializes *done* to *False* indicating that no valid transition has been executed yet, and searches for a valid transition by calling Algorithm 1; if *done* is still false, then executes the during action *dur* and all of its sub-diagrams. Note that for an OR diagram, the execution of the virtual state is essentially to execute the sub-diagram directly. Finally, the monitor is notified about completion of the broadcasting and outputs the shared data.

Likewise, each sub-diagram (represented by P_{diag}) may be AND or OR diagram. Different from an outermost AND diagram, for simplicity, we define an AND sub-diagram in terms of a sequential composition of its parallel states. This is reasonable because there is no true concurrency in Stateflow and the parallel states are actually executed in sequence according to their priorities. The OR diagram is encoded as a sequential composition of the connecting states, guarded by a condition $a_{\mathcal{S}_i} == 1$ indicating that the i-th state is active.

Note that in the above, **TTN** returns an HCSP process corresponding to both outgoing and ingoing transitions of $\mathcal{S}_i$. Local events may be emitted during executing transition or state actions. In such a case, the current execution of the diagram needs to be interrupted for broadcasting the local event, and will be resumed after processing the broadcast is completed. For modeling this kind of preemption, we use general recursion of the form $\mu X.(P_1; X; P_2)$, X referring to the place where the local event is emitted.

$$\mathcal{D} \;\widehat{=}\; \mathcal{M}\|\mathcal{S}_1\| \cdots \|\mathcal{S}_n,$$
$$\mathcal{S}_i \;\widehat{=}\; P_{init}; P_{entry}; (BC_i?E; VOut_i?sv_i; \mathcal{S}_{du}; BO_i!; \quad VIn_i!sv_i)^*,$$
$$\mathcal{S}_{du} \;\widehat{=}\; done = False; \textbf{TTN}(\mathcal{S}_i, E, done); \neg done \rightarrow (dur, P_{diag}),$$
$$P_{diag} \;\widehat{=}\; P_{and} \mid P_{or}, \quad P_{and} \widehat{=} \mathcal{S}_{1_{du}}; \cdots ; \mathcal{S}_{m_{du}},$$
$$P_{or} \;\widehat{=}\; (a_{\mathcal{S}_1} == 1 \rightarrow \mathcal{S}_{1_{du}}); \cdots ; (a_{\mathcal{S}_k} == 1 \rightarrow \mathcal{S}_{k_{du}}).$$

3.4 Handling Advanced Features of Stateflow

In this section, we discuss how to handle special features of Stateflow in the translation, including *early return logic*, *history junctiona*, *nontermination*, and so on. As discussed above, a Stateflow digram is translated into $\mathcal{D} \;\widehat{=}\; \mathcal{M}\|\mathcal{S}_1\| \cdots \|\mathcal{S}_n$. In the following discussion, we only consider how to revise the translation of $\mathcal{S}_i$ accordingly in order to address these advanced features, as the coordinated processes stay the same.

Early return logic prevents execution of an interrupt from returning to the interrupted action, thus discarding the rest of the execution of the interrupted action. E.g., in Fig. 4, activity in $A1$ is interrupted by broadcasting the local event e, which results in the control shifting to B. Thus, $A1$ becomes inactive. After the execution of B, the control will be shifted to A rather than $A1$, discarding $A2$.

We use the example in Fig. 4 to demonstrate how to deal with early return logic in our setting. By using activity control variables a_A, a_{A1}, a_{A2} and a_B, we revise the translation for the example diagram as follows:[1]

$S_1 = a_A := 0; a_B := 0; a_A := 1; a_{A1} := 1;$

$\quad \mu X.\,(BC_1?E1; done_1 := False; (a_A == 1) \rightarrow ((\neg done_1 \wedge E1 == e) \rightarrow ($

$\quad (a_{A1} == 1) \rightarrow a_{A1} := 0; (a_{A2} == 1) \rightarrow a_{A2} := 0; a_A := 0; a_B := 1; done_1 := True);$

$\quad (\neg done_1) \rightarrow ((a_{A1} == 1) \rightarrow ((\neg done1) \rightarrow (BR_1!e; X; (a_{A1} == 1) \rightarrow ($

$\quad\quad\quad a_{A1} := 0; a_{A2} := 1; done_1 := True))); (a_{A2} == 1) \rightarrow skip));$

$\quad (a_B == 1) \rightarrow skip; BO_1!)$

Fig. 4. Early return logic   **Fig. 5.** Nontermination

A **history junction** memoizes control flow in an OR diagram for later reactivation. With a history junction in an OR diagram, the state marked by the default transition is only relevant for the first activation. Upon subsequent activation, control on te OR diagram returns to where the diagram was last left. To translate a *history junction*, we revise the definition of P_{entry}: We introduce a variable *history* to record the active state interrupted in the previous execution, and initialize it to the state pointed to by the default transition. P_{entry} is implemented simply by setting the active state to *history*.

Nontermination of Stateflow transitions is difficult to formalize and often not considered, like in [19]. Consider Fig. 5, where the statechart will exhibit nontermination whenever process S_1 receives an event e. In our approach, nontermination can easily be coped with. Regarding Fig. 5, we can translate it into an HCSP process as:

$S_1 = a_A := 0; a_B := 0; a_A := 1;$

$\quad \mu X.\,(BC_1?E1; done1 := False; (a_A == 1) \rightarrow ((\neg done1 \wedge E1 == e) \rightarrow (BR_1!e; X;$

$\quad (a_A == 1) \rightarrow (a_A := 0; a_B := 1; done1 := True))); (a_B == 1) \rightarrow skip; BO_1!)$

---

[1] Please note that the example is an OR-diagram.

3.5   Combination of Simulink and Stateflow

Given a Simulink/Stateflow model, its Stateflow parts are translated into separate processes by the above algorithms. These processes are put in parallel with the processes obtained from the Simulink part, together forming the complete model of the system. The Simulink and Stateflow diagrams in parallel transmit data or events via channels. The communications between them are categorized into the following cases:

– As defined in Sect. 3.2, the input (and output) variables from (and to) Simulink will be transmitted through the monitor process to (and from) Stateflow;
– The input events from Simulink will be passed via the monitor to Stateflow;
– as defined in Sect. 3.3, the output events (i.e. the ones occurring in $\mathcal{S}_1, \cdots, \mathcal{S}_n$ in the Stateflow diagram) will be sent directly to the Simulink processes;
– the input/output variables and events inside Simulink part are handled as in our previous work [23].

3.6   Implementation

We had already implemented a tool **S2H** translating Simulink diagrams into HCSP processes as part of our previous work [23]. We have now extended **S2H** to support the translation of Stateflow diagrams, and we have named the new tool **Sim2HCSP**. For each Stateflow diagram, it generates three files that correspond to the definitions of variables, processes, and assertions respectively. To use **Sim2HCSP**, the user has to install the Java Runtime Environment and has to set two environment variables to point to the paths of Isabelle and HHL prover, respectively.

4   Case Study: Revisiting the Combined Scenario of CTCS-3

In our previous work [23], we modeled a combined operational scenario of Chinese Train Control System level 3 (CTCS-3) as a pure Simulink model, in which all the control behaviors of Radio Block Center (RBC), Train Control Center (TCC), Driver and so on are abstracted away as assumptions, as it is impossible to model such event-driven control behavior using Simulink. In this paper, we will revisit this example by modeling the event-driven control behaviour as Stateflow diagrams, and therefore give a complete Simulink/Stateflow model of this scenario by dropping the assumptions. In addition, we formally prove the Simulink/Stateflow model against the System Requiement Specification (SRS) by HHL Prover.

According to the SRS, a train needs to apply for movement authority (MA) from RBC under CTCS-3 or TCC under the backup system CTCS-2. If it succeeds, the train gets permission to move within the geometric extent of its MA. An MA is composed of a sequence of segments, each of which is associated with two kinds of speed limits $v_1 > v_2$, respectively for emergency brake intervention and service brake intervention, the end point e of the segment, and the operating mode *mode* of the segment.

Given an MA, as shown in Fig. 6, the static speed profile (solid line) is the region formed by the two speed limits, i.e., $v \leq seg.v_1$ and $v \leq seg.v_2$, where *seg* represents the current segment the train is running on; while the dynamic speed profile (dotted line) is calculated according to $v^2 + 2b\,s \leq next(seg).v_i^2 + 2b\,seg.e$ for $i = 1, 2$, where b represents the train's maximum deceleration and $next(seg)$ the next segment ahead of the train. At any time, the train must move within the static and dynamic speed profiles. For simplicity, in our modeling, we assume that each MA contains 3 segments, and whenever there is only one segment left, the train must apply for another MA extension.

The *combined scenario* is shown in Fig. 7: the train has got the MA till x_3; the control system is CTCS-2 before x_2, while CTCS-3 after x_2; and meanwhile, the moving mode is Full Supervision (FS) before x_2, while Calling On (CO) after x_2. So, in this scenario, the level transition and mode conversion will occur at x_2 simultaneously. By SRS, the train starts to apply for level transition from RBC at location ST. If RBC approves the request, the train will start the level upgrade from x_1, and when it reaches x_2, its control system is upgraded to CTCS-3, and the level transition completes. It should be noticed that, when the train moves between x_1 and x_2, it will be co-supervised by CTCS-2 and CTCS-3, thus it must follow the speed profiles of both control systems. In addition, under CTCS-3, a train is required to fully stop before starting a CO segment, and ask for the confirmation of the driver in order to enter the CO segment. As a result, both the speed limits at x_2, the starting point of a CO segment, will be 0 initially. Under CTCS-2, in contrast, the train will convert the mode to CO directly at x_2.

4.1 Modeling in Simulink/Stateflow

The top-level view of the Simulink model for the combined scenario is shown in Fig. 8. It consists of two sub-systems: the *plant* sub-system models the movement of the train by using the differential equation $\dot{s} = v$ and $\dot{v} = a$, with input a from the control sub-system; the *control* sub-system reads s and v from the plant periodically (every 0.125 s in our setting), based on which it computes the new acceleration a and sends it back to the plant; they together constitute a closed loop.

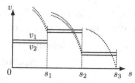

Fig. 6. Static and dynamic speed profiles

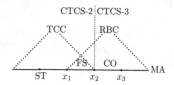

Fig. 7. Level and mode transition

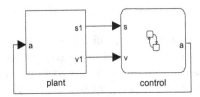 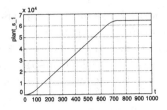

Fig. 8. The top-level view of Simulink model   **Fig. 9.** The result of simulation

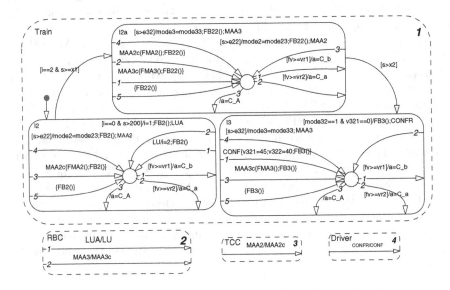

Fig. 10. The control model in Stateflow

The control sub-system is modeled as a Stateflow model, shown in Fig. 10. It is an AND diagram with four parallel states modeling the four components (i.e. *Train, RBC, TCC,* and *Driver*) involved in the scenario. A set of events, variables, and functions are introduced, for which we assume a naming convention that the first and second numbers always refer to the level and the MA segment on which the train is moving, resp., and the third to the type of speed limits, if existent. E.g., $e22$ represents the end of the second segment at level 2 (i.e. location x_2), etc. The *Train* state, featuring highest priority 1, contains three sub-states: $l2$ corresponding to the cases when the train is under CTCS-2, $l3$ to the case when the train is under CTCS-3, and $l2a$ the case when the train is co-supervised by CTCS-2 and CTCS-3. By performing the default transition, $l2$ becomes active first, and will check the following transitions in sequence:

- The outgoing transition goes to $l2a$, and becomes enabled when the train reaches x_1 and gets permission from RBC to start level transition (i.e., $i == 2$);

- The ingoing transitions 1 and 2 represent the application for level transition from RBC. Obviously 2 will be enabled first, when the train is approaching ST. It starts to apply level transition by setting i to 1 and sending LUA to RBC. Accordingly, RBC will be triggered and then approve the request by emitting LU back. As a result, transition 1 in $l2$ will be enabled and then set i to 2. This will enable the outgoing transition to $l2a$. The action $FB2()$ models the supervision of CTCS-2.
- The transitions 3 and 4 represent the application for MA extension from TCC. Transition 4 will be enabled first, when the train reaches e_{22}, and it will first update the mode to CO and then start to apply MA extension by sending $MAA2$ to TCC. Accordingly, TCC will be triggered and then agree on the request by emitting $MAA2C$ back. As a result, transition 3 in $l2$ will happen and extend the MA correspondingly. $FMA2$ models MA extension under CTCS-2.
- The transition 5 represents the supervision of CTCS-2 and is always enabled.
- When reaching the junction, there are three outgoing transitions, which by comparison with the speed limits $vr1$ and $vr2$, update the acceleration a correspondingly. Here C_b, C_a and C_A represent the maximum deceleration, a random deceleration, and a random acceleration respectively.

As the train moves, the outgoing transition of $l2$ will be taken, and state $l2a$ will become active. $l2a$ has one outgoing transition targeting $l3$, which is enabled when the train reaches beyond $x2$. $l2a$ has a similar structure to $l2$, except that it is not involved in the level transition, but enriched with transitions 1 and 4 representing the application for MA extension from RBC in the co-supervised area. $l3$ also has a similar structure to $l2$, except that it will ask for confirmation of mode conversion from the driver, via transitions 1 and 2.

Results. The simulation result is shown in Fig. 9, which indicates that the train will stop at location x_2 (thus state $l3$ is never reachable). Applying the tool **Sim2HCSP** to translate the Simulink/Stateflow model, it generates seven files, corresponding to the variable, processes, and assertion definitions of the Simulink and Stateflow models resp., and the *goal* to be verified. Together, they contain 1351 lines of code in total. We use P to denote the resulting HCSP model for the combined scenario. Using HHL prover, we prove the following goal for P as a theorem (T stands for **True**):

```
lemma goal :"{T,T,T,T,T,T} P {plant_s_1<=64000, T,T,T,T,T;
              (1 = 0) | (high (plant_s_1<=64000)), T,T,T,T,T}"
```

Obviously, the postcondition together with the history formula indicate that the train never moves across location x_2, i.e., 64000 here.

All the files related to the case study including the translation and formal interactive proof can be found at https://github.com/submission/Sim2HCSP.

5   Conclusion and Future Work

The combination of Simulink and Stateflow provides a seamless integration of hierarchical and parallel state machines into a control-oriented block-diagram formalism involving both discrete and continuous behaviors. Extending our previous work on translating pure Simulink models into the hybrid-state process calculus HCSP, this paper presents the translation of Simulink/Stateflow to HCSP. Based on this translation, full formal verification of Simulink/Stateflow diagrams can be achieved using the Isabell/HOL-based interactive verifier HHL Prover. We demonstrate our approach on the case study of a combined scenario from the Chinese Train Control System CTCS-3. In comparison to our previous work, more complex discrete control is involved, and as a consequence more complex interactions between the controllers and continuous plant are covered by the proof certificate obtained.

Acknowledgements. This paper is supported partly by "973 Program" under grant No. 2014CB340701, by NSFC under grants 91118007 and 91418204, by CDZ project CAP (GZ 1023), by the CAS/SAFEA International Partnership Program for Creative Research Teams, and by Deutsche Forschungsgemeinschaft as part of the Transregional Collaborative Research Center SFB/TR 14 AVACS.

References

1. Simulink User's Guide (2013). http://www.mathworks.com/help/pdf_doc/simulink/sl_using.pdf
2. Stateflow User's Guide (2013). http://www.mathworks.com/help/pdf_doc/stateflow/sf_ug.pdf
3. Agrawal, A., Simon, G., Karsai, G.: Semantic translation of Simulink/Stateflow models to hybrid automata using graph transformations. Int. Workshop Graph Transform. Visual Model. Tech. **109**, 43–56 (2004)
4. Cavalcanti, A., Clayton, P., O'Halloran, C.: Control law diagrams in circus. In: Fitzgerald, J.S., Hayes, I.J., Tarlecki, A. (eds.) FM 2005. LNCS, vol. 3582, pp. 253–268. Springer, Heidelberg (2005)
5. Chen, C., Dong, J.S., Sun, J.: A formal framework for modeling and validating Simulink diagrams. Formal Asp. Comput. **21**(5), 451–483 (2009)
6. Clarke, E.M., Zuliani, P.: Statistical model checking for cyber-physical systems. In: Bultan, T., Hsiung, P.-A. (eds.) ATVA 2011. LNCS, vol. 6996, pp. 1–12. Springer, Heidelberg (2011)
7. Hamon, G., Rushby, J.: An operational semantics for Stateflow. Int. J. Softw. Tools Technol. Transf. **9**(5), 447–456 (2007)
8. He, J.: From CSP to hybrid systems. In: A Classical Mind, Essays in Honour of C.A.R. Hoare, pp. 171–189. Prentice Hall International (UK) Ltd (1994)
9. Herde, C., Eggers, A., Fränzle, M., Teige, T.: Analysis of hybrid systems using HySAT. In: ICONS 2008, pp. 196–201 (2008)
10. Hoare, C.A.R.: Communicating Sequential Processes. Prentice-Hall Intl, Upper Saddle River (1985)

11. Liu, J., Lv, J., Quan, Z., Zhan, N., Zhao, H., Zhou, C., Zou, L.: A calculus for hybrid CSP. In: Ueda, K. (ed.) APLAS 2010. LNCS, vol. 6461, pp. 1–15. Springer, Heidelberg (2010)
12. Meenakshi, B., Bhatnagar, A., Roy, S.: Tool for translating simulink models into input language of a model checker. In: Liu, Z., Kleinberg, R.D. (eds.) ICFEM 2006. LNCS, vol. 4260, pp. 606–620. Springer, Heidelberg (2006)
13. Miller, S.P., Whalen, M.W., Cofer, D.D.: Software model checking takes off. Commun. ACM 53(2), 58–64 (2010)
14. Moore, R.E.: Interval Analysis. Prentice Hall, Upper Saddle River (1966)
15. Moszkowski, B., Manna, Z.: Reasoning in interval temporal logic. In: Engeler, E. (ed.) Logic of Programs 1979. LNCS, vol. 125. Springer, Heidelberg (1981)
16. Rauh, A., Sibert, C., Aschemann, H.: Verified simulation and optimization of dynimc systems with friction and hysteresis. In: Proceedings of ENOC 2011 (2011)
17. Scaife, N., Sofronis, C., Caspi, P., Tripakis, S., Maraninchi, F.: Defining and translating a "safe" subset of Simulink/Stateflow into Lustre. In: EMSOFT 2004, pp. 259–268 (2004)
18. Tiwari, A.: Formal semantics and analysis methods for Simulink/Stateflow models. Technical report, SRI International (2002)
19. Tripakis, S., Sofronis, C., Caspi, P., Curic, A.: Translating discrete-time Simulink to Lustre. ACM Trans. Embedded Comput. Syst. 4(4), 779–818 (2005)
20. Zhan, N., Wang, S., Zhao, H.: Formal modelling, analysis and verification of hybrid systems. In: Liu, Z., Woodcock, J., Zhu, H. (eds.) Unifying Theories of Programming and Formal Engineering Methods. LNCS, vol. 8050, pp. 207–281. Springer, Heidelberg (2013)
21. Zhou, C., Wang, J., Ravn, A.P.: A formal description of hybrid systems. In: Alur, R., Sontag, E.D., Henzinger, T.A. (eds.) HS 1995. LNCS, vol. 1066, pp. 511–530. Springer, Heidelberg (1996)
22. Zou, L., Lv, J., Wang, S., Zhan, N., Tang, T., Yuan, L., Liu, Y.: Verifying chinese train control system under a combined scenario by theorem proving. In: Cohen, E., Rybalchenko, A. (eds.) VSTTE 2013. LNCS, vol. 8164, pp. 262–280. Springer, Heidelberg (2014)
23. Zou, L., Zhan, N., Wang, S., Fränzle, M., Qin, S.: Verifying simulink diagrams via a hybrid Hoare Logic prover. In: EMSOFT 2013 (2013)

Decidability of the Reachability for a Family of Linear Vector Fields

Ting Gan[1], Mingshuai Chen[2], Liyun Dai[1], Bican Xia[1], and Naijun Zhan[2(✉)]

[1] LMAM & School of Mathematical Sciences, Peking University, Beijing, China
{gant,dailiyun,xbc}@pku.edu.cn
[2] State Key Laboratory of Computer Science, Institute of Software,
CAS, Beijing, China
{chenms,znj}@ios.ac.cn

Abstract. The reachability problem is one of the most important issues in the verification of hybrid systems. Computing the reachable sets of differential equations is difficult, although computing the reachable sets of finite state machines is well developed. Hence, it is not surprising that the reachability of most of hybrid systems is undecidable. In this paper, we identify a family of vector fields and show its reachability problem is decidable. The family consists of all vector fields whose state parts are linear, while input parts are non-linear, possibly with exponential expressions. Such vector fields are commonly used in practice. To the best of our knowledge, the family is one of the most expressive families of vector fields with a decidable reachability problem. The decidability is achieved by proving the decidability of the extension of Tarski's algebra with some specific exponential functions, which has been proved in [21,22] due to Strzebonski. In this paper, we propose another decision procedure, which is more efficient when all constraints are open sets. The experimental results indicate the efficiency of our approach, even better than existing approaches based on approximation and numeric computation in general.

Keywords: Tarski's algebra · Polynomial-exponential function · Reachability · Real root isolation · Cylindrical Algebraic Decomposition (CAD)

1 Introduction

Hybrid systems (HSs) integrate computation with physical processes: embedded computers and networks monitor and control physical processes and feedback loops continuously influence computations, which are known as Cyber-Physical Systems (CPSs) nowadays. Applications of CPS span over many safety-critical domains, including communication, healthcare, manufacturing, aerospace, transportation, etc. To guarantee the correctness of these systems is vital so that we can bet our lives on them, and challenging [24]. Therefore, formal methods have been widely used in the verification of HSs. The reachability problem of HSs is

© Springer International Publishing Switzerland 2015
B. Finkbeiner et al. (Eds.): ATVA 2015, LNCS 9364, pp. 482–499, 2015.
DOI: 10.1007/978-3-319-24953-7_34

to verify that unsafe states are not reachable from the set of initial states for a given HS, which is one of most important issues in the verification of HSs.

As HSs consist of deep interaction between continuous evolutions and discrete transitions, the reachability problem of most of HSs is undecidable [12], except for some simple cases, either their vector fields, *i.e.*, their continuous evolution parts, are quite simple such as timed automata [4] and multi-rate automata [3], or there are very restrictive constraints on their discrete transitions like o-minimal HSs [15].

In [16], Lafferriere et al. investigated vector fields of the following form

$$\dot{\xi} = A\xi + \mathbf{u}, \tag{1}$$

where $\xi(t) \in \mathbb{R}^n$ is the state of the system at time t, $A \in \mathbb{R}^{n\times n}$ is the system matrix, and $\mathbf{u} : \mathbb{R} \to \mathbb{R}^n$ is a piecewise continuous function which is called the *input*. They obtained the decidability of the reachability problems of the following three families of vector fields:

1. A is *nilpotent*, i.e. $A^n = 0$, and each component of $\mathbf{u}$ is a polynomial;
2. A is *diagonalizable* with rational eigenvalues, and each component of $\mathbf{u}$ is of the form $\sum_{i=1}^{m} c_i e^{\lambda_i t}$, where λ_is are rationals and c_is are subject to semi-algebraic constraints;
3. A is *diagonalizable* with purely imaginary eigenvalues, and each component of $\mathbf{u}$ of the form $\sum_{i=1}^{m} c_i \sin(\lambda_i t) + d_i \cos(\lambda_i t)$, where λ_is are rationals and c_is and d_is are subject to semi-algebraic constraints.

The above results are achieved by reducing the problems into Tarski's algebra [23]. To the best of our knowledge, these results are the strongest ones on the decidability of the reachability problems of HSs obtained so far.

However, in practice, there are many linear HSs, whose reachability problem is out of the above three families. For instance,

Example 1. Consider an LDS $\dot{\xi} = \begin{bmatrix} \sqrt{2} & & \\ & -\sqrt{2} & \\ & & -1 \end{bmatrix} \xi + \begin{bmatrix} 1-t \\ te^t \\ e^{-t} \end{bmatrix}$. Let $\mathrm{X} = \{(x_1, x_2, x_3)^T \mid 1 - x_1^2 - x_2^2 - x_3^2 > 0\}, \mathrm{Y} = \{(y_1, y_2, y_3)^T \mid y_1 + y_2 + y_3 + 2 < 0\}$. The problem we are concerning is to check if some state in Y is reachable from X. Obviously, this problem is not in any of the above three cases.

In this paper, we will generalize the case 2 above by allowing:

- A is *diagonalizable* with *real* eigenvalues, and each component of $\mathbf{u}$ is of the form $\sum_{i=1}^{m} c_i e^{\lambda_i t}$, where λ_is are *reals* and c_is are subject to semi-algebraic constraints.

Such extension is substantial, as the new family is strictly more expressive than the case 2, for instance, Example 1 falls into this family. In addition, the reachability problem cannot be reduced to Tarski's algebra any more as in [16].

To obtain the decidability, we have to resort to the decidability of the extension of Tarski's algebra with functions of the form

$$f(t, \mathbf{x}) = \sum_{i=0}^{m} f_i(t, \mathbf{x}) e^{\lambda_i t}, \tag{2}$$

where $m \in \mathbb{N}$, $f_i(t, \mathbf{x}) \in \mathbb{R}[t, \mathbf{x}]$, $\lambda_i \in \mathbb{R}$, $i = 0, 1, \cdots, m$ and the e is the natural logarithm. We denote the extension by $\mathcal{T}_e$.

Tarski's algebra is the first-order theory of reals over the structure $\langle \mathbb{R}; +, -, \cdot, 0, 1 \rangle$, which is also called the elementary algebra and geometry. In [23], Tarski showed the decidability of Tarski's algebra. But whether the extension of Tarski's algebra with exponentiation is decidable (so-called "Tarski's conjecture") is still open. In [2], Weispfenning et al. gave a partial solution to Tarski's conjecture by showing the decidability of the extension of Tarski's algebra by allowing terms of the form $f(t, \mathbf{x}, e^t)$, where $f(t, \mathbf{x}, y) \in \mathbb{R}[t, \mathbf{x}, y]$. In [25], Xu et al. considered how to generalize Weispfenning et al's approach by allowing functions of the form (2), but with the restriction that all the λ_is are nonnegative integers. While in [21,22], Strzebonski presented a decision procedure for $\mathcal{T}_e$ under the assumption of *Schanuel's conjecture*.

In this paper, we first show how to reduce the reachability problem under consideration to the decidability problem of $\mathcal{T}_e$, therefore obtain its decidability due to Strzebonski's result [21,22]. Then, we give another decision procedure based on a new real root isolation algorithm for functions of (2) using *Rolle's theorem* and openCAD [20] or CAD [7], depending on if all constraints are open sets. The complexity of our algorithm is nearly same as Strzebonski's in general, but more efficient than his if all constraints are open sets. The experimental results indicate the efficiency of our approach, which is better than existing approaches based on approximation and numeric computation in general, e.g., HSolver [18], FLOW* [6], dReach [14], etc., given that most of them can only be used to compute reachable sets in bounded time.

2   Problem Description

In this section, we describe the problem to be solved.

As a convention, we use $\mathbf{x}$ to stand for a vector variable $(x_1, \ldots, x_n)$, $\mathbb{N}, \mathbb{Q}, \mathbb{R}$ for natural, rational and real numbers respectively, $\mathbb{R}[\mathbf{x}]$ for the polynomial ring in $\mathbf{x}$ with coefficients in $\mathbb{R}$ in what follows.

A term with the form (2) is called *polynomial-exponential function* (PEF). A *linear differential system* (LDS) is of the form (1). We say an LDS is a *linear differential system with polynomial-exponential input* (LDS$_{\text{PEF}}$) if every component of $\mathbf{u}$ is a PEF.

A set $X \subset \mathbb{R}^n$ is said *semi-algebraic* if it is defined as $\{\mathbf{x} \in \mathbb{R}^n \mid p_1(\mathbf{x}) \triangleright 0, \cdots, p_j(\mathbf{x}) \triangleright 0\}$, for some polynomial $p_1(\mathbf{x}), \cdots, p_j(\mathbf{x}) \in \mathbb{R}[\mathbf{x}]$, where $\triangleright \in \{\geq, > \}$, $j \in \mathbb{N}$. A semi-algebraic set X is said to be *open* if all $\triangleright$ are instantiated to $>$.

Given an initial state $\xi(0) = \mathbf{x}$, the solution of (1) at time $t \geq 0$ is denoted by $\xi(t) = \Phi(\mathbf{x}, t)$. Then the *backward reachable set* $Pre(X)$ and the *forward reachable set* $Post(X)$ of the LDS (1) from a given set X are defined as follows:

$$Pre(X) = \{\mathbf{y} \in \mathbb{R}^n \mid \exists \mathbf{x} \exists t : \mathbf{x} \in X \wedge t \geq 0 \wedge \Phi(\mathbf{y}, t) = \mathbf{x}\} \tag{3}$$

$$Post(X) = \{\mathbf{y} \in \mathbb{R}^n \mid \exists \mathbf{x} \exists t : \mathbf{x} \in X \wedge t \geq 0 \wedge \Phi(\mathbf{x}, t) = \mathbf{y}\} \tag{4}$$

Now, the problem under consideration is formulated as follows: Given an LDS$_{PEF}$ in which A is diagonalizable with real eigenvalues, an initial set X and an unsafe set Y, the problem is to verify whether any unsafe state in Y is not reachable by some trajectory starting from X, *i.e.*, whether $Post(X) \cap Y = \emptyset$, or dually $Pre(Y) \cap X = \emptyset$, or

$$\mathcal{F}(X, Y) = \exists \mathbf{x} \exists \mathbf{y} \exists t : \mathbf{x} \in X \wedge \mathbf{y} \in Y \wedge t \geq 0 \wedge \Phi(\mathbf{x}, t) = \mathbf{y}.$$

3   Reduction to the Decidability of $\mathcal{T}_e$

For a given LDS$_{PEF}$ (1) and a given initial state $\mathbf{x}$, the solution can be represented by

$$\xi(t) = \Phi(\mathbf{x}, t) = e^{At}\mathbf{x} + \int_0^t e^{A(t-\tau)}\mathbf{u}(\tau)d\tau, \tag{5}$$

where the matrix exponential e^{At} is defined as $e^{At} = \sum_{k=0}^{\infty} \frac{t^k}{k!}A^k$.

Suppose the matrix A can be diagonalizable with real eigenvalues, then there exist a diagonal matrix D and an invertible matrix Q in $\mathbb{R}^{n \times n}$ such that $A = QDQ^{-1}$. The matrix D is formed with the eigenvalues of A along the diagonal and the columns of Q form a basis of eigenvectors of A. For brevity, we denote

$$A = (a_{ij}), \quad Q = (q_{ij}), \quad Q^{-1} = (q_{ij}^-), D = diag(\lambda_1, \cdots, \lambda_n),$$

where a_{ij}, q_{ij}, q_{ij}^- and $\lambda_1, \cdots, \lambda_n$ all are reals.

So, the input of the LDS$_{PEF}$ can be reformulated as

$$\mathbf{u} = (u_1, u_2, \cdots, u_n)^T, \text{ where } u_i = \sum_{k=0}^{r_i} g_{ik}(t)e^{\mu_{ik}t} = \sum_{k=0}^{r_i}\sum_{l=0}^{d_{ik}} g_{ikl} \cdot t^l e^{\mu_{ik}t}, i = 1, 2, \cdots, n,$$

in which $\mathbf{v}^T$ means the transposition of $\mathbf{v}$, $r_i \in \mathbb{N}$, $\mu_{ik} \in \mathbb{R}$, $g_{ik} \in \mathbb{R}[t]$, $d_{ik} \in \mathbb{N}$ is the degree of g_{ik}, $g_{ikl} \in \mathbb{R}$, for $i = 1, \cdots, n$, $k = 1, \cdots, r_i$, $l = 1, \cdots, d_{ik}$.

Now, let us further discuss the solution given in formula (5) with an initial state $\mathbf{x} = (x_1, \cdots, x_n)$. First of all, note that $e^{At} = e^{QDQ^{-1}t} = Q \begin{bmatrix} e^{\lambda_1 t} & & \\ & \ddots & \\ & & e^{\lambda_n t} \end{bmatrix} Q^{-1}$.

Thus,

$$(e^{At})_{ij} = \sum_{k=1}^n q_{ik}q_{kj}^- e^{\lambda_k t}, \tag{6}$$

$$(e^{At}\mathbf{x})_i = \sum_{j=1}^n (e^{At})_{ij}x_j = \sum_{k=1}^n (\sum_{j=1}^n q_{ik}q_{kj}^- x_j)e^{\lambda_k t} = \sum_{k=1}^n \alpha_{ik}(\mathbf{x})e^{\lambda_k t}, \tag{7}$$

where $\alpha_{ik}(\mathbf{x}) = \sum_{j=1}^{n} q_{ik}\bar{q}_{kj}x_j$, $i = 1, \cdots, n$.

Besides, for the second summand in the right side of (5), we have

$$\Psi(t) = \int_0^t e^{A(t-\tau)}\mathbf{u}(\tau)d\tau,$$

$$(\Psi(t))_i = \int_0^t (e^{A(t-\tau)}\mathbf{u}(\tau))_i d\tau = \sum_{k=1}^{n}(e^{At})_{ik}\int_0^t (e^{-A\tau}\mathbf{u}(\tau))_k d\tau$$

$$= \sum_{k=1}^{n}(e^{At})_{ik}\int_0^t \sum_{j=1}^{n}\sum_{m=1}^{n} q_{km}\bar{q}_{mj}e^{-\lambda_m\tau}\sum_{h=0}^{r_j}\sum_{l=0}^{d_{jh}} g_{jhl}\tau^l e^{\mu_{jh}\tau}d\tau$$

$$= \sum_{k=1}^{n}\sum_{j=1}^{n}\sum_{m=1}^{n}\sum_{h=0}^{r_j}\sum_{l=0}^{d_{jh}}(e^{At})_{ik}q_{km}\bar{q}_{mj}g_{jhl}\int_0^t \tau^l e^{(\mu_{jh}-\lambda_m)\tau}d\tau.$$

Now, we consider the following two cases:

$\mu_{jh} - \lambda_m \neq 0$: Then $\int_0^t \tau^l e^{(\mu_{jh}-\lambda_m)\tau}d\tau = \sum_{w=0}^{l}(-1)^w \frac{l!}{(\mu_{jh}-\lambda_m)^{w+1}(l-w)!}t^{(l-w)}$
$e^{(\mu_{jh}-\lambda_m)t} + (-1)^{l+1}\frac{l!}{(\mu_{jh}-\lambda_m)^{l+1}}$.

$\mu_{jh} - \lambda_m = 0$: Then $\int_0^t \tau^l e^{(\mu_{jh}-\lambda_m)\tau}d\tau = \frac{t^{l+1}}{l+1}$.

So, $(\Psi(t))_i$ can be reformulated as: $(\Psi(t))_i = \sum_{j=0}^{c_i}\psi_{ij}(t)e^{\theta_{ij}t}$, where $\psi_{ij}(t) \in \mathbb{R}[t]$, $\theta_{ij} \in \mathbb{R}$ and $c_i \in \mathbb{N}$, for $i = 1, \cdots, n$, $j = 1, \cdots, c_i$. Thus, we have $(\Phi(\mathbf{x}, t))_i = \sum_{k=1}^{n}\alpha_{ik}(\mathbf{x})e^{\lambda_k t} + \sum_{j=0}^{c_i}\psi_{ij}(t)e^{\theta_{ij}t}$, which is a PEF.

Therefore, (3) and (4) can be reformulated accordingly as

$$Pre(X) = \{\mathbf{y} \mid \exists\mathbf{x}\exists t : \mathbf{x} \in X \wedge t \geq 0 \wedge \bigwedge_{i=1}^{n}\sum_{j=1}^{s_i}\phi_{ij}(\mathbf{y}, t)e^{\nu_{ij}t} = x_i\} \qquad (8)$$

$$Post(X) = \{\mathbf{y} \mid \exists\mathbf{x}\exists t : \mathbf{x} \in X \wedge t \geq 0 \wedge \bigwedge_{i=1}^{n}\sum_{j=1}^{s_i}\phi_{ij}(\mathbf{x}, t)e^{\nu_{ij}t} = y_i\} \qquad (9)$$

Likewise, our problem considered in this paper is elaborated as: Given two semi-algebraic sets $X = \{\mathbf{x} \in \mathbb{R}^n \mid p_1(\mathbf{x}) \rhd 0, \cdots, p_{J_1}(\mathbf{x}) \rhd 0\}$, $Y = \{\mathbf{y} \in \mathbb{R}^n \mid p_{J_1+1}(\mathbf{y}) \rhd 0, \cdots, p_J(\mathbf{y}) \rhd 0\}$, where $\rhd \in \{\geq, >\}$, whether

$$\mathcal{F}(X, Y) = \exists\mathbf{x}\exists\mathbf{y}\exists t : \mathbf{x} \in X \wedge \mathbf{y} \in Y \wedge t \geq 0 \wedge \bigwedge_{i=1}^{n}\sum_{j=1}^{s_i}\phi_{ij}(\mathbf{x}, t)e^{\nu_{ij}t} = y_i \qquad (10)$$

Hence, by Strzebonski's result [21, 22], we can conclude that

Theorem 1. *The reachability problem (10) is decidable if $\mathcal{T}_e$ is decidable.*

4 Decision Procedure for $\mathcal{T}_e$

In this section, we give a decision procedure for $\mathcal{T}_e$ based on *cylindrical algebraic decomposition* (CAD), due to Collins [7].

The basic idea of CAD is: Given a set S of polynomials in $\mathbb{R}[\mathbf{x}]$, CAD is used to partition $\mathbb{R}^n$ into connected semi-algebraic sets, called *cells*, such that each polynomial in S keeps constant *sign* (either $+$, $-$ or 0) on each *cell*. As CAD plays a fundamental role in computer algebra and real algebraic geometry, in the literature, a numerous works are done on improvement of CAD, e.g., [5,8,10, 11,13,17]. When constraints are open sets, GCAD [20] or openCAD [11] is enough, which partitions the space $\mathbb{R}^n$ into a set of *open cells* instead of *cells* (i.e., takes sample points from open cells only), such that on each of which every polynomial in S keeps constant nonzero *sign* (either $+$ or $-$). For example, suppose $f_1 = y - x, f_2 = y + x$. The graphs of $f_1 = 0$ and $f_2 = 0$ decompose $\mathbb{R}^2$ into 9 cells with different dimensions: four of which are 2-dimensional (open) cells (i.e., $f_1 \sim 0 \wedge f_2 \sim 0$, where $\sim \in \{>,<\}$); four of which are 1-dimensional cells (i.e., $f_1 \sim 0 \wedge f_2 = 0$, $f_1 = 0 \wedge f_2 \sim 0$, where $\sim \in \{>,<\}$); and one of which is 0-dimensional cell (i.e., $f_1 = 0 \wedge f_2 = 0$). Complete CAD takes at least one sample point from each of the 9 cells, while GCAD or openCAD takes at least one sample point only from each of the four 2-dimensional (open) cells. Formally,

Definition 1. *For a polynomial $f(x_1, ..., x_n) \in \mathbb{R}[x_1, ..., x_n]$, a CAD (openCAD) defined by f under the order $x_1 \prec x_2 \prec \cdots \prec x_n$ is a set of sample points in $\mathbb{R}^n$ obtained through the following three phases:*

Projection: *Apply CAD (openCAD) projection operator on f to get a set of projection polynomials $\{f_n = f(x_1, ..., x_n), f_{n-1}(x_1, ..., x_{n-1}), ..., f_1(x_1)\}$;*

Base: *Choose a rational point in each of the (open) intervals defined by the real roots of f_1;*

Lifting: *Substitute each sample point in $\mathbb{R}^{i-1}$ for $(x_1, ..., x_{i-1})$ in f_i to get a univariate polynomial $f_i'(x_i)$, and then, as in Base phase, choose sample points for $f_i'(x_i)$. Repeat this process for i from 2 to n.*

Using CAD (openCAD), we develop a decision procedure for $\mathcal{T}_e$ as follows:

Step 1. Check whether $X \cap Y = \emptyset$, if not, it's easy to see that (10) holds.

Step 2. Translate the problem to an **openCAD** solvable problem if X and Y are open sets, otherwise a **CAD** solvable problem. By (9), $y_i(\mathbf{x}, t) = \sum_{j=1}^{s_i} \phi_{ij}(\mathbf{x}, t) e^{\nu_{ij} t}$. So, we can replace $p_j(\mathbf{y})$ with $p_j(y(\mathbf{x}, t))$, which is polynomial in $\mathbf{x}$ and polynomial-exponential in t, abbreviated as $p_j(\mathbf{x}, t)$, for $j = J_1 + 1, \cdots, J$. Simply, we define $p_j(\mathbf{x}, t)$ as $p_j(\mathbf{x})$, for $j = 1, \cdots, J_1$. Thus, $\mathcal{F}(X, Y)$ in (10) can be reformulated as $\mathcal{F} = \exists \mathbf{x} \exists t \bigwedge_{j=1}^{J} p_j(\mathbf{x}, t) \rhd 0 \wedge t \geq 0$.

Step 3. Eliminate $x_1, \cdots, x_n$ one by one using CAD (openCAD) projection operator on $\prod_{j=1}^{J} p_j$ and obtain a set of projection polynomials $\{q_n(x_1, \ldots, x_n, t) = \prod_{j=1}^{J} p_j, q_{n-1}(x_2, \ldots, x_n, t)\}, \ldots, q_0(t)\}$.

Step 4. Isolate the real roots of the resulted PEF q_0 based on *Rolle's theorem*, which will be elaborated in the next section.

Step 5. Lift the solution using openCAD or CAD lifting procedure corresponding to Step 2 according to the order t, x_n, $\cdots$, x_1 based on $\{q_0, \cdots, q_n\}$, and obtain a set S of *sample points*.

Step 6. Check if $\mathcal{F}$ holds by testing if there exists α in S such that $\wedge_{j=1}^{J} p_j(\alpha) \triangleright 0$.

In [22], Strzeboński presented another decision procedure for $\mathcal{T}_e$ completely based on CAD. Our decision procedure differentiates from Strzeboński's in the following points:

– When all constraints are open sets, our method is based on openCAD, which requires less computation compared to the corresponding complete CAD. Therefore, our decision procedure is more efficient (see Sect. 6) in this case. But the two decision procedures share the same complexity in general case.

– In [22], an algorithm for isolating real roots of a given PEF based on *weak Fourier sequence* [21] is given. It is claimed that the algorithm is *complete* under the assumption of *Schanuel's conjucture* [19]. While, in this paper, we give another algorithm to isolate real roots of the resulted PEF $q_0(t)$ based on *Rolle's theorem*. We prove that our approach is also *complete* under the assumption that $q_0(t)$ does not have any multiple real roots, which can be implied by *Schanuel's conjecture*.

5   Isolating Real Roots of PEFs

In this section we give an algorithm PEFIsolation to isolate all real roots for a PEF.

Definition 2. *Consider a PEF in t as*

$$f(t) = \sum_{i=0}^{s} f_i(t) e^{\nu_i t}, \tag{11}$$

where $s \in \mathbb{N}$, $0 \neq f_i \in \mathbb{R}[t]$ and $\nu_i \in \mathbb{R}$ are pairwise different. Real root isolation of the equation $f(t) = 0$ is to obtain a set of intervals $\{I_j = (a_j, b_j) \mid a_j, b_j \in \mathbb{R} \wedge a_j < b_j, j = 1, \ldots, J\}$ such that $I_i \cap I_j = \emptyset$ if $i \neq j$, in each I_j there exists only one real root of $f(t)$, and all real roots of $f(t)$ are contained in $\bigcup_{j=1}^{J} I_j$.

Given an open interval I, *real root isolation* of $f(t)$ over I can be defined similarly. Without loss of generality, in (11), we can assume

$$0 = \nu_0 < \nu_1 < \nu_2 < \cdots < \nu_s, f_i(t) \not\equiv 0, \text{ for } i = 0, 1, \cdots, s. \tag{12}$$

When $s = 1$ or every ν_i ($0 \leq i \leq s$) is a positive integer, in [2] an algorithm named ISOL was proposed to isolate all real roots of $f(t)$. This algorithm can be easily extended to the case when all ν_i ($i = 0, \cdots, s$) are rationals or there exists a nonzero real number κ such that for every $0 \leq i \leq s$, $\nu_i \kappa$ is a rational.

5.1 Lower and Upper Bounds on Real Roots

Similar to [2], we can prove the following theorem, which indicates that there is a lower and upper bound on real roots for any given PEF.

Theorem 2 (upper bound). *Let $f(t)$ be a PEF of the form (11). Then we can obtain an upper bound C on its real roots through the following procedure:*

1. *Find $C_1 \geq 0$, $M > 0$ such that for all $t > C_1$, $|f_s(t)| > \frac{1}{M}$;*
2. *Find $C_2 \geq 0$ and $k \in \mathbb{N}$ such that for all $t > C_2$ and for all $0 \leq i < s$, $|f_i(t)| < \frac{t^k}{sM}$;*
3. *Find $C_3 \geq 0$ such that for all $t > C_3$, $t^k < e^{(\nu_s - \nu_{s-1})t}$;*
4. *Set $C = \max\{C_1, C_2, C_3\}$.*

Proof. Let $t > C$, then we have $|f_s(t)| > \frac{1}{M}$, $t^k < e^{(\nu_s - \nu_{s-1})t}$, $|f_i(t)| < \frac{t^k}{sM}$, for $i = 0, \cdots, s-1$. Whence

$$
\left| f_0(t) + \sum_{i=1}^{s-1} f_i(t) e^{\nu_i t} \right| \leq |f_0(t)| + \sum_{i=1}^{s-1} |f_i(t) e^{\nu_i t}| < \frac{t^k}{sM} + \sum_{i=1}^{s-1} \frac{t^k}{sM} e^{\nu_i t}
$$

$$
< \frac{t^k}{sM} e^{\nu_{s-1} t} + \sum_{i=1}^{s-1} \frac{t^k}{sM} e^{\nu_{s-1} t} = \frac{1}{M} t^k e^{\nu_{s-1} t} < \frac{1}{M} e^{\nu_s t} < |f_s(t) e^{\nu_s t}|.
$$

This implies $f(t) \neq 0$ for any $t \geq C$. So C is an upper bound on the real roots of $f(t)$. □

In order to get a lower bound, a commonly used method is to replace $f(t)$ with $g(t) = f(-t) e^{\nu_s t}$. Then, by Theorem 2, there is an upper bound B on the real roots of $g(t) = 0$. It's easy to see that $-B$ is a lower bound on the real roots of $f(t) = 0$. Thus, we see that all roots of $f(t) = 0$ are in the interval $(-B, C)$. In what follows, we denote by $L(f) = -B, U(f) = C$, the lower and upper bounds on the real roots of $f(t)$, respectively.

5.2 Algorithm

In this subsection, we present our algorithm PEFIsolation for isolating all real roots of a given nonzero PEF $f(t)$ of the form (11).

Definition 3. *Let $f(t)$ be a nonzero PEF of the form (11). We define*

$$
\mathrm{coff}(f) = (f_0, f_1, \ldots, f_s)^T, \quad \mathrm{nu}(f) = (0, \nu_1, \ldots, \nu_s)^T,
$$

$$
\deg(f) = (\deg(f_0), \deg(f_1), \ldots, \deg(f_s))^T,
$$

where $\deg(g)$ means the degree of g, and as a convention, $\deg(0) = -1$. So, (11) can be shorten as $f(t) = \mathrm{coff}(f)^T \cdot e^{\mathrm{nu}(f)t}$, where $e^{\mathrm{nu}(f)t} = (1, e^{\nu_1 t}, \ldots, e^{\nu_s t})^T$, $\mathbf{a} \cdot \mathbf{b}$ stands for the inner product of the two vectors, i.e., $\sum_{i=1}^{n} a_i b_i$.

From Definition 3, it follows

$$
\mathrm{coff}(f') = (f_0', f_1' + \nu_1 f_1(t), \ldots, f_s' + \nu_s f_s(t))^T, \quad \mathrm{nu}(f') = (0, \nu_1, \ldots, \nu_s)^T,
$$

$$
\deg(f') = (\max\{\deg(f_0) - 1, -1\}, \deg(f_1), \ldots, \deg(f_s))^T,
$$

where f' denotes the derivative of f w.r.t. t.

In the following, we will explain the basic idea behind `PEFIsolation` through the following simple example.

Example 2. Consider $\hat{f}(t) = t + 1 + e^{\sqrt{2}t} - (t+2)e^{\sqrt{5}t}$.

Firstly, in order to isolate the real roots of $\hat{f}(t) = 0$, we need to calculate the upper and lower bounds on all its real roots according to Theorem 2.

Regarding the upper bound of $\hat{f}(t) = 0$, we have: (i) $C_1 = 0$ and $M = 1$ as $\forall t \geq 0.|t+2| > 1$; (ii) $C_2 = 4$ and $k = 2$ as $\forall t \geq 4.|t+1| < \frac{t^2}{2} \wedge 1 < \frac{t^2}{2}$; (iii) $C_3 = 12$ as $\forall t \geq 12.t^2 < e^{(\sqrt{5}-\sqrt{2})t}$. Thus, we obtain $U(\hat{f}) = 12$.

In order to obtain the lower bound, we have to calculate the upper bound $U(g)$ of $g(t) = \hat{f}(-t)e^{\sqrt{5}t}$, i.e., $g(t) = t - 2 + e^{(\sqrt{5}-\sqrt{2})t} - (t-1)e^{\sqrt{5}t}$. Because (i) $\overline{C}_1 = 3$ and $M = 1$ as $\forall t \geq 3.|t-1| > 1$; (ii) $\overline{C}_2 = 4$ and $k = 2$ as $\forall t \geq 4.|t-2| < \frac{t^2}{2}$ and $1 < \frac{t^2}{2}$; (iii) $\overline{C}_3 = 1$ as $\forall t \geq 1$ and $t^2 < e^{\sqrt{2}t}$, we obtain the upper bound $U(g) = 4$.

Therefore, the lower bound $L(\hat{f}) = -U(g) = -4$ is obtained. Obviously, all real roots of $\hat{f}(t) = 0$ should be in the interval $(-4, 12)$, which implies that we just need to isolate all real roots in $(-4, 12)$.

From *differential mean value theorem* (i.e., *Rolle's theorem*), we know there must exist at last one real root of $f'(t) = 0$ between every two real roots of $f(t) = 0$, if $f(t)$ is continuous differentiable. In order to obtain the real roots of $f(t) = 0$, we can try to get the real roots of $f'(t) = 0$ first. Likewise, in order to obtain the real roots of $f'(t) = 0$, we can try to get the real roots of $f''(t) = 0$ first. We can repeat the above procedure until the real solutions of the ith derivative of $f(t)$ for some i can be achieved. Then, we lift the real solutions of the respective derivative in the inverse order until $f(t)$ itself. We illuminate the procedure by continuing the running example.

At the beginning,

$$S_0 = \hat{f}(t) = t + 1 + e^{\sqrt{2}t} - (t+2)e^{\sqrt{5}t},$$
$$\text{coff}(S_0) = (t+1, 1, -t-2)^T, \text{nu}(S_0) = (0, \sqrt{2}, \sqrt{5})^T, \deg(S_0) = (1, 0, 1)^T.$$

Then, we obtain the derivative of $\hat{f}$ is

$$S_1 = \hat{f}'(t) = 1 + \sqrt{2}e^{\sqrt{2}t} - (\sqrt{5}t + 2\sqrt{5} + 1)e^{\sqrt{5}t},$$
$$\text{coff}(S_1) = (1, \sqrt{2}, -\sqrt{5}t - 2\sqrt{5} - 1)^T, \text{nu}(S_1) = (0, \sqrt{2}, \sqrt{5})^T, \deg(S_1) = (0, 0, 1)^T.$$

Furthermore, the derivative of $\hat{f}'$ is

$$\hat{f}''(t) = 0 + 2e^{\sqrt{2}t} - (5t + 2\sqrt{5} + 10)e^{\sqrt{5}t},$$
$$\text{coff}(\hat{f}'') = (0, 2, -5t - 2\sqrt{5} - 10)^T.\text{nu}(\hat{f}'') = (0, \sqrt{2}, \sqrt{5})^T, \deg(\hat{f}'') = (-1, 0, 1)^T.$$

Clearly, $\hat{f}''$ and the following S_2 share the same real roots:

$$S_2 = \hat{f}''(t)e^{-\sqrt{2}t} = 2 - (5t + 2\sqrt{5} + 10)e^{(\sqrt{5}-\sqrt{2})t}, \tag{13}$$
$$\text{coff}(S_2) = (0, 2, -5t - 2\sqrt{5} - 10)^T, \text{nu}(S_2) = (0, 0, \sqrt{5} - \sqrt{2})^T, \deg(S_2) = (-1, 0, 1)^T.$$

Now, the derivative of S_2 is

$$S_3 = S_2' = 0 + 0 + he^{(\sqrt{5} - \sqrt{2})t},$$
$$\text{coff}(S_3) = (0, 0, h)^T, \text{nu}(S_3) = (0, 0, \sqrt{5} - \sqrt{2})^T, \deg(S_3) = (-1, -1, 1)^T.$$

where $h = -(5(\sqrt{5} - \sqrt{2})t + 15 + 10\sqrt{5} - 2\sqrt{10} - 10\sqrt{2})$. Obviously, $S_3 = 0$ if and only if $h = 0$, while the real zeros of h can be easily achieved by any real root isolation procedure for polynomials (*e.g.*, cf. [9]).

Remark 1. In general, suppose $S_i(t) = f_0(t) + \sum_{j=1}^{J} f_j(t)e^{\nu_j t}$ with $0 \not\equiv f_j(t) \in \mathbb{R}[t]$, $0 < \nu_1 < \cdots < \nu_J$, and $0 < J \in \mathbb{N}$, then we define $S_{i+1}(t) = S_i'(t)$ if $f_0'(t) \not\equiv 0$; otherwise, $S_{i+1}(t) = S_i'(t)e^{-\nu_1 t} = (f_1'(t) + \nu_1 f_1(t)) + \sum_{j=2}^{J}(f_j'(t) + \nu_j f_j(t))e^{(\nu_j - \nu_1)t}$. It's obvious that $S_{i+1} = 0$ shares the same real roots of $S_i'(t) = 0$. We construct S_{i+1} from S_i, for $i = 0, \cdots$. This procedure terminates when S_k is a polynomial for some k.

Theorem 3. *Let $f(t)$ be a PEF, $f'(t)$ the derivative of $f(t)$ w.r.t. t, $I = (a, b)$ a non-empty open interval, and $\mathcal{L}_I(f') = \{I_j | j = 1, \ldots, J\}$ a real root isolation of f' in I, in which $I_j = (a_j, b_j)$ with $a = b_0 < a_1 < b_1 < \cdots < a_J < b_J < a_{J+1} = b$. Furthermore, $f(t)$ has no real roots in any closed interval $[a_j, b_j]$, $1 \le j \le J$. Then, $\{ (b_j, a_{j+1}) \mid f(b_j)f(a_{j+1}) < 0, \ 0 \le j \le J \}$ is a real root isolation of $f(t)$ in I.*

Proof. Since $f(t)$ has no real roots in any closed interval $[a_j, b_j]$, $1 \le j \le J$, all real roots of $f(t)$ are in $\bigcup_{j=0}^{J}(b_j, a_{j+1})$ and $f(b_j)f(a_{j+1}) \ne 0$. Moreover, $f(t)$ has at most one real root in each (b_j, a_{j+1}), otherwise, there must be at least one real root of $f'(t) = 0$ on it by *Rolle's theorem*, which is a contradiction with the definition of $\mathcal{L}_I(f')$. So, if $f(b_j)f(a_{j+1}) < 0$ then there exists only one real root of $f(t)$ in (b_j, a_{j+1}), otherwise no real root of $f(t)$ in (b_j, a_{j+1}). This completes the proof. $\square$

Now, let's continue the running example. As $e^{(\sqrt{5} - \sqrt{2})t} \ne 0$, by $S_3 = he^{(\sqrt{5} - \sqrt{2})t} = 0$, it follows $h(t) = 0$. Thus, $t = -\frac{15 + 10\sqrt{5} - 2\sqrt{10} - 10\sqrt{2}}{5(\sqrt{5} - \sqrt{2})} \in (-5, -4)$. As $(-5, -4) \cap (-4, 12) = \emptyset$, there is no real root of $S_3 = 0$ in $(-4, 12)$. Hence, we have $\mathcal{L}(S_3) = \emptyset$. In addition, from (13), we have

$$S_2(-4) = 2 + (10 - 2\sqrt{5})e^{-4(\sqrt{5} - \sqrt{2})} > 0, S_2(12) = 2 - (70 + 2\sqrt{5})e^{12(\sqrt{5} - \sqrt{2})} < 0.$$

Thus, there exists only one real root of S_2 in $(-4, 12)$ by Theorem 3. Clearly, the real root isolation of S_2 in $(-4, 12)$ is same as that of $\bar{f}''$.

In order to construct $\mathcal{L}_{(-4,12)}(S_1)$, a real root isolation of S_1 in $(-4, 12)$, from $\mathcal{L}_{(-4,12)}(S_2)$ by Theorem 3, the condition that there is no real root of S_1 in $[a, b]$ for any (a, b) in $\mathcal{L}_{(-4,12)}(S_2)$ should be guaranteed. This means that we have to refine the intervals in $\mathcal{L}_{(-4,12)}(S_2)$ until the condition holds. This is achieved by Algorithm 2 below (see lines 2-13).

The following table is the bisection procedure (line 2-13) in Algorithm 2 to refine the interval $(-4, 12)$, in which '∃' (resp. '¬∃') means there exists (no) a real root in the observed interval.

	(-4,12)	(-4,4)	(-4,0)	(-2,0)	(-2,-1)
S_2	∃	∃	∃	∃	∃
S_1	∃	∃	∃	∃	¬∃

Finally, a refined interval $(a, b) = (-2, -1)$ is obtained, which satisfies the condition of Theorem 3. Thus, $(-4, -2)$ and $(-1, 12)$ are two intervals that may contain at most one real root of $S_1(t) = 0$. In addition, as $S_1(-4)S_1(-2) > 0$ and $S_1(-1)S_1(12) < 0$, $(-1, 12)$ contains a real root of $S_1(t) = 0$, but $(-4, -2)$ does not by Theorem 3. Thus, we get a real root isolation for $S_1(t) = 0$ in $(-4, 12)$, i.e., $\mathcal{L}_{(-4,12)}(S_1) = \{(-1, 12)\}$.

In order to compute $\mathcal{L}_{(-4,12)}(S_0)$, we repeat the above procedure, and finally obtain

$$\mathcal{L}_{(-4,12)}(\hat{f}) = \{(-4, -0.59375), (-0.390625, 12)\}.$$

Up to now, we have already explained the main idea of our approach how to isolate real roots of a PEF by the running example. This procedure is implemented in Algorithm 1, whose main steps are understood as follows:

Step 1: At line 1, compute the upper and lower bounds of $f(t)$;

Step 2: At line 1, construct a sequence $S_0(t) = f(t)$, $S_1(t)$, $S_2(t)$, ..., $S_r(t)$, where S_i is a PEF which has the same real roots as the derivative of S_{i-1}, $i = 1, 2, \ldots, r$, $r \in \mathbb{N}$, and $S_r(t)$ is a polynomial in t.

Step 3: Isolate all real roots of $S_r(t)$ by calling UPIsolating($S_r(t)$) in line 1. Note that there are lots of work on isolating real roots of a univariate polynomial (e.g., cf [9]).

Step 4: At line 1, for $i = r - 1$ down to 0, construct a real root isolation of S_i from that of S_{i+1} using Theorem 3 by calling PEFI. Note that during this procedure, we use $\mathcal{I}_1$ to record all subintervals in which $f(t)$ has no real roots, while $\mathcal{I}_2$ to record all subintervals in which $f'(t)$ has no real roots. So, we only need to construct a real root isolation of S_i from that of S_{i+1} on the remainder part of the considered interval by excluding all subintervals in $\mathcal{I}_1$ and $\mathcal{I}_2$, and accordingly update $\mathcal{I}_1$ and $\mathcal{I}_2$ in each iteration, see the detail in Algorithm 2.

Theorem 4 (Correctness of PEFI). *Algorithm PEFI always terminates correctly.*

Proof. The termination of PEFI is obvious because $f_1(t) = 0$ and $f_2(t) = 0$ have no common real roots. Then we prove its correctness.

$\mathcal{I}_1'$ and $\mathcal{I}_2'$ are updated in line 5 and line 7, respectively. Obviously, after every update, the properties of $\mathcal{I}_1'$ and $\mathcal{I}_2'$ still hold, i.e., $f_1(t)$ has no real roots in $\cup \mathcal{I}_1'$, $f_2(t)$ has no real roots in $\cup \mathcal{I}_2'$, and $\cup \mathcal{I}_1' \cap \cup \mathcal{I}_2' = \emptyset$. It is also easy to see that, after the second *for loop* at lines 15-18, $\mathcal{L}'$ is a real root isolation of $g_1(t)$ on $(a, b) \setminus \cup(\mathcal{I}_1' \cup \mathcal{I}_2')$. □

Theorem 5 (Correctness of PEFIsolation). *Algorithm PEFIsolation always terminates and returns a real root isolation for a given PEF f, if f does not have multiple real roots.*

Algorithm 1. PEFIsolation

Input: $f(t)$, a PEF of the form (11) with the assumption (12), which has no
    multiple real roots
Output: $\mathcal{L}$, a real root isolation of $f(t)$

1 Calculate a lower bound a and an upper bound b on real roots of $f(t) = 0$;
2 set $\mathcal{I}_1 \leftarrow \emptyset, \mathcal{I}_2 \leftarrow \emptyset$;
    /* $\mathcal{I}_1$ records all closed subintervals of $[a, b]$ in which $f(t)$ has no
    real roots, while $\mathcal{I}_2$ records all closed subintervals of $[a, b]$ in
    which $f'(t)$ has no real roots.   */
3 Construct a sequence, $S_0(t) = f(t)$, $S_1(t)$, $S_2(t)$, $\ldots$, $S_r(t)$, where S_i is a
    PEF, which shares the common real roots with the derivative of S_{i-1},
    $i = 1, 2, \ldots, r$, $r \in \mathbb{N}$, and $S_r(t)$ is a polynomial;
4 $\mathcal{L}_{(a,b)}(S_r) := \texttt{UPIsolating}(S_r(t))$, a real root isolation of $S_r(t)$;
5 **for** $i = r - 1; i \geq 0; i - -$ **do**
6     $\lfloor \quad [\mathcal{I}_1, \mathcal{I}_2, \mathcal{L}] \leftarrow \texttt{PEFI}(S_0, S_1, S_i, S_{i+1}, (a, b), \mathcal{I}_1, \mathcal{I}_2, \mathcal{L})$;
7 **for** $[c, d] \in \mathcal{I}_2$ **do**
8   **if** $S_0(c)S_0(d) < 0$ **then**
9         $\lfloor \quad \mathcal{L} \leftarrow \mathcal{L} \cup \{(c, d)\}$;
10 **return** $\mathcal{L}$;

Proof. Termination is immediately obtained from Theorem 4. Then we prove its correctness. After the *for loop* in line 2, $\mathcal{L}$ is a real root isolation of $S_0(t) = 0$ (i.e., $f(t) = 0$) on $(a, b) \setminus \cup(\mathcal{I}_1 \cup \mathcal{I}_2)$. Because $f'(t)$ has a constant nonzero sign in each interval of $\mathcal{I}_2$, $f(t)$ has at most one real root in each interval of $\mathcal{I}_2$ and this can be decided by checking the signs of $f(t)$ at two endpoints of the interval. Moreover, since there is no real root of $f(t) = 0$ in $\cup \mathcal{I}_1$, so $\mathcal{L}_2$ is a real root isolation of $S_0(t)$ in (a, b). $\qquad \square$

5.3 Complexity Analysis of PEFIsolation

Here we give a rough complexity analysis of PEFIsolation. Suppose $f(t) = f_0(t) + f_1(t)e^{\nu_1 t} + \cdots + f_s(t)e^{\nu_s t}$, $L(f)$ and $U(f)$ are respectively a lower bound and an upper bound on real roots of $f(t)$, $\deg(f) = (d_0, d_1, \cdots, d_s)$. PEFIsolation computes all real roots for a PEF chain $f(t) = 0$, $f'(t) = 0$, $f''(t) = 0$, $\cdots$, totally, $d_0 + \cdots + d_{s-1} + s + 1$ such PEFs at most, with the corresponding degree. The last element in the chain is a polynomial with degree d_s, so it has at most d_s real roots. Clearly, for each function in the chain, the number of intervals in its real root isolation is at most $d_0 + d_1 + \cdots + d_s + s + 1$. In addition, suppose the lower bound on the distances between real roots of S_i and those of S_{i+1} is δ, then *the while loop* (line 3-13) in Algorithm 2 always terminates after the length of an interval is less than δ. Since the length of every interval is less than or equal to $U(f) - L(f)$, *the while loop* must terminate in $\log_2 \frac{U(f) - L(f)}{\delta}$ steps. In a summary, the complexity of PEFIsolation is about $\mathcal{O}((\sum_{i=0}^{s} d_i + s + 1)^2 \log_2 \frac{U(f) - L(f)}{\delta})$.

Algorithm 2. PEFI

Input: (1) PEFs $f_1(t), f_2(t), g_1(t), g_2(t)$ s.t. $f_2(t)$ and $f_1'(t)$ share same real zeros, $g_2(t)$ and $g_1'(t)$ share same real zeros, and $f_1(t)$ and $f_2(t)$ have no common real zeros;

(2) an open interval (a, b);

(3) $\mathcal{I}_1, \mathcal{I}_2$, two sets of closed intervals contained in (a, b), s.t. $f_1(t)$ has no real zeros in $\cup \mathcal{I}_2$, $f_2(t)$ has no real zeros in $\cup \mathcal{I}_2$, $\cup \mathcal{I}_1 \cap \cup \mathcal{I}_2 = \emptyset$;

(4) $\mathcal{L}$, a real root isolation of $g_2(t)$ on $(a, b) \setminus \cup(\mathcal{I}_1 \cup \mathcal{I}_2)$.

Output: (1) $\mathcal{I}_1'$ and $\mathcal{I}_2'$ with the same properties as $\mathcal{I}_1$ and $\mathcal{I}_2$, respectively;

(2) $\mathcal{L}_2$, a real root isolation of $g_1(t)$ on $(a, b) \setminus \cup(\mathcal{I}_1' \cup \mathcal{I}_2')$.

1   $\mathcal{I}_1' \leftarrow \mathcal{I}_1, \mathcal{I}_2' \leftarrow \mathcal{I}_2$;

2   **for** (l, u) *in* $\mathcal{L}$ **do**

3   **while** $0 \in g_1([l, u])$ **do**

4   **if** $0 \notin f_1([l, u])$ **then**

5            $\lfloor$ $\mathcal{I}_1' \leftarrow \mathcal{I}_1' \cup \{[l, u]\}$;   break;

6   **if** $0 \notin f_2([l, u])$ *and* $f_1(l)f_1(u) \neq 0$ **then**

7            $\lfloor$ $\mathcal{I}_2' \leftarrow \mathcal{I}_2' \cup \{[l, u]\}$;   break;

8   **if** $g_2(l)g_2(\frac{l+u}{2}) < 0$ **then**

9            $\lfloor$ $u \leftarrow \frac{l+u}{2}$;

10   **else if** $g_2(\frac{l+u}{2}) = 0$ **then**

11           $\lfloor$ $l \leftarrow \frac{3l+u}{4}$; $u \leftarrow \frac{l+3u}{4}$;

12   **else**

13           $\lfloor$ $l \leftarrow \frac{l+u}{2}$;

14   $\mathcal{L}_1 \leftarrow \mathcal{L}$; $\mathcal{L}_2 \leftarrow \emptyset$; $\mathcal{L}_3 \leftarrow \{(a_1, b_1), \ldots, (a_m, b_m)\}$;

    /* where $a_1, b_1, \cdots, a_m, b_m$ are the endpoints of the intervals in $\mathcal{I}_1$
    and $\mathcal{I}_2$ s.t. $a \leq a_1 < b_1 < \cdots < a_m < b_m \leq b$, $(a_i, b_i) \subseteq (a, b) \setminus \cup(\mathcal{I}_1 \cup \mathcal{I}_2)$
    for $i = 1, \ldots, m$, and $\cup_{i=1}^m (a_i, b_i) = (a, b) \setminus \cup(\mathcal{I}_1 \cup \mathcal{I}_2)$.   */

15   **for** (c, d) *in* $\mathcal{L}_3$ **do**

16      $\mathcal{L}_{1(c,d)} \leftarrow \{I \mid I \in \mathcal{L}_1 \text{ and } I \subset (c, d)\}$;

17   Obtain a real root isolation $\mathcal{L}_{(c,d)}$ for $g_1(t)$ on (c, d) from $\mathcal{L}_{1(c,d)}$ by Theorem 3; $\mathcal{L}_2 \leftarrow \mathcal{L}_2 \cup \mathcal{L}_{(c,d)}$;

18   **return** $\mathcal{I}_1', \mathcal{I}_2', \mathcal{L}_2$;

---

6   Implementation and Experimental Results

We have implemented the proposed approach in *Mathematica* as a prototype, called *LinR*[1], which takes a specific **LDS** reachability problem as input, and gives either *False* if the problem is not satisfiable, or *True* otherwise associated with some valid sample points.

Remark 2. When we implement the above algorithms, some optimizing strategies are adopted for improving efficiency. For example, if the input function can

---

[1] Both the tool and the case studies in this section can be found at http://lcs.ios.ac. cn/~chenms/tools/LinR.tar.bz2.

be factorized, then we isolate the real roots of each factor rather than the input function itself, and then refine the resulted intervals if necessary. We omit the implementation details here.

In the following, we report some experimental results with *LinR*.

Example 3. Let us continue Example 1 given in the introduction first.

Obviously, $X \cap Y = \emptyset$, and $\xi(t) = \begin{bmatrix} x_1 e^{\sqrt{2}t} + \frac{\sqrt{2}t - \sqrt{2} + 1}{2} + \frac{\sqrt{2}-1}{2}e^{\sqrt{2}t} \\ x_2 e^{-\sqrt{2}t} + \frac{(1+\sqrt{2})t-1}{3+2\sqrt{2}}e^t + \frac{e^{-\sqrt{2}t}}{3+2\sqrt{2}} \\ x_3 e^{-t} + te^{-t} \end{bmatrix}$ is the solution

of the LDS. Thus, the reachability problem becomes

$$\mathcal{F} = \exists x_1 \exists x_2 \exists x_3 \exists t. \ \Phi(x_1, x_2, x_3, t);$$

$$\Phi(x_1, x_2, x_3, t) = 1 - x_1^2 - x_2^2 - x_3^2 > 0 \wedge x_1 e^{\sqrt{2}t} + x_2 e^{-\sqrt{2}t} + x_3 e^{-t} + h(t) < 0 \wedge t > 0,$$

where $h(t) = \frac{e^{-\sqrt{2}t}}{3+2\sqrt{2}} + te^{-t} + \frac{\sqrt{2}t - \sqrt{2}+5}{2} + \frac{(1+\sqrt{2})t-1}{3+2\sqrt{2}}e^t + \frac{\sqrt{2}-1}{2}e^{\sqrt{2}t}$.

Then, using *Brown's projection operator* [11] to eliminate x_1, x_2, x_3 successively (**Step 3** in Sect. 4), we have

$$q_3(x_1, x_2, x_3, t) = (x_1^2 + x_2^2 + x_3^2 - 1)(ax_1 + bx_2 + cx_3 + h)$$

$$q_2(x_2, x_3, t) = a(x_2^2 + x_3^2 - 1)$$
$$(-a^2 + a^2 x_2^2 + a^2 x_3^2 + b^2 x_2^2 + 2bcx_2 x_3 + 2bhx_2 + c^2 x_3^2 + 2chx_3 + h^2),$$

$$q_1(x_3, t) = a(x_3 - 1)(x_3 + 1)(a^2 + b^2)(2chx_3 + h^2 - b^2 + b^2 x_3^2 + c^2 x_3^2)$$
$$(-a^2 + a^2 x_3^2 + 2chx_3 + h^2 - b^2 + b^2 x_3^2 + c^2 x_3^2),$$

$$q_0(t) = ab(c - h)(c + h)(a^2 + b^2)(b^2 + c^2)(b^2 + c^2 - h^2)(a^2 + b^2 + c^2)$$
$$(a^2 + b^2 + c^2 - h^2),$$

where $a = e^{\sqrt{2}t}$, $b = e^{-\sqrt{2}t}$ and $c = e^{-t}$.

Isolate all real roots of $q_0(t) = 0$ in $(0, +\infty)$ (as we only care $t > 0$) (**Step 4** in Sect. 4), and obtain $\mathcal{L}(q_0) = \{(1.08, 1.29)\}$.

Lift the real root isolation in the order t, x_3, x_2, x_1 successively using the openCAD lifting procedure (**Step 5** in Sect. 4), finally, we obtain 48 sample points, $\{-0.835, -0.212, 0.184, 2.\}$ satisfies Φ, which implies that the safety property is not satisfied with the counter example starting from $(-0.835, -0.212, 0.184, 2) \in X$, and ending at time $t = 2$.

Example 4 (Adapted from [1]). Consider a vessel of water containing a radioactive isotope, to be used as a tracer for the food chain, which consists of aquatic plankton varieties phytoplankton A and zooplankton B. Let $\xi_1(t)$ be the isotope concentration in the water, $\xi_2(t)$ the isotope concentration in A and $\xi_3(t)$ the isotope concentration in B. The dynamics of the vessel is modelled as $\dot{\xi} = A\xi$, where $A = \begin{bmatrix} -3 & 6 & 5 \\ 2 & -12 & 0 \\ 1 & 6 & -5 \end{bmatrix}$. The initial radioactive isotope concentrations $\xi_1(0) = x_1 > 0, \xi_2(0) = 0, \xi_3(0) = 0$.

The safety property of our concern is whether $\forall t > 0 \ \xi_1(t) \geq \xi_2(t) + \xi_3(t)$. To this end, we consider a more general problem: For which $n_1, n_2 \in \mathbb{N}$ s.t. $\mathcal{F}(n_1, n_2) = \exists x_1 > 0 \ \exists t > 0 \ \xi_1(t) < n_1 \xi_2(t) + n_2 \xi_3(t)$ holds.

It is easy to see that the matrix A is diagonalizable with eigenvalues $0, -10 + \sqrt{6}, -10 - \sqrt{6}$. When $(n_1, n_2) = (1, 1)$, using the method in Sect. 4, we obtain two sample points for (x_1, t), i.e., $(-0.1, 1), (0.1, 1)$. But none of them satisfies $\mathcal{F}(1, 1)$, which simply implies the safety property holds. When $(n_1, n_2) = (2, 2)$, similarly, we obtain four sample points for (x_1, t), i.e., $(-0.1, 0)$, $(0.1, 0)$, $(-0.1, 1)$, $(0.1, 1)$, in which $(0.1, 1)$ satisfies $\mathcal{F}(2, 2)$. It can be proved that $\xi_i(t) \geq 0$ for any $t > 0$ and $i = 1, 2, 3$. So, it is clear that, if $\mathcal{F}(n_1, n_2)$ holds, $\mathcal{F}(m_1, m_2)$ holds for $m_1 \geq n_1$ and $m_2 \geq n_2$. Then, by checking some pairs of $(n_1, n_2) \in \mathbb{N} \times \mathbb{N}$ in a similar way as above, we conclude that all pairs $(n_1, n_2) \in \mathbb{N} \times \mathbb{N}$ satisfy $\mathcal{F}(n_1, n_2)$, except for the pairs $\{(0, 0), (0, 1), (0, 2), (1, 0), (1, 1), (1, 2), (2, 0), (2, 1), (3, 0), (3, 1), (4, 0), (5, 0)\}$.

Example 5 (Adapted from [1]). Consider a typical home with attic, basement and insulated main floor. Let $x_3(t), x_2(t), x_1(t)$ be the temperature in the attic, main living area and basement respectively, and t is the time in hours. Assume it is winter time, the outside temperature is nearly $35°F$, and the basement earth temperature is nearly $45°F$. Suppose a small electric heater is turned on, and it provides a $20°F$ rise per hour. We want to verify that the temperature in main living area will never reach too high (maybe $70°F$). Analyze the changing temperatures in the three levels using Newton's cooling law and given the value of the cooling constants, we obtain the model as follows:

$$\dot{x}_1 = \frac{1}{2}(45 - x_1) + \frac{1}{2}(x_2 - x_1), \dot{x}_2 = \frac{1}{2}(x_1 - x_2) + \frac{1}{4}(35 - x_2) + \frac{1}{4}(x_3 - x_2) + 20,$$

$$\dot{x}_3 = \frac{1}{4}(x_2 - x_3) + \frac{3}{4}(35 - x_3),$$

with the initial set $X = \{(x_1, x_2, x_3)^T \mid 1 - (x_1 - 45)^2 - (x_2 - 35)^2 - (x_3 - 35)^2 > 0\}$ and the unsafe set $Y = \{(y_1, y_2, y_3)^T \mid y_2 - 70 > 0\}$. The safety property we are concerning is to check if some state in Y is reachable from X, which holds by using *LinR*.

The above three examples are verified by *LinR*. Both the time and memory costs on a 64-bit Linux computer with a 2.93GHz Intel Core-i7 processor and 4GB of RAM are shown in Table 1. Besides, we have also compared on the same platform with the performances of Strzebonski's approach (i.e., CT1D) [22], as well as verification tools dReach [14], HSolver [18], and Flow* [6] on these examples. Note that, both dReach and Flow* cannot handle unbounded model checking, and even for BMC, they are less efficient than our tool in many cases (see Example 3 and Example 4)[2]. In particular, Flow* accepts only rectangular initial set, i.e. each variable needs to be specified within a closed interval and polynomial constraints are not allowed, and thus we tried different cube to approximate the spherical initial set in Example 3, while none of them can derive a desired result ("unsafe"). As for HSolver, due to the rejection of "*sqrt*", we simplify the original model by replacing all the irrational numbers with their approximate decimals, however, 2 of the 3 examples still can not be answered by HSolver in reasonable time and memory.

---

[2] Here, we set the time bounds 2s, 2s, and 5s resp. for Examples 3, 4, and 5 when using dReach and Flow*.

Table 1. Evaluation results of different methods

LDS	Time (sec)					Memory (kb)				
	LinR	*CT1D*	*dReach*	*HSolver*	*Flow**	*LinR*	*CT1D*	*dReach*	*HSolver*	*Flow**
Example 3	1.35	×	37.36	–	–	112	×	3812	–	–
Example 4	0.03	0.20	0.71	–	–	131	2018	3816	–	–
Example 5	1.68	×	0.05	0.72	16.50	166	×	3812	1076932	113492

× : the verification fails by non-termination within reasonable amount of time (10 hours)
– : the verification fails because of giving an answer as "safety unknown"

Table 2. Time consumption (in milliseconds) on Example 3.4 from [16]

LinR	CT1D	QEPCAD	dReach	HSolver	Flow*
39	33	57	110	–	–

Remark 3 In the above examples, all constraints are open sets. Actually, more general initial and unsafe sets, i.e., when either $Pre(X)$ or $Post(X)$ is not *open semi-algebraic*, can be coped with in our approach also, as we have implemented CAD in the algorithms. For the Example 3.4 in [16], where A is diagonalizable with rational eigenvalues and $Pre(X)$ and $Post(X)$ are both closed sets, it takes 57 milliseconds using Lafferriere et al's approach based on quantifier elimination by QEPCAD. In contrast, LinR takes 39 milliseconds, and CT1D takes 33 milliseconds. In brief, our approach shares nearly same complexity as Stzebonski's in general case, but is still better than other approaches, see Table 2 (QEPCAD stands for Lafferriere et al's approach).

7   Conclusion

In this paper, we proved the decidability of a family of vector fields whose state parts are linear, while input parts are non-linear, (possibly) with exponential expressions. Such vector fields are commonly used in practice. To the best of our knowledge, this family is one of the most expressive families of vector fields with a decidable reachability problem. The decidability is achieved by reduction to the decidability of the extension of Tarski's algebra with some specific exponential functions. Experimental results indicate our algorithm is more efficient than Strzebonski's if all constraints are open sets, better than existing approaches based on approximation and numeric computation in general, e.g., HSolver [18], dReach [14], FLOW* [6], etc.

In addition, similar as in [22], our decision procedure can be extended without any substantial change to deal with logarithm functions as well as the composition of logarithmic and exponential functions.

Acknowledgements. The first, third and fourth authors are supported partly by NSFC under grants 11290141 and 11271034; the second and fifth authors are supported partly by "973 Program" under grant No. 2014CB340701, by NSFC under grants

91118007 and 91418204, by CDZ project CAP (GZ 1023), and by the CAS/SAFEA International Partnership Program for Creative Research Teams.

References

1. http://www.math.utah.edu/~gustafso/s2013/2250/systemsExamplesTheory2008. pdf
2. Achatz, M., McCallum, S., Weispfenning, V.: Deciding polynomial-exponential problems. In: ISSAC 2008 (2008)
3. Alur, R., Courcoubetis, C., Halbwachs, N., Henzinger, T., Ho, P.-H., Nicollin, X., Olivero, A., Sifakis, J., Yovine, S.: The algorithmic analysis of hybrid systems. Theoret. Comput. Sci. **138**(1), 3–34 (1995)
4. Alur, R., Dill, D.L.: A theory of timed automata. Theoret. Comput. Sci. **126**(2), 183–235 (1994)
5. Brown, C.W.: Improved projection for cylindrical algebraic decomposition. J. Symb. Comput. **32**(5), 447–465 (2001)
6. Chen, X., Ábrahám, E., Sankaranarayanan, S.: Flow*: an analyzer for non-linear hybrid systems. In: Sharygina, N., Veith, H. (eds.) CAV 2013. LNCS, vol. 8044, pp. 258–263. Springer, Heidelberg (2013)
7. Collins, G.E.: Quantifier elimination for real closed fields by cylindrical algebraic decompostion. In: Brakhage, H. (ed.) Automata Theory and Formal Languages 2nd GI Conference. LNCS, vol. 33, pp. 134–183. Springer, Heidelberg (1975)
8. Collins, G.E., Hong, H.: Partial cylindrical algebraic decomposition for quantifier elimination. J. Symb. Comput. **12**(3), 299–328 (1991)
9. Collins, G.E., Loos, R.: Real zeros of polynomials. In: Computer Algebra - Symbolic and Algebraic Computation, pp. 83–94. Springer (1982)
10. Davenport, J.H., Heintz, J.: Real quantifier elimination is doubly exponential. J. Symb. Comput. **5**(1), 29–35 (1988)
11. Han, J., Dai, L., Xia, B.: Constructing fewer open cells by gcd computation in cad projection. In: ISSAC 2014, pp. 240–247. ACM (2014)
12. Henzinger, T.A., Kopke, P.W., Puri, A., Varaiya, P.: What's decidable about hybrid automata? J. Comput. Syst. Sci. **57**(1), 94–124 (1998)
13. Hong, H.: An improvement of the projection operator in cylindrical algebraic decomposition. In: ISSAC 1990, pp. 261–264. ACM (1990)
14. Kong, S., Gao, S., Chen, W., Clarke, E.: dreach: Delta-reachability analysis for hybrid systems. In: TACAS 2015 (2015)
15. Lafferriere, G., Pappas, G.J., Sastry, S.: O-minimal hybrid systems. MCSS **13**(1), 1–21 (2000)
16. Lafferriere, G., Pappas, G.J., Yovine, S.: Symbolic reachability computation for families of linear vector fields. J. Symb. Comput. **32**, 231–253 (2001)
17. McCallum, S.: An improved projection operation for cylindrical algebraic decomposition of three-dimensional space. J. Symb. Comput. **5**(1), 141–161 (1988)
18. Ratschan, S., She, Z.: Safety verification of hybrid systems by constraint propagation based abstraction refinement. In: Morari, M., Thiele, L. (eds.) HSCC 2005. LNCS, vol. 3414, pp. 573–589. Springer, Heidelberg (2005)
19. Richardson, D.: How to recognize zero. J. Symb. Comput. **24**, 627–645 (1997)
20. Strzeboński, A.: Solving systems of strict polynomial inequalities. J. Symb. Comput. **29**(3), 471–480 (2000)
21. Strzeboński, A.: Real root isolation for exp-log functions. In: ISSAC 2008, pp. 303–314 (2008)

22. Strzeboński, A.: Cylindrical decomposition for systems transcendental in the first variable. J. Symb. Comput. **46**, 1284–1290 (2011)
23. Tarski, A.: A Decision Method for Elementary Algebra and Geometry. University of California Press, Berkeley (1951)
24. Wing, J.: How can we provide people with cyber-physical systems they can bet their lives on? Computing Research News, 20(1) (2008)
25. Xu, M., Li, Z.-B., Yang, L.: Quantifier elimination for a class of exponential polynomial formulas. J. Symb. Comput. (2015). doi:10.1016/j.jsc.2014.09.015

Stochastic Local Search for Falsification
of Hybrid Systems

Jyotirmoy Deshmukh[1]([✉]), Xiaoqing Jin[1], James Kapinski[1],
and Oded Maler[2]

[1] Toyota Technical Center, Gardena, CA, USA
{jyotirmoy.deshmukh,xiaoqing.jin,jim.kapinski}@tema.toyota.com
[2] Verimag, Gières, France
Oded.Maler@imag.fr

Abstract. Falsification techniques for models of embedded control systems automate the process of testing models to find bugs by searching for model-inputs that violate behavioral specifications given by logical and quantitative correctness requirements. A recent advance in falsification is to encode property satisfaction as a cost function based on a finite parameterization of the (bounded-time) input signal, which allows formulating bug-finding as an optimization problem. In this paper, we present a falsification technique that uses a local search technique called *Tabu search* to search for optimal inputs. The key idea is to discretize the space of input signals and use the *Tabu list* to avoid revisiting previously encountered input signals. As local search techniques may converge to local optima, we introduce stochastic aspects such as random restarts, sampling and probabilistically picking suboptimal inputs to guide the technique towards a global optimum. Picking the right parameterization of the input space is often challenging for designers, so we allow dynamic refinement of the input space as the search progresses. We implement the technique in a tool called SITAR, and show scalability of the technique by using it to falsify requirements on an early prototype of an industrial-sized automotive powertrain control design.

1 Introduction

Embedded control systems governing safety-critical aspects in medical devices, avionics and automotive systems are increasingly being designed using the model-based development (MBD) paradigm. The early phase of MBD involves rapid iterations to check the correctness of the control software or to check the feasibility of a new control algorithm. Design models are usually closed-loop models, i.e., a plant model in a feedback loop with a controller model. Plant models represent the dynamic, physical behavior of the environment that is to be controlled (e.g., an engine, a powertrain system, a human heart, an avoinics

Oded Maler's research was supported in part by the ANR project CADMIDIA and Toyota.

B. Finkbeiner et al. (Eds.): ATVA 2015, LNCS 9364, pp. 500–517, 2015.
DOI: 10.1007/978-3-319-24953-7_35

power-distribution system). Controllers are modeled as a reactive computer program interacting in real-time with the plant, and are typically designed in a visual block-diagram based language such as Simulink®. The closed-loop system also has exogenous inputs, usually modeling user events or other disturbances from the environment. As fixing software issues in late design stages is expensive, identifying such bugs in the early phase of the design cycle is valuable.

Closed-loop models can be modeled as hybrid dynamical systems, and it is well-known that for even simple hybrid systems, the verification problem is highly undecidable [4,11]. Prevalent practice in industry is extensive model-based testing, where control designers use heuristics and previous experience to pick a set of test input signals and system parameters to stimulate the system-under-test. Modeling environments usually have numerical simulation to estimate the system behavior for such inputs. Designers typically perform a finite number of such simulations over the chosen set of inputs and parameters, and identify undesirable behaviors by manual inspection of the resulting outputs. These techniques are incomplete in the sense that they provide no guarantees on whether a bug is found; however, they significantly increase the possibility of identifying problems early in the system design.

Recently developed falsification techniques seek to automate this process in many ways. First, they allow the designer to express correct behavior as a set of logical or quantitative requirements on the inputs and outputs in a machine-checkable format. Second, they allow formulating the search for errors as an optimization problem by encoding property satisfaction by a function that maps a given input/output signal and a logical requirement to a real number. A recent development is the advent of quantitative semantics for real-time temporal logics. Fainekos and Pappas define a robust semantics for metric temporal logic (MTL) [10], which allows to quantify *how much* a signal satisfies a specification. Similarly, Donzé and Maler define robust semantics for signal temporal logic (STL), which permits a similar analysis [8].

A core step in falsification is thus to find a (bounded-time) input signal that minimizes the cost function. Falsification tools typically rely on a global optimization algorithm to perform this task. Most falsification techniques are often ineffective when the cost function is nonconvex or discontinuous, or if the underlying model has discontinuous dynamic behavior. The S-TaLiRo tool has several algorithms to perform global optimization including simulated annealing, ant-colony optimization, and the cross-entropy method among others [2,3,15,18]. The Breach [7] tool provides a similar framework but uses nonlinear-simplex optimization, also known as the Nelder-Mead algorithm. Other falsification tools such as those based on the RRT algorithm [9,16,17], multiple-shooting [20], combined global and local search [14] and gradient descent-based local search [1] have also shown promise in exploring hybrid state-spaces and complex, nonlinear cost surfaces.

In this paper, we continue the quest to find an effective global optimization algorithm. In particular, we focus on addressing models whose structure reflects typical control designs found in industrial systems. Common features of some of these systems include: presence of Boolean combinations of predicates on real-valued input signals (typically to decide an operating mode of the system), discrete switching influenced strongly by the shape of the input signal and to a lesser extent by the state of the sytem, and highly nonlinear and occasionally discontinuous dynamics in the plant models. We present an adaptation of a discrete optimization technique known as Tabu search to address systems with such features, and make a case for the effectiveness of our technique with experimental evidence.

Tabu search is a *meta heuristic* applied to a lower-level heuristic method used to solve an optimization problem. It essentially restricts the search of a discrete decision space so that particular valuations of the decision variables are not revisited once they have been evaluated using a data structure known as the *Tabu list*. The technique has been applied to integer programming problems and is mainly used to prevent cycling that would eventually occur while searching finite spaces [6].

In applying Tabu search, we handle the continuous input signals by discretizing the solution space. In Sect. 3, we explain how the algorithm locally searches in a neighborhood of an input signal (i.e., neighboring points on the discrete parameterization of the input signals) and follows a descent direction obtained by stochastically approximating the gradient of the cost function. Naïve local search techniques can converge to local optima. Also, an interesting case is when the output signals are Boolean or if their values are closely dependent on some internal Boolean conditions in the models. Here, the cost function has "plateaus" and "narrow valleys," i.e., the surface of the function to be optimized has regions that are flat with narrow regions where the cost is significantly lower. By adding stochastic aspects such as random restarts, and allowing the algorithm to pick sub-optimal inputs with a small probability, we allow the Tabu search to escape local optima and increase its chances of reaching the global optimum.

A key consideration for us is the ease of use of the tool by control designers; hence, we avoid techniques that seek user annotations to assist extraction of the underlying hybrid structure of the model [5]. Furthermore, when engineers use falsification tools like S-TaLiRo or Breach, they must parameterize the space of inputs to their models for the tools to work. This parameterization is usually in the form of a list of uniformly spaced control points, i.e., a list of times at which the optimizer is free to pick a value for the input signal. For the intermediate times, a suitable interpolation scheme is used to define a continuous input signal. A key challenge in using such tools is that the verification engineers need to have good insight into how many control points to choose. If too many control points are chosen, then the input search space becomes large, and the efficiency of the optimizer suffers. On the contrary, if too few control points are chosen, then the tool may be unable to find problematic behaviors that rely on having flexibility in the shape of the input signal. In Sect. 4, we show how we can allow designers to specify a coarse discretization of the input space, and we provide a mechanism to automatically refine the discretization to incrementally increase the accuracy of the optimization.

We have implemented stochastic local Tabu search with refinements in a tool named SITAR. In Sect. 5, we show how we use SITAR in a falsification framework and demonstrate its efficacy on a range of benchmarks, starting from toy models that pose challenges to existing falsification engines to industrial-sized benchmarks. Finally, we conclude with some promising future directions in Sect. 6.

2 Preliminaries

We denote the system under test S. We assume that S is given by some model of an embedded control system and is equipped with a *simulator*, which is capable of computing *typed* output sequences generated by S under a given *typed* input sequence. A typed input sequence is a sequence of time-value pairs, where the values lie in a set known as the domain. We note that input domains can be finite, i.e., finite subsets of sets such as $\mathbb{Z}$ and $\mathbb{B}$, or could be compact (i.e., bounded and closed) subsets of sets such as $\mathbb{R}$. Let $\mathcal{W} = \mathcal{W}_1 \times \ldots \times \mathcal{W}_m$, where each $\mathcal{W}_i \subseteq \mathbb{R}$ is a dense domain. Let $\mathcal{V}$ be a subset of the Cartesian product of some finite domains. Then, in general, the domain of values is $\mathcal{U} = \mathcal{W} \times \mathcal{V}$. Let $\mathcal{U}_T$ be the set of all input sequences over time bound T. An input sequence is defined as:

$$\mathbf{u} = (u_0, t_0), (u_1, t_1), \cdots, (u_N, t_N),$$

where $u_i \in \mathcal{U}$, $t_i \leq t_{i+1}$ for each $0 \leq i < N$, and $t_N \leq T$. Note that input sequences are often used to represent continuous-time signals; sequences can be used to represent a strictly discrete-time signal or can be used to represent the parameterization of a continuous-time signal[1]. We similarly define $\mathcal{Y}$ as an output set and $\mathcal{Y}_T$ as the set of all output sequences. Outputs are given as a sequence

$$\mathbf{y} = (y_0, \tilde{t}_0), (y_1, \tilde{t}_1), \cdots, (y_M, \tilde{t}_M),$$

where $y_i \in \mathcal{Y}$, $\tilde{t}_i \leq \tilde{t}_{i+1}$ for each $0 \leq i < M$, and $\tilde{t}_M \leq T$. We use the notation $S(\mathbf{u})$ to mean the output sequence given by S under input $\mathbf{u}$. Note that the sequence of time instants associated with a given $\mathbf{u}$, t_i, does not necessarily match the time instants associated with the corresponding $\mathbf{y}$, $\tilde{t}_i$.

We define a property that should hold for S in terms of a property function. Let $\varphi : \mathcal{U}_T \times \mathcal{Y}_T \to \mathbb{R}$ be a function that maps an input and output sequence to a real value that determines whether system S under a given input sequence satisfies the desired property. Positive valuations of φ indicate that the desired property is satisfied and negative values of φ indicate that the desired property is not satisfied. Furthermore, the magnitude of the valuation indicates *how much* the property is satisfied. This function provides the cost used by an optimization tool to search for input sequences that give rise to output sequences that

---

[1] For inputs representing continuous functions over dense time, the actual input signal to S is obtained by interpolating across the sequence $\mathbf{u}$ using a user-specified interpolation scheme.

demonstrate incorrect behavior from $\mathcal{S}$. The falsification problem can then be cast as the following optimization problem.

$$\min_{\mathbf{u} \in \mathcal{U}_T} \varphi(\mathbf{u}, \mathbf{y}) \quad \text{subject to} \quad \mathbf{y} = \mathcal{S}(\mathbf{u}) \tag{1}$$

Any assignment of the decision variable $\mathbf{u}$ that produces a negative value from the cost function is an input sequence that demonstrates a behavior from $\mathcal{S}$ that fails to satisfy the desired property defined by φ.

3   Stochastic Local Tabu Search

Local search is the discrete/combinatorial variant of steepest-descent, gradient-based methods for solving global optimization problems, such as the optimization problem indicated in (1). Local search is based on defining a distance function on the solution space, where typically the distance between two points is related to the number of modifications needed to transform one point into the other. The neighborhood of a point is typically the set of neighbors at distance 1 or some subset of this set. A key feature of Tabu search (a variant of local search) is to utilize a data structure called a *Tabu list*, to avoid repeated computations on visited points. In this section, we present a modification of the Tabu search procedure that allows systematic exploration of a finite parameterization of the input sequences of a model with the goal of falsifying a given quantitative property specification. We first introduce some required terminology.

3.1   Discretization and Neighborhoods

Note that, in general, the space of input sequences $\mathcal{U}_T$ is infinite. Without loss of generality, we can assume that the dense input domain ($\mathcal{W}$) is the set $[0, u_{\max}]^m$. For ease of exposition, we will start with a discretized representation of signals and a fixed discretization scheme. We assume a time step ε and space increment δ. See Fig. 1 (a) for an illustration.

Definition 1 (Uniform δ-Discretization of Input Domain). *For a given* δ, *let* $\ell = \lfloor \frac{u_{\max}}{\delta} \rfloor$. *Let* $\Delta_{\mathrm{u}}(\delta, \mathcal{W})$ *denote a uniform grid over* $\mathcal{W}$, *i.e.,* $\Delta_{\mathrm{u}}(\delta, \mathcal{W}) = \{j \cdot \delta \mid 0 \leq j \leq \ell\}^m$. *A uniform δ-discretization of the input domain* $\mathcal{U}$ *is then defined as* $\Delta_{\mathrm{u}}(\delta, \mathcal{U}) = \Delta_{\mathrm{u}}(\delta, \mathcal{W}) \times \mathcal{V}$.

Definition 2 (Uniform (δ, ε)-Discretization of Input Sequence Space). *Let* $\tau = \lfloor \frac{T}{\varepsilon} \rfloor$. *We abuse notation and let* $\Delta_{\mathrm{u}}(\varepsilon, T)$ *denote a uniform discretization of time, i.e.,* $\Delta_{\mathrm{u}}(\varepsilon, T) = \{j \cdot \varepsilon \mid 0 \leq j \leq \tau\}$. *A uniform (δ, ε)-discretization of* $\mathcal{U}_T$, *denoted* $\Delta_{\mathrm{u}}(\delta, \varepsilon, \mathcal{U}_T)$ *is defined as the finite set of sequences* $\hat{\mathbf{u}}$ *of the form* $(\hat{u_0}, \hat{t_0}), \ldots, (\hat{u_N}, \hat{t_N})$, *where for each i,* $\hat{u}_i \in \Delta_{\mathrm{u}}(\delta, \mathcal{U})$, *and* $\hat{t}_i \in \Delta_{\mathrm{u}}(\varepsilon, T)$.

Having fixed the search-space, we define distance and neighborhoods in this space. For the finite input domain $\mathcal{V}$, we assume that there is function $N_{\mathcal{V}}(v)$ mapping each element $v \in \mathcal{V}$ to a set of neighbors in $\mathcal{V}$. For example, if $\mathcal{V}$ is the following set of integers: $\{1, 3, 5, 8\}$, then $N_{\mathcal{V}}(5)$ may be defined as $\{3, 8\}$.

Definition 3 (Neighborhood in Input Domain). *Consider a* $u = (w^1, \ldots w^m, v) \in \Delta_u(\delta, \mathcal{U})$. *For a given* δ, *the* $(i, \delta, \mathcal{W})$-*neighbor of* u *is defined as:*

$$nb_{\mathcal{W}}(i, \delta, u) = (w^1, \ldots, w^i + \delta, \ldots, w^m, v).$$

Let $D = \{-\delta, +\delta\}$. *The* $\mathcal{W}$-*neighborhood of* u *is defined as:*

$$N_{\mathcal{W}, \delta}(u) = \bigcup_{i=1}^{m} \bigcup_{\delta \in D} nb_{\mathcal{W}}(i, \delta, u).$$

We abuse notation and let the $\mathcal{V}$-*neighborhood of* u *be defined as:*

$$N_{\mathcal{V}}(u) = \{(w^1, \ldots, w^m, v') \mid v' \in N_{\mathcal{V}}(v)\}.$$

Finally, we define the neighborhood *of* u, $N_{\mathcal{W}, \delta, \mathcal{V}}(u) = N_{\mathcal{W}, \delta}(u) \cup N_{\mathcal{V}}(u)$, *and say that* u' *is a* neighbor *of* u *if* $u' \in N_{\mathcal{W}, \delta, \mathcal{V}}(u)$.

Definition 4 (Neighborhood in Input Sequences). *Given an input sequence* $\mathbf{u}$, *its* j-*neighborhood* $N_{\mathcal{U}_T}(j, \mathbf{u})$ *is the set of sequences:*

$$N_{\mathcal{U}_T}(j, \mathbf{u}) = \{(u_0, t_0), \cdots, (u'_j, t_j), \cdots, (u_N, t_N) \mid u'_j \in N_{\mathcal{W}, \delta, \mathcal{V}}(u_j)\}.$$

Given a time horizon T, *the* neighborhood *of* $\mathbf{u}$ *is defined as:*

$$N_{\mathcal{W}, \delta, \mathcal{V}, \varepsilon}(\mathbf{u}) = \bigcup_{0 \le j \le \tau} N_{\mathcal{U}_T}(j, \mathbf{u}).$$

For an illustration of neighbors, see Fig. 1. Uniform discretizations provide a simple way to define a quantization of the decision space for the falsification problem, but it produces a decision space that increases exponentially as δ decreases, and it does not provide the flexibility to define a refinement of the decision space in specific regions. To address these deficiencies, we define a generalization of the uniform discretization notions that permits uneven discretizations. See Fig. 1(b) for an illustration.

Definition 5 (Nonuniform $\boldsymbol{\delta}$-Discretization of the Input Domain). *Let* $\boldsymbol{\delta}$ *be a nonuniform grid over the input domain, i.e.,* $\boldsymbol{\delta} = (\widehat{\mathcal{W}_1}, \ldots, \widehat{\mathcal{W}_m})$, *where each* $\widehat{\mathcal{W}_i}$ *is a finite set of elements of* $\mathcal{W}_i$. *A nonuniform* $\boldsymbol{\delta}$-*discretization of* $\mathcal{U}$, *denoted as* $\Delta_{\mathrm{nu}}(\boldsymbol{\delta}, \mathcal{U})$ *is the set* $\widehat{\mathcal{W}_1} \times \ldots \times \widehat{\mathcal{W}_m} \times \mathcal{V}$.

Definition 6 (Nonuniform $(\boldsymbol{\delta}, \boldsymbol{\varepsilon})$-Discretization of the Input Sequence Space). *Let* $\boldsymbol{\varepsilon}$ *denote a nonuniform discretization of the time domain, where* $\boldsymbol{\varepsilon}$ *is a finite set of elements from* $[0, T]$. *Given a nonuniform* $\boldsymbol{\delta}$-*discretization of* $\mathcal{U}$, *and* $\boldsymbol{\varepsilon}$, *a nonuniform* $(\boldsymbol{\delta}, \boldsymbol{\varepsilon})$-*discretization of* $\mathcal{U}_T$, *denoted* $\Delta_{\mathrm{nu}}(\boldsymbol{\delta}, \boldsymbol{\varepsilon}, \mathcal{U}_T)$, *is a finite set of input sequences* $\hat{\mathbf{u}} = (\hat{u_0}, \hat{t_0}), \ldots, (\hat{u_N}, \hat{t_N})$, *such that for all* i, $\hat{u_i} \in \Delta_{\mathrm{nu}}(\boldsymbol{\delta}, \mathcal{U})$ *and* $\hat{t_i} \in \boldsymbol{\varepsilon}$.

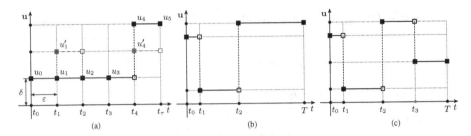

Fig. 1. Fig. (a) shows an instance of $\Delta_u(\delta, \varepsilon, \mathcal{U}_T)$. For the input sequence $\mathbf{u} = (u_0, t_0),(u_1, t_1),(u_2, t_2),(u_3, t_3),(u_4, t_4),(u_5, t_\tau)$, the sequences $\mathbf{u}_1 = (u_0, t_0), (u'_1, t_1), (u_2, t_2), (u_3, t_3), (u_4, t_4), (u_5, t_\tau)$ and $\mathbf{u}_2 = (u_0, t_0), (u_1, t_1), (u_2, t_2), (u_3, t_3), (u'_4, t_4), (u_5, t_\tau)$, are two neighbors, shown in blue and red resp. Figure (b) and (c) show an instance of $\Delta_{nu}(\delta, \varepsilon, \mathcal{U}_T)$, where (c) shows a refinement of the space in (b) by adding a new time (t_3).

The notion of neighborhoods easily extends to nonuniformly distributed input spaces and input sequence spaces, and we denote them as $N_{\mathcal{W},\delta,\mathcal{V}}$ and $N_{\mathcal{W},\delta,\mathcal{V},\varepsilon}(\mathbf{u})$ respectively.

In the sequel, we describe an implementation of the stochastic local Tabu search method that can be configured to use either uniform or nonuniform discretizations of the decision space. In Algorithm 1, we show the basic steps of the search algorithm. The innermost while-loop (Lines 8–19) implements a stochastic local search scheme, augmented with a Tabu-list. A run of this while-loop to completion is called a single *local improvement*. The main steps executed in the loop are as follows: (1) Select a neighbor of the current input $\mathbf{u}$ (Line 11) that is not in the Tabu list. (2) Evaluate the cost of $\mathbf{u}_{nb}$ (by running a simulation with $\mathbf{u}_{nb}$ as input and computing the value of $\varphi(\mathbf{u}_{nb}, \mathcal{S}(\mathbf{u}_{nb}))$) (Line 15). (3) Add each $\mathbf{u}_{nb}$ not previously in the Tabu list to the list (Line 16). (4) Once the desired number of neighbors have been visited, pick the minimal-cost neighbor as the next point in the search (Line 19). (5) Terminate when the stopping condition is reached (Line 17); typically this is $c_{nb} < 0$. The while-loop from Line 3 to Line 23 iterates over the maximum number of local improvements permitted. The number `maxLocalImprovements` provides the user control over how much they wish to utilize the stochastic gradient-descent. A larger number is useful when the surface of the cost function is smooth, while a smaller number is better to use when the cost function is highly discontinuous or with sharp valleys (as gradient-descent has less chance of success in this scenario). The outermost while-loop (Lines 2–27) iterates over the maximum number of random restarts permitted. We explain the purpose of random restarts in Sect. 3.3.

3.2 Local Search by Stochastic Gradient-Descent

The size of the neighborhood for a given point is $2m|\mathcal{V}|\tau$ and depending on m, $|\mathcal{V}|$, $\tau = \lfloor \frac{T}{\varepsilon} \rfloor$, and the cost of simulation, it might be too large to explore the entire neighborhood in each step. The procedure for selecting a subset of the neighborhood is stochastic: we sequentially sample up to `maxNeighbors` number of neighbors of $\mathbf{u}$ from $N_{\mathcal{W},\delta,\mathcal{V},\varepsilon}(\mathbf{u})$. The actual sampling is effected

---

Algorithm 1. Stochastic Local Tabu Search over given discretization of $\mathcal{U}_T$.

Input: Model $\mathcal{S}$, Input Sequence $\mathbf{u}$, grid over input domain δ, time domain discretization ε, Property function φ, maxLocalImprovements, maxRestarts

Output: Minimum cost $c_{\min}$, Minimizing input $\mathbf{u}_{\min}$

```
 1  cmin,cprev := ∞ ; i, j := 0; TabuList := ∅
 2  while i < maxRestarts do
 3      while j < maxLocalImprovements do
 4          TabuList.add(u)
 5          y := Simulate(S, u) ; c := φ(u, y)
 6          if c < cmin then cmin:=c; umin:=u
 7          neighborsVisited := 0
 8          while neighborsVisited < maxNeighbors do
 9              k := 0
10              do
11                  | unb := pickNeighbor(δ, ε, u) ; k := k + 1
12              while unb ∈ TabuList ∧ k < |N_{W,δ,V,ε}(u)|
13              if unb = ∅ then break
14              neighborsVisited := neighborsVisited + 1
15              ynb := Simulate(S, unb), cnb := φ(unb, ynb)
16              TabuList.add(unb)
17              if StoppingCondition(cnb) then halt
18              if cnb < cmin ∨ with probability P_subopt then
19                  | cmin := cnb ; umin := unb
20          u := umin
21          if slowConvergence(cmin, cprev) ∨ localOptimum(c, cmin) then
22              | break
23          j := j + 1; cprev := cmin
24      do
25          | u := pickRandomInput(δ, ε, U_T)
26      while u ∉ TabuList
27      i := i + 1
```

---

by randomly selecting a j, and for the chosen u_j, randomly picking either a $\mathcal{V}$-neighbor or a $\mathcal{W}$-neighbor from $N_\mathcal{V}(u_j)$ or $N_{\mathcal{W},\delta}(u_j)$. If the latter is picked, the $\mathcal{W}$-neighbor $nb_\mathcal{W}(i, \delta, u_j)$ is obtained by randomly picking an $i \in [0, \lfloor \frac{u_{\max}}{\delta} \rfloor]$ and a $\delta \in \{+\delta, -\delta\}$. The random choice can be performed based on any distribution function on the set of i, j indices or on the $\mathcal{V}$-neighborhood. In our implementation, we use uniform random sampling. This general technique of obtaining a stochastic approximation of the gradient is called the finite-difference stochastic approximation (FDSA) method [19], and is the technique currently implemented in our tool. The algorithm then moves to the neighbor with the lowest cost in the neighborhood (thus performing the steepest descent along the stochastically approximated gradient). If there is no neighbor with a lower cost, the algorithm infers that a local optimum has been reached (Line 21).

3.3 Random Restarts and Stochasticity

Like any local search method there is a risk of getting stuck in a local optimum. We use two mechanisms to help the search procedure escape a local optimum:

1. We introduce jumps in the search procedure stochastically: If the algorithm detects a local optimum or slow convergence, or once it has exhausted the maximum permitted local improvements, it restarts the local search from a randomly chosen point in the input search space that is not in the Tabu list (Line 21).
2. In the phase where the algorithm is performing local search, we allow the algorithm to select a neighbor that is not optimum with a small probability (Line 18) in spirit of techniques such as simulated annealing [13].

To provide the control over termination of the algorithm, we permit the user to limit the number of random restarts (maxRestarts). Together, maxRestarts, maxNeighbors, and maxLocalImprovements influence the number of simulations performed by the algorithm. The performance of Algorithm 1 depends on several factors. The *size* of the search space influences how much we can explore it in finite time. Given a time horizon T, the search space defined by $\Delta_u(\delta, \varepsilon, \mathcal{U}_T)$ or $\Delta_{nu}(\boldsymbol{\delta}, \boldsymbol{\varepsilon}, \mathcal{U}_T)$ is finite and of size $O(\tau^{m|\mathcal{V}|\ell})$, i.e., it depends exponentially on m, the dimension of the dense input domain, maximum number of neighbors in the finite input domain (which in the worst case is $|\mathcal{V}| - 1$), and exponentially in ℓ or the number of discretizations of the signal domain, and linearly in τ, i.e., the length of the input sequence. The efficiency of the operations depends on the *inner-most loop* of the procedure, which includes application of the mutation operations, the cost of running a single simulation and the size of the neighborhood (which determines the number of simulations in each step).

4   Search Space Refinement

We intend our technique to be used by designers who may not have good insight into the optimal discretization of the input space needed to find a falsifying $(\mathbf{u}, \mathbf{y})$ pair. A conservative assumption is that designers start with a coarse discretization of the input space. There are distinct advantages to starting with a coarse level of discretization: as the cardinality of the decision space is given by $\tau^{m|\mathcal{V}|\ell}$, larger values of δ and ε result in a smaller search space; however, in most cases, the initial discretization is too coarse to be able to find the $(\mathbf{u}, \mathbf{y})$ with the optimal cost. To address this, our tool supports automatic and heuristic refinement of the discretization of the input space. We describe this procedure in Algorithm 2. In Algorithm 2, the key procedure is Refine. This is a heuristic step to increase the number of elements in the quantized search space. The Refine procedure currently supports the following heuristics:

Algorithm 2. Input Search Space Refinement Procedure

Input: Model $\mathcal{S}$, Initial grid over input domain δ_0, Initial grid over time
domain ε_0, Property function φ, User-defined parameters:
`maxRefinements, maxLocalImprovements, maxRestarts`

Output: Minimum cost c_{min}, Minimizing input $\mathbf{u}_{min}$

1   `refinementNum` := 0
2   $\delta, \varepsilon := \delta_0, \varepsilon_0$
3   $\mathbf{u}$:= pickRandomInput$(\delta, \varepsilon, \mathcal{U}_T)$
4   **while** `refinementNum` < `maxRefinements` **do**

5      $(c_{min}, \mathbf{u}_{min})$:= StochasticLocalTabuSearch $\begin{pmatrix} \mathcal{S}, \mathbf{u}, \delta, \varepsilon, \varphi, \\ \texttt{maxLocalImprovements}, \\ \texttt{maxRestarts} \end{pmatrix}$

6   **if** $c_{min} < 0$ **then**
7        $\lfloor$ Report violation found, violating input: $\mathbf{u}_{min}$
8   **else**

9        $\begin{matrix} \delta, \varepsilon, \mathbf{u}, \texttt{TabuList}, \\ \texttt{maxLocalImprovements} \end{matrix}$:= Refine $\begin{pmatrix} \delta, \varepsilon, \mathbf{u}, \texttt{TabuList}, \\ \texttt{maxLocalImprovements} \end{pmatrix}$

10   `refinementNum` := `refinementNum` + 1

---

1. Naïve Refinement: For uniform discretization, in each refinement iteration, we can set $\delta = \frac{\delta}{2}$, $\varepsilon = \frac{\varepsilon}{2}$. Note this quadratically increases the search space for each input dimension in each iteration, and can cause an exponential blowup in the number of refinements.

2. Input Domain Random Refinement: For a given discretization $\Delta_{nu}(\delta, \varepsilon, \mathcal{U}_T)$, we choose (at random) an index i, and for the corresponding dense input domain $\widehat{\mathcal{W}}_i \in \delta$, we add at random a new value in $[0, \mathbf{u}_{max}]$ to $\widehat{\mathcal{W}}_i$. In other words, we increase the number of quantization levels in the ith dense input domain.

3. Time Domain Largest Gap Refinement: For a given discretization $\Delta_{nu}(\delta, \varepsilon, \mathcal{U}_T)$, where $\varepsilon = \{t_0, \ldots, t_N\}$ and $t_N = T$, we find the index j corresponding to the largest time-gap in ε, and add a time-point there. Formally, $j = \arg\max_{0 \le j \le N-1} \{t_{j+1} - t_j \mid t_j, t_{j+1} \in \varepsilon\}$. Then, we add the time-point $\frac{1}{2}(t_j + t_{j+1})$. E.g., if $\varepsilon = \{0.0, 1.1, 5.3, 7.3, 10.0\}$, then we add the time 3.2 to ε. We can combine this heuristic with the heuristic above or the one below. (See Fig. 1 (c) for an illustration).

4. Input Domain Largest Gap Refinement: We can use a similar scheme as the above heuristic to refine the input domain for a particular dense input domain. We first choose (at random) an index i, and then for the corresponding input domain $\widehat{\mathcal{W}}_i \in \delta$, we add a value to $\widehat{\mathcal{W}}_i$ where the distance between adjacent elements is the largest.

Definition 7 (Dense Neighborhoods). *Given a point* $u = (w^0, \ldots, w^m, v)$ *in the input domain* $\mathcal{U}$ *and a* δ, *a dense neighborhood of* u *is defined as follows:*

$$DN_{W,\delta}(u) = \{(w^0 + \delta^0, \ldots, w^m + \delta^m, v) \mid |\delta^i| \leq \delta\}.$$

Given an input sequence $\mathbf{u} = (u_0, t_0), \ldots, (u_N, t_N)$, *and a time perturbation step* ε, *a dense neighborhood of the input sequence* $\mathbf{u}$ *is defined as follows:*

$$DN_{W,\delta,\varepsilon}(\mathbf{u}) = \{(u_0', t_0 + \varepsilon_0), \ldots, (u_N', t_N + \varepsilon_N) \mid u_j' \in DN_{W,\delta}(u_j) \text{ and } \forall j : |\varepsilon_j| \leq \varepsilon\}.$$

Definition 8 (Robust Violation). *We say that an input* $\mathbf{u} = (u_0, t_0), \cdots,$ (u_N, t_N) *robustly violates a property* φ *if the following conditions hold:*

1. *The model interprets* $\mathbf{u}$ *as a piecewise constant function[2]* $\mathbf{u}_c$ *over* $[t_0, t_N]$, *where* $\mathbf{u}_c$ *is defined s.t.* $\forall j \in [0, N-1]$, $\forall t \in [t_j, t_{j+1})$, $\mathbf{u}_c(t) = u_j$, *and* $\mathbf{u}_c(t_N) = u_N$.
2. $\mathbf{y} = \mathcal{S}(\mathbf{u}) \wedge \varphi(\mathbf{u}, \mathbf{y}) < 0$,
3. $\exists \delta^* > 0, \varepsilon^* > 0$, *s.t.* $\forall \mathbf{u}' \in DN_{W,\delta^*,\varepsilon^*}(\mathbf{u})$ *it is true that* $\mathbf{y}' = \mathcal{S}(\mathbf{u}') \wedge$ $\varphi(\mathbf{u}', \mathbf{y}') < 0$.

In other words, a violation is robust if for a given input sequence that violates the property, all sufficiently nearby input sequences also violate the property. In the following theorem, we characterize the asymptotic behavior of Algorithm 2. The inputs to Algorithm 2 include user-defined constants `maxLocalImprovements`, `maxRestarts`, and `maxRefinements`; we show that as the user makes these constants arbitrarily large, the probability of finding a robust violation goes to 1.

Theorem 1. *If the given system* $\mathcal{S}$ *has an input* $\mathbf{u}^*$ *that robustly violates the property* φ, *then as the choice for the parameters* `maxLocalImprovements`, `maxRefinements`, *and* `maxRestarts` *tend to* ∞, *with a suitable refinement scheme, the probability that Algorithm 2 finds an input* $\mathbf{u}'$ *such that* $\varphi(\mathbf{u}', \mathbf{y}') < 0$, *where* $\mathbf{y}' = \mathcal{S}(\mathbf{u}')$, *tends to 1.*

Proof. Due to lack of space, we give only a proof sketch for the case when we choose the naïve refinement scheme. Let $\mathbf{u}^* = (u_0, t_0), \ldots, (u_L, t_L)$ for some L, where $t_L = T$, and let δ^* and ε^* be values that satisfy Condition 3 from Definition 8. We first show that as we increase `maxRefinements`, there is some (large enough) `refinementNum` (Line 10) for which the refinement generates uniform discretization $\Delta_u(\delta, \varepsilon, \mathcal{U}_T)$, such that

1. For every point t_i in $\mathbf{u}^*$, there is a corresponding point t_j in $\Delta_u(\delta, \varepsilon, \mathcal{U}_T)$ such that $|t_j - t_i| < \varepsilon^*$. (Note that the number of time-points in $\Delta_u(\delta, \varepsilon, \mathcal{U}_T)$ may be much larger than L);
2. Let $u_j = (w_j^1, \ldots, w_j^i, \ldots, w_j^m, v_j)$. Then, $\forall j, i$ there is a $(\omega^1, \ldots, \omega^m, v)$ in $\Delta_u(\delta, \mathcal{U})$ such that $|w_j^i - \omega^i| < \delta^*$, and $v_j = v$.

---

[2] We can also use piecewise linear interpolation to define $\mathbf{u}_c$.

Table 1. Results of comparison between SITAR approach and S-TaLiRo tool. For model RD, we allow refinement of the control points of the input state space, we report the initial control points in the table and mark these with a *.

Model	Requirement	SITAR						S-TaLiRo			
		Δ	$|\mathcal{U}|,|\varepsilon|$	Falsified?	Time (sec)	Sim.	$|T|$	Falsified?	Time (sec)	Sim.
AFC	(2); ζ=0.024	U	4,3	y	23	18	7	y	13	5
	(2); ζ=0.028	U	4,3	y	3	2	7	y	19	7
	(2); ζ=0.032	U	4,3	y	102	71	7	y	79	32
MRS	(3)	NU	35,3	y	50	233	40	n	745	1000
	(3)	U	35,3	y	241	2058	40	n	2121	3000
RD	(5)	NU	3,2*	y	17	206	2	n	141	2000
	(5)	U	3,3*	y	47	575	4	n	141	2000
	(5)	U	3,4*	y	28	575	8	y	1	17
PTAC	(6); $\zeta = \zeta_1$	U	3,3	y	3996	18	6	y	2448	6
	(6); $\zeta = \zeta_2$	U	3,3	y	8424	31	6	y	21348	51
	(6); $\zeta = \zeta_3$	U	3,3	y	8784	39	6	y	26568	71

Next we show that at this level of discretization, the algorithm can asymptotically find an input sequence $\mathbf{u}'$ in $DN_{\mathcal{W},\delta^*,\varepsilon^*}(\mathbf{u}^*)$, which guarantees that $\varphi(\mathbf{u}',\mathbf{y}') < 0$. The following observations are used to complete the proof: Under Condition 1 in Definition 8, any L-length sequence of the form $(u_0,t_0),\ldots,(u_L,t_L)$ in $\mathbf{u}^*$, can be found embedded in a sequence over more time points. For any given $\Delta_u(\delta,\varepsilon,\mathcal{U}_T)$, there is a finite number of input sequences. The Tabu list ensures progress as it disallows visiting the same sequence twice; thus, the probability that a certain neighbor in $DN_{\mathcal{W},\delta^*,\varepsilon^*}$ is *not* picked goes to zero as the user-defined parameters `maxLocalImprovements` $\to \infty$ and `maxRestarts` $\to \infty$.

5   Experimental Results

We implemented Algorithm 2 with support for refinement heuristics and both uniform and nonuniform discretization in a tool named SITAR (**S**tochast**I**c **T**abu-search **A**nd **R**efinement). We present the results of comparing the performance of our method with a state-of-the-art falsification tool S-TaLiRo on multiple academic and industrial system models. For each model, we give requirements in temporal logic and compare the performance of SITAR and S-TaLiRo.

We pick S-TaLiRo for comparison as our tool SITAR shares several features with S-TaLiRo: (1) both tools use a property function φ to guide the search over the input space (S-TaLiRo uses robustness degree of a requirement specified using Metric Temporal Logic), (2) both tools support a finite parameterization of the input sequence space, (3) both tools use heuristic global optimization relying on black-box simulations of a given Simulink®model. A key difference is that S-TaLiRo allows a fixed parameterization of the input signals, where users choose a number uniformly spaced time-points in the time domain (known as

control points), and the optimizer is free to pick any input value in the range
$[0, u_{max}]$ for each dense input dimension. In contrast SITAR also uses a grid over
the dense input domain, and search is restricted to be over the grid elements.
Further, SITAR supports automatic refinement of the input discretization and
allows nonuniform control points in the time domain.

In the results reported in the sequel, we highlight the input sequence discretization method (Δ), which is either uniform (U) or nonuniform (NU), size of
the input sequence discretization ($|\mathcal{U}|$), number of control points in time domain
($|T|$), the result of whether faslficiation was successful, total computation time,
and the total number of simulations (Sim.). For comparison between SITAR and
S-TaLiRo, we use a fixed number of control points for three of the four cases and
demonstrate the refinement capability of SITAR on one model. All requirements
used are of the form $\Box_I(\mathbf{y} < \mathbf{c})$ (specifying that over the interval I, the output
signal $\mathbf{y}$ remains less than $\mathbf{c}$). We use a property function similar to the robust
satisfaction degree of STL [8].

5.1   Air-Fuel Control System (AFC)

Our first case study is an automotive air-fuel control (AFC) model [12]. The
model is a representation of a closed-loop embedded control system, and contains several challenging features that are commonly found in industrial systems.
It consists of a plant that describes physical phenomena such as fuel injection
dynamics, exhaust gas transport dynamics, and sensor dynamics. While some
aspects of the plant dynamics are derived using first principles, others aspects
are captured with multi-dimensional lookup tables. One challenging aspect of
the system dynamics from an analysis perspective is the presence of a *variable
transport delay*; this effectively models dynamics containing a delay differential equation. The controller contains two parts: (1) an open-loop feedforward
observer, and (2) a Proportional + Integral (PI) controller that regulates the
air-fuel (A/F) ratio. For detailed description of this model, please refer to [12].
The controller has several modes, but for the purpose of this case study, we
restrict ourselves to the normal mode of operation.

The paper [12] describes a safety requirement in the normal mode: in the
time range $[T_{nom}, T_{hoz}]$ the normalized A/F ratio should remain within a given
threshold ζ. The requirement can be described in temporal logic as following:

$$\Box_{[T_{nom}, T_{hoz}]}\mathbf{y} < \zeta. \tag{2}$$

We use $\min_{t_i \in [T_{nom}, T_{hoz}]}(\zeta - \mathbf{y}(t_i))$ as the property function. The results shown in
Table 1 show that both SITAR and S-TaLiRo can falsify the property for all three
choices of the ζ parameter for the requirement. Two out of three requirements
can be falsified by S-TaLiRo faster than SITAR. For the case when $\zeta = 0.028$,
SITAR outperforms S-TaLiRo. The main lesson from this case study is that,
although SITAR uses an essentially discrete optimization based technique, it can
still search over a continuous state space relatively well.

5.2   Mode-specific Reference Selection Model (MRS)

In [9], the authors observe that current falsification tools became trapped at a local optimum due to the structure of the model, which contains complex discrete and temporal behaviors. The model selects an operating mode based on a region in the dense input state space. The mode is defined as a Boolean combination of conditions arising from 8 input signals $w^1, \ldots, w^8$ being compared to a threshold. The output is some function of a ninth input w^9, with a different function for each operating mode. The range for inputs in $w^1, \ldots, w^8$, is $[0, 100]$ and the range for w^9 is $[-5, 5]$. The safety property requires the output $\mathbf{y}$ to remain above -8. The temporal logic requirement is defined as follows, and the property function can be derived as before:

$$\Box_{[\tau, T_{hoz}]}(y_i > -8). \tag{3}$$

In the above, we use $\tau = 5.1$ s, and $T_{hoz} = 10$ s. According to [9], in order to falsify the requirement, the system has to select the mode corresponding to the satisfaction of the following condition:

$$\bigwedge_{i \in [1..4]} \left((w^{2i}(t) > 90) \wedge (w^{2i-1}(t) < 10) \right). \tag{4}$$

The probability of hitting the right combination of the w^i values that falsify the property is 10^{-8} (8 inputs, and for each input there is a probability of $\frac{1}{10}$). Given the right combination, a tool such as S-TaLiRo can quickly falsify the requirement. However, it is not practical to expect that the designer to provide this insight to the tool, as a Boolean circuit of arbitrary complexity could be embedded in the given Simulink®model. In our opinion, the value of the falsification tool is to automatically explore the search space to identify the problematic input sequences with minimal user input.

As shown in Table 1, SITAR can falsify the requirement. When we discretize the input space in a nonuniform fashion, SITAR can falsify the requirement in less than one minute. Here, we choose the partition for w^i where $i \in [1, ..., 8]$ as $\{0, 10, 90, 100\}$ and $\{-5, 0, 5\}$ for w^9. One may claim that through this nonuniform discretization, we give extra information to the search algorithm; however, we argue that this information is related to the domain of the inputs and representative operating conditions, and such knowledge can be provided by design engineers with relative ease. Even with uniform gridding, SITAR is still able to falsify the requirement, with a moderate increase in computing time. For this example, S-TaLiRo (using the simulated annealing optimization heuristic) could not find a falsifying input sequence after 3000 simulations.

5.3   Rate Detection (RD) System

Next, we describe the performance of the SITAR algorithm with refinement. We choose to use a simplified model originating from a rate detection system. The rate detection system checks if the rate of decrease of the signal is within a certain threshold $[\zeta_1, \zeta_2]$ in a given time window $[\tau_1, \tau_2]$, and if yes, causes the

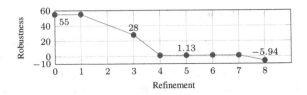

Fig. 2. The robustness value changes during the refinement process.

output $\mathbf{y}$ to be less than -0.001. For different values of $\zeta_1, \zeta_2, \tau_1, \tau_2$ the difficulty of finding the violating input varies. We picked the values $[\zeta_1, \zeta_2] = [2.2, 3.2]$ and $[\tau_1, \tau_2] = [5, 7]$, which present a reasonable level of difficulty for both SITAR and S-TaLiRo.

The safety requirement can be expressed as

$$\Box_{[\tau, T_{hoz}]}(\mathbf{y} \geq -0.001). \tag{5}$$

Here, $\tau = 0.1$ is some initial time where the output behavior is ignored. For a falsifier like S-TaLiRo that uses a fixed parameterization of the input state space if the falsifier fails to find a falsifying input sequence using an initial input parameterization, the algorithm may be run again using an input parameterization corresponding to a finer resolution in the time domain. This approach is inefficient for this example, because it is not possible to find a falsifying input sequence unless discrete time instants exist near the required window of $[\tau_1, \tau_2]$, meaning computational effort is wasted on parameterizations of the time domain that are too coarse (and thus cannot possibly result in falsifying traces for this example). This explains why S-TaLiRo fails if the number of input parameters is less than 8, in Table 1. When using the appropriate number of input parameters, S-TaLiRo can trivially falsify the requirement; however, knowing the appropriate number of parameters requires significant user insight.

On the other hand, SITAR dynamically refines the discretization of the input space as needed. If combined with nonuniform input discretization, the SITAR algorithm can falsify the requirement in less than 20 s. In Fig. 2, we show how the robustness value decreases over the 8 refinement steps. Although SITAR could be trapped in a local optimum (in refinements 4 to 7), it eventually escapes from the local optimum and falsifies the requirement. Even with a uniform input discretization, as SITAR introduces time discretization, it can find a falsifying input sequence.

5.4 Powertrain Air Control (PTAC) System

To illustrate the scalability of our algorithm, we consider a powertrain air control subsystem (PTAC). This is a prototype model, developed during the early design phase of an advanced powertrain project. It has a complex, high fidelity plant model that is able to generate accurate simulation results, which correlates closely with data collected from the actual powertrain components. The controller contains logic for two of the system's electronic control units (ECU).

Because of the complexity of the model, simulations are computationally expensive (simulating 1 s of real operation requires almost 5 s, so 5x slower). Although simulation is usually light-weight, in this case, it is crucial for the falsification tool to use fewer simulations. The safety requirement for this system, obtained from design engineers, is expressed as follows in temporal logic:

$$\Box_{[\tau, T]}(\mathbf{y} < \zeta). \tag{6}$$

Due to proprietary reasons, we suppress the values of ζ. As shown in the last few rows in Table 1, both S-TaLiRo and SITAR can falsify all requirements successfully. We use three values of threshold ζ_1, ζ_2, and ζ_3, where $\zeta_1 < \zeta_2 < \zeta_3$. Note that falsifying the requirement becomes harder with increasing ζ value. For the last two values of ζ, SITAR can falsifiy the requirements much faster, using less than half the time and a lower number of simulations. When $\zeta = \zeta_1$, S-TaLiRo can falsify the requirement faster, partly because SITAR performs thrice the number of simulations.

6   Conclusions and Future Work

Conclusion: Given a model of an embedded control system, and a (quantifiable) property over its input/output behaviors, we present a technique to find robust violations of the property. The key idea is to transform the problem of searching over an infinite set of timed input sequences to the system to a finite search over a discretized version of the input space using a Tabu list to avoid repeated computations. The search proceeds in the fashion of a stochastic gradient descent, with random restarts to perturb the system away from local optima. We wrap the search procedure in an outer loop that dynamically refines the input space discretization. This removes the burden of providing a clever discretization from the system designers, shifting it to the refinement heuristics employed by the tool. Our technique shows promise on industrial-sized benchmark problems, as well as toy problems that pose a challenge to existing falsification tools.

Future Work: In this paper, the technique to perform stochastic gradient descent involves computing finite differences of a point's cost with its neighbors' costs ($k + 1$ valuations for a k-dimensional space). Each cost computation requires a simulation with the neighboring sequence as input. We can instead use the simultaneous perturbation stochastic approximation technique (SPSA), where the effect of a gradient descent is converged upon using a stochastic result [19]. In the SPSA approach, only 3 valuations are made, regardless of the dimension. Each computation of a cost function requires a simulation; thus, the SPSA scheme would help reduce the number of simulations.

In our current implementation, the Tabu list is stored as a simple list data structure in MATLAB®; an alternative is to use spatial data structures such as k-d trees. Currently, the random restarts in our technique are chosen based on a uniform random distribution over the points in the discretization of the input space. An interesting direction to pursue is that of coverage metrics such as the star-discrepancy metric [9] to cover the input sequence space.

Acknowledgments. The authors would like to thank the anonymous reviewers for constructive feedback that helped improve this paper.

References

1. Abbas, H., Fainekos, G.: Linear hybrid system falsification through local search. In: Bultan, T., Hsiung, P.-A. (eds.) ATVA 2011. LNCS, vol. 6996, pp. 503–510. Springer, Heidelberg (2011)
2. Annapureddy, Y.S.R., Fainekos, G.E.: Ant Colonies for Temporal Logic Falsification of Hybrid Systems. In: Proceedings of the IECON, pp. 91–96 (2010)
3. Annapureddy, Y.S.R., Liu, C., Fainekos, G.E., Sankaranarayanan, S.: S-TaLiRo: a tool for temporal logic falsification for hybrid systems. In: Proceedings of the Tools and Algorithms for the Construction and Analysis of Systems, pp. 254–257 (2011)
4. Asarin, E., Maler, O.: Achilles and the tortoise climbing up the arithmetical hierarchy. JCSS **57**(3), 389–398 (1998)
5. Hoxha, H.A.B., Fainekos, G.: Using S-TaLiRo on industrial size automotive models. In: Worskhop on Applied Verification for Continuous and Hybrid Systems (2014)
6. Cordeau, J.-F., Laporte, G., Mercier, A., et al.: A unified tabu search heuristic for vehicle routing problems with time windows. J. Oper. Res. Soc. **52**(8), 928–936 (2001)
7. Donzé, A.: Breach, a toolbox for verification and parameter synthesis of hybrid systems. In: Touili, T., Cook, B., Jackson, P. (eds.) CAV 2010. LNCS, vol. 6174, pp. 167–170. Springer, Heidelberg (2010)
8. Donzé, A., Maler, O.: Robust satisfaction of temporal logic over real-valued signals. In: Chatterjee, K., Henzinger, T.A. (eds.) FORMATS 2010. LNCS, vol. 6246, pp. 92–106. Springer, Heidelberg (2010)
9. Dreossi, T., Dang, T., Donzé, A., Kapinski, J., Jin, X., Deshmukh, J.V.: Efficient guiding strategies for testing of temporal properties of hybrid systems. In: Havelund, K., Holzmann, G., Joshi, R. (eds.) NFM 2015. LNCS, vol. 9058, pp. 127–142. Springer, Heidelberg (2015)
10. Fainekos, G.E., Pappas, G.J.: Robustness of temporal logic specifications for continuous-time signals. Theor. Comput. Sci. **410**(42), 4262–4291 (2009)
11. Henzinger, T., Kopke, P., Puri, A., Varaiya, P.: What's Decidable about Hybrid Automata?. In: Proceedings of the Symposium on Theory of Computing, pp. 373–382 (1995)
12. Jin, X., Deshmukh, J.V., Kapinski, J., Ueda, K., Butts, K.: Powertrain Control Verification Benchmark. In: Proceeding of Hybrid Systems: Computation and Control, pp. 253–262 (2014)
13. Kirkpatrick, S., Vecchi, M., et al.: Optimization by simmulated annealing. Science **220**(4598), 671–680 (1983)
14. Kuřátko, J., Ratschan, S.: Combined global and local search for the falsification of hybrid systems. In: Legay, A., Bozga, M. (eds.) FORMATS 2014. LNCS, vol. 8711, pp. 146–160. Springer, Heidelberg (2014)
15. Nghiem, T., Sankaranarayanan, S., Fainekos, G.E., Ivancic, F., Gupta, A., Pappas, G.J.: Monte-carlo techniques for falsification of temporal properties of non-linear hybrid systems. In: Proceeding of Hybrid Systems: Computation and Control, pp. 211–220 (2010)
16. Plaku, E., Kavraki, L.E., Vardi, M.Y.: Hybrid systems: from verification to falsification by combining motion planning and discrete search. Formal Methods Sys. Design **34**(2), 157–182 (2009)

17. Plaku, E., Kavraki, L.E., Vardi, M.Y.: Falsification of ltl safety properties in hybrid systems. Softw. Tools Technol. Transfer **15**(4), 305–320 (2013)
18. Sankaranarayanan, S., Fainekos, G.E.: Falsification of temporal properties of hybrid systems using the cross-entropy method. Computation and Control. In: Proceeding of Hybrid Systems (2012)
19. Spall, J.C.: Introduction to Stochastic Search and Optimization, 1st edn. Wiley, New York (2003)
20. Zutshi, A., Sankaranarayanan, S., Deshmukh, J.V., Kapinski, J.: Multiple shooting, cegar-based falsification for hybrid systems. In: Proceedings of the 14th International Conference on Embedded Software, p. 5 (2014)

Author Index

Printed in the United States
By Bookmasters